The Failure of the
Muslim Brotherhood
in the Arab World

In memory of my late grandfather, late father, and late grandmother.

The Modern Arab World (Economic and Social Commission for Western Asia, Map No. 3978, Rev. 13, October 2015). Used by permission of the UN Publications Board.

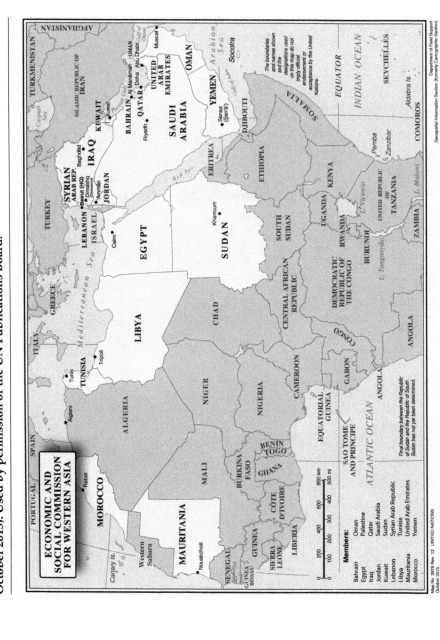

Contents

Preface

After over fifteen years of working in various advisory positions within the administration of the Saudi Arabian government, where I had experienced and worked on numerous issues involving the Muslim Brotherhood (MB) organization, I began to document their destructive actions across the Arab world. After the Arab revolutions in 2011, their influence sharply increased in various Arab countries of consequence, especially in Egypt, and that's when their objectives and aims were laid bare to the world to witness. The initial euphoria of President Hosni Mubarak's downfall in Cairo gave the leaders and supporters of the MB the false belief that they were on the cusp of a historic takeover of most of the Arab world.

Ultimately, the goal of this book is to tell a compelling—and ultimately very tragic—tale of the Muslim Brotherhood from its origins in Egypt nearly one hundred years ago right up to the present day. What began as a local religio-political mobilization by a young average schoolteacher, Hassan Al-Banna, meant to return a transitioning Egyptian society to Islam and sharia soon expanded into a global organization with affiliate entities around the Arab and Muslim worlds.

Then, in 2011, when the eruption of what came to be known as the so-called Arab Spring occurred, the Brotherhood—whose leaders, organization, and media activities were now primarily funded and sheltered by the Qatari authorities—launched a daring grand project to overtake a vast majority of Arab countries. Through a long-standing alliance between leading MB cleric, Yusuf Al-Qaradawi, and Qatar's Sheikh Hamad bin Khalifa Al-Thani, father of the current Amir, the two attempted to use the infrastructure of the Brotherhood to foment and capitalize on the upheavals.

The main reason for me to write this book was to expose and explain why this MB "conspiracy" ended in such an unmitigated disaster. The Brotherhood failed for the same reasons that the organization had been struggling for decades—an inconsistent political platform, a penchant for violence, the lack of a clear vision of their own, and an inability to permanently capture popular support among an Arab population increasingly resistant to the Islamization of politics and society without any tangible solutions to the rampant underdevelopment, unemployment, stagnation, and poverty seen across the Arab world.

Before concluding, I wish to point out that there are three Arab countries located in the three regional poles of the Arab world that have been assessed differently from the others: Lebanon in the Levant, Yemen in the Gulf, and Sudan in Africa, as well as their respective MB affiliates. The reasoning is twofold. First, these states present uniquely complex domestic political landscapes due to histories and demographics that have led to lengthy bouts of conflict and political instability, which have in turn exposed them to considerable regional geopolitical jockeying. Second, although Lebanon's Jemaah Islamiya, Yemen's Al-Islah, and Sudan's National Congress Party are all based on MB-inspired political theology and dogma, they are not currently true MB affiliates.

As a result of these realities, Lebanon, Sudan, and Yemen have in recent years been the sites of conflicting and crisscrossing loyalties that, while not unconnected to the broader regional Brotherhood battle led by Turkey and Qatar on the one side and the Saudi-led bloc on the other, are not representative of that conflict.

In the nearly three years it has taken me to complete this long and complicated project, I have learned a lot. What inevitably appears is a picture of a tragically flawed organization. While its members have long believed themselves to be acting on pure motives and for good reasons—as tragic characters often do—those motives and reasons have consistently given way to thoughts and actions that have launched a long series of flawed and fatal decisions with enormous geopolitical repercussions. In that sense, this book is a classic story of failure due to hubris, or an excessive pride and self-confidence, that necessarily detaches the actors from reality and leads to unwanted results at the hands of an ever-growing opposition with devastating strategic consequences.

Acknowledgments

I would not have been able to complete this book without the love, support, and understanding of my adorable daughter, Dalal.

My wife, mother, aunt, and especially my two brothers have been wonderful and limitlessly supportive of my work, and for that I am and will always be grateful.

I also thank my former colleagues at Harvard University with whom I worked for six years, where I got all the support I needed to complete a first detailed study on the MB that served as the foundation for this book—Dr. Gary Samore (Harvard Kennedy School), Brigadier General Kevin Ryan (Harvard Kennedy School), Josh Burek (Harvard Kennedy School), Sharon Wilke (Harvard Kennedy School), Professor Joe Nye (Harvard Kennedy School), Professor Alex Whiting (Harvard Law School), Professor Graham Allison (Harvard Kennedy School), and Professor Tarek Masoud (Harvard Kennedy School).

I thank my colleagues at the other Boston area universities as well—Professor Nadim Shehadi (Tufts Fletcher School), Professor Ibrahim Warde (Tufts Fletcher School), Professor Shai Feldman (Brandeis Middle East Center), Professor Steven Van Evera (MIT Political Science Department), and Professor Richard Shultz (Tufts Fletcher School).

Thank you to all my friends and colleagues in Saudi Arabia and across the Arab world who have helped me immensely with the research and translation of numerous important documents that I have relied on in the book.

And thank you to the staff that has taken care of my family, especially during the difficult times, while I was away on my numerous research trips for this book.

Last but not least, a special thank you to my longtime editor, Kirk Bromley, who while working on this project with me was diagnosed with lymphoma. He fought against all odds with ironclad determination. He fortunately recovered from his illness, and his contribution was vital in helping me complete this daunting task.

Introduction

While in one sense this book is a piece of politico-historical analysis that relies heavily on various religious components unique to Islam, in another sense it is simply a story. And a very human (or, in the words of Nietzsche, an "all too human") story at that. In fact, were it to be categorized on the shelves with the other stories, it should probably be labeled "tragic non-fiction," because it is a true story, and it bears the classic arc of the tragic tale.

The protagonist of the story is not a person but an organization—the MB, or *Al-Ikhwān Al-Muslimūn* as it is called in Arabic. And the story starts, as does this book, in Egypt in 1928, with the founding of the MB by a devout Muslim, a former student at Cairo's Dar Al-Ulum university, and later a primary school teacher in Ismailia, by the name of Hassan Al-Banna. Al-Banna was greatly concerned with what he saw as the moral, religious, and political degradation that was happening to the Muslim world as a result of Westernization and modernization. He felt that Islam was being sold for cheap to an a-religious global elite political class that was corrupting the youth with popular media and music. He believed a new religio-political mobilization was needed to bring Muslim society back to a traditional, respectful state that put Islam—and its proper legal code "sharia"—first in everything, especially practical actions of the state and their ramifications on the overall culture. And he felt change needed to happen quickly, drastically, and broadly.

Of course, such a task was a huge one, and it pitted Al-Banna and his Brothers against massive planetary forces, so the implementation of his ideas would not come easily—or certainly not as easily as he might have liked—and so this is where the first bit of tragedy leaks in. As Chapter 1 makes clear, Al-Banna and his followers soon found it expedient to call all Muslims to jihad, or, in their limited definition of that term, an armed insurrection against unbelievers. And thus begins the MB's long history with political violence, that great tragic flaw that can be traced all the way up to our present day as the primary cause of its incessant and continuing failure as a political project.

As Chapter 1 concludes its look at the MB's early history in Egypt, its efforts to export its ideology to affiliate organizations in other Arab countries, and its life under different leaders, including Ayman Al-Zawahiri, an acolyte of radical cleric Sayyid Qutb, one begins to see that violent revolution in an attempt to set up a pan-Arab caliphate that defies the system of Westphalian sovereignty is hard-wired into the genetics of the Brotherhood. As I later point out, Al-Banna's Brotherhood had two main goals: "that the Islamic fatherland be freed from foreign domination" and "that a free Islamic state may arise,"[1] with laws based on sharia. Despite occasional respites in order to garner some political power, it has not strayed far from these founding principles.

After explicating the birth of the group in Egypt up to the so-called Arab Spring and the fall of Mubarak, the book takes a multi-chapter look at the MB's presence in the many nations in which its affiliate organizations have taken root. For this purpose, I break these nations into three groups: Northern Africa (Algeria, Libya, Morocco, Tunisia, and Sudan), the Levant (Syria, Jordan, Palestine, Iraq, and Lebanon), and the Gulf (Oman, Bahrain, Kuwait, the UAE, Saudi Arabia, Qatar, and Yemen).

I also spend an entire chapter on post-Mubarak Egypt, primarily because it has been such a disaster for the MB and is thus indicative of many of the larger problems touched on throughout the book. The July 3, 2013, deposition of then Egyptian president Mohammed Morsi demonstrates the Brotherhood's unpreparedness to rule the people with set guidelines, despite the fact that it had waited years—over eighty—to put someone in power. But it also demonstrates the ease with which such a government could become corrupt. While Mubarak's role as a puppet for the United States was widely accepted by Egyptians tired of the ruler's abuse of power, Morsi and his ties to the Brotherhood did not present itself as enough of a contrast. The acquisition of power by the Brotherhood simply resulted in a continuance of the "systematic subversion" that Egyptians had endured for years, oppressing them with even more hegemony.[2]

Thus, when Morsi came into rule, his consulting with the Brotherhood appeared to be questionable, and his later declaration of absolute rule affirmed the perception of the Brotherhood as overbearing. Had the group developed a less hegemonic approach, it could have perhaps maintained a more serious stance in the public's eye. Further undermining its seriousness was the Brotherhood's constant reconstruction of its viewpoints. For example, during his oath of office in Tahrir Square in 2012, Morsi promised to work toward the freeing of Sheikh Omar Abdel Rahman, an Islamist convicted of planning to bomb various NYC landmarks. Following this, however, a Brotherhood spokesman said that Morsi "intended to ask federal officials in the United States to have Mr. Abdel Rahman extradited to Egypt on humanitarian grounds. He was not seeking to have Mr. Abdel Rahman's convictions overturned or calling him a political prisoner."[3]

The verbal redaction made by the Brotherhood member was just one more representation of an Egyptian ruler being inconsistent, ruled by yet another overpowering party. As Dr Khalil Al-Anani, Resident Senior Fellow at The Middle East Institute, has said, "The Brotherhood interfered in the presidency, issuing statements and adopting positions that conflicted with it."[4] This was harmful to the image of Morsi, and rendered him, in the people's eyes, as "subordinate to the Brotherhood. In a country where the office of president has historically enjoyed considerable prestige, the Brotherhood made many political and strategic errors that helped to prematurely bring their rule to an end."[5]

Following the military coup led by President Abdel Fattah El-Sisi and his presidency, tens of thousands of Brothers were exiled or fled Egypt. El-Sisi—who, let it be known, is in the opinion of this author a strongman whose methods are entirely questionable and often destructive to true progress in Egypt—has made it clear that he does not wish to stamp out Islam; rather, he opposes those who abuse it for their own best interests. His insistence on claiming Islam and redefining it has sent a positive message to many others who have grown tired of watching Islamists kill in the name of their religion. For instance, after the Charlie Hebdo shooting, El-Sisi made a claim for a "religious revolution," suggesting that the "contemporary understanding of [Islam] is infected with justifications for violence, requiring the government and its official clerics to correct the teaching of Islam."[6] El-Sisi has even exerted his control over the dissemination of Islam in Egypt by establishing imams in mosques who are aligned with the will of the government, and dictating sermons.[7]

El-Sisi's rhetoric has been aptly applied—much more aptly than the Brotherhood is generally able to do—and has been enhanced by convenient timing. From 1993 to 2008, Islamist militants were behind 60 percent of the terrorist bombings with the highest casualties.[8] For years, headlines have presented the Islamist extremists of the Taliban and Al-Qaeda as the enemy, and the ties between the Brotherhood and such groups, even if tenuous, have been enough to create pushback against them.

In Algeria, Libya, Tunisia, Morocco, and Sudan, Brotherhood affiliates have taken on different names in order to conceal their links to the leading organization in Egypt—the Movement of Society for Peace, the Justice and Construction Party, Ennahda, The Justice and Development Party, and the National Congress Party, respectively. While levels of government participation have varied in each country, the overall picture is one of organizations struggling to shed their connection to violence, to maintain a coherently progressive narrative that does not seem overly religio-fanatic, and to seem amenable to working within the confines of an established governmental system.

In Algeria, the Movement of Society for Peace has been able to enjoy some governmental representation since a multiparty system was established in the early 1990s as part of various coalitions by shedding its Islamist image, giving up on its goal of radically transforming society according to strict religious dictates and distancing itself from the Front Islamique du Salut and the armed Islamic groups that started staging postcoup uprisings in 1992.

Libya's MB affiliate, the Justice and Construction Party, has not fared well. King Idris and Muammar Qaddafi banned the group entirely and lived in a constant state of war against all forms of Islamism. The so-called Arab Spring gave new life to the organization, which held its first press conference on November 17, 2011, but it did not do well in elections and has since faced constant widespread criticism for its links to political violence and terror groups. In 2014 elections, the MB won only 25 of 200 parliamentary seats.

In Sudan, the MB started as it has in many countries—through exchange students in Cairo—but it has suffered greatly in the last two decades due to its ties to Omar Al-Bashir and the twenty-year civil war that has engulfed the nation. Turkey, Saudi Arabia, and the UAE have been providing financial assistance, but only recently, with the shuttering of Al Jazeera's offices in Khartoum and the recalling of its ambassador from Doha, has Sudan been able to maintain the dedication of the latter two important funding partners along with help from the United States. It seems now that many in the country are realizing that if they want a prosperous future, they must steer clear of the MB.

Morocco's Islamist movement is composed of the political group Al Tawhid (which formed the Justice and Development Party, or PJD) and the non-political group Al-Adl Wal Ihsan. PJD's desire to remain valid within the Moroccan political sphere has led to the stripping away of any overtly religious aspects. It has pressured the key political actor in the country—the Monarchy—but it has refrained from clashing with it by making alliances with other opposition movements to facilitate such pressures and avoid isolation. The PJD has secured a foothold in government through an accommodationist posture toward the monarchy and by making such strict renunciations of Islamist positions that it has been largely discredited as a legitimate MB group.[9]

In Tunisia, the perception of Ennahda has changed with the government's agenda. Zine El-Abidine Ben Ali, suspecting Ennahda of plotting to overthrow him, arrested roughly 8,000 members between 1991 and 1992.[10] The government modified schools, newspapers, and books, and banned headscarves and long beards in Ben Ali's attempt to "religiously cleanse" Tunisia.[11]

When jihadists started going to fight for ISIS after the so-called Arab Spring, Ennahda leaders, who had long been trying to distance themselves from terror in the hopes of political inclusion and socioeconomic development, seemed stumped. With jihadism on the rise throughout the Middle East, it became harder and harder for Ennahda to maintain a soft-touch, inclusion-driven approach. In August 2013, the group declared Ansar Al-Sharia a terrorist organization. However, for many Tunisians, Ennahda's response was too little too late, and like Nidaa Tunis, they criticized the party for adopting a sluggish and vague approach to jihadism.

In the wake of the so-called Arab Spring, dissatisfaction—political and economic—remained high. Then came the assassination of secular human rights activist Chokri Belaid and, five months later, his fellow leftist Mohamed Brahmi.[12] Both were critics of Ennahda, raising questions of the groups' lax responses to radical Islamist violence. These assassinations created a rallying cry throughout Tunisia for change. Following the murder of Belaid, Ennahda surrendered the interior ministry. Under Ennahda's rule, countless terrorist cells had formed along the Algerian border in the mountainous areas.[13]

In mid-May 2016, Ennahda held a three-day congress, the first of its kind since 2012, and emerged with the announcement that it would separate the religious (al-da'awi) from the political (al-siyasi).[14] While some might see this as organizational and political evolution, it is similar to developments in other countries—the more an affiliate tries to distance itself from the core MB tenets, the less it actually remains an MB affiliate but instead becomes an example of the failure of the MB objective.

The next region discussed is the Levant, or Syria, Jordan, Palestine, Iraq, and Lebanon. The MB has a long history in Syria. The group rose indigenously in the wake of the failed Great Syrian Revolt of 1925–1927.[15] A loose network of religious associations, referred to as the "Jamiyyat Al-Gharra," sprang up to counter the French Mandate's secularizing influences. The Egyptian Ikhwan provided ideological and organizational inspiration, and although the Syrian Brothers considered Hassan Al-Banna to be the spiritual leader of the movement, the group retained its operational independence, unlike the affiliate in Jordan.

For many years, the Syrian MB struggled to be seen as more than just a strictly Islamic party. However, when the neo-Baathists seized power in 1966, they began a process of secularization.[16] The aim was to replace Islam with Arab nationalism. Then, in 1976, militant Muslims who had broken away from the MB mounted a violent struggle against the government. The rank-and-file MB had to decide whether or not to join. From 1976 to 1982, it waged a violent campaign against the Baath regime, and they succeeded in mobilizing significant backing.

In 1979 the Ikhwan launched an attack on the Aleppo Artillery School and massacred thirty-three Alawis. The MB then took partial control of several Syrian cities in 1980. In June of that year, it attempted to assassinate president Hafez Al-Assad. This resulted in a major punitive campaign against the movement that included the murder of 1,000 inmates who had been members of the MB. Emergency Law 49 was passed in late 1980, which enacted the death penalty for any member of the MB. Then, in February 1982, the government attacked the city of Hama in order to quell an MB uprising, and—while figures differ—many thousands of Syrians were killed.

There was a cooling of relations between the MB and the government in the 1990s, but when Bashar Al-Assad came to power in 2000, the failure of the Islamic rebellion in Syria became clear. The radical religious groups had failed to break out of the traditional circles of support and gain it from other sectors of the population. Further, the government was able to create the image of positive state-religion relations, with a Syrian ethnic-Alawite secular state dressed up in Islamic symbols and gestures of cooperation. Now that Syria has been ripped apart by civil war, the MB has entered into a fully violent relationship with the government as it funds fighters seeking to overthrow the Assad regime.

The Islamic Action Front, Jordan's branch of the MB, has built coherent internal political structures, but it has also developed its own internal faults, which have led to the decline of the Islamist movement in Jordan. Many of these faults have come as a price the group has paid for shifting its focus from social issues to political affairs, particularly Palestine.

In 2006, the MB found itself divided upon the death of Abu Musab Al-Zarqawi.[17] Even though the Brotherhood refused to apologize for the visitation of four of its members to Zarqawi's funeral tent, it did issue two statements clarifying its positions. Some saw this as an attempt to pacify the government, and this led to eighteen out of the forty of the MB's consultative council members submitting their resignations.

Then on April 3, 2016, the government shut down the group's headquarters, as well as branches in Irbid, Ramtha, Mafruq, Madaba, and El Karak. While the reason given was that the MB lacked a renewed license according to the law of associations and parties that was passed in 2014,[18] Ali Abu Al-Sukkar, a former chairman of the Brotherhood's Shura Council, describes the current relationship between the Brotherhood and the government as "tepid," pointing out "the rise of the Islamist movement in the region has raised fears here, and the presence of Daesh [the Islamic State] has created a fear of Islamist parties."[19]

In Palestine, Islamism was originally represented by the Islamic Jihad, which had been founded in opposition to the Brotherhood's gradualist ways in 1980, yet the Islamic Jihad did not catch on the way its members would have liked; it remained small and could not garner a following resembling the likes of the Brotherhood. So, to address the criticisms that the Brotherhood was not doing enough to resist Israeli occupation, Hamas was established.

Hamas's charter contains the philosophy of the movement, its rationale, and its positions on central issues, such as social welfare, the role of
women, and other Islamic movements like the Palestine Liberation Organization (PLO). Its position on most of these issues doesn't differ from that
of the Brotherhood, but it pays less attention to transforming society and
much more to the Palestinian cause and jihad.

As a branch of the Brotherhood, Hamas has been able to build on the
mother organization's extensive infrastructure in expanding its public
base of operations, facilitating useful vehicles for spreading its ideas and
influence and enlisting supporters. Hamas's nonparticipation in the political process has led it to concentrate its efforts on Intifada activity. It has
become the party most engaged in armed actions against Israeli targets,
and thus it is widely recognized as a terrorist organization and shunned
on the world diplomatic stage.

As for Iraq, the MB goes all the way back to the mid-1940s, and the official branch was opened in 1951. Facing a strong local communist threat,
the Iraqi MB—called the Iraqi Islamic Party, or IIP—conjoined politics
and religion and began working for a state ruled by sharia. Following the
Baath Party taking power in 1968, crackdowns against the MB followed
and the group basically went dormant until after the first Gulf War, when
it began working to oust Saddam Hussein.

Hussein's response was to embrace Islam and mosque building, but he
was inevitably removed by the United States in 2003. As the country rebuilt, the IIP played a significant role in the political development process.
This has meant, however, that Sunni support for the IIP has waned significantly. Further, its decision to align itself with Qatar, Iran, and Turkey, as
opposed to the Saudi-led bloc that is opposing Qatar's support of the MB,
has affected it financially and politically. Finally, its failure to deliver on
security, economic, and services policy promises has led to a dramatic loss
of political power. As a result, the IIP has started to distance itself from
the MB and the turmoil caused by ISIS, which many in the country see as
MB-linked.

Lastly, Lebanon is home to the smallest MB affiliate in the Levant,
Jemaah Islamiya. The group dates back to 1964 and was pioneered by
Muslim scholar Fathi Yakan, a staunch disciple of Qutb, who opposed secularism, communism, and the West, and wanted Islam to be the basis of
society and law. To this day, Jemaah has only one member of parliament.
The group's decision to oppose Assad and Iran in the Syrian Civil War
led to a split with Hezbollah, with which it had launched joint operations
against Israel in the past. Ultimately, due to Lebanon's demographics and
religio-political history, Jemaah is likely to remain a fringe group in the nation's political scene for the foreseeable future.

The third region discussed in the book is the Gulf. The nations covered include Oman, Bahrain, Kuwait, the UAE, Yemen, Saudi Arabia,
and Qatar. The MB in Oman is very small, and various crackdowns in the

1990s and 2000s have led to the nation being largely free of Ikhwani activity. The nature of religion in the country has something to do with it—the Omanis are not Sunni or Shia but Ibadi, which is a highly tolerant form of Islam. Nevertheless, the government remains vigilant against radical scholars, and recently evicted one for denouncing the Saudi-led blockade against Qatar.

In Bahrain, which is a majority Shia nation with a ruling Sunni family, the local MB—called Al-Menbar—has been co-opted by the state for years to act as a foil to Shia opposition. Al-Menbar has supported the government often, even as recently as the 2011 protests. But following what became clear in Egypt about the group, the Bahraini government made moves to diminish the group's power, though it seems likely that Al-Menbar will stay involved in Bahraini politics to some extent for the foreseeable future as long as it can continue to show that it is distancing itself from the ideologies and actions of the central organization.

Like Bahrain, Kuwait has come to a relatively comfortable living arrangement with its MB affiliate, which is the oldest in the Gulf. The greatest tension between the Kuwaiti government and the MB occurred when the group expressed its support for Saddam Hussein's invasion of the country. After the liberation, the Kuwaiti MB re-branded itself as Hadas and started moving more aggressively into government agencies. The response was a purge and Hadas boycotting elections, but then in 2016 the group took four of the five seats contested by its candidates. At this point, it has settled into the political establishment in Kuwait and has assumed a largely neutral, unthreatening stance.

The UAE MB was late to the game—originating in 1974—as Al-Islah. By the late 1980s, the group began raising concerns over links to the Egyptian MB and various political reform agendas. This brought about Crown Prince Sheikh Mohammed bin Zayed Al-Nahayan's "drying the springs" initiative to remove Islamist influence from society. Crackdowns following the 2011 turmoil and the discovery of an MB coup plot brought the group's growth to a severe halt. With the persistence of Sheikh Mohammed's efforts, including the ordering of an assassination attempt on the leader of the Yemeni branch of the MB, it has become clear that the group is not welcome in the country and can only persist under severely limiting draconian pressure.

As for Yemen, the MB affiliate there, Al-Islah, is a mash-up of groups and positions. Moderates, socialists, businessmen, tribal leaders, and Arab nationalists have all been related in some way to the organization. Like Sudan, the country is split and currently involved in an internal conflict. In Yemen, however, the source is Iran and its Houthi proxies. Saudi Arabia is strongly backing Al-Islah, which has been involved in the conflict from the start. The UAE is also backing Al-Islah, but more hesitantly. Once the smoke from the civil war there clears, Al-Islah will have a role to play in the reconstruction of the country but not as a leader.

Next Saudi Arabia is covered. The Kingdom is unique in the Arab world as the epicenter of Islam due to its being the Custodian of the Two Holy Mosques. Al-Banna came to the Kingdom in 1936 in search of new followers, and Brotherhood members enjoyed a relatively welcoming environment in the kingdom. And while it welcomed the MB in the early years, the relationship soon soured, especially once the MB was shown to be involved in the Sahwa movement during the first Gulf War, and both entities made it clear that they supported Hussein's invasion of Kuwait and strongly criticized the Saudis' decision to host the American military to help repel the Iraqis.

Thus came the crackdown, which only intensified following the so-called Arab Spring of 2011. A government decree was issued in 2014 that leveled strict and lengthy prison sentences at those supporting terrorists, and then, only a month later, the MB was designated as a terrorist group. Now, with Crown Prince Mohammed bin Salman in place, who is collaborating with Emirati crown prince Mohammed bin Zayed, the Saudis have largely obliterated the group from the country.

Finally in the Gulf there is Qatar, which stands in stark contrast to every country covered in this book. The marriage between Qatar and the MB has been going on for more than six decades, and it has resulted in the Qatari social and political scene—its schools, its media, its financial endowments, its foreign policy—being dominated by the MB ideology as designed by its leaders, who enjoy carte blanche residence in Qatar and top-level influence in its ruling class. At the heart of the Qatari embrace of the Brotherhood is the fact that the Qatari leadership has long come to feel ideologically controlled by the Saudis, and this lack of agency and status has chafed hard and long enough to lead them to their current situation— a total alliance with Saudi Arabia's arch enemy, the MB.

To give a sense of the history and the deeply entrenched nature of the MB in Qatar, Abdulbadi Al-Saqr, a former student of Al-Banna, arrived on the run from Egypt in 1954 and founded Qatar's Ministry of Education. A wave of MB scholars followed. Yusuf Al-Qaradawi arrived in 1961, and has lived in Qatar ever since, serving as the head religious and political counselor to the ruling emir. His long-running and highly popular talk show *Sharia and Life*, which aired on Al Jazeera, is indicative of the full support Qatar's media gives to the Brotherhood.

MB ideology has also greatly influenced Qatari foreign policy. As Dr. Abulaziz Khoja, former Saudi Minister of Information, said in 2016, "Qatari foreign policy has in recent years become a tool for exportation of MB ideology." In 2008, Qatar pledged $250 million to Hamas, a year after the MB-inspired terror group took control of the Gaza Strip. This financial flow has not stopped.

Then, when the so-called Arab Spring occurred in 2011, Qatar and its MB associates went into high gear. Qatar began helping finance and plant MB uprisings and influence in Syria, Libya, Tunisia, Egypt, and elsewhere.

Qatar became so Brotherhood focused that in 2013, Andrew Hammond, former Reuters bureau chief in Saudi Arabia, called the country "a mini Ikhwanistan."

But the chickens came home to roost when, in the summer of 2017, Saudi Arabia and three allies—Bahrain, the UAE, and Egypt—announced an embargo against Qatar that would not end until thirteen demands were met, many of which involved Qatar breaking ties with the MB. As of the publishing of this book the standoff shows no signs of abating, and King Salman even recently told French president Emmanuel Macron that a Saudi military invasion is being considered.

Why would the Saudis go to such lengths to sway the politics of a tiny neighboring nation? Because they, like this book, view Qatar's actions as indicative of a general conspiracy to overthrow various Arab governments in order to transplant an international MB-inspired Islamist leadership. In short, the Saudis see the Qataris as the primary financial backer of the most dangerous political organization in the region that has, again and again, made it very clear that it wishes a widespread revolution by any means necessary.

This view was particularly confirmed after the so-called Arab Spring and Qatar's extensive support of the uprisings. The tiny nation's engagement with the MB suddenly grew into a region-wide issue that the Saudis felt needed to be addressed. Lines were drawn, allies assembled, and a campaign to alert the world to the fact that the MB is an international terrorist organization on par with ISIS and Al-Qaeda began, leading to the Saudi-led boycott of Qatar in 2017.

As the renewed focus on Qatar has now shown the global community, Qatari MB support has gone beyond its hosting of MB leader, Qaradawi, its billions sent to various Middle Eastern MB affiliates (especially its propping up of Hamas and the Morsi regime), and its hosting of the Al Jazeera network as a regional mouthpiece for MB's racist, violent ideology. Qatari efforts now reach beyond the Middle East, into Europe, Asia, and the United States. Qatari activity in these areas is largely the story of maintaining financial sources that fund MB activities in the MENA region.

The Qatari royal family funded Qaradawi's globe hopping in the early years by paying for his recruiting adventures in Pakistan, Malaysia, Indonesia, Europe, North America, and even as far afield as Japan and South Korea. In recent years Qatar has given more than $175 million to Brotherhood-linked groups in France, the UK, Italy, and Denmark. It has also heavily funded the Geneva-based Alkarama Foundation run by Abdulrahman Al-Nuaimi under the guise of a charitable foundation supporting Muslim causes. However, the United States and the UK have both designated Alkarama as a terrorist organization due to its support for Al-Qaeda and the MB.

In addition, Qatar is now using Turkey as a proxy for its MB efforts and growing closer to Iran. As far as Qatar and Turkey, the struggling

Turkish economy needs an infusion of cash, and Qatar is able to provide it. Turkey also still holds dreams of control over the Arab world and is very open to the destructive tendencies of the MB and its sponsor, Qatar. Finally, president Recep Tayyip Erdogan is highly competitive with the Saudi Kingdom, and Qatar is a great player on his team. As far as Iran and Qatar, the relationship seems an almost natural one. MB thinking inspired the Islamic Revolution, together the two countries would hold the largest natural gas reserves in the world, and Iran's rivalry with Saudi Arabia fits hand-to-glove with Qatar's. This entire Qatar conspiracy and its ramifications are discussed heavily in Chapters 5, 6, and 7.

Then, in Chapter 8, an important and, I believe, novel distinction is made in the arena of understanding the MB, and that distinction is between what I call quietist Salafism and the jihadi Salafism of the MB. While it is common among journalists and analysts to label the MB and the terror groups it has inspired "Salafi," this is actually a misnomer. True Salafism is the result of Islamic scholar Sheikh Muhammad bin Abdul Wahhab and his eighteenth-century efforts to return Islam to its original state as based on its ancestors (or Salaf). It is a peaceful strain of Islam that stresses loyalty to the ruler and an aversion to violence. Wahhab's alliance with Imam Muhammad Ibn Saud led to the first (and eventually the contemporary) Saudi state.

As such, quietist Salafism has no qualms with sovereign states. (In fact, it thoroughly supports them.) It believes that Saudi Arabia is the center of the Islamic world due to its king being the Custodian of the Two Holy Mosques at Makkah and Madinah, and it thus has no urge for—and is deeply inimical to the ambition of—tearing down all Arab governments and placing all Muslim peoples under the single rule of a caliphate run by the Al-Ikhwān Al-Muslimūn. Because this is the MB's central objective, Salafism and the MB ideology have basically been at war—with intermittent periods of peaceful tolerance—since the organization began.

In original Islamic scriptures, the highest authority is the "caretaker" of the Umma, or the *wali al amr*. All religious, political, and military powers are concentrated under this authority, and in return for his protection and leadership the people show their acceptance of his rule by swearing an oath of loyalty (*baya*h) to him. This oath, which is an act of obedience (*ta'ah*), is fundamental to Salafism, and anyone that breaks the oath —as the MB has done and encouraged others to do—can never again be considered a true Salafi.

In short, comparing the quietist Salafism of the Saudis and the jihadi Salafism (which is in fact best described as Kharijite) of the MB highlights the theological reasons behind the political differences between much of the Arab world, which is religiously centered on Saudi Arabia, and the MB.

This emphasis on Salafism segues into my penultimate chapter, which profiles a longtime friend and colleague of mine who struggled between his loyalty to quietist and jihadi Salafism as typified by Saudi Arabia and the MB: Jamal Khashoggi. I not only discuss Jamal's life, our association, and his assassination from both a personal and professional perspective but also show how it serves as a metaphor for the MB and its members in general. In essence, many MB members are stuck between two worlds—they are loyal to their country, yet believe in a group that seeks its destruction; they want more democracy in the Arab world, yet support an organization that has failed again and again to participate in democracy; they believe that violence and suppression are tearing the Middle East apart, yet they adamantly march in lock step with a group that practices political terror and suppresses dissent. Jamal lived this struggle, and my look at his productive life and tragic death shines an important light on the MB.

Finally, in the last chapter, various geostrategic consequences of the failure of the MB project are discussed. Covered are the current situations in Egypt, Syria, and Yemen; political collapse in Algeria, Libya, and Sudan; U.S. president Donald Trump's plan to designate the MB a terrorist organization; the problems inherent in Gulf security what with Qatar's continued resistance to the demands of the Arab Quartet; Iran's persistent meddling in the region and what can be done about it; Saudi Arabia's role and objectives; the continued disaster that is Hamas in Palestine; and what America's role, in alliance with the Saudis and their allies, might be in helping resolve various crises in the region.

After over ninety years, it seems that the MB's chances at participating in political power in the MENA region are largely dead. While some loosely affiliated MB groups have been able to participate in parliamentary politics by stripping away their entire Islamist agenda, the MENA nations, especially after the so-called Arab Spring, seem politically closed to the MB. Its next phase will have to involve social and political ambitions of a different order from those in the past.

The Qatari crisis appears to have produced a kind of breaking point. The crisis represents a major challenge for Saudi-Qatari relations, the coherency of the GCC, the Saudi-Iranian rivalry, Saudi-American relations, Qatari-American relations, and the different possible solutions to the problems in the many crumbling states of the region. But what is also clear is that the MB has, at least vis-à-vis global awareness, been finally lifted out of the shadows and is likely to be addressed with as much regional and international vehemence in the coming decade as Al-Qaeda and ISIS have been over the last two decades.

Finally, the entire Islamist agenda that the MB has represented for nine decades seems to be on its last legs, partly due to the MB's many political failures, partly due to Islamism becoming synonymous with terror and religious fanaticism as a result of Al-Qaeda and ISIS, and partly due to the renewed attention and energy that Saudi Arabia is now paying to the problems inherent in the Ikhwani project. One might even go so far as to say MENA has become far too secular as a result of globalization for the religio-political ideology that is central to the MB agenda. How it will navigate this new alienation from political hope remains to be seen.

The MB emerged in a time very different from the twenty-first century. When a young Hassan Al-Banna looked around the Arab world in 1928, he saw the ravages of European imperialism, he saw a region with almost no economic development, and he saw the hopes of an emerging Islamic sociopolitical ideology that could give Muslims pride and progress. Yet there had been no World War II, no American century, no oil boom, no Iran-Iraq War, no Israel, no Israeli-Palestine issue, no GCC, no Islamic Republic, no Al-Qaeda, no ISIS, no Arab Spring, and no Qatari funding. That is where the story began, and it could have ended happily had his organization been able to adjust its expectations, act patiently, emphasize compromise, and mature and evolve politically with the times.

But instead, the MB has remained for almost a century an inflexible, impatient, uncompromising, and out of touch revolutionary organization that has again and again showed that it is incapable of "playing well with others." It has too often been linked to or responsible for terrorism. It has too often sided with the idea of government overthrow. And it has too often forced the idea that the social and political orders should bend to the rules of a strict Islamist worldview. The vast majority of the people and the leaders of the Arab world have outgrown the MB—and many of them have worked together across borders and sects to destroy it—which is why its story is a tragedy.

And it is to that tragic story we now turn.

CHAPTER 1

The Birth of the Muslim Brotherhood in Egypt

The Muslim Brotherhood Motto:
God is our goal.
The Prophet is our leader.
The Quran is our constitution.
Jihad is our way.
Death in the service of God
is the loftiest of our wishes.
God is great, God is great.[1]

The Muslim Brotherhood (MB) has now been around for more than ninety years, and in that time we have learned a great deal about it. Foremost among these lessons is that its ideology and vision represent a chimera, a fantastical dream of Muslim life in the modern world. Precisely why this is so will be detailed in this book.

For now, suffice it to say that the Brotherhood is a chameleon, constantly shape-shifting and altering its stripes to fit into its surroundings. Even more, it's amoeba-like, with no clearly defined shape. Only one overriding element has remained through all the years and all the turmoil: the revolutionary foundation, the idea of coming to power through violence. That has been present since the beginning.

THE BROTHERHOOD BEGINS

As the twentieth century dawned, the Ottoman Empire had lost not only influence but also vast swathes of territory in Eastern Europe and the Middle East. The faded superpower, which had since the fourteenth century claimed the caliphate and served as the global face of Islam, staggered on its last legs. A World War I alliance with Germany would prove its final undoing, as the victors partitioned the remnants of the Ottoman Empire.

Only the heroics of Mustafa Kemal (later given the surname Ataturk, or "Father of the Turks"), who built the Turkish army that forced out the Greeks, would save Turkish lands. His Republic of Turkey, born via National Assembly vote on October 29, 1923, was created to be modern and secular, with religion separated from the state. Thus, four months later, the assembly abolished the caliphate: the rise of a Western-leaning state marked the end of the primary Islamic one.

Though it had long been largely symbolic, the caliphate's end sparked a crisis in certain corners of the Muslim world. Hassan Al-Banna, a promising and devout eighteen-year-old student at Cairo's Dar Al-Ulum at the time, viewed it as a "calamity" and "declaration of war against all shapes of Islam."[2] Three years later, he became a primary school teacher in Ismailia, a mid-sized city in northeast Egypt.

Since it served as the Egyptian headquarters of the Suez Canal, Ismailia had a stronger foreign presence than the rest of the country. The UK had given Egypt its independence in 1922, but Britain still controlled the Canal Zone with thousands of troops and expat managers mostly from France and the UK. Many Egyptians in the area became disenchanted with cultural colonialism, fearing the foreigners' efforts to modernize Egypt and undermine Islamic traditions. In addition, many Egyptians were unhappy with the country's most popular party at the time, Wafd, in part for its support of secularism.

Al-Banna began speaking in coffeehouses and mosques about creeping Western influence and the need for Islamic renewal. Then, one day in March 1928, six Suez Canal workers came to him complaining about mistreatment by their French and British bosses.[3] They asked him to become their leader. He accepted and dubbed their group the Society of Muslim Brothers, a.k.a. the Muslim Brotherhood.

The Brotherhood gave him a platform to denounce moral depravity and anti-religious education as part of a European strategy to subjugate the Muslim world. He started an evening school, focused on Islamic education. By 1931, the group had raised enough to build a mosque and launch a Cairo branch. Al-Banna relocated to Cairo the following year, as did the Brotherhood headquarters. The group initially acted much like an Islamic welfare outfit, doing social work among the poor, repairing mosques, building schools, and setting up workshops and clinics. But its founder envisioned a great deal more.

THE FOUNDER'S VISION

The son of a popular imam, Al-Banna had from an early age been concerned with Egyptian society's declining respect for religion and rising enthusiasm for Western culture. He was born in 1906 outside Cairo and moved to the capital to study in 1923, arriving in a period of political and cultural ferment. What he found there shocked him. In Al-Banna's view, the eagerness of the country's political elite to "ape" Western ways signaled their betrayal of the country's Islamic heritage. He saw an East versus West, "clash of civilizations" dynamic, with the latter representing depravity and the former morality and spirituality. In denouncing the British, he referenced the Crusades, stirring up the age-old Islam-Christianity rivalry.

Further, the secular models of law and education borrowed from Europe were out of touch with the religious beliefs and sentiments of Egyptian society.[4] Al-Banna viewed secularization as "perhaps the most insidious and devastating weapon ever devised by Europeans"[5] and believed its goal was the end of Islam. He saw Westernization slowly and inevitably destroying Islamic traditions, spurring licentiousness and greed. This perception became "an integral part of the Brotherhood's belief system," according to Martyn Frampton, a historian at Queen Mary University of London, in his 2018 book *The Muslim Brotherhood and the West*.[6] This idea drove the Brotherhood's first major initiative: the creation of schools to counter Christian missionaries and to raise a new generation of pious Muslims.

Al-Banna believed that Egyptian youth had become corrupted; they were overwhelmed by doubt and perplexity that stimulated apostasy rather than faith as well as by the lewd popular media and music that undermined traditional values and created moral problems. He sought to reverse these trends. "The long-term goal of establishing an Islamic state in Egypt is derived from Hassan Al-Banna's proscription against the 'vices' of the modern world," the CIA said in a 1986 report.[7] As a counselor and teacher, he would give himself the task of teaching "the objectives of religion and the sources of their wellbeing and happiness in life." He would bring to this mission "perseverance and sacrifice," study and understanding, and a body willing to face hardship and a soul that had been "sold to God."[8]

This new generation would build Al-Banna's vision of a modern society renewed by Islam. He saw early twentieth-century Egypt as defined by two great failures: the hidebound, traditional Islam of Al-Azhar University and other revered institutions (like those in Makkah and Madinah) and the greedy, foreigner-dominated economy. In Cairo, he saw firsthand the extent to which Egyptian youth had drifted away from Islam and how Islamic culture and traditions were losing out to Western ideas, modernization, and rapid urbanization. He saw in Cairo "a wave of atheism and indecency"[9]—largely the result of the creeping influence from a Western civilization in steep decline:

> Its political foundations are being destroyed by dictatorships, and its economic foundations are being swept away by crises. The millions of its wretched, unemployed and hungry offer their testimony against it. . . . Their congresses are failures, their treaties are broken and their covenants torn to

pieces: their League of Nations is a phantasm, possessing neither spirit nor influence, while their strongmen, along with other things, are overthrowing its covenant of peace and security.[10]

In his memoirs, Al-Banna pointed out how the rise of Western-leaning Kemalism in Turkey had led to the end of the caliphate: a Muslim country embraced Western ideas and lost touch with Islam and its traditions and morality. He envisioned a modern Islam of "Din Wa Dawla"—it should shape not just day-to-day society but political and economic spheres as well, providing the basis for national rebirth. He saw Islam as "creed as well as worship, homeland and race, religion and state."[11]

Al-Banna believed that the interpretations of generations of Islamic theorists had turned Sharia into an edifice of sterile erudition inapplicable to real life. His answer to this was to go "back to the Quran and the Sunna."[12] He did not want to return to the pre-industrial past as the Salafi Ulama in Saudi Arabia had done. Instead, he wanted to use the new technical and scientific resources that the modern West could provide in order to renew the Ummah, or global Muslim community. Like most Muslim reformers from the early nineteenth century, he believed it was possible to pick and choose the aspects of Western civilization compatible with Islamic doctrine and morality and neatly excise the rest.

Though framed as a return to "pure" and "true" Islam of the prophet's time, the MB's understanding of Islam was a product of modern times, influenced by the ideas of Islamic modernists like Rashid Rida, Mohammed Abduh, and Muhibb Al-Din Al-Khatib.[13] Historians and MB scholars generally agree that Al-Banna was no great thinker or scholar of Islam. "It is probably fair to say that Al-Banna's personal qualities were more impressive and left a greater impression than his ideology," Alison Pargeter, senior research associate at the Royal United Services Institute, writes in her book *Muslim Brotherhood: From Opposition to Power*. "Although he was able to tap into the grievances of a generation, he can hardly be considered to have been a major intellectual force or even a scholar. As Egyptian philosopher Hassan Hanafi has argued, 'to say the truth, the ideas of Hassan Al-Banna probably may not amount to much.' "[14]

Within those ideas, the misty vision of the MB was sometimes combined with spiritual elements from Sufism, although these gradually became less pronounced. As veteran *New York Times'* correspondent David Kirkpatrick explains in his bestselling 2018 book, *Into the Hands of the Soldiers*, MB ideology was a confused grab bag from the start:

Hassan Al-Banna, who was born in 1906 and founded the Brotherhood at the age of twenty-two, had a knack for paradox. He was the son of a rural imam who owned one of Egypt's first phonograph shops, and both father and son had a keen interest in Sufi mysticism—even though both Sufism and music were deemed heretical by the most orthodox Sunni Muslims. The son trained as an Arabic teacher and worked in state schools. But he also briefly took over publication of the flagship of Abduh's Islamic modernist movement—Al-Manar, or the Lighthouse. More than anything else, he dedicated the Brotherhood to Abduh's idea that returning to the roots of Islam was the only way to catch up with the West in rationalism and progress. Into that core concept Banna mixed themes of Islamic traditionalism and anti-Western nationalism borrowed from some of Abduh's intellectual successors. Then Banna harnessed their abstract ideas to his own zeal for organizing. "If the French Revolution decreed the rights of man and declared for freedom, equality and brotherhood, and if the Russian Revolution brought closer the classes and social justice for the people," Al-Banna once wrote, "the great Islamic revolution decreed all that thirteen hundred years before." Would it be a movement for spiritual renewal or political power? Militant or peaceful? Egyptian nationalist or pan-Islamic? Democratic or authoritarian? Al-Banna took both sides of every argument, and he bequeathed to his acolytes decades of internal debate over their goals.[15]

Still, Al-Banna's overarching objective seemed to be to unite the Ummah into a single state defined by their faith. In essence, the MB sought to revive the caliphate with the Quran as the determinant for daily lives and government and with Jews and Christians as second-class citizens. "Islam does not recognize geographical boundaries, nor does it acknowledge racial and blood differences, considering all Muslims as one Ummah," Al-Banna said in 1938. "The Muslim Brethren consider this unity as holy. . . . They see the caliphate and its re-establishment as a top priority."[16]

VIOLENCE AND POLITICS

To achieve these ends, Al-Banna called all Brotherhood members, indeed all Muslims, to jihad. To abstain would be a mortal sin. The concept of jihad has two distinct meanings in Islam: a personal journey toward growth and an armed struggle against unbelievers. The latter became central to MB ideology; Al-Banna made it clear that the Brotherhood's jihad would involve "fighting and soldiering"[17] against the imperialists. "The tongue of force is the most eloquent tongue,"[18] he wrote in the late 1930s.

Al-Banna cited the military foundations of Mussolini's fascism and Hitler's Nazism, concluding that those "were inferior to the 'militarism of Islam,' which enjoyed divine sanction."[19] The Brotherhood had more direct connections to the Axis Powers. Its paramilitary units, known as the Rovers and the Battalions, had been inspired by European fascists. Hitler and Al-Banna were both anti-Semites: just as the Nazis began to hint at their plan for European Jews, in 1938, Brotherhood newspaper Al-Nadhir called for Jews' expulsion from the Muslim world.[20] Around the same time, Egyptian police discovered documents showing the Brotherhood had received payments from Nazi Germany. These funds were most likely an incentive for the Brotherhood to increase its calls for jihad in Palestine, which would of course help keep the Jews from gaining their own state.[21]

Right from the outset, the concept of violence was enshrined in the MB's motto: "Allah is our objective. The Prophet is our leader. Qur'an is our law. Jihad is our way. Dying in the way of Allah is our highest hope."[22] Pargeter stressed this element in her book: "Fighting jihad has been core to the Ikhwan's political ideology since its very inception."[23] She points to Palestine, where the MB had 1,500 fighters at one point, despite travel restrictions, and even Al-Banna's son-in-law Said Ramadan led a brigade.[24]

Christopher Dickey, foreign editor for the *Daily Beast* and author of several best sellers about terrorism, wrote about the group's dual nature, balanced between politics and violence, stretching back to its beginnings:

> The Muslim Brotherhood is not a benign political organization, but neither is it Terror Incorporated. It was created in the 1920s and developed in the 1930s and '40s as an Islamic alternative to the secular fascist and communist ideologies that dominated revolutionary anti-colonial movements at the time. From those other political organizations the Brotherhood learned the values of a tight structure, party discipline, and secrecy, with a public face devoted to conventional political activity—when possible—and a clandestine branch that resorted to violence if that appeared useful.[25]

Unlike other Islamic organizations at the time, which remained strictly apolitical, the Brotherhood encouraged its young, educated members to take on political causes. From the group's earliest days, Brotherhood members campaigned strongly against colonialism, in Egypt and later in other Muslim countries. Their anticolonial, anti-Western view spurred growth, rallying resentment at the British presence and the wealth of foreigners running the Suez Canal. The call of pan-Islamic nationalism found a receptive audience and created a sizable, angry organization that posed a danger to British occupation and the Egyptian monarchy.

"The Ikhwan were never non-political for a single day," Al-Banna wrote in March 1938. "Their call never distinguished between politics and religion."[26] At that time, the group had 300 branches across the country and printed its own newspapers; a decade old, it was already a major opposition group with mass appeal and a diverse membership. Around 1936, when Al-Banna decided to support jihad against the British and Zionists in Palestine, the Brotherhood began sending weapons to Arabs fighting there. It could thus be said that the West has been fighting the MB for more than eighty years.

In August 1938, Brotherhood members were involved in their first violent street clashes with Egyptian police, during which they denounced Britain and the Jews and distributed pamphlets calling for "holy war" against infidels and colonizers.[27] This led to Al-Banna's imprisonment, at the urging of the British, in late 1941. But this time, he was in regular contact with Egyptian authorities—friendly with Ali Maher Pasha, head of the royal cabinet, and Sheikh Al-Magrahi, a top religious leader, and meeting with Prime Minister Muhammad Mahmud Pasha to discuss Palestine—and there were rumors that the Brotherhood received palace funding.[28] As a result, Al-Banna was released after a month, infuriating the British.

By then, the British had begun to grasp the Brotherhood's legitimate threat: a British intelligence report from December 1942 labeled it an "exceedingly dangerous" "extremist organisation"[29] of up to half a million members. British authorities even began talks with Al-Banna to reach an agreement, a promise of peace during World War II. The fact that nothing came of it underscores the group's deep anti-Western bias. In 1942, the Brotherhood established a separate unit known as the Nizam Al-Khass, or "special apparatus," which was responsible for the assassination of a prominent judge, among many other violent attacks.[30]

TERRORIST BROTHERS

The Brotherhood had begun to change its stripes. During World War II, rumors emerged of MB suicide squads. Salah Shadi, a police officer and Brotherhood leader at the time, has said that the group's first terrorist attack was when MB members threw a bomb at a British club toward the end of World War II, aiming not to kill but to "terrorise."[31] In the end, Britain's wartime desperation, and the Egyptian government's instability, empowered the MB.

By the end of the war, the group was larger and more militant, with a sizable propaganda arm, and became increasingly geared toward violence. Even a January 1945 cartoon in the MB's weekly newspaper that appeared to be about election campaigns was also subtly about making the ultimate sacrifice for the *Ikhwan*, as Tarek Masoud details in his 2014 book *Counting Islam*:

> In it, we see two candidates addressing the same constituency. In the first panel, the (presumably secular) candidate proclaims, "I'll dig irrigation canals and drainage ditches for you. I'll get you more rations. I'll get your sons government jobs. Etc. Etc." The voters, however, appear unmoved. Turning their backs on the candidate, they grumble, "We have had our fill of such promises." In the second panel, we see the Muslim Brotherhood candidate. "God is our destiny!" he declares, reciting the first item from the Muslim Brotherhood catechism. "The Prophet is our leader! The Qur'an is our constitution! And death in the path of God is our fondest wish!" The voters lean toward him intently, smiling in approval, exclaiming, "What is more beautiful than such talk?"[32]

Why, in Allah's name, would a candidate need to exhort his constituents to die for the cause if he's only asking for their votes? Because it was in the

MB's very DNA, and by 1945 the group could see the violence and martyr-dom just up the road. Their leaders knew the way ahead would not be easy.

The Brotherhood's daily newspaper, launched in 1946, was fiercely anti-British. One piece argued that all pro-British Egyptians should be hanged.[33] In the years after the war, the Brotherhood executed a series of attacks: the bombing of a Cairo train thought to be carrying British sol-diers; bomb attacks on police stations and bars frequented by the British; a failed assassination attempt on the leader of a liberal political party; and the bombing of Ismailia's King George Hotel, a British intelligence base.

By this time, the special apparatus had begun to focus on committing violence to further the group's agenda. "The Brotherhood's special appa-ratus cooperated with [Colonel Gamel] Abdel Nasser's Free Officers to fight against the fledgling state of Israel and to plot against the British oc-cupation. Anwar El-Sadat was the Free Officers' liaison to train and equip the Brothers."[34] El-Sadat and the special apparatus recruited and sent vol-unteers to fight against the new state of Israel.

Al-Banna wrote to the head of the Arab League offering up to 10,000 men for Palestine's "army of salvation."[35] In the end, the MB helped sev-eral thousand Egyptians fight for Palestine, a huge number considering the travel restrictions laid down by the British. American journalist John Roy Carlson visited Cairo around this time. He met Brotherhood lead-ers, wrote of their "special assassin squad," and said the Brothers had a "strong militarist, terrorist aspect" and were committed to a "religious to-talitarianism" meant to "smash modernism in government and society."[36]

In the fall of 1948, Egyptian authorities found a great cache of weap-ons and explosives at the home of the MB leader in Ismailia. Weeks later, the MB bombed the Cairo home of Egypt's ambassador to London, then the publisher of the pro-British *Egyptian Gazette*. On December 8, 1948, Prime Minister Mahmoud El-Nuqrashi Pasha ordered the dissolution of the Brotherhood. Egyptian authorities quickly arrested hundreds of mem-bers. Within weeks, the prime minister had been assassinated by a student Brotherhood member. According to Kirkpatrick,

> On December 28, a twenty-three-year-old student veterinarian who belonged to the Brotherhood's paramilitary dressed up as a policeman and snuck in-side the Interior Ministry when the prime minister, Mahmoud el-Nuqrashi, was visiting. The impostor saluted, shot the premier in the back, and then finished him off with a bullet to the chest when Nuqrashi turned to see what hit him.[37]

January brought another major bombing attack by an MB member, this time on the office of the prosecutor examining the murder of Nuqrashi. The bomb killed two people and injured more than twenty. Thus, over a six-month period, the Brotherhood executed more than half a dozen major bombings. There was no point in denying it: the MB had become a deadly terrorist organization that used bombings and assassination to fight enemies and overthrow governments. Perhaps inevitably, this led to the assassination of Al-Banna by government agents, on February 12, 1949. He was just forty-three.

Brotherhood newspapers blamed the Americans, French, and British—whose ambassadors reportedly met shortly before the killing, agreeing to destroy the MB—and swore vengeance.[38] If it hadn't had one before, the Brotherhood now had its bogeyman: the West. Decades later, Brotherhood spiritual leader Yusuf Al-Qaradawi maintained a similar narrative: that a Western-Zionist cabal had conspired to assassinate the Brotherhood founder while MB members fought for Palestine.

Egyptian authorities cracked down, leading to hundreds of arrests and the seizing of Brotherhood property. By July 1949, some 4,000 MB members were in prison and the group was in shambles. Still, some observers knew it would survive. Arabist and author James Heyworth-Dunne believed Al-Banna's ideas would last longer than "any Egyptian Ministry." He saw a clash between the Brotherhood and the ruling classes of the Arab world as inevitable—the only way "the movement could remain true to its 'revolutionary' spirit."[39]

NEW LEADER, NEW ERA

In 1948, Egypt's government sent a school inspector named Sayyid Qutb to the United States to study the American education system—a fateful decision, to say the least. Two years later, Qutb returned to Cairo bemoaning Americans as "numb to faith in religion, faith in art, and faith in spiritual values altogether"[40] and calling for an Islamic renewal. He soon left his Ministry of Education post and joined the Brotherhood, becoming head of propaganda. His extremist, deeply anti-Western views took root within the group and deepened its commitment to violence.

Back before Al-Banna's assassination, the British embassy had reported "much talk of guerrilla warfare" among Brotherhood members aiming to liberate the country from British rule.[41] By late 1951, the Brotherhood had regained strength and called for jihad against the British in Egypt. Its Liberation Battalions, with some 1,000 MB members, began spearheading a guerrilla war in the Canal Zone, inciting riots, evacuating Egyptian workers, and launching bomb attacks on British installations (the group continued through 1953 to attack British military positions in the Canal Zone). Then came Black Saturday, January 26, 1952: a day of riots and arson attacks that devastated vast chunks of Cairo, destroying British-friendly shops, bars, clubs, and hotels and leaving dozens of people dead. No conclusive evidence has been found, but most historians believe MB members were involved and likely among the ringleaders.[42]

A quarter century after its birth, the Brotherhood had survived the killing of its founder and a harsh crackdown to build a vast organization focused mainly on terrorism and revolution. Some reports had Egyptian Brotherhood membership at two million in the early 1950s—or 10 percent of the country's population,[43] though the actual number was probably half that.

The Egyptian monarchy had been wise to crack down on Brotherhood efforts to send soldiers to fight in Palestine. While fighting there in 1948, a group of Brotherhood-linked officers formed a cell called the Free Officers Movement. It was led by Nasser and El-Sadat, two figures who had been close to Al-Banna for years. Upon their return to Egypt, the Free Officers talked of ousting the corrupt monarchy and installing democracy and began working with the MB to plan the coup.[44]

On July 23, 1952, while King Farouk was away in Alexandria, several dozen officers under the command of the Free Officers commandeered the government. Three days later the king sailed to Italy amid farewell salutes and Mohammad Naguib became the first president of modern-day Egypt. Shortly after the revolution, Nasser visited Al-Banna's tomb and swore his allegiance, saying: "Do not think, oh *Ikhwan* ["Brotherhood"], that I am a foreigner to you, for I am one of you."[45] Less than a quarter century after its birth, the MB had pulled off, or at least inspired, its first successful revolution. "Brotherhood leaders saw themselves as having provided the 'inspiration' for the rebellion and saw the establishment of the new regime as a fulfillment of the aspirations of the Brotherhood itself," Carrie Rosefsky Wickham writes in her 2013 book, *The Muslim Brotherhood: Evolution of an Islamist Movement*.[46]

By this time, Nasser had become close to Qutb, starting with meetings before the coup to bemoan the corrupt, un-Islamic monarchy. Post-coup, Nasser continued to meet and talk with Qutb for hours, seeking his advice on building a new state. But soon, this new government, created by former Brotherhood members, turned against the MB and instituted a secular constitution. Nasser outlawed the Brotherhood in January 1954 and arrested hundreds of Brothers, including Qaradawi. Another purge followed in September, with Qutb among the hundreds of Brothers rounded up.

Nasser sought to destroy the organization once and for all. Though its leaders denied involvement, the Brotherhood responded by attempting to assassinate him. But the eight gunshots fired by Brotherhood member Mahmud Abd Al-Latif at an October rally in Alexandria all missed their target. Nasser suddenly appeared heroic and invincible. The very next day, a mob set fire to Brotherhood headquarters in Cairo. Nasser arrested hundreds more Brothers every month and executed a handful of its leaders, along with Al-Latif.

Tens of thousands of MB members fled Egypt in the wake of Nasser's crackdown, mainly to Saudi Arabia and the Levant, creating the Brotherhood diaspora we know today, and that is outlined in the subsequent chapters. But by 1970, when the crackdowns eased under Anwar El-Sadat, the movement had branches and affiliates in Palestine, Syria, Kuwait, Jordan, Iraq, and Sudan. Before his death, Al-Banna had broadened his attacks to include the French, the Italians, the Dutch, and even India's policy in Kashmir—wherever Muslims were oppressed. This is in part because the Brotherhood ran a so-called foreign ministry that sent delegations to Muslims across Europe, Africa, China, and beyond, looking to harness opportunities wherever the group had a presence.

Al-Banna's son-in-law, Said Ramadan, emerged in this period as a key public face of the MB and de facto foreign minister. He later fled to Saudi Arabia, and in 1958 King Saud bin Abdulaziz Al-Saud forced him out. Ramadan moved to Geneva, where he founded the Islamic Center, a mosque, a think tank, and a community center. Later on, with help from the CIA, which saw him as assisting in the fight against communism, he spearheaded the construction of a mosque in Munich that would provide refuge for exiled MB members and become a hotspot for radicalism in Europe.[47] Ramadan's opening of Islamic centers in Europe was seen by the group's Egyptian leaders as an opportunity to use media freedom there to promote their cause internationally, though the differing perspectives of the Egyptian Brotherhood and its foreign branches would soon come to a head.

Back in Egypt, the Brotherhood splintered under Nasser's pressure, leading to schisms. Many Brothers lost faith in education as the best means to revolution and began to re-embrace violence. By late 1955, many observers believed the Brotherhood to be in its death throes in Egypt, as most of its key figures either had been killed or imprisoned or had fled. But the group quietly recovered.

Al-Banna's successor as the Brotherhood's general guide was a former judge, Hassan Al-Hudaybi, who "made it his top priority to purge violence from the organization and eradicate its secret apparatus," writes Kirkpatrick.[48] But, in the early 1960s, a splinter group led by Qutb concluded that any regime that could inflict such suffering on Muslims was irredeemably corrupt and could only be combated by arms. They sought to reestablish a secret paramilitary unit, in defiance of Al-Hudaybi, and smuggled weapons in from Sudan. In September 1965, Egyptian state media began reporting on a Brotherhood-run terrorist cell, known as Organisation 1965, that had plotted to kill Nasser and overthrow the regime.

Some doubted the accusations of a coup plot by a Nasserite regime that had become increasingly paranoid, but Israel, the United States, and the UK all believed the plot to be real.[49] Evidence revealed that the Brotherhood had been discussing a coup at least since Qutb's release from prison in May 1964, with a commando group organizing paramilitary training and stocking arms. It was during his time in prison, from 1955 to 1964, that Qutb wrote his landmark book, *Milestones along the Path*. This work would later become the foundation stone for extremist groups, including Egyptian Islamic Jihad, Al-Qaeda, and ISIS. "Some of Qutb's ideas—specifically

about the apostasy of dictatorships like Mubarak's—became a starting point for the thinking of Salafi jihadists like Ayman Al-Zawahiri of
Al-Qaeda," Kirkpatrick acknowledges.[50]

One of Qutb's key innovations in *Milestones* was how he expanded the
traditional Muslim concept of *Jahiliyya*, which refers to the "ignorance" of
pre-Islamic Arab lands, to modern times. Qutb extended the term to refer
to any state of blindness to God's power, applying it not only to the West
but also to Muslim countries that embraced secularism and capitalism.
The opposite of this is *Hakimiyyat*, which refers to the sovereign power of
God and the imposition of Islamic law. Qutb called on Muslim youth to
launch a jihad against the *Jahili* system exemplified by Nasser's regime
and establish his utopian model of a *Hakimiyyat* state. In 1965 Egypt, he
and his followers had sought to do precisely that. "But they were too
slow," writes Fitzpatrick. "Abdel Nasser learned of the scheme, broke up
the plot, and, in 1966, executed Qutb."[51]

RESURRECTED: A RETURN TO VIOLENCE

By mid-1968, with Nasser teetering in the wake of the disastrous Six
Day War, reports suggested that the MB was again plotting a coup. Yet, the
fact that the Brotherhood made no waves when Nasser died in September
1970, allowing Anwar El-Sadat to easily take power, underscored the reality: the group was a ghost of its former self. The most influential Islamic
group in Egypt, and perhaps the whole Muslim world, had been nearly
liquidated.

But El-Sadat proved friendlier to the Brotherhood, thanks to his long-
acknowledged connections to the group. He instituted a new constitution
that named Islam the official state religion and *Sharia* a source of law.[52]
He fired dozens of powerful Nasserite generals and released Brotherhood
members from prison if they agreed to not criticize him. This tacit approval of Islamism, combined with fewer restrictions on college campus
life, created an environment more conducive to Brotherhood growth. The
MB spent the next few years slowly regaining its strength, focusing on social work and community development and playing nice with the El-Sadat
regime. The Brotherhood needed to rebuild its structures after the evis-
cerations under Nasser and appreciated El-Sadat's disavowal of much of
what Nasser stood for.

During this time, a potent Islamist student movement emerged,
Al-Jama'at Al-Islamiya. Inevitably, these youth made their way to the
Brotherhood. Kirkpatrick recalls one momentous meeting:

One evening in 1974, a tall, slender medical student slipped into a busy shoe
store on Qasr el-Aini Street, not far from the hospital where he worked as a
resident. He did not need shoes; he was asked there to meet a Muslim Brother who had been released that year after twenty years in prison in Qena,

a six-hour drive south of Cairo. The storekeeper was another Muslim Brother. Shoe shopping was a pretense to allow them to speak outside the earshot of the secret police. The medical student, Abdel Moneim Aboul Fotouh, was then the leader of a new and independent Islamist student movement that was sweeping campuses. He was a born politician, handsome and articulate, with a round face and a ready smile. . . . At the moment of the meeting in the shoe store, Aboul Fotouh might have been the most influential Islamist in Egypt, or possibly in the region.[53]

Aboul Fotouh, then the head of Al-Jama'at, soon brought his student Islamists into the MB. They revitalized the movement after the dark years under Nasser, while Aboul Fotouh became, in the decades that followed, one of the Brotherhood's most prominent figures.

The October 1973 Yom Kippur War against Israel, which El-Sadat portrayed as a religious war, marked a key turning point. Islamists believed that the conflict restored Egypt's honor, just as "Abdel Nasser's promises of national greatness were shattered by his humiliation in the Six-Day War with Israel in 1967."[54] Echoing the ideas of Qutb, Brotherhood leaders began referring to Nasser's reign as a time of *Jahiliyya*, or ignorance, which by default meant that El-Sadat had brought enlightenment. But this did not cow Aboul Fotouh. In 1977, he attended a televised forum at Cairo University with El-Sadat, who was still riding high after the victory over Israel. At one point, Aboul Fotouh raised his hand:

> He wanted to know why El-Sadat's security agents had barred a popular sheikh from speaking in public. Was it because he criticized the government? Mr. President, Aboul Fotouh told El-Sadat, you are surrounded by "sycophants" and "hypocrites." "Stand right there, stop!" Sadat shouted. "I am the president of the family, the president of the country!" "I am standing, sir," Aboul Fotouh replied evenly. Many had gone to prison for less. Aboul Fotouh became an Islamist icon.[55]

The MB appealed to many of the new members from Al-Jama'at because of their more militant stance. "They felt much closer to the ideas of the Nizam Al-Khass [special apparatus] than they did to the more traditional Ikhwani school," Pargeter writes. "As Aboul Fotouh has said: Our ideas and our methodology was close to the methodology and the way of thinking of the Organisation 1965."[56]

Still, with this injection of young blood, the Brotherhood re-entered public life in Egypt in 1975 with a newspaper, *Al-Da'wa*, in which its leaders argued against the use of violence, portraying themselves as "preachers" rather than "revolutionaries."[57] Officially, the MB had renounced violence, but senior leaders like Mustafa Mashhur held the following view:

> Brotherhood leaders were clear that physical-force jihad—in some form— remained an eternal obligation for Muslims, prescribed in the Quran. Without

it, Mashhur stated, Muslims faced "conquest, humiliation, and extermination," whereas jihad secured their dignity and empowered Islam.[58]

The 1970s saw a resurgence of Qutbist thought among some MB members, which led to further splintering. One Brotherhood leader of that time was Ayman Al-Zawahiri, an acolyte of Qutb. Hassan Al-Hudaybi, supreme guide of the Muslim Brotherhood until his death in 1973, took issue with some members turning away from the gradual reformist approach of the Islamist movement. He outlined his arguments in his 1971 book *Preachers, Not Judges.* For obvious reasons, the increasingly militant presence of members of the Brotherhood who favored a more aggressive stance resulted in a crackdown by El-Sadat.

Around this time, Zawahiri left the Brotherhood to help establish Egyptian Islamic Jihad, a terrorist group with the same original objective as the Brotherhood: establishing Islamic rule in Egypt. Two decades later, Egyptian Islamic Jihad and Al-Zawahiri would join forces with Osama bin Laden and Al-Qaeda, etching into the history books an unavoidable reality: Al-Qaeda was cofounded by a former Brotherhood member.[59]

BROTHERS OF THE REVOLUTION

This is another reminder that, almost since its founding, the Brotherhood has been a group that has advocated violence and revolution. In his 1957 novel *Sugar Street*, Nobel Prize–winning Egyptian author Naguib Mahfouz sketched a vivid portrait of an MB member explaining the group's political stance during World War II:

> Islam is a creed, a way of worship, a nation and a nationality, a religion, a state, a form of spirituality, a Holy Book, and a sword. . . . Let us prepare for a prolonged struggle. Our mission is not to Egypt alone but to all Muslims worldwide. It will not be successful until Egypt and all other Islamic nations have accepted these Quranic principles in common. We shall not put our weapons away until the Quran has become a constitution for all Believers.[60]

From its inception, the group has been on the attack against secular society and democracy. In its very DNA, the MB is a revolutionary organization, primarily outfitted for turning against and seeking to overthrow the government through violence. Sometimes called the Brotherhood's "second founder,"[61] Qutb took the ideas of Al-Banna and extended them, arguing that Westernization and modernity were not only a threat to the Muslim way of life but threatened humanity with "complete annihilation." Only Muslims committed to violence and revolution could overcome this reign of ignorance.

In other words, they are revolutionaries, bent on using whatever means necessary to undermine governments and ultimately seize power. We know this because of their history, in which they have attacked and re-volted again and again, and because nothing in the Brotherhood platform or ideology suggests any real plan for governance. As Wickham notes in her 2013 book, "The Brotherhood never offered a detailed and coherent vision of the Islamic order it sought to create."[62]

Hassan Al-Banna took great pains to build an organization that stood in opposition to Western culture and ideas, to modernity and materialism. He spent his adult life calling for a return to the origins of Islam, to a state ruled by Islamic law—an end goal that would of course involve taking the reins of government. His call attracted thousands, tens of thousands, millions, across more than a dozen countries, who listened and spread the word. But over several decades, neither Al-Banna nor his successors ever laid out their vision for an Islamic state, took the time to bring the laws of the Prophet Mohammed and his followers into the modern day, or explained what the state might look like, how it might work, if their vision were to ever become reality. Scholar after analyst, journalist after researcher have found this to be the case. Kirkpatrick may have summed it up best:

> I would spend seven years studying debates about the true nature of the Brotherhood. What real agenda was it hiding behind its slogans? I learned that that question was all wrong. There never was a single, essential charac-ter of the Muslim Brotherhood, because the Brothers themselves never fully agreed with one another about any of these issues. Their ideology was not just ambiguous to the public; it was ambiguous even to them. Vagueness and flux, in fact, were the keys to the endurance of their movement. . . . [Al-Banna] pledged to work for a new caliphate and declared that the "Quran is our constitution." But he made clear that he regarded the caliph-ate as only a gauzy, end-of-history paradise. He denounced theocratic rule and "ecclesiastical tyranny." At times he said the best model for Islamic government was a democracy with the sort of written constitution found in the West. What might an Islamic state or society look like in practice? Al-Banna mostly avoided the question, or insisted that the answer would vary with time, place, and public consensus. [That is part of the reason Brotherhood-inspired groups differ from one country to the next.] His by-laws demanded absolute obedience, but the first internal rebellions, splits, and defections broke out within four years of the founding. They were still roiling when I lived in Cairo. The Muslim Brotherhood was tethered to a core vision and history, to be sure. But it was always changing and never monolithic. Should I fear the Muslim Brothers? Their reputation for vio-lence was so pervasive in the West that I took special care to understand that legacy. Al-Banna had talked avidly of jihad, martyrdom, and "the art of death" in defense of Islam.[63]

This fact, that the MB never knew its own vision for an Islamic state, proves more than anything else that the Brotherhood is, always has been, and always will be more focused on revolution than rule. What's more, MB discourse on state institutions presents several contradictions and ambiguities. There's tension between the ultimate authority of God as expressed by Sharia and the authority of the nation's elected representatives in parliament or local councils in accordance with the popular will. The main known element of any possible Brotherhood state is that it would be unable to accept any accepted leader or monarch. "The MB mimics some central features of a state in its hierarchical structure and the requirement for members to swear an exclusive oath of loyalty to the Murshid. However, it repudiates national identity and any loyalty other than that to the Murshid and God," Sir John Jenkins, former British ambassador to Saudi Arabia and author of the British government's strategic assessment of the MB, wrote in an Oxford commentary paper in November 2017.[64]

The group's position on the rights of those who do not subscribe to its agenda is also unclear—for example, its stance on the right of the private citizen to choose his or her own values and lifestyle. In claiming to represent all Muslims and portraying its message as the only true and correct understanding of Islam, the MB exhibits intolerance toward dissent—which gives its ideology a rigid and coercive tone. Its ambivalence toward formal political institutions like parliament and political parties is also unsettling. The Brotherhood participated in electoral politics as early as 1941, but due to disappointing election results its members gave it up, only to re-embrace it decades later.

Furthermore, MB operations and ideology have much in common with revolutionary socialism. In Ismailia, the Brotherhood contained both middle- and lower-class elements. But eventually people from the lower middle class occupied the top positions, giving the Brotherhood the popular and non-elitist character that it retained even after it had become an influential political force. In addition, protecting the organization's financial independence was a major concern for Al-Banna. He advocated a policy of non-reliance on local authorities for financial aid to welfare projects and relied on benefactors who were not in a position to dominate the movement. Thus, the Brotherhood's professed nonalignment with the dominant political forces, underpinned by its financial independence, added much credibility to its ideological program—and its revolutionary agenda.

Put another way, all the bombings and coup plotting leading up to 1965 were not out of character for the group. Its primary agenda is establishing an Islamic state under its own precepts. Al-Banna described the Brotherhood's two main goals thusly: "According to Al-Banna, the Brotherhood's main goals were freeing the Islamic fatherland from foreign control and the establishment of a free Islamic state under the rule of Sharia."[65]

But what, exactly, is the Islamic fatherland? Al-Banna sought to restore an "Islamic Empire" that included parts of Spain, Italy, and Eastern

Europe and then expand to the whole world. Who decides what qualifies as foreign domination? Does the U.S. Air Force base at Al-Udeid qualify as foreign domination of Qatar? It very well might, and thus Doha would be ripe for revolution. Who knows what other states, in the Gulf or beyond, might qualify. Perhaps Al-Banna and later Qutb sought to free all Muslim countries from Western influence and put non-Muslim countries under Muslim control. By the beginning of the twenty-first century, the Brotherhood had Europe in its sights.

CHAPTER 2

The Muslim Brotherhood in Northern Africa—Algeria, Libya, Morocco, Tunisia, Sudan

From its founding in Egypt, the Brotherhood soon spread westward across the Maghreb, with Islamists building beachheads in every country in the region. The tales of these affiliates vary considerably, and in this chapter I'll detail the experiences of the Brotherhood in Algeria, Libya, Morocco, Tunisia, and Sudan.

In these countries and in accordance with the MB's clandestine practices, MB affiliates have often taken on different names to conceal their links to the leading organization in Egypt. While levels of political participation vary, the overall picture is one of organizations struggling to distance themselves from the Egyptian MB and its connections to violence and revolution while attempting to maintain a coherently progressive narrative and to appear amenable to working within an established governmental system.

ALGERIA

Islam and Muslim identity have been a crucial part of the Algerian character since before the state's founding in 1962. Standing against the Christian colonizer, France, in a years-long struggle for liberation, became in part about embracing an Arab-Muslim identity: those who died in the war are still called *chouhada*, or martyrs. This is largely thanks to Sheikh Ahmed Sahnoun, the godfather of Algerian Islamists and a Brotherhood leader who, along with the MB in Egypt, called for jihad against the French occupiers.[1] The National Liberation Front, or FLN, spearheaded Algeria's revolution, but this explains why Algerians were so ready for Islamism when it arrived in the 1960s.

It should be noted, however, that political Islam in Algeria has always been deeply fragmented into various factions and that many have embraced radicalism and turned to violent jihad. Over the decades, no charismatic leader has emerged to unite them under a single vision. As a result, the country's military, which has dominated power almost since independence, has been able to skillfully manipulate Algeria's various Islamist parties and render them nearly a non-factor—either toothless government backers or greatly marginalized terrorists.

As in most countries across the region, the MB made its way into Algeria via education. In the years surrounding independence, many Egyptians were brought on to teach at Algerian universities—a good number of these men were MB members. Mahfoud Nahnah, an Arabic professor at the University of Algiers at the time, fell in with some MB-member colleagues, paid a few lengthy visits to Egypt, and soon joined the movement.

The Algerian state, dominated at that time by the FLN, attempted to control Islam through its new Religious Affairs Ministry. As in Turkey, Islamic scholars and imams were state employees, and religious conservatives bridled against the state's yoke, viewing a series of policies as overly liberal and secular.

This frustration prodded the ruling party to bring in two Islamic scholars to boost its religious credentials: Mohammed Al-Ghazali and Yusuf Al-Qaradawi, both MB members. They called for an Islamic revival in Algeria, largely ignoring the FLN. Still, the frustrations of conservatives built and boiled over in 1988, with violent protests and rioting across northern Algeria. The clashes only ended after President Chadli Bendjedid met with MB members.

The next year, the state abolished the single-party system, sparking a burst of new political parties. In 1990, Al-Qaradawi was named to a position of some influence: Chair of Algeria's Scientific Council of Islamic University and Higher Institutions, and from there he continued to spread MB ideas.[2] That same year, with the coming of the country's first multi-party elections after decades of single-party rule, Nahnah created his own party, known as Hamas (though later renamed the Movement of Society for Peace, or MSP). Hamas adopted much of the Brotherhood's organizational model and many of its religious ideas, including its commitment to a pan-Islamic state based on Sharia.

However, it was not Hamas that emerged as Algeria's leading Islamist political group. Rather, the Islamic Salvation Front, or FIS, won most mayoral offices and municipal majorities in the 1990 local elections. The group was not completely disconnected from the MB; Ali Belhadj, one of the co-founders of the FIS, had been educated by MB teachers and embraced a similar ideology. The party's goals were to eliminate French language and culture and install an Islamic state. A charismatic speaker, Belhadj saw secular democracy as a threat to Sharia and often preached to thousands of frustrated youth.

After winning the local elections, FIS also took the first round of 1991 parliamentary elections, gaining 54 percent of the vote. Faced with an Islamist party taking power, the military canceled the results and the second parliamentary round and reclaimed power.

Enraged with the generals' dismissal of the electoral process, various radical elements within the FIS and other Islamist parties banded together to launch a guerilla war on the military state.

Hamas stayed out of the fray, aligning with the government during the conflict and remaining a peaceful organization. As a reward, and a way to co-opt the Islamists, Algeria's military government appointed several MSP members to the cabinet in 1995 during the height of violence.[3] Some members of Hamas joined the insurgents, however, notably the armed wing of FIS, known as the Islamic Salvation Army, or AIS, and the more radical Armed Islamic Group, or GIA. Some rebel leaders were strongly influenced by the MB. AIS leader Madani Mezraq, for instance, cited Hassan Al-Banna's collection of letters as one of his most important Islamist influences.[4] Around 1998, the GIA became the Salafist Group for Call and Combat, which later evolved into Al-Qaeda in the Islamic Maghreb.[5]

Throughout this "Black Decade" of violence, MB leaders in Egypt called for dialogue while quietly backing the Islamist rebels. In one interview, Al-Qaradawi argued that their violent struggle was legitimate.[6] The brutal civil war took hundreds of thousands of lives. Unsurprisingly, the military crushed the AIS and other rebel groups, leaving Nahnah's MSP in an entirely new political landscape with just one Islamist rival: Al-Nahda.

Violence declined following the election of Abdelaziz Bouteflika as president in 1999, as many Islamists de-radicalized and returned to politics. The MSP emerged from the civil war as Algeria's most popular Islamist party. But after Nahnah's death in 2003, the party shed its Islamist image, giving up on creating a Sharia-based society and becoming largely co-opted by the government. The next year, MSP joined an alliance with two secular parties that helped keep Bouteflika in power.[7]

In addition to their failure to influence policy, corruption scandals eroded the party's credibility further still—the most sordid being MSP vice president Boujerra Soltani's using his position as Minister of Labor and Social Security to help embezzle $1.5 billion and generate kickbacks. "The party seemed to have little in the way of concrete proposals on economic, social, and other policies being debated in the post-conflict period," writes Fellow at the Foreign Policy Research Institute's Program on the Middle East, Vish Sakthivel, in 2017; hence, "party unity suffered, rival splinters multiplied, and serial defections ensued."[8]

This is a good description of Algeria's Islamist politics at the time. An array of Islamist parties emerged in the late 1990s and 2000s, dividing and joining forces, often confusing voters; for instance, Abdallah Djaballah founded the MB-linked party Al-Nahda in 1989, then founded El-Islah years later after he was ejected from Al-Nahda, and finally created a third party, the Justice and Development Front, or Adala, in 2011. One hardly knew who hailed from which party, much less what that party stood for.

In 2009, several key members of MSP broke away, alleging that the group had achieved nothing after fourteen years in government.[9] Three years later, the MSP merged with Ennahda and El-Islah to form the Green Algeria Alliance, which lost the election that year and broke up. MSP then merged with the small Islamist party, Front for Change (FC). The duo boycotted the 2014 vote, but took part in 2017, coming in third place. However, the MSP-FC alliance refused to join the government, citing electoral fraud.

In the last two decades, MSP has been in a position of potential influence, in large part because it has been able to distance itself from the armed radicals of the civil war years. However, it has achieved very little. During the so-called Arab Spring it also distanced itself from the government, which made little difference.

Due to decades of colonial dominance by France, Algerians are loathe to see signs of a foreign hand. Thus, Nahnah's Hamas and then MSP have tended to downplay the role and influence of the Egyptian MB. However, after the ousting of Mohammed Morsi in July 2013, MSP president Abdul-Razzaq Al-Maqri said, "This is not a coup against Morsi, but against democracy."[10] Nevertheless, MSP's interactions with the Egyptian MB are very careful—and it has even discussed dropping the label of "Islamist," as Tunisia's Ennahda has done.[11] In May 2017, Al-Maqri, after refusing to join the government and maintaining his party's position that it must remain in opposition to "keep up with the democratic logic," said that his movement is not an MB branch and is not affiliated with Ennahda or Morocco's Justice and Development Party.[12]

The YouTube channel QatariLeaks tells a different story, however. It calls the Algerian Muslim Brotherhood "Qatar's devastating tool."[13] It highlights how Qatar uses the MB to penetrate Arab societies and, in the case of Algeria, to control its gas and financial assets. In order to do this, it uses the tactic of "igniting strife between the state and extremists led by the MB."[14] It also points out that its tool for this penetration is Al Jazeera and that the MSP supported Qatar against the so-called Boycott Quartet (Saudi Arabia, Egypt, the UAE, and Bahrain). Al-Maqri criticized Algeria's position toward Qatar and support of the Quartet, created a committee of solidarity with the Hamadein of Qatar over and against the Arabs of the Quartet, and lashed out at Saudi Arabia for its "normalization" of Israel.

"The Algerian MB has received considerable support from Qatar, both financial and ideological, via Al Jazeera," a former director of DGSE, France's foreign intelligence agency, told me, "and Al-Maqri's statements against the Saudi-led blockade clearly show which side they are on."[15] Qatar has provided funding for Al-Maqri's campaign[16] and the Brotherhood affiliates in Algeria.[17] In turn, Prime Minister Ahmed Ouyahia spoke out against Qatar's divisive tactics and said Doha sought to destroy Algeria the way it had Libya.[18]

The MSP's support for Qatar was a common reaction among Northern African MB affiliates.[19] The Algerian Parliamentary Committee, made up of MB members, quickly went to Doha to try to end the crisis. Rached Ghannouchi, the Tunisian politician and co-founder of the Ennahdha Party, requested that Turkey step in and try to help Qatar out of its bind, given Turkey and Tunisia's close relations. These efforts by the Brotherhood's North African branches came at the same time as the MB's claim that the boycott was "haram" (religiously forbidden), as well as "an official statement it issued threatening the countries that abide by the act."[20]

In further indication of its Ikhwani roots, MSP has embraced its links to the Palestinian terror group Hamas, an MB spawn. The MSP provides aid to Hamas, such as the construction of Gaza's Mahfoud Nahnah High School.[21] Its connections to the other Hamas have boosted its status and reputation within Algeria, which is more openly pro-Palestine than other North African states. For one thing, stressing its strong bond to Hamas has been a boon to MSP recruitment. As Abdellah Yousfi, the MSP official responsible for Palestine in Blida, told Sakthivel: "Hamas and MSP are the same movement: we are Hamas Algeria; they are Hamas Palestine."[22]

With signs of the FIS returning to the political playing field in Algeria, the prospects of MB-linked MSP have dimmed further still. Today, Algeria's main Brotherhood party risks fading into irrelevance, as the influence of the country's Islamists continues to decline. As Algerian extremism researcher Dr. Dalia Ghanem-Yazbeck says:

> The MSP has always been pragmatic and favored dialogue and compromise with the regime. But while this approach sustained the MSP as a key player in Algeria for decades, it may no longer be effective. Instead, after years of working with what is known as le pouvoir (the power)—the country's main nationalist party, the National Liberation Front (FLN), together with the bureaucracy and the military—the party has been co-opted. This has weakened its claim to be an opposition force, cut its support among the public, and led it toward a political dead end.[23]

LIBYA

If Algeria's Islamists lost influence because they changed their stripes, moving away from the MB's revolutionary ideals, Libya's MB affiliate has failed for the opposite reason—embracing the extremist violence that is part of the MB's heritage.

Muslim Brothers fleeing Nasser's crackdown in Egypt arrived in Libya in the 1950s. Their first real organizational system had to wait until 1968, and even that effort was disrupted the following year by the coup of Colonel Qaddafi.[24] The MB had hoped to establish a new branch, yet it was unable to operate openly for decades, as King Idris and then Qaddafi banned the group.

Qaddafi-run media referred to them as "deviant heretics" and "stray dogs" and hung the heads of their members from lampposts in the mid-1980s.[25] After that, the Libyan MB largely became an in-exile organization, with the "Islamic Group—Libya" being reborn in the United States and elsewhere. Upon their return, jail and severe repression were all that greeted them.

In 1999, the Libyan MB began a dialogue with the regime, largely due to Saif Al-Islam Qaddafi's efforts to co-opt Islamist groups in the country. This was part of a larger effort to allow MB members back into the country via an amnesty policy that would pardon opponents and dissidents that had been fighting with the Libyan Mujahideen in Afghanistan. Qaddafi and his advisers feared their return as armed professionals who might threaten the government and instead wanted to invite them to return with the hopes of neutralizing their rebellious intentions and abilities.[26]

In 2009, the former general observer of the Libyan MB, Soliman Abd Al-Qadr, "estimated the numbers of MB figures in exile to be around 200 and inside Libya to be a few thousands, mainly concentrated in the professional and student sectors."[27] Then with the arrival of the so-called Arab Spring and the killing of Qaddafi, Libya's MB could finally come out of the shadows: the group held a press conference in November 2011 to announce the creation of the Justice and Construction Party, which would contest the next year's elections and quickly became Libya's largest Islamist party.

Yet even this move was marred by contradictions inherent to so much of the MB's history. For instance, Abdel Latif Karmous, head of the Libyan Muslim Brotherhood's Shura Council, said at the time, "the party is separate from the Brotherhood because lots of people say the party is the Brotherhood which is not the case. The Justice and Construction Party (JCP) is a different organization. Unfortunately the JCP has been damaged by its association with the Brotherhood because of Qaddafi's propaganda against us."[28]

Widely expected to perform well, the JCP disappointed, taking just 10 percent of the vote and gaining seventeen out of eighty seats. But the worst was yet to come. As Libya devolved into chaos, its MB affiliate soon began working with other Islamist terrorist groups. The militias caused the secular government to flee the capital in 2014. The country then split into two rival factions—the Tobruk government and the National Salvation Government—each a tenuous coalition of militias and tribes.

By 2014, the militias had grown to over 300,000 members. The strongest of them were the Islamists in Misrata, who represented the MB; were armed with heavy artillery, tanks, and missiles; and received their funding from theft, salaries the government paid them, the so-called Loyalty to Martyrs group, and the MB:

> These two blocs used threats and outright force to pass the controversial Political Isolation Law . . . with the outward aim of removing leaders with ties to the Qaddafi regime, but the real intention was excluding competitors from the political process. [This law] cast a wide net with a very negative impact on the administration of the country, removing many qualified officials with unblemished records other than holding high government positions under Qaddafi's 42-year rule.[29]

The United States' "Muslim Brotherhood Terrorist Designation Act of 2015" accused Libyan MB units of "joining forces with United States-designated terrorist organizations, particularly Ansar Al-Sharia."[30] Ansar Al-Sharia is the group the United States blames for the 2012 attack on the U.S. consulate in Benghazi in which Ambassador Christopher Stevens was killed. Reports have suggested that it was MB members who were guarding the Benghazi consulate on the night of the attack.

As a result, secular Libyan politicians repeatedly accused the JCP of links to extremist groups, and the party fared poorly—winning just 25 of 200 parliamentary seats in the 2014 election. In October 2017, Colonel Ahmed Al-Masmary, spokesman for the Libyan National Army, announced that ISIS and MB affiliates linked to Al-Qaeda were working together in Libya.[31] The Libyan military commander, Khalifa Haftar, said around the same time that the Brotherhood was "a terrorist group and alleged that it constitutes the greatest threat to the country."[32]

As is common with MB affiliates, this terrorist threat to Libya was financed by none other than Qatar. Just as Saudi Arabia, the UAE, Bahrain, and Egypt have supported the country's legitimate government based in the East, Doha has backed the radical Islamists seeking to destabilize the country and wreak havoc. These efforts began during the 2011 revolution to oust Muammar Qaddafi, according to David B. Roberts, reader at King's College London and author of *Qatar: Securing the Global Ambitions of a City-State*. "Qatar was a particularly enthusiastic partner," he wrote for Foreign Affairs in September 2011.

> The Arab emirate of just 1.6 million people, rich in oil and gas, was the first Arab country to recognize the rebel government, the Transitional National Council. It sold Libyan oil on behalf of the rebels to avoid sanctions and supplied them with gas, diesel, and millions of dollars in aid. And Al Jazeera, the satellite broadcaster based in Doha, covered the struggle of the Libyan rebels in even greater detail and depth than it has the Arab world's other revolutionary movements. . . . This move signaled a qualitative change in Qatari foreign policy. . . . Never before has Qatar so overtly supported one side or made such an active intervention.[33]

Roberts goes on to add that Qatar sent arms, including anti-tank mis-siles, brought Libyan fighters back to Doha for training, and took part in front lines fighting in the final assault on Qaddafi's compound at Bab Al-Aziziya.[34] And this committed backing from Doha didn't end with the fall of Qaddafi. Since the revolution, Qatar "has been sending massive amounts of weapons and cash to Islamist militants battling the Western-backed government in Libya," Jonathan Schanzer, senior vice president at the Foundation for Defense of Democracies, wrote for *Newsweek* in August 2017.[35] "Massive amounts" seems an apt phrase. As of June 2017, Qatar had sent more than $850 million in funds and supplies to Al-Qaeda–linked fighters in Libya.[36] As of early 2019, the number is likely over a bil-lion dollars.

None of this is secret. In October 2011, the Qatari chief-of-staff, Major General Hamad bin Ali Al-Attiyya, acknowledged his country's close sup-port for the rebels. "We were among them and the numbers of Qataris on the ground were hundreds in every region. Training and communications had been in Qatari hands," he told AFP, adding that Qatar "supervised the rebels' plans because they are civilians and did not have enough military experience."[37] Less than two years later, the UN Security Council cited Qatar for violating the UN arms embargo by "providing military material to the revolutionary forces through the organization of a large number of flights and the deliveries of a range of arms and ammunition."[38]

This funding did not go toward supporting legitimate rebels but to hardcore Islamist radicals. In his *Newsweek* article, Schanzer states: "Arab states are not simply bothered by Qatar's support for garden variety Islamists. They allege that Qatar is directly backing the worst of the worst. And they appear to be correct."[39]

According to Kristian Coates Ulrichsen of the Baker Institute for Pub-lic Policy, Qatar maintains close ties with the leader of the Libyan Islamic Fighting Group, Abdelhakim Belhadj, who has twice met with Osama bin Laden.[40] Al Masry Al Youm cited connections between Doha and Al-Qaeda–linked outfits Ansar Al-Sharia and the Benghazi Revolution-ary Shura Council.[41] In August 2018, Qatari MB figures spoke at a funeral prayer for a slain Libyan jihadi with connections to ISIS.[42]

In May 2018, France attempted to initiate a conference that would help fashion a political road map for Libya. No military figures were invited, however, in a clear exclusion of Commander Haftar. Khaled Al-Mishri, head of the High Council of State, said that only Prime Minister Al-Sarraj, President of the House of Representatives Aguila Saleh, and the High Council of State should attend the conference.

The fourteen militias seeking Islamist rule, including the MB and Al-Qaeda, voiced their rejection of the initiative, because "it is a call that aims 'to nationalize military rule,' and asserted the significance of 'a civil state and the peaceful devolution of power.'"[43] As has so often been the case throughout the MB's history, the group's willingness to abide, and even support, jihadi violence while claiming a desire for "a civil state and the peaceful devolution to power" has undermined its impact and outlook.

It's clear that Qatar supported militias linked to the MB and Al-Qaeda since the start of the revolution, spending countless millions to spur continued violence and greater destabilization in Libya. More recently, Doha may have handed this responsibility to Ankara—to which it appears to have given much of its MB support duties since the imposition of the blockade in mid-2017. On consecutive days in December 2018, arms shipments from Turkey were stopped at Khoms port, near Tripoli, carrying 3,000 guns and more than 4 million bullets.[44] The United Nations called the discovery "extremely disconcerting."[45] An Algerian security official said Turkey's shipments were meant to destabilize Libya and further undermine an unstable region.[46]

Khoms is a relatively minor port, likely chosen because controls there might be less rigorous and thus might allow the secrets arms shipments to slip through, according to Zvi Mazel, former Israeli ambassador to Egypt, Romania, and Sweden and senior researcher at the Jerusalem Center for Public Affairs.[47] "From the nature of the contraband weapons, it is fairly obvious they were not intended for a regular army, but rather for terrorist activities of armed groups, most probably Islamic organisations linked to the Muslim Brotherhood," Mazel wrote in the *Jerusalem Post* in January 2019.[48]

The shipments violate a UN Security Council weapons embargo on Libya in place since the start of the civil war in 2011. As of early 2019, the country remains split between the pro-Islamist Government of National Accord, led by Fayez al Sarraj in Tripoli and recognized by the UN, and the Tobruk government, led by General Khalifa Haftar, de facto ruler of eastern Libya and head of the Libyan National Army.

As violence continued, dozens of radical Islamist militias emerged, with some being linked to the MB. The local branch of the Islamic State (ISIS) is still active, though greatly diminished. Both Libyan governments condemned the arms shipments from Turkey, and Haftar demanded an investigation from the UN Security Council.

The fact that Ankara was helping Islamic organizations involved in Libya's civil war was already known. In 2013, Greek customs agents found Turkish-made weapons in a Libya-bound ship that had sought shelter from a storm in a Greek port. "Turkey had sided with Islamic parties led by the Muslim Brotherhood immediately after the fall of Qaddafi," wrote Mazel. "Those parties won the first parliamentary elections held the following year. Ankara maintained its support when they lost the subsequent elections in 2014."[49]

Two weeks after the Khoms discovery, officials in Misrata intercepted another shipment of Turkish weapons in a container marked as carrying children's toys.[50] This came the day after an assassination attempt on the lead Libyan investigator into the Khoms shipment.[51] Also, in late 2018, police in Tobruk recently chased down two Land Cruisers and found them packed with Turkish weapons.[52]

Ankara, which is in cahoots with Qatar, likely sees an opportunity in the chaos of Libya to create a safe space for MB-linked groups now that Egypt is basically a no-go zone. "Turkey's goal might not only be the empowerment of radical groups to destabilize Libya," Michael Rubin, resident scholar at the American Enterprise Institute, wrote for the *National Interest* in January 2019: "An Islamist Libya could provide refuge for groups dedicated to undercutting Egypt's stability and returning Islamists to power."[53]

MOROCCO

Abdelkrim Al-Khatib, Morocco's first surgeon and a well-known political figure, founded Morocco's first Brotherhood-linked group in 1967. But the group did next to nothing in its early decades. Its political edition, the Justice and Development Party (PJD), was born in 1994, after members of *Chabiba Islamia*, a secret radical Islamist group, and the Movement for Unification and Reform, or MUR (previously Jama'at Al-Islamiyya and also known by a shortened version of its Arabic name, *Al-Tawhid*), united with Al-Khatib. MUR had been led by Abdelilah Benkirane, who continued to hold a leadership position in the new party and later became Morocco's prime minister.

Another MB-affiliated movement, the Justice and Charity Group (JCG, also known by a shortened version of its Arabic name, *Al-Adl*), emerged in 1987, founded by a Sufi leader, Sheikh Abdessalam Al-Yassin. Both JCG and the PJD are said to have been influenced by Turkey's Islamists, led by Necmettin Erbakan, who in turn had been heavily influenced by the MB. But while JCG rejects the monarchy and refuses to participate in politics, calling for full democracy, the PJD ran in the elections of 1997 and won nine parliamentary seats.

From 1997 to 2002 the party focused on reducing corruption and promoting ethical and religious issues. But a great deal of antagonism developed between the PJD and the leftist and secular parties in parliament, with the latter scrutinizing the party's relationship with MUR, its ideological arm, and orchestrating an anti-PJD media campaign following the 2003 terrorist attacks in Casablanca—even though PJD condemned the attack.

The PJD participated in politics according to the dictates of the constitution and at the same time maintained links with MUR. Some MUR members felt their political participation compromised the religious and social character of the movement; others felt that while Islam was all encompassing, this functional separation made sense.[54]

The PJD limited candidates to 18 percent of electoral districts— and remarkably won the presidency of seventeen municipalities. The leadership shifted its focus to management and administrative decisions. It also dropped its unconditional support for Islamic identity and lost MUR's support as a result. The PJD refashioned itself into a party less concerned with theological issues and more involved in social and economic issues.

Over the years, the party has made tremendous efforts to present itself as an exemplary block in parliament by implementing initiatives for attendance, questions, training, and legislation. Its vision of constitutional reform included new mechanisms to secure the independence of the judiciary, the expansion of supervisory and legislative prerogatives of the House of Representatives and a review of those of the House of Councilors, and a guarantee that the executive branch was accountable to parliament.[55]

In order to promote constitutional and legal reforms, the PJD had to form coalitions with other opposition forces—and thus took a mild approach in its platform. For example, instead of referring to Sharia, the PJD's 2007 electoral platform mentioned "the protection of Morocco's Islamic identity" as its main religious-based priority.

The party promoted a healthy, competitive, and open economy, as well as a generous redistribution of wealth to combat poverty, deal with the negative consequences of unemployment, and cover the costs of a universal healthcare system. The PJD positioned themselves as "the good men"— pragmatic managers of local issues, fostering good neoliberal governance.[56] Their religiosity became less marked, with emphasis placed on the needs of the local population. This accommodation and integration strategy, however, turned out to be politically costly for the party, as it lost votes in the 2007 legislative elections.

The next year, Benkirane won an internal vote and became the party's secretary-general. His election to head the PJD was a bit of a surprise, as he was known for his polemical declarations and hopes to "moralize political life."[57] But he was also known for being an accommodationist, advocating gradual reform and compromise with the monarchy despite his sometimes hawkish rhetoric.

Benkirane confirmed his commitment to the convention's political hypothesis, which included a democratic struggle with an eye on participation in governance. With the economic argument taking prominence, the party's relationship with Islam was largely euphemized. References were rarely made to Sharia, the MB, or MUR. In addition, like traditional political parties, the PJD put in place forms of personalized social and institutional mediation with voters. It emphasized its availability to constituents and its readiness to serve and insisted that services provided were not subject to favoritism but were rather normal services that citizens had the right to claim.

After the stinging disappointment of 2007, the PJD came out strongly against the 2008 budget law, arguing that it showed the government's lack of concrete plans to resolve the country's economic issues to help the common person. This message was well received, but it did not bear full fruit until the arrival of the so-called Arab Spring, with its theme of opposition to unfeeling, authoritarian states.

The Arab uprisings played in favor of the PJD, as the monarchy learned from the protests that it needed to broaden its democracy to include the Islamists. The PJD depicted Moroccan politics as displaying worrisome signs of an entrenched authoritarianism encompassing the judiciary, the bureaucracy, and the Sahara cause. But the PJD did not participate in the February 20, 2011, protests, rather choosing to support them from a distance.

When the protests snowballed, it became apparent that the monarchy would wisely not respond with force. The PJD began to highlight the accuracy of its previous agenda, which stressed slow but sure reforms.[58] This approach helped the PJD win a plurality (27 percent) in the elections and win the prime ministership, making Morocco the first Arab country to have an Islamist head of government.

Overall, the PJD succeeded because it played it smart, running on an inclusive style of governance predicated on gradual societal and state change while campaigning on a record of socioeconomic stability, justice, and transparency. Using social media wisely, it pressured the key political actor in the country (the monarchy), yet refrained from clashing with it by making alliances with other opposition movements to facilitate such pressures and avoid isolation.[59]

The party has led the country's coalition government ever since. Its performance has not been perfect: public frustration has increased with the Benkirane government's incremental reforms and apparent scandals, including a massive drug bust and two party vice presidents found in a "sexual position" on the beach.[60] Protests have erupted sporadically to condemn government decisions and lack of progress.

But the party seems to be effectively changing the political calculus in Morocco by presenting a positive governance alternative and operating within the political system. By following the rules of the game and openly seeking to mitigate the authoritarian features of the state, the PJD is pressing forward improvements in major socioeconomic issues. The Moroccan model of political Islamism is one that is "characterized by molding specific state religious policy, deploying Islam selectively and strategically, resetting the power relationship between political party and allied religious wings, and proactively navigating domestic and international competition."[61]

Some might say Morocco's Islamists have carved their own path and countered the predictions that mainstream political Islam is on the wane. But can the PJD even be considered Islamist? The group has found some measure of success by giving up its Islamist ideals. As a result, it should really no longer be seen as a Brotherhood affiliate. "Religious authority is

with his majesty as the commander of the faithful," Benkirane said to Mohamed Daadaoui, Assistant Political Science Professor at Oklahoma State
University.[62] No leader of a Brotherhood party, or any serious Islamist, for
that matter, would ever make a statement like that.

"While Morocco is often viewed in the West as one of the region's more
secular countries, the very fact that the monarchy is so intimately involved
with religious initiatives both at home and abroad belies this," Senior
Brookings Institute Fellows Shadi Hamid and Peter Mandeville wrote in
November 2018.

> With this in mind, the country's main Islamist party, the Justice and Devel-
> opment Party (PJD), entered into a bargain: it could participate and even
> govern—of course under the watchful eye of the royal court—as long as
> it accepted that religious legitimacy resided in the king and only the king.
> To question his role as commander of the faithful was tantamount to her-
> esy. As scholar of Middle Eastern and North African politics Avi Spiegel
> writes, "PJD officials still evoke religion, but almost never in opposition to
> the state."[63]

PJD's desire to remain valid within the Moroccan political sphere has led
to the stripping away of any overtly religious aspects. It has pressured the
key political actor in the country—the king—but refrained from clashing
with him, making alliances with other opposition movements to avoid
isolation. Unsurprisingly, the extremists of ISIS and Al-Qaeda, originally
descended from the MB, have taken issue with the PJD, claiming that "no
type of Islam nor Islamism in Morocco is haqiqi," or authentic.[64] In a July
2014 video, an ISIS leader referred to JCG founder Al-Yassin as a "polythe-
ist." The same reasons have largely led to the absence of Qatar—the main
supporter of MB affiliates around the world—in Morocco and the PJD.

"The case of the PJD in Morocco offers a clear example of an MB-
inspired group that continues to struggle to separate itself from Islamism,"
a former director of DGSE, France's foreign intelligence agency, told me
in November 2017. "The more it moves away, the less it has anything to
stand for, so while it might gain some votes in elections, it has effectively
pulled its own platform out from underneath itself."[65]

In Morocco, at least, MB-linked organizations face a stark choice: either
sacrifice the MB vision and embrace a monarch-dominated political system or remain on the margins, making little to no impact. JCG is outlawed,
and many of its members have been arrested, particularly after protests
demanding reform in the wake of regional uprisings.[66] Despite thousands
of followers, the JCP's influence has fallen considerably since Al-Yassin's
death on December 25, 2012. Today it's all but irrelevant. The PJD may
have secured a foothold in government, but due to its accommodationist
posture toward the monarchy and strict renunciations of Islamist positions, it has been largely discredited as an MB group.[67]

TUNISIA

The establishment of Tunisia as a French protectorate in the late nine-teenth century brought about a new social and economic order. More importantly, it also bifurcated Tunisian society into the elites, who were heavily influenced by the French colonialists, and the poorer, more con-servative majority, who tended to be more deeply religious and became essentially second-class citizens.

Over time, upper class, urban Tunisians who sought a Western edu-cation for their own children were granted access to French institutions. Naturally, this altered the Muslim learning institutions that were already in place, secularizing a significant part of Tunisian society. Side by side, two different societies operated—the rural countryside that strove to pre-serve traditional Tunisian values and a modern society that reflected a French way of life. Unsurprisingly, the relationship between the Muslim and French enclaves became strained.

Rached Ghannouchi, the figurehead of Tunisian Islamism, was born to a poor farming family in the south in 1941. With financial help from an older brother, he graduated from the prestigious Zaytouna University, in Tunis, in 1962. Frustrated with Tunisian president Habib Bourguiba's aping of the West, Ghannouchi left for Cairo in 1964 to study agriculture and learn about Arab nationalism, but the Bourguiba regime soon called all Tuni-sians back from Egypt. It was just as well, for Ghannouchi had quickly become "appalled by Nasser's crackdown on the Muslim Brotherhood."[68]

Ghannouchi moved to Syria, where he began to study Islamism in 1966. His timing was prescient: after the Arabs' swift and stunning defeat in the Six-Day War the following year, many began to abandon Arab na-tionalism and move toward Islam as a uniting force. As Habib Ellouze, a Tunisian Arab nationalist–turned Islamist, put it: "1967 was a turning point; it left deep scars among the youth and an identity problem began to emerge."[69]

Ghannouchi and others came to believe that the nationalist way was wrong. Even though his heart was perfectly reassured of Islam, he realized that what he had been following "was not the right Islam but a traditional and primitive version of it. The traditional model was not ideological, nor did it represent a comprehensive system. It was a conventional and reli-gious sentiment, a set of traditions, customs, and rituals that fell short of representing a civilization or a way of life."[70]

Ghannouchi left for Paris for his postgraduate studies. There he became more deeply involved in Islam, eventually toiling as an imam in a poor suburb. He returned to Tunis in 1970 to launch a loose, underground or-ganization called Al-Jama'a Al-Islamiyya (the Islamic Group), with Abdel-fattah Mourou. The movement focused on greater religiosity and public morality rather than political issues. Ghannouchi delivered courses on the Quran and traveled the country conducting *dawa*.[71] "Our work focused on the development of ideological conscience and consisted essentially of a critique of the Western concepts which dominate the spirit of youth," Ghannouchi said.[72]

In 1978 there was a violent clash between the leftist trade union and the government. The Islamic movement, which had previously only talked about social issues, started writing about politics—in particular the conflict between the government and the labor union. It backed the government, as Islamists regarded the left as the traditional enemy of Islam.

With Bourguiba's regime focused on curbing leftists, the Islamists were able to flourish. Due to its authenticity and ability to bind communities together, and as a rejection of Bourguiba's modernization drive, Al-Jama'a quickly gained followers. Then the Iranian Revolution came along, further enabling the rise of Islamism in Tunisia. Ghannouchi went to great lengths to associate the MB with the Islamic movement in Iran:

> Speaking about the contemporary history of the Islamic Movement, it should be remembered that there was a close relationship between the Martyr Imam Hassan Al-Banna and Imam Kachani, the ex-leader of the Islamic Movement during the 1940s and 1950s in Iran, when they established a cooperation program to found the Islamic State and to gain social support for it. In addition, the movement of Nawab Safawi in Iran was much influenced by the Muslim Brotherhood Movement in Egypt.[73]

Thanks to the spread of Brotherhood literature, Tunisian college campuses had become hotbeds of Islamist activism in the 1970s. In 1977, Tunisian students involved in Al-Jama'a changed their name to the Islamic Tendency Movement (MTI) to contest student union elections and take action against state secularization. Al-Jama'a leaders knew a winner when they saw one, and decided to follow suit, changing the group's name to MTI in 1979.[74] Because they had sided with the government during the conflict with the union, they found they had been granted more space for political activism. As the organization grew, they decided that it was time to organize a founding congress.

In 1980, the Tunisian Congress decided it would openly apply for official registration as a political party, and the next year it officially became the MTI.[75] Some observers have questioned MTI's connections to the Brotherhood, but they were always strong. Although Ghannouchi, elected as MTI leader, remained intellectually independent, the vast majority of MTI members swore allegiance to the international MB, Al-Tanzeem Al-Dawli. In addition, Salah Karker, Ghannouchi's deputy, was a fierce MB supporter, and the group itself was aligned with the MB from the start.[76] Like the Brotherhood, MTI's program opposed secularism and highlighted the evils of the West.

However, Ghannouchi had a political ideology distinct from the MB and his Iranian counterparts. Ghannouchi asserted that a violent revolution was not the answer. Rather, change would be most successful if it came from the bottom up—a slow process that gradually transformed society and used increased political participation and democratic principles to bring about a desired goal: a state that was both democratic and Islamic in nature.

He held an open commitment to democracy as a viable "method of preventing those who govern from permanently appropriating power for their own ends." It was a "system of governance in which rulers are held accountable for their actions in the public realm by citizens, acting indirectly through the competition and cooperation of their elected representatives." He also believed that if "by democracy, one means the liberal model of government prevails in the West, a system under which the people freely choose their representatives and leaders, and in which there is an alteration of power as well as freedoms and human rights for the public, then the Muslims will find nothing in their religion to oppose democracy, and it is not in their interest to do so anyway."[77]

This, of course, did not keep Tunisia's government from fearing an Islamic Revolution a la Iran and cracking down on Islamists. Bourguiba imprisoned many members and rejected MTI's directing of the mosques, believing that they were set on seizing power. The crackdown quickly degenerated into a full-blown attack on Islam and public expressions of religion: praying, mosques, veils, and beards were all banned.

At one point police nabbed Karker and another member and tortured the two until they revealed the names of the MTI leaders.[78] Now officially on the government's radar, Ghannouchi and Mourou shifted MTI activities back underground, dissolving prominent committees while remaining quietly active. In the 1980s, as the crackdown accelerated, some MTI members responded to the repression by joining violent groups and even plotting a coup.[79] They believed that the end of the Bourguiba government was coming. Therefore, when Prime Minister Mohammed Mzali's government fell in 1986, a new wave of Islamist persecutions emerged, culminating in a death sentence for Ghannouchi in 1987.

Zine El-Abidine Ben Ali preempted the coup plotters, engineering a bloodless coup and making himself president in 1987. He soon freed all arrested MTI members and tried to position himself as a reformer. His initial months in office looked promising:

- He let MTI take part in the High Council of the National Pact.
- He allowed MTI representation in the Islamic High Council through their leader Abdel Fatah Mourou.
- He allowed MTI an Islamic student union and granted them the right to publish a magazine (Al-Fajr).
- He allowed the movement to take part in the parliamentary elections of 1989. [80]

Until late 1989, the Islamists played their cards carefully, intent on maintaining their dialogue with the government. Further, in response to Ben

Ali's requirement that no party try to monopolize Islam, MTI agreed to change its name to Ennahda (Renaissance). But the group's 1989 application to become a political party was rejected because some of its members had spent significant time in prison.

The Islamist independents, which included Ennahda candidates, failed to win any seats in parliament that year. They still won 17 percent of the vote, displacing the secular left—their main opposition. However, Ennahda's participation in the parliamentary elections spelled the end of the period of participation. Because its candidates put forward proposals that denounced women's rights and would exploit religion in political life, Ben Ali deemed Ennahda too dangerous for public order, reversed his strategy, and reneged on promises to initiate democratic change in Tunisia.[81]

Ennahda soon began to give greater autonomy to local branches, allowing them to decide policy and strategy. The government modified schools, newspapers, and books, and banned headscarves and long beards in Ben Ali's attempt to "religiously cleanse" Tunisia.[82] The result of these two factors (repression and autonomy), perhaps unsurprising to those who know the MB and its affiliates, was that Ennahda splintered into a moderate branch and a radical one, and the latter began to embrace violence. Thousands of Ennahda activists were arrested around this time, and the group's leadership went into exile in Europe.

Arriving in London, Ghannouchi created a new Executive Bureau of Ennahda to complement the Political Bureau, based in Paris. Still, the international movement remained weak, spread as it was across France, the UK, Germany, and Switzerland. Political repression in Tunisia increased in the 1990s, spurring an anti-Ben Ali alliance between Islamists and secular activists.

The Call of Tunis Agreement, signed by Ennahda and three secular parties in June 2003, called for true democracy, anti-corruption measures, religious freedom, and respect for Arab-Muslim values.[83] This was among the first signs that Ennahda was willing to compromise—even contradict—the MB's vision of an Islamic state ruled by Sharia.

Tunisia witnessed a deepening of religiosity in the 2000s, as citizens reached for tradition in response to the rise of consumerism. Ennahda had been working for years to bolster its reputation, aiming for a comeback, when, on December 13, 2010, a fruit seller named Mohamed Bouazizi set himself on fire in front of the governor's office in Sidi Bouzid.

Passersby helped douse the flames, and Bouazizi was rushed to the nearest trauma center in Ben Arous. His self-immolation became national news, a symbol of the country's frustration, and Ben Ali paid Bouazizi a visit in the hospital. According to the patient's mother, the president promised to send her son to France for treatment, but that never happened.

On the afternoon of January 4, 2011, days after doctors declared his condition stable, Bouazizi passed away. The protests that had simmered on the streets as he lay in the hospital quickly exploded, in Sidi Bouzid and across Tunisia, with hundreds of thousands calling for justice. Ten days later, the people's rage prodded Ben Ali to flee Tunisia with his family to Saudi Arabia, giving up power after 23 years.

One of the most important issues in post-revolution Tunisia concerned the relationship between Islam and politics. Should Tunisia allow religious political parties, or should the country maintain its longstanding practice of separation of religion and politics? The answer soon became apparent. Riding the deepening appeal of Islam, along with the wave of anti-Western sentiment that attended the exit of U.S. ally Ben Ali, Ennahda quickly rose to the fore of Tunisia's political scene. Ghannouchi and Ennahda had a long history as the primary opposition to Bourguiba and Ben Ali. They bore the battle scars that gave them popular legitimacy, despite returning to politics amid deep suspicions regarding their democratic claims.

Up until the Arab Spring, tens of thousands of Islamists were jailed, and the party was largely absent from the Tunisian political scene. Ennahda's luck changed, however, following the ousting of Ben Ali. Ghannouchi was welcomed back into the country, and Ennahda was legalized on March 1, 2011. Following this move, the Islamists gained in popularity, and when the Constitutional Assembly election was held on October 23, 2011, Ennahda won 89 of 217 seats (37 percent of the vote), winning a plurality.

This victory came as a result of extensive and costly campaigning, increased voter turnout, especially from poorer citizens, and the handout of meals and gifts, a tactic used consistently by the MB in Egypt to win allegiance. Ennahda's electoral platform had reflected Ghannouchi's long-held progressive views about reform, democracy, equality, civil state, pluralism, and human rights. The 2011 political transition gave the group the opportunity to test this commitment. Overall, in interaction with other groups, the leaders of Ennahda insisted on democratic commitment.

After its victory, Ennahda formed a government with two secular parties. By this time, the party had been swept up in the revolutionary fervor, and began to move away from Islamism. "We salute Sidi Bouzid and its sons who launched the spark and we hope that God will have made Mohamed Bouazizi a martyr," Ghannouchi said after Ennahda's victory. "We will continue this revolution to realize its aims of a Tunisia that is free, independent, developing and prosperous."[84]

In March 2012, Ennahda announced that the constitution, which was being written at the time, would not include Sharia law. This step prodded a sizable chunk of Ennahda's younger members, as many as 10 percent, to leave the party. Many joined radical Islamist groups.[85] Here we see the frequent pragmatism of supposed Islamists: at the first opportunity to take power, the Islamists of Ennahda shed the wolf's clothing of the MB and turn into docile democratic sheep.

This is what we've seen time and again with the Brotherhood and its affiliates across the region: either they hold fast to their initial values and vision, remain politically marginalized, and tend toward violence and revolution, or they sacrifice their Islamist ideals to gain broader acceptance and potentially take power. The former are the true MB, and when they do come to power, as in Egypt, the threat to democracy and stability is unmistakable. The latter are neither Islamists nor politicians of any real integrity.

After the July 2013 coup removed the MB's Mohammed Morsi from power in Egypt, Ennahda's leaders moved to "become a 'true' Tunisian party, openly dissociating themselves from the international ambitions entrenched in the Muslim Brotherhood's ideology."[86] But then a wave of fear regarding Islamization began to erode Ennahda's position of power in the predominantly secular country.

The party assigned Hamadi Jebali as prime minister, but with the February 2013 assassination of Chokri Belaid, the leader of the left-secular Democratic Patriots' Movement, and the news that radical Islamists had carried it out, Jebali resigned. Ali Laarayedh of Ennahda then took over as prime minister, but then Mohamed Brahmi, another opposition leader, was assassinated by the same extremists in July 2013.

Though Ennahda was forced to relinquish power in January 2014, the party came in second in parliamentary elections that October (with 32 percent of the vote) and formed a coalition government with the secular Nidaa Tunis party that remains in power to this day. Some took this result as evidence that secularism had won out against Islamism. However, polling shows that Tunisians did not change their views about the role of religion in life between 2011 and 2014 but rather voted on economic and security issues and ended up holding their government responsible for not fulfilling its promises. Thus, the 2014 defeat of Ennahda was not entirely a moratorium on Islamism. Rather, "the democratic process triumphed, and therefore, every Tunisian, of every ideological persuasion triumphed too."[87]

Tunisia, the only Arab country to have a democratic government, has been considered by many to be an exception to the trend of unsuccessful Islamist movements in the Middle East. Tunisia's Muslim Brotherhood sister organization, Ennahda, has succeeded despite the relatively unpopular status of political Islam in Tunisia prior to the revolution and the tremendous loss of cultural Islam that Tunisia suffered as a byproduct of French colonization and then—following its independence—as a secular government. However, Ennahda's success has come at a price.

As was the case with several other MB affiliates, such as Morocco's PJD, Ennahda needed to make major concessions in order to gain a foothold in politics. And as in Morocco, these major concessions have led to the conspicuous absence of Qatar, the primary supporter of the MB in most Arab nations, in Tunisian politics. Indeed, one can say that the cases of Morocco and Tunisia show that the farther an MB affiliate strays from actually following the leadership of the Murshid, the less Qatar is interested in supporting that affiliate.

In May 2016 Ennahda moved even further from its MB roots. In an interview with the French newspaper *Le Monde*, Ghannouchi announced that the party was breaking its historical ties with Islam. "Political and religious activities must be independent from one another," he said. "We are Muslim democrats who no longer claim political Islam."[88] Two weeks later, at the party's annual conference, Ghannouchi confirmed Ennahda's new position: "We are keen to keep religion far from political struggles, and we call for the complete neutrality of mosques away from political disputes and partisan instrumentalisation, so that they play a role of unification rather than division."[89]

Ghannouchi acknowledged that the decision was made in part due to ISIS and Al-Qaeda, which, particularly in Tunisia, had corrupted the concept of Islamism and linked it with violent jihad. Whatever the motivation, it appears to have been a smart move. In May 2018, Ennahda won Tunisia's first municipal elections since the ouster of Ben Ali, putting itself back in the driver's seat for the November 2019 presidential election. But it is not an Islamist party.

Indeed, when various Ennahda leaders, members, and supporters were asked what kind of Islamist party Ennahda aspired to emulate after the revolution, none said the Egyptian Muslim Brotherhood. In fact, the majority said Turkey's Justice and Development Party (AKP). Ghannouchi in particular believed the "AK Party will gradually make Turkey a more Muslim country through education, building the economy, and diversifying the media. That's our model—not law. Make people love Islam. Convince, don't coerce them."[90]

The problem with that model is that it doesn't work. According to a survey published in January 2019 by leading Turkish pollster Konda, the share of Turkish citizens who call themselves religious fell from 55 percent to 51 percent from 2008 to 2018, while the share of those who see themselves as extremely religious dropped by nearly a quarter, from 13 percent to 10 percent.[91] Although the number of those who believe in God increased slightly, Turks are worshiping less than they were a decade prior, according to the survey. The share of those who fast for Ramadan fell from 77 percent to 65 percent, the study found, while Turks are having fewer arranged marriages.[92] Finally, the number of atheists in Turkey has tripled, from 1 percent in 2008 to 3 percent in 2018.[93]

Of course, these numbers do not represent a major drop in religiosity, merely a minor decline. But President Recep Tayyip Erdogan's AKP has been in power in Turkey for seventeen years. If the party's "long-game" project to engineer a more Islamic—even Islamist—society were succeeding, we would surely see it in the data by now. Turks' commitment to Islam would be increasing, or at the very least holding steady, if the AKP model were working. That is not the case. Ghannouchi's trust in Turkey's Islamists seems misplaced.

Still, while some might see Ennahda's move away from Islamism as part of an organizational and political evolution, it is similar to developments in other countries—the more an affiliate tries to distance itself from the core MB tenets, the less it actually remains an MB affiliate but instead becomes an example of the failure of the MB objective. In addition, the shift away from Islamism is in fact part of the traditional MB evolution, one that has happened elsewhere and tends to spur many members to seek out more revolutionary forms of political Islam.

In fact, in the years since Tunisia's revolution, with Ghannouchi moving away from traditional MB ideology and embracing compromise and consensus, many younger Ennahda members have left the group in frustration, believing it has moved away from true Islam, or that it was never zealous enough. Similarly, many Tunisian Islamists, particularly Salafis, felt Ennahda failed to embrace Islam. Ahmed Nadhif, journalist and author of *Tourist Rifles: Tunisians in World Jihadist Networks*, argues that Ennahda exploited the Salafis:

> Having come to power, Al-Nahda opened the way for radical Salafi movements to enter the political arena. It also encouraged the Salafis to engage in politics as it believed their impact would ensure Al-Nahda a grass-roots base and abundant votes in the elections. At this time, several religious fatwas were issued by the Salafi tendency necessitating engagement in politics to support Al-Nahda as the "standard bearer of Islam in the fight against the secular infidel trend." During Al-Nahda rule, the traditional Salafis were supportive of the Muslim Brotherhood and dedicated their platforms, popularity and mosques to promote its message.[94]

Yet, having encouraged the Salafists, Ennahda did not then enact policies that reflected its stated commitment to Islamism. Instead, it advised Salafists to go slowly and to respect Ghannouchi's "gradual" approach.[95] A twenty-four-year-old student who identified as a Salafi jihadi and a member of Ansar Al-Sharia told Oxford scholar Monica Marks in a 2015 Brookings Institute report:

> Go slowly, they say. But all their going slowly hasn't brought any results. They gave up Sharia, they listen to the West. . . . I don't see what makes them so Islamic. They use lies to manipulate people just like any other party. Maybe they should be listening to us! We're going to make a change.[96]

This helps explain the high incidence of Tunisians among those who joined ISIS in the years after the so-called Arab Spring—long-frustrated Islamists looking for a deeper commitment, and finding it in a Qutbist offshoot. As Pulitzer Prize–winning *Washington Post* reporter Kevin Sullivan wrote in October 2014:

Tunisia, a small North African country of 11 million people, has become the largest source of foreign fighters joining the Islamic State and other extremist groups in Syria and Iraq, according to estimates by the Tunisian government and private analysts. As many as 3,000 Tunisians, most of them men under 30, have joined the battle. . . . That flow of Tunisian fighters is partly an un-intended consequence of the Arab Spring uprising in 2011 that overthrew longtime dictator Zine El-Abidine Ben Ali and touched off popular revolu-tions across the region. The moderate, Islamist-led government elected after the revolution granted new religious freedom after a half-century of harshly enforced secularism, when the state banned women's veils and almost all other displays of piety and jailed thousands of people it suspected of holding Islamist beliefs. That freedom was quickly exploited by Islamist radicals, who killed two politicians and at least 25 police officers and soldiers, and used newly free mosques to incite a rising tide of violence that now reaches as far as Islamic State strongholds in Syria and Iraq.[97]

Now, you might ask, is all this necessarily the fault of the MB's Tunisia affiliate, Ennahda? Some might argue that taking the lid off following de-cades of repression would necessarily lead to a flowering of expression, which for some people would include greater religiosity and even extrem-ism. That perspective would largely relieve the MB of any blame for the explosion of jihadism in post-Ben Ali Tunisia.

But most observers blame Ennahda and Tunisia's Islamists in two ways. First, as Sullivan suggests, when Ennahda was in power it was particu-larly lax with the country's extremists, who in 2013 took advantage of the freedom to assassinate two progressive politicians, Chokri Belaid and Mohamed Brahmi, as mentioned earlier in this chapter. The day before Belaid was killed, a meeting of his supporters was attacked by Islamists, and he accused Ennahda of giving a "green light" to political violence.[98] Brahmi, too, was a vocal critic of Ennahda. Both of their wives and their supporters blamed Ennahda for the killings, either because the Islamists were unable to ensure security in the country or because they are actively collaborating with extremist elements to target their opponents.[99]

The assassinations created a rallying cry for change, sparking wide-spread protests that ultimately forced Ennahda to relinquish power in January 2014, "amid criticism that its failure to control its most extreme sup-porters had led to the rise in violence."[100] Under Ennahda's lax oversight rule, countless terrorist cells had formed, mainly along the Algerian border in the mountainous areas.[101] Tunisia's new government cracked down—banning more than 150 Muslim organizations and arresting more than 2,000 people on terrorism charges,[102] but by then it was too late. "Human rights organizations and lawyers say the government has overemphasized security, creating a climate of repression and anger that is fueling the flow of Tunisian fighters to the Islamic State," Sullivan wrote in October 2014.[103]

Then interior minister Lotfi Ben Jeddou told Sullivan that the Ennahda government allowed the Islamist group Ansar Al-Sharia, formed by some of the 3,000 men released from Tunisian prisons immediately after the revolution, to hold public meetings and do social work in poor neighborhoods. "But by the end of 2012," the former interior minister added, "they showed their true face."[104] Ansar Al-Sharia was widely blamed not just for the attack on the U.S. Embassy in late 2012 but also for the 2013 assassinations of Belaid and Brahmi, after which the government labeled it a terrorist group and arrested dozens of its members.[105]

"This ended an anomaly in the history of Tunisian Jihadism whereby for the two and a half years following the revolution, individuals in Tunisia had been allowed to openly proselytize, recruit, conduct events, and provide social services that promoted Jihadi ideology," writes Aaron Zelin, Richard Borow Fellow at the Washington Institute for Near East Policy and author of *Your Sons Are at Your Service: Tunisia's Missionaries of Jihad*.[106] Who oversaw the Tunisian government and security services during the vast majority of that anomalous period? Ennahda, of course. This underscores how Tunisia's MB affiliate enabled radical Islamism. However, others say it went much further than that.

Five years after the murders, the defense team for the two assassinated politicians put Ennahda firmly in their crosshairs. In October 2018, the team charged Tunisia's MB affiliate of creating a "secret apparatus" that had orchestrated the assassinations and stole thousands of documents from government institutions to cover it up.[107] Among the team's evidence is a document titled "Motorcycle Fighting skills," which provides training for assassinations using motorcycles, which were used in the Brahmi and Belaid killings.[108]

In November 2018, the defense team met with President Beji Caid Essebsi and revealed new data accusing Ennahda's secret organization of planning in 2013 to assassinate Essebsi and then president Francois Hollande of France.[109] Days later, the defense team said it planned to file a lawsuit against Ennahda accusing it of terrorism links and released a list of twenty-six Ennahda leaders, including Ghannouchi, whom it said were behind the secret apparatus.[110] A member of the team said it would soon call for Ennahda's dissolution, based on Tunisian counterterrorism law that allows up to a five-year ban for any party linked to terrorism.[111] Ennahda denies these claims, arguing that the defense team is a political committee linked to the leftist Popular Front coalition, seeking to tarnish Ennahda's name in the lead-up to November 2019 elections.[112]

The country is a mess politically and economically. Eight years after the ouster of Ben Ali, Tunisia seems no better off than when he was in power. Protests fill Habib Bourghiba Avenue nearly every day, according to a January 2019 story from *Bloomberg*, and that's just the tip of the iceberg:

> Hundreds of thousands of public servants demanding higher salaries went on strike on Thursday in the latest expression of organized rage over political

and economic stagnation. . . . Inflation is near a 25-year high, the dinar is weakening, tourism hasn't fully recovered from jihadist attacks in 2015 and foreign investors are staying away. Almost a third of the youth population is without work, double the national level. . . . Tunisia has been running a current-account deficit of about 10 percent of its economic output for the past two years, meaning the country is already dependent on foreign financing and going deeper in debt. The size of the economy has shrunk since the revolution in 2011, sending average annual incomes down by more than 10 percent to about $3,500.[113]

Meanwhile, Ansar Al-Sharia, which Ennahda enabled before banning, has emerged as a key conduit for the thousands of Tunisians who joined terrorists groups abroad. The group helped incubate, sanction, and promote the idea, according to Zelin, writing in a 2018 Washington Institute report:

AST [Ansar Al-Sharia in Tunisia] leader Abu Iyad Al-Tunisi became an early advocate of joining with ISI. In supporting this travel to the east, he was on the vanguard of world jihadist leaders. . . . In February 2013, Abu Iyad exclaimed in an interview with Mosaique FM journalist Nasr Al-Din bin Hadid that "Tunisians can be found everywhere in the land of jihad. The ways of going are easy and we don't stop our people from leaving."[114]

Ansar's media outlet released a video praising the jihad as a gift to the leader of Al-Qaeda–linked Jabhat Al-Nusra. When Ansar members died fighting in Syria, the group's Facebook page would "glamorize their martyrdom," according to Zelin, while "AST members like Bilal Chaouachi served as a public face for Jihad promotion in Syria. Chaouachi did this through his rhetoric on the streets of Tunisia, in interviews with foreign journalists, and on Tunisian television debates."[115]

These efforts made a real impact. As of September 2018, the UN says some 5,500 Tunisians had gone off to join ISIS or Al-Qaeda in Iraq, Syria, or Libya.[116] Zelin estimates that a total of 30,000 Tunisians had tried to join the fighting, but the vast majority were stopped before they were able to leave the country.[117] These problems, of economic troubles, unemployment, youth frustration, and jihadism, are not unique to Tunisia, but they seem to fester in countries that have experienced Brotherhood rule.

SUDAN

Countries that have experienced Brotherhood rule include Sudan, a majority-Arab African nation and another example, after Egypt and Tunisia, that wherever an MB-linked leadership takes power, trouble is sure to follow. Omar Al-Bashir, the founder of the National Congress Party, came to power in 1989 with the help of leading MB ideologue Hassan Al-Turabi and was removed from office in 2019. Al-Turabi had for years been the leader of Sudan's MB affiliate, the Islamic Charter Front.[118]

As in many countries across the region, the Brotherhood's history in Sudan begins with exchange students in Cairo. Sudanese students in Egypt's capital fell in with MB ideas in the 1940s and decided against joining the Egyptian main branch.[119] In 1952, they founded the Islamic Liberation Movement, which two years later became the Sudanese MB.[120] Most of its members were university graduates, including from what would become the University of Khartoum, and some were from a Sufi sect, Khatamiyya.[121] Hasan Al-Banna appointed the group's second leader Ali Talib-Allah, replacing Sheikh Umar Al-Imam, which soon led to complaints about Egyptian control over the Sudanese MB, particularly as the group also used Egyptian MB literature.[122]

Fighting off British and Egyptian influence, many young Sudanese at this time wanted independence and felt Islam might be the solution. The Brotherhood was of course campaigning to institute a state and a society based on Islam, and backed by a revolutionary ideology. Independence came in 1956, and by 1958 president Ibrahim Abboud led a military regime in Khartoum. Dissatisfaction with Abboud grew, particularly with the violence in the country's south, and in 1964 Khartoum University students set up a series of debates that spurred broader criticism of the regime, which in turn spurred protests and major strikes.

By this time, Al-Turabi's popularity and skill as an orator had begun to peak, and he emerged as the voice of the MB in Sudan, which by then was known as the Islamic Charter Front. He had earned a law degree from Khartoum University, had obtained a PhD from the Sorbonne in Paris, and was fluent in English, French, and German.[123] Spurred by Al-Turabi, the Brotherhood "played a central role in the downfall of the Abboud military regime in the October Revolution in 1964," Stig Jarle Hansen, international relations professor at Norway's University of Life Sciences and an expert on Islamism in the Horn of Africa, and Atle Mesoy, researcher on political Islam and co-editor of *The Borders of Islam*, wrote in a 2009 report for the Norwegian Ministry of Foreign Affairs.[124]

> The Brotherhood gained considerable power, gaining five representatives and one minister in the parliament. . . . Hassan Turabi, who had joined the movement in 1951, was at the centre of events, attempting to modernise the movement, to politicise Islam and to promote independence from the Egyptian Brotherhood and their ideology. Turabi's goal was to create a strong multi-party front that would be able to make a political and ideological difference.[125]

Soon an anti-Turabist faction emerged, advocating education and Da'wa rather than politics. In 1969, the group split, with the anti-Turabists leaving to create what would later emerge as the Sudanese branch of the Brotherhood.[126] Supported for the moment by the Egyptian MB, Al-Turabi's Islamic Charter Front grew into a legitimate political party, thanks mainly to its leader's dedication, charisma, and political skill. The ICF joined forces with the Gaafar Nimieri regime in 1977, gaining members appointments in the judiciary, as well as education and financial systems.[127] But this compromise drove away many members who left to join the anti-Turabists.[128] Sudan's MB affiliate was slowly losing its MB credentials.

Still, Al-Turabi and Nimieri began to introduce Islamic law, until the latter was ousted in 1985. That year, Al-Turabi created the National Islamic Front, which supported Al-Bashir after he came to power after a 1989 coup.[129] Al-Bashir and Al-Turabi instituted Sharia law, yet nearly a decade after Al-Bashir became the country's leader, the National Islamic Front split, with Al-Turabi and Al-Bashir launching the National Congress Party.[130]

This led to a distancing from the central MB institution. "Although Turabi brought the Brotherhood in Sudan to the highest position of political power in the country, he also managed to fall out of favour with the leaders of the international Muslim Brotherhood," wrote Hansen and Mesoy.[131] "He wanted to lead the Brotherhood members away from any influence from Cairo and to lead them according to his vision," they said. "Eventually the Turabi group stopped using the name 'The Muslim Brotherhood.'"[132]

Al-Turabi told the Sudanese people that Islamism would unite the country.[133] Instead, under Al-Bashir and National Congress, Sudan suffered through a brutal twenty-year civil war, which included the genocide in Darfur and ended with the secession of South Sudan. During this period Sudan hosted the likes of Osama bin Laden and Al-Qaeda's current leader, Ayman Al-Zawahiri. The waves of violence and instability, in addition to the corruption, devastated the country's economy, leading to mass protests that began months before and continued months after Al-Bashir's ouster in April 2019. Meanwhile, the new Brotherhood that developed by those who left the Al-Turabi–led groups came to embrace more of the ideas of Sayyid Qutb and openly supported Hamas in Palestine.[134]

Essentially a failed state by 2018, Sudan became the site of a geopolitical tussle, with Saudi Arabia and the UAE seeking to wield increasing influence while Turkey and Qatar established a beachhead there through hundreds of millions worth of investments and later used it to funnel Al-Qaeda–linked militants to the Brotherhood-friendly government in Tripoli.[135] After pivoting away from Iran, Sudan became one of the very few states able to balance friendly ties with both Ankara and Riyadh. But behind the scenes, one emerged as the more influential player: "Turkey has been betting on a lame duck for a decade: Al-Bashir's regime has brought about dire economic conditions, while greedy warlords and world-class kleptocrats rose to the highest echelons of power. They proved ready to sell out the Islamist ideology, and anything else, in their own self-interest. Saudis understood this well and exploited the cracks in Al-Bashir's Sudan,"

Mustafa Gurbuz, Middle East Fellow at the Arab Center in Washington, DC, wrote in June 2019.[136]

Turkey has since late 2017 invested significantly in Sudan, including plans to build a new airport in Khartoum and a free-trade zone in Port Sudan and to establish a naval dock on Suakin Island, the former site of an Ottoman port.[137] Yet by enticing Sudan's Al-Bashir to send troops to Yemen and offering, in exchange, to make Sudan's case in Washington, it was Saudi Arabia, along with the UAE, that enabled those Turkish investments.[138] "By March 2016, Al-Bashir agreed to send 6,000 elite troops," wrote Gurbuz. "His reward, thanks in part to Saudi-Emirati lobbying in Washington, was that in October 2017 the United States lifted a raft of two-decades-old sanctions, saying that Sudan had begun to address concerns about terrorism."[139]

That initial troop commitment also spurred significant investment and financial aid from Saudi Arabia and the UAE and has since mushroomed to 14,000.[140] Since Al-Bashir's ousting, the Saudi-led bloc and the Ankara-Doha alliance have competed to gain influence over Lieutenant General Abdel Fattah El-Burhan, head of the military council overseeing Sudan's transition to democracy, and the former appears to have the advantage, in part because El-Burhan and his deputy have both commanded Sudanese troops in Yemen.[141] Within days of the overthrow of Al-Bashir in April 2019, Sudanese officials made clear that the troops would continue fighting in Yemen.

This likely helped spur a $3 billion aid package from Saudi Arabia and the UAE, including $500 million to stabilize Sudan's economy.[142] In late May, the transitional military council shuttered the Khartoum offices of Al Jazeera, and two days later Sudan recalled its ambassador from Doha.[143] By June 2019, some analysts believed Sudan was preparing to dismiss dozens of MB members from its state institutions and deport hundreds of Brotherhood members who had fled Egypt after the ouster of Morsi.[144] Either way, the jockeying for influence in a deeply troubled post-Bashir Sudan, where Islamists, including the splintered MB, still play a key political role, is sure to continue for some time.[145]

CHAPTER 3

The Muslim Brotherhood in Post-Mubarak Egypt

> I've heard this from President Mubarak, if you sort of open it up and the Muslim Brotherhood were legitimate, that you would in fact have a more radical outcome and greater instability in Egypt.
>
> —John Kerry, Senate confirmation hearing, 2008[1]

In the book's first chapter we learned how Hassan Al-Banna had been inspired, by the end of the Caliphate and the incursion of Western people and ideas, to create the Muslim Brotherhood nearly a century ago and how from the group's earliest days it tilted toward violence and revolution.

This chapter picks up back in Egypt where that one left off, following the MB's return to strength after the lean years under Nasser and the group finally coming to power after the fall of Hosni Mubarak. It is precisely this that the Arab world, the entire Ummah, had been waiting for, for so long. Today we all know how the MB fared in power and what came next. This chapter analyzes why the MB fell, what it meant, and what is the current status of the MB in Egypt.

FROM EL-SADAT TO MUBARAK

Thanks to the addition of Aboul Fotouh and his student Islamists, as detailed in Chapter 1, the Brotherhood returned to prominence in the 1970s under El-Sadat, following the harsh crackdown of the Nasser years. By the end of 1977, the prisons were full of Nasserites, communists, and MB members. Communists went underground and lost their effectiveness, as did the MB. However, as the Egyptian journalist, Muhammad Hasanayn Haykal writes:

> The regime put them [communists and Nasserites] in one basket. . . . It was logical for El-Sadat to look for allies to support him. The Right was the natural

direction in which he needed to search, not only the political right but also the religious right. El-Sadat released MB members from prisons and allowed it to be active in universities under the supervision of Mohamed Othman Ismail, the Governor of Assiut at that time, with the aim of using the MB against the Nasserites and the leftists. In the Autumn of 1978, members in the Islamist groups were able to win all the 60 seats of the Student Union in the Faculty of Medicine and Faculty of Engineering. And they won most seats in the Faculty of Law and the Faculty of Pharmacy. This sweeping victory gave these student groups the upper hand in running student life in universities.[2]

Since these student groups were sure of the support of the regime, they started acting as if they were responsible for managing the universities and the various curricula.[3] This was an astute strategy on the part of the MB, focusing on frustrated youth, engaged students, and future teachers to help spread their message.

"We believe the MB's potentially most effective tactic in ensuring its long-term strength is infiltration of the Egyptian educational system. The MB recognizes that Egyptian youth face deteriorating social conditions and dim economic prospects, and it offers to a receptive audience its version of fundamentalism as a panacea," the CIA said in a report from that period. "The US Embassy in Cairo reports that the MB targets, recruits, and financially supports pious university students who plan to become primary and secondary teachers. The MB believes these future teachers will infill the organisation's values in their pupils. It also believes other disciples will eventually carry MB ideals to business, government, and the professionals."[4]

Then, in 1979, the MB received two boosts. First, Iran overthrew the shah, which meant that an Islamist movement (though Shiite) had seized power. To the MB, this marked the dawn of a new age. "Khomeini's proclamation of an Islamic state gave a major fillip to Islamist movements of all stripes," Martyn Frampton, historian at Queen Mary University, London, and a former research fellow at Cambridge, writes in his 2018 book *The Muslim Brotherhood and the West*.[5] Later that year, the Soviet war in Afghanistan and the resulting calls for jihad further boosted Islamists. The MB helped thousands of young men heed the call and travel to Afghanistan for holy war. This helped establish its reputation as a potent and competent Muslim organization willing to wage jihad far beyond the borders of Egypt and challenge global powers.

The decision to mobilize Cairo's Islamist groups was bolstered by the success of the Iranian Revolution and the jihad in Afghanistan. This inspired some Brothers to embrace violence wholeheartedly and splinter off. By 1981, when the dangerous role of these student groups and other MB factions became public, a socialist prosecutor warned El-Sadat of their danger. But the Egyptian president was in no hurry to deal with the situation; he even released twelve students who were imprisoned after being caught carrying knives.[6] Former MB member Ayman Al-Zawahiri's terrorist group Egyptian Islamic Jihad (EIJ) assassinated El-Sadat in October 1981, attacking him during a victory parade in Cairo and opening the way for Hosni Mubarak to take power.

By this time, the violence of the MB and its radical offshoots was globally known. "Islamic radicals, inspired by the Iranian model, believe that an Islamic revolution is necessary to solve Egypt's social, spiritual, and economic problems,"[7] the CIA said in its 1986 report on the MB. "The radicals' violent and utopian ideology stems from the writings of Sayyid Qutb, a Muslim Brother executed in 1966 for plotting against [Egyptian president] Nasir. The radical groups [under heavy influence from Qutb's writings] such as Al-Jihad, and Islamic Liberation Army have been involved in terrorist activities including the assassination of President El-Sadat in 1981."[8]

Mubarak quickly cracked down on EIJ and the Brotherhood, which was, yet again, officially banned. MB leaders and members shifted their activities underground. And while their political influence may have suffered, the group's provision of local social services, such as healthcare and education, meal handouts, and food staples, earned it considerable support and credibility—and provided a sharp contrast to Mubarak's corruption.

The MB's stand against the economic policies and political meddling of Mubarak-allied Western countries also played well among educated Egyptians. By the mid-1980s, the MB had again consolidated a strong base of influential supporters across the country. "The MB has been successful in building a fundamentalist network in Egypt, through the recruitment of educators, students, journalists, other professionals, and businessmen," the CIA wrote in a 1986 report.[9] "Despite cooperation with [the Egyptian] government, the stand of the Brotherhood against Camp David accords, the Agency for International Development, and Western cultural penetration of Egypt makes it a potential anti-US force."[10]

Yet even as Mubarak amassed despotic power and great wealth, he occasionally used the MB to counter the secular opposition. He liked to frame Egypt as an Arab leader and guarantor of regional stability, thanks to its powerful military. Following the Iranian Revolution and assassination of El-Sadat, Islamists were of course seen as one of the key regional threats. To the West, Mubarak played up the potential threat of the MB—a radical Islamist menace—if he were to be removed from office. He thus used his ability to keep a lid on the dangerous MB as evidence of Egypt's crucial stability under his rule. "State media under Mubarak portrayed the concept of a religious state as intolerant and extremist and its proponents as extremist," scholars Elizabeth Monier and Annette Ranko wrote for the Middle East Policy Council.[11]

In this way, the MB was portrayed as a domestic and regional security threat, even after being officially disbanded and disavowing violence.

Yet many observers felt confident that the group had not completely up-rooted its embrace of violence. "We believe that Brothers who advocate more confrontation with the [Mubarak] government have defied the leadership's instructions and have maintained a covert military capability," the CIA wrote in 1986.[12]

Dozens of MB leaders were arrested in the early years under Mubarak, and Zawahiri and others were tortured, much like their hero Qutb. But by the time Mubarak came to power, the Brotherhood had become more potent and influential than it had ever been. As it continued to develop internationally, Cairo came to act as a natural arbiter and leader and intervened to resolve local issues. However, these interventions were spontaneous and were done without any real organizational formality until after 1980.

Facing the Mubarak crackdown, the Brotherhood felt compelled to establish an international body, Tanzeem, which formalized the relationship between Cairo and other chapters and laid out a new leadership structure (detailed in Chapter 9). New insistence was placed on the obedience that other Brotherhood groups should display toward the Egyptian Murshid in order to strengthen control over existing branches in the Arab world. The highly centralized system gave Egyptians control of the group and its finances, yet proved problematic for the branches, as explained in Chapter 2.

Throughout the 1990s in Egypt, Islamist candidates and their allies swept elections in all the major professional unions. So Islamist politicians were ever-present, even though the Brotherhood was often banned. Occasionally, it was allowed to resume activities, existing in a sort of legal limbo that allowed the government to periodically arrest its otherwise law-abiding members on charges of being part of an illegal organization. This status enabled it to call itself an "outsider party" and run on that platform. The MB painted Mubarak allies—the United States and Israel—as the real threat and quietly gained influence, making alliances with several leading political parties and emerging by the 1990s as the largest opposition group. Once in parliament, they did not always play nice with other parties. "The Brotherhood has been an unreliable political partner from the beginning. Its members in parliament have ignored the New Wafd leaders, discussed political issues only at Brotherhood headquarters, and voted exclusively in the Brotherhood's own interest regardless of the views of the Wafd," the CIA said in its 1986 report.[13]

FROM 9/11 TO REVOLUTION

The attacks of September 11, 2001, changed the game for the MB, particularly due to its role in the Afghanistan conflict, its links to terrorist groups like Al-Qaeda, and its stated commitment to Sharia. Yet in some ways, the increased international scrutiny, particularly from the West, helped the MB, forcing the group to haul itself into the Internet era. According to Alison Pargeter, senior research associate at RUSI and former fellow at Cambridge and King's College London,

> The fear of being labelled as a terrorist organisation prompted a greater urgency to be seen as willing to work within the political framework of the state. In spite of the Ikhwan's deep reservations about the War on Terror and the role of the West in the Islamic world, it seems that the reformist current within the Egyptian Ikhwan somehow received a boost from this new international climate. It was as if now the world was watching if they could come into their own and find a truly appreciative audience. The reformists, many of whom speak English, took advantage of renewed interest by scholars and journalists and were keen to engage in interviews and debates as a means of demonstrating their commitment to reform. In line with the globalised age they also began promoting themselves through the Internet, setting up their own English language website.[14]

These interviews and the online presence began to erode the image of the MB as secretive and aggressive, a shift that was buoyed by the elevation of Mehdi Akef to Murshid, or MB leader, in 2004. The MB soon issued a series of documents outlining the group's moderate stance on a handful of issues, from political and legal reform to education. Yet even while these new documents marked a more open and progressive approach, they suffered from a long-running MB problem: a lack of clarity and vision. As the scholar Alison Pargeter explains in her 2013 book *The Muslim Brotherhood: From Opposition to Power*, the initiative promoted democratic principles, yet restricted individual freedoms; advocated the rights of non-Muslims, yet stressed the state's Islamic nature; and stressed the value of elections and the civic nature of political authority while asserting that the MB would strive to install Sharia.[15]

Still, by the time of the 2005 elections, the MB had accrued significant support from across Egypt. Still banned from politics, MB politicians ran as independents and won eighty-eight parliamentary seats, or about 20 percent. Mubarak responded aggressively, detaining hundreds of MB members and adding an amendment to the constitution that banned parties with a religious affiliation. That worked, but only until he went too far. For the 2010 elections, the government turned to blatant vote rigging, sparking widespread public anger. This of course spurred the mass protests of January 2011, which led to the overthrow of Mubarak on February 11, just weeks after Ben Ali's fall in Tunisia.

A key question about the Egyptian Revolution has been to what extent the Brotherhood took part in or guided the demonstrations that brought down Mubarak. It's true that many top MB leaders did not participate in the early protests, like the Police Day protest of January 25, but that does not mean MB members were not present in considerable numbers early on. Younger Muslim Brothers were among the core organizers of the Police

Day protests, thousands of other MB members joined the marches as individuals, and a female MB parliamentarian led a group of MB-supporter women all the way to Tahrir Square.[16]

The Police Day protests, that year dubbed the Day of Rage, seemed to mark a shift, after which the demonstrators began to feel they had the upper hand on the government—and the Brotherhod stepped to the fore. "The success of Police Day convinced MB leaders to go all in and call on all members to march on Tahrir Square and stay there."[17] The next day, nearly 150 MB members were among the protesters arrested by the police.[18] Egypt's Interior Ministry blamed the MB for riots on the streets and said its members infiltrated the crowds in order to wreak havoc.[19]

By the first days of February, the MB had become central to the revolutionary movement to oust Mubarak. "The group's famed discipline and organizational skill gave a structural integrity, a backbone to the defense of Tahrir Square."[20] In the wake of Mubarak's fall, the MB was legalized, and it established a political wing: the Freedom and Justice Party. By this time, the Brotherhood had learned to use its superior organizational and get-out-the-vote skills. The imperative of vote maximization led the Brotherhood to shed its ideological baggage, move to the center, and woo the elusive median voter—all elements that resulted in the temporary repudiation of Qutb and the apparent adoption of democratic ideals.

THE BROTHERHOOD GAINS, FUMBLES POWER

In Egypt's parliamentary elections held from November 2011 to January 2012, the Brotherhood won 235 of the 488 parliamentary seats, or nearly 50 percent. "The Egyptian Salafist parties' winning a quarter of the seats may have been the surprise of the vote, but few disputed that the MB emerged as the clear winner. Finally, nearly eighty years after Brotherhood founder Hassan Al-Banna first envisioned the group in power, that goal was within reach."[21]

Before we examine how the MB all but encouraged its own decimation and the massacre of many of its supporters in the summer of 2013, it is crucial that we review the errors that led to its political demise. The troubles began on the first day of the MB-controlled parliament: January 23, 2012, saw backbiting and in-fighting as MB members argued with their fellow Islamist lawmakers, the Salafists. That old bugaboo of indecision and uncertainty regarding the MB's ideology and political vision soon emerged. During the uprising, the MB said it would not seek more than a third of parliamentary seats; it contested almost all of them and won nearly half. Then the MB said it wouldn't offer a presidential candidate; it did and, of course, won. But that's getting ahead of ourselves. First, let's look at how the MB selected its presidential candidate.

Considering how he had emerged in the 1990s as the most prominent MB leader, many might view Aboul Fotouh as the most likely MB candidate. In reality, he had been shifting away from the MB's conservative stance for years.[22] The MB governing board even voted to expel him from his seat back in 2009 in retaliation for his dissent of a party platform declaring that only a male Muslim could serve as president and that parliament should be required to listen to a council of Muslim scholars.[23] Two years later, as discussions heated up regarding Egypt's first democratically elected president, the MB's powerful conservative faction put their foot down about Aboul Fotouh. The leaders who had evicted him from the governing board went one step further, expelling him entirely from the MB because he had defied their orders by running for president.[24]

This might be the first of many political mistakes the MB made on their road to perdition. Aboul Fotouh was the movement's best hope for moderation, for building consensus and shaping an Islamic democracy, and the MB forced him out, apparently because he was not radical enough, or not obedient enough. The real reason may have been something else entirely. The crucial question is, who was behind the decision? None other than Aboul Fotouh's old friend, Khairat El-Shater, a wealthy financier and the MB's deputy general guide.[25]

In the years before Mubarak's overthrow, El-Shater had reorganized the group as Aboul Fotouh injected it with new life. El-Shater funded its political efforts, its embrace of digital tools, and its outreach to Western countries.[26] After Mubarak's overthrow, MB members charged that El-Shater began to run the group like the country's longtime dictator, suppressing dissent and debate and prodding many to leave. "During this period there was an exodus of MB members, leaving out of frustration mainly due to an inability to express their political views."[27] Of course, considering the group's strict discipline, MB members had to follow the movement's political path; joining another political party meant leaving the MB. For all intents and purposes, internal debate was banned—which is to some extent the MB modus operandi (see Chapter 9). Yet this seems a poor way for the MB to put itself on the road to democracy.

El-Shater soon broke the pledge for which Aboul Fotouh had been expelled: in March 2012, the MB's internal assembly nominated him as their candidate.[28] Technically, he was no longer an MB member; he had resigned from the group in order to avoid violating the movement's vow not to field a candidate. But that was window dressing. In the end, El-Shater was unable to run. Two weeks after his nomination, Egypt's election council barred his candidacy because he had been released from prison the year before, and the law states that a presidential candidate must not have been in prison for at least six years.[29] Suddenly, an uncharismatic technocrat and former parliamentarian named Mohammed Morsi was thrust forward to run as the MB candidate against Ahmed Shafik, Egyptian Air Force commander under Mubarak.

The presidential election took place on June 16 and 17, with votes counted in the precincts after polls closed. When word began to spread, on the evening of the 17th, that Morsi appeared to have won by a relatively slim margin, U.S. intelligence agencies reported that the electoral commission wanted to invalidate the results and declare Shafik the winner. But in the end, pressure from the United States and an MB threat to take to the streets if an attempt was made to steal the election settled it. Morsi became Egypt's first democratically elected president, with nearly 52 percent of the vote. The Brotherhood had come to power, without the need for violence.

> Morsi's electoral victory was without question the greatest democratic success in the history of the Brotherhood, and modern Islamism, and all the more stunning because it was achieved by a relative unknown. Suddenly he found himself in charge of the largest country in the Arab world, a bellwether for the region and the Muslim world. Many hoped he could lead Egypt toward democracy and freedom. Unfortunately, he was woefully unprepared for the position.[30]

Within days, Morsi and the MB began to fumble away their dream. Part of the problem was Morsi's character. He lacked charisma and stifled debate. He would often tell his audience what *they* had done wrong.[31] He could be autocratic, rarely offering concessions to critics or trying to gain new allies.[32] Morsi spent very limited time behind bars. He was in prison for two days and then escaped with other MB members—a de rigueur experience for the underground hero. He was long-winded, unpredictable, and uninspiring on the stump.[33] Even while Morsi was president, El-Shater continued to work behind the scenes to explain the president's policies and maintain the group's support.[34]

Morsi was sworn in on June 30, 2012, but he delivered his de facto inaugural address at Tahrir Square the night before. "You have the power! You grant power to whoever you choose, and you withdraw power from whomever you choose," he told the huge crowd.[35] Then he stepped to the front of the stage and opened his sports coat, to show he was not wearing any body armor at a public event, unlike Mubarak.[36] He called on the people to work with him to ensure the integrity of the state against the possible will of the military. "Are you ready? Will you stand by me to fully regain our rights?"[37]

Morsi soon met with General Abdel Fattah El-Sisi, who reportedly won the president's trust by warning him of a looming assassination attempt.[38] In addition, El-Sisi undermined his second-in-command, General Hussein Tantawi, by handing Morsi evidence of Tantawi's corruption. Within hours, Tantawi and Sami Hafez Anan, his military chief of staff, had resigned and relinquished legislative authority, handing it to Morsi.[39] It was August 12. The MB had gained control of parliament, of the presidency, and now they seemed to have overtaken Egypt's long-dominant military as well.

That was just the beginning. On November 22, Morsi's spokesman suddenly appeared on state television. "The president is authorized to take any measures he sees fit in order to preserve and safeguard the January revolution," the spokesman said, adding that Morsi's decisions could not be appealed, cancelled, or legally challenged.[40] Egypt's president had suddenly decreed that his decisions were beyond judicial review until a new constitution was ratified. In essence, he declared himself pharaoh, even as his reasoning was about protecting the people's voice. "This is a way of recreating a dictatorship, of giving executive power to one person, with no regulation from the law," Rami Shaath, one of the founders of the Free Egyptian Movement, said at the time.[41] The move took even MB leaders by surprise. "If I were not in my place, I would think he wants to be a dictator," El-Shater said as he watched the declaration on television.[42]

It took just five months in office for a Brotherhood president to declare absolute power, and this happened right around the time when Morsi and MB parliamentarians had slipped numerous Islamic references into their latest draft constitution. If signs of disillusionment had already begun to emerge among many Egyptians regarding the MB and its ability to govern, this cemented them. "The constitution-drafting process was flawed and Morsi's presidential decree of November 2012 was perceived as a step towards establishing a new MB-style authoritarian system," Elizabeth Monier, Middle Eastern Studies fellow at Cambridge, and Annette Ranko, former fellow at the German Institute of Global and Area Studies, wrote in 2013.[43]

The next day, tens of thousands of Egyptians turned out to protest across the country. Again Tahrir Square filled with demonstrators, while MB offices across Egypt were attacked and torched.[44] When Morsi spoke outside the presidential palace that afternoon, he did not calm the angry masses by stressing that his expanded powers would last only a short period of time, maybe a few weeks, until the constitution was ratified. Instead he talked about rebellions and martyrdom, the occupation of Gaza, and conspiracy theories, painting himself as the brave strongman standing against Egypt's myriad enemies.

A few weeks later, grasping the public anger, Morsi rescinded his decree. But the damage had been done. "Though Morsi was ultimately forced to rescind that decree, to many it revealed something fundamentally authoritarian about the president and the movement of which he was a part, and thus legitimated a popular, extra-constitutional movement to oust him," Tarek Masoud, Sultan of Oman Professor of International Relations at Harvard's Kennedy School, writes in his 2014 book *Counting Islam: Religion, Class and Elections in Egypt*.[45] Protests again became a regular occurrence, particularly in Cairo, and particularly in front of the presidential palace. MB offices were regularly attacked and burned down. Shater and other MB leaders began to grow frustrated with Morsi's stubbornness, as the group was forced to defend his unpopular decisions. Another draft constitution, delivered on November 30, was met with even broader protests and public anger, particularly about threats to free expression. By early December, the presidential palace "felt under siege."[46] Morsi turned to the MB for help, urging Brothers to come defend the palace. Many MB members sided with Morsi's power grab and took it upon themselves to undertake a "cleansing" of those who stood against the president.[47]

What happened on December 5, 2012, around Egypt's presidential palace has been the subject of much debate, but what is clear is that there was then and remains today an effort among Western voices to promote the story that the MB was besieged and victimized. For example, Human Rights Watch and the UK's Special Panel of the House of Lords on the MB could not bring themselves to make a pronouncement of guilt against the MB in this case. Yet what transpired has been made clear via video documentation and reports by several journalists on the scene.[48] That afternoon, hundreds of MB members poured out of a nearby mosque and converged on the sit-in, pulling up tents and aggressively chasing away protesters. Police general Khaled Amin said the Brothers "looked euphoric, high on their own power, like they were invincible."[49] Here's how the *Guardian* reported it:

> Clashes began when thousands of Islamist supporters of Morsi descended on the area around the palace where some 300 of his opponents were staging a sit-in. Members of the Brotherhood chased the protesters away from outside the main gate and tore down their tents. The protesters fled into side streets where they chanted anti-Morsi slogans. . . . By nightfall, there were about 10,000 Morsi supporters outside the palace.[50]

There is no question that Morsi and the Islamists were instigators of violence, with several reported instances of assault. One case was activist Awatef Salem Ali, who was slapped by a Morsi supporter while attending a trial in support of the military.[51] This explains why "the Brotherhood's attack on protesters became a rallying cry for the anti-Morsi opposition."[52]

December 5 was merely the first of what would be many examples of Morsi's inability to maintain security and stability. Six weeks later, thousands gathered at Tahrir Square to mark the second anniversary of Mubarak's overthrow. With no police presence, at least eighteen women were sexually assaulted, including journalist Hania Moheeb, who was stripped of her clothes and raped. Many Egyptians blamed the Islamists for the assaults, and their response, blaming the government for failing to protect its citizens, left most unsatisfied. "How do they ask the Ministry of Interior to protect a woman when she stands among men?" wondered Reda Saleh Al-Hefnawi, an MB parliamentarian.[53]

The next day, Port Said, at the northern end of the Suez Canal, exploded in violence after a judge sentenced twenty-one soccer fans to death for the murder of seventy-four people in a stadium riot a year earlier. Somebody among the hundreds gathered there shot a prison guard after the announcement, and police opened fire, killing more than twenty people and wounding dozens. The city was soon engulfed by violence. With hospitals overwhelmed, doctors pleaded to the media for help. Rioters attacked television cameras, and the army deployed troops to secure the port.[54] Morsi declared a state of emergency for Port Said and neighboring areas. The next day, El-Sisi warned for the first time of the collapse of the state.[55]

Indeed, already Egypt's intelligence and security agencies appeared to be working against Morsi. Police had begun to refuse to provide security for MB offices, which continued to suffer attacks across the country, with burglaries, ransacking, and arson. "By December, the people had lost all confidence in Morsi and the MB leadership. The groups leaders seemed pathetic, and couldn't even guard their own offices against attack."[56]

By early March, people began calling for a coup and police went on strike to protest the MB government.[57] So, after five months in office, Morsi sought to grab absolute power. After six months, the country had begun to spin out of the government's control. And within eight months, amid riots, protests, and violence in the streets, people were calling for his removal. By April, gas lines stretched for miles, the central bank's reserves were dwindling, inflation and unemployment were on the rise, and blackouts got longer every week as the spring heat gripped Cairo.[58] Around this time, a leaked presidential report revealed that Egypt's armed forces committed forced disappearances, torture, and killings during the 2011 revolution, even as military leaders declared their neutrality.[59] The leak seemed perfectly timed to erode rising confidence in the military, which had a history of coming to the rescue of the troubled state.

Things were coming to a head for the MB, as U.S. officials began to get a clear picture of the situation. In March, U.S. secretary of state John Kerry met with Morsi in Cairo. "He is the dumbest cluck I've ever met," Kerry told his chief of staff after the meeting. "This isn't going to work. These guys are wacko."[60] Kerry said all the problems started with the November decree. "That is where we just said, 'This stinks, these guys aren't doing anything productive and ultimately they are going to be anti-democratic.'"[61]

At the end of April, three freelance journalists banded together to form *Tamarrod*, or Rebellion, which sought to collect fifteen million signatures to get Morsi to step down on the one-year anniversary of his inauguration, June 30.[62] Leaked documents later revealed that top generals including

El-Sisi were behind *Tamarrod*, with possible funding from the UAE.[63] But this made little difference. The group expressed a widespread desire for change among the Egyptian people.

In the spring of 2013, Morsi made blunder after blunder, almost as if he were begging to be seen as incompetent and removed from office. On June 26, he delivered a rambling speech in which he blamed everybody for Egypt's problems: his opponents, enemies of the revolution, media moguls, and judges. He named a member of a political party linked to an Islamist militant group as governor of Luxor, where a wing of the same group had massacred more than sixty people at a tourist site in 1997. Protesters blocked the governor from his office, and he resigned.[64]

Once the protests began, it was only a few days before Morsi was out, despite his efforts to compromise. On the morning of Sunday, June 30, Tahrir Square quickly filled with tens of thousands of protesters, many chanting "Down with Morsi! Down with the MB!"[65] The next day, the Egyptian army issued an ultimatum: Morsi had forty-eight hours to come with a plan to address the country's problems or it would intervene. Cheers broke out across Tahrir Square when the ultimatum was announced.[66] On Tuesday, Morsi delivered his proposal, which offered a new prime minister and a reconciliation committee along with constitutional amendments to address opposition complaints, to the military.[67] Yet by the early morning of Wednesday, July 3, the pressure on Morsi to step down or for the military to remove him had become acute.

That morning, the army took control of state television—often one of the first steps in a coup.[68] Soon after, former UN nuclear watchdog Mohamed ElBaradei called on the military to remove an unhinged Morsi from office. "We ask the army to protect the souls of Egyptians after Morsi lost his mind and incited bloodshed of Egyptians," the Dustour Party, led by ElBaradei, said in a statement.[69] Military vehicles and security forces surrounded Tahrir Square as the ultimatum deadline approached. By that evening, top MB leaders had been arrested as Egypt's army forced Morsi out and took him into custody.[70] The military suspended the constitution and installed an interim government led by a senior jurist.[71] Some 300 arrest warrants were issued for MB members as tens of thousands of people celebrated the coup in Tahrir Square.[72,73] Saudi Arabia's King Abdullah was the first to congratulate Egypt's new leadership and express hope that it could shoulder the responsibility.[74] Within days, Saudi Arabia ($5 billion in aid) and the UAE ($3 billion) stepped in to help prop up the Egyptian economy during a highly unstable period.[75]

On July 3, as word spread, President Barack Obama issued a statement that refrained from using the word "coup" and expressed deep concern about the military's decision to remove Morsi.[76] Michael Morrell, deputy director of the CIA, expressed a different view. He was asked at the time how Morsi's overthrow boded for Egypt. "This is a good thing," he said. "Morsi was leading the country to ruin, to instability, and to extremism. Now Egypt has a chance again."[77] Nagla Rizk, an Egyptian economics professor who has spent time at Harvard and Yale, agreed with that assessment:

> This is the best thing that can happen. . . . I am worried about safety. I am worried about terrorism. I am worried about somebody trying to bomb himself in a jihad move in the name of Morsi. I don't want my kids to get bombed in the streets by some Morsi supporter who wants to defend Islam. That is my worry. This is a movement for an Islamic caliphate, so for them Egypt is just a detail. [The Brothers] were taking us back to the Dark Ages, at all levels. [Violence is] the only language that they know how to speak.[78]

The anti-MB rhetoric soon became overheated, as Egyptians began to call them cockroaches who sought to destroy Egypt. This led, almost inevitably, to a series of massacres, culminating in the horrific violence of August 14, detailed later in this chapter. In some ways, it was MB founder Hassan Al-Banna's lack of vision that caught up with the group. As detailed in Chapter 1, neither Hassan Al-Banna nor any of the MB leaders who came after ever laid out their vision for governance or outlined how the MB would act once in power. After four-score years struggling to come to power, the MB performed miserably once they finally achieved it—because they weren't adequately prepared.

The failure of the MB in this case typifies what the group has got wrong again and again in its attempts to participate in legitimate governance. Ashraf El-Sherif, a former associate at the Carnegie Endowment for International Peace, argues that the MB failed to democratize and moderate, as many predicted it would, showed an inability to win over elites and other key players as well as an ideological hollowness and opportunism that undercut its goal of Islamic democracy, and thus was never able to gain sustainable political control.[79] Essentially, the Brotherhood was done in by its very character, as El-Sherif described in 2014:

> Politically, the Brotherhood misread the situation. It moved toward political domination too quickly, making a series of tactical mistakes in the process. It failed to either appease or successfully confront institutional power bases, and, believing its electoral victory to be an irreversible popular mandate, it was reluctant to make the concessions necessary to avoid alienating crucial secular elites. The Brotherhood waged an unwinnable battle, driven more by ideological zeal and delusions of grandeur than by a realistic assessment of the political environment.
>
> Ideologically, the Brotherhood was shallow and opportunistic. It proved too willing to sacrifice elements of its ideology for short-term political victories. Furthermore, fundamentally antidemocratic components of Brotherhood dogma and the disconnect between the group's professed ideology and the policy positions it assumed highlighted its incompatibility with modern democratic politics.

Organizationally, the Brotherhood was incapable of adaptation. Its rigid, hierarchical structure prevented it from successfully reacting to rapid societal changes. The Brotherhood's attempts to promote organizational unity, while successful at muting the impact of intragroup differences, contributed to the exodus of fresh talent and ideas. Its organizational introversion and conspiratorial mindset also undermined its ability to build a broad network of support.[80]

An important sidenote is that Egyptians did not vote for the MB's Freedom and Justice Party because of its commitment to Islam. "Citizens voted for that party not because of its stance on the application of Islamic law, but because they believed it would pursue economic policies on behalf of the poor," Harvard scholar Tarek Masoud writes in his 2014 book *Counting Islam*.[81] Why does this matter? Because many observers linked the MB's electoral victory to its presence in the community—setting up local clinics, charitable work at the mosque and in schools, and so on—believing that the MB had over the years won the commitment of a vast base largely because of its conservative social credentials.

In reality, many voters chose the MB merely because they believed, in the moment, that it had the best chance of delivering prosperity—which is precisely why they were willing to move on from the MB when Morsi's government failed to deliver. "The fundamentally economic nature of voting for the Muslim Brotherhood in the aftermath of Mubarak's overthrow helps us to understand how an organization that seemed to have won hearts and minds across classes and ideological affiliations could lose all but its most hard-core supporters scarcely a year after assuming power," writes Masoud.[82]

Despite having had eighty years to create a vast following across Egypt, to win hearts and minds and generate widespread support for a state based on Islam and Sharia, the MB failed miserably—not only at governance but at building up a reliable political base. Egyptians' backing of the MB was not about a commitment to their conservative credentials or Islamist vision, which never really existed, but about a vague expression of hope. This may be because MB members are a great deal more passionate about jihad and revolution than they are about political campaigning and institution building.

This showed in polling data as well. The Egyptian Research and Training Center conducted surveys in November 2011, just before the parliamentary elections and in June 2013, as the mass protests swelled against Morsi. In the first, more than 40 percent of Egyptians said they were "very confident" in the MB, while about a quarter had "no confidence" in the movement. In the second, more than 60 percent had "no confidence" in the MB. What's more, 63 percent said their lives had worsened since Morsi's election as president, while just 11 percent said their lives had improved.[83]

As Masoud explains,

> If a passion for Islam is what drove voters in Egypt's founding elections, the
> Muslim Brotherhood and its allies might still be in power today. Instead, we
> saw that voters defected from Islamists almost as soon as they elected them,
> once the Brotherhood and its allies began to build up a record of policymak-
> ing that could be assessed against their outsized oaths.[84]

In the place of strong policy, Morsi and other MB leaders seemed to offer
obfuscation and secrecy, paired with an inability to connect with the people, to relay their strategy, vision, and potential. As Egypt's economy collapsed, so did the MB's hopes. "The network of the Muslim Brotherhood,
in all ways, is closed," Mohammed Menza, a professor of Middle East politics at the American University in Cairo, told Emirati newspaper *The National* in July 2013.[85] Menza said a lack of transparency about investments,
campaign spending, and goals for Egypt fuelled fears of a secret MB plot
to take control of the country (more on this below).[86]

MB leaders had long argued that letting the people choose freely would
put the Islamists in charge, leading to agreement between the citizens
and the regime, a counter to the United States and Israel and an independent Egypt's return to prominence. But it is one thing to be an opposition
group pointing out the flaws of the current regime. It is entirely another
to be in power and expected to lead—especially for an organization that
has never been able to articulate a solid vision. Monier and Ranko echo
Masoud:

> With its rise to power after the revolution, the onus was on the MB to live
> up to its promises to eliminate authoritarianism and establish Egypt as an
> independent regional power. This level of expectation meant that the Broth-
> erhood began suffering damage to its credibility because of perceived po-
> litical incompetence soon after becoming the largest bloc in parliament in
> early 2012.[87]

While Mubarak's role as a U.S. puppet was widely accepted by Egyptians
tired of the ruler's abuse of power, Morsi and the Islamist vision of the
MB did not present itself as enough of a contrast. The acquisition of power
by the Brotherhood simply resulted in a continuance of the "systematic
subversion" that Egyptians had endured for years, oppressing them with
even more hegemony.[88] As Monier and Ranko put it:

> The MB failed to convince either domestic audiences or regional actors that
> it was able to realize a viable or attractive transition for Egypt. Part of this
> was due to a lack of sufficient planning and part to the tension between Is-
> lamism as a transnational project and the regional system of sovereign Arab
> states. . . . Political incompetence and the perception of a hidden agenda con-
> cerning the MB's vision for Egypt and the Middle East undermined support.

This lack of clarity did not fit with the assertive "Egypt first" climate that emerged from the 2011 uprising. Mubarak was ousted because Egyptians saw him as serving his own interests; Morsi was overthrown for seeming to prioritize the MB's Islamic project. . . . Morsi soon became a symbol of both authoritarianism and the continuing weakness of Egyptian regional leadership that the MB had criticized while in opposition.[89]

The MB brought disaster upon itself, starting way back in late 2011, when General Guide of the Egyptian Muslim Brotherhood, Mohammad Badie declared that the ultimate MB goal of establishing the caliphate was near.[90] Domestic and international resentment had started to build even before Morsi became president—and only increased from there as the MB failed to move Egypt toward true democracy or implement its social justice agenda. As a result, the *Tamarrod* campaign, organic or not, generated considerable momentum and brought great numbers of protesters onto the streets, ultimately enabling the army and General Abdul Fattah El-Sisi to marginalize Morsi and push him and the MB from power on July 3, 2013.

As Sir John Jenkins says, "What happened between 2011 and 2013 is that the Brotherhood thought its moment had come. It had not, any more than it had in 1953. That does not tell us they are martyrs for freedom. It tells us that while they are good at playing games, when reality hits, they do not know what they are doing."[91]

THE REAL STORY BEHIND RABA'A

In response to Morsi's overthrow, the Brotherhood mobilized its masses, initiating a large sit-in at Cairo's Raba'a Square and a smaller gathering at nearby Al-Nahda Square. By early August, a huge tent city had been built at Raba'a, and thousands of protesters were ignoring government orders to disperse and were calling for Morsi to be reinstated as president. Many had been camped there for weeks and thought they might never leave. "Young Muslim Brotherhood members, some of them still in college, told me of that mix of adrenaline and dread they felt as they drafted their wills and bid their families goodbye," wrote Senior Brookings Fellow Shadi Hamid, detailing the mood in the square.[92]

One first-hand account from a former top UN official relates the preparedness for battle, the religious delusion, and the speeches of insurrection that typified the sit-in:

Raba'a is a major street with high-rise buildings on all sides full of residents. . . . They tore up the sidewalks and put in portable latrines and a stage. . . . It had six levels of sand bags piled up with a small opening to allow a car to go in, and there were four "thugs" holding sticks that I imagine can crack a head. . . . The poor residents of the surrounding buildings could not come out of their homes. And if they did, they were taken to questioning. . . . What was said from the podium was very dangerous and implicating. . . . For example Al Baltagi, one of the MB leaders, said that what is happening in Sinai will stop as soon as Morsi can go back as president. In other words, terrorism in Sinai is under the MB control. Then there were crazy and funny things from my point of view but the poor people in the camp believed it. One of the sheikh leaders said that he dreamt that the Prophet Mohammed came at the time of prayer but he asked Morsi to lead him and others for prayer. Another one said that the angel Gabriel was with them physically and interacted with them.[93]

The Interior Ministry reportedly developed a plan to disperse the protests at Raba'a and Al-Nahda Square by cordoning off the sites to block any new arrivals, then using water cannons and teargas. But when news of the plan leaked, on August 12, thousands more MB supporters flooded into the camps, prodding police to cancel their assault.[94] It was clear that the MB did not want the protest to be peacefully dispersed; it almost seemed MB leaders were hoping for violence.

What happened on the morning of August 14, 2013, is now known as the Raba'a Massacre, and has been described as "a crime against human-ity equal to, or worse, than Tiananmen Square"[95] and the "single biggest killing of protesters in modern history."[96] After encircling the camps, El-Sisi's security forces opened fire on thousands of pro-MB demonstrators at Al-Nahda and Raba'a Square, killing some 900 people and injuring 4,000. The scene was one of chaos and mass murder, according to an Egyptian journalist:

> In the halls [of the nearby hospital], in every corner, on every floor, the dead and wounded were sprawled; and there was an incessant flow of more being carried inside. The stairs were slippery with blood. It was stiflingly hot. All the windows had been shut to keep the tear gas out and the air, pungent with chemicals and sweat, hung heavy. The cacophony of shouting and moaning and sobbing rose above the mechanical crackle of the machine guns doing their work outside. Mass death assaults all the senses at once.[97]

While El-Sisi's forces undoubtedly fired upon civilians, what has been lit-tle reported on is the role the MB played in the bloodshed. This has be-come clear thanks to Emad Abo Hashim, an Egyptian judge who fled to Turkey after Morsi's ouster.[98] Hashim had long been a member of the MB in Egypt, but by the time of the interview, he had left the group. He starts by saying:

> All their words are lies, misguidance, illusions, rumours and rubbish that is being promoted from the door of religion or using religion as means to promote these lies. Therefore . . . when you know that the things they used to put forward about the June revolution are lies and you delete them from the information system of your brain or head, then the picture will be completely clear and the facts will be very clear; you will be able to find the truth.[99]

He makes clear that the MB knew the army was going to move in, and it kept the protesters there with the knowledge that blood would be shed. According to Hashim, Ashraf Abdel Ghaffar, a senior Egyptian MB leader, "was responsible for the dispersal of the Raba'a sit-in." Now in exile in Turkey, Ghaffar gave a July 2015 interview in which he defended the Brotherhood's sabotage of power stations and high-voltage pylons to punish Egyptian citizens for their support of the government.[100]

Hashim spent time at the Raba'a sit-in and said MB leaders lied to the protesters about the government's likely use of force in order to create a massacre. In fact, just two weeks before the massacre, a Brotherhood spokesperson, Gehad El-Haddad, outlined the group's willingness to die for the cause. "If they want to disperse the sit-in, they'll have to kill 100,000 protesters," the spokesman told journalist Maged Atef. "And they can't do it—we're willing to offer one hundred thousand martyrs."[101] To achieve this end, MB leaders had to convince the protesters that continuing the sit-in would lead them to no harm. Hashim said MB leaders told the protesters:

> That the government will not use force to disperse the sit-in. If [those in Raba'a] had known . . . they would have returned from where they came and only a few would remain. Al-Ikhwan hid the information that the government informed them of the zero hour of the dispersion of the sit-in because . . . they wanted this sit-in to continue to witness the hour of the dispersion in this manner, in order to maximize the number of victims that will fall among the demonstrators . . . and win political gains through pressure of number, through human sacrifices.[102]

Hashim also said that "a judge who is not a member of Al-Ikhwan but who is sympathetic to them . . . discovered that some elements in these demonstrations carried arms and they shot at the security forces and; therefore, it was natural that the security forces responded to the hail of fire directed at the soldiers and elements who were doing their job."[103]

Meanwhile, we now have a clear picture of growing tensions between then president Morsi and then military chief El-Sisi in the weeks leading up to Morsi's overthrow, thanks to documents released by then major general Muhammad Mostafa with the approval of the General Intelligence Directorate of Egypt.[104] Conversations between the two show the extent to which the MB, supported by Morsi and international collaborators, had infiltrated the country and meant to seize not just power but also territory and key bits of infrastructure, and how Morsi and MB leaders were well aware that any public challenge to the people's will would face the wrath of Egypt's military.

The meetings also revealed another important element. "They show the cool El-Sisi trying to convince Morsi of the early elections and Morsi's refusal. In addition, they evince El-Sisi's insistence that the army will not side against the demonstrators even as Morsi insists that he is the General Command of the Army in his capacity as the President of the Republic. Ultimately, it's clear that El-Sisi was trying to avoid a confrontation with the MB and find a peaceful solution," Thoraya Obaid, former Executive Director of the United Nations Population Fund, told me during an October 2018 interview.[105]

In early summer 2013, El-Sisi met with Morsi and with Khairat El-Shater and repeatedly stressed his desire to find a peaceful solution and avoid confrontation with the MB. Meanwhile, Morsi reiterated his belief that he was the general commander of the army in his capacity as president of the Republic.

Morsi: What about your position and that of the Army?

El-Sisi: We are warning against confronting the people and the peaceful demonstrations. The army will not allow this to happen.

Morsi: Are you going to stand with the saboteurs against legitimacy?

El-Sisi: We are always with the people; this is our mission and our creed. The demands of the people are just and we ask you to respond to their demands before it is too late.

Morsi: I do not accept your threat.

El-Sisi: We are not threatening but we are trying to save whatever can be saved.

Morsi: I know whatever concerns governing and I am the President and I warn you against continuing in this road.

El-Sisi: You know that our purpose is to protect the country and we do not have any other objective. We have a hope that you and your groups will respond to the voice of the people until we can get past the present crisis, especially that we have information that millions of Egyptians are coming out to demonstrate on 28 June.

Morsi: Your information is incorrect. We are confident that the demonstrators will be groups of subversives and thugs and they will not exceed a few thousand and we will deal with them.

El-Sisi: And we warn against attacking them because the army will not allow that. And we hope for our quick intervention to end this crisis.[106]

When Speaker of Parliament Saad El-Katatni interrupted and claimed that there was a conspiracy against the legitimacy of the president, El-Sisi countered:

The conspiracy is only in your minds. The people are peaceful but they have become tired of being underestimated and waiting for prosperity coming through you; however, they faced death, sickness, hunger and destruction. They waited for the building of the nation but they faced the rule of the MB and a President who talks only to his supporters from the MB and the Islamists among your family and tribe and forgot that there is a people of 90 million.[107]

Then, El-Sisi outlined a grand MB plot to overtake the country:

> The Military Council realized that there is no possibility of any moderation
> by the MB (Ikhwan) and all of Egypt was on sale by foreign dictation in
> exchange for the protection of the throne that they have stolen. He [Morsi]
> promises them Halayeb and Shalateen in Sudan and agrees with Ethiopia
> about the Millennial Dam and he suggests that it is called Al-Nahdha Dam.
> And he promised Al-Zawahiri to rule Sinai and he promised Qatar the right
> to make use of the Pyramids and Sphinx for 99 years for US$ 200 billion,
> equivalent to US$2 billion annually. The more dangerous was allowing
> ownership in Sinai and the naturalization of many members of Hamas and
> giving Qatar the right to use Suez Canal.[108]

Facing a military crackdown, the MB had devised a plan that would
involve confrontation with the demonstrators and the regime's forces.
Called the Ikhwan Plan in the documents, it details an extensive takeover of the country by the MB in collaboration with Qatar and Turkey.
Due to its audacious nature, the plan deserves to be nearly fully repro-
duced here:

- Dr. Mahmoud Izzat goes immediately to Al-Arish to prepare the Islamic forces
  with four-wheel drives carrying middle and heavy arms. The first group would
  liquidate all the military checkpoints on the way to Cairo and would control
  Martyr Ahmed Hamdi tunnel, in order to move to the Suez-Cairo road. The second group will control Al-Salam Bridge and will move to the Ismailia—Cairo
  road to enter Cairo the night of 19 June. The first group will move towards
  Al-Itihadiya [Presidential Palace] and the second one to Tahrir Square to stop
  the demonstrations, no matter how big are the losses and it would coordinate
  with Brother Haniya and Al-Qassam regiment.
- Brother Mohamed Kamal will assemble the Tanzeem under his leadership and
  they would be deployed in Cairo, Giza and the roads leading to Tahrir Square,
  destroying a lot of buses and microbuses, mining El-Sadat metro station and the
  tunnels and exploding them when needed to stop the flow of demonstrators.
- Brother Khairat Al-Shater is tasked with Brother Dr. Issam Al-Iryan to present
  the case to the American Ambassador and to the British Ambassador, requesting their support and explaining the seriousness of the situation.
- Brother Issam Haddad will meet with Sheikh Hamad bin Khalifa in Qatar,
  requesting his support and to pressure the Americans to intervene.
- Brother Jihad Haddad will travel to Turkey to meet with Brother Erdogan
  requesting his support of military forces in the case of the assassination of the
  leaders of the army and the police, as per the plan.
- Brother Biltagi and Essam Yassin and Asaad Sheikha will undertake an opera-
  tion for limited explosion of the back western runway. An invitation will be
  extended to the Salfist Brethren to attend the Presidential speech and issuing
  the permits for Al-Qassam brigade members, who will be responsible for liqui-
  dating the military leadership, especially El-Sisi, and Sidki Subhi and the Minister of Interior Mohamed Ibrahim.[109]

Learning of this plot, El-Sisi and the military decided it was time to move to save the country from a full-blown MB takeover. The July 3 ousting of Morsi and the ensuing Raba'a protesters—who were encouraged by the MB to stay and turn themselves into martyrs when the government's security forces arrived after numerous requests to disperse—demonstrated the Brotherhood's unpreparedness and failure to deliver its promise, among other things, to restructure the government institutions and protect the religious rights of the Copts and their right to their own religious laws. Instead, the MB leaders hatched a plan to fleece the country and empower themselves.

Jason Brownlee, professor of government at the University of Texas, wrote for the Middle East Institute that during his year in power, "Morsi used a familiar bag of dirty tricks against his opponents while his partisans captured the state. A caretaker legislature, dominated by the Muslim Brotherhood, tried to weaken the judiciary, thugs menaced television stations critical of Morsi, and the public prosecutor targeted the country's most trenchant dissidents."[110]

By early 2013, seeing that their efforts were failing, Morsi and his team began talking about calling for early elections. Tharwat Al-Kharabawi, a former MB member, warned in March 2013 that the MB planned to rig parliamentary elections.[111] Just after the coup, the writer Waḥid Abd Al-Magid echoed this view: "No one outside the Muslim Brotherhood and its supporters trusted in the fairness of any parliamentary elections under Morsi. . . . It is clear enough that preparations for rigging these elections had begun in earnest through the Ikhawn's hegemony over the relevant ministries and executive agencies."[112]

In the end, none of the MB's plans worked—it failed to take absolute power, to rig elections, and to use a massacre to return to prominence. In fact, the massacre "reflected the total failure of the Brotherhood's post-Morsi strategy, and its defeat in the power struggle with the military-backed government that assumed control following Morsi's ouster."[113] It also failed in its effort to remake Egypt into an Islamic state. In a 1992 speech in Washington, D.C., longtime U.S. diplomat Edward Djerejian explained how Islamists sought to exploit democratic elections to replace democracy with Islamic theocracy. Instead of "one man, one vote," he said, Islamists would lead to "one man, one vote, one time."[114] In Egypt, that appears to be precisely what the MB sought to do, until they were thwarted.

RETURN TO QUTBISM

In just over a year, the MB had taken and subsequently lost power due to a series of political blunders and had been absolutely decimated, largely thanks to its own mistakes. Then things got even worse. In late 2013, the El-Sisi government launched a massive crackdown, designating the MB a terrorist group, arresting hundreds of MB members, and blaming the group for the December 2013 bombing of a police station, which Al-Qaeda had claimed. MB members faced mass trials, which led to at least a thousand death sentences—though only two executions have been carried out, and those men confessed to their crimes. One was Abel Habbara, who killed several Egyptian security officers in the Rafah massacre in Sinai and who said that if released from prison he would kill them again.[115] The other was Mahmoud Hassan Ramadan, who confessed to throwing a teenager from a roof to his death.[116]

Campaigning for Egypt's May 2014 presidential election, which he won with 97 percent of the vote, El-Sisi declared: "There will be nothing called the Muslim Brotherhood during my tenure."[117] As of early 2019, he had nearly achieved this wish. Estimates of MB members behind bars ran from 30,000 to as many as 60,000.[118] Egypt's Interior Ministry had even built new jails to hold all of them.[119] "Even Muslim Brotherhood leaders acknowledge that the campaign against it has been effective in the sense that it has been devastating, breaking the organization into multiple pieces," Hassan Hassan, senior fellow at the Tahrir Institute for Middle East Policy and author of *ISIS: Inside the Army of Terror*, wrote in *The Atlantic* in November 2018. "Precisely because crackdowns have worked, the regime and its supporters also back their continuation. Now that a final victory against the Muslim Brotherhood is within reach, why let up?"[120]

In May 2019, to stress that it remained vigilant against the MB threat both at home and abroad, the Egyptian government blacklisted 600 people for funding MB-linked entities.[121] El-Sisi continued to make it clear that he does not wish to stamp out Islam. Rather, he opposes those who abuse it for their own best interests. His insistence on claiming Islam and redefining it has sent a positive message to many others who have grown tired of watching Islamists kill in the name of their religion. El-Sisi's rhetoric has been aptly applied and enhanced by convenient timing. From 1993 to 2008, Islamist militants were behind 60 percent of the terrorist bombings with the highest casualties.[122] In a speech James Mattis gave before taking office as President Trump's secretary of defense, he said of El-Sisi, "it's time for us to support him."[123]

The main risk in again pushing the MB to the margins, in blocking the group's path to politics and labelling it a terrorist organization, is that it will again go down that dark road, as Harvard's Tarek Masoud explains:

> Some have worried that the Muslim Brotherhood will now conclude that democracy is a fool's game, that future elections that might bring them once again to power will never be respected by so-called liberals or by the men with guns. One commentator fretted that . . . the Brothers will conclude "violence is the only path." Despairing of the ballot box, the Brothers, in this telling, would finally return to the path of violent revolution, fully embracing the jihadist ideology of Sayyid Qutb, who preached that this thing called

democracy was an abomination and an illusion. Events in Egypt in the aftermath of Morsi's overthrow seemed to confirm these fears, as a spate of church-burnings, police station firebombings, and other acts of violence have been attributed to supporters of the ousted president.[124]

Controlled by the El-Sisi regime, the narrative inevitably became that ousting Morsi and the MB was a part of confronting terrorism in the region, which soon became the truth. In the wake of the Raba'a massacre and the government crackdown, frustrated MB members turned again to violence and revolution. Some left the group to join more violent outfits, like Egyptian Islamic Jihad, while the main Egyptian MB soon moved in the same direction. In May 2015, a hundred Egyptian imams and Islamic scholars signed a letter declaring, "The aggrieved party has the right to fight back against the aggressor."[125] The letter said "a murderous regime" ruled Egypt, and its collaborators—"rulers, judges, officers, soldiers, muftis, media professionals, and politicians"—should be punished as "murderers" under Islamic law. The next day, the Brotherhood's leadership-in-hiding endorsed the declaration.[126]

Around the same time, the MB's Sharia Committee released a book, *The Jurisprudence of Popular Resistance to the Coup*, which provides Islamic justification for terrorist attacks on the state as a legitimate form of defensive jihad.[127] The authors argue that Egypt's people had sworn allegiance (*Bayah*) to Morsi, that his overthrow represented a violation of the people's will, and that the military's treachery and treason against a president they had sworn to protect made the new regime enemy combatants, according to an analysis and translated excerpts by Mokhtar Awad, research fellow at George Washington University's Program on Extremism: "The rule of the putschists over President Morsi in Egypt is not legitimate rule in any way as outlined by Islam in reaching power. Therefore, they are usurpers, thieves, thugs, and killers."[128] The book echoes both Qutb and Al-Qaradawi, at one point blaming the Egyptian government's collaboration with the Zionist and Crusader powers.

By this time, ISIS jihadis had begun to recruit heavily among MB members and other persecuted Egyptians imprisoned under El-Sisi.[129] Fall 2013 to early 2016 was a period of heavy MB-linked violence and disruption across Egypt, according to the scholars Monier and Ranko:

> In the immediate aftermath of Rabaa, the Brotherhood went on a rampage attacking and burning police stations, killing personnel, taking weapons, and releasing prisoners. In the town of Kerdassa they killed fourteen police officers and their bodies were mutilated. Forty-four churches were burned down and the newly built Museum of Antiquities was robbed and torched. Between June 2013 to the end of February 2016, the Muslim Brotherhood and ISIS killed nine hundred police officers and committed 1,494 acts of violence across Egypt. Brotherhood members have worked to sabotage Egyptian electricity grids and disrupt traffic.[130]

By the end of 2016, the Brotherhood had begun to crack and splinter under the pressure, amid endless debates about who should lead the group and whether they should embrace violence and confrontation. A period of reevaluation again led to an embrace of violence as the surest route to change. Though not all MB leaders agree, the view gained traction among at least one major faction in Egypt. After Morsi's overthrow, a senior MB leader from Upper Egypt named Mohamed Kamal formed his own splinter group and in early 2014 gave the green light to violence.[131] Kamal created a group called Revolutionary Punishment, which in 2015–16 carried out some 150 armed assaults on police and security checkpoints.[132] Researcher Ahmad Al-Tilawy, who self-identifies as a "loyal Brother," wrote in February 2016 about the internal discussions, and even mentioned:

> A project adopted by the [Brotherhood] leadership which is the creation of "strong arms," which is a special apparatus inside the Muslim Brotherhood that is meant to carry out specific special operations during the stage of Hassm [decisiveness] with the regime. This is after the stages of disorienting and attrition [of the enemy]. These are the three stages that the [Brotherhood] specified in its literature following the coup in order to overthrow the military regime and bring back legitimacy [Morsi].[133]

Shortly after this was written, a new terrorist group called *Hassm*, suspected of ties to the MB, began a campaign of violence across the country. Many older MB leaders disagreed with the violent tactics of Kamal and others and made this plain. So, in December 2016, two months after Kamal was killed in a security forces raid, his faction launched a coup inside the Egyptian MB, assuming all leadership positions. According to George Washington's Mokhtar Awad, as of late 2017, there were two distinct Egyptian MB factions claiming the mantle of MB leadership, both with their own constituencies inside and outside Egypt.[134]

The MB had suddenly found itself on a dark road, with violent splinter factions and ideological rifts and debates about vision and mission. What's clear is that Qutb and his extremist ideology, and advocacy of violent jihad, have reemerged in recent years as the group's motivating force. Egypt's President of Supreme Council for Islamic Affairs, Dr. Mohamed Mokhtar Gomaa, has called the Brotherhood "harmful to Islam," adding that it is "the progenitor of the Islamic State and similar terrorist groups."[135] It's a sign of how deeply embedded Qutb's thinking became that still today these are the animating ideas behind the diatribes of MB spiritual leader Yusuf Al-Qaradawi. "After the destruction of the Egyptian Ikhwan in 1954," writes Frampton, "it was Qutb who rebuilt the organization at an intellectual level."[136] This explains why Cambridge scholar Hazem Kandil, in his 2014 book *Inside the Brotherhood* calls Qutb the group's second founder.[137]

Shortly after Mohamed Kamal's death, his daughter told the news site Masr Al-Arabia that he had been seeking a "third founding" of the MB, which would again require the use of violence.[138] But in a way this third founding had already happened, in 2015, with the release of the jurisprudence book and when the MB approved a statement that called for aggression to overthrow El-Sisi:

> Everyone must realise that we are embarking upon a new phase. We gather all our strengths; recount the meanings of jihad; prepare ourselves, families and those who support us for a long-term jihad; and aspire to reach the ranks of martyrs.[139]

In addition to Revolutionary Punishment, violent MB factions included the Arms of Egypt movement and the Revolutionary Brigade. In December 2018, ISIS profiled three Egyptian Army officers under Morsi who joined ISIS following the Raba'a massacre, as detailed in a tweet by Hassan, of the Tahrir Institute.[140] The former MB members were soon incorporated into ISIS' military planning department.[141]

All of this is of a piece with the MB's re-embrace of revolutionary violence in recent years. Shadi Hamid, one of the foremost analysts of Islamism, has noted within the Egyptian MB a broader shift toward Qutbist ideas in the wake of Morsi's overthrow. "After the Egyptian coup of July 2013, a process of radicalization began at the individual level, with a growing minority of younger Brotherhood members advocating 'defensive violence' and, more recently, economic sabotage to the dismay of an older, more conservative leadership-in-exile," he wrote for the Brookings Institute in December 2015.[142]

> Younger Brotherhood members have adopted a more revolutionary posture, seeing the Egyptian state not as something to be reformed (the group's pre-2013 position), but as an enemy to be overhauled, purged, or even destroyed.... These changing attitudes toward state institutions suggest a potentially deeper, philosophical shift, with profound long-term implications. This new, revolutionary politics has, over time, seeped up to the Brotherhood's leadership and organizational structures. It reflects not just a critical mass of individual Brotherhood members adopting different attitudes toward political change, but an *organizational* shift as well.[143]

A few weeks after Hamid's piece was published, senior MB leader Abdul Ashraf Ghaffar—whom former MB member Hashim blames for the Raba'a massacre—said the MB would soon overthrow El-Sisi. "A new revolution is coming today and we will end this system of Abdel Fattah El-Sisi," he said in a January 2016 interview with Turkish state broadcaster TRT World. "We are in a difficult position, but we are coming to the streets again. We are coming to clean our country again."[144] Two years later, Ghaffar was said to be in charge, along with the head of the international MB, Ibrahim Mounir Mustafa, of MB-linked terrorist operations in Sinai and beyond.[145]

As poorly as the Brotherhood served Egypt during its short time in power, and however much the group may have earned the harsh crackdown under El-Sisi, two concerns should be expressed here. First, while there are undoubtedly thousands of MB members deserving of arrest and detention—Egypt, like Saudi Arabia and the UAE, has declared the group a terrorist outfit, which means its members are by definition enemies of the state—the El-Sisi government has gone too far in its willingness to imprison all who disagree with the official narrative, including those who have nothing to do with the MB, ISIS, or Al-Qaeda.

The second, closely related point is that an overly aggressive crackdown could be worse than no crackdown at all. Of course the group needs to be silenced and marginalized, as it is inherently violent and revolutionary, as has been detailed repeatedly in this book. However, when government efforts to stamp out the group appear in the public eye unjust and brutal, they are liable to have precisely the opposite impact as had been intended. As one can see by the several-year spate of attacks, the heavy ISIS recruitment in prisons, the splintering off of several terrorist cells, and the apparent organizational shift toward violence, this newly Qutbist MB in Egypt is growing more dangerous than ever. There is a line beyond which an oppressor begins to further the cause he seeks to destroy, and El-Sisi may have crossed it.

THE CURSE OF MB-LINKED RULE

In the wake of the Arab uprisings of 2011, many thought the region was witnessing the resurrection of political Islam. Egypt's MB and Tunisia's Ennahda joined Turkey's AKP as Islamist parties in power, leading some to argue that Islamism would be the next great political wave to wash over the region. But with the AKP losing favor as Turkey turns authoritarian and its economic star fades, Ennahda uncertain about its role, Sudan's Islamists turfed out, and Egypt's MB ousted and returned to its radical roots, those predictions have proven wrong. The Muslim world, along with Western observers, has begun to grasp that the MB's Islamism, lacking the requisite concern for governance, is far from enough. "The MB is inimical to independent states, to the independence of the Arab people, to their right to control their own destiny. Their strict religio-ideological approach to politics leaves no room for a population to determine its own destiny. It must march in step with the MB vision, or it must be destroyed," Bahrain's national security adviser told me in 2018.[146]

Indeed, putting an MB-linked leader in power seems to put a country on the road to ruin. As detailed earlier, today's Egypt is overrun with terrorist groups. It's also deep in debt, facing rampant unemployment, and run by a dictator that has drawn vast criticism for his abuses of power and human rights violations. After decades of rule by MB-friendly Omar Al-Bashir, Sudan is a highly unstable economic disaster following his overthrow.[147] Tunisia, the darling of Western liberals a few years ago, has taken a similarly sharp downturn since Ennahda came to power in 2012. Political assassinations have returned, the economy has collapsed, and tens of thousands of Tunisians signed up for ISIS' jihad—more than any other country in the region. Meanwhile, tens of thousands more took to the Mediterranean, hoping to reach the Italian island of Lampedusa and opportunity in the EU. "Tunisia's democracy on life support," declared the headline of a January 2019 *Al-Monitor* story.[148] "Many of the chronic ills that triggered the revolution and the lack of democratic institutions have thrust this North African nation of 11.7 million back into a crisis with no ready fixes in sight," according to the article. "Young people are stuck having to choose between Lampedusa and DAESH," said the country director of an international nongovernmental organization.[149]

Turkey, while not ruled by an MB affiliate, has since 2002 been run by the MB-friendly Justice and Development Party (AKP)—and has also lost its way of late. A decade ago, Western analysts and U.S. president Barack Obama were hailing "the Turkish model" of President Recep Tayyip Erdogan for his successful blend of Islam and democracy. By the end of the U.S. president's second term, he had a different view: "Obama now considers Erdogan a thuggish autocrat who threatens Turkey's democracy."[150] Since the failed July 2016 coup attempt, Erdogan has unleashed several purges, dismissing some 130,000 public servants, putting more than 50,000 people behind bars, including prominent politicians, and closing more than 150 news outlets while imprisoning some 200 journalists. His government has also turned to terrorism and begun detaining Americans visiting Turkey to use as diplomatic leverage. "They are engaging in Hezbollah-like behavior and taking hostages to use as trade bait," Eric Edelman, who served as U.S. ambassador to Turkey from 2003 to 2005, told *Bloomberg*.[151]

By early 2019, the Turkish lira had fallen sharply and inflation and unemployment peaked.[152] As in Tunisia, all of this trouble spurred a mass exodus. "Spurning Erdogan's Vision, Turks Leave in Droves, Draining Money and Talent," declared a *New York Times* headline in January 2019. The article pointed out that more than 113,000 Turkish nationals had emigrated in 2018, up by more than 60 percent from the previous year, and that many were well-educated professionals, top scientists and academics, and wealthy businesspeople.[153] That March, this all appeared to catch up with Erdogan's party, as voters turfed out AKP mayors in the capital, Ankara, and the country's economic powerhouse, Istanbul, shortly after Turkey had fallen into a recession. "The party suffered its most serious electoral setback in its 16 years in power, as an unusually united opposition tapped into widespread economic discontent to flip control of Ankara and nine provincial capitals," according to *Foreign Affairs*.[154]

Turkey had seen this movie before. Some fifteen years before the rise and fall of the MB in Egypt, something similar happened in Turkey. In 1996, Necmettin Erbakan, founder of the MB-inspired Welfare Party, became the country's first Islamist prime minister, after a close national election. "He declared Turkish politics a pitiful imitation of the West and announced a campaign for worldwide Muslim solidarity," according to a 2003 *New York Times* magazine profile of Erbakan's prize pupil, Erdogan. "He overreached. After 12 months, the military forced him to resign."[155]

These examples show us yet again, if any further proof were needed, that Islamism is incompatible with democracy. Whenever an MB-type ideology is given power, that country's institutions, if not its economy, begin to rot from within. This is likely because, returning again to a point that has been stressed throughout this book, the Brotherhood has never had any vision for governance and never imagined how it might run a state should it ever get the opportunity. This is why it has never been a true political entity but a revolutionary movement. As Abdel Monem Said Aly, senior fellow at the Crown Center for Middle East Studies at Brandeis University, wrote for *Cairo Review* in Spring 2018:

> The historical evolution, ideological doctrine, and organizational structure of the Brotherhood all reveal a movement that is as politically totalitarian as it is religiously extreme. The notion that the Brotherhood can ever be a force for pluralism and political openness if only the "root causes" that have driven them to extremism are addressed belies their violent history, their frequent resort to terrorism, and the inescapable reality that it has spawned countless terrorist groups that today continue to afflict Egypt and the region. . . . Brotherhood members strive to create a theocratic regime not so different from the Iranian political system. In their actions, organization, and ideology, the MB acts as an incubator of terrorists, a mobilizer of human and material resources to fund and to defend terrorism, whether directly or indirectly.[156]

This echoes prominent Western voices. Dennis B. Ross, former U.S. envoy and negotiator to the Middle East and a fellow at the Washington Institute for Near East Policy, wrote in *The New York Times* in September 2014: "Do not reach out to Islamists; their creed is not compatible with pluralism or democracy."[157] The CIA has held a similar view for decades. "Increased strength of the Brotherhood . . . will tend to make Egypt less sympathetic to US goals in the Middle East," its intelligence directorate wrote in a 1986 report on the group. "The Egyptian MB's long term goal is to build a fundamentalist Muslim society by sweeping out Western influence and implementing Islamic law."[158] The British government's 2015 report on the group, co-authored by former ambassador Sir John Jenkins, pointed to its tendency for violence, a tendency he saw making a return in the wake of Morsi's overthrow:

> The Muslim Brotherhood historically focused on remodelling individuals and communities through grassroots activism. They have engaged politically

where possible. But they have also selectively used violence and sometimes terror in pursuit of their institutional goals. . . . There is little evidence that the experience of power in Egypt has caused a rethinking in the Muslim Brotherhood of its ideology or conduct. UK official engagement with the Egyptian Muslim Brotherhood produced no discernible change in their thinking. Indeed, even by mid-2014, statements from Egyptian Muslim Brotherhood-linked media platforms seem to have deliberately incited violence.[159]

Sir John Jenkins also reminds us that this dangerous, revolutionary vision is not just a threat to Egypt but to the entire Arab region, even the Muslim world, and beyond. "Events in Libya, Tunisia, Jordan and Yemen showed the MB would not have stopped at the Red Sea. Nasser had the same hegemonic ambitions—this was an Islamist reboot," he wrote in 2017.[160]

Again and again over the past half century, the MB has proven to be an organization that in its truest incarnation embraces not democratic moderation but violence and revolution. This is because the only Islamic ideology the Brothers have to turn to is that of Qutb. Al-Banna was no scholar of Islam and never laid out his interpretation of the Quran or other scholarly works. This is why the MB has been so keen to claim Qutb, who inspired the creation of Al-Qaeda and ISIS, as their own. "He is essentially the only true scholar that the Ikhwan produced," writes Pargeter, "the only thinker whose ideas have really gone beyond the confines of the movement."[161]

The problem is that the ideas of Qutb led directly, again and again, to abominable acts of terrorism. It is these ideas, and their influence, that inspired Saudi Arabia and other Gulf states, in the 1970s and in the decades since, to push back against the Brotherhood influence that had taken root in their countries.

CHAPTER 4

The Muslim Brotherhood in the Levant

This chapter looks at the MB in the Levant, specifically Syria, Jordan, Palestine, Iraq, and Lebanon. MB affiliates in this region are generally older and are more closely aligned with the mother organization than those of the Gulf and North Africa, due to proximity and direct connections with MB founder Hassan Al-Banna.

As a result, the history of the MB in the Levant contrasts considerably with that in North Africa, largely due to regional circumstances. In Syria, civil war and social strife have severely curbed the MB's ability to gain power. In Jordan, the monarchy's relation with the MB has consistently been uneasy. In Palestine, the Israeli-Palestinian conflict and the role of Hamas have severely limited the MB's ability to present itself as a viable governing alternative. In Iraq, the MB's political party has failed to capture Sunni hears in the post-Saddam era. And in Lebanon, the Brotherhood's experience has been greatly influenced by regional conflict and the presence of Hezbollah. Each of these affiliates, and territories, has their own unique history, though today the outlook for all seems increasingly bleak.

SYRIA

Syria's Brotherhood affiliate is one of the region's oldest and most established, beginning back in the 1930s. The Syrian religious scholar Mustafa Al-Sibai was studying in Egypt when he came under the influence of MB founder Hassan Al-Banna, who had recently moved the group to Cairo. Al-Sibai took part in MB activities in Egypt, and when he returned to Syria in 1941 he began drawing together the country's various Islamist groups to create a single organization like Egypt's MB. With help from his friend Muhammad Al-Mubarak Al-Tayyib, Al-Siba founded the Syrian

MB in 1945, a year before the country's independence from France. Alison Pargeter, senior researcher at the Royal United Services Institute with a focus on Islamist movements, takes a close look at the group's early days in her 2013 book *The Muslim Brotherhood: The Burden of Tradition*:

> Al-Sibai soon gained a reputation for his level-headed and enlightened approach, as well as for his openness to others. What he shared in particular with Al-Banna was his strong sense of pragmatism. Although he was personally less interested in working in the political sphere, believing that the primary duty of the movement was dawa rather than politics, he was willing for the Ikhwan to contest the 1947 parliamentary elections, in which it won three seats to the parliament.[1]

With an agenda focused on ending Syria's dependence on foreign powers and the domination of the upper class elite, the Syrian MB grew quickly.[2] By 1954, as the Egyptian MB faced Nasser's wrath, the Syrian affiliate was even able to offer support to the mother organization and refuge to exiled leaders. It's important to note that unlike the Egyptian MB, the Syrian chapter was not a mass movement in its early years. "It was actually a rather elitist organization with followers who were typically educated members of the traditional Sunni urban middle class and the sons of religious scholars, merchants, or craftsmen," Thomas Pierret, author of *Religion and State in Syria* and lecturer in contemporary Islam at the University of Edinburgh, wrote in August 2015.[3]

This helps explain why, unlike Egypt's MB, the group showed surprising flexibility and a willingness to embrace fashionable ideas, such as giving up its 1950 proposal to make Islam the official state religion and later adapting Arab nationalism and even bits of socialism.[4] As a result, the Syrian MB steadily gained political clout, taking three seats again in 1949, five seats in 1954, and an impressive ten seats in 1961, with ministers in two governments.[5]

But everything changed on March 7, 1963, when the secular Baath Party, dominated by Alawites, came to power in a coup and quickly sought to weaken the Sunni merchant class that backed the MB.[6] The next year, Syria's MB was banned and its leader, Issam Al-Attar, forced into exile. "The immediate impact of Al-Attar's banishment was to create a vacuum inside the movement that not only led to a leadership crisis but also enabled more militant elements within the group to flourish," writes Pargeter.[7]

More radical scholars soon began to take the lead, starting with Said Hawa. The charismatic Hama native joined the MB in the 1950s and supported the idea that Muslims had abandoned Islam. He advised his followers to distance themselves from the heathen and impure, to stay away from radio, television, newspapers, and theater and advocated jihad against "impure" Muslims including Shiites and Sufis.[8] "Hawa's book *Soldiers of Allah: Culture and Manners*, which called for jihad against the regime, was distributed in its thousands in bookshops, street stalls and mosques and became a major point of discussion for all Syrian Ikhwanis," writes Pargeter, again highlighting the MB's tendency toward violence and revolution:

> He called upon the Syrian Ikhwan to restructure itself so that it could move away from being a party of dawa to one of jihad. Hawa was a charismatic figure who, because of his scholarly achievements, had more influence than other leading figures within the Ikhwan. As such his call to turn the Brotherhood into a jihadist party that could lead a rebellion against the Baathist regime could not be ignored. His comments provoked a major internal debate within the Syrian Ikhwan and exacerbated the factionalism that was already present. Whilst the traditional leaders were calling on the Brotherhood to work behind the scenes and to focus their efforts on dawa, Hawa instigated his followers to prepare for military action. He allegedly involved his young followers in physical training including wrestling, boxing and street fighting, and he divided those who followed him into family units and fighting brigades.[9]

Hawa's ideas likely helped spur the first Hama revolt, in 1964, which the new Baath Party leadership quickly put down.[10] Hawa's thinking also contributed to the creation—spurred by the death of fellow Hama native Marwan Hadid, who led the initial revolt against the Baathists in 1964—of an armed splinter group called the Fighting Vanguard, which led an assassination campaign against top officials.[11] This cemented the radicalization of the Syrian MB, as with other MB affiliates around the same time. The major difference in Syria was that the jihadis remained connected to the MB, instead of leaving to form their own organizations, which made it much more difficult to prevent a broader radicalization of the group.[12]

Yet the movement was growing, thanks to a new strategy that resulted from the oppression of military rule. The Syrian MB began systematically recruiting and proselytizing via a network of informal study circles, which enabled it to take advantage of the Islamic revival sweeping the Muslim world in the 1970s.[13] Hafez Al-Assad took power in 1970, spurring tensions that erupted into violence sanctioned by the Syrian MB, which refused the legitimacy of the Alawite regime. By 1976, the Syrian MB had embraced full-on rebellion and embarked on a violent insurgency. In June 1979, perhaps inspired by the Islamist revolution in Iran a few months prior, the group attacked the Aleppo Artillery School, massacring as many as eighty cadets, and assassinated prominent academics.[14] Al-Assad responded with a massive crackdown and death sentences for fifteen suspected MB members already in prison. Terrorist attacks became a near daily occurrence, with many launched by the Syrian MB, though the exact share is impossible to determine as the resistance soon gained broad support.

By March 1980, Syrian cities were paralyzed by protests and strikes as the seventeenth coup anniversary approached. The Assad regime responded with great force, unleashing tanks and helicopters along with thousands of troops. Hundreds of protesters were killed in the Aleppo area alone, and the uprising was silenced. A June assassination attempt on Al-Assad resulted in authorities massacring as many as 1,000 inmates at Tadmur prison, where many MB members were being held.[15] In July 1980, the Assad regime introduced Law 49, which made MB membership not just illegal but punishable by death.[16] In the months that followed, the government committed horrifying acts of collective punishment—80 executed in Aleppo, then 400 in Hama—as a warning to those who would challenge Al-Assad's rule.

The next year, more than a thousand, mostly young MB members turned themselves in to the authorities, looking to avoid the death penalty. Despite the loss of these members, in the second half of 1981 the Syrian MB carried out a series of car bomb attacks against government and military targets in the capital. The state-run press claimed the attacks killed hundreds of people. Flush with confidence, the Syrian MB launched an insurrection in Hama on February 2, 1982, and quickly gained control of the city. The military responded with wave after wave of bombing runs, killing as many as 38,000 people in a city of 250,000.[17] Remaining MB members left the country, fleeing to Iraq, Jordan, and beyond, and that was the end of the MB in Syria, for a time.

"The uprising in Hama went far beyond the Muslim Brotherhood and represented a much wider general dissatisfaction with the ruling regime. However, it is obvious that when the time came the Ikhwani were willing to support the use of violence in order to achieve change," writes Pargeter.[18] The Syrian MB failed spectacularly in that effort and became a movement in exile, focusing its efforts on evaluating what went wrong and negotiating a return. Even its own internal evaluation proved as contentious as most MB efforts at governance, and took twelve years.[19] As for making its way back to Syria, a key element of this was a shedding of the years of militancy and a return to the more moderate stance of the affiliate's early days.

Crucial to this makeover was the new supreme guide of the Syrian Muslim Brotherhood, appointed in 1996, Ali Sadreddine Al-Bayanouni, who initiated secret negotiations with the Assad government and was behind the issuance of several reform platforms.[20] The National Honour Pact of late 2001 called for broad political dialogue and rejected taking up arms against one's own government.[21] Unsurprisingly, the document also asserted that the Syrian MB "had no hand in creating or initiating" the violence that led to the Hama massacre.[22] The charter went on to support elections as a means to determine leadership, but remained ambiguous on the envisioned interaction of Sharia and democracy. Still, the charter represented a major shift from the radical ideas that held sway in the 1970s, including a willingness to start a dialogue with Europe and the United States. But this may have been posturing, in part, as after September 2001 the Syrian MB became just as interested as the Egyptian MB in proving to the world that it was not a terrorist organization.[23]

Shortly after the U.S. invasion of neighboring Iraq in 2003, Al-Bahanouni called for a comprehensive reconciliation as the Syrian MB began to be taken more seriously.[24] This is how the Syrian MB survived in exile, shifting away from violence and offering compromise with the regime in order to request the release of MB prisoners, the right to return, and the revocation of Law 49. Hafez's son Bashar Al-Assad came to power in 2000 and quickly freed several hundred MB prisoners and allowed the publication of several out-of-print works by Al-Sibai, hoping to foster an image of friendly relations between Islam and the state.[25] In 2005, opposition groups and the Syrian MB, still outlawed and predominantly in exile, signed the Damascus Declaration, calling for a peaceful transition to democracy in cooperation with the regime.

But a few months later the Syrian MB made a surprising decision, aligning itself with former vice president Abd Al-Halim Khaddam, who had been until his defection a few months prior one of the most powerful figures in Syria, to launch the National Salvation Front, which called for peaceful regime change. "The SMB alliance with Khaddam was deeply unpopular among the movement's rank and file and was roundly criticized by prominent Damascus declaration signatories," Yvette Talhamy, former teaching fellow in the University of Haifa's department of Middle Eastern studies, wrote for *Middle East Quarterly* in Spring 2012.[26]

The Syrian MB had made a serious miscalculation. "Khaddam was also far from being the right horse to back, despite his former position. He was perceived in Syria as one of the regime's most corrupt figures. He had been marginalized for several years, leaving him little leverage inside the state apparatus," according to Perriet.[27] By fall 2008, it was clear that Arab and Western states were willing to engage with Bashar Al-Assad. The next year, when Al-Assad's government backed MB-linked Hamas in its war with Israel, the Syrian MB was forced to break from the Khaddam alliance. The three-year union had brought little more than problems: "The alliance with Khaddam damaged the SMB's credibility in the eyes of many Syrians, and for very little return," said Talhamy.[28]

In 2010, the Syrian MB elected a new leader Riad Al-Shaqfa, a hardliner who had led the group's military unit in the 1980s.[29] Al-Shaqfa urged Turkey's Islamist Justice and Development Party (AKP), which had long been friendly with the MB, to liaise with the Assad regime to ease restrictions on the group's activities.[30] "We would like the Turkish government to intervene to solve the problems," he said in October 2010, adding later that the Syrian MB was even willing to stop calling itself the "Muslim Brotherhood" if allowed to return to Syria.[31]

A few months afterwards came the Arab uprisings, for which the Assad regime largely blamed the MB, at least domestically. Syria descended into a bloody civil war, which spurred the Syrian MB to attempt a return.

In fact, a key domestic result of the Syrian civil war is the resurrection of the MB. "Much like the MB in Egypt, once the Syrian Brotherhood understood what was happening, they knew they had to jump into the conflict as well as the political negotiations if they sought any real say in the country's future."[32]

In April 2011, the Syrian MB issued a statement in support of the uprisings. At the first conferences to organize the country's opposition groups, in Antalya and Brussels a few months later, the Syrian MB jostled for political influence. These conferences led to the formation of opposition groups in which the MB pushed for an outsized presence. These groups later aligned with other anti-Assad forces to create the Syrian National Coalition. The SNC set aside seats for both the MB and the Damascus Declaration group, which itself had a significant MB presence.[33] Here's how the Syrian MB put its finger on the scales of political influence, according to Hassan Hassan, a Syrian author and senior fellow at the Tahrir Institute for Middle East Policy:

> The Brotherhood's political domination became more pronounced in late September 2011, when opposition figures and forces met in two separate hotels in Turkey to form a political body representing all opposition forces. In an early sign of its organizational skill, the Brotherhood divided itself into two groups, one in each hotel, to influence both sides of how the body was to be shaped: The Brotherhood's leader, Riad Al-Shaqfa, was in one hotel while his deputies, Tayfour and Ali Sadreddine Al-Bayanouni, were in the other. . . . The strategy paid off: A list of agreed-upon members was altered in one of the hotels, and more Brotherhood members and Brotherhood-affiliated groups were added before the creation of the [Syrian National Council] was announced on Oct. 2.[34]

Saudi Arabia, the UAE, and Jordan worked to reduce MB influence in the coalition, pushing for the inclusion of secular Syrians and more rebel representatives. This led to the selection of Ahmad al Jarba and Hadi Al-Bahra, two pro-Saudi figures, who led the SNC for nearly two years.[35] Still, the Syrian MB was able to avoid confrontation with its foes and retain its key positions. In addition, several other opposition groups were essentially fronts for the Syrian MB, including the Levant Ulema League, the Hama Revolution Gathering, and the Commission for Civilian Protection, which generates foreign funding to help Syrians inside the country.[36] The MB also gave activists media training in Turkey and then returned them to Syria to create coordinating committees.

At the same time, the MB reactivated contacts across Syria and began to put together fighting battalions. The group found and met with early defectors from Al-Assad's military and gained significant influence within the Free Syrian Army, as well as within the Tawhid Brigade, Jaysh Al-Mujahideen, and other rebel groups. "Brotherhood exiles have been funding armed groups since late 2011. The organization now controls or sponsors dozens of small paramilitary units inside Syria," Aron Lund, former fellow of the Middle East Program at the Carnegie Endowment, wrote in May 2013.[37]

In addition, the chaos of the war has allowed many exiled Syrian MB members to return to the country, filtering back into rebel-held areas to reestablish the movement and rebuild influence. "We are encouraging people to go back to Syria," Mohammed Walid, who heads the Syrian Brotherhood, told Reuters in 2015. "I would say hundreds."[38]

If any opposition group could be said to have overseen the first years of the Syrian civil war, it was the MB. This was thanks in part to its good relations with Turkey, which provided meeting places and staging areas along the border, and Qatar, which offered predominantly positive coverage on Al Jazeera. But as of mid-2019, with the war winding down, the Brotherhood's reputation had fallen across the region. As its Islamist competitors have gained a greater profile in Syria, the outlook for the Syrian MB has become cloudy at best. "They don't have a young generation and although there's some recruitment, they're not popular," Adib Shishakly, Gulf envoy of the Syrian National Coalition, said in 2015. "People supported them because they were the only religious option, now there will be lots."[39]

Still, assisted by the government of neighboring Turkey, which is influenced by Qatar, the MB hopes to wield some real influence in the Syrian state. "[Turkish President] Erdogan, acting through the so-called opposition, the majority of which is, of course, loyal to him, is seeking to . . . ensure that the Muslim Brotherhood has a voice in the Syrian government," Bouthaina Shaaban, an adviser to Syrian president Bashar Al-Assad, said in a February 2019 interview.[40] This helps explain why, in October 2018, Saudi Arabia provided $100 million to the United States for stabilization projects in Syrian territories formerly held by ISIS but now under the control of U.S.-allied Kurdish militias.[41]

Though the civil war enabled the Syrian MB to return to a position of influence, the group remains a long way from making any real political impact. As of mid-2019, Bashar Al-Assad had retaken some 90 percent of the country's territory and the war had all but ended in favor of a leader with little history of warm relations with the MB or acceptance of challengers. Perhaps more importantly, all those years in exile have left the aging Syrian MB leadership out-of-touch and still clinging to an outdated, undemocratic system.

Consider that the Syrian MB leader Al-Shaqfa is seventy-five years old in a country where two-thirds of the population are under thirty. "They've become too old," a young Syrian activist who is sympathetic to the Brotherhood told Lund:

> His family is closely associated with the group, but he has opted not to join it. "Frankly, the Muslim Brotherhood in Syria is a pensioners' club. . . . I myself

could be considered part of the second, or even third, generation of Brotherhood families, but I grew up outside of Syria, so I don't have the same attachment to the group. And I'm not alone, there are thousands of us." This generation gap has led many young Islamist Syrians to feel excluded from the Brotherhood as an organization. "We may know more than they do about a great many things, but it's very hard to become one of them," the activist complains. And in turn, the older generation has become disconnected from realities on the ground. "When they talk about Syria, they think of Syria thirty years ago. I think they're finally beginning to realize this now. . . . But I haven't seen any real steps to address the problem."[42]

JORDAN

As in Syria, Jordan's MB came into existence before the state itself. Abdel Latif Abou Qura, an Islamic scholar from the town of Salt, founded the group in 1945 in what was then the Emirate of Transjordan. The next year marked the creation of the Hashemite Kingdom of Jordan, followed soon after by the traumatic creation of Israel and the influx of thousands of Palestinian refugees.

Jordan's King Abdullah was assassinated in July 1951, and his son Talal acceded to the throne. But Talal was soon diagnosed with schizophrenia and forced to abdicate to his own son Hussein, who took the throne in August 1952, still just sixteen years old. The young monarch's legitimacy immediately came into question, and to present a show of strength Hussein decided to co-opt rather than combat the MB—beginning a cooperative relationship that lasted decades. Of course, Jordan's monarchy derived its legitimacy from Islam: the Hashemite kings claim to descend from the Prophet Mohammed. It is thus not surprising that a succession of Jordanian kings maintained predominantly friendly relations with the pre-eminent Islamist group.

Even after the British withdrew in 1956 and Jordan came under martial law, Hussein allowed the MB to continue its charitable work.[43] In this way, Jordan's king used the movement to solidify his own legitimacy, while the Jordanian MB flourished as a charitable and social organization, though not politically. The two found common ground in opposing liberation movements such as the Palestinian Liberation Organization and pan-Arab groups. In 1982, the MB established its offices in the new Islamic Hospital in Amman. But by this time, after the Iranian Revolution and with Arabs joining the jihad in Afghanistan, questions had begun to swirl around Islamist movements and the potential threat they posed to the region's leaders.

The First Intifada against occupying Israeli forces in 1987—Intifada is an Arabic word that literally means to "shiver" or "shake off"—marked the arrival of another Brotherhood affiliate—the Palestinian Movement of Islamic Resistance, or Hamas (see more in next section of this chapter). The Jordanian MB and Hamas soon built strong ties, with the latter even setting up an office in Amman and beginning to influence the Jordanian MB. This connection provided a larger stage for and gave more attention to the Jordanian MB just as the country moved toward legislative elections. In the 1989 elections, the MB performed well, taking twenty-two of eighty seats, though political parties remained banned. A 1992 law enabled the formation of parties, and the MB created a political wing, the Islamic Action Front (IAF), which was immediately a significant player on Jordan's political scene.

In the years that followed, thanks to the MB's network of charitable giving and conservative credentials, the IAF was the only party with a parliamentary bloc that could weigh in on key issues, whereas other parties remained independents. The Jordanian MB had brilliantly taken advantage of a particular moment, wielding its Islamic bona fides in the wake of the Intifada, according to Hana Jaber, senior fellow at the Arab Reform Initiative: "The mythical sense of belonging to the despoiled land of Palestine was a recurring theme in the Brotherhood's rhetoric. Questions that were inherently of national concern were not a main feature of the Brotherhood's daily agenda."[44] Over the years, the MB became not so much an opposition group and a threat, as in most other regional states, but an ally to the monarchy.

Still, fearing an Islamist takeover of the lower chamber of parliament, King Hussein introduced his "one man, one vote" law before the 1993 elections. This meant that instead of voters casting votes for every parliamentary seat in their district, they were allowed to cast only one. The MB criticized the new system as unjust because it favored tribesmen and government loyalists, and in the years that followed went on to call for boycotts and reform. A rift soon emerged within the Jordanian MB between those who sought to align with the king ("doves") and those who sought to remain close to the MB vision of an Islamic state ("hawks").

King Hussein died in February 1999, and the throne passed to his son, Abdullah II. The new monarch sought to create a modern, business-friendly state and thus had little use for the conservative MB. Later that year, King Abdullah closed Hamas's Amman office, arguing that the group had broken an agreement that forbade it from practicing politics or directing military action from Jordan. This pointed toward growing tensions between the Jordanian MB and their new king, which had been further exacerbated by the 1998 Al-Qaeda attacks on U.S. embassies in Dar Es Salaam and Nairobi. With the September 11, 2001, attacks on the United States, King Abdullah began a crackdown on the group and saw all Islamists with grave suspicion—a necessary move to maintain strong relations with his key ally, the U.S. Relations between the king and the MB soured further after the November 2005 hotel bombings in Amman, which killed sixty people and were masterminded by Jordan native Abu Musab Al-Zarqawi.

The hawks and doves engaged in intense internal debate about how to proceed and ultimately put together an official narrative: the Vision of the Islamist Movement on Reform, which focused on domestic issues and sought to distance the movement from Al-Qaeda and the question of Palestine.[45] But in 2006, the MB found itself divided about Al-Zarqawi's death.[46] The group refused to apologize for the visitation of four of its members to Al-Zarqawi's funeral tent, but did issue statements clarifying its positions. Some saw this as a weak attempt to pacify the government rather than stick to MB ideology. Frustrated, eighteen of the MB's forty consultative council members resigned as Jordan's MB hit a new low. In the 2007 elections, IAF candidates took just 6 of 110 seats—the poorest MB showing in decades.[47]

The so-called Arab Spring arrived in 2011, ultimately weakening the Jordanian MB even though the wave barely touched the kingdom. Even before the Arab rebellions, Jordanians had been calling for greater labor rights, less corruption, and more political participation, such as with the 2009 Constitutional Monarchy initiative led by Ryhayyel Gharaibeh, a prominent MB member.[48] The Arab rebellions merely added fuel to this fire, though the MB's demands were quite moderate: constitutional reform and taking away the king's ability to dissolve parliament and appoint a prime minister.[49] The MB never called for regime change, though the protests did build momentum. "This dissent came to a head in Amman in November 2012, where a protest of several tens of thousands of Jordanians in which the Brotherhood had decided to massively mobilize forced the government to engage in constitutional reforms," writes Jaber. "Nonetheless, these reforms remained at best negligible."[50]

The IAF boycotted the January 2013 elections, looking to take a stand against the government's lack of serious reforms. But that summer, after General El-Sisi pushed out Egyptian president Mohammed Morsi and purged the Egyptian MB, altered the landscape for Islamists. Amman began to view the Jordanian MB as an enemy and shifted from coexistence to repression. After the UAE declared the MB a terrorist organization in November 2014, Jordanian MB leader Zaki Bani Irshid criticized the decision on Facebook. He was criticized for endangering the more than 200,000 Jordanians living in the Emirates and put on trial in February 2015 for disrupting relations with a foreign state.[51]

Around this time, King Abdullah embarked on a new policy toward the MB that sought to gradually fragment the group[52]—and it worked. In February 2016, Jordan declared the MB illegal, primarily for its links to the Egyptian MB. After decades of solid relations with the regime, leading public opinion, and organizing protests and blocs of votes, the Jordanian MB faced an existential threat for the first time since its creation seventy years ago. Would its leaders accept the government's demands, cut ties with Egypt, and place itself under the Ministry of Social Affairs? Or could they find another solution?

While heated internal debates ensued, MB member Abdel-Majid Thneibat proposed the creation of a second movement, the Muslim Brotherhood Society, unconnected to Egypt. He'd been brewing the idea for some time. Back in January 2015, Thneibat had secretly met with King Abdullah, who warned of the coming terrorist organization label for the Egyptian MB and urged Thneibat to de-link Jordan's MB to the mother organization to help Jordan avoid any embarrassment. After meeting the king, Thneibat met with other members of the Jordanian MB, according to Nael Masalha of the Brookings Institution:

> They discussed possible ways forward, arriving at a decision to register the group under the name "Muslim Brotherhood Society," and to appoint an interim leadership for six months until elections were held to choose a new leadership. They would then be in compliance with Jordanian law.[53]

The Jordanian MB ultimately shifted most of its membership into the new MB Society and put new leadership in place, even as a hardcore group of loyalists sought to create their own organization. The original Jordanian MB was thus largely abandoned, and in April 2016 Jordanian security services closed the MB's Amman headquarters; offices in Jerash, Madaba, Karak, and Mafraq followed.[54] The next month, the government barred the MB from holding internal elections.[55] The baton had been passed to the MB Society.

The results of the September 2016 elections appear to have proven the wisdom of the MB's maneuvering, with the MB-led Reform Coalition taking a respectable 15 out of 130 seats. But the next year told a different story. MB-backed groups lost their lead roles within Jordan University and in the Jordan Engineers' Association, after decades of dominance. These changes may seem minor, but they underscore the MB's internal problems and point toward a broader shift. "As universities and unions are bellwethers of social change, the JU and JEA losses reveal Islamist influence may be declining," Sean Yom, political science lecturer at Temple University, and Wael Al-Khatib, an Amman-based anthropologist, wrote in May 2017.

> Our research, including interviews with political activists, suggests disenchantment with Islamism has been years in the making. . . . [We] see a new wave of mobilization that is youth-driven, highly informal and reform-oriented. Examples such as Nashama and Numuw are also unfazed by identity debates like the Palestinian-tribal divide and suspicious of all parties and ideologies, including Islamism.[56]

Yom and Al-Khatib found that Islamist participation hadn't fallen; rather youth participation had spiked, significantly altering the results. They view these two votes as part of a broader trend: Islamists have also lost ground at several other universities and within the Jordan Bar Association and Teachers Association. The Islamic Action Front built solid internal political structures, but it also developed internal flaws that have led to the decline of the Islamist movement in Jordan; the group has paid for shifting its focus from social issues to political affairs, particularly Palestine. The recently formed MB Society has thus failed to gain any traction. Nael Masalha of Brookings writes of "a decline in support for the Muslim Brotherhood Society, due to its inability to formulate a new and inspiring political project. It is currently lost, having failed to distinguish itself from various other emerging ideas and political parties."[57]

The Islamic Action Front claimed victory in the local and provincial elections of August 2017, winning seventy-six seats. But it's important to point out that more than 2,400 seats were contested, making this a total of about 3 percent.[58] Ali Abu Al-Sukkar, a former chairman of the Brotherhood's Shura Council, describes the current relationship between the Brotherhood and the government as tepid, pointing out "the rise of the Islamist movement in the region has raised fears here, and the presence of Daesh [the Islamic State] has created a fear of Islamist parties."[59]

The Jordanian MB's splintering into several groups—the MB Society, the old Jordanian MB, a Group of Elders, and the Zamzam group that aims to promote unity and diversity[60]—has also undermined the movement. "Despite decent relations with the state, these internal disputes expose the Brotherhood to further restrictions and severely undermine its hopes of gaining any real political influence."[61]

The splintering has led to a loss of traction, which has muddied the MB's message for a new generation that is constantly connected and informed. "Jordanian youths are the raw materials for political mobilization, but they are more cynical and less ideological than ever," Yom and Al-Khatib write. "For them, Islamism is simply another failed product in an obsolete marketplace of ideas."[62]

PALESTINE

Unique among countries outside Egypt, the MB in Palestine emerged largely thanks to the direct efforts of founder Hasan Al-Banna. As detailed in Chapter 1, Al-Banna made the fight for freedom in Palestine one of the Brotherhood's first major issues. As early as 1936, the MB backed the jihad in Palestine and sent weapons to Arabs fighting the British and Zionists there. Decades later, it's no surprise the Palestinian MB has violent insurrection in its very DNA. By 1950, the Egyptian MB's jihad-focused "special apparatus" had recruited and sent thousands of Egyptian volunteers to fight for Palestine. MB members in Palestine soon began setting up branches. Over the years, as Egypt, Jordan, and Israel snatched sizable chunks of Palestinian territory, the MB flourished in a troubled land.

Meanwhile, as Israeli authorities cracked down on resistance organizations, the Brotherhood's lack of involvement allowed it to build up an institutional structure with little interference. When Egypt confronted its most severe challenges during the 1950s and 1960s, the MB stood aloof, a position that allowed it to operate in many social spheres and even run for parliament. The Brothers employed scores of people through Waqfs and used mosques for recruitment. In 1973, Sheikh Ahmed Yassin launched the MB charity Mujama Al-Islamiya (Islamic Center), which served as a social organization, building schools and mosques, delivering healthcare, and spreading Islamic values. With this group, Yassin centralized the Brotherhood's command and organization across Gaza, the West Bank, and Jordan.

In Palestine, in particular, there was disillusionment with the PLO-led resistance movement, making people more amenable to alternative approaches. The 1970s witnessed the rise of Israel's conservative Likud party along with a settler movement, which was convinced that territorial gains from the Arab-Israeli wars evinced a divine mandate to reclaim the entire biblical land of Israel. These domestic, regional, and international shifts lent an increasingly religious cast to the conflict, laying the groundwork for a decisive turn in Palestinian politics toward Islamism and hinting at the violence to come.[63]

In the 1970s, Palestinian medical student Fathi Shaqaqi moved from Gaza to Cairo to continue his studies and joined the Egyptian MB. He quickly decided the MB was too moderate and left with his fellow Palestinian Abd Al-Aziz Awda to join Egyptian Islamic Jihad. Expelled from Egypt after the assassination of El-Sadat, Shaqaqi and Awda returned home to launch Palestinian Islamic Jihad (PIJ) in 1981. The group began using violence, mostly in shooting attacks, to fight Israel and carve out an Islamic Palestinian state.

In August 1987, a PIJ assassin killed the commander of Israel's military police in a shooting in the Gaza Strip.[64] Inspired in part by this successful attack, as the First Intifada began in 1987, Sheikh Yassin launched Hamas,[65] which sought to liberate Palestine from Israeli occupation. The Brotherhood had fully embraced violence in Palestine, and from the start, Hamas was not particularly shy about it. "In early 1988, Hamas began operating as the military arm of the Muslim Brotherhood in the territories," writes Boaz Ganor, the Dean and Ronald Lauder Chair for Counter-Terrorism at the Lauder School of Government, Diplomacy & Strategy at the Interdisciplinary Center in Herzliya, Israel.

> Hamas' activities were directed against both Israelis, military and civilian, and local Palestinians—"collaborators" or those "acting contrary to Islamic values." . . . A few months after the outbreak of the intifada, Hamas was already playing a central role in the various protest and terrorist activities in the territories, while movement activists began to carry out terrorist attacks against Israeli civilian and military targets.[66]

Around this time, the PIJ was exiled to Lebanon, where it linked up with Hezbollah and began to receive training and financial support from Iran (though the group was Sunni, PIJ took inspiration from the Iranian Revolution). In 1989, PIJ relocated to Damascus, where it remains—though small in numbers—to this day. Meanwhile, the newer group filled the void of a violent MB outfit in Palestine.

Hamas, which has been labeled a terrorist group by the United States, and by the EU and Israel, launches frequent attacks on Israeli soldiers and civilians, including suicide bombings and, since 2001, rocket attacks. In late March 2019, a rocket apparently fired by Hamas wounded seven people after it struck a home in central Israel, near Tel Aviv. The missile had traveled some 120 kilometers—showing the group's expanded reach.[67] Human Rights Watch has condemned Hamas' attacks on Israeli civilians as war crimes.[68] The leaders of the Egyptian MB, on the other hand, applaud the group and its killing of Israeli civilians, viewing their violence as justified resistance to an illegal occupation.[69]

On this issue, the MB has a point. For more than half a century, Israel has ignored and eroded the rights of Arab and Palestinian citizens within Israel, and all but ignored the humanity of the Palestinians living within its occupied territories. In Israel proper, rights watchdog Amnesty International cites Israeli authorities' "ill-treatment and torture of detainees, excessive use of force, the detention of conscientious objectors, and forced evictions and home demolitions."[70] Regarding what it calls "the Israeli occupation of Palestinian territory (the West Bank including East Jerusalem and the Gaza Strip)," Amnesty sees even more problematic behavior:

> Human rights violations by Israeli forces in the Occupied Palestinian Territories (OPT) have included, but are not limited to, home demolitions and the forced eviction of Palestinian families; punitive arrests, unfair trials, ill-treatment and torture of detainees and the use of excessive or lethal force to subdue nonviolent demonstrations as well as the use of restrictive legal means. In contravention of international law, Israel continues to build parts of the wall/fence in the OPT, expand settlements and use draconian restrictions on the movement of Palestinians with some 600 roadblocks and checkpoints. Amnesty International is also concerned about discriminatory policies affecting access to water for Palestinians. . . . Israel maintains effective control over Gaza, controlling all but one of the crossings into the Gaza Strip, the airspace, territorial waters, telecommunications and the population registry which determines who is allowed to leave or enter Gaza.[71]

Israel's illegal and deeply problematic treatment has only gotten worse in recent years as governments under Binyamin Netanyahu have become increasingly hawkish, in part in response to the presence of Hamas. Israeli politics and rhetoric have also seen a considerable shift to the right. Consider that in May 2003, Israeli prime minister Ariel Sharon, one of the country's more hawkish leaders and a military general, criticized the "occupation" in a press conference, using the word repeatedly.[72] Today, though critics and rights groups freely invoke the "O" word, neither Israeli officials nor their allies in Washington are willing to go anywhere near it. The State Department, for instance, prefers "Israeli-controlled."[73] This sort of language leads to what happened in January 2019, when Israel passed the nation-state law. This established national self-determination as a Jewish right and Hebrew as the official language, downgrading Arabic, and encouraged Jewish settlement. Israeli Arabs make up a fifth of Israel's population, yet their country "passed a law of Jewish supremacy and told us that we will always be second-class citizens," said Ayman Odeh, an Arab-Israeli politician who leads a coalition of mostly Arab parties.[74]

This was merely a continuation of Israel's oppression of Arabs within its territory and the occupied territories over the past dozen years. In the December 2008-January 2009 conflict between Israel and Hamas, Israeli attacks killed some 1,200 Palestinians, most of them innocent civilians, while just 13 Israelis died in the fighting.[75] In 2014, it was more of the same, as more than 2,200 Palestinians were killed, including nearly 1,500 civilians, compared to about 70 Israelis.[76] Israel also uses deadly force and other unlawful policies on non-combatants during times of relative peace, as Human Rights Watch wrote in 2018:

> The Israeli government continued to enforce severe and discriminatory restrictions on Palestinians' human rights; restrict the movement of people and goods into and out of the Gaza Strip; and facilitate the unlawful transfer of Israeli citizens to settlements in the occupied West Bank. Israeli forces stationed on the Israeli side of the fences separating Gaza and Israel responded to demonstrations for Palestinian rights on the Gaza side with excessive lethal force.[77]

As of April 2019, Israeli security forces had killed more than 270 Palestinians in just over a year of weekly "March of Return" protests at the Gaza border crossing.[78] But those protests, and that death toll, hide an insidious Hamas' strategy. At the end of 2008, when the first Hamas-Israel conflict flared up, journalist Matti Friedman was working as an editor for the Associated Press in Jerusalem when he first got a glimpse of this. "Early in that war, I complied with Hamas censorship in the form of a threat to one of our Gaza reporters and cut a key detail from an article: that Hamas fighters were disguised as civilians and were being counted as civilians in the death toll," Friedman wrote in a May 2018 op-ed in *The New York Times*:

> We used that same casualty toll throughout the conflict and never mentioned the manipulation. Hamas understood that Western news outlets wanted a simple story about villains and victims and would stick to that script, whether because of ideological sympathy, coercion or ignorance. The press could be trusted to present dead human beings not as victims of the terrorist group that controls their lives, or of a tragic confluence of events, but of an unwarranted Israeli slaughter. The willingness of

reporters to cooperate with that script gave Hamas the incentive to keep using it. The next step in the evolution of this tactic was visible in Monday's awful events. If the most effective weapon in a military campaign is pictures of civilian casualties, Hamas seems to have concluded, there's no need for a campaign at all. All you need to do is get people killed on camera. The way to do this in Gaza, in the absence of any Israeli soldiers inside the territory, is to try to cross the Israeli border, which everyone understands is defended with lethal force and is easy to film. About 40,000 people answered a call to show up. Many of them, some armed, rushed the border fence. Many Israelis, myself included, were horrified to see the number of fatalities reach 60.[79]

On Monday, May 14, U.S. officials including Treasury Secretary Steve Mnuchin and the president's daughter Ivanka Trump opened the new embassy in Jerusalem just as, some 50 miles away, so-called protesters clashed with Israeli security at the Gaza border. Many U.S. news outlets showed the two events simultaneously, on a split screen, which seemed to create a troubling juxtaposition. But it became less troubling when the truth was revealed that Hamas organized the protest, that it seeded the lead protesters with its members, and that fifty of the sixty protesters killed were from Hamas, with three from Islamic jihad.[80] That protesters threw stones and Molotov cocktails and used kites to drop incendiary devices on the Israeli side of the border. In fact, the day before this deadly clash, Hamas leader Mahmoud Al-Zahar acknowledged the deception in a television interview. "This is not peaceful resistance. Has the option [of armed struggle] diminished? No. On the contrary, it is growing and developing," he told Al Jazeera. "So when we talk about 'peaceful resistance,' we are deceiving the public."[81]

Hamas continues to argue that it fights for Palestinians, but Palestinians may be starting to disagree. In a September 2018 report, the World Bank described Gaza's economy as "in free fall," with minus 6 percent growth in the first quarter of 2018 and indications of further deterioration since then. Every second person lives in poverty, the unemployment rate is the world's highest, at 50 percent, with youth unemployment rate over 70 percent.[82] "The economic and social situation in Gaza has been declining for over a decade but has deteriorated exponentially in recent months and has reached a critical point," said Marina Wes, World Bank Country Director for the West Bank and Gaza. "Increased frustration is feeding into the increased tensions which have already started spilling over into unrest and setting back the human development of the region's large youth population."[83]

The situation has got so bad that Gazans are leaving in droves. A UN report found that at least 35,000 people left Gaza in 2018, with most seeking a better life elsewhere in the hope of sending money back to help their families.[84] Some 150 doctors were among those who fled, a finding that spurred Hamas to ban the departure of medical professionals.

By early 2019, Hamas had become so desperate that it turned to bitcoin to solve its financial troubles: an Al-Qassam Brigades spokesman urged all Hamas supporters to support "the resistance" financially via the troubled cryptocurrency.[85] Many blame the economic troubles at least partially on Hamas. In addition to taxes paid to Israel and the PA, Gaza residents must pay an additional Hamas tax on all goods that come into the territory, driving up the cost of many items as much as 20 percent.[86] Hamas has stolen several tons of food and other aid from humanitarian shipments, which in 2009 forced the UN to halt aid shipments.[87]

More recently, the Gaza branch of Turkey's aid agency (TIKA) was found to have direct connections to Hamas' military wing. In February 2017, Israeli police arrested Muhammad Murtaja, Gaza coordinator for TIKA. Years before he had taken part in Hamas military training, manufacturing bombs and weapons, and digging tunnels, and maintained those connections long after accepting the TIKA position in 2012. "Murtaja deceived TİKA by misusing the organization's resources and funds, which were intended for substantial humanitarian projects in the Gaza Strip, by diverting them to Hamas's military wing. This fraud was carried out in collusion with the senior ranks of Hamas in Gaza," according to an Israeli government report.[88]

Hamas' aggression, combined with an economic crisis that has led to the world's highest unemployment rate, has become so unpopular that a majority of Palestinians polled in a 2017 Palestinian Center for Public Opinion survey preferred that Hamas "accept a permanent two-state solution on the 1967 borders."[89] The polling took place just weeks after Hamas released a new policy document, dropping its longstanding call for Israel's destruction and agreeing to a transitional state within the 1967 borders. Hamas, which continued to support armed struggle against Israel, also ended its association with the MB.[90] This move was apparently aimed at improving ties with Egypt and Gulf states, which have labeled the MB a terrorist group.

"This delinking is largely about appearances: whatever its leaders claim, Hamas is rooted in the Muslim Brotherhood and the MB ideology."[91] The group's charter contains the philosophy of the movement, its rationale, and its positions on central issues, such as social welfare, the role of women, and other Islamic movements like the PLO. "Hamas' position on most issues differs little, if at all, from that of the Brotherhood, though it does pay less attention to transforming society and more to the Palestinian cause and jihad."[92]

Furthermore, Hamas has long held deep ties with the Jordanian MB, to the point that it is almost more of a regional organization. This is largely because of the sizable Palestinian presence in Jordan—some estimates say up to 60 percent of Jordanians are of Palestinian origin.[93] In addition, the Jordanian MB, having long had the support of the monarchy, has generally had solid financial backing. Particularly combined with the Jordanian

MB's weak and splintered leadership, it was an easy decision for Hamas to reorient toward the MB's Jordan branch and wield its influence there. Nael Masalha cited:

> Hamas's ability to penetrate and consequently exert control over all aspects of the Jordanian Brotherhood. In so doing, they were able to make it seem that if you were not with Hamas, you were against the Islamic movement overall. . . . Hamas worked in an organized fashion within the Jordanian Brotherhood and its affiliated institutions, injecting huge amounts of money to recruit members—some of Jordanian origin—who became increasingly active and engaged in the Brotherhood's projects. This resulted in Hamas consolidating control over the Brotherhood's organization in Jordan.[94]

At the same time, as a branch of the Brotherhood, Hamas has been able to build on the mother organization's extensive infrastructure in expanding its public base of operations, facilitating useful vehicles for spreading its ideas and influence and enlisting supporters. As mentioned in an earlier chapter, Hamas has emphasized Intifada activity over participation in the political process. It has become the party most engaged in armed actions against Israeli targets, and thus it is widely recognized as a terrorist organization and shunned on the world diplomatic stage.

Hamas's profile had been on the wane in recent years until the Trump administration decided to move the U.S. embassy to Jerusalem. In January 2017, thousands of Gazans protested against Hamas's governance and, in a Palestinian Center for Policy and Survey Research (PCPSR) poll, Palestinians chose Palestinian Authority president Mahmoud Abbas over Hamas's Ismail Haniyeh at 50 to 42 percent. Shortly after Trump's Jerusalem decision in May 2018, a new PCPSR survey found that Haniyeh topped Abbas, 53 to 41 percent, while the share of Palestinians calling for Hamas-style resistance spiked from 35 to 44 percent. "Hamas benefits from being able to say that they were the ones who were right to be opposed to the peace process," Shadi Hamid, senior fellow at the Brookings Institute, said in December 2017. "They can point to this announcement as the evidence of the failure of the peace process."[95]

IRAQ

In the mid-1940s, several Egyptian lecturers in Baghdad began to recruit conservative-minded, well-educated young locals to disseminate the ideas of Egypt's MB and create the first Iraqi cells of the Islamist group. By 1948, the group was promoting Muslim unity and Islamic morality and was mobilizing Iraqis to fight in Palestine, and the Iraqi monarchy enabled members to officially register their organization.[96] Yet because Iraqi law at the time forbade political groups from registering as branches of foreign entities, the Iraqi MB registered as the Islamic Brotherhood Organization.[97]

The formal MB branch in Iraq was established in 1951, and it quickly emerged as the country's largest Sunni Islamist movement. According to an Iraqi MB leader at the time, Basim Al-Azami, the main ideological concern of the group in this early period was not Palestine, as it was for so many Arabs back then, but a swelling communist movement in the country.[98] Still, the Iraqi MB supported the liberation struggles in Palestine and Algeria. The group emphasized education and Dawa and initially rejected political participation to focus on society. Iraq's MB affiliate was thus able to function peacefully, until the overthrow of the Hashemite monarchy in July 1958, installing Abd Al-Karim Qasim as prime minister. Leftist parties attacked the MB offices in Baghdad and forced its leader, Sheikh Mohammed Al-Sawwaf, into exile.[99] As in several regional countries around this time, the MB moved its operations underground.

But in 1960, the Iraqi MB decided that political action was a religious duty and founded the Iraqi Islamic Party.[100] The party manifesto said that Muslims and non-Muslims should enjoy the same rights and that the democratic state should be ruled by Sharia while stressing the importance of national unity.[101] In a move that might sound surprising today, Iraqi MB leaders actually called for Shias to join the IIP. But the top Shia cleric at the time, Sayyid Muhsin Al-Hakin, forbade Shia from joining or cooperating with the party.[102] IIP still exists today and is widely seen as an MB front despite its denials, according to Muhanad Seloom, a lecturer at the Institute of Arab and Islamic Studies at the University of Exeter.[103]

Soon after the Baath Party took power in July 1968, MB and IIP figures faced a number of harsh crackdowns. Many of the group's leaders were jailed and tortured, spurring others to flee the country. Decades of suppression under Saddam Hussein forced top MB and IIP figures into exile, or forced them to change their position. These iron-fisted policies curbed the expansion of the MB and Islamists in Iraq from the 1970s through the 1990s. "The Brotherhood believed that the Baath Party had seized power from the pro-communist Qasim regime with CIA backing and concluded that the Brotherhood would not be capable of overcoming Baath power. The leadership of the Brotherhood remained in exile thereafter," Graham Fuller, former vice chairman of the National Intelligence Council at the CIA and professor of history at Simon Fraser University, wrote for the U.S. Institute of Peace in August 2003.[104]

The MB's Iraqi arm lay dormant until just after the first Gulf War, when IIP resumed operations in exile, in London. It began to work with other groups to remove the Iraqi dictator, even while remaining skeptical of the United States. "In 1991, one of the stated aims of the party was to save Iraq from succumbing to a 'U.S.-led western conspiracy which was plotting to destroy it in the interests of Israel and ensuring oil supplies to the western world,' " Fuller wrote in 2003, "a commentary with disturbingly current relevance."[105]

During this period the Iraqi MB shifted away from traditional MB ideology and took a more political stance in opposition to the regime while emphasizing the suffering of Iraqi people under the UN sanctions. The IIP accepted that an Islamic state could only be implemented gradually after many years and supported a pluralist democracy.[106] "Particularly in the late 1990s, the IIP began to morph away from its Islamic roots and increasingly adopted unprincipled pragmatism due to their hatred of Saddam Hussein," Tallha Abdulrazaq, researcher at the University of Exeter's Strategy and Security Institute, wrote in May 2015.[107]

Meanwhile, back in Iraq, a chastened Hussein after 1991 began to embrace Islam in an effort to boost his legitimacy. The Baath Party's top ideological institution had called for a policy reorientation toward Islamists, and an accompanying Islamization, back in 1986.[108] But Saddam seemed not to embrace the idea domestically until after the Gulf War. He opened hundreds of new mosques and established a new theological school, unsurprisingly called Saddam University.[109] In the months before the U.S. invasion in early 2003, Hussein even began to pull back on his persecution of the Brotherhood, possibly out of fear that the group should not be alienated at a time when he needed all the backing he could get, particularly among his core supporters, Sunnis.[110] "It is of course, notoriously difficult to judge the level and depth of Brotherhood supporters within Iraq during this period of harsh regime crackdown on all political opposition," wrote Fuller, acknowledging that it had long been entirely underground. "Nonetheless, given the strength of the Brotherhood in other Arab states—Syria, Jordan, Egypt, and in the Gulf—it is highly likely that the nucleus of an underground Brotherhood remained in place—now free to emerge."[111]

Indeed, the Iraq War marked an awakening of sorts for the MB in Iraq. After the U.S.-led coalition ousted Hussein and took power in April 2003, many top MB figures returned to take part in the country's new political system, which seemed to favor the country's Shia. In a May 2003 interview with Al Jazeera, the head of the Iraqi MB, Usama Al-Tikriti, acknowledged that the group faced several problems heading into the post-Hussein era, including sorting out the leadership between the exiles and those who stayed underground in Iraq.[112] Still, the IIP came to play a significant role within Iraq's postwar political process based on an ethno-sectarian quota system. "Between 2004 and 2018, IIP members were given senior positions under this system, including the speakership of parliament and the vice presidency, and others were appointed ministers or deputy ministers. The IIP had transitioned from an Islamist opposition party in exile to one involved in national decision-making," Seloom wrote in November 2018.[113]

But the price has been a vast decline of IIP support among Sunnis amid independent Iraq's struggle toward democratic maturity. "It was perhaps one of the singularly best-placed parties that could have made a significant difference in post-Saddam Iraq," wrote Abdulrazaq, an MB sympathizer who has attended IIP meetings. "Instead, I have spent years watching in dismay as the party has blundered from one disaster to another, failing its core Sunni constituents (especially Arabs, but also Kurds and Turkmens). Sadly, rather than being a part of the solution, they abandoned their principles and became a part of the problem."

The IIP, though an MB affiliate and thus to some extent an anti-Western movement, opposed violent resistance to the U.S.-led occupation and joined the Iraqi Governing Council, unlike other Sunni groups. From the Sunni perspective, the IIP aligned with the West and the Iran-backed Shia. Meanwhile, the Sunni-led resistance enabled extremist groups like Al-Qaeda in Iraq and ISIS to take root. These jihadis, and many Sunnis, viewed the IIP "as a puppet of the occupying powers and a weak representative of Sunnis," according to Seloom.[114] In his party's defense, IIP leader Mohsen Abdul Hamid "stated that the IIP had to deal with the inevitable fact that Iraq was under American occupation and, if they did not participate in the political process, the Sunni voice would lack representation."[115]

Though coalition forces withdrew from Iraq in 2011, the disagreement over whether to use violence to end the occupation or embrace the political process and the coalition still polarizes the country's Sunnis. IIP opponents point to the party's significant drop in popularity in Sunni-majority cities, highlighted by the results of January 2009 elections, as proof that it no longer reflects the will of the community.[116] This may help explain why the IIP soon chose Ayad Al-Samarrai, who had long rejected the presence of U.S. troops, to lead the party.[117] This, however, did not change the fortunes of the party, or of the MB in Iraq, in the next few years. "Given that the revived Sunni insurgency is expected to take several months if not years to quell at the minimum," Iraqi analyst Aymenn Jawad Al-Tamimi wrote in January 2014, "the Muslim Brotherhood as a whole in Iraq is likely to remain on the peripheries for quite some time."[118]

More than five years later, his prediction has proved accurate. Following the overthrow of Egyptian president Morsi in the summer of 2013, the IIP's clear MB links placed it at the center of the broader regional conflict. The IIP predictably aligned itself with the MB, Turkey and Qatar, in opposition to Saudi Arabia, the UAE, and Egypt, and suffered after the blockade of Qatar. "Following the blockade of Qatar in mid-2017, the IIP was no longer able to receive any support from its main Gulf backer, Qatar, and found itself increasingly isolated. The result was the further erosion of its popularity and influence."[119] These rifts and regional divides have hurt IIP at the polls, as it took fewer seats in the May 2018 elections than it had since the 2003 invasion.

The MB's party in Iraq has also suffered from its failure to deliver on promises of security and services. Many Sunnis blame the IIP for the thousands of Sunnis executed by government-linked Shia militias from 2006 to 2009, as this occurred while a top IIP leader, Tariq Al-Hashimi, was Iraq's co-vice president. During this period of violence, predominantly Sunni cities lacked crucial services like water, electricity, and reliable healthcare, and these same cities tended to have the highest rates of unemployment.[120]

In December 2011, Al-Hashimi was charged with financing terrorism and assassinating two prominent Shia figures, a female lawyer and an army general. He fled and ultimately found refuge in Turkey. But back in Iraq, he was convicted in absentia and sentenced to death.[121] It was yet another example that the MB and its affiliates will find a way to embrace terrorism, targeted violence, and rebellion.

As recently as 2014, the military councils for Sunni revolutionaries viewed "the IIP as a collaborator with (Iraqi President Nouri Al-) Maliki, deriding it as the 'Party of Surrender,' " according to Syrian journalist Aymenn Jawad Al-Tamimi.[122] These military councils also accused IIP-linked militants, known as Iraqi Hamas, of siding with militias supportive of Maliki.[123] As a result, the IIP has suffered a massive decline of influence among Iraq's Sunnis, and is now seen as dishonest, self-serving, and incompetent, according to Seloom:

> Making things worse is the perception that the IIP has failed to effectively influence government policies, undermining its strategy of seeking to share power with the leading Shia political parties. . . . Unless these trends change, the IIP will be unlikely to regain an important role in the governance of Iraq.[124]

Abdulrazaq goes even further, arguing that the political failures of the MB's Iraq affiliate drove Sunnis to embrace armed resistance and helped lay the groundwork for the creation of the Islamic State, or ISIS.

> The IIP must share in the blame for the growth of extremists such as the Islamic State (IS) group, as well as state-sponsored Shia extremist groups. They abandoned principled and measured Islamic politics that appealed to a large segment of the Iraqi population in favour of immoral pragmatism, stood by a corrupt and violent regime, and failed to engage with their core constituents, the vast majority of whom have abandoned them.[125]

As a result, the IIP has of late sought to distance itself from the MB, in the hope of boosting its outlook domestically and internationally.

LEBANON

Last, and perhaps least, we have the smallest MB branch in the Levant, Lebanon's Jemaah Islamiya. The group was founded in 1964 at the height of Nasser's MB crackdown in Egypt. But its roots go back to an earlier group founded by Mohammad Omar Al Daaouk in Beirut in 1950. That group, actually called the "Muslim Brotherhood," had no connection to the mother organization in Egypt, but it did lay the groundwork for a significant Islamist organization in Lebanon.

The figurehead for Lebanon's Islamists is the prominent Muslim scholar Fathi Yakan, who helped pioneer the Islamic movement in the 1950s and played a key role in the founding of Jemaah Islamiya. He later dabbled in politics, but Yakan was never a moderate Islamist. "As a disciple of the radical Egyptian Islamist thinker Sayyid Qutb, he opposed secularist and communist ideology and he considered Islam to be the basis of the sociopolitical order," according to Lebanon Support, a research organization. "In the wake of the 1967 Arab-Israeli war, Yakan joined Said Hawa of Syria's Muslim Brotherhood to advocate jihad against the West and Israel."[126] As with other MB affiliates, Jemaah Islamiya aims to establish an Islamic state based on Sharia. Jemaah strongly supports the Palestinian cause and has had some success with youth recruitment across Lebanon, largely thanks to its network of mosques, schools, and healthcare facilities.[127]

The MB has generally played a smaller role in Lebanon than in other regional states, mainly due to the country's demographics (27 percent Sunni, 27 percent Shia, 40 percent Christian). For instance, Jemaah has only one member in Lebanon's parliament, and he is a minor member of Saad Hariri's Future Movement coalition. But the election of Azzam Ayyoubi, a school inspector and political operative, to lead Jemaah in early 2016 may have signaled a shift in ambition.[128] Carnegie analyst Rafael Lefevre sees Jemaah moving away from an old guard focused on establishing the group into the hands of a new generation looking to embrace greater openness and political participation.[129]

One crucial issue is the war in neighboring Syria, to which Jemaah has given humanitarian assistance. Some observers say it has also taken up arms against Al-Assad, but Jemaah leaders say they have stayed out of the fighting. Ayyoubi appears willing to be more critical of the Assad regime, which may exacerbate Jemaah's recently troubled relations with Hezbollah, the Iran-backed Shia militia based in South Beirut. Although Jemaah is a Sunni group, it had long been friendly with Hezbollah. Jemaah's military wing and Hezbollah have launched joint operations against Israel in the past, and in 2006 Fathi Yakan and others left Jemaah to form the Islamic Action Front, a Sunni group closely aligned to Hezbollah.[130]

The outbreak of war in Syria changed all that, as Jemaah members generally stood against Al-Assad and his Iranian backers, while Hezbollah became one of the regime's fiercest fighting forces. Since taking up his leadership role, Ayyoubi has walked the tightrope of denouncing Al-Assad while not spurring sectarian violence, even while becoming a more aggressive and transparent political player. "Jemaah may yet gain a greater profile. But it seems unlikely, given Lebanon's fraught history and religious makeup, that the group could ever be more than a fringe participant in the country's political scene, as was clearly demonstrated in the parliamentary summer elections of 2018 where Jemaah fared very badly."[131]

CONCLUSION

As across North Africa, the MB chapters of the Levant are generally flailing and have failed to establish strong political roots. In Syria, historical violent tendencies led to decades in exile that even the opportunity of the Syrian civil war seems unlikely to fully reverse. In Jordan, the MB has splintered almost to the point of disintegration, allowing itself to be commandeered by Hamas. Hamas, for its part, has overseen the worst economic collapse in the Levant in decades, and is fast losing support, while in Iraq and Lebanon the MB is a negligible presence and has little chance of gaining traction anytime soon.

Despite having a significant presence in every mainly Muslim territory in this region, the MB is a marginal entity, likely to play a role only in Syria in the years ahead. And even there its impact and influence are sure to be circumscribed. The MB's experience in the Levant in this century is largely indicative of its fate across the region.

CHAPTER 5

The Muslim Brotherhood in the Arab Gulf

The Muslim Brotherhood has a long history in the Gulf, beginning with the 1936 meeting between Hassan Al-Banna and the founder of the modern Kingdom of Saudi Arabia. King Abdulaziz Al-Saud (known as Ibn Saud in the West) was friendly to the MB founder, but he decided against an MB branch in his country, telling Al-Banna, "We are all Muslim Brothers."[1]

But regional geopolitics soon shifted, as detailed in previous chapters, and the MB came to the Gulf. "Although the movement was never allowed to organize inside Saudi Arabia, the MB's links to the Gulf [and especially the Kingdom] go back to the organization's founding," according to Sir John Jenkins, former British ambassador to Saudi Arabia.[2]

In the 1950s and 1960s, as Arab nationalism swept the region, leaders in Egypt, Syria, and Iraq cracked down on the group, sidelining, imprisoning, and torturing dozens of its leaders and key players. Driven by the Islamic belief in charity, the Saudis (the Gulf Cooperation Council had not yet been created and most Gulf countries were still part of the British Empire) saw their fellow Muslims in need and responded. Saudi Arabia and other Gulf states would ultimately provide refuge to thousands of MB members as they fled persecution. Many of the new arrivals found work in education and prospered.

However, their troubling ideology and political stance soon became clear. A sea change occurred in 1990, when Iraqi dictator Saddam Hussein occupied Kuwait. The international MB took a stance in opposition to Saudi Arabia and its ally, the United States, creating a divide between the Brotherhood and Gulf leaders that would only expand in the following years. After the attacks of September 11, 2001, the world learned of the MB's crucial role in the rise of international terrorism, from jihadi theorist Sayyid Qutb to Al-Qaeda's current leader Ayman Al-Zawahiri. In the wake of the so-called Arab Spring, when the MB won elections in Tunisia and Egypt and became a key political player in Morocco, Jordan, Sudan, Yemen, Libya, and Syria, the threat to the Gulf States, and even Saudi Arabia, was no longer in doubt.

Ultimately, the MB failed to take root in the Gulf as it had in Egypt and in parts of the Levant for several reasons. The first is these states' growing wariness. A second is that GCC states are not plagued by the instability found in much of the region; government largesse combined with political and financial stability means that citizens tend to have less interest in new and novel ideologies, or indeed in upending the political order. Former Qatari Brotherhood leader Jassim Sultan put it this way: "Nobody will listen to any radical ideas when their needs are fulfilled."[3] Long before the MB's arrival, the vast majority of Saudi and Gulf citizens already identified strongly with deeply conservative Islamic beliefs and lived in an Islamist environment.

Qatar has long been the exception. Fueled by an abiding desire to wield outsized influence and an overinflated sense of Islamic importance, the small peninsular state has for decades harbored MB leaders and supported the group's attempts to seize power around the region. This affiliation has of late led Qatar into great trouble with its neighbors. This chapter details the MB's history in each of the Arab Gulf States, with a focus on the countries where its presence has been most strongly felt.

OMAN

Like other Gulf states, Oman experienced an influx of MB members in the mid-twentieth century. Within a generation, these new arrivals had become a threat to the state. In the summer of 1994, Omani authorities arrested more than 200 people for plotting to use violence to destabilize the country, linking the subversives to the MB.[4] Those arrested included a former ambassador to the United States, a former air force commander, and leading religious scholars such as Salah Soltan,[5] a prominent MB figure close to Sheikh Yusuf Al-Qaradawi. That November, 135 of the accused were sentenced to lengthy prison terms, though a year later they were freed as part of an amnesty.

Following the 1994 crackdown, MB activists worked in secret to keep their Oman chapter alive. But the state cracked down again a decade later. In December 2004 and January 2005, authorities detained hundreds of Islamists, accusing them of plotting to destabilize the state. Ultimately, just thirty-one of them were arrested, tried, and sentenced to jail.[6] A month later, as in the previous case, they were freed. In both cases, the release of the purported MB subversives suggests the crackdowns were deterrents rather than interruptions—meant to frighten Omanis away from the MB, rather than stop actual plots. If so, they appear to have had the intended impact. In the past dozen years Oman has been all but free of MB activity.

Some regional observers see a reason for less concern in Oman. "The MB threat is less dangerous in Oman because of the country's religious leanings," Dr. Omar Al-Zawawi, advisor to Sultan Qaboos, said in an interview with the author. "Most Omanis are neither Sunni nor Shia, but Ibadi, which is a less stringent strain of Islam. This limits the MB's appeal there."[7] Indeed, in part because MB members are predominantly Sunni, Omanis have historically been less prone to extremism. As of early 2019, in fact, no Omanis had been convicted of terrorism or captured in Afghanistan, Iraq, or Syria, fighting for Al-Qaeda or ISIS.

This of course does not mean the country has no need to be wary. Omani authorities continue to be on the hunt for potential MB-linked troublemakers. In September 2017, the Ministry of Foreign Affairs asked a prominent Indian Muslim scholar to leave the country after he denounced Saudi Arabia for the Kingdom's blockade of Qatar, which he referred to as a Muslim country that "harbors Hamas and the Muslim Brotherhood."[8]

BAHRAIN

Bahrain is unique in the Gulf: the majority of its citizens are Shiite, while its ruling Al-Khalifa family is Sunni. For decades, the state enabled and co-opted the local MB chapter, using it as a proxy to offset the Shiite opposition. In fact, an uncle of Bahrain's Emir, Sheikh Isa bin Muhammad Al-Khalifa, helped establish Bahrain's MB affiliate in 1984.[9] Also, as predominantly Shiite protesters filled the streets of Bahrain's capital, Manama, in 2011, Sheikh Mohammed Khalid, a parliamentarian from MB-affiliated Al-Menbar, called the protesters "traitors" and "agents of Iran," essentially assisting the regime in silencing a potential threat.[10]

For years, Al-Menbar politicians have generally supported the government's agenda. Indeed, along with military forces from Saudi Arabia and the UAE, MB-linked figures played a key role in helping quell the protests that shook the regime in 2011. But as the true threat of the MB has emerged, the government's stance has changed. Just before November 2014 parliamentary elections, Bahrain redrew its electoral boundaries in an effort to squeeze out Islamist parliamentarians and reduce MB influence.[11] The government also dropped Al-Menbar cabinet ministers and curbed MB influence within the Ministry of Education.

Al-Menbar leaders took pains to distinguish their organization from the suddenly poisoned Brotherhood. "All eyes of the voters are on us as they say we are the Muslim Brotherhood, which is not right," Al-Menbar president Ali Ahmed said in 2014.[12] "It is the ideology that we follow, but we do not have the organization in Bahrain—neither do we support it." As part of its effort to keep a low profile, Al-Menbar decided not to run any candidates in municipal elections, where it previously had strong representation.[13] In the end, Islamists lost two of their five seats, with Al-Menbar losing one of two.[14]

"Bahrain understands that more important than immobilizing the Brotherhood and other Islamists is weakening them so they pose no threat," Sheikh Fawaz bin Mohammed Al Khalifa, Bahrain Ambassador to the UK, told me in July 2018.[15] Bahrain depends on Saudi Arabia and, to a lesser extent, on the UAE, for energy and security, and needs to maintain those crucial friendships. In the years ahead, Al-Menbar is likely to persist, with Bahrain remaining one of only a few Gulf countries where an MB-linked group maintains a social and political entity. At the same time, Bahraini authorities will continue to freeze out MB-linked citizens from public platforms, continuing to reduce their influence and presence.

KUWAIT

Much like Bahrain, Kuwait accepts the existence of a local MB affiliate, but for a different reason. While Bahrain has a Shiite majority to offset, Kuwait has a diverse population and is home to the oldest MB-linked group in the Gulf. Abdulaziz Al-Mutawa founded Kuwait's MB chapter back in 1951, mainly to counter Western influence. By the 1960s, the group, first known as the Social Reform Organization and later Al-Islah, had made a considerable impact on Kuwaiti society and education, mainly by working with impressionable youth.

Members of the Kuwaiti Brotherhood soon began to rise through the government ranks—Abdulrahman Al-Atiqi became minister of oil and finance in 1971; Yusuf Al-Hajji was named justice minister the following year—and used their positions to advance the Brotherhood's agenda. By the 1980s, with its influence growing thanks to a few parliamentary posts, an internal split divided the group into moderates and fundamentalists. "The greatest actual enemy to the Islamic movement is the regimes," former Al-Islah parliamentarian Dr. Abdullah Al-Nafisi said at the time.[16] But his perspective quickly lost ground. "Al-Nafisi's radical anti-regime perspective soon lost out to that of the 'gradualist reformer' Ism'il Al-Shatti," a former chief of Kuwait's National Security Agency told me.[17]

Saddam Hussein's invasion and occupation of Kuwait remade Gulf relations with the MB, and nowhere more than in Kuwait. Iraqi forces entered Kuwait in August 1990, quickly overwhelming Kuwaiti forces, many of which fled to neighboring Saudi Arabia and Bahrain. Emir Sheikh Jaber Al-Ahmed Al-Sabah joined them, fleeing to Saudi Arabia in a helicopter, while his younger brother, Fahd, was shot and killed by Iraqi forces in Dasman Palace in Kuwait City.[18]

Hussein annexed the Gulf state, claiming it was a part of Iraq that had been carved off by the British decades before. Iraqi officials also argued that the Kuwaiti Emir was highly unpopular and that his overthrow would mean an increase in freedom.[19] So Hussein's Iraq became the first Arab state in modern history to invade another Arab country without provocation, and its reasoning was that the leader of that state, Kuwait,

deserved to be overthrown. Thinking about it now, it's no surprise the MB
supported Hussein's occupation and planned overthrow—the violent assault and coup dovetails with their usual modus operandi.

Yet Iraq's invasion of Kuwait was a horrific act of aggression and a
shock to the region and much of the world. Here's how London's *Sunday
Times* described it, a few days after it all began:

> It was a strategy on Hitlerian lines: the annexation by blitzkrieg of a weak
> neighbour in defiance of the great powers, whose likely reaction he expected
> to be little more than pious hand-wringing. It was not just the Arabs who
> would be caught off guard. Western leaders, basking in the peace of a post-
> cold war summer, did not expect him to invade either.[20]

Most observers viewed the occupation as an attempt to seize Kuwait's oil
assets, about which Baghdad had been complaining for some time.[21] Two
weeks prior to the act, Hussein accused Kuwait and the UAE of stabbing
Iraq with a "poisoned dagger" by driving down the price of oil.[22]

Global powers lined up in opposition to the invader. The United States
and the Soviet Union, which would last one more year, joined forces
for the first time since World War II. (News of the invasion broke while
U.S. secretary of state James Baker was meeting Soviet foreign minister
Eduard A. Shevardnadze in Siberia.)[23] Washington imposed a trade ban
and moved a group of aircraft carriers to the Gulf, while Moscow, the
main arms supplier to Iraq, suspended all shipments. Britain and France,
along with India, Saudi Arabia, the UAE, Bahrain, Egypt, and dozens of
other countries, all stood against Hussein's act of military aggression.[24]
The UN condemned the invasion, urged the removal of all Iraqi forces,
and placed sanctions on Iraq, which later led to the U.S.-led military
response.

Within Kuwait, life was turned upside down. In the early weeks, a protest movement was able to organize rallies and build some momentum,
but then Iraq's puppet regime began to crack down. Freedom of movement and assembly were severely restricted, media outlets were censored,
and Iraqi secret police seemed to lurk around every corner.[25] Food became
scarce, spurring stories of Kuwaitis trading television sets for vegetables.[26]
By November it was unsafe to go out during daylight hours, and Iraqi
authorities' looting had gone beyond brazen. "Where they had originally
confined themselves to stealing from vacant houses and stores," said *The
New York Times*, "they were now driving up to occupied dwellings, empty-
ing them of furniture and belongings at gunpoint."[27]

By January, more than half of the population had fled the country, while
thousands of people had been arrested and hundreds publicly executed.[28]
Often, Iraqi authorities would deposit the bodies of executed resistance
leaders on their family's front lawn, where they remained for hours, to
serve as a painful warning. Human Rights Watch found that many of the
bodies showed signs of torture.[29] Hundreds of Kuwaiti men were shipped

to Baghdad prisons and were never heard from again.[30] "All of a sudden our entire world collapsed," Luwa Al-Iwayed, a thirty-year-old administrator in a travel agency, told *The New York Times* days after the occupation ended. "We found ourselves waiting for anything to happen to us at any time. Life was not natural."[31]

Despite these horrors, the MB continued to support the Iraqi takeover, which some compared to Hitler's conquest of Poland in 1939. Citing the problem of U.S. troops on Saudi soil, the MB continued to support the deprivation, the absence of freedom, and the rule of law in occupied Kuwait, even when most of the Arab region and traditional Iraqi allies like France and India stood against Saddam Hussein. To Gulf states that had welcomed exiled MB members fleeing oppression in Egypt a few decades ago, this support of Saddam's horrifying and unjust oppression, including summary executions, disappearances, torture, and widespread destruction, was an act of betrayal.

The experience of occupation brought Kuwaitis closer together as they found ways to survive. Moved by the strength of resistance, a new generation of Kuwaiti MB members emerged and came to prominence. "During the Iraqi occupation, the MB called for liberation, organized resistance activities, and delivered services. It also cut ties with the international MB (Tanzeem) for its unwillingness to denounce Saddam Hussein's occupation. This obviously went far with Kuwaiti authorities," a former chief of Kuwait's National Security Bureau told me in September 2018.[32]

To clarify, starting in early 1991, the Kuwaiti MB was no longer connected to the main MB organization, based in Egypt. This does not mean that it was no longer an MB-linked group, potentially prone to violence and revolution. But it was a meaningful step, as the group no longer took orders or direction from Cairo, and was thus free to take positions and political stances more suited to domestic and Gulf realities. Following the liberation of Kuwait in March 1991, the Kuwaiti MB launched a political arm, known as Hadas.[33] Prior to this, MB members had run for office as individuals, not as part of an organization.

Hadas began working with non-Islamist opposition parties and during the 1990s established itself as a legitimate political party, regularly winning parliamentary seats.[34] In the wake of the so-called Arab Spring, Hadas won an impressive four seats in the February 2012 vote. The Constitutional Court declared those results unconstitutional. Hadas boycotted elections in December 2012 and July 2013 and joined a coalition calling for greater political reform. Hadas also criticized the Kuwaiti government for its support of the removal of Egyptian president Mohammed Morsi. Kuwaiti politicians responded strongly, arguing that Hadas is corrupt, is involved in terrorism, and is a disciple of Egypt's MB—and that it had been plotting a coup.[35] "Hadas also sought to infiltrate government ministries and expand its influence with the authorities," according to a senior advisor within the National Security Bureau in July 2017.[36]

The government responded with a purge. Local newspapers reported that MB supporters in the Ministry of Religious Endowments and Islamic Affairs, the Zakat House, and other government bodies had been forcibly retired or were moved to less prominent posts. The government also constrained MB charities and arrested and deported an Egyptian accused of being an MB member.[37] Hadas's boycott of parliamentary elections in 2012 and 2013 had eroded its influence and prominence, so the party changed its mind for the 2016 vote—and took four of the five seats its candidates contested.

This political resurrection did not worry the leaders of neighboring countries like the UAE and Saudi Arabia, which by that time had designated the MB a terrorist organization, for several reasons. First, as detailed earlier, the Kuwaiti MB, and thus Hadas, had since 1991 been de-linked to the Egyptian and international Brotherhood. As a result, it had no broader regional agenda. In addition, Kuwaiti politics had always been rather different from that of its neighbors. Here's how Giorgio Cafiero, CEO and founder of Gulf State Analytics, described the situation, in February 2017:

> Most leaders in the Gulf accept that Kuwait's political life is uniquely democratic and transparent, and trust that Kuwaiti authorities have their country's Islamists "under control." For the most part, there appears to be a mutual understanding in the G.C.C. that as long as Kuwaiti Islamists limit their goals to domestic issues . . . the presence of Hadas' parliamentarians in the National Assembly is acceptable and not a threat to the GCC's collective security.[38]

Today, the Kuwaiti MB has embraced a pragmatic approach, refraining from denouncing the monarchy or calling for further Islamization of society and instead focusing on stamping out corruption and greater political openness. "Privileging pragmatism over ideology, perhaps having learned lessons from the Brotherhood's failure in Egypt," is how Courtney Freer, Middle East research fellow at the London School of Economics, put it in a 2015 Brookings report.[39]

As a result, the Kuwaiti MB is likely to maintain its role in Kuwaiti government and society. "A crucial aspect of the Kuwait government's detente with the MB is the group's respect for the legitimacy of the country's leadership and its commitment to Kuwait's national interests, rather than the agenda of the international MB. In fact, the Kuwaiti Emir [Sheikh Sabah Ahmad Al-Jaber Al-Sabah] regularly meets with MB leaders and attends their diwan gatherings," the former security chief claimed in an interview.[40] Essentially, Kuwait's MB affiliate continues to exist because it toes the line. "We are 100 percent loyal to [the ruling family]," former Hadas parliamentarian Usama Al-Shahin said in 2015.[41] "We want reform, repair—not change."

THE UNITED ARAB EMIRATES

The United Arab Emirates' MB affiliate officially came into existence in 1974, when the Reform and Social Counseling Association, or Al-Islah, registered as an NGO. Muslim Brothers had been present in the UAE for decades, with many working as teachers. Yet no MB-linked group had received the approval of the state, which gained independence in 1971. With assistance from Kuwaiti Brothers, Al-Islah became the second civil society organization given a license to operate in the UAE. The group focused on sports and culture and charity and social activities, and in its early years, it had strong relations with government officials: the first chairman of its management council was Sheikh Mohammed bin Khalifa Al-Maktoum, cousin of Dubai's current ruler, Sheikh Mohammed bin Rashid Al-Maktoum.[42]

In the 1980s Al-Islah gained prominence in the education and justice sectors, and added a political reform agenda, aiming to provide Emiratis with moral guidance. Many Emiratis began to wonder whether Al-Islah was directed by the MB in Egypt, particularly as many MB members had studied there. In the early 1990s, Sheikh Mohammed bin Zayed, son of then Emirati ruler Sheikh Zayed and today the crown prince of Abu Dhabi, led a crackdown on Islamists.[43] "Sheikh Mohammed had long been suspicious of the MB, viewing them as a creeping Islamist threat, due partly to his very bad academic experience with Ezzedine Ibrahim, an MB teacher and Sheikh Mohammed's former tutor," a former counter-terrorism director of the UK's Secret Intelligence Service told me in April 2016. The British counter-terrorism officer pointed to a 1994 Egyptian investigation that found that Al-Islah's charity arm had funded Egyptian Islamic Jihad as a clear early sign.[44]

Not long after, Sheikh Mohammed implemented a plan called "drying the springs" to curb Islamist influence. Authorities shut down Al-Islah (in all emirates except Ras al Khaimah), banning its members from public office, firing its board of directors and placing it under the supervision of the Ministry of Social Affairs. Suspicious charities and NGOs were closed, including the Islamic Relief Committee, and Koranic study circles were banned from mosques. Al-Islah members in prominent posts in media and academia soon lost their jobs.[45] Influential Islamist foreigners were also targeted: a Palestinian suspected of links to MB-affiliated Hamas was arrested; Iraqi MB scholar Sheikh Abd Al-Munim Al-Ali, who wrote a great deal of Brotherhood literature, was deported.[46]

For Emirati Islamists, life with Sheikh Mohammed as the ultimate authority responsible for his country's defense became increasingly difficult, as crackdown followed crackdown, each worse than the last. Then, the world changed for the worse for the MB. "The attacks of September 11, 2001, highlighted the MB's links to Al-Qaeda. Two Emiratis were involved in the attacks—a member of Ras Al-Khaimah's most powerful tribe piloted one of the planes—and Dubai was found to be a hub for terror financing," a former British ambassador to the UAE said in July 2016.[47] The UAE's National Security Agency quickly detained and questioned hundreds of suspected terrorists and MB members. Within a year, authorities had transferred or forced the retirement of some seventy educators and government officials thought to be linked to the MB.[48]

The most disruptive crackdown came in the wake of the so-called Arab Spring. In March 2011, shortly after Egyptian protesters toppled Egyptian president Hosni Mubarak, dozens of Al-Islah members signed a petition calling for comprehensive elections. Authorities seized on the opportunity: Sheikh Mohammed met with the leaders of Al-Islah, telling them to disband the group and provide a list of their associates. They refused, citing their record as peaceful activists. UAE authorities stripped seven MB leaders of their citizenships, expelled them, and detained more than fifty Islamists.[49]

The government launched a $1.6 billion infrastructure plan for its poorer and more conservative northern emirates, home to the majority of Al-Islah supporters, and neutered two major Brotherhood-dominated groups, the Jurist Association and the Teachers' Association, by dismissing their board members.[50] At a January 2012 security conference, Dubai's police chief Dhahi Khalfan clarified the position of Emirati authorities: "The Muslim Brotherhood is a security threat to the Gulf, and is no less dangerous than Iran."

Within months, an MB coup plot emerged in the UAE, sealing the fate of Al-Islah. "By late 2012, Emirati authorities had arrested nearly 100 alleged MB members and charged them with 'forming a secret organization plotting to overthrow the regime.' Even royal status failed to protect offenders: Al-Islah chairman Sheikh Sultan bin Kayed Al-Qasimi, cousin of the ruler of Ras Al-Khaimah, was among those arrested," the British former counterterrorism director said.[51]

The leaders of the group, known as UAE94, signed a document promising never to make political demands again, and the government introduced an anti-terrorism law likely to keep MB members in prison or in exile.[52] Authorities said several imprisoned Al-Islah members confessed to a detailed plan to create an armed wing with the goal of seizing power in the UAE.[53] Al-Islah denied these claims.

The British former counterterrorism director explained the plot this way:

> The so-called activists had sworn their loyalty to the MB Murshid and this, for them, transcended their loyalty to their respective countries. Therefore, the foreigners were expelled to where they came from and the Emiratis were detained on sedition and treason charges. Further, the Al-Islah leaders were shown evidence of their cooperation and collusion with associates of the MB's Murshid in Cairo while preparing their demands and what their follow-up steps should be. In short, the case is clear that there was a conspiracy to hold the UAE hostage to the demands of Al-Islah and that the primary orders were coming from the MB in Cairo at the time. This level of international meddling in the state's affairs has had a huge negative effect on the MB's chances in UAE.[54]

In 2014, the UAE recognized Al-Islah, along with the international MB, as a terrorist organization, making clear that it viewed the group as a national security threat.[55] Many UAE citizens, including tribal leaders and businessmen who fear instability, support this view. UAE foreign minister Sheikh Abdullah Bin Zayed Al-Nahyan has described the Brotherhood as "an organization which encroaches upon the sovereignty and integrity of nations,"[56] urging Arab Gulf states to cooperate against it.

In recent years, Sheikh Mohammed and UAE national security authorities have worked closely with Saudi Arabia's Crown Prince Mohammed bin Salman and other allies to curb Brotherhood groups across the Gulf and beyond. In July 2013, after the Egyptian military forced President Mohammed Morsi out of power, the UAE, as part of a Saudi-led plan, gave Egypt's new government $3 billion in aid, along with $5 billion from the Saudis.[57] Egypt soon launched a crackdown on the MB, detaining thousands (see Chapter 3 for more details).[58] By 2016, Egypt had received $23 billion in aid from Saudi Arabia, the UAE, and Kuwait, and across the Arab world the MB was withering.[59]

Emirati authorities have continued to keep an eye out for Brotherhood activity around the region. In January 2014, when Al-Qaradawi described the UAE as being "against Islam," the UAE's foreign ministry summoned Qatar's ambassador to ask why his government had not denounced the statement.[60] In December 2015, the UAE hired a private U.S. security firm to assassinate a leader of the Yemeni branch of the MB, hoping to turn the war against the Iran-backed Houthis and in favor of the U.S.- and Saudi-backed fighters.[61] The mission failed, but it highlights the lengths to which the Emirates is willing to go to stop the MB. And after prominent Kuwaiti MB member Mubarak Al-Duwailah said the UAE's Sheikh Mohammed harbored "extreme hostility" toward the Brotherhood, the UAE tried him for insulting the Emirati leadership and, in 2016, sentenced him to five years in prison, in absentia.[62]

Still, when it comes to Brotherhood activity in the Gulf, one neighbor receives the lion's share of the UAE's attention. UAE's ambassador to the United States Yousef Al-Otaiba recently accused Qatar of "funding, supporting, and enabling extremists from the Taliban to Hamas and Al-Qaddafi, inciting violence, encouraging radicalization, and undermining the stability of its neighbors."[63] The UAE has also lobbied Western governments to stand strongly against the Brotherhood, and Qatar, which has hosted and supported MB members for decades.

SAUDI ARABIA

Saudi Arabia's MB experience began in 1936, when Hassan Al-Banna visited the Kingdom in search of new followers eight years after he founded the group. King Abdulaziz welcomed him to Riyadh. When the two leaders met, Al-Banna proposed the establishment of a Brotherhood branch in Saudi Arabia.[64] The king politely declined, as detailed at the beginning of this chapter.

Outsider Islamists like the Brotherhood face a fundamental problem in the Kingdom. "In almost all countries in the Muslim world, Islamism arose and developed outside the state,"[65] writes Sciences Po professor Stéphane Lacroix. "The converse was true of Saudi Arabia: from the beginning, Islamism was integrated into the official institutions."[66] As will be detailed in Chapter 9, the Islamist idea is embedded within the Kingdom's centuries-old alliance between the ruling Al-Saud family and the Al-Wahhab Ulema. The visions and goals of the MB hold much less appeal in Saudi Arabia, as they are a poor reflection of the status quo in the Kingdom. This is one reason why Saudi Ulema, trained in true Salafism, were among the first to see the problems inherent in the Brotherhood project.

Still, King Abdulaziz remained cordial to Al-Banna and the Brotherhood, and the MB founder began to visit Makkah during Hajj, meeting delegation leaders there and preaching to the pilgrims. Relations between the two men, and consequently the Kingdom and the Brotherhood, began to sour in 1948.[67] In neighboring Yemen, the Brotherhood backed the revolutionaries who overthrew and killed Imam Yahya that February, while King Abdulaziz stood against it, and supported Crown Prince Ahmad's retaking of Sanaa a month later.

Despite these tensions and disagreements, Saudi Arabia opened its doors to the MB, according to Dr. Abdullah Al-Uthaymin, former secretary general of the King Faisal International Prize:

> The Saudi Kingdom refused to turn a cold shoulder to suffering Muslims, even if they were MB members. In 1952, a group of nationalist military officers within the Brotherhood overthrew Egypt's King Farouk and established a militant Arab nationalist government. Soon after, President Gamal Abdel Nasser turned on the Brotherhood, and in 1954 a Brotherhood member attempted to assassinate him. The group was swiftly outlawed and its leaders jailed. Saudi Arabia offered refuge to the fleeing members.[68]

Countless MB members fled not just Egypt but also Syria and Iraq, as the Brotherhood ideology lost out to Arab nationalism. Even though the Egyptian Brotherhood had recently attempted a coup, Saudi Arabia offered refuge.[69] As in other Arab Gulf states, many of the new arrivals accepted teaching jobs and helped develop the Kingdom's nascent education system.[70] King Faisal bin Abdulaziz viewed the MB scholars as an acceptable counter to communism and Arab nationalism, which by the 1960s had swept the region.[71]

Brotherhood figures like Muhammad Qutb, Sayyid's younger brother, and Abdullah Azzam established a foothold within academia, outside the Kingdom's religious establishment, to indoctrinate young Saudis.[72] It was the teachings of Qutb and Azzam that influenced a student named Osama bin Laden and laid the groundwork for Al-Qaeda. And it was the ideas of these same figures that laid the groundwork for the Sahwa, or so-called

Islamic Awakening, an Islamist movement heavily influenced by the Brotherhood.[73] As detailed by Thomas Hegghammer, senior research fellow at the Norwegian Defence Research Establishment who has held fellowships at Harvard, Princeton, and Stanford, and Stéphane Lacroix, political science professor at Sciences Po, in their 2011 book *The Meccan Rebellion*:

> In the climate of the policy of "Islamic Solidarity" put into effect by King Faisal to fight against Gamel Abdul Nasser and his 'progressive' allies, the Kingdom at that time became a veritable religious melting pot where all those who were being persecuted for their Islamic activism could find refuge. Among those who found refuge were, first of all, a large number of members of the Muslim Brotherhood. The hybrid that took shape when the political and cultural aspects of their ideology encountered the religious concepts of Wahhabism is called Al-Sahwa Al-Islamiyya (the Islamic Awakening), shortened simply to the Sahwa.[74]

In essence, the way the Brotherhood thanked Saudi leaders for their kindness in welcoming them and giving them refuge and prominent jobs was to create a movement that would ultimately undermine the religious and educational foundations of Saudi Arabia. This underscores why Saudi leaders view the Sahwa, and MB, response to the Iraqi occupation of Kuwait as a betrayal.

But even before then, the storm clouds were gathering. As the Saudi interior minister, late Crown Prince Nayef bin Abdulaziz, has said, "Whenever they got into difficulty or found their freedom restricted in their own countries, Brotherhood activists found refuge in the Kingdom, which protected their lives. . . . But they later turned against the Kingdom."[75] By the 1980s, MB and Sahwa figures came to dominate much of academia and the education system.

Appearing on a Saudi talk show in May 2019, Ali Faghassi Al Ghamdi, former chief of Al-Qaeda's military council in Saudi Arabia, spoke of the nefarious influence of the MB-inspired Sahwa leaders during the 1980s and 1990s, as well as their hypocrisy. "I was brought up and educated on the tapes of the poisonous public discourse that the Sahwa leaders in Saudi Arabia espoused. They radicalised entire generations of Saudis to send them to fight in Afghanistan, Chechnya and elsewhere," he said on Al Liwan. "The same Sahwa leaders that encouraged and theologically supported generations of Saudi youths to go and fight in Afghanistan and elsewhere are the same ones that then condemned us for doing so."[76]

After Saddam Hussein occupied Kuwait in 1990, Brotherhood members and supporters criticized the American military presence, which had been requested by King Fahd. Prominent Sahwa leaders denounced the position of the Saudi leadership in regard to Iraq. This took the Saudis by surprise. "The group's support for the Iranian Revolution in 1979 and then the Iraqi invasion of Kuwait in 1990 came as shocks to Gulf leaders," according to Jenkins.[77]

As detailed earlier in the section on Kuwait, the Brotherhood supported Hussein's invasion, even as it became clear that life under Iraqi occupation had become deeply dangerous and all but intolerable. To the leaders of Saudi Arabia, which hosted the exiled Kuwaiti Emir during the months of occupation and had always been a steadfast ally to Kuwait, this was a clear act of betrayal. In an instant, MB members within the Kingdom went from being Islamist allies to supporting Saddam's horrifying and unjust oppression of loyal Kuwaiti citizens, including summary executions, disappearances, and torture.

The Brotherhood stood with Saddam, which meant that Riyadh's position inspired protests led by the MB-linked Sahwa movement (more on Sahwa in Chapter 8). "Key Brotherhood figures inspired the Sahwa movement, which organized protests of the US military in the Kingdom and submitted petitions demanding broad political reform," AbdulMohsen Al-Akkas, former Saudi Minister of Social Affairs, told me in a 2008 interview. "The threat to the Saudi leadership was clear, and the Brotherhood was behind it."[78]

This moment, this juxtaposition—Saudi leaders supporting their suffering Khaleeji brethren while the MB took the side of the oppressive dictator—marked the beginning of the end for the Brotherhood in the Kingdom. This was the origin of the final divergence, when the true political colors of Brotherhood were revealed. No longer would MB members be seen as trusted fellow Muslims and Islamist allies. By 1995, Saudi leaders had snuffed out the Sahwa campaign, mainly by jailing leaders such as Sheikh Salman Al-Awda.[79] In the years that followed, the government expelled many prominent Brotherhood members, including Muhammad Qutb.[80] Ridding the Saudi education system of MB influence, however, would take a great deal more work. Key MB figures like Qutb and Azzam had for decades been seen as guiding lights of Islamic education in Saudi Arabia. They had implanted MB thinking deep within Saudi society and the education system, and their impact would not be easily erased.

Still, the crackdown intensified in the next decade. In the wake of the attacks of September 11, 2001, the world learned that the MB had been a key driving force behind the creation of Al-Qaeda. Along with the teachings of Muhammad Qutb and Azzam, the 1964 book *Milestones*, written by leading Brotherhood figure Sayyid Qutb while in prison (see Chapter 1), served as inspiration for Osama bin Laden and his right-hand man, Ayman Al-Zawahiri, another Brotherhood figure.

Back in the 1980s, Brotherhood members in the Kingdom and around the region had spearheaded donation collection and mobilization efforts to support Afghan mujahideen, helping create the "Afghan Arabs," which later formed the core of Al-Qaeda.[81] Since fifteen of the nineteen September 11 hijackers were Saudi nationals, the Kingdom had to respond swiftly and harshly. In early 2002, Prince Nayef bin Abdulaziz threw down the gauntlet, declaring the MB the "root of all our problems."[82] Saudi leaders initiated their broadest crackdown yet on the Brotherhood.

Then came the Arab uprisings, which led to renewed tensions with MB-linked clerics. "After the so-called Arab Spring, Sheikh Salman Al-Awda wrote a book in favor of the Arab uprisings, and he and other Sahwa leaders petitioned the government for political reform," Dr. Al-Uthaymin told me. "It is however a sign of the weakness of anti-government sentiment in the Kingdom that none of the Sahwa leaders supported the call for an Egypt-like 'Day of Rage,' which ultimately failed to materialize."[83] King Abdullah presented a $130 billion aid package, including new housing and tens of thousands of jobs, and dissent subsided.[84]

Two years later, after Egypt's military forced out President Mohammed Morsi, the Kingdom gave billions in aid to help stabilize Egypt's new government. More than fifty Saudi clerics linked to the Brotherhood criticized the Kingdom's support for the El-Sisi regime, describing the overthrow of Morsi as against the will of the people.[85] Saudi authorities clamped down on domestic support of the MB. Posting the four-finger symbol of the Raba'a Square massacre on social media, for instance, became a crime. MB-friendly instructors were removed from their university posts, and MB-linked books were banned from the Riyadh bookfair, the largest and most important in the Arab world.[86]

Throughout this extended period, from the early 1990s to the present day, the MB supported the leading Saudi dissident group, based in London. In an interview on Rotana's Al Liwan talk show in May 2019, Kassab Al-Otaibi recounted his twenty years in exile with the Saudi opposition—the Islah Islamic Movement (IIM), led by Mohamed Al-Masairi and Saad Al-Faqih—before he returned home to the Kingdom in 2015.[87] He said he was recruited from central Qassim province because his tribal background and his religious scholarship were lacking within the IIM leadership in London.[88]

The relationship between Al-Faqih and the Ikhwan started in the early 1990s and continues to this day. MB members linked to ousted Egyptian president Mohammed Morsi regularly meet Al-Faqih in London, according to Al-Otaibi. "Al-Faqih receives logistical, monetary and spiritual support from the MB and is committed to the ideology," he said. According to Al-Otaibi, the rift between the movement's leaders was largely a result of Al-Faqih being a follower of MB ideology, while Al-Masairi followed Salafist ideas, which ultimately led to the group's unraveling.[89] Al-Otaibi said Al-Faqih was financially supported by several groups that shared his opposition to the Saudi leadership, including Al-Qaeda. Al-Faqih maintained regular connections with Al-Qaeda's leaders, Al-Otaibi said, including through his television station, Al-Islah.[90] During the Al Liwan interview, a recording was played of current Al-Qaeda chief, and former MB member, Ayman Al-Zawahiri responding to a question regarding his thoughts on IIM, which aims to overthrow the Saudi monarchy and assume power. "We have seen huge progress in the movement under the leadership of Saad Al-Faqih and by many known religious figures joining the movement as well as tribal leaders that are to join as well," said Al-Zawahari. "My position on the IIM is that of support, blessing, honour and respect."[91]

Al-Faqih was close to MB senior leader Azzam Tamimi. "The Ikhwan leader was the spiritual godfather of Faqih and shaped the IIM's ideology and inspired it politically," Al-Otaibi said.[92] During the interview, a recording was played in which Azzam Tamimi is heard calling "for the fall of the corrupt regimes in the Gulf, chief among them the Saudi regime." Tamimi also says that the "crises after the murder of Jamal Khashoggi should be utilised to the maximum to topple the Al-Saud regime."[93] As a senior analyst, Al-Otaibi had rare insight into the IIM's transactions and business dealings, and was well aware of Qatari support for the movement. "From 1994, the IIM received £300,000 every 3 months personally delivered by Sheikh Hamad Bin Thamer Al-Thani," said Al-Otaibi, referring to the chairman of the board of Al Jazeera Media Network.[94] In addition, Al-Otaibi received a million Qatari riyals from the Qatari Embassy in London to oversee an anti-Saudi and anti-UAE social media campaign, as revealed in a leaked cable from the Qatari embassy.[95]

Back home, Saudi authorities have continued to take steps to cleanse the country of Brotherhood influence. In February 2014, the government issued a decree that those who expressed sympathy or support for a terrorist group could face three to twenty years in jail.[96] A month later, the government named the MB, and all groups that resemble it, a terrorist organization. Suddenly, even posting the Raba'a sign on one's Twitter or Facebook page could land a Saudi in jail for a long time. The result was that, within Saudi Arabia, support for the Brotherhood vanished and in turn the Sahwa's outspokenness and visibility decreased considerably.

This is when things began to turn, highlighting how Saudi authorities had begun to subdue the internal Brotherhood threat. King Salman launched a bold foreign policy move just two months into his reign: intervention in Yemen, in March 2015, to crush the Houthis and reinstall the government of Abdrabbuh Mansur Hadi. There was broad Islamist backing for the intervention in Yemen, as well as for the crackdown on Shia protests against the intervention, which sprang up in eastern Saudi Arabia. In an interview on Al Jazeera, Sheikh Salman Al-Awda argued that since Iran was taking over Arab lands, it needed to be punished; thus, the Saudi intervention was legitimate.[97] The idea that Iran was behind both of these problems—backing the Houthis in Yemen and assisting Saudi Shias—may have helped bring the two sides together. Either way, since late 2014, Saudis linked to the Brotherhood have been mostly silent, or supportive of government policy. For the moment, the internal threat appears to have been squelched.

Yet the government's work is far from over. In 2015, authorities removed some eighty religious books from Saudi schools, including those by Hassan Al-Banna, Al-Qaradawi, and Sayyid Qutb. In the fall of 2017, the government arrested some thirty clerics and scholars suspected of links to the Brotherhood, including Salman Al-Awda, and the Islamic University of Imam Muhammad bin Saud began to dismiss any employees connected to the Brotherhood. Shortly thereafter, Saudi education minister Ahmad Al-Issa vowed that the Kingdom would eliminate any trace of the influence of the MB in the education curricula.[98] A year later, the job had been completed. "The books and the curricula in our schools have no link with the Muslim Brotherhood dogma," Al-Issa said. "The past issues about the Brotherhood's influence were linked to the extra-curricular activities in some schools and to the mentality of some teachers. The ministry had dealt with both."[99]

Crown Prince Mohammed bin Salman went even further, saying he would terminate the MB from his country. He has repeatedly discussed the issue with President Trump, linking Al-Qaeda to the Brotherhood and urging the American leader to designate the Brotherhood a terrorist group.[100] This is far from the only time Saudi leaders have taken their fight against the Brotherhood beyond the borders of the Kingdom. Crown Prince Mohammed bin Salman has often worked closely with Emirati crown prince bin Zayed, who has led one of the harshest crackdowns on the Brotherhood in the Gulf.

Under the watch of Mohammed bin Salman, Saudi authorities have moved beyond mere categorization and are now treating the Brotherhood as a legitimate terror organization. "Working with the UAE, Saudi Arabia has weakened the position of the Syrian Brotherhood within the Syrian opposition—the Brotherhood has lost considerable influence among insurgent groups in that conflict. In Egypt, the Kingdom strongly supported the ousting of Brotherhood President Mohammed Morsi, and along with the UAE has over the past five years given tens of billions of dollars in aid and fuel to the El-Sisi regime," a former GCC Secretary General told me in 2017.[101]

QATAR

No Gulf country has a greater MB presence—and no nation has more fully supported the group outside its borders—than Qatar. For more than six decades, the Brotherhood has been influencing Qatari policy and decision-making, mainly through education, Islamic endowments, and the media. Further, it can be said that since the late 1990s, there has been a conspiracy by the Qatari rulers to aid the MB coming to power in the Arab world and quietly putting down roots in the West (see Chapter 6). The architect of this policy is former Qatari Emir Sheikh Hamad bin Khalifa

Al-Thani. Al-Thani and his Qatari cohorts have long believed that the Arab world can only develop through a group of individuals that come to power through the ballot box who have deep Islamic conservative roots, and the only group that meets this criterion is the MB.

"In my frequent discussions with him, Sheikh Hamad always made clear his belief that the future of the Arab world lies with the MB and its affiliate religious offshoots in the Arab countries," Bertrand Besancenot, former French ambassador to Qatar and Saudi Arabia and current Special French Presidential Envoy to the GCC, claimed in July 2018.[102] The Qataris have been supporting MB-based infiltration for many years, culminating in the Morsi government in Egypt, which, according to the Qataris, inevitably failed only because Saudi Arabia and its allies conspired to take Morsi down.

Like Saudis, Qataris practice Salafism. The country's ruling family, the Al-Thanis, hail from Najd, the same Central Arabian region as Sheikh Muhammad bin Abdul Wahhab himself, and citizens generally support the monarchy. Thus, when Qatar began welcoming MB members in the 1950s, the Islamist ideas of the new arrivals often fell on deaf ears. "Though the state overall was receptive to the influx of the Ikhwan," Gulf political analyst David B. Roberts explained in a 2014 lecture, "the ground for proselytization was not so accepting."[103]

Still, the monarchy found an important use for the MB. In subscribing to Salafism, Qatari leaders believed they had exposed their country to a degree of theological ideological control from Saudi Arabia. Sheikh Jassim Al-Thani, the founder of modern-day Qatar, sought a way to keep Riyadh at arm's length, even from the country's early days, as Roberts detailed in his talk:

> To augment the status of Wahhabism in Qatar, to explicitly instill it through education systems in schools or to give its religious scholars an official place in government, would have been to intractably instill the necessary deference of Qatar to Saudi Arabia as the custodian of the Two Holy Places and the Al-Wahhab legacy. Instead, supporting the Ikhwan allowed a different group to develop Qatar's systems. This avoided a reliance on Saudi-scholars or jurists to design and staff Qatar's systems in a Wahhabi image inevitably tilting toward Riyadh. Also, Qatar's leadership was in a stronger position and could set and enforce guidelines as to the group's limitations to a greater degree.[104]

Thus, from the beginning, Qatar viewed the Brotherhood as a tool to wield against Saudi Arabia, to minimize the influence of the Kingdom. Never mind the threat the MB might pose internally, or to Qatar's neighbors— the ruling family decided the Brotherhood could shape the country's education system, and enable it to keep Saudi Arabia at arm's length. "Qatar's over-inflated sense of its Islamic importance and desire to wield outsized influence and distinguish itself from Saudi Arabia have spurred its decades-long support for the Muslim Brotherhood," a former French ambassador to Qatar and Saudi Arabia stated in September 2018.[105]

In 1954, Abdulbadi Al-Saqr, a former student of Hassan Al-Banna, arrived from Egypt and established Qatar's Ministry of Education, becoming its director. Al-Saqr hired many MB teachers, who soon "stamped the education system with their Islamic ideology," Abdulla Juma Kobaisi wrote in 1979.[106] Qatar imported MB scholars from Egypt, including Abdelmoaz Al-Sattar, Hassan Al-Banna's emissary to Palestine, and Kemal Naji, who served fifteen years as Qatar's director of education (1964–1979). Palestinian Brothers also arrived, including Muhamad Yusuf Al-Najjar, a founding member of Fatah, and current Fatah leader and Palestinian president Mahmoud Abbas, who worked in the education department for a dozen years and signed the paperwork for the most notable name to settle in Qatar in this period.

Sheikh Yusuf Al-Qaradawi arrived from Egypt in 1961 and has lived in Qatar ever since. The Brotherhood's spiritual leader regularly advised the former Emir, Sheikh Hamad bin Khalifa Al-Thani, father of the current Emir, Sheikh Tamim bin Hamad Al-Thani. "Sheikh Hamad accepted Al-Qaradawi as one of his primary religious counselors and bent much of Qatari policy to his MB-centered aspirations," a former French ambassador in the Gulf said during a 2018 interview.[107] According to a former Senior Case Officer in the CIA's Near East Directorate, the two developed a scheme to influence and even control the region. "This grandiose and delusional plan of domination over the Arab world grew out of this very personal relationship between Hamad of Qatar and Al-Qaradawi of the Brotherhood movement," the former case officer told me.[108]

In the 1970s, Al-Qaradawi established and led the College of Sharia at Qatar University. Today, even at the age of ninety-two, he remains one of the most prominent thinkers on Islam, thanks in part to his long-running Al Jazeera talk show *Sharia and Life*, which went off the air in 2014. Al-Qaradawi often makes controversial statements in support of jihad and, more specifically, the killing of Jews. "Oh Allah, take this oppressive, Jewish, Zionist band of people," he said in 2009, "do not spare a single one of them. Oh Allah, count their numbers, and kill them, down to the very last one."[109]

Today, though the MB ideology helped shape the school curriculum and the country's education system, the Brotherhood is little involved in Qatar's domestic affairs. In other states, the Brotherhood used benign social activities, like running local sports clubs and food banks, to become part of the community. In Qatar, such activities were not possible because of a tacit agreement between the Qatari leadership and the Brotherhood that goes back decades: you can stay in our country as long as you focus your energies outside Qatar. This outward focus led to the closing of the MB's Qatar branch in 1999.[110] "The Ikhwan soon began to use Qatar as a launching pad for its expansion into the Emirates and especially Dubai," says Roberts.[111]

YEMEN

For nearly a century, Yemen has been the laggard in the Gulf, far behind its neighbors in terms of development and political stability. In addition to a lack of natural resources, this is a result of endemic tribal conflict enabled by long-lasting British colonial rule, which did not end until 1967, along with a twisted history of political leanings and a complex religious makeup that includes a significant Zaydi Shia minority. A variety of clans have emerged to fight for power since Yemen declared independence in 1962, and Arab nationalism and Marxist-Leninism have also had their heydays, particularly the latter in South Yemen.[112]

In the 1940s, Algerian Muslim Brotherhood leader Fudai Al-Wartilani played a key role in bringing MB ideas to Yemen, where he was involved with anti-Shia activities connected to the Egyptian MB.[113] The ideology spread, and a number of MB-linked organizations came and went until 1969, when the MB-affiliated Islamic Front was established and soon led by Abdul Majeed Al-Zindani.[114] Al-Zindani, who in 2004 was designated by the United States as a terrorist and loyalist of Osama bin Laden,[115] was seen as too radical and soon replaced by Yassin Abd Al-Aziz Al-Qubati.[116] Yet Al-Zindani continued to serve as advisor and later speaker of the group's Shura Council.[117]

In the 1970s, with Soviet-backed Marxists in control of South Yemen, the northern Yemen Arab Republic of Ali Abdullah Saleh funded the Islamic Front militia to halt the advance of communists on the Arabian Peninsula.[118] Buoyed by this kind of support, the group expanded in the 1980s, launching its own newspaper and winning several seats in the consultative council. With the reunification of Yemen in 1990, the Islamic Front merged with one of the country's largest tribes, the Hashid confederation, to create the Yemeni Congregation for Reform, or Al-Islah.

As many scholars have pointed out, Al-Islah is much less a political party than a loose, complicated coalition of tribal leaders, Islamists, and businessmen. Writing in the *International Journal of Middle East Studies* in 1995, Paul Dresch, a Yemen-focused cultural anthropologist at Oxford, and Bernard Haykel, professor of Near Eastern studies at Princeton, called Al-Islah a "broad church" of groups that share a wide range of interests and opinions.[119] It has at times aligned with leftists and non-Islamists.[120] "Al-Islah had and still has some very clear non-Brotherhood components," Hansen and Mesoy wrote in 2009.[121] Due to this history, Al-Islah views Saudi Arabia as a sister Kingdom and sees maintaining strong ties with Riyadh as one of its primary objectives.[122]

Somewhat contradictory for an MB affiliate, Al-Islah was close to Yemen's Arab nationalist ruling party, the General People's Congress, led by

President Saleh. This was largely a result of the history of Al-Islah members, many of whom fought alongside Saleh's forces in North Yemen and worked with the regime for decades. This cooperation and support continued after reunification, ultimately leading to the implementation of Sharia law.[123] "Far from being a force for peace, Al-Islah was a willing partner in the ruling regime's war efforts," Hansen and Mesoy wrote, referring to the short-lived 1994 conflict.[124]

A few years later, marginalized by the Saleh regime, Al-Islah joined a political cooperative that included the Yemeni Socialist Party, mainly made up of remnants of southern Yemen's communist period, which is to say former battlefield foes of some members of Al-Islah. Despite their vast differences, Al-Islah soon accepted the socialists as allies, perhaps seeing them as less autocratic than the ruling party.

A group of moderates, such as Mohammed Qahtan, emerged within the organization in the late 1990s. Although they failed to get any female candidates nominated to run in the 2003 elections, by 2007 they were able to replace Al-Zindani as speaker of the Shura and elect 13 women into the 130-member council. This was a first. "Zindani became a liability to the party when he was accused by the United States of funding Al-Qaeda," wrote Hansen and Mesoy.[125] By 2008 he was out, though he still had his Imam University to oversee in Sanaa, an institution attended by American Al-Qaeda figures John Walker Lindh and Anwar Al-Awlawki, who also lectured there.[126]

By this time, conflict was brewing in the south, mainly due to frustration on the part of Houthi Shias with the government in Sanaa. The Houthis had begun to spread the Iranian ideology, and various Al-Islah groups began working to avoid conflict and to build militias to fight the Houthis. Amid the violence and instability, the group emerged as one of the country's key actors. "Al-Islah remains one of the few stable organisations in Yemen, and must be part of any solution to the various Yemeni conflicts. It is also more moderate than most Islamist organisations in Yemen," Hansen and Mesoy wrote in 2009, adding that the group will "be an important partner in any peace process that takes place in Yemen. However, it is doubtful that in itself it can contribute directly to peacemaking as its tribal links and ideological platform make it too controversial."[127]

The group's relative stability and influence, as well as its opposition to the Iran-backed Houthis, helps explain why Saudi Arabia has backed Al-Islah-linked militias in recent years. Two months into his reign—in March 2015—King Salman launched an intervention in Yemen to crush the Iran-backed Houthis and reinstall the Abdrabbuh Mansur Hadi government. As of mid-2019, the conflict raged on, with the UN describing the situation in Yemen as the world's worst humanitarian crisis, with four of every five Yemenis said to be in need of assistance or protection.[128]

Of course, Riyadh did not go into Yemen alone. The Saudi-led intervention, jointly with the UAE, received strong domestic backing from

MB-linked Islamists, including leading Sahwa figure Salman Al-Awda, who said Iran was looking to conquer Arab lands and needed to be pushed back.[129] The intervention has also benefited from significant and steady support from the United States. Without billions of dollars' worth of American arms, as well as training and intelligence, the death toll in Yemen would likely be much higher.[130]

Saudi leaders have expressed a desire to find a way to end the violence. "They just don't know how to do so without basically leaving a major beachhead for Iran in that country in the form of the Houthi rebels, who would take over the country," Princeton University Yemen scholar Bernard Haykel told *The New Yorker* in April 2019.[131] While Haykel states that the Saudi leadership shouldered some responsibility for the situation, he also points out that the Kingdom and other Gulf states had provided hundreds of millions in aid and were prepared to pay for Yemen's reconstruction.[132] "But you have to remember there is also a civil war that predates the Saudi involvement there. So it is more complicated than just attributing everything that happens there to Saudi Arabia," he said.[133]

Haykel was referring to the Houthi insurgency that began around 2004, when the group's leader, Hussen Al-Houthi, was killed as a part of a crackdown by the Saleh government. By 2009, the conflict had heated up enough to draw in the Kingdom, but only until a ceasefire was signed the following year. These tensions simmered through the Yemeni revolution in 2011, which toppled the Saleh government. In January 2015, a counter-revolution led by the Houthis ousted Hadi, forcing the Saudi leadership to intervene. For Riyadh, Yemen had by mid-2019 become something like the U.S. war against Al-Qaeda in Afghanistan, but in a neighboring state, not some far-flung corner of the world. "If they just drop the war and withdraw, that country would become a threat to the national security of Saudi Arabia," Haykel said.[134]

This statement is more true today than at the start of the conflict. As Anchal Vohra, fellow at Indian think tank Observer Research Foundation, wrote for *Foreign Policy* in June 2019, Tehran's relations with Hezbollah had chilled due to economic troubles in Lebanon. "There are a growing number of signs that Tehran now believes the Houthi insurgents of Yemen should be their preferred regional proxy in the growing confrontation with the United States and its allies," wrote Vohra.[135] By May 2019, as Houthis began to withdraw from the crucial Hodeidah port, implementing the UN-brokered agreement in Sweden, there were signs that the conflict could be coming to an end.[136]

Yet it was not Hezbollah or Shiite militias in Iraq that struck back when the United States sent an aircraft carrier group to the Gulf later that month, but Houthis, attacking a Saudi pipeline via drone and a Saudi arms depot near the Yemen border, re-escalating the conflict.[137] This was followed by not one but two drone attacks on Saudi Arabia's southern airports, with one missile injuring dozens of civilians in the Abha arrivals hall.[138] The

UN swiftly condemned the Houthi attacks.[139] It's telling that Tehran's rising proxy in Yemen has begun funding its troubled, formerly powerful proxy in Lebanon. "Houthis of Yemen raised funds for Hezbollah during the month of Ramadan," Fatima Alasrar, a senior analyst at the Arabia Foundation and a former fellow at Harvard's Kennedy School, tweeted in May 2019, citing a Houthi news agency report about a fundraiser in Yemen that collected millions of riyals.[140] "It's not the first time," she added.

Al-Islah has been involved in the conflict from the start and is now strongly backed by Saudi Arabia. Riyadh has a long history with Al-Islah and sees the group as a tool to help unite Sunni forces against the Houthis. The UAE had been supporting the Southern Transitional Council's so-called Security Belt, which has fought against Al-Islah forces. But at a late 2017 meeting in Riyadh with Crown Prince Mohammed bin Salman and Sheikh Mohammad bin Zayed, Al-Islah leader Mohammad Al-Yadoumi agreed to officially and publicly cut the group's ties to the Brotherhood.[141] This enabled the UAE to join Saudi Arabia and essentially align behind the Al-Islah militia to more forcefully confront the Houthis and their militias across central Yemen. However, the UAE is not yet fully convinced that supporting Al-Islah is the right path, even though "the UAE's military and infrastructural interests in southern Yemen are on the rise" as part of a general cultivation of a military ethos in Abu Dhabi as a way to strengthen national cohesion.[142]

CONCLUSION

Saudi Arabia and its Gulf partners have worked to curb the influence of the MB in the region, yet the fight is far from over. As Jenkins wrote in 2017, "For the Saudis, the MB has come to represent a profound ideological threat to the basis of their state. For them, it is a secretive, partisan and divisive organization dedicated to a self-defined renewal of Islam and the establishment of a transnational Islamic state through incremental but ultimately revolutionary political activism, using tactical violence if necessary."[143]

Though the Brotherhood's size, reach, and influence have waned in Egypt, Syria, and the Gulf, it remains the only organized alternative to the ruling governments in these states. Across the region, Arab citizens are less likely to submit to authoritarian leadership after the so-called Arab Spring. What's more, Tunisia's Ennahda, still involved in government there, offers a successful model. In the Gulf, Brotherhood ideas have spread in varying degrees to all GCC states and influenced generations of students. Yet there is a reason the MB has not made the same impact in the Gulf as it has elsewhere. "Long before the MB's arrival, the vast majority of Saudi and Gulf citizens already identified strongly with deeply conservative Islamic beliefs and lived in an Islamist environment. Therefore, the MB was partly irrelevant to the region, and partly an affront to its already established core belief system," former Saudi information minister Dr. Abdul Aziz Khoja told me in 2012.[144]

Ultimately, the movement will not be completely eradicated from the Gulf until Qatar changes its policies, banning all support for the Brotherhood, its affiliates, and its members. Not only is Qatar the primary supporter of the MB, but its "financial support for Al-Qaeda and Daesh affiliates enables them to terrorize innocents everywhere," former Saudi intelligence director Prince Turki Al-Faisal Al-Saud stated in late 2017.[145] In the next two chapters, we will learn much more about Qatar's support for the MB and terrorism at home and abroad.

CHAPTER 6

Muslim Brotherhood Reach in the West Backed by Qatar and Turkey

Thus far, we have seen how the Muslim Brotherhood has largely failed in its quest to seize power in the Arab world and the devastating impact of that failure in many countries. Yet even as the MB sought to overthrow governments in the Middle East, it was also making inroads across the West, and into Asia, starting more than half a century ago.

In the past decade, these efforts have been ramped up, as the MB and its affiliates have expanded deeper into Europe, the United States, and beyond, putting down roots, often with several MB-linked organizations in a single country. These groups have become deeply embedded in their adopted societies and political scenes, even while their political influence and impact have remained limited.

Unsurprisingly, Qatar has created a vast funding network to provide backbone for this outreach, spending hundreds of millions of dollars, either directly or indirectly, to back MB-linked groups around the world and in support of Turkey's efforts to extend its policy. Doha has funded decades of globe hopping by Yusuf Al-Qaradawi, paying for trips to Turkey and Pakistan, across Europe and North America, and even as far afield as Japan and South Korea. Doha has also been financing dozens of European organizations linked to the MB, keeping the ideology alive even as its influence fades in the Middle East.

Qatar's deep connection to the MB is now a matter of fact and has spurred a major rift in the GCC nations and the Middle East in general. This connection begins at the very top. As Sheikh Hamad bin Khalifa Al Thani, former Amir of Qatar and father of current Emir Tamim bin Hamad Al-Thani, told a former prime minister and foreign minister of an Arab gulf state, "I used to be a Baathist in my youth, but after the Arab defeat of 1967, I became a member of the Muslim Brotherhood."[1]

However, as I was recently told by a former counterterrorism director in France, "the Qatari authorities have been playing a very dangerous game with their deliberate funding on MB activities across Europe. The time will come when they will pay heavily for having ignored the repeated French and British warnings to end this misguided policy."[2]

THE UNITED STATES HELPS CREATE
GLOBAL BROTHERHOOD

As newly installed Egyptian president Hosni Mubarak began to crack down on the Brotherhood, the group's leaders, mostly exiled to Europe, adopted a strategic plan that laid out a "cultural invasion" of the West aiming to "establish an Islamic government on earth."[3] The scheme, widely known as "The Project" and detailed in a 1982 MB document found in Switzerland, involved immigration, infiltration, surveillance, protest, political involvement, and more to gain influence and ultimately control.[4] A decade later, at an Islam conference in Ohio, Yusuf Al-Qaradawi reiterated the group's agenda, declaring that the MB would "conquer Europe . . . America, not through sword, but through Da'wa."[5]

In reality, the Brotherhood's efforts to conquer the West had started decades before. Over the past seven decades, the MB has successfully put down roots in dozens of countries outside the Middle East. It all started in the United States, where in 1953 the government welcomed the wolf into its home. As a counterterrorism advisor said to me, "The US invited Said Ramadan, Hassan Al-Banna's son-in-law and by that time the de facto MB foreign minister, to Washington for a series of meetings. The Americans viewed Islamism as a crucial counter to Soviet communism, and within a few years the CIA was supporting Ramadan's efforts to build an Islamist beachhead in Europe, from his base in Geneva."[6] Like most MB members, Ramadan opposed communism because it rejected religion. This made him a natural U.S. ally.

In the decades following this meeting, American support for Islamists, and particularly Ramadan, would help the MB establish and develop Islamist groups across Europe and beyond. Many of the Afghan leaders backed by the United States in the anti-Soviet jihad were MB members and helped build Al-Qaeda. State Department memos at the time even warned of the potential future threat of MB members.[7] The leader of an MB affiliate in Iran called the Devotees of Islam mentored Ayatollah Ruhollah Khomeini, who spurred the 1979 Iranian Revolution.[8] Ramadan himself would often play a key role in this outreach. For instance, the Islamists of Pakistan led by Abul-A'la Maududi, a scholar Ramadan visited repeatedly, created the Taliban.[9]

"Ramadan, who had always had international ambitions, arrived in Europe in 1958. There, according to his son, Tariq, he was generally considered to be in charge of the Ikhwan abroad," Alison Pargeter, senior researcher at RUSI, writes.[10] He settled in Geneva, where he published Islamist literature and in 1961 set up the Islamic Centre of Geneva, which soon became a gathering place for Islamists from around the world and an MB publishing house.[11] The center's mission was to promote the MB ideology. "The creation of the Islamic Center was supposed to realize my father's desire of creating a center from which he could spread the teachings of Hassan Al-Banna," Hani Ramadan, Said's son, who took over after his father's death, said in 2016.[12]

MB leaders fleeing oppression in the Arab world were surprised at the welcome they received in Europe. They "found an environment where they could operate with a relative degree of freedom and where they could take advantage of the media opportunities that were on offer to promote their cause," writes Pargeter. "Indeed, this group of highly ambitious and hawkish Ikhwani saw possibilities in Europe that they could not even dream of inside Egypt."[13] The MB felt so comfortable in Switzerland that it launched its own Swiss bank, Al Taqwa. The bank was not an official MB entity, but many prominent MB figures soon became investors and clients. As of April 2000, for instance, Yusuf Al-Qaradawi held more than 5,000 shares in Al Taqwa.[14] After the attacks of September 2001, the United States listed the bank as a terrorist sponsor.[15]

THE BEACHHEAD

Said Ramadan's greatest success came in Munich. Starting in the mid-1950s, the United States backed his effort to build a mosque there, initially proposed for the Central Asian and Caucasus Muslims who had turned against the Soviet Union in World War II and fought alongside German troops. This would be Germany's first mosque for a permanent Muslim population. At the initial gathering of the mosque commission, in 1962, Ramadan showed up and gave 1,000 marks to the construction fund, much more than any other contributor present.[16]

Working with local Arab MB members, Ramadan gradually gained control of the mosque effort, with backing from the American Committee for Liberation, an anti-Soviet CIA effort that also ran Radio Free Europe. "Documents and interviews show how the Muslim Brotherhood formed a working arrangement with U.S. intelligence organizations, outmaneuvering German agencies for control of the former Nazi soldiers and their mosque," Pulitzer Prize–winning journalist Ian Johnson wrote in 2005.[17] "But the U.S. lost its hold on the movement, and in short order conservative, arch-Catholic Bavaria had become host to a center of radical Islam."[18] By the time the Munich mosque finally opened, in August 1973, one of Ramadan's lieutenants, Syrian-born Ali Ghaleb Himmat, had taken over. He also managed Al Taqwa Bank, usually from a villa in Campione d'Italia. Himmat had established the bank in 1988 with the help of influential Egyptian businessman and MB figure Yusuf Nada, who after the Iranian Revolution of 1979 arranged for key MB leaders to visit the new regime in Tehran.[19]

The Munich mosque soon came to play a crucial role in building a Europe-wide network of MB-linked organizations, such as the UK-based Federation of Islamic Organizations in Europe. It's no coincidence that several of the MB's murshids, or supreme guides, spent significant time in Munich. One of them, former MB Supreme Guide Mahdi Akef, who died in 2017 at the age of eighty-nine, has said that while he was there, leaders and top officials from across the Muslim world would visit the mosque to pay their respects to the world's most powerful Islamic organization.[20]

The Munich mosque first appeared on German authorities' radar after the 1993 car-bomb attack on New York's World Trade Center. One of the plotters, Mahmoud Abouhalima, had attended the mosque. The Germans began watching the mosque, but found no terror links and ended the surveillance. The ground shifted with the attacks of September 2001, which ultimately linked the Brotherhood, the Munich mosque, and Al Taqwa, which is accused of sending money to Hamas, and possibly Al-Qaeda.[21] The 9/11 attackers spent time in Munich, and Europe has seen terrorist attack after terrorist attack in the past decade, many of which can be traced back to visitors of the Munich mosque. This is a much more subtle and insidious edition of the American backing of anti-Soviet jihadis in the 1980s, which led to blowback in the form of Al-Qaeda, Osama, and 9/11. "The parallels between the 1950's and today are striking," Johnson writes in *A Mosque in Munich*, his 2005 bestseller. "Now like a half century ago in Munich, western societies are seeking Muslim allies. . . . Munich shows the danger of doing so without careful reflection and scrutiny."[22]

Today, Himmat is under investigation for terrorist links, while the Islamic Community of Germany (IGD), as the Munich mosque is now known, is one of the country's leading Muslim organizations, representing sixty German mosques.[23] After several raids and close surveillance, it's no longer a center of radical activity, but it remains a key MB center in Europe. In 2007, the Interior Ministry of Bavaria branded IGD an MB branch and an extremist organization.[24] This happened not long after the state closed an IGD school. "We are afraid that the group running the school, which belongs to the Islamic Community of Germany, is using the school to spread Islamist ideology," a spokesman for the government of Upper Bavaria told the *Wall Street Journal* in 2005.[25]

Yet, because the MB gained control of the Munich mosque in the early 1970s, before the flowering of renewed faith in political Islam and had U.S. backing in the Cold War, it was able to put down roots and make Munich the nexus of a fast-growing network. "Political and social groups affiliated with the Muslim Brotherhood now dominate organized Islamic life across a broad swath of Western Europe," writes Johnson.[26] The German city of Aachen, on the Belgium border, also emerged as an MB hub around the same time, mainly because it was home to Syrian MB leader Issam

Al-Attar. After the Syrian MB had been crushed and forced into exile in the early 1980s (see Chapter 4), Al-Attar settled in Aachen and created a new organization, Al-Talia, which was independent but essentially carried on the MB ideology.[27]

Yet even today, BfV, the German intelligence agency, still views IGD as the country's MB headquarters.[28] In early 2019, a top official in the state of North Rhine-Westphalia said that the MB threat to Germany is greater than that of ISIS or Al-Qaeda.[29] Throughout the Rhine region, the state estimates that 109 places of worship promote the MB ideology.[30] In addition, in 2017 German intelligence warned that the MB was working to recruit refugee arrivals in the eastern state of Saxony while also buying up property in order to build mosques and increase its presence.[31]

The MB also put down roots in Austria. MB networks first appeared there in the 1960s, with branches in Egypt, Syria, and Palestine. After suffering under Nasser, Egyptian MB member Yussuf Nada arrived in Vienna in 1969 and built a multimillion-dollar cement business. He soon became the head of MB external relations and welcomed all variety of Muslim business and political figures to his mansion in Campione d'Italia, which became an unofficial MB foreign ministry.[32] "Nada spent only limited time in Austria," writes Lorenzo Vidino, director of the extremism program at George Washington University and author of a 2017 report on the MB in Austria, "but enough to set up the embryo of a Brotherhood presence in the country and to establish a link" to the Munich hub.[33]

Several top MB figures spent time in Austria, including Ahmed Mahmoud El-Abiary. As of late 2018, an Austrian citizen and longtime Vienna resident, El-Abiary lived in London and serves as a senior member in what has become the MB's headquarters outside Egypt.[34] As I have been told, "Another Austrian MB regular is Egyptian-born Ayman Ali. During the Bosnian War he ran the Bosnia branch of a Tirana-based aid agency, which was designated a terrorist outfit by the US in 2004."[35] He moved his family to Graz, where he became an imam and set up an import-export firm Austrian authorities believe has been used for money laundering. He later served as deputy secretary-general of the MB's pan-European organization, the Federation of Islamic Organizations in Europe, then returned to Egypt to serve as senior advisor to President Mohammed Morsi during his one-year tenure.[36] Today, MB-linked organizations are the Austrian government's main interlocutors with the country's Muslim communities.[37]

France and the UK also became key MB outposts in Europe during this time. In 1963, an Indian academic named Muhammad Hamidullah, linked to the MB via ties to Said Ramadan and Issam Al-Attar, established the Islamic Students Association of France (AEIF).[38] The AEIF set up branches at universities in the largest French cities and emerged as one of the country's strongest Islamic organizations. In 1983, the AEIF, the Islamic Group of France, seen as the Tunisian MB arm in France, and other Islamic groups joined forces to create the Union of Islamic Organizations in

France (UOIF), which is today the country's largest Islamic organization and is widely seen as France's MB branch.[39]

Some have questioned the UOIF's connection to the MB, but it has strong links to Algerian Hamas and Yusuf Al-Qaradawi, leaving little doubt as to its ideological leanings.[40] Ennahda's Rached Ghannouchi regularly visited Qatar in the 1990s, helping to convince Doha to finance the expansion of his movement to Europe, particularly the founding of the Paris-based UOIF, for which he wrote the charter.[41] "This organisation of the Brotherhood in France, with its large North African minority, politically and ideologically dominates the more than 500 Brotherhood-affiliated organisations under its umbrella and serves as the Brotherhood arm for expansion in Europe," writes Tarek Dahroug, PhD graduate in international affairs from the Sorbonne.[42]

Although French Muslims were back then, and remain today, largely of North African origin, a handful of Muslims from the Levant have taken prominent roles. Lebanese scholar Faisal Al-Mawlawi, leader of the Islamic Group, delivered a lecture in 1984 detailing, according to Pargeter, "how to be a Muslim in France whilst at the same time pursuing one's own jihad in order to bring down impious powers and establish an Islamic state."[43]

France, however, has started to realize the problems inherent in allowing Islamist organizations to run free. As one source told me, in recent years, "the French services have launched a comprehensive investigation on the MB sources of funding and discovered among other troubling things that Qatar had supported Islamic Centres and Mosques in cities such as Lille, Bordeaux and even Mulhouse." Qatar's supporting a mosque in Lille at first didn't make sense to the investigators, but "it was soon discovered that all these projects were heavily influenced and led by known MB leaders and sympathisers, even some that were under investigation for their relationships with the Al-Qaeda affiliate in Syria."[44] Further, "since the arrival of President Macron at the Élysée, the Qataris have been warned several times to stop their financial support of certain Mosques and Centres in specific large French cities that we (DGSI) deemed to be problematic."[45]

In the UK, the first MB groups were also student groups and were also launched in the early 1960s. Their leaders came from Egypt, Syria, and Iraq, as well as from India. Here, too, Said Ramadan helped lead the way, setting up the Islamic Center of London in 1964. The center emerged as a key node of MB activity in the country.[46] But the arrival of Egyptian MB figure Kamal Helbawy in the 1970s marked the start of a bold new approach. He acted as the MB's main representative in Europe and worked with the Afghan mujahideen from the early 1980s.[47] Helbawy set up an MB media center in London, even going so far as declaring it an MB office, before establishing the Muslim Association of Britain (MAB), which quickly came to be known as the MB arm in the UK.[48]

Around this time, the Islamic Society of Britain and the Muslim Council of Britain also emerged, similarly dominated by MB thinking.[49] "As the Muslim Brotherhood, we have never seen a Muslim state," a young member of the MAB, Jamal El-Shayyal, said in 2003. "Officially, we emerged in the mid-1990s. Every single Muslim organisation in Britain—apart from three—was set up under the influence of the ideology of the Muslim Brotherhood. We have gone from strength to strength."[50] By the late 1990s, according to James Brandon and Rafaello Pantucci of King's College, "London was home to the general secretaries of the Muslim Brotherhood branches of Iraq, Syria and Tunisia, as well as to hundreds of lower-level activists."[51]

Former MAB leader Anas Al-Tikriti is the founder-CEO of the Cordoba Foundation, which former British prime minister David Cameron has called a "political front for the Muslim Brotherhood."[52] In 2003, the United States designated the London-based charity Interpal a terrorist entity for its links to Palestinian Hamas. The Islamic Society, the Muslim Council, and MAB have lost some influence in recent years, as more MB members have arrived from Arab countries. In 2013, after the ouster of Morsi in Egypt, many Egyptian MB members arrived and began delivering MB communications out of London, supported by protest movements like R4BIA.[53] MB members also arrived from the Emirates and the UAE, according to the 2015 UK government report.[54] While still highly active in Europe, Helbawy remained connected to the Egyptian MB, and in the days following the toppling of Mubarak, he was describing himself as a senior member of the Egyptian Brotherhood and was serving as one of the group's most public faces on regional news outlets.[55] "Britain is the command and control centre for the Brotherhood in Europe," Steven Merley, the editor of Global Muslim Brotherhood Watch, said in 2017. "Nowhere else comes close—that is undeniable."[56]

Many top Tunisian MB members came to play a key role in Britain's Brotherhood community. Ennahda's Rached Ghannouchi, for instance, worked with the Dublin-based European Council for Fatwa and Research, which Brandon and Pantucci describe as "an important Brotherhood initiative led by Yusuf Al-Qaradawi that has attempted to make the Brotherhood's version of politicized Islam the default interpretation of the religion among European Muslims."[57] Ghannouchi confidant Said Ferjani became involved with the MAB, using his post as head of media relations to shape Britain's relations with its Muslims. "Ferjani's networking and advocacy work led to the MAB becoming one of four Muslim organizations chosen to act as founders of the Mosques and Imams National Advisory Board (MINAB), a UK government-funded body intended to address radicalization and poor governance in British mosques," wrote Brandon and Pantucci.[58]

Much of this work, extending the MB's networks and branches in Europe from the 1970s through the early 2000s, was overseen by the MB's international arm. Capitalizing on the Islamic revivalism sweeping the region, particularly after Iran's revolution, Tanzeem spotted opportunities and helped funnel funding and key MB figures to where they were most needed. "As well as strengthening their control over existing branches in the Arab world, the group also sought to harness opportunities on offer in other parts of the world where the Ikhwan had a presence. Many of these openings were in Europe," writes Pargeter.[59] "By the end of the 1990s the Ikhwan had in many countries been able to establish itself as the primary Islamic organisation, quietly dominating religious institutions across the continent."[60] Nevertheless, over time, "the MB financial network has become problematic for several European governments that they have begun to actively share information on MB affiliated individuals and bodies. Even the Swiss authorities have become much more proactive in clamping down on accounts linked to known MB activists across the EU."[61]

THE TROJAN HORSE

Like the fabled frog carrying the scorpion on its back because it's "in its nature," Western countries have made a mistake over and over again. It started with Eisenhower and Said Ramadan, as detailed earlier, assisting him and enabling his nefarious designs. Later, it was Eritrean-born U.S. citizen Abdurahman Alamoudi. For years, as the founder of the American Muslim Foundation, he served as a key Muslim voice in the U.S. capital, meeting regularly with top officials under presidents Bill Clinton and George W. Bush. The latter even invited him to speak at a Washington memorial event for the victims of 9/11. Soon after, the Pentagon hired Alamoudi to train imams to serve as military chaplains.[62]

Then, in August 2003, he was stopped at London's Heathrow airport with $336,000, which he said he had received from a Libyan charity.[63] He was soon found to be part of a plot to kill then Saudi crown prince Abdullah ordered by Libyan dictator Muammar Qaddafi. He later told U.S. investigators that he had twice met Qaddafi.[64] "I want the Crown Prince killed either through assassination or through a coup," Qaddafi told him, according to Alamoudi.[65] He also linked two leading Saudi dissidents, Mohamed Al-Masairi and Saad Al-Faqih, who received support from the MB (see Chapter 5), to the assassination plan.[66]

Alamoudi pled guilty and was sentenced to twenty-three years in federal prison and stripped of his citizenship. All the while, there had been signs of his true loyalties. In 1997, for instance, he called Hamas Deputy Musa Abu Marzook "among the best people in the Islamic movement."[67]

The list goes on. In December 2001, the U.S. Treasury designated the Holy Land Foundation for Relief and Development, the United States' largest Muslim charity at the time, as a terrorist group. After a lengthy trial, Holy Land was found guilty of funneling $12.4 million to Hamas to support its goal of creating an Islamic Palestinian state.[68] For years, a terrorist MB affiliate had been receiving funds from a major American charity. Holy Land leader Ghassan Elashi, who was sentenced to sixty-five years in prison, was also a leading member of the Council on American-Islamic Relations, one of the most prominent Muslim organizations in the United States.

That MB figures like Elashi, Alamoudi, and Ramadan emerged as favored Muslim voices in the West is no accident, but rather part of the MB's modus operandi, according to Lorenzo Vidino, author of the 2010 book *The New Muslim Brotherhood in the West*. Unlike Islamist movements that seek to maintain some distance from Western culture, the MB does not advocate isolation from society but rather urges participation while maintaining conservative traditions. Al-Qaradawi has called this "openness without melting."[69]

This approach has helped the MB put down deep roots across the United States. "Some went to Europe, some went to America," Al-Qaradawi said to a Muslim group in Toledo, Ohio, in 1995, "and they began to establish Islamic activity, with low volume at first. And they continued to work and now we see what we see in the West: the Muslim student associations."[70] In 1963, the Brotherhood helped establish the Muslim Students' Association (MSA) at the University of Illinois, Urbana-Champaign, which spurred hundreds of chapters across the country.[71] A decade later, the MSA set up a holding company, the North American Islamic Trust, which soon came to oversee mosques and Islamic centers across the country.[72] Finally, in 1981, the MSA created the Islamic Society of North America. All three were later investigated by the FBI for foreign financing.[73]

Many observers have commented on how the wolf-like MB slips into sheep's clothing when the situation dictates. Abdel Monem Said Aly, founding director of the Arab Gulf States Institute, a think tank in Washington, DC, addressed this in the Spring 2018 issue of *Cairo Review*:

> When the balance of power with other political forces—whether they are in government or in the opposition—is not in their favor, the Muslim Brotherhood exhibits an image of moderation. This is particularly evident in the United States, Europe, and generally in Western countries where the Brotherhood succeeded in mastering the representation of Muslims and speaking on their behalf. These include in the United States virtually all major entities representing Muslims in contemporary American politics: The Islamic Society on North America (ISNA), the Muslim Student Association (MSA), the Muslim Public Affairs Council (MPAC), the Muslim American Society (MAS), and the Council on American—Islamic Relations (CAIR). Under such conditions, the Brotherhood discourse will emphasize democracy (Shoura), human rights, civic society, equality, and condemnation of violence.[74]

This enables MB leaders to publicly speak in favor of Western states and society, currying favor with prominent political figures in order to become representatives of the Muslim community. This is a key goal of the MB in the West, presenting themselves as moderate and emerging as partners of governments and elites, as with Alamoudi and Said Ramadan. This helps them to not only gain financial and political backing and better spread their ideology through, potentially, the crafting of Islamic curricula, but also influence foreign policy. In 2017, UAE foreign minister Sheikh Abdullah bin Zayed warned European leaders about the dangerous Islamists they had welcomed and encouraged:

> There will come a day that we will see far more radical extremists and terrorists coming out of Europe because of lack of decision-making, trying to be politically correct, or assuming that they know the Middle East, and they know Islam, and they know the others far better than we do. I'm sorry, but that's pure ignorance.[75]

HIDING IN PLAIN SIGHT

It's crucial to keep in mind that although MB voices modify and moderate when in the West, they do not adapt Western cultural mores but rather strive to maintain their own traditions. Thus, even while appearing to integrate, they hold onto their world and their beliefs, through connections to the homeland, culture, and the movement, ala Qaradawi's openness without melting. An excellent example of this is the Euro Fatwa App, launched in April 2019 by the Dublin-based European Council for Fatwa and Research. The app's introduction is written by MB spiritual leader Al-Qaradawi, who references previous fatwas including one with derogatory remarks toward Jews. Weeks after its release, Google removed the app from its online store for this anti-Semitic language.[76] Here, we can see the MB being open to the technology and culture of their adopted home, even while holding fast to their outdated and dangerous practices and beliefs.

Vidino divides MB members and organizations in the West into three categories: pure Brothers, who are part of the MB structure and dependent on it; Brotherhood spawn, which have been created by MB members but remain independent; and MB-influenced groups, which are founded by people linked to the MB but have no direct ties to the group. He finds this hierarchy across the West:

> Individuals and organisations that belong to each of the three categories have operated for decades in Austria, creating a sophisticated web of entities, charities, educational academies, and businesses, and obtaining a disproportionate level of visibility and power, considering the small number of Brotherhood members and sympathizers in the country. This pattern is common to most Western countries, as organisations linked to the Brotherhood have often managed, thanks largely to their access to large resources and organisational skills, to become privileged interlocutors of Western elites within Western Muslim communities. Western observers tend to overestimate the representative nature and underestimate/ignore ties between the MB and these organisations.[77]

Starting in the 1960s and 1970s in many Western countries, like Germany and Austria, small MB groups and student organizations grew rapidly in many cities, along with increased mosque attendance. The groups continued to expand and develop, following Al-Banna's model, and ultimately found such fertile ground they decided to call the West *dar al dawa*, a new term between *dar al harb* (land of war) and *dar al Islam* (land of Islam) that means the land of preaching.[78] This oriented their activities toward gaining new followers and spreading their ideology, and that's precisely what they've been doing for decades, with considerable success.

A few years ago, police found a document dated from 1982 in the villa of Al Taqwa manager Ghaleb Himmat. As mentioned in the opening of this chapter, it outlined the MB's methods in the West, advising Ikhwan to know the terrain, remain flexible, accept temporary cooperation with nationalists without forming alliances, develop a strong MB network, support jihadi movements across the Muslim world, and employ surveillance systems.[79] As many analysts have pointed out, the document fell far short of advocating violent resistance or calling for toppling Western governments. Yet it very clearly outlined an agenda of deception and subversiveness that sought to develop strength and maintain vigilance for some undescribed future endeavor, presumably the creation of an Islamic state.

In its 2015 report on the MB, led by Sir John Jenkins, former British ambassador to Saudi Arabia, the British government laid out a similarly slippery modus operandi:

> Engagement with government has at times been facilitated by what appeared to be a common agenda against Al-Qaeda and (at least in the UK) militant Salafism. But this engagement did not take account of Muslim Brotherhood support for a proscribed terrorist group and its views about terrorism which, in reality, were quite different from our own; aspects of Muslim Brotherhood ideology and tactics, in this country and overseas, are contrary to our values and have been contrary to our national interests and our national security.[80]

The vast majority of MB-linked organizations in the West deny those links, for several reasons. First, members would prefer to not be tied to an organization with such a negative reputation. Not only does the MB have a reputation for violent radicalism and revolution, but it envisions the imposition of Sharia and the creation of an Islamic state, denounces Western wars, and calls for the elimination of Israel. Official MB membership not only would draw the attention of authorities in their adopted home but also could spur the security services in their homeland to act, on them or on loved ones still living there. The latter is not unprecedented: in 1981, when Hafez Al-Assad was decimating all remnants of the Syrian MB, Syrian agents targeted Issam Al-Attar in Germany, killing his wife.[81]

One factor that continues to limit the reach, impact, and influence of MB groups in the West, and particularly Europe, is a lack of diversity and integration. Western Ikhwan are primarily new arrivals or first-generation residents and are mainly from one region of the world. "Due to the fact that many Ikhwan-oriented organisations are still dominated by first-generation immigrants, their preoccupations are in many cases still centred on the Arab world," writes Pargeter. "Ikhwani organisations in Europe have remained mostly the domain of Arab communities; despite their desire to represent European Muslims, they are still unable to reach out beyond their own ethnic groups."[82]

Generally, MB leaders in Europe have a more traditional perspective, and feel they are not part of European society. As a result, they tend to frame debates as "us versus them," or Muslims versus the West. "These organisations repeatedly stress the need to refrain from being 'contaminated' by Western values," writes Pargeter.[83] This is how MB Supreme Guide Mehdi Akef describes it: "Our mission is immense, at the forefront of which is educating the lost youths on the streets and confronting the corruption that comes to us from the West to destroy our families and values."[84]

Thus, even as the MB is putting down roots and infiltrating various Western institutions, it is also maintaining its own traditions, stressing the importance of Islamic education and staying connected to the homeland. In 2009, for example, Usama Al-Tikriti, the father of Anas Al-Tikriti, director of the MB-linked, London-based Cordoba Foundation and then head of the MAB, was named leader of the Iraqi MB.[85] And in 2014, the imam of the MB-linked mosque in Manchester, England, which had been frequented by the 2017 Manchester Arena bomber, urged authorities to allow him to make decisions for his worshippers based on Sharia law.[86]

Still, as detailed throughout this book, the MB has always had great difficulty breaking completely from its violent, revolutionary past. Certainly a note of caution is required when considering their ultimate agenda in the West. As the 2015 UK report led by Sir John Jenkins noted, "Their public narrative—notably in the West—emphasised engagement not violence. But there have been significant differences between Muslim Brotherhood communications in English and Arabic."[87]

Internally, MB groups in the West often promote a narrative of victimhood that can spur radicalization, according to Vidino. They tend to exaggerate anti-Muslim incidents and attitudes, which do exist, "to foster a siege mentality within local Muslim communities, arguing that the government and Western societies are hostile to them and to Islam in general." Thus, violence becomes a legitimate response, especially when Muslims are under threat or occupation. This explains how many MB groups in the West, including Al Taqwa Bank and Holy Land Foundation, raise funds for violent MB affiliates while flying under the radar of authorities. Vidino advises:

> The spread of this narrative of victimhood mixed with a justification of violence should be seen with concern given the massive rise in radicalisation

seen throughout Europe during the last five years. The Brothers' narrative is also problematic when it comes to its impact on integration and social cohesion. While Western Brotherhood spokespeople tend to publicly adopt more nuanced and less controversial views, their representatives in the Middle East or some of the less visible members of the milieu in the West condemn Western societies as corrupt, immoral, and unjust, as well as inferior to Muslim societies.[88]

Vidino calls MB leaders in Europe "short-term firefighters," putting out the flames of radical violence with moderate public stances, and "long-term arsonists," encouraging internally the sort of frustration and anger that can radicalize. Anas Al-Tikriti, the British MB leader, played to his crowd at a 2017 event at Georgetown University by calling the Brotherhood "the most important democratic voice that espouses multiculturalism, human rights and basic freedoms."[89] Like other shrewd MB leaders in the West, Al-Tikriti has repeatedly sought to encourage Western officials to back Islamists like the MB. "Support them," he said he told a group of Washington figures after the Arab uprisings. "Unless we encourage them and offer them an incentive, their own crop of hard-liners will have been proven right."[90]

Indeed, as I've been told, "since the Brotherhood officially rejected violence in the 1970's, its rejections have been filled with qualifications that offer loopholes—for Muslims under attack and defending themselves, for example."[91] In Austria, Germany, and other European countries, MB-linked groups exaggerate public offenses to the extent that they could be seen as being under attack, which leads to this question: Don't Muslims in these countries, like Palestinians, have the right to defend themselves? And even if they never choose to "defend themselves" in their adopted home, many will support Muslims fighting jihad elsewhere, as the MB urges them to do. And even if most European MB organizations have yet to embrace or fund violence, they may have begun to undermine their host countries in more subtle ways. A 2005 report from the BfV warns:

> These "legalistic" Islamist groups represent an especial threat to the internal cohesion of our society. Among other things, their wide range of Islamist-oriented educational and support activities . . . are used to promote the creation and proliferation of an Islamist milieu in Germany . . . [that could] form the breeding ground for further radicalisation.[92]

We have seen similar concerns expressed by the intelligence agencies of Belgium ("a clandestine structure") and the Netherlands ("trying to pave the way for ultra-orthodox Islam").[93] The reality is that it's all but impossible for Western analysts and intelligence agencies to know for certain the objectives of these groups, if only because they never state them clearly, or publicly. As a result, there is a great deal of educated guesswork involved. The fact that MB-linked organizations have become intertwined with open-minded and largely democratic Western societies, while staying linked to possibly extremist Islamist ideas, makes any sort of collective assessment and response incredibly difficult. Leading American counter-terror official Juan Zarate once said, "They [Muslim Brothers] are a political movement, an economic cadre and in some cases terrorist supporters. They have one foot in our world and one foot in a world hostile to us. How to decipher what is good, bad or suspect is a severe complication."[94]

The surest way to decode the signs is via close examination. Let us consider one of Europe's most prominent MB figures, Ibrahim El-Zayat. The son of an Egyptian engineer, he was born in Germany in 1968 and gained an economics master's at Marburg before emerging within the MB. He founded several Muslim youth groups and led the FIOE youth organization, then Munich's famed Islamic Community of Germany, succeeding Himmat. In recent years, he has been advising wealthy Arabs on investing in real estate in Germany and snapping up properties on which he then helps Islamic organizations build mosques. He sits on the board of Europe Trust, the MB's London-based financial arm, and has spoken publicly in support of the Brotherhood, but denies being a member.

Crucially, he encapsulates the growing links between the MB and Turkey's Islamists: El-Zayat is married to Sabiha Erbakan, the German-born niece of Necmettin Erbakan, founder of the Turkish Islamist organization *Milli Görüş* and mentor to Turkey's president, Recep Tayyip Erdogan. Erbakan is esteemed among Arab Islamists, particularly leading MB figures. "In the Arab world, in my generation," Ennahda's Ghannouchi said after Erbakan died in 2011, "when people talked about the Islamic movement, they talked about Erbakan . . . it is comparable to the way they talked about Hassan Al-Banna and Sayyid Qutb."[95] Indeed, Erbakan is known to have shared Qutb's anti-Westernism and anti-Semitism.[96] El-Zayat sits on the board of the German firm that oversees *Milli Görüş'* mosques across Europe. A 1999 report by BfV, Germany's domestic intelligence agency, on the Turkish nationalist-Islamist group sounded a note of caution that echoed its concerns about the MB: "Although *Milli Görüş* in public statements pretends to adhere to the basic principles of Western democracies, abolition of the *laicist* government system in Turkey and the establishment of an Islamic state and social system are, as before, among its goals."[97] A 2005 report by the German Ministry of the Interior identified *Milli Görüş* as an "Islamist extremist group."[98]

THE PROXY

These developments should come as no surprise, since Turkish organizations in Europe are taking orders from an increasingly conservative government at home. The AKP is the most successful of today's MB-linked groups, having held power in Turkey since 2002. Yet it's crucial to point out that the AKP has never been an MB affiliate, and it's no longer a true Islamist party, if it ever was. As of mid-2019, Erdogan's party has been in power for seventeen years, yet not only has it failed to implement Sharia law, it has barely discussed the possibility. It's meaningful that in a November 2018 report, Brookings fellow Shadi Hamid, a leading expert on Islamism, refrains from calling the AKP an "Islamist party" or "MB-affiliated." Rather, he refers to it as "the Islamically oriented Justice and Development Party," which seems an apt label.[99]

As detailed in Chapter 3, religiosity has decreased slightly in Turkey in the past decade. If the AKP's project to engineer a more Islamic, even Islamist, society were succeeding, we would see it in the data by now. Thus, Erdogan's AKP has relinquished any right it may have once had to call itself an Islamist party. Hamid of Brookings said in a May 2019 interview that while some may question whether the AKP is even Islamist, "Erdogan shares a similar school of thought to the Brotherhood, with some Turkish modifications."[100] It is sympathetic to the MB cause, and has openly supported the group politically. But it cannot be considered an MB success because it is not an MB affiliate, like Hamas or Ennahda. Rather, it is an indigenous Turkish Islamist movement that took some inspiration from the MB and has now significantly watered down its revolutionary ideology. To put it another way, Turkey's AKP has likely been able to stay in power precisely because it is not an MB affiliate.

Still, Erdogan has been influenced, and even funded, by the MB, since back in the 1990s when he was Istanbul mayor. "In Erdogan's early years, he needed money and support, so the Tanzeem [MB network] connected him to several Saudi businessmen in Jeddah who provided him with the bulk of funds he needed to politically succeed as mayor of Istanbul," a former senior case officer for the Middle East in the DGSE, France's foreign intelligence agency, told me.[101] "After 9/11, the Saudis went into war mode and took down this particular Tanzeem network that Erdogan was still shockingly benefiting from. Soon after, when the funds dried up, in came Al-Qaradawi's Syrian boys with a lot of Qatari money."[102]

Erdogan sees the world through the prism of Al-Qaradawi and his Qatari backers, in part because he owes his political longevity to them. Tharwat Al-Kharabawi, former leader of the Egyptian MB's International Committee, confirms Erdogan's longtime anti-Saudi stance. "While he was mayor of Istanbul, the Tanzeem began to assist him and we quickly found out that his intentions were very revolutionary at their core," he said. "He had a lot of contempt for Saudi Arabia and privately was very clear about how he challenged the legitimacy of the Saudi monarchs. He was explicit in saying that the Saudis should not be guarding the Two Holy Mosques."[103]

This thinking, this vision of Erdogan's, has shaped Turkish foreign policy in the past decade, particularly since the ousting of Egyptian president

Morsi remade regional geopolitics. Hamid and Mandeville, in their Brookings report, take this thinking further:

> Turkey under Erdoğan has sought to position itself as a leader in the Sunni Muslim world and to compete—sometimes quite directly—with the likes of Saudi Arabia. The religious dimensions of neo-Ottomanism therefore seem less about the projection of any specific theological or ideological model (per Saudi Arabia and Iran), and more to do with revitalizing a distinctly Turkic model of civilizational Islam in which economic and geopolitical power go hand in hand with Muslim identity. Turkey's current policy of supporting Muslim Brotherhood movements and parties in the Arab world is ideologically consistent with the roots of the ruling AKP but also—and perhaps more importantly—emblematic of Ankara's desire to challenge the religious legitimacy and political influence of regional monarchies.[104]

Indeed, over the past decade, Turkey has undergone a transformation, increasingly promoting Islam abroad as a soft power tool while aligning itself closely with Qatar and the MB, for economic and geopolitical reasons. It's important to break down these developments separately before bringing them together to highlight how they have dovetailed in the last few years.

Under Erdogan, Turkey's religious institutions have expanded considerably while becoming more internationally focused in an effort to promote Turkey's unique brand of Islam and claim a Muslim leadership role. Ankara has built mosques across the Balkans, in Asia, in the United States, and in Western Europe, such as the massive Cologne mosque Erdogan inaugurated in late 2018.[105] This neo-Ottoman policy is largely about beating Saudi Arabia in the regional competition for Sunni Muslim hearts and minds. "The AKP has taken Turkey's religious outreach to unprecedented levels," Gonul Tol, founding director of the Middle East Institute's Center for Turkish Studies and adjunct professor at George Washington University, wrote in *Foreign Affairs* in January 2019.[106] "In the minds of those executing the policy, Turkey, as heir to the Ottoman Empire, is Islam's last fortress and the natural leader of a revival of Muslim civilization."

Not coincidentally, it all goes back to the end of the caliphate. In 1924, one year after founding modern Turkey, Mustafa Kemal Ataturk abolished the caliphate and created the Diyanet, or government directorate of religious affairs, in its place. Instead of making Islam the law of the land, as the caliphate sought to do, the Diyanet would manage mosques and religious education in a way that would make Islam subservient to the ostensibly secular state.[107] With the founding of modern Saudi Arabia in 1932, the Kingdom soon reclaimed the mantle of Islamic leadership.

According to a former Lebanese prime minister, "today Erdogan's AKP uses the Diyanet to encourage a conservative lifestyle within Turkey and promote Turkey's MB-friendly Islam abroad, often directly challenging the Saudi Kingdom."[108] On a 2015 visit to Makkah, then Diyanet head Mehmet Gormez announced plans for an Islamic university in Istanbul, arguing that highly regarded institutions such as Saudi Arabia's Madinah Islamic University had failed to stop the violent extremism troubling the Muslim world. "The scholars who graduate from these universities are becoming the problem themselves, rather than solving the problems," said Gormez.[109]

Back in the 1980s, the Diyanet began assisting Turkish communities in Europe. Those efforts have increased exponentially under the AKP. DITIB, formerly the Diyanet's German arm and still overseen by Turkey's government, is today one of Germany's most influential Muslim organizations, overseeing some 900 mosques. The Diyanet's French arm ranks among the country's top Muslim groups, even though Turkish-origin Muslims represent just a sliver (8–10 percent) of France's seven million Muslims.[110] The Diyanet runs the Dutch Islamic Foundation, which oversees more than 140 mosques and maintains a sizable Belgian arm as well. "The Diyanet pays the salaries of imams who are sent from Turkey, and it tightly controls the messages they deliver," wrote Tol. "The weekly Friday sermons are the same as the ones delivered in Turkey, issued from the Diyanet's headquarters in Ankara."[111]

Turkish Islamists connected to Erdogan's ruling Justice and Development Party (AKP) have also made headway in European Muslim communities in recent years. In June 2016, after overseeing the Turkish government's Islamic affairs arm in Austria, Ibrahim Olgun was elected president of the Islamic Religious Authority of Austria. He now serves as the voice of the country's Muslims, the key interlocutor with the government and the public. In May 2018, Erdogan publicly urged Turks in Europe to "take an active part in politics—become a member of parliament,"[112] which dovetails with the MB goal of helping to shape the country's affairs.

This is merely the tip of the iceberg of Turkey's MB-linked efforts in Europe. As Lorenzo Vidino, director of Georgetown's program on extremism, wrote for *Foreign Policy* in May 2019:

> Lately, the AKP's attempts to exert influence on European Muslim communities have gone beyond taking over Turkish diaspora organizations and extended to forming a close partnership with European Muslim organizations and individuals with ties to the Muslim Brotherhood. As a result of these changes, the Turkish government or nongovernmental organizations and financial institutions close to the government and the AKP began to provide ever growing support to Brotherhood-linked networks, which, in turn, vocally promote the AKP government. . . . It is increasingly clear that Turkish embassies, religious organizations, and businesses, acting in coordination with the comparatively broad network of entities linked to the Brotherhood, are pursuing interests and promoting views within Muslim communities that are on a collision course with those of European governments.[113]

In addition to the Diyanet, AKP officials, Muslim organizations, and intelligence services, Ankara also uses its aid and development arm, TIKA, to achieve this vision. TIKA promotes Turkey's Ottoman and Islamic heritage abroad by restoring mosques and fortresses in former Ottoman lands, such as Sudan's Suakin Island.[114] Pro-government humanitarian organizations also promote Turkish Islam abroad, and some, like the Human Rights and Humanitarian Relief Foundation (IHH), have been linked to the MB.[115] Religious NGOs affiliated with the AKP regularly host Istanbul conferences and forums on Islam, making the city an important MB hub. In addition, state-run institutions and educational foundations promote Turkish religious education abroad, particularly in Africa, the Balkans, and South Asia.[116]

This outreach has been less successful across the Middle East. This is mainly because most Arab countries have long viewed Turkey as an imperial power, thanks to their time under Ottoman rule. Turkey has sought to change this in recent years. "To enhance its soft power in the Middle East, the AKP has primarily relied on its ties to the Muslim Brotherhood, which does not have a chapter in Turkey but is closely aligned ideologically with the AKP," wrote Tol.[117] Al Jazeera, backed by MB-friendly Qatar, has also helped promote Turkey as a model Muslim country.

This highlights the growing bond between Qatar and Turkey, which is built upon Brotherhood support. Ankara's MB backing began around 2007, when it sought to support blockaded MB affiliate Hamas in the Gaza Strip, looking to gain a greater profile in the Arab world as part of its neo-Ottoman outlook. This connection exploded into public view with the Gaza Flotilla incident of May 2010. MB-linked Turkish non-profit IHH backed a flotilla of six ships carrying aid and construction materials that sought to break the blockade of Hamas-controlled Gaza, spurring a violent altercation when Israeli forces boarded one of the ships, the Mavi Marmara, killing nine IHH activists, including a Turkish-American.[118]

Within months, the Arab uprisings had toppled Ben-Ali and Mubarak and pushed the MB to the regional fore, much to the delight of Ankara and Doha. Following the election of the MB's Morsi in mid-2012, Turkey negotiated two dozen trade and aid deals with Cairo.[119] Following Morsi's overthrow a year later, Turkey welcomed many prominent MB members who fled El-Sisi's crackdown and soon emerged as the MB's new regional hub, hosting MB meetings and conferences. Among those who settled in Turkey was MB leader Amr Darrag, who established the Egyptian Institute for Political and Strategic Studies (EIPSS), a think tank that often promotes violence in the name of Islam, according to Eric Trager, a fellow at the Washington Institute for Near East Policy and author of *Arab Fall: How the Muslim Brotherhood Won and Lost Egypt in 891 Days*. In a September 2017 article for The Hill, Trager cited recent EIPSS writings that called for waging jihad to reform tyrannical and un-Islamic regimes.[120]

Turkey had made clear which side it was on, and has continued to do so in the years since, emerging along with Qatar as a leading terrorist sponsor. Qatar began backing Islamist militia in Libya as far back as mid-2011, even before the killing of Muammar Qaddafi.[121] In early 2015, Libya's internationally recognized prime minister Abdullah Al-Thinni denounced Turkey's arms shipments to Libya. "Turkey is a state that is not dealing honestly with us. It's exporting weapons to us so the Libyan people kill each other," he told Egyptian TV.[122] In June 2017, a Libyan Army spokesman described Turkey, Qatar, and Sudan as "the triad of terrorism in Libya."[123]

Around that time, following the imposition of the blockade, Doha receded, handing its duties of supporting the Tripoli-based Islamist government to Ankara. In March 2018, the counter-terrorism department of the General Khalifa Haftar-led government in western Libya said detained Jabhat Al-Nusra militants had told them during interrogation that the Turkish government had flown them from Turkey to Sudan, from where they had been smuggled to Libya's Mediterranean port of Sirte to join Al-Qaeda forces.[124] That December, some 3,000 Turkish-made guns and more than 4 million bullets were found hidden in shipping containers in the Libyan port of Khoms. A relatively minor port, Khoms was likely chosen because controls might be less rigorous there, according to Zvi Mazel, former Israeli ambassador to Egypt, Romania, and Sweden and senior researcher at the Jerusalem Center for Public Affairs.[125] "From the nature of the contraband weapons, it is fairly obvious they were not intended for a regular army, but rather for terrorist activities of armed groups, most probably Islamic organisations linked to the Muslim Brotherhood," Mazel wrote.[126] The shipments violated a UN Security Council weapons embargo on Libya since 2011. Libyan and Algerian officials denounced them as a "declaration of war" meant to further destabilize the region.[127]

Ankara's true intention was simply to support the Islamist side in the conflict for control of Libya. "While Egypt, Saudi Arabia, Jordan and the United Arab Emirates support the more secular, anti-Islamist Tobruk government, Turkey has joined Qatar and Sudan to prop up Libya's Islamists," Michael Rubin, resident scholar at American Enterprise Institute, wrote in January 2019 for *National Interest*. "It is against this context that Turkish weapons entered the scene. Simply put, as Qatar has become the go-to financier of the Muslim Brotherhood and its more radical offshoot groups around the globe, Turkey has become their armorer."[128]

Other analysts have confirmed this view. "Turkey has long been associated with backing Islamist organisations in Libya, especially groups that are tied into the Muslim Brotherhood," Nicholas Heras, Middle East Security Fellow at the Center for a New American Security, said in April 2019, days after General Haftar's forces launched a major assault on the Islamist government in Tripoli. "In this effort, Turkey and Qatar have been partners and there is no mistake that significant financial resources from Qatar and Turkey have made it over to Islamist groups in Libya."[129]

Nor is there any mistake about Turkey's involvement in the conflict in Syria, particularly its enabling of Islamist extremists to build up and ultimately create ISIS. In November 2018, the Dutch intelligence service (AIVD) published a report detailing ISIS' use of Turkey as a base to reorganize in the wake of its defeat in Syria and Iraq.[130] AIVD noted that Turkey "was for a long time a springboard" for foreign fighters traveling to join ISIS, adding that Ankara did not consider jihadi groups a security threat. At least 4,000 people joined ISIS via Turkey, where more than 20,000 people are in contact with Salafi jihadis, according to Turkish journalist Dogu Eroglu, author of *ISIS Networks: Radicalisation, Organisation, Logistics in Turkey.*[131]

A few months later, Abu Mansour al Maghrebi confirmed this view in an interview for *Homeland Security Today*, which called him an ISIS ambassador. He said that ISIS had no armed groups in Turkey but that many ISIS jihadis had been living in Turkey, with tacit government approval. "There were some agreements and understandings between the Turkish intelligence and ISIS," said Abu Mansour, adding that he met regularly with the Turkish intelligence agency, MIT, as well as other branches of Turkey's government, including the military.[132]

Most meetings were in the border regions, but some were in Turkey's capital, Ankara. One time he nearly met Turkey's president. "One of his intelligence officers said Erdogan wants to see you privately, but it didn't happen," said Abu Mansour, who explained the policy goal for Turkey. "Turkey wants to control its borders—to control Northern Syria. Actually they had ambitions not only for controlling the Kurds, they wanted all the north. . . . This is the Islamists' ideology of Erdogan. . . . In our meetings, we talked about re-establishing the Ottoman Empire. This was the vision of Turkey."

Funding that vision is Qatar. In 2017 and 2018 alone, Qatar bought $800 million worth of defense materiel from Turkish companies, including armored vehicles, tanks, drones, and various ships.[133] In August 2018, as the Turkish lira plunged to record lows, Qatari Emir Tamim bin Hamad Al-Thani pledged Turkey $15 billion in investment to curb the country's economic decline.[134] By this time, Turkey had largely become a tool of Qatari and MB policy. And Erdogan has vowed to continue to increase cooperation with Qatar, in defense, trade, energy, and more. "We have never forgotten and will never forget the solidarity shown to our country by our Qatari brothers on nearly all issues," he said in early 2019.[135]

The next month, after criticizing Egypt's El-Sisi for the execution of nine people, Erdogan called for the release of the country's MB prisoners.[136] Most likely, Erdogan had been compelled to make clear his position regarding the Egyptian leader and the Egyptian MB because of an incident a few weeks prior. In mid-January, Turkish authorities at Istanbul's Ataturk airport had extradited Egyptian MB member Mohamed Abdelhafiz Ahmed Hussein, spurring some to wonder whether Turkey had shifted away from Qatar and the MB.[137] Concerns within the Turkish government about this perception were so strong that Erdogan advisor Yasin Aktay appeared on the Istanbul-based Brotherhood TV station Mekameleen to state that a security error had occurred and Turkey had not changed its stance toward Egypt.[138]

Indeed, Doha's backing of Turkey is absolutely crucial to Ankara's regional policies. "Without Qatar's moral support, as an Arab country, along with its financial assistance, Turkey would not have been able to fund its existence in Libya," says Joumana Gebara, president of consulting group MidEastAnalyst.[139] No surprise, then, that Erdogan's government has become increasingly populated by officials with pro-Qatari and MB views. As veteran Turkish journalist Yavuz Baydar wrote in February 2019, "It's clear that sections loyal to Turkish President Recep Tayyip Erdogan within the security apparatus, as well as political appointees to official posts, identify with the Muslim Brotherhood."[140]

The feelings of respect and admiration are mutual. Just as Turkey sought to assist the MB and promote its agenda in order to gain a greater regional profile, MB leaders found in Turkey a powerful ally, according to Ahmed Charai, who sits on the board of directors for the Atlantic Council and advises the Center for Strategic and International Studies:

> Its relationship with the Muslim Brotherhood fits the AKP's world view that considers the end of the Ottoman caliphate as the main cause of the decline of the Muslim world. Whatever their country of origin, the Muslim Brotherhood (which has chapters in every Muslim land) goes beyond nationalism and projects as leaders of all Muslims. Turkey's military power, its history, and its ruler's speech are an attractive magnet for Brotherhood support.[141]

Writing in *National Interest* in February 2019, Charai argued that this MB-linked grassroots support for Erdogan across the Arab world is a tool with which Turkey's leader is unwilling to part. "Without the Brotherhood to magnify its power, Turkey cannot be a regional powerbroker. Therefore, it is very difficult to imagine that Ankara abandons an influential movement in the region for seventy years. It would lose much and gain nothing."[142]

Yet Arab countries remain deeply skeptical of Turkey and its foreign policy. "Turkey's damaging engagement in Syria and its authoritarian turn under Erdogan have shattered its image in neighboring countries. Moreover, the Muslim Brotherhood—which Turkey relies on heavily to accomplish its goals—is now considered a failure by many Muslims and labeled a terrorist organization in Egypt, Saudi Arabia, and the United Arab Emirates," Tol wrote in *Foreign Affairs*.[143] Similarly, Rubin argues that Turkey's support for Islamist militias in Libya highlights Ankara's new foreign policy direction, "not as a bridge between East and West, but rather as a catalyst for insurgency and Islamist terrorism . . . a sponsor of radicalism on a global scale."[144]

DOHA'S DEEP POCKETS

"For now nearly a decade, Turkey has championed the Palestinian cause, looking to regain its Ottoman prominence and take a regional leadership role,"[145] a former Lebanese prime minister recently told me. Ankara has given aid to the poor and fixed up roads and buildings in the Old City, and tens of thousands of Turks have visited the city of late. "Erdogan's focus on Jerusalem is part of a broader ambition to establish Turkey as the world's foremost proponent of political Islam," Bloomberg News argued in September 2018, adding that Ankara's effort "presents a challenge to Saudi Arabia."[146] These efforts require funding, and since Turkey has been mired in a currency crisis, it has been forced to turn to others for help. MB backer Qatar has of course stepped up, pledging $15 billion in investment in mid-2018.[147]

This is just the tip of the iceberg in terms of Doha's global financial backing of Islamists. Qatar's engagement with the MB, in particular, reaches far beyond the Middle East. In recent years, it has given more than $175 million to Brotherhood-linked groups across Europe, according to Belgian parliamentarian Koen Metsu. At an October 2017 forum on terror financing in Europe, Metsu said Qatar had sent at least that much to MB-linked groups across Europe and provided ideological support.[148] With this funding and guidance, Doha aims "to use MB groups in Europe as its own pressure groups to increase its power and . . . influence decision-makers," Metsu explained. "Security and financial reports in Europe show the MB controls many of the Islamic organizations that are supposed to defend Muslim communities."[149]

In their 2019 book *Qatar Papers: How the Emirate Finances Islam in France and Europe*, French journalists Christian Chesnot and Georges Malbrunot highlight more than 140 Qatar-financed projects across the continent in the past eight years, with 90 percent supporting MB-linked bodies. With its vast funding to European MB groups and sizable backing of Turkey, Qatar largely controls Europe's powerful MB networks and pulls the strings of Europe's Muslim communities. In an April 2019 interview with France Inter, Malbrunot said Doha is pursuing "a political initiative in order to ensure global hegemony of the Brotherhood project."[150]

Qatar Papers "documents payments of €72 million (Dh296m) to groups in seven European countries. In just one region of France, the payments have totalled €4.6m." It also names "a long-standing employee of the Qatari embassy in Paris as the key link in the money chain in Paris. The employee is described as a protege of the ideological leader of the group, Qatar-based Yusuf Al-Qaradawi."[151] Also from France, my source tells me that "the father of the current Qatari Emir is especially duplicitous and cannot be trusted. Against our repeated warnings, he was behind the covert support his country provided l'Union des Organisations Islamique de France (UOIF). In doing so they turned this organ into a mouthpiece for the MB."[152]

"For more than two decades now, Doha has spread its investment far and wide to reach effective and influential MB-linked groups,"[153] the Bahraini Ambassador to the UK has told me personally. Back in the early 1960s, Qatar financed Said Ramadan's trips to Geneva to open the Islamic Cultural Centre, as well as to Munich and beyond.[154] Today Qatar is supporting the son of Said Ramadan, and the grandson of MB founder Hassan Al-Banna. When rape allegations emerged against Oxford scholar Tariq Ramadan in November 2017, Qatar quickly stepped up and began paying him €35,000 a month as a consultant to the Qatar Foundation, an organization run by Sheikha Moza bint Nasser, wife of former Emir Sheikh Hamad.[155] Jailed and put on indefinite leave by Oxford, Ramadan has since his bail been living in Doha and teaching at Hamad bin Khalifa University, which is funded by the Qatar Foundation.[156]

Qatar's push into Europe in recent decades was largely shaped by a 1992 book by Al-Qaradawi, *The Priorities of the Islamist Movement in the Coming Phase*. The MB's spiritual guide outlined a middle path between extremism and secularism and urged Muslim communities in the West to manage their own jurisprudence or risk assimilation. Qatar founded Al Jazeera a few years later, in 1996, and Al-Qaradawi's popular show, *Sharia and Life*, quickly became "one of the most effective instruments for Qatari policy in Europe," writes Tarek Dahroug, Muslim scholar and Sorbonne PhD.[157] Qatar financed Al-Qaradawi's 1996 launch of the Dublin-based European Council for Fatwa and Research. The council gave the MB Islamic legitimacy in Europe and proved a key tool of MB expansion in the continent. In 2004, Al-Qaradawi created the London-based International Union of Muslim Scholars, which brings together prominent MB members from around the world.

As my contact, a counterterrorism advisor at the Federal Department of Foreign Affairs, told me in Bern in late 2018, "After the 9/11 attacks, the U.S. froze the assets of Al Taqwa Bank, so Doha stepped forward to fill the financing void for MB organizations in Europe. Qatari Emir Hamad bin Khalifa (father of current Emir) zeroed in on North African communities in France, Belgium, Italy, Spain, and Switzerland, as well as the de facto MB European headquarters in UK."[158] His first move was to boost financing for Ghannouchi's Union of Islamic Organizations, in France.[159] Doha also funded MB-inspired initiatives and federations, including a campaign to oppose the 2003 U.S.-led invasion of Iraq, which was inspired by

Al-Qaradawi and ultimately evolved into a movement to oppose Western aggression against Muslims. Other Qatar-backed MB entities include the Cordoba Institute, a London-based research center, the Consultative Centre for Research and Rights, and the Geneva-based AlKarama Foundation, which was founded by Qatari Abdulrahman Al-Nuaimi and financed by Qatari businessman Khalifa Al-Raban.[160]

"The AlKarama Foundation in Geneva is one of the best examples of how the Tanzeem infrastructure in Europe was used, with Qatari funding, to undermine Arab governments, under the guise of education, human rights and political activism," a former Swiss special envoy and, as of early 2019, a Swiss ambassador in the Middle East told me in March 2018.[161] How does AlKarama achieve this? The former Swiss official explained:

> AlKarama funded pretty much every single prominent dissident in most Arab countries to come to Geneva or Vienna and be given executive courses of how to challenge their respective governments, how to avoid and flee security forces and even how to mount campaigns of civil disobedience. Karama even gave their "pupils" encrypted phones, computers and listening devices that were at the time state of the art and in most Arab countries not available to carry out their covert activities. Karama's leader at the time was Abdulrahman Al-Nuaimi, an active Qatari MB member, who was subsequently linked to organizing financial and material support campaigns for Al Qaeda's affiliate in Syria. Al-Nuaimi has since been put on the American and British terrorist list and returned to Qatar. He's currently being protected by the father of the Qatari Emir, though the Americans and the British would like to arrest him.[162]

A charity that purports to back Muslim causes, AlKarama is also an MB promotional tool supported by Doha, funding these training programs for dissident activists, as detailed by the Swiss ambassador and elsewhere.[163] These seminars occurred both before and after the 2011 Arab upheavals, so it is no surprise that its Qatari financier has a less than stellar reputation. "Al-Nuaimi is a known entity within violent Jihadi circles and his role in Syria with Al-Nusra cannot be disputed," Sheikh Fawaz bin Mohammed Al Khalifa, Bahraini Ambassador to the UK, told me in November 2017.[164] Qatar spent some $4 million on the May 2016 establishment of the Museum of Islamic Civilizations in Jura, Switzerland, which includes works by Hassan Al-Banna and Al-Qaradawi, and $4.5 million for the Al-Houda Centre in Rome.[165] It funded the construction, in Sicily, of a religious center for Italy's 1.5 million Muslims, and gave €20 million for the construction of the largest mosque in Copenhagen, to be used by the Danish MB branch.[166] Doha also donated half a million euros for a new mosque in the Netherlands and 300,000 more to the Islamic League for Dialogue and Coexistence, in Spain, which works with an MB relief organization in London. Documents signed by Al-Qaradawi supported the construction of an Islamic center in Milan, as well as a mosque and schools.[167] Qatar has also funded major mosques in Ireland and Islamic activities at Oxford University. Dahroug writes:

> Sheikh Hamad bin Khalifa, the former Qatari ruler, donated around 11 million pounds sterling in the post-Arab Spring period for the renovation of St Anthony's College in Oxford. The donation was made on behalf of the Sheikh Hamad Chair for Islamic Studies at the college, which is held by Brotherhood member Tariq Ramadan, grandson of Hassan Al-Banna and Qatar's lynchpin for the Brotherhood project in Europe in the post-Arab Spring period.[168]

This placed Tariq Ramadan—who has advised British prime ministers Tony Blair and David Cameron—as the voice of Qatar's MB project within British academia, which made his fall from grace in late 2017 all the more difficult for Doha. Ramadan, a married father of four, was jailed and forced to take a leave of absence after two women accused him of rape and provided evidence.[169] Qatar has continued to back him, hoping he will be acquitted and return to a position of influence in Europe. Either way, the Oxford anecdote shows how Qatar has a variety of methods for delivering financing. Sometimes it does so directly, with government funds. But because it wants to avoid being seen as a backer of Islamists, Doha often uses other channels.

Qatar's main tool for financing MB activity in Europe is Qatar Charity, founded in 1992 to help Afghan children orphaned by the war.[170] Perhaps no nongovernment entity in the world has provided more funding to Islamists in recent decades. Belgian parliamentarian Metsu estimates Qatar Charity has financed 60 percent of the Islamic institutions in Europe.[171] Since 2009, Qatar Charity has handed at least €12 million to the 150,000-strong Muslim community in Alsace to build an Islamic religious and cultural center and an Islamic academy.[172] In 2012, Qatar Charity brought the MB into the French education system, spending €1.5 million for a building to house France's first Islamic school, the Al-Razi School in Lille. The initiative had been proposed by the Union of Islamic Organisations, which has received more than €18 million from several Qatari sources.[173] In 2014, Qatar Charity handed €1.1 million to the Belgian MB branch, the League of Belgian Muslims. The next year it funded Luxembourg's first Islamic center.[174] It funded the creation of the Islamic museum in Jura, Switzerland, and according to *Qatar Papers*, planned to expand it with more than $20 million for a prayer hall and a swimming pool.[175] Qatar Charity spent some $1.7 million on a sociocultural center for Muslims in Lausanne and also backed the Eman Trust, which supports Yemen MB members in the UK, and on various centers that provide religious education to British converts to Islam.[176] Ahmed Al-Hammadi, a Qatari scholar of Islam and for several years the director of legal affairs at the Qatari embassy in Paris, oversaw a Qatar Charity program in France. He also had strong ties to Al-Qaradawi and had been linked to radical groups, according to French intelligence.[177]

Wealthy private Qatari funders, some from the ruling family, such as Sheikha Moza Al-Misned and her husband, former Emir Sheikh Hamad, also invest in MB initiatives abroad. In addition, Doha uses more subtle ways to channel money to MB supporters. For instance, Qatar has partnered with the French government to set up a €100-million fund to back Muslim start-ups in poor neighborhoods. Doha also finances the activities of the European Institute of Human Sciences, which sounds like a modern, liberal body but is in fact a training institute for preachers and imams, with an academic board headed by Al-Qaradawi.[178] In 2012, a Qatari businessman funded the construction of a mosque in Nantes for the MB-linked Islamic Society of Western France.

In the past couple of years, momentum against all this foreign support of MB-linked networks in Europe has begun to swell, as European officials have become increasingly concerned about Qatar and Turkey's Islamist meddling. "It will not be possible in the future to have imams employed by the Turkish government," Austria's then foreign minister Sebastian Kurz, later the country's chancellor, said in 2015, after Austria banned foreign funding for mosques.[179] Three years later, Vienna announced a plan to shut down mosques and expel dozens of imams paid by the Turkish government.[180]

As of early 2019, Germany was considering banning foreign funding for its mosques, which are of course mainly run by Turkey-backed DITIB, as well as requiring that imams speak German.[181] German intelligence is mulling whether to put DITIB, which oversees some 900 mosques, under official surveillance.[182] In 2017, DITIB, a former arm of Turkey's government and still essentially run by Ankara, refused to take part in an anti-terrorism march in Cologne, drawing criticism for its unwillingness to denounce extremism.[183] In January 2019, DITIB organized a conference in Cologne on the future of Islam in Europe. Among the attendees was Egyptian native Imam Hussein Halawa, secretary-general, under Al-Qaradawi, of the Dublin-based European Council for Fatwa and Research.[184] "What is especially alarming is the invitation sent to representatives of the Muslim Brotherhood," Bavaria's interior minister Joachim Herrmann said in a statement following the event.[185]

French president Emanuel Macron has questioned Qatar's funding for Islamic bodies in his country and urged Qatari leaders to put an end to it.[186] Italian parliamentarians have urged Italian prime minister Giuseppe Conte to ban foreign funding for Islamic institutions in the country— where Qatar funded more projects in recent years (50 projects) than in any other European country.[187] "We have been reporting Doha's ideological and religious penetration for years. In the form of investments and financial operations, Qatar extends its proselytizing network every day, with serious damage to European societies," Souad Sbai, the Moroccan-born president of Italy's Averroes Studies Center and former Italian parliamentarian, said in April 2019.[188]

TENTACLES REFLECT DESPERATION

Lest we forget, all this Qatari investment in global MB activity is a reminder of the group's failure in the region of its birth. In Egypt, the MB has been banned and turned once again to terrorism. In Saudi Arabia, the UAE, and Kuwait, it's little more than a social group. It's been cowed into submission and marginalized, or turned to radicalization, across North Africa and the Levant.

While the rest of the Gulf and indeed the whole Arab region have accepted the Brotherhood as a political failure and an extremist group, Doha has not. "Certain Gulf and Arab countries have finally realised that, by backing extremist Islamists, they were, in fact, on the wrong path," says Karim Ifrak, a founding member of the Federation of Muslim Republicans in France. "Qatar is not among these countries. It continues to protect Yusuf Al-Qaradawi and to send money to the Muslim Brothers."[189]

As detailed in the previous chapter, "Qatar initially embraced the Brotherhood as a way to break free from the regional control of Saudi Arabia and expand its foreign policy capabilities."[190] That embrace has long extended far beyond the Gulf and the Arab region, but even more so in recent years, as the Islamist agenda has lost traction in the Arab world. The MB's appeal among Arabs has fallen precipitously, and the group has desperately sought to find a foothold beyond the region, largely thanks to Qatar.

In many Western countries, the MB has put down roots. Yet even after half a century, its political and social impact has never been more than negligible. As Vidino wrote in August 2017,

> Despite their unrelenting activism and ample resources, the Brothers have not been able to create a mass movement and attract the allegiance of large numbers of Western Muslims. While concepts, issues, and frames introduced by the Brothers have reached many of them, most Western Muslims either actively resist the Brothers' influence or simply ignore it.[191]

Nonetheless, Qatar has shown no intention of backing down in its support of the MB, across the Middle East and across the world.

The MB, meanwhile, has shown little ability to integrate fully into Western societies without having a hand in terrorist activities, either in their adopted home or in Muslim countries. In February 2019, U.S. secretary of state Mike Pompeo was asked about the Brotherhood being a terrorist organization. "The Muslim Brotherhood has many faces, most of which are not in the American people's best interests to allow them to advance," he said in response. "Whether the Muslim Brotherhood's efforts take place in Egypt or in Turkey or wherever it is in the world, President Trump's been unambiguously clear terrorism, extremism in whatever form will be defeated."[192]

CHAPTER 7

The Qatar Crisis

In November 2015, U.S. secretary of defense Ashton Carter pointed to Iran's increased strength and urged Arab Gulf nations to rely less on Washington and "get in the game"[1]—by which he meant that the United States wanted them to take on a bigger role in their neighborhood, particularly in the fight against terrorism.

Since Carter's call, most have indeed done that, particularly Saudi Arabia. The Kingdom has taken the lead in the regional conflict against Iran and in the fight to put down the Muslim Brotherhood, focusing on MB-aligned Qatar. This chapter will focus on the showdown between Qatar and the Saudi-led blockade group—how the diplomatic crisis began, the boycotters' justification, the crisis's impact on the region and the world, and finally how it might play out and eventually be resolved.

Qatar's overinflated sense of Islamic importance and desire to wield outsized influence and distinguish itself from Saudi Arabia have spurred its decades-long support for the MB. In the wake of the so-called Arab Spring, this marriage has placed Doha in dire straits and thrown Gulf relations into crisis, particularly as other GCC states have put their houses in order. Two and a half years into the blockade, neither side has shown a willingness to budge, making it all the more crucial that we take a closer look at this cold war in the Gulf and consider what might come next.

QATAR IN BED WITH THE MB

It is understandable that the Gulf states, with their conservative Muslim societies, view Islam as a crucial aspect of domestic and foreign policy and a key security issue. "Islam is such a resonant political currency and resource," Senior Brookings Institute fellows Shadi Hamid and Peter

Mandeville write in their November 2018 report *Islam as Statecraft*. Muslim states, they continue,

> have a strong interest—and a strong security interest—in engaging with religious ideas. . . . Once "Islam" is inserted into public debates, how citizens interpret their religion becomes, in effect, a matter of national security. If these governments didn't directly involve themselves in debates around the nature and purpose of Islam, they would be leaving an ideological vacuum that domestic challengers can take advantage of.[2]

This describes well the view of Saudi Arabia and the other Gulf states that see the MB, which infiltrated Gulf societies decades ago, as a threat to national security. In Bahrain, MB-affiliated Al-Menbar remains a social and political entity that could potentially run for and gain greater parliamentary representation. This could lead to instability and put a strain on relations with neighboring Saudi Arabia. Fortunately, Manama understands the importance of its relationship with the Kingdom and is likely to continue to freeze out the group, making Al-Menbar less and less politically relevant. Similarly, in Kuwait, MB-linked Hadas is a legitimate political entity, with members in parliament.

What's more, as recently as five years ago, there were rumors that Hadas members had been plotting a coup (see Chapter 5). Yet, as in Bahrain, the Kuwaiti government has purged the troublesome elements, and in recent years the MB-linked group has shown deference to the country's leadership. In the UAE, Abu Dhabi ruler Sheikh Mohammed bin Zayed has made sure the MB and its political arm Al-Islah, both of which he's designated as terrorist groups, have little influence in the country. In the Kingdom of Saudi Arabia, Crown Prince Mohammed bin Salman has completed a decades-long purge of MB members and literature to the point that MB influence has largely been eradicated.

It is in Qatar where the problem remains acute. "Qatar, by contrast, has seen support of Brotherhood movements as a source of its distinctive foreign policy orientation, setting it apart in its long-running rivalry with Saudi Arabia," Hamid and Mandeville explain.[3] Exhibit A is that Doha has harbored longtime MB spiritual leader Yusuf Al-Qaradawi—an outspokenly anti-American and anti-Semitic voice—for nearly half a century, and continues to do so. Although there is no MB arm within the country, Doha has allowed MB ideas to infiltrate its government, its policies, its academic system, its institutions, and its mouthpiece, Al Jazeera, largely thanks to the spiritual leader.

This all started in the 1990s, when Al-Qaradawi and then Emir Sheikh Hamad met to discuss political Islam and regional concerns. "Sheikh Hamad bin Khalifa Al-Thani accepted Al-Qaradawi as one of his primary religious counselors and bent much of Qatari policy to his MB-centered aspirations," a former French ambassador to the Middle East told me.[4] Al-Qaradawi agreed to support the Emir and his regime, while in return the Emir gave him a base of operations, funding, and a regional mouthpiece. This was the foundation for the deep partnership between Qatar and the MB, which only grew more ambitious with the arrival of the so-called Arab Spring.

On his Al Jazeera show *Sharia and Life*, in books, in speeches, and in his regular Friday sermons, Al-Qaradawi spoke about the latest developments in Tunisia, Libya, Egypt, and Syria. He stood against dictators like Ben Ali, Mubarak, and Qaddafi and foresaw Islamists in power across the region. Qatari Emir Sheikh Hamad helped promote these views, and by early 2013, Qatar had become so Brotherhood-focused that Oxford scholar Andrew Hammond, a former Reuters bureau chief in Saudi Arabia, called the country "a mini Ikhwanistan."[5] "Islamists from around the region are a notable presence in university departments, think tanks and other non-government organisations," Hammond wrote, "and there is a constant flow of Islamist politicians to Doha seminars and forums." Dr. Abdullah Al-Uthaymin, the former secretary general of the King Faisal International Prize, confirmed this view: "Qatar has allowed most of its social institutions to be infiltrated by MB members and their ideological positions," he told me in 2014.[6]

Supporting this Ikhwanistan is the leading Arab news outlet, Doha-based Al Jazeera. The state-owned network has long provided a global platform for Al-Qaradawi and other MB leaders. Speaking on Al Jazeera in March 2012, Al-Qaradawi vowed that UAE leaders would "face the wrath of God" after they deported a group of Syrians to Egypt.[7] Following Morsi's overthrow, Qatar allowed Egyptian MB leaders to regroup in Doha. Al Jazeera put them up in a five-star hotel and gave them airtime to promote their cause.[8] Around that same time, twenty-two Al Jazeera journalists resigned en masse, "citing what they said was the station's biased coverage of the Brotherhood," according to *The New York Times*.[9]

Beyond its borders, Qatar's support for the MB largely determines foreign policy, and much of its international spending is for MB affiliates. "Qatari foreign policy has in recent years become a tool for exportation of MB ideology," Dr. Abdulaziz Khoja, former Saudi Minister of Information, told me in 2016.[10] In 2008, a year after the MB-inspired terror group Hamas took control of the Gaza Strip, Qatar pledged $250 million to aid the group. The assistance has since continued unabated (see Chapter 4), and Doha's backing is a key reason Hamas remains in power in Gaza today. In 2012, then Emir Hamad bin Khalifa became the first head of state to visit Hamas-run Gaza, pledging $400 million. Two years later, in the wake of the most recent Gaza-Israel war, Qatar pledged $1 billion toward Gaza reconstruction.[11] In 2016, Qatar paid $30 million to Hamas-hired workers in Gaza.[12]

Back home, Qatar has long hosted a Hamas delegation and even allowed the group to set up an office in Doha. Khaled Meshaal, former

Hamas leader, has lived in Qatar for lengthy stretches and owns commercial buildings in Doha.[13] He has held Hamas press conferences in Doha and has been called a "dear guest of Qatar" by the government.[14] Other Hamas figures have spent time in Qatar, including former disputed Palestinian Authority prime minister Ismail Haniyeh and military leader Saleh Al-Arouri.[15] "Doha has managed to attract a number of controversial politically-driven Islamist organisations such as Hamas, the Taliban, and the Muslim Brotherhood. Through these affiliations, Qatar has bolstered its influence over a wider sphere regionally and internationally," Sheikh Fawaz bin Mohammed Al-Khalifa, Bahraini ambassador to the UK, told me in early 2018.[16] He continued: "The problem, of course, is that these organisations are run by interest groups that seek to overthrow governments, often through violent means. Meaning that Qatar is not playing the stabilizing role it seeks to portray."

Remember, MB ideologue and so-called second founder Sayyid Qutb inspired the creation of Al-Qaeda, while Egyptian MB member Ayman Al-Zawahiri played a crucial role as Osama bin Laden's right-hand man in the terrorist organization's early years and leads the group today. These ties, between the MB and the world's top terror groups, Al-Qaeda and its offshoot, ISIS ("Daesh" in Arabic), reach all the way to Doha. "Qatar's financial support for Al-Qaeda and Daesh affiliate groups permits them to terrorize innocents everywhere," said Prince Turki Al-Faisal, former Saudi intelligence director and former Saudi ambassador to the United States and the UK.[17]

With the arrival of the Arab uprisings, Qatar found itself well positioned to become the enabler of a broad variety of MB-affiliated groups, from terrorist outfits to political parties. "After the so-called Arab Spring uprisings, there was an uptick in Qatari efforts to help implant MB influence in Syria, Libya, Tunisia, and elsewhere,"[18] a former French ambassador who wished to remain anonymous told me. "When the events of 2011 began, the pair [Emir Sheikh Hamid and Qatari prime minister Sheikh Hamad bin Jassim] and some of their close family members and advisors were euphoric at the prospect of Mubarak falling and then Qaddafi," according to a former British ambassador in the region. "For them, it was the beginning of a new era where they would be considered the royalty of royals, so to speak."[19]

Qatar and its MB allies had a very specific vision for how this era would unfurl. They sought to take advantage of the protests to remake the region, gaining greater influence and control, according to Prince Turki Al-Faisal, chairman of the King Faisal Center for Islamic Studies and Research. "Qatar's plan has been clear from the beginning: exploit the destabilized environment of the Middle East after the so-called Arab Spring in order to foment Muslim Brotherhood infiltration into various Arab countries," he told me in 2018. "Following that, state instability is sought, the MB seizes control, and the Islamist agenda is used to eradicate any semblance of legitimacy in the sovereign nations of the region."[20]

The former British ambassador to several Middle Eastern countries from 2005 to 2015 said Sheikh Hamad saw Al-Qaradawi and the MB as a way to extend his authority and become a sort of modern-day sultan. The Qatari Emir was the architect of the plan, while Hamad bin Jassem bin Jaber Al Thani was tasked with carrying it out. "On more than one occasion when I served in the region, the British Government very subtly tried to convince him and HBJ [Hamad bin Jassem] to back off from their doomed grand project. The problem with the pair is that they never listened to anyone and always believed they knew better."[21]

The former president of Bahrain's National Security Agency (NSA), Sheikh Talal bin Mohammed Al-Khalifa, painted this scheme in darker colors. "I think it is appropriate to call Qatar's approach to the Arab world after the turmoil of 2011 a take-over conspiracy. The MB is their tool and the destruction of independent nations is their goal. It is a violent, distorted, self-appointed mandate that seeks to install religious rule over diverse peoples that we all must oppose if peace and prosperity are to take root in the region."[22]

Qatar's position, on the other hand, is that the political and security changes that arrived with the Arab uprisings have remade the regional playing field, putting forth Islamists like the MB as legitimate alternative political options. In addition, younger regional leaders like Saudi crown prince Mohammed bin Salman and the UAE's Sheikh Mohammed bin Zayed are less cautious than the older generation, and view Doha's policies as problematic because they support democratic change in the region, according to Majed Al-Ansari, a professor of political sociology at Qatar University. "The Saudi and Emirati leaders have led a coalition of Arab regimes that supported the reversal of gains made by Arab societies during the Arab Spring upheavals and the restoration of authoritarian rule in the region," he told Al Jazeera in April 2019.[23]

Yet it is Qatar's pro-MB agenda that has failed in recent years. "Sheikh Hamad's blind support of the Muslim Brotherhood in Egypt and [Al-Qaeda-affiliated] Jabhat Al-Nusra group in Syria is a historic and catastrophic mistake for him and Qatar," Bertrand Besancenot, France's presidential envoy to the GCC, explained in July 2018.[24] The Morsi regime failed so badly that it needed to be removed from office after one year, while Al-Nusra contributed to the mayhem in northern Syria that enabled ISIS to carve out its so-called caliphate.

During the Brotherhood's year in power in Egypt, Qatar loaned the government of President Mohammed Morsi $7.5 billion and provided grants and energy supplies.[25] "In Egypt, after the elections of Morsi, is where the Qataris overplayed their hands, and it's where their grandiose plan began to fall apart," according to a former British ambassador to several Middle Eastern countries. "They were warned repeatedly by King Abdullah of Saudi Arabia to stop their interference in Egypt. They ignored his advice and repeated warnings—and looking back at it now, to their detriment."[26]

The British ambassador pointed to Qatar's financial support of armed vigilantes that supported the MB president as particularly troubling. "The Qatari funding of Morsi brigades will haunt them for a long time to come. Morsi's armed street vigilantes committed atrocities in Cairo and Alexandria before and after the election of Morsi. These armed groups had a command structure that linked them directly to the senior leadership of the MB."[27] *The Guardian* says Doha "bankrolled Egypt during Morsi's year in power."[28] Prime Minister Sheikh Hamad bin Jassim Al-Thani appears to have secretly sent several million dollars to various MB officials after Morsi's election victory,[29] while an Egyptian court later convicted Morsi of sharing state secrets with Qatar.[30] When Morsi was overthrown, Al-Qaradawi appeared on Al Jazeera urging Muslims to fight to restore the deposed Egyptian president to power.[31]

Doha funded and supplied Islamist extremists in Syria and Libya, even hosting several key Libyan terrorist leaders. Qatar coordinated with the Syrian Brotherhood to push aside the head of the Syrian National Coalition, Moaz Al-Khatib, who favored negotiations with the Assad regime, and appointed MB figure Ghassan Hito as head of Syria's government-in-exile. Rached Ghannouchi, founder of Tunisia's MB-inspired Ennahda Party, has been a regular visitor to Doha in recent years, meeting with Al-Qaradawi, among others. He has called Qatar a partner in Tunisia's revolution. Doha has invested billions to help boost Tunisia's post-revolution economy, and Al Jazeera has provided extended and predominantly friendly coverage.[32]

The problem is that these investments and support, in Syria, Libya, Tunisia, Egypt, and elsewhere, ultimately undermine state sovereignty. "The MB is inimical to independent states, to the independence of the Arab people, to their right to control their own destiny," a former senior White House advisor told me in September 2018. "Their strict religio-ideological approach to politics leaves no room for a population to determine its own destiny. It must march in step with the MB vision, or it must be destroyed."[33]

As the uprisings gripped the region, Saudi Arabia and its Western allies attempted to steer Qatar away from its alignment with the MB. "There is a very long, special and close relationship between Sheikh Hamad and Al-Qaradawi. In 2011, I repeatedly warned Sheikh Hamad to disassociate himself from Al-Qaradawi and his group's sinister objectives and stop his funding and support plan for the groups affiliated with the MB intent on overthrowing Arab regimes," Ambassador Besancenot said in July 2018.[34] "He categorically rejected my advice and told me I would be proven wrong. They had a grand plan for the region, and it had to start with Egypt for other affiliated groups to feel emboldened and carry on their respective national campaigns."[35]

Their shared vision inspired the duo to craft a plan in the early days of the so-called Arab Spring to help the MB and its affiliates gain power in Egypt and other regional states, resulting in greater influence for both.

The former senior case officer in the CIA's Near East Directorate says at least three foreign intelligence agencies had "specific, actionable data" on Sheikh Hamad and Al-Qaradawi's joint vision for the region.[36] "Their dumb plan ultimately failed," the former CIA officer said. "Hamad gave up power to his son Tamim, and Al-Qaradawi is less powerful. But the rot at the Qatari center remains."

BATTLE LINES ARE DRAWN

Riyadh and Doha have had tense relations for decades, partially due to their differing views on Islamism. Qatar has long been driven by what it sees as an intense rivalry with the Kingdom, driven by deep-seated hostility and distrust. "Sheikh Hamad has not forgiven Saudi Arabia and its allies for their support for the failed counter coup against him when he deposed his father in June 1995," an advisor in Qatar's Emiri Court said in an interview in March 2018. "There was clearly a plan hatched up by Bahrain, the UAE, and Egypt, with the vital support of Saudi Arabia, to dethrone him and bring back his father. The counter coup was planned very badly and failed. But this has had a big psychological effect on him to this day."[37]

As the two Gulf neighbors diverged in regard to the MB in the wake of the Arab uprisings, relations declined further still. Recordings leaked in 2011 contain conversations between Libya's Qaddafi and Qatar's former foreign minister and prime minister Hamad bin Jassem from 2008 and give a glimpse of Doha's view of Saudi Arabia, which is at the heart of Qatar's support of the MB. Bin Jassem begins by telling Qaddafi that British and American intelligence had asked him to assess the situation in Saudi Arabia, which he had done.[38] "The government is senescent, and it is not allowing anyone to run the affairs," bin Jassem said of the Saudis. "OK, it can be an old government, but at least allow people to run the country. I told them that if someone cannot work for eight hours a day, he should leave it to someone else to work and oversee the affairs. They haven't even allowed the youth to work."[39]

In May 2019, Ayidh Al-Qarni, one of the Islamic scholars of Saudi Arabia's Sahwa movement, apologized during a television interview about his ties with Qatar in previous decades. From 1990 to around 2010, Al-Qarni often appeared on religious shows on Al Jazeera, and at one point he met Sheikh Hamad. He learned that Qatar was conspiring against Saudi Arabia, encouraging Saudi dissidents in the hopes of overthrowing the Saudi leadership someday.[40] In that 2008 conversation, bin Jassem touched on this same vision, detailing how Qatari authorities sought to find and encourage Saudis willing to turn against the leadership in Riyadh:

Hope in the front line [generation], even in the army, is lost. Hope should be vested in the second line. . . . One should develop personal relations with them, those who are in between. This, in my personal view, is an important aspect of the process. These people [holiday] in London, Paris, Rome. They are known. These are the ones we need to work on. Our embassies should quietly [work on them]. This won't cost us a lot.[41]

Finally, Hamad bin Jassem mentioned Qatar's drive to pull American bases from the Saudis and the threat of Islamists in the Kingdom: "The second point is that the English told me that they will stand with the Al Saud [ruling family] to the end because the alternative—Islamists, is dangerous. We don't want that. They're tired of them [Al Saud] but they can't find an alternative. We succeeded when we took away their [American] bases [and brought them] to Qatar. We created a [security] deficiency. Now they [Saudis] have given them again paid-for bases."[42]

Hamad bin Jassem goes on to say that Qatar had broken the Saudi monopoly over the Gulf. "Look at how many heads of state attended in Damascus," he said, a reference to the 2008 Arab League summit in the Syrian capital, which was undermined by political instability in Lebanon. Riyadh and Cairo sent only low-level representatives.[43] "We, the Kuwaitis and the Emiratis attended," Jassem continued. "This was a major setback for Saudi Arabia. They [Saudis] no longer have control over the Arab League."[44]

He goes on to explain that Saudi Arabia often works to undermine Qatar and that Doha would be better able to gain U.S. support on a variety of issues if Qatar's perspective hadn't become increasingly idiosyncratic in the region. "They [U.S. officials] ask us for our opinions on many things," he told Qaddafi. "But the problem is that we don't have many Arab states that will [publicly stand with us]."

Hamad bin Jassem's approach to the conversation makes clear that much of Qatari policy—toward the United States, the Arab League, and regional allies like Libya—is about beating Saudi Arabia. At one point, he acknowledges that the Saudis have had some success in persuading the United States to see Al Jazeera as problematic. "The Americans are upset with Al Jazeera," he admits. "They [the Saudis] piled significant pressure on us [through] the Americans. We were steadfast in the face of this for three years and did not change our positions."[45]

Unsurprisingly, the recordings upset Saudi leaders and were likely among the reasons the Kingdom downgraded ties with Qatar in late 2011. When a supposed ally and regional partner is actively working against you, actively working to undermine your standing with one of your strongest and longest-standing allies, and actively encouraging treason and revolt, the response must be strong, making clear that such behaviors are unacceptable. This is how Saudi leaders responded to Doha, which still remained steadfast in its support for terrorism and efforts to undermine the Kingdom.[46]

Qatar's rivalry with Saudis has been a major impetus to the tiny nation's dedication to the MB, which the Saudis have long viewed as a threat. Amid the uprisings in 2011, Qatari MB leader Jassim Sultan's Nahda initiative sought to organize an Islamist conference in Kuwait. But Saudi Arabia stepped in and pressured Kuwaiti leaders to cancel it, which they did.[47]

Still, Doha continued its embrace of the Brotherhood even after the downfall of the Morsi regime, hosting and giving a platform to MB figures exiled from Egypt and the UAE. At a GCC summit in November 2013, as the anti-MB momentum swelled, Qatar agreed to end its support of Brotherhood affiliates. But the Saudis and Emiratis quickly grew frustrated with Doha's failure to live up to this commitment. Incensed with Qatar's continued embrace of the Brotherhood and its affiliates, Saudi Arabia, the UAE, and Bahrain withdrew their ambassadors in March 2014 and demanded Qatar change its ways or face economic blockade.[48]

After months of acrimonious discussions, Sheikh Tamim agreed in September 2014 to relocate MB members to Turkey, force Emirati Al-Islah members out of Qatar, and close Al Jazeera's Egypt bureau.[49] Qatar also committed to end its support for the MB and agreed to cooperate more closely with GCC partners on hunting down and taking action against MB members in the Gulf, including pursuing across borders and extraditing. Following this agreement, Qatar expelled seven Egyptian citizens suspected of Brotherhood ties. "We and our allies were glad that Qatar relocated its MB members to Turkey in 2014," a former Saudi cabinet minister said in a January 2018 interview. "But we soon discovered that this was a merely symbolic move and did not represent a true repudiation of the MB."[50]

Qatar maintained its backing of the MB, even flaunting it. MB figures continued to appear on Al Jazeera. Hamas stayed in its Doha offices. And in April 2017, Qatari official Mohammed Al-Emahdi visited Gaza and was photographed shaking hands and smiling with Hamas leader Ismail Haniyeh.[51] The visit came shortly after Doha announced $100 million in aid for Gaza reconstruction.[52] The next month—more than three years after its GCC partners pulled their ambassadors and threatened a blockade if Doha didn't stop supporting MB-affiliated groups—Qatar hosted a press conference at which Hamas presented a charter that demanded Palestinian control of Israel and advocated "all forms of resistance."

A few weeks later, on May 24, the final straw arrived: a video, which Qatar officials quickly called a fake, appeared on the website of Qatar's state-run news agency.[53] "No one has the right to accuse us of terrorism just because they declare the Muslim Brotherhood a terrorist group," Emir Sheikh Tamim said in the video, which included a not-so-subtle attack on Saudi Arabia. "The real danger lies in the behavior of certain governments which have bred terrorism themselves, by adopting an extreme version of Islam that does not correspond to the truth."[54]

THE BOYCOTT BEGINS

About ten days after the release of the video, on June 5, 2017, the Kingdom accused Qatar of "dividing internal Saudi ranks, instigating against the state, infringing on its sovereignty, adopting various terrorist and sectarian groups aimed at destabilizing the region."[55] Over the next twenty-four hours, Saudi Arabia, the Emirates, and Bahrain (along with Egypt, Yemen's government-in-exile, and Libya's Council of Deputies) broke off diplomatic relations and blockaded Qatar via air, land, and sea.

In the days that followed, some observers speculated that the Saudis and their allies planned to invade Qatar and topple the Emir, commandeering a wealthy state of just 300,000 citizens. And indeed, as my source makes clear, "a plan was drawn up for a 'tactical invasion of Qatar' by Saudi-led forces to capture and detain certain individuals, including Al-Qaradawi."[56] The only reason the plan wasn't followed through on was that former U.S. secretary of state Rex Tillerson and Former UN secretary of defense James Mattis intervened with the Saudi leadership. Of course, it is "ironic that it was the Americans that saved Al-Qaradawi and his followers from being captured by the Saudis."[57]

As for the possible outcome of such a battle, "the Qataris were and still are awfully ill prepared to repel a Saudi invasion. If the Saudis put enough brigades on the ground, even the Turkish contingent won't matter in military terms." In addition, the Trump administration has "made it clear to all sides that in case of military conflagration, the US won't be taking sides" and that "US forces won't be firing at a Saudi invading force as long as the American base is not attacked."[58]

The Saudi-led group did make demands of Qatar, including the following:

- Declare the MB a terrorist organization and sever all ties to terrorist organizations, "specifically the Muslim Brotherhood."
- Shut down Al Jazeera, its affiliate stations, and other pro-MB outlets.
- Terminate military partnership with Turkey, which has voiced support for the Brotherhood.
- Stop all funding for individuals and groups designated as terrorists by GCC states, the United States, and other countries, such as Hamas.
- Hand over terrorists and other wanted individuals to their countries of origin; the list includes Al-Qaradawi.
- End interference in internal affairs of GCC states, particularly support for MB affiliates.[59]

All of this came just two weeks after a summit in Riyadh, at which Saudi leaders discussed counter-terrorism with President Trump and other global leaders. The summit concluded with the opening of a pan-Arab, pan-Muslim center for fighting terrorism. Bahrain's MB-affiliated political party, Al-Menbar, issued a statement after the event, commending "the strenuous efforts led by the Kingdom of Saudi Arabia to unify the stances of all Islamic states that attended the Riyadh summit."[60]

Saudi leaders appear to have made a strong impression on Trump with their case against the MB. A few days after the imposition of the blockade, then U.S. secretary of state Rex Tillerson said that listing the MB as a terrorist outfit was problematic because some of its affiliates had gained political power by "renouncing violence and terrorism."[61] But Tillerson was soon fired and John Bolton brought on as President Trump's National Security Adviser.[62] Days after that Riyadh summit, Bolton argued that it was time to cut off all terrorist support and financing in the region. "Let's declare the Brotherhood a terrorist organization," he said, referring to U.S. policy. "Having done that, we turn back to Qatar and say, 'Now you follow suit.' "[63] In April 2019, the Trump administration began openly discussing its plan to designate the MB a terrorist organization, marking a major policy shift.[64]

QATAR'S RESPONSE

Qatari officials said the video posted on Qatar News Agency was fake and that the site had been hacked, which was confirmed several weeks later. U.S. intelligence officials revealed in July 2017 that the UAE had orchestrated the hacking of the news site and posted the video of Sheikh Tamim.[65] Senior Emirati officials led by Sheikh Mohammed bin Zayed had met the day before the hack and discussed the plan. Also, according to investigations by Qatar and the FBI, users from two IP addresses in the UAE accessed and refreshed the QNA site many times just before the video appeared online.[66] UAE officials denied any role in the alleged hacking.[67] Saudi Arabia, the UAE, and Bahrain also argued that, regardless of the reliability of the video, Qatar had not lived up to its 2014 deal, and that this reality, not the statements made in the video, is what had necessitated the blockade and accompanying demands.

Qatar remained intransigent, if slightly confused in its messaging. Foreign Minister Sheikh Mohammed bin Abdulrahman Al-Thani said his country had the right to support groups like the MB, calling Hamas "a legitimate resistance movement."[68] A spokeswoman at the Qatari Embassy in Washington said Qatari officials would respond to the allegations by "reaching out to both the administration and Congress to provide them with the facts. These facts prove that these countries' allegations are not true."[69] A few weeks after the blockade began, Qatar's Director of Communications, Sheikh Saif bin Ahmed Al-Thani, stated: "Qatar does not fund terrorism whatsoever," adding, "We do not support the Muslim Brotherhood. . . . We do not have a relationship with the Muslim Brotherhood."[70]

Both of these last statements are demonstrably false, as the foreign minister suggested in his statement, and as this and other chapters have already made clear. Qatar has invested billions of dollars in MB-linked Islamist groups across the Middle East, according to some estimates.[71] In recent years, Qatar has given more than $175 million to Brotherhood-linked groups across Europe, according to Koen Metsu, a Belgian parliamentarian and head of the Belgian committee fighting terrorism (see Chapter 6).

At a May 2017 event focused on Qatar, terrorism, and the MB, former U.S. secretary of defense Robert Gates urged Qatari leaders "to pick up the ball and be as aggressive as some of their neighbors have been"[72] in taking on the MB. The likes of Saudi Arabia and the UAE, he added, "have become aggressive and unambiguous in their willingness to take on the terrorism problem, and I think that's what we need to expect from Qatar."[73] Qatari foreign affairs minister Al-Thani responded soon after the start of the blockade: "Qatar's priorities in the region and beyond are to maintain an open-door policy, and to encourage dialogue and political settlements," he said in an interview.[74] "Qatar's regional positions, particularly in Yemen, Syria and Libya, have been in coordination and in line with the positions of the international community and United Nations resolutions": an apparently appeasing statement, but an inaccurate one as well.

Qatar's positions, particularly in Syria and Libya, have mainly encouraged violence and gone against the international community. Doha has funded Turkey's arms shipments to the Islamist Libya Dawn coalition in Libya, in direct violation of a UN embargo. This policy is also in direct contrast to those of Saudi Arabia, the UAE, Egypt, France, and Russia, who have supported General Haftar's army.

The world is still waiting for Doha to change its stripes. In October 2018, Doha pledged $150 million in aid to Gaza on the orders of the Emir.[75] The United Nations' Development Program is to oversee distribution of the funds, but wherever it ends up the Qatari money will help prop up Hamas. That same month, shipments of Qatari fuel began arriving in Gaza to power the devastated region's power plant. "These Qatari efforts that started months ago ended successfully," a Hamas spokesman told CNN.[76] The next month, Doha handed out $15 million to thousands of Gazan civil servants, paying employees of the Hamas-controlled government as part of a $90 million commitment.[77] And now that Hamas is accepting cryptocurrencies, tracking Qatari transfers to the group is going to become even more difficult.[78]

As the blockade hit the two-year mark, Qatar had done little to satisfy the demands of the Saudi-led bloc. It has not declared the MB a terrorist organization. It continues to support Hamas and fund MB-linked groups across Europe and Asia. Al Jazeera coverage continues to favor MB-linked groups. Al-Qaradawi did resign as MB spiritual leader in November 2018, but that was likely due to health reasons: he is in his nineties and has appeared frail.[79] Qatar's leaders seem convinced that the Brotherhood poses no threat. Some, like Washington Institute for Near East Policy senior fellow Eric Trager, have argued that, in the wake of Arab uprisings, "the Brotherhood presented no internal risk to the Qatari regime, because Doha had dissolved the domestic Brotherhood chapter in 1999."[80]

This may be true, but it is largely irrelevant. "The fact that the Brotherhood aims to establish a global caliphate means it poses a threat to not only Qatar but to all the Gulf states, and to countries beyond," a former Jordanian prime minister told me in September 2017.[81] Al-Qaradawi himself has admitted as much: though the Brotherhood scholar denies the account, Russia's former ambassador to Qatar, Vladimir Titorenko, says Al-Qaradawi told him several years ago that "corrupt and bloody" regimes in Arab countries must be replaced, including the rulers of Qatar.[82] Even if the Brotherhood poses no threat to Qatar, its threat to the region is eminently clear: "The Ikhwan's importance has transcended from a potentially influential group to one with demonstrable capabilities in a revolutionary era," writes Gulf analyst David Roberts, lecturer at King's College. "Qatar's policies seem to underestimate the depth of antagonism they create."[83]

So why hasn't Qatar cracked down fully? Why hasn't it cleaned house at Al Jazeera, halted its support for Hamas and other MB-linked groups and individuals—made a clean break from its Brotherhood connections and support? Is it because, as Roberts suggests, it doesn't appreciate the trouble they create? Or is it that Qatar believes this connection is in fact worth the trouble? Ambassador Besancenot believes the MB is deeply embedded in Doha's thinking:

> The architect of the policy that was adopted by the Qataris vis-a-vis the MB since the late 1990's is Sheikh Hamad bin Khalifa Al Thani. It has since evolved into Qatar's main foreign policy base to exert outsized influence and perceived power throughout the Arab world. Sheikh Hamad inherently believes that the Arab world can only develop through a group of individuals that come to power through the ballot box but have deep Islamic conservative roots, and for him the only group that can claim this mantle is the MB. He believed it then and still believes in the MB project and clearly has no regrets. For him, the Egyptian MB experience failed because Saudi Arabia and its allies conspired to bring down the MB government of President Mohammed Morsi. But he insists that Qatar will continue to fund and support the various MB-affiliated political parties in the region.[84]

Qatari MB leader Jassim Sultan has echoed this view. He runs an initiative called Nahda, which means rebirth and is a key term for the Brotherhood, used in the name of Tunisia's Ennahda Party and in the slogan for Mohammed Morsi's election campaigns. "From the start, Qatar has had very good relations with the Muslim Brotherhood," Sultan told Gulf analyst

Courtney Freer in 2018. "They put them in a frame where they are part of the system but cannot disrupt it."[85]

After nearly seven decades of cooperation, the Brotherhood may be in Qatar's nature. "The Muslim Brotherhood is the DNA of Qatar," French journalist Christian Chesnot, co-author of the *Qatar Papers*, said in 2017.[86] For starters, Qataris are steeped in MB ideology from an early age; with decades of leadership in Qatar's education system, MB-inspired academics have created a heavily Brotherhood-influenced curriculum. In addition, Doha has always sought to maintain a certain distance from Riyadh and endeavored to be beyond the Kingdom's control. The country's leaders believe their relations with the Brotherhood and its various offshoots— and their half-embrace of their non-Wahhabi ideology—achieve that end. It's an assertion of independence, and another strike in what Doha sees as its great rivalry with Riyadh.

What's more, Qatar has always moved to its own beat. In December 2015, the entirety of a Qatari royal family hunting party, some twenty-eight people, was kidnapped in Iraq. The crisis lasted for some 16 months, until shortly before the imposition of the blockade, in fact, and reportedly ended when Qatar paid a billion dollars to free the people. According to the BBC, the money may have ended up going to the Quds Force of Iran's Revolutionary Guard, which is subject to U.S. and EU sanctions and led by General Qassim Suleimani, and to Hayat Tahrir Al-Sham (HTS), the leading Al-Qaeda–linked jihadist outfit in Syria.[87] As my source reports, "The Qataris managed to pay just about a $1 billion to Shia militias that were directly being funded and controlled by Suleimani."[88]

These are the kinds of erratic, irresponsible policies and behavior the Qataris have come to be known for over the years, and that continue to this day to undermine regional security. Support for the MB should be seen in this context. Qatari leaders have always worked to punch above their weight, to wield more than expected influence in the region and beyond. Again, they believe supporting Islamists achieves that end, that it makes Qatar special and independent.

Lastly, Sheikh Jassim bin Mohammed Al-Thani, the founder of Qatar, once wrote a poem that referred to Qatar as "the Kaaba of the dispossessed."[89] He meant that just as the Kaaba in Makkah will always be a true north for all Muslims, Qatar will always be a place of refuge for the world's exiles. Just now, members of the MB are unwelcome across much of the Arab world. As its political asylum law attests, Qatar seems to believe that it stands for something good and that it stays true to its foundation in continuing to welcome and assist the Brotherhood and its affiliates.[90] "Many leaders in Qatar do view their small nation as unique in its willingness to shelter MB thinkers, and they view this willingness as a kind of Islamic charity," Sheikh Fawaz bin Mohammad Al-Khalifa, Bahraini Ambassador to the UK, said in a March 2018 interview. "The problem, of course, is that they are offering charity to revolutionaries who are looking to overthrow governments, often through violent means."[91]

IMPACT IN THE GULF, AND BEYOND

The Saudi side has refused to budge, and two years on the crisis shows no signs of ending, as Doha continues to underestimate the problematic nature of the MB and refuses to meet the blockade's demands. If supporting the MB has indeed become second nature to Qatar, part of its very character as a state, then this division could last years, even decades. Crown Prince Mohammed bin Salman visited the Egyptian capital in March 2018, his first foreign trip as heir to the Kingdom. When reporters asked about the rift with Qatar, the crown prince said the dispute could last generations, but that he remained unconcerned because Qatar is "smaller than a Cairo street."[92]

Qatar's position, as outlined earlier, is that the Arab uprisings remade the regional playing field and that in combating the MB and Doha Saudi and UAE leaders are seeking to suppress not terrorism but freedom and democratic change. Tharwat Al-Kharabawi, former senior member to the Egyptian MB's International Committee, sees the situation rather differently. In a November 2017 interview, he explained how Sheikh Hamad believed the Arab world's future rested with the radical change advocated by the MB. As a result, with the guidance of Al-Qaradawi, the duo supported MB figures and affiliates across the region, focusing in particular on one state.

"The priority was always Saudi Arabia," Al-Kharbawi told the Syrian television station Al-Ikhbariya.[93] "Supporting Saudi activists and religious leaders was a primordial necessity for the Qataris. We did though very politely remind them that they were playing with fire but all our suggestions were ignored repeatedly." Ambassador Besancenot confirmed this perspective, regarding Sheikh Hamad's animosity toward the Kingdom. "He was repeatedly counseled by several wise close friends of his to drop this vendetta against Saudi Arabia because it would have devastating consequences for him and Qatar, but he never listened," he told me.[94]

In June 2018, a year after the imposition of the blockade, Qatari Emir Sheikh Tamim underscored his stubborn defiance of Gulf neighbors by placing Al-Qaradawi in the seat of honor at an iftar dinner in Doha.[95] Sheikh Tamim also took the time to embrace Al-Qaradawi, a moment that was captured on social media for all to see.[96] More than likely, this was directed at the Kingdom and the UAE, in an attempt to send the message: "We will not change our behavior or our policies, despite your demands."

Indeed, leaders in Doha and Riyadh seem unlikely to change their views any time soon, which forces us to consider: what would it mean for the GCC and for Gulf trade and relations, if the rift between Doha and other Gulf states is long lasting? As of mid-2019, Saudi Arabia, the UAE, and Bahrain have already adapted their economies and foreign policies to a world without trade or relations with Qatar, while Doha has sought to do the same.

In December 2018, Qatar announced that it would be leaving Saudi-dominated OPEC. Doha had accounted for just 2 percent of OPEC's crude output.[97] But as the world's largest exporter of liquified natural gas, Qatar has real clout in energy markets, so its departure was meaningful. "After almost 60 years of membership, the move underscored Qatar's discovery that it can survive in separation from its neighbors," *Bloomberg* analyst Marc Champion wrote of the decision.[98] Qatar does appear to be riding out the blockade better than its neighbors had envisioned. In November 2018, the IMF announced that Qatar's economy continues to expand despite the blockade and predicted 3 percent growth for 2019.[99]

Might we expect to see deeper enmity develop and lead to conflict within the GCC? It's highly unlikely that Doha would ever consider an attack on more powerful Riyadh, and all the main players are U.S. allies, so direct conflict seems unlikely. At the same time, the trio does see the MB as an existential threat, so if Qatar remains recalcitrant, push may come to shove. In July 2018, the unprecedented happened in the Gulf. Emirati prince Sheikh Rashid bin Hamad Al-Sharqi, second in line to rule Al Fujayrah, defected to Doha amid a dispute with the rulers of Abu Dhabi.[100] It appeared to be the first time in the UAE's nearly fifty-year history that a member of one of its royal families criticized the country's rulers.

In late 2018, Qatari Emir Sheikh Tamim offered a rather disingenuous solution to the crisis. "This can be achieved by lifting the 'siege' and resolving differences through dialogue and non-interference in other countries' internal affairs," he said at the Doha Forum.[101] UAE State Minister for Foreign Affairs Anwar Gargash responded in a tweet: "The Emir of Qatar at the Doha Forum refuses interference in his internal affairs, but he is adamant about his country's policies of interfering in the internal affairs of his neighbours and the countries of the region. This is duplicity that bears the influence of the former Emir."[102]

Two years in, it appears that one of the biggest potential trouble spots of the rift is a fractured GCC. This would be problematic for trade, tourism, and diplomatic relations but not apocalyptic. Strong linkages remain between Saudi Arabia and Qatar, which could eventually lead to understanding. Both countries' ruling families—the Al-Thanis in Qatar and the Al-Sauds in Saudi Arabia—originally hail from Nejd, the vast, central region of the Arabian Peninsula. Qatar's religious beliefs and traditions are heavily based on the Wahhabi doctrines of the Kingdom. "Qatar's religious establishment, for example, has long been influenced by scholarship and religious trends from Saudi Arabia," Hamid and Mandeville point out, "and its national mosque is named in honor of Muhammad ibn Abd Al-Wahhab."[103]

AN EMERGING ALLIANCE

Yet some see Doha shifting its loyalties in the great Saudi-Iranian regional conflict to side with Tehran. After all, MB ideology helped lay the foundation for the Iranian Revolution, and Qatar has long been friendly with Iran, despite Saudi rejections. The duo's combined natural gas reserves would be unrivalled, easily topping second-place Russia and giving them significant global and regional influence. In addition, thanks to Tehran's development program, Iran could potentially be just a few years away from having nuclear weapons, with which it could threaten Israel, Saudi Arabia, and other regional rivals.

Soon after the start of the blockade, Qatar foreign affairs minister Mohammed bin Abdulrahman Al-Thani talked about relations with Iran:

> We are concerned about the security, peace and stability of the region, which is precisely what drives us to work responsibly on converging the views of the two countries together despite all differences. This approach helps assure desirable outcomes for the entire region. The State of Qatar refuses to look at Iran through the sectarian lens or to frame the region's conflicts in the Sunni vs Shia paradigm.[104]

A Qatari-Iranian partnership may not be so far-fetched. The two already share the world's largest gas field, which holds some 43 trillion cubic meters of reserves deep under the Gulf.[105] When the blockade began, Qatar turned to Iran for help, quickly rerouting flights over Iranian airspace.[106] According to Giorgio Cafiero, chief executive of Gulf State Analytics, a Washington-based political risk consultancy, the blockade has convinced Doha's leaders that they face a bigger security threat from Saudi Arabia and the UAE than from Iran.[107]

Many MB and Qatari leaders have a soft spot for the Iranian regime. In the video that spurred the blockade, Qatar's Emir highlighted his country's strong relations with Iran, adding that "escalation with Iran is unwise, for it is a big power that guarantees stability in the region."[108] In a May 2018 speech at Tehran's Amirkabir University of Technology, Iranian foreign minister Javed Zarif argued that Saudi Arabia's leaders were not as powerful as many believed. "They aren't even able to overcome Qatar," he said. "Qatar has brought Saudi Arabia to its knees, because the sources of power and the tools for reaching power have changed."[109] Also, the theocracy in Tehran represents a different kind of power structure, one that leans toward the MB vision. "The Iranian Revolution was welcomed by many mainstream Sunni Islamists, who might have otherwise been suspicious of Shia Islam," write Hamid and Mandeville of the Brookings Institution.[110] They argue that Tehran, as an Islamist revolution, offers an alternative to U.S. capitalism and Gulf monarchies like that of Saudi Arabia.[111]

In late 2018, sensing an opportunity, Iran offered to host some of the thirty-two teams expected to play in the 2022 World Cup, which Qatar will host. Event organizer Hassan Al-Thawadi said that Qatar is considering the offer and that other countries had also offered to help. Further, he expressed hope that Gulf nations could end the boycott and allow their citizens to enjoy the World Cup in person. "I hope the blockading nations can see the value of this major tournament and can allow for their people to benefit from this tournament," he told *The National* in November 2018.[112]

In reality, an Iran-Qatar military alliance could never happen. In any potential conflict between the Kingdom and Iran, the United States is going to side with its longtime ally, Saudi Arabia. In addition, Qatar hosts Al-Udeid Air Base, the forward headquarters of U.S. Central Command and one of the largest U.S. military bases in the region. In 2018, in fact, Qatar began upgrading and expanding the U.S. base, in the hopes of making it permanent.[113] "A strong relationship and partnership between the United States and the State of Qatar has been developing for decades, and it is characterized by an exceptional and a distinguished strategic bilateral political, military and economic relationship," Qatar foreign affairs minister Mohammed bin Abdulrahman Al-Thani said soon after the start of the blockade.[114]

The minister pointed to the United States' largest military base in the region, at Al-Udeid, and a recently signed counter-terrorism cooperation agreement, which he said "sets a precedent for other countries in the region."[115] With such strong military cooperation, Washington would never allow Doha to join a military partnership with Iran, at least not any time soon. In the video that spurred the blockade, Sheikh Tamim underscored American military support for Qatar, citing Al-Udeid as a "protective shield for Qatar from the greed of some neighbouring countries."[116]

Yet we have begun to see signs of an alliance between Qatar, Turkey, and Iran, which enables Qatar to gain militarily without importing soldiers from a U.S. and Saudi enemy. Since Qatar is no longer able to support MB-related causes as freely and openly as it had in years past, the blockade has forced it to find a proxy or conduit to carry on these efforts. It has found precisely that in Recep Tayyip Erdogan's Turkey. Although Erdogan's ruling Justice and Development Party (AKP) is not an MB affiliate, the party is rooted in MB thinking, thanks to Erdogan's mentor Necmettin Erbakan, a revered figure among MB leaders (see Chapter 6). Ankara has long had close, friendly relations with Doha and supported MB causes, including welcoming dozens of exiled MB figures after the ousting of Morsi in Egypt and more recently, from Qatar. For Doha, this makes Turkey a safe base from which to operate.

Turkey's economic crisis means it is unable to fund MB projects on its own. This makes it all the more willing to serve as Qatar's conduit for international MB support and to accept Qatari direction and financing for

MB-aligned policies. In the previous chapter, I detailed Doha's considerable financial backing for the Erdogan regime, including a commitment of $15 billion in investment in mid-2018.

With Qatari and MB backing, Turkey has begun to emerge as the leader of a new regional alliance. "Ankara is turning into a major regional player with its own agenda, ambitions, ideology and allies," Hussein Ibish, senior resident scholar at the Arab Gulf States Institute in Washington, wrote for *Bloomberg* in March 2019.[117] The region's anti-Iranian group is led by Saudi Arabia, the UAE, Egypt, and Israel, and has U.S. backing. On the other side is Qatar, which shares a gas field with Iran, and its ally Turkey, which has come to view Iran as an occasional partner. "Turkey's role at the epicenter of a new Middle East alliance was consolidated by the 2017 boycott of Qatar by Saudi Arabia, the UAE, Bahrain and Egypt," wrote Ibish. "Qatar has relied on Turkey, which maintains a military base in that country, for support against the boycott."[118] The money comes from Qatar, while Turkey serves as a safe base from which to operate. Hamas, too, has also begun renewing its ties to Tehran. Saudi Arabia and its allies "not only have to deal with expanding Iranian influence, but now face a Sunni Islamist alliance led by Turkey and financed by Qatar."[119]

This makes it all the more fitting that Turkey, Qatar's new MB conduit, was the site of the killing of Jamal Khashoggi, an international incident that transfixed the world and significantly impacted relations between Turkey and Saudi Arabia, Saudi Arabia and the United States, and perhaps ultimately between Saudi Arabia and Qatar. Certainly the Khashoggi killing drove Qatar and Turkey closer together (as detailed in Chapter 9), but the two had taken steps toward closer relations long before this gruesome incident. One of the demands that came with the Saudi-led blockade was for Qatar to stop hosting a Turkish military base, which the two agreed to set up in 2014.[120] Doha instead took the opposite step, urging Turkey to complete the base and deploy more troops as a way to bolster its defenses.[121] The two countries held their first joint exercises on August 1, 2017, less than two months after the imposition of the blockade.[122]

This is just the tip of the iceberg in terms of defense cooperation. Qatar's military procurements from Turkey increased sharply after the blockade. At the 2018 International Maritime Defence Exhibition in Doha, for instance, Turkey's defense firms signed deals worth $800 million with Qatar.[123] Turkey has also been commissioned to build a naval base in Qatar, and agreed to a multimillion-dollar deal to send Doha at least 250 of its next-generation battle tanks.[124]

Meanwhile, Turkey has risked sanctions and imperiled the NATO alliance, as well as Ankara's involvement in the United States' advanced F-35 fighter jet program, with its purchase of Russia's S-400 missile defense system. Analysts and officials have said the S-400 could compromise the security of the F-35 if the two systems are deployed together.

Turkey's top regional ally, Qatar, has also expressed interest in buying the Russian missile system.[125] Saudi Arabia has expressed interest in the S-400 as well, but the Kingdom is not a regional sponsor of terrorism that hosts a U.S. military base. In June 2018, King Salman made clear in a letter to French president Emmanuel Macron that Qatar must never be allowed to deploy Russia's S-400 system. "The kingdom would be ready to take all necessary measures to eliminate this defence system, including military action," King Salman wrote.[126]

There have been further areas of policy alignment between Turkey and Qatar that stand in opposition to those of other GCC states. In Somalia, Turkey and Qatar have been supporting the Islamist-leaning government in Mogadishu, while the UAE has backed the country's federal states.[127] In Iraq, where the Kingdom has been supporting Prime Minister Haider Al-Abadi and his anti-Iranian partners, Qatar and Turkey have been backing more Iran-friendly elements, including former prime minister Nouri Al-Maliki. "It is very clear the internal Gulf rift is also playing out in Iraq," Renad Mansour, research fellow in the Middle East and North Africa Program at Chatham House, told *Bloomberg*.[128]

This helps explain why Turkey and Qatar have added Iran to their alliance. The connections between Qatar and Iran have already been described in this chapter. For their part, Iran and Turkey share a level of distrust with the West and the United States. They also share a common border, which has seen increased trade of late, including an estimated $12 billion from May 2018 to March 2019.[129] Both are home to substantial Kurdish minorities, and neither would ever allow the creation of a Kurdish state in the area. They also share a common antipathy toward Saudi Arabia, with Turkey looking to reclaim Ottoman glories and Iran aiming to promote Shia causes.

In the first days of the blockade, with Qatar facing a possible crisis, it was Turkey and Iran that rushed to fly in essential commodities.[130] By ratcheting up the desperation, the blockade appears to have driven Qatar into their embrace, as Iman Zayat, *Arab Weekly* managing editor, wrote in December 2018:

> Doha has gradually slid into an unofficial yet open alliance with Iran, the arch-rival of Saudi Arabia, and Turkey, one of the few remaining havens for Islamist groups, notably the Muslim Brotherhood. Iran, Turkey and Qatar quietly struck a deal in late November in Tehran to create a "joint working group to facilitate the transit of goods between the three countries." While the agreement seemed like a modest effort to streamline trade flow to Qatar, which can no longer access air, land and sea routes to neighbouring Arab countries, it has proven to be a mechanism to further the agendas of Ankara and Tehran, which are at loggerheads with Saudi Arabia. . . . Qatar has irrevocably joined with Ankara and Tehran against its former Arab allies. It has conclusively positioned itself in a regional alliance that pursues geopolitical dominance by driving instability.[131]

The opposing sides—the United States-Saudi-UAE and Turkey-Qatar-Iran—have clashed most visibly in Syria. Turkey has long opposed U.S. support for the People's Protection Units (YPG), a Syrian Kurdish militia Ankara views as an extension of Kurdish insurgents in Turkey. Yet the YPG have been widely praised, by U.S. officials and a variety of analysts, as having played a crucial role in defeating ISIS in Syria.[132&133] After Trump announced, in December 2018, the planned withdrawal of U.S. forces from Syria, Turkey and the United States began discussing the creation of a buffer zone that would isolate the YPG, likely exposing it to attacks from Turkey. In January 2019, UAE State Minister for Foreign Affairs Gargash condemned the plan, arguing that Ankara was conflating Kurdish nationalism with terrorism.[134]

This was not the UAE's first criticism of Turkey's policies in Syria. A year prior, in January 2018, Emirati officials had condemned Turkey's military intervention in the mainly Kurdish region of Afrin. A few months later, as Emirates-run media outlets portrayed the Kurdish militias as U.S.-allied freedom fighters, the UAE went one step further. In coordination with Saudi Arabia, UAE military advisers held a series of meetings with YPG and Kurdistan Workers Party (PKK) officials at a U.S. base in northeast Syria to help prepare the Kurdish militias for a possible Turkish military intervention, according to an Al-Monitor report in February 2019.[135]

By late 2018, Saudi Arabia and the UAE had invested $150 million in areas held by Kurdish militias, which inspired pro-government Turkish newspapers to accuse them of sponsoring terrorism in northeast Syria.[136&137] By mid-2019, some observers expected Ankara, thanks in part to improved relations with Tehran, to reach out to Bashar Al-Assad—whose relations with Erdogan had been icy since the start of the war—to negotiate a plan for northeast Syria and the Kurds.[138] Meanwhile, another MB-linked terrorist group sought to join the emerging alliance: "Just as Turkey and Qatar are growing closer to Iran, Hamas is renewing its Iranian ties," Hussein Ibish wrote for *Bloomberg* in March 2019.[139]

It comes as no surprise that Russian president Vladimir Putin, friend to any and all efforts to foment anti-Western instability, supports this emerging Turkey-Qatar-Iran alliance, which is likely to undermine U.S. and Saudi influence in the region and potentially become problematic for NATO, of which Turkey is a leading member. "Turkey, Iran and Qatar are moving in a direct course towards creating a full-fledged alliance in the Middle East, threatening to make serious adjustments to the status quo in the region," declared a December 2018 article at the pro-Putin think tank Katehon.[140]

Some fear the Turkey-Qatar-Iran alliance could also draw in other Gulf and Arab states, like Kuwait—where nearly two-thirds of those surveyed (64 percent) in late 2018 chose Erdogan as their favorite leader.[141] Ankara and Tehran are increasingly in opposition to Washington. Thus, Doha's alignment with them could undermine its standing in the United States. For one thing, the Qatar-Turkey-Iran grouping is likely to submarine U.S.

efforts to create a broad Middle East alliance to counter Iran. Now the United States, Saudi Arabia, and their allies "not only have to deal with expanding Iranian influence, but now face a Sunni Islamist alliance led by Turkey and financed by Qatar," according to Ibish.[142]

Souad Sbai, former Italian parliamentarian and head of the Averroes Studies Center, has repeatedly urged Western countries to follow the so-called Quartet (Saudi Arabia, the UAE, Egypt, and Bahrain) and crack down on Qatar's terrorist backing. "Instead of contributing to the isolation of Qatar—as the Quartet has done for more than a year when it carried out an air, land and maritime embargo against Qatar—the West closes its eyes and prefers to give in to the temptation of economic and 'investment' financial institutions. Especially in Europe, Qatar is buying everything and everyone in exchange for silence regarding its policies of destabilization of the Middle East and its support for terrorism," she said in December 2018.[143]

This came just a few months after Trump hosted the Qatari leader in Washington. Emir Tamim highlighted U.S.-Qatari cooperation on counter-terrorism and expressed his wish that bilateral trade would soon double.[144] Yet at some point the United States will likely need to grapple with maintaining a military base on the territory of a state that has opposing policies, according to American security analyst Richard Miniter, who has reported widely on terrorism and wrote the 2004 bestseller *Losing bin Laden*. "Qatar's support for terrorist groups, like Hamas, is not in doubt," he wrote in April 2017:

> Hosting a U.S. air base also gives Qatar enormous stature across the region. That the tiny Gulf state enjoys America's protection, while openly feting (sic) and funding America's enemies, only enhances its prestige. This state of affairs signals that Qatar is so special that even the world's only remaining superpower must meekly tolerate its two-faced foreign policy. . . . The question is: Why do we continue to put up with Qatar's double-game?[145]

This may be in part due to a Qatari campaign. For several years, and particularly since the imposition of the blockade, Qatar has sought to buy influence in Washington, hiring lobbyists to solidify pro-Qatar narratives in the minds of influential U.S. figures. Doha spent $16.3 million in 2017 alone, according to the *Wall Street Journal*, in an attempt to save face amid the crisis.[146] Doha paid lobbying firm Stonington Strategies $300,000 a month for two years, a substantial sum that may well have helped convince a number of U.S. officials to soften their stance on Qatar's support for terrorism and Islamism.[147] A lawsuit filed in Washington in January 2019 alleges that Qatar hacked the email of a former Republican official known for standing against the MB and terrorism and supporting the UAE. Private details of Elliott Broidy's business dealings and personal affairs were revealed in mid-2018 after his email accounts were hacked and his emails made public. Many view Qatar as behind the attack, as alleged in the suit. *Politico* called it "the latest salvo in a proxy war between Arab Gulf states that has played out in Washington in recent years."[148]

ALLIANCE AS MIRAGE

Still, the United States has begun to apply some regional pressure. In March 2019, the United States acted against twenty-five people and businesses based in Iran, Turkey, and the UAE that had transferred more than a billion dollars to the IRGC and Iran's military, in violation of U.S. sanctions.[149] The next month, Trump declared Iran's Islamic Revolutionary Guard Corps a terrorist organization, marking the first time the United States had declared part of another country's government a terrorist group.[150] Trump said the IRGC "actively participates in, finances and promotes terrorism as a tool of statecraft."[151] A Saudi official called the move a "practical and serious step" to address Iran's support of regional terrorism.[152]

Unsurprisingly, Qatar and Turkey stood against the U.S. move. "No country can declare another country's armed forces a terrorist organization," Turkish foreign minister Mevlut Cavusoglu said at a joint press conference in Ankara with his Qatari counterpart Mohammed bin Abdulrahman Al-Thani.[153] Tehran has used the IRGC, which has 125,000 personnel as well as a paramilitary force, to train foreign militias like Hezbollah, in Lebanon, and Iran's critics say it has plotted and carried out assassinations on foreign soil. The IRGC is also linked to a vast business network worth some $20 billion annually, according to the *New York Times*.[154]

This reality reminds us that the sudden Qatar-Turkey-Iran alignment may be less a legitimate alliance than signs of increasing desperation. The sanctions laid down by the Trump administration in late 2018 and early 2019, on oil, mining, and metals, have begun to bite the Iranian economy. Oil exports have been cut in half, as of May 2019, and were expected to decline further.[155] The country's GDP shrank nearly 4 percent in 2018, and was headed for a 6 percent decline in 2019, according to the IMF.[156] Unemployment was expected to climb over 15 percent in 2019 and above 16 percent in 2020.[157] The terrorist designation for the IRGC is likely to further undermine the Iranian economy. Former CIA Director and top U.S. general David Petraeus, who now analyzes geopolitical trends and risk as chairman of the KKR Global Institute, told CNN in May 2019 that Iran's economy was headed into "a tailspin."[158]

Iran's troubles are also hurting its neighbor, Turkey, which entered recession in late 2018 and relies heavily on Iranian oil. Or at least it had, until the United States decided in April 2019 to not extend Turkey's sanctions waiver on its purchases of Iranian oil.[159] The next month, Turkey's lira fell to more than 6.20 to the U.S. dollar, a seven-month low, amid concerns of further political instability. Unemployment has reached its highest rate in more than a decade and Moody's predicted a 2 percent contraction for Turkey's economy in 2019.[160] This is how Axios' Markets Editor Dion Rabouin described the situation in May 2019: "Turkey's outlook got worse on Monday as the country continues slipping into dictatorship, under a dictator who doesn't seem to care much for laws or macroeconomics."[161]

Qatar, meanwhile, remains deeply isolated under the embargo. Thus, all three are in dire straits and in need of a helping hand, and find themselves agreeing at least on the goal of greater regional instability. At least one academic in Doha views the Qatar-Iran-Turkey alliance as a "marriage of convenience" unlikely to last, as detailed in a March 2018 report by Bulent Aras, international relations professor at Istanbul's Sabanci University and global fellow at the Wilson Center, and Emirhan Yorulmazlar, a fellow at Johns Hopkins' School of Advanced International Studies.[162] "The ongoing blockade against Doha necessitates utilizing Iranian geography in the short term. Yet association with Iranian interests would further aggravate the Qatari isolation," Aras and Yorulmazlar wrote. "Qatar cannot take the risk of espousing a minority position and marginalize its interests in broader Gulf and Arab politics."

Indeed, Qatar's cozying up to Iran and the MB may have already begun to shift perspectives in Washington. U.S. Congressman Roger Marshall, who has made several trips to the Middle East in recent years, spoke out against Qatar at a Washington conference in early 2019:

> Iran isn't alone, its promotion of radical terrorism. Across the Persian Gulf sits the nation Qatar, whose well documented support for terrorism and extremist groups have fueled violence, civil war and bloodshed. Its blind eye to the terrorist financing within its own borders continues to undermine security and cause them to question the long-term partnership of the U.S. operated base within the country.[163]

Despite all this, Saudi leaders have continued to keep the door open to rapprochement and a renewed alliance in the Gulf. In late October 2018, Crown Prince Mohammed bin Salman listed Qatar among the regional countries capable of positive change. "Even Qatar, despite our differences with them, has a very strong economy and will be very different" in the years to come, he said during an investment summit in Riyadh.[164]

Yet if Doha continues on its current course, the time may come for the United States, which as of May 2019 had begun moving to designate the MB a terrorist organization, to remove its military forces from Qatar. This, along with Doha's continued efforts to support terror outfits and undermine regional stability, could lead to a military conflict. As a Senior Political Advisor for United States Central Command told me, "Depending [on] how long this lasts, and how willing Qatar is to change its stripes, the only way to resolve the Gulf dispute may be with a credible military threat."[165]

CHAPTER 8

Understanding Salafism

One sunny afternoon in London several years ago, I was having a cup of tea with a friend at a café overlooking a busy square in Mayfair. A Gothic-style church loomed nearby, and talk turned to personal belief and the complexities of Islam. Our discussion lasted most of that afternoon, during which I came to understand the extent to which my friend saw two of the most powerful forces in the Muslim world as two sides of the same coin. Both offered considerable appeal, my friend explained, while both had their drawbacks. And that was precisely his problem: even after years of analysis and contemplation, he struggled to decide which he preferred, which addressed more completely his needs and concerns as a Muslim, his vision of Islam.

For many years, he ended up toggling between the two—leaning toward one this month, the other the next—leaving his friends and acquaintances, if not himself, unsure where his loyalties lay. Through this conversation, I came to better understand my friend and his worldview, as well as why so many across the Arab region seemed for so long drawn to, yet uncertain about, political Islam. That friend was Jamal Khashoggi, the prominent Saudi journalist who was killed in Istanbul in October 2018 (see Chapter 9) and a close friend and colleague of mine for nearly two decades. And the two forces with which he wrestled were the ideology of the Muslim Brotherhood and the theology of Salafism.

His ultimate choice, in 2017, to move away from the Salafi perspective and toward the MB view, likely precipitated his killing: not because such a choice was deserving of death—far from it; but rather because by that time, the Brotherhood was seen in Saudi Arabia and across most of the Arab Gulf as a grave terrorist threat that sought to undermine regional stability. As a result, the Kingdom's leaders, and its people, had embraced broader security measures to defend against it.

This chapter examines the underlying ideas that led to the MB's marginalization, detailing the connections, and more importantly the considerable contrasts, between the MB ideology and the ideology of Salafism as exemplified in the Saudi state. It puts forth the assertion that there are in fact two kinds of Salafism: one true and one false. The true could be called mainstream, or quietist, Salafism, while the other is MB-inspired, or jihadi, Salafism.

In the following pages, I compare their histories and divergent ideologies and theologies to reveal how the latter ended up embracing violence and revolution as one of its defining principles, while the former created a nation-state based on an Islamic reform movement.

SALAFIST STIGMA

In the book's first chapter we laid out the creation and early history of the Brotherhood, but we have yet to examine the group's theology. In pre-Mubarak Egypt, we saw how the MB shed its pacifist cocoon and emerged as a violent, revolutionary ideology centered on the overthrow of governments and sovereign religious establishments. The question is why, and the answer lies in the inherent weakness of the MB's Islamic thought and the absence of any real vision.

MB thinking is flimsy and largely empty, a stark contrast with the legitimate religio-historical revival known as Salafism. Salafism is a millennium-plus-old Islamic theology, established by the religion's great innovators in the birthplace of Islam. It should come as no surprise that it has now spread across much of the globe. The Brotherhood ideology, on the other hand, was created less than a century ago by a schoolteacher and lacks a broad interpretation of political Islam or guidance on how to govern. Essentially, it's more of a resistance movement than guidelines for Muslim living.

Despite all this, Salafism has somehow emerged in recent years as the Muslim ideology most often tied in the common mind (incorrectly) to extremism and violent jihad. That could hardly be further from the truth. Confusion and misunderstanding about Salafism are so widespread that one often sees, in popular books, academic journals, and mainstream news, terrorists labeled "Salafi Jihadists" and the like. For example:

- "The United States is losing the war against an enemy it has misunderstood for decades. Al-Qaeda, the Islamic State of Iraq and al Sham (ISIS), and the Salafi-Jihadi groups that threaten the United States are stronger, smarter, and more resilient than they were on September 11, 2001."[1]

- "Qatar has emerged as a key financier of the Syrian opposition, including Salafi Jihadist groups as well as Sunni Islamist organizations."[2]

- "Accurately labeling the nature of Salafi-Jihadist doctrine as a religious ideology is not merely an exercise in academic theorizing, but has important policy implications. Most importantly, it should be obvious that the United States and its allies are not facing a religion—Islam—as their main enemy, but an ideology, namely the Salafi-Jihad."[3]

Branding all terrorists who kill in the name of Islam "Salafists" is not only an inaccurate use of the term, but it also lacks the kind of intellectual subtlety that can easily recognize, for instance, that Irish Catholic terrorists of the IRA do not represent—and are in fact widely denounced by—the main body of Catholics. More importantly, this misconception loops the wrong interpretation of Islam in with terrorism, as detailed in the pages to come.

The reality is that Salafism is practiced by Muslims in almost every country in the world, and it contains great diversity. "There are many peace-loving and even quietist Salafis around the world," writes Matthew D. Taylor, scholar at the Institute for Islamic, Christian, and Jewish Studies in Baltimore, Maryland. "While these folks might have rigorous religious standards for themselves that guide their behavior, there are plenty of Salafis who have no intention of imposing those standards coercively on anyone else."[4] Dr. Abdullah Al-Uthaymin, secretary general of the King Faisal International Prize, put it to me this way in August 2015:

> Some people think Salafism is synonymous with Sunni Islamic terror, but that is only in its bastardized form, which various terrorists have used to recruit enraged radicals obsessed with revolution. In fact, Salafism urges us to live in accord with the principles of the early Muslim elders, whose Islam was one of peace, acceptance, and unity. In the Kingdom, it's understood to be through the preservation of the Saudi state as the Custodian of the Two Holy Mosques.[5]

To gain a clearer picture of what exactly the MB ideology aims to overthrow—and to offer a deeper perspective on the theological underpinnings of the MB by comparing it to a specific historical, political, and religious alternative—this chapter presents the origins of modern-day Salafism in Saudi Arabia and highlights the ways in which the Saudi state embodies—if not always perfectly—the dynamics of those origins. In comparison, the seeds of the MB's failure can be found in its turn away from Salafism and its embracing of revolutionist, anti-Salafist views.

DEAL IN THE DESERT

The Najd plateau stretches across the center of the Arabian Peninsula, from the jagged mountains of the Hejaz in the west to the red dunes of Ad-Dahna in the east. Along its northeastern rim are a series of oases, including Buraydah, Diriyah, and Riyadh, that served as the fount of pre-Islamic Arab culture. "In this group of oases," the British scholar and adventurer T. E. Lawrence wrote a century ago, "lay the true centre of Arabia, the preserve of its native spirit, and its most conscious individuality. The desert lapped it round and kept it pure of contact."[6]

Barren, hot, dusty, and unwelcoming, the Najd was never colonized by Europeans, nor conquered by the Ottoman Turks. A handful of tribes cobbled together a life in its Hobbesian wasteland, including Bedouin nomads and the sedentary Bani Hanifa tribe, forebears of the Saudi royal family. In the late sixth century, in the Hejaz along the Red Sea coast, the Prophet Mohammed was born. Around 622, he and dozens of followers left Makkah and founded the first self-governing Muslim community, in Yathrib, a predominantly Jewish town. It was later named Madinah, or "city of the prophet," as Islam flourished across the peninsula and beyond.

The religion is thus deeply intertwined with the Arabian Peninsula, its place of birth, and with the three successive Saudi states. Yet by the early eighteenth century, Islam had been corrupted and bastardized; people embraced palm trees, chanted spells, and prayed to saints. The Arabian Peninsula turned lawless, with small oasis-states battling tribal fiefdoms. Adultery and theft were common and rarely punished. Few knew the Quran.

Then, a scholar of Islam emerged. Sheikh Muhammad bin Abdul Wahhab hailed from a family of Muslim scholars and gained a following by calling for a return to the Islam of the Prophet's time, urging strict adherence to the original Islamic scriptures and traditional religious practices. His Islam came to be called Salafism, in reference to the "ancestors" or "salafs"—the original Muslim converts who were contemporaries and followers of the Prophet, along with a few succeeding generations.

In 1744, at Diriyyah (the capital of the first Saudi state), Sheikh Abdul Wahhab met a local Emir, Imam Muhammad Ibn Saud, who received him graciously. "I usher in for you glory and power," the Sheikh told the Emir. "For whosoever holds fast to the affirmation, 'There is no God but Allah' and labors for it and supports it, through it he will achieve dominion over lands and people."[7] The two agreed on a partnership to bridge tribal divisions and help settle Najdis in cities and towns. Sheikh Abdul Wahhab endorsed Imam Ibn Saud and his state of united tribes, while Imam Ibn Saud promised to support and propagate Salafism under all the domains he would rule. The duo was well received. "The peoples of this part of the world had become fed up with the lawlessness, the violence, and the chaos of their lives," said Prince Amr bin Mohammad Al-Faisal. "[They] wanted to practice their faith in a proper way, and . . . not just to practice it as a custom without knowing what they were doing."[8]

The peninsula's tribal heterogeneity, with differing cultures and lifestyles, and the era's false, malleable religion, made state-building a great challenge. But conservative Islam helped establish a shared ethos, a cohesiveness and trust, enabling locals to move from a state of *jahiliyya* toward one of *hakimayyat*. "Relations between the rulers of Al-Dir'iyya and the Shaykh were deeper than the ordinary ties between a secular ruler and a spiritual leader. These rulers seem to have believed implicitly in his doctrines and the cause that he was proclaiming," writes Al-Uthaymin.[9]

The newly settled towns engendered familiarity and understanding. In turn, the popularity of Sheikh Muhammad bin Abdul Wahhab and his teachings enhanced the legitimacy and influence of Imam Ibn Saud. If Salafism sedated the warring tribes, the first Saudi state united them. "The deal that was struck," writes prominent legal scholar Dr. Abdul Aziz Al-Fahad, "reflects that the two parties, the Sheikh and the Amir (Imam), clearly understood the political goal they sought: the establishment of a single polity in the area that would unite the warring towns, villages, and tribes into a realm with one imam and where the Sharia would reign supreme."[10]

The success of the Saud-Wahhab partnership marked a major turning point for the Arabian Peninsula and Islam. Today's Islamists have dreamt of creating a state based on Sharia for more than a century, but, in essence, the Saud-Wahhab deal achieved the feat nearly three centuries ago.

The partnership was sealed when Abdul Aziz, the eldest son of Imam Muhammad Ibn Saud, married the daughter of Sheikh Muhammad bin Abdul Wahhab. The families have intermarried regularly ever since, dissolving clan affiliations and joining their power and influence. Their first state slowly expanded across the peninsula, nearly reaching the Kingdom's current size. But Saudi princes grew overconfident, and in 1812 raided villages near Baghdad and Damascus and attacked Hajjis they believed had shown inadequate Islamic devotion. Enraged, the Ottoman sultan backed Egyptian leader Muhammad Ali's campaign to retake Makkah and Madinah, ending the first Saudi state. The second Saudi state lasted from 1830 to 1891 and fell prey to family infighting and succession issues.

ISLAMIC LEGITIMACY OF THE SALAFIST SAUDI STATE

Imam (later King) Abdulaziz ibn Abdul Rahman ibn Faisal Al Saud planted the flag for the third and current Saudi state in 1902, taking Riyadh from the rival Al-Rasheed clan during a surprise midnight raid. In the years that followed, King Abdulaziz used theological persuasion, political wisdom, and force to ensure the loyalty of peoples from Hejaz, Najd, Hassa, Jouf, Assir, and other provinces. He gave Bedouins great chunks of land, dispatched clerics and teachers to educate nomads, and created the beginnings of a central administration.

These moves unified the tribes and helped establish a third state. "As revenues started to increase in the central coffers, he began to build hospitals, schools, social services centers, roads and more," Sheikh Mohammad bin Abdullah Al-Suweilem, president of Citizens (and Tribal) Affairs at the Saudi Royal Court, told me in 2010. "Now more than 70 years later, the children and grandchildren of these nomadic Bedouin tribes are engineers, doctors, leading businessmen, and senior government officials and military officers."[11] In this way, King Abdulaziz defused a potential threat, united the tribes under the Saudi umbrella, and laid the foundation for the state that is to Islam what the Vatican is to Christianity—a historical, administrative, and spiritual epicenter.

In many respects, the Islamic legitimacy of the Saudi state is due to its deeply rooted Salafism. The Saudi king's official title is Custodian of the Two Holy Mosques, and the second most powerful body in Saudi Arabia, after the monarch, is the Ulema—the educated class of Muslim scholars who ideologically descend from Wahhab and who theologically determine and assess the law. The head of the Ulema, the Grand Mufti, is the top advisor to the king on religious matters. "Religion is the law," columnist Prince Amr bin Mohammad Al-Faisal said in 2001. "It permeates the culture. It is rooted in the history. It is part of the DNA, if you like, of the Saudis. Any response to any challenge has to go through the Islamic filter, has to be dealt with from an Islamic point of view."[12]

In original Islamic scriptures, the highest authority is the caretaker of the Ummah, known as *Wali al amr* in Arabic. All religious, political, and military powers are concentrated under this authority. In one of his better known works, Sheikh Abdul Wahhab relayed the key factors that distinguished Muslims from the followers of other systems of belief, which included: "Obedience to rulers has to be observed, [and] the *wali* is the individual who works according to the commands of God."[13] In a later book on ethical behavior, the Sheikh stressed that "rebellions and disturbances should be avoided . . . and the ruler should be sincere and kind toward his subjects."[14]

King Salman's legitimacy is contingent on his being first and foremost *Wali al amr* of the Saudi people, and in return the people show their acceptance of his rule by swearing an oath of loyalty, or *Bayah*, to him. This oath, which is an act of obedience, is fundamental to Salafi Islam (the Arabic word "Islam" means "submission"). Anyone who breaks the oath —as the MB regularly does and encourages others to do—can never be considered a true Salafi. As Sir John Jenkins, former British ambassador to Syria, Iraq, and Saudi Arabia, wrote for Oxford University's Gulf and Arabian Peninsula Studies Forum,

> The Saudis believe [the MB] outlook represents a dangerously radical misreading of Islamic history in the service of "anarchy" (their term). Their Islam needs no *tajdeed* [renewal]—the kingdom is a legitimate Islamic state, with a religiously legitimate ruler, and all Saudis owe absolute loyalty to him as *wali al amr*. Any advice to him from the ulama should therefore be discreet. . . . Anyone who acknowledges fealty to another is considered disloyal to the king by definition . . . for the Saudis, it is above all a question of territorial allegiance and loyalty to a sovereign individual.[15]

Compared to the Salafist ideology of the Kingdom, the Brotherhood offers a displaced revolutionary ideology that lacks even a vision for its ideal state. "If there is one Islamic theological thread that has historical legitimacy, stands opposed to the Muslim Brotherhood, and can unite the Muslim world against terrorism, that thread is Salafism as it is practiced in and represented by Saudi Arabia," Dr. Abdullah Al-Otheymeen told me in 2015.[16]

And the MB is fully aware of its natural opposition to the Saudi state and its Salafist essence. The group openly seeks to provide a religio-political structure with the potential to delegitimize the Kingdom and any other Islamist government, which is precisely why it has been widely rejected by governments in the Gulf, across the Muslim world, and beyond. "The MB denies state sovereignty and demands loyalty to its Murshid, thereby negating the legitimacy of heads of state and their respective governments," Prince Turki Al-Faisal, former Saudi intelligence director and former ambassador to the UK and the United States, stated in a 2017 interview.[17]

KINGDOM AND BROTHERHOOD DIVERGE

How and when did these ideologies diverge? The final and most telling rupture began around the time of the first Gulf War. "The beginning of the real break with the organisation happened in the late 1990s," writes former British ambassador Sir John Jenkins, "when then-Grand Mufti of Saudi Arabia, Sheikh Abdul Aziz bin Baz, stigmatized the MB as deviationists. In 2002, the late Prince Nayef spoke bitterly about the Saudi and Kuwaiti experience in 1990–91, and accused the MB of betraying the trust of [Saudi] and Gulf states."[18]

Yet the origins of the modern-day divergence between the two can be traced much further back, to the 1950s, when the MB took a dark road toward violence and terrorism. These were the Brotherhood's first years in the wilderness, during Nasser's harsh reign; the group was lost and rudderless, with Al-Banna assassinated several years before and most of its leadership in jail or exile. The result was the emergence of Qutb.

The Kingdom of Saudi Arabia spied an opportunity to boost its status and influence among the world's Muslims. In 1954, just as Nasser launched a sweeping crackdown on the Brotherhood in Egypt, King Saud visited Pakistan, Jordan, and Egypt and spoke of his desire to strengthen "the spirit of true Islamic brotherhood"[19]—a comment that clearly suggested the MB could not provide that spirit given that Qutb was in prison, Al-Banna long gone, and his twenty-something son-in-law Said Ramadan still finding his footing on the world stage.

The Brotherhood had embraced violence before, but it was during Qutb's time in prison that he began to reshape the legacy of the MB and the world's vision of radical Islam. As mentioned in Chapter 1, while in prison he wrote *Milestones on the Path*, an extension of Al-Banna's ideas and the wellspring for Islamic extremism today. In *Milestones*, Qutb called on Muslim youth to launch a jihad against the *jahili* system and establish a *hakimiyyat* state. He did not go all the way to invoking *takfir*, the Islamic concept in which a Muslim is labelled a non-Muslim after committing some forbidden behavior. But he did say that if people insisted on living "the life of *jahiliyyah*," they were "not Muslims," which is equivalent to calling them infidels.[20]

Consider in comparison the view of Sheikh Abdul Wahhab: "Regarding *takfir*, I consider to be an infidel the person who has known the religion of the Prophet and yet stands against it, prevents others from accepting it and shows hostility towards those who adhere to it. As for fighting, until today we have not fought anyone except to protect our own lives and honor."[21] Abdul Wahhab also argued that the ideas of true Islam should first be explained to people, and only if they were to then decide against it could they be seen as infidels.[22]

It is important to note that Qutb was the first to extend the concept of *jahiliyya* to Muslim countries; previous Islamic thinkers had applied it only to the West. For Qutb, even the claims to Muslimhood of Egyptians, Iraqis, and other Arab citizens were dubious if their state and their lives had been infected by Western ideas. Ironically, since at the time he was writing thousands of Muslim Brothers had recently found refuge in the Kingdom and other Gulf countries, Qutb even included Saudi Arabia in the list of *jahili* countries because of its relationship with the United States.[23] These were the ideas behind Qutb's 1965 organization, which plotted the assassination of Egyptian leaders in a planned overthrow of the state.

None of this marks as great a shift from the ideas and policies of Al-Banna's Brotherhood as some might believe. It was there in some of the founder's earliest statements on jihad, in which he could often sound like Qutb and his terrorist descendants. "According to Al-Banna, there is little textual support for the idea that self-improvement is a greater jihad than fighting Islam's enemies. He says that the tradition of the prophet on which it is based is allegedly apocryphal," Tarek Masoud writes:

> Instead, Al-Banna argues, Jihad is to be undertaken for two reasons—first, to spread the faith, and second, to defend the lands of the faithful from invaders. In the first instance, Jihad is a farḍ kifāya—an obligation that individual Muslims are relieved of if enough of their number undertake it. In the second instance, defense against encroachers, Jihad is a farḍ ʿayn—incumbent on all Muslims. It is to this latter form of Jihad that he devotes the greatest attention. He writes: "Muslims today as you know are subjugated by others and ruled by nonbelievers. Their lands have been trampled and their sanctities violated. Their enemies govern their affairs, and their faith is disrupted in their own homes, in addition to their neglect of spreading their faith. And so it is incumbent on all Muslims without exception to prepare, and to settle upon the intention of Jihad and prepare for it until the opportunity arises that Allah might accomplish that which must be done."[24]

Again, compare this to the sayings of Sheikh Abdul Wahhab, who, on the other hand, noted four categories of jihad (which means "struggle" in Arabic), only one of which necessarily included violence: against oneself, which is about learning to live like the Prophet; against the devil, which is about resisting doubt and temptation; against infidels and hypocrites, which should be done with every part of one's being; and against oppressors and Islamic innovators, which can be done only with the heart.[25] What's more, in a later work, the sheikh delineated only three situations under which violent Jihad was obligatory: "at times of actual battle, when an enemy enters the country and when the imam calls people to fight."[26] Sticking to these conditions would exclude the vast majority of the MB's calls for jihad over the years.

ISLAM OF REBELS

This is likely because Al-Banna and Qutb's ideas about jihad and violence in the name of Islam come from a much older ideology, which takes its very name from the concept of rebellion. Next to Sunnism and Shiism, a third ideological tradition emerged in the early days of Islam, arguing that neither did power come from the bloodline of the Prophet nor should it be handed to those in political power. This tradition holds that true political power comes only from God and that those who did not rule according to his word are infidels. "Adherents of this tradition became known as *Khawarij*, or rebels," Abdel Monem Said Aly, senior fellow at the Crown Center for Middle East Studies at Brandeis University, wrote for *Cairo Review* in Spring 2018. "As the word '*Khawarij*' denotes, it is a group that rebelled against that political order that emerged from both Sunnism—the Caliphate—and Shiism—the Imam."[27]

In their earliest days, there were similarities between the followers of Sheikh Abdul Wahhab and the Kharijites, as they are also known, such as their stated commitment to the original Islam and the intensity of their devotion. But the traditions diverged on two crucial points: respect for authority and the impact of a mortal sin. "Unlike the Kharijites, the Wahhabis respected all the Companions and never disowned Uthman or Ali (the third and fourth Caliphs, respectively), on this question, as well as on the matter of *imama* (Imamate, leadership of the Muslims)," writes Al-Otheymeen. "The Wahhabis advocated complete obedience to the ruler . . . unless he were to order the ruled to commit sins."[28]

This is of course in great contrast to a group that is in large part defined by rebellion, in particular their rebellion against Ali, the rightful successor to Mohammed in the Shia tradition. The second point of departure is their attitude toward a Muslim who commits a grave sin. "To the Kharijites such a person is an infidel," Al-Otheymeen adds, "but the Wahhabis adhered to the views of the orthodox in maintaining that the person is merely sinful, and should not be excluded from Islam but left to the mercy of God."[29] The gap here is vast: in the world of Wahhabis, the sinner would face justice, which could be anywhere from a slap on the wrist to one hundred years in prison; in the Kharijite world, the sinner would be killed.

These three traditions, Shiism, Sunnism, and the Kharijites, have defined the political rivalries within Islam for centuries, with one crucial difference among them in recent decades. "Only the third group had sanctioned assassinations and different forms of political violence to achieve its objectives, while branding their opponents as infidels," writes Said Aly.[30]

> It was this third strand of Islamic political thought that would constitute the ideological basis for the emergence of the Muslim Brotherhood in the wake of the ideological and political vacuum left after the dissolution of the Islamic Caliphate in 1924 after the collapse of the Ottoman Empire. Four years later the Society of Muslim Brothers was born in Egypt espousing the fundamental tenets of the *Khawarij* paradigm of power and authority not only for Egypt but for the entire Islamic World.[31]

Along with Al-Banna, both Sheikh Abdul Wahhab and Sayyid Qutb sought "to convert jahili society to Islam," writes David Commins in his 2006 book *The Wahhabi Mission and Saudi Arabia*. "But Qutb diverged from Wahhabism in defining exactly what conversion entailed. Furthermore, Qutb's method for interpreting the Qu'ran and the Sunna was utterly unacceptable to Wahhabi ulama. . . . Some of the lessons he drew from the Qu'ran and his theological views appalled the Wahhabi ulama."[32]

This explains why even in the 1980s—the peak decade of Islamic revivalism in the Muslim world—Saudi Arabia only published one Qutb book, and that book was not his iconic *Milestones*, but his reflections on visiting the United States.[33] This should come as no surprise, as the motivating ideas and vision of Qutbism and Al-Qaeda contrast starkly with those of Saudi Salafism. Commins goes on:

> The set of issues and ideas that matter most to Osama bin Laden are those of modern Islamic revivalism dating back to the early twentieth century: resisting western domination and combating regimes that fail to rule according to Islamic law. By contrast, the Wahhabi mission essentially aims to institute correct performance of worshipping God, to eliminate idolatry and to ensure compliance with Islamic law and morality. Mohammad ibn Abd Al-Wahhab and his followers made correct understanding of *tawhid* the centre of their mission and their adversaries were other Muslims who rejected their views on tawhid. . . . Bin Laden's point of reference is not a rigorous dogma of tawhid but the community of believers, the umma, whose rights and lives are trampled by Washington and its servant regimes. . . . His language is that of an injured party retaliating against an aggressor, not a vigilant theologian eager to stamp out idolatry.[34]

In a nutshell, the MB-inspired ideas of Al-Qaeda and other violent ji-hadis are not about Islam but about vengeance. Salafism, in contrast, is about instituting a religion and state whereby Muslims can live by proper Islam. Al-Banna and Qutb took this original Salafist idea and twisted it into something that stood in angry opposition to modernity and the West. The MB ideology and the Qutbism that came later were never meant to be guidelines for running an Islamic state but rather in-structions for insurrection.

One of the leading twentieth-century proponents of purist Salafism and a major influence on Saudi religious thinking was Muhammad Nasir-ud-Dīn Al-Albani, an expert on the Hadith and Islamic law. Origi-nally from Albania and educated in Syria, he taught at Madinah's Is-lamic University in the 1960s and served as head of higher education in Islamic law in Makkah in the 1970s. Al-Albani advocated a quietist, nonviolent form of Salafism, and thus tended to side against the MB. He denounced the ideas of Qutb and urged the Sahwa to revive, not Jihad, but Ijtihad, which refers to the use of independent reasoning to make de-cisions on Islamic law.

"At a time when all the Islamic currents . . . paid homage to the 'mar-tyred' radical Muslim Brotherhood ideologue Sayyid Qutb, Al-Albani was one of the first shaykhs to openly risk criticism of him," Hegghammer and Lacroix wrote in their 2011 book. "Yes, he must be refuted, it is a duty,"[35] Al-Albani said of Qutb. Al-Albani also saw Hassan Al-Banna as problem-atic, because he was not a religious scholar, yet he had taken positions that contradicted the Sunna.

For true Salafists like Al-Albani, the Islam of the MB represents a dan-gerous form of hypocrisy, about which the Prophet had warned his follow-ers. In his *Book of Divine Unity*, Sheikh Abdul Wahhab explained that there is only one sin Allah could never forgive, though it had several forms: "A person should be vigilant in regard to matters that may vitiate his faith and lead him to polytheism, which is the sin that God hates most and will not pardon."[36] The Sheikh goes on to describe "a tradition that says that hypocrisy (riya)—explained as a minor form of polytheism—was the trend the Prophet most feared that Muslims become involved in."[37]

Thus, MB ideas represent a bastardization of Islam, or an Islamic in-novation that serves as a means to an end. As any Islamic scholar would argue, no man-made organization should be free to reinterpret and alter the fundamental concepts of Islam to fit its own acts and designs, as the MB wants to do. "We Muslims have seen many terrorists who tried to fal-sify and distort religious texts and twist their historical facts," Moham-med Al-Issa, secretary-general of the Muslim World League, said in 2018. "There is no authority on religions except correct religious texts free of misleading, false, and distorted interpretations."[38]

This explains why the theories of Al-Banna and Qutb remain the driv-ing vision behind Al-Qaeda today and why that leading terrorist outfit has long stood against true Salafism, especially as it is typified by the Kingdom: it feels threatened by the true Islam. "Since the early 1990s, Al-Qaida has routinely vilified the Saudi royal family and its government for being un-Islamic and illegitimate, describing the monarchy and the princes as apostates who should be attacked and toppled from power," Bernard Haykel, professor of Near Eastern Studies at Princeton University, and Cole Bunzel, editor of *Jihadica* and a research fellow in Islamic Law and Civilization at the Yale Law school, wrote in January 2019.[39] This is Khajirite thinking par excellence: an attempt to rebel, to upend the powerful without justification. Al-Qaeda argues that Saudi leaders "only pretend to be Muslim" and "have consistently undermined Islam from within," Haykel and Bunzel said.[40] "Anti-Saudi messaging [which is, in essence, anti-Salafi messaging] is indeed a central element of Al-Qaeda's propaganda, and Al-Qaida does not conceal its ambition to seize control of Arabia's spiritual and material resources."[41]

Indeed, Al-Qaeda has in recent years found a new reason for attacks on the Kingdom: Crown Prince Mohammad bin Salman and his social reforms, like the mixing of sexes at live concerts. A recent Al-Qaeda newsletter depicted the crown prince as "the devil incarnate . . . spreading the symbols of Westernization, the rituals of secularism, and liberal values."[42] A December 2018 audio address by Al-Qaeda leader and former MB member Ayman Al-Zawahiri went into great detail explaining how Muslims in Arabia should resist the Saudi government:

> In keeping with his roots in the Muslim Brotherhood, Al-Zawahiri offers a conspiratorial narrative to explain regional and global politics over the last century. . . . Al-Zawahiri asserts that the Saudi ruling family, from the time of its founder King Abdulaziz Ibn Saud (r. 1902–1953) until MBS today, are concealed Zionists who pretend to be Muslims. They have ceaselessly plotted to destroy Islam in alliance, first with the British, and since WWII with the United States.[43]

Al-Zawahiri went on to urge Saudis to leave the country in order to learn jihad and unite with other Muslims so as to ultimately return and launch their violent resistance.

One of the Kingdom's leading Islamic scholars, Sheikh Abdul Aziz bin Baz, who rose through the ranks to serve as the Kingdom's Grand Mufti until his death in 1999, knew right away that Qutb's works were blasphemous—and dangerous. "Whereas other sheikhs saw some merit in Qutb's works," David Commins writes, "Ibn Baz argued that they contained so many gross errors that they could easily lead astray those lacking deep training in religious sciences."[44]

That is precisely what came to pass. Qutb expanded on the ideas of Al-Banna, then mentored a young Ayman Al-Zawahiri. Inspired by Qutb's passionate advocacy of violence, Al-Zawahiri left the MB to launch Egyptian Islamic Jihad, then signed on with Al-Qaeda and Osama bin

Laden—who had received instruction from Ayman's brother, Muhammad Al-Zawahiri. As former Kuwaiti education minister Ahmad Al-Rubai wrote in 2005,

> The beginnings of all of the religious terrorism that we are witnessing today were in the Muslim Brotherhood's ideology of *takfir* [accusing other Muslims of apostasy]. . . . Sayyid Qutb's book *Milestones* was the inspiration and the guide for all of the *takfir* movements that came afterwards. The founders of the violent groups were raised on the Muslim Brotherhood, and those who worked with bin Laden and Al-Qaeda went out under the mantle of the Muslim Brotherhood.[45]

In the last two decades, Al-Qaeda and its angry stepchild, the Islamic State, or ISIS, have led astray tens of thousands of Muslim men and women who never knew the real Islam, only Qutb's fire and brimstone version. The result is countless dead and endless havoc across the Muslim world and beyond—all originating with the MB—not Wahhabism, not Salafism, not Saudi Arabia—as Commins explains:

> Because Osama bin Laden and most of the hijackers are Saudi nationals, it was assumed that Al-Qaeda is an expression of Wahhabism. That is not the case. . . . Al-Qaeda is part of the Jihadist tendency whose intellectual roots go back to Sayyid Qutb. . . . Its advocates include Sheik Omar Abd Al-Rahman, best known for his role in plotting the 1993 World Trade Center bombing, and Ayman Al-Zawahiri, the former Egyptian surgeon and deputy to Osama bin Laden.[46]

Khalid Sheikh Mohammed, mastermind of the 9/11 attacks, and Mohamed Atta, one of the leaders of the attacks, had both been MB members before joining Al-Qaeda.[47] Though fifteen of the nineteen hijackers in the September 11 attacks on the United States were from Saudi Arabia, this fact has proven to be much less an indictment of Saudi Salafism than a revelation about the extent to which MB-style thinking had taken root in the Kingdom. "[There is] no evidence that the Saudi government as an institution or senior Saudi officials individually funded [Al-Qaeda]," said the 9/11 Commission report.[48]

Many observers blame Saudi Arabia for extremist terrorism, but the United States might well have played a greater role, particularly with its considerable support of MB-linked groups and individuals, starting with President Eisenhower and Said Ramadan back in the 1950s (see Chapter 6). As Chris Hedges, a best-selling author and Pulitzer Prize–winning journalist who has taught at Princeton and Columbia universities, wrote in April 2019,

> From the CIA's funneling of over a billion dollars to Islamic militants in the 1970s war in Afghanistan against the Soviet Union to the billion dollars spent

on training and equipping the radical jihadists currently fighting in Syria, the United States has repeatedly empowered extremists who have filled the vacuums of failed states it created. The extremists have turned with a vengeance on their sponsors. Washington's fueling of these conflicts was directly responsible for the rise of figures such as Ayman Al-Zawahiri and Osama bin Laden and ultimately laid the groundwork for the 9/11 attacks.[49]

Certainly, there is a difference between Salafism and Saudi Arabia, but the point being made is that the incorrect blame at times hurled at Saudi Arabia, which is the de facto epicenter of Salafism, for extremist terrorism—blame that is far more correctly hurled at the MB—shows the way in which the MB is in fact a break from Salafist beliefs and how the United States and the West have for decades often been backing the wrong horse. For half a century, in the Arab world and beyond, MB-linked groups have repeatedly revealed their proclivity for terrorism and political violence, which has gone a long way in preventing the group from developing into an organization able to put forth and implement a viable form of governance.

As shown earlier, the original MB, in Egypt, funneled jihadis to Palestine to fight the British starting in the 1940s and has plotted and executed terrorist attacks in nearly every decade since. In the 1970s and early 1980s in Syria, the MB often attacked the Baathist government of Bashar Al-Assad's father, Hafez. The Islamic Action Front, an MB-linked political group in Jordan, has expressed support for Hamas and ISIS. The Palestinian Islamic Jihad, another MB offshoot, has carried out dozens of attacks against Israeli citizens since the 1980s, including deadly bombings of a commuter bus and another on a shopping mall.[50]

And then there is Hamas, the Palestine branch of the MB, which is responsible for countless acts of violence over the years. Mohammed Louizi, a forty-year-old Moroccan now living in France, was a member of the MB for fifteen years, from 1991 to 2006. "That the Muslim Brotherhood are dangerous, it's a fact," Louizi said in a 2018 short film about his life. "That the Muslim Brotherhood feed Islamist radicalization, by their talks of hate and rupture, it's a fact."[51]

Appearing on a Saudi talk show in May 2019, Ali Faghassi Al-Ghamdi, former chief of Al-Qaeda's military council in Saudi Arabia, highlighted the links between the MB and the dominant terrorist outfits of today, Al-Qaeda and ISIS. "Al-Qaeda and the Muslim Brotherhood have the same strategy (to achieve their objectives), but disagree on the tactics to achieve them," he said. "The core tenants of the Muslim Brotherhood are the same as Al Qaeda's. The difference is that when Al-Qaeda began its terrorist operations the MB distanced itself."[52]

Yet that same month, a respected U.S. think tank reiterated the outdated view of many Western analysts, blaming Saudi Arabia—in effect, Salafism—for exporting terrorism. The report from the Foundation for Defense of

Democracies called Wahhabism "the ideological tinder . . . for the jihadi fire that the United States has been battling for 20 years."[53] Astute observers quickly pointed out the oversight. "This is a weird and outdated take," Josh Hammer, editor-at-large for *The Daily Wire*, tweeted in response to the FDD report, using the common acronyms for the Kingdom of Saudi Arabia and Crown Prince Mohammed bin Salman. "KSA has largely (not wholly) cleaned up its act. And MBS's KSA is now a key strategic ally against the real U.S. regional foe: The Iran-Qatar-Turkey-Muslim Brotherhood axis of destructive Islamism."[54]

The MB's support for violence took only a brief pause during the Mubarak years and has resumed again more recently, spreading far beyond its country of origin. Having inspired the deadliest terrorist groups of our age, the Brotherhood has been designated a terrorist organization by Saudi Arabia, Egypt, the UAE, and Russia. This is the Brotherhood's legacy. The anti-Western, anti-modernity ideology of Al-Banna evolved into the angry, extremist militarism of Qutb and infected much of the Muslim world, inspiring countless Muslims to attack both the West and Islamic regimes seen as sullied by alliances with Western states. This is not Salafism.

TERROR, FOR OR AGAINST

To take the comparison farther, a stark contrast to the MB's embrace of terror can be seen in Saudi Arabia's struggles against it, which provide a further example of the tenets of the Salafist reform. In the early 2000s, the Kingdom faced a spate of terrorist attacks by Al-Qaeda in the Arabian Peninsula (AQAP), an offshoot of Brotherhood-inspired Al-Qaeda. The largest took place on May 2003 in Riyadh and killed 39 people and injured 160. Under the guidance of then interior minister Prince Mohammed bin Nayef bin Abdul Aziz Al-Saud, Saudi Arabia launched a massive counterterrorism program to weed out and dismantle terrorist networks and de-radicalize and reintegrate terrorist fighters. The Kingdom's military and security budget more than doubled, and within a decade Saudi Arabia was largely secure.[55]

Then, on the afternoon of May 22, 2015, during Friday prayers at the Imam Ali mosque in Al-Qadeeh in the Shia enclave of Qatif in the east of the Kingdom, a suicide bomber exploded his vest, killing 21 people and injuring more than 100. ISIS had come to the Kingdom and delivered the country's deadliest terrorist attack in a dozen years. More attacks followed, killing dozens more Saudis and proving without a doubt that ISIS had a foothold in the Kingdom. Once again, as with Al-Qaeda, Saudi Arabia was not the source of the group, as some claimed, but one of ISIS's main targets.

In fact, in 2014, ISIS leaders switched their approach to a campaign called "qadimum" and started telling radicals living in the Kingdom to stay put and await plans to strike.[56] As detailed earlier in the chapter, ISIS accuses Saudi Arabia of hypocrisy for guarding the Two Holy Mosques while also being allied with the United States. Like the MB, it aims to re-store the caliphate. In order to do so, it would need to depose the Saudi leadership and gain control of Makkah and Madinah.

As of early 2019, the Kingdom had all but snuffed out ISIS domestically, as it had with AQAP. Riyadh has also cracked down on terrorist financiers and criminalized ISIS funding with stiff penalties. Saudi authorities have arrested hundreds of ISIS supporters and operatives since 2014. Many end up at the Prince Mohammed bin Nayef Center for Counseling and Care, just north of Riyadh, where Islamic extremists undergo de-radicalization treatment that involves counseling and religious instruction. Some 86 per-cent of the thousands who had gone through the program have returned to normal lives, while only a handful have relapsed.[57]

That battle begins with the Kingdom's Prevention, Rehabilitation and Aftercare Campaign (PRAC) program. A complement to the hard mili-tary element, PRAC targets the ideological and intellectual foundation of Islamic terrorism, based on the ideas of Qutb, and incorporates a peace-ful Salafist counterpoint to extremist ideology. Its emphasis on deterrence, rehabilitation, and reintegration has helped stop the dissemination of ter-rorist ideology. In addition, the Ministry of Islamic Affairs has its *Sakinah* ("Tranquility") counter-radicalization campaign. Agents of that program take to online forums, chat rooms, and social media to find potential ex-tremists and walk them back from the ledge, as well as sniff out terrorist networks and attack plans.

The Kingdom's Salafist approach has even taken the ideological battle to the airwaves, as detailed in a June 2015 story on National Public Radio:

> A new Saudi TV series created by a popular comedian, Nasser Al Qasabi, mocks ISIS and religious extremists. The title is *Selfie*, which suggests holding a camera to the country. The satire pokes fun at mindless militants who are interested only in sex and violence. It's attracted so much attention that the hashtag *#selfie* is now trending on Twitter across the Middle East.[58]

In years past, the Saudi government may have been expected to frown on a show that made light of extremist Islam, if not shut it down. No longer. When an imam called out Al Qasabi as a heretic, the government called for an investigation and the imam publicly apologized. This shows precisely where Saudi leaders stand in regard to ISIS and Qutbist interpretations of Islam and highlights an important Saudi effort to promote social and re-ligious tolerance. The PRAC and *Sakinah* campaigns, and a willingness to embrace non-traditional voices, evince the pliability of Salafism.

MB RIGIDITY

While Salafism welcomes debate and is willing to embrace new ideas, the MB's main problem beyond its proclivity for violence, according to Cambridge University scholar Dr. Hazim Kandil, is that it is anti-intellectual and resistant to change. The MB's lengthy screening and initiation process, known as *Tarbiya* ("cultivation"), is as much brainwashing as it is indoctrination, which is one reason it lasts so long. It takes four years, in all, to become a Muslim Brother. A candidate for membership spends one year under examination. If he proves himself, he then spends three years as an initiate before he is welcomed as a full and active Brother.[59] Through this process, the MB squelches dissent before it arises by producing "a new kind of person," says Kandil.[60] Tarek Masoud put it this way: "One of the most common slurs against the movement, particularly in vogue after the January 25 revolution, is to twist their moniker from 'Al-Ikhwān' (Brothers) to 'al-Khirfān' (sheep)—a backhanded testament to the unity of the movement and the absolute obedience of its members to their superiors."[61]

Since the time of the autocratic Al-Banna, MB leaders—who are mainly educated university graduates (primarily physicians, engineers, and lawyers)—have favored obedience over enquiry and argumentation and developed internal systems of pressure and marginalization to stifle intellectual and ideological debate. "As is evident in the Brotherhood's loyalty oath, unquestioned obedience (*al-sam' wa al-ṭā'a*) is a value to which the movement attaches a great deal of importance. Hasan Al-Banna spoke of obedience as 'total compliance with and immediate execution of commands,'" writes Masoud.

Every MB member is part of a "family" of five to six members who often live in the same area and meet weekly to share their lives and discuss the latest news. Families are grouped into branches, which are grouped into areas, the administrators of which report to the MB secretary.[62] Within families, Brothers are to become close to each other, share secrets and personal concerns, and even be responsible for one another. "Al-Banna did not call this the 'system of families' by accident," writes Masoud. "It was his intention to bind his men emotionally as well as organizationally."[63]

Of course, the family system is also used to generate funding for the organization. "Each member contributes 10 percent of his income to the Brotherhood. These funds, in addition to donations from wealthy sympathisers, are sent to Islamic Charities that manage investment portfolios whose profits are returned to the MB," the CIA wrote in a 1986 report on Egypt's MB.[64] "The Brotherhood receives funds from sympathisers and expatriates in Saudi Arabia, other Arab Gulf states, and Western Europe or through black-market currency exchange operations."[65]

Meanwhile, Brothers are urged to reach out across their personal and professional networks for potential backers, particularly keeping an eye out for businesses run by men with MB sympathies. "To avoid government interference or takeover of their enterprises, the MB usually forms partnerships with sympathetic businessmen who are not members of their organisation," said the CIA report. "Part of the companies' profits—including money from overstated expenses—is donated to the MB."[66]

These firms tend to hire MB members, and their financial support enables the MB to build hospitals and schools, publish books, and proselytize outside Egypt.[67]

The great advantage of this system, according to Richard Mitchell, one of the top historians on the MB's early years, is how it enabled the group's leaders to exert control over subordinates. It gave MB authorities a strong, clearly defined chain of command, and kept recruits and new members in lockstep.[68] This system of purely top-down leadership likely played a part in the MB's lack of a coherent ideology, its absence of a vision for an Islamic state, according to Pargeter:

> This lack of clarity about how the Ikhwan envisages the relationship between Sharia and the democratic political process has done little to assist it in its bid to be seen as a truly progressive and democratic movement. . . . The Brotherhood has hardly been a bastion of democracy itself. Whilst members of the movement regularly assert that they have their own kind of democracy through the use of *shura* (consultation), some Islamic scholars complain that the Ikhwan's talk of *shura* has become more propaganda than reality, and more mechanical than functional, given that the leaders do not allow any space for criticism or evaluation.[69]

Thus, we have an organization that seeks to create an Islamic state but is unable to outline the makeup of that state, its institutions and outlook; an organization that claims a commitment to parliamentary structures as well as to Sharia law; and an organization that says it is committed to democracy while being wholly undemocratic itself.

This undemocratic internal structure does however have at least one benefit: the MB is a disciplined institution, particularly so in a country and a culture marked by inefficiency. In fact, it is all too disciplined. "Rather than constituting a force for political pluralism or ideological moderation, a close examination of [MB] tenets reveals the Brotherhood as a totalitarian organization that is irreconcilable with the fundamental pillars of a modern democratic polity," writes Said Aly.[70]

Emad Abo Hashim—who lives in Turkey, is a member of Judges for Egypt (which supported Morsi's return), and, as a dissident, has been putting his observations about the MB and the way it functions on his website in recent years—has written about what it means to be an MB supporter. Despite the rigorous system of discipline, many Ikhwan are able to fake their commitment to the group:

> Be comforted, the Al-Ikhwan will not look into your past to see if it is prideful or shameful; they will not examine if your motives are noble or low and they will not analyze whether your character is healthy or sick. Al-Ikhwan will not make you take a lie test and will not test your abilities or knowledge even in your area of specialization. It is not necessary for you to be outstanding in your skills or super intelligent or knowledgeable about the rules of political

science and law. It is enough for you to be a brilliant actor, mastering your role as a free revolutionary and capable of repeating revolutionary slogans with fervor and strength. If you want to get integrated into Al-Ikhwan, you need to pose as a "brother" who is experienced in the religious discourse and to repeat their words and to wake up for the fajr prayer on time. If you did not pray before or if you were not basically a [real] Muslim, it is enough for you to publish on your social media sites your comments at the time of the fajr prayers to prove that you pray it on time. If you do this, you have reached perfection in terms of your relationship with the Ikhwan, and they will consider you—truly—one of them.[71]

These tendencies were solidified in the early years by the dominance of rural, working-class members, as opposed to highly educated intellectuals. Still present among the group today, though rarely within the leadership, they have long been used as foot soldiers, as shown by the masses bussed from villages and poor communities to the Raba'a sit-in in 2013 and paid a daily allowance. In fact, early MB ideology had many similarities to revolutionary socialism, or Soviet communism: it sought to tear down existing power structures and empower the disenfranchised; it emerged as the voice of the lower classes, workers, and peasants, demanding nationalization of industries and generous social welfare; and it did not abide serious inquiry, seeking to attract and mobilize in the spirit of an idea and emphasizing action and organization over vision.

The MB organizational model takes some of these socialist ideas and adds in a healthy dose of fascism. It is important to remember that Al-Banna honed and developed his model precisely at the time Hitler and Mussolini were emerging in Europe. Much like the MB, those two leaders oversaw political movements that had little need for policy prescriptions or any serious vision for governance. "They ask us what is our program," Mussolini said in 1922. "Our program is simple: We want to govern Italy."[72] What mattered was not the ideas of the movement but that it had an all-powerful leader and foot soldiers who followed his orders without question.

In fact, the MB and its descendants share a great deal with the genocidal maniacs of the 20th century. This is not a new idea: in its 1949 obituary of Al-Banna, *The New York Times* said his movement had "fascist overtones."[73] And when he spoke to Congress ten days after the September 2001 attacks, President George W. Bush described MB-inspired Al-Qaeda this way: "We have seen their kind before. They are the heirs of all the murderous ideologies of the 20th century. By sacrificing human life to serve their radical visions, by abandoning every value except the will to power, they follow in the path of fascism, Nazism and totalitarianism."[74] Abdel Monem Said Aly, the Brandeis scholar, takes this thinking even further:

The MB follows the traditions of totalitarian organizations of the communist and fascist brands which are based on secrecy and a rigidly hierarchical pyramid-like structure composed of a base of small cells reporting to provincial chapters and then finally to a powerful and highly centralized political organ at the top. . . . Throughout the history of the Muslim Brotherhood, the organization has been run by iron-clad rules of "Listening and Obedience," a rigorous system of socialization and indoctrination into the ideology of the movement that initially was based on the writings and speeches of the original founder Hassan Al-Banna, but since the 1950s has expanded to include the writings of Sayyid Qutb.[75]

The Brotherhood has developed an organizational system in which members are taught how to be obedient soldiers for the cause. As mentioned earlier in this chapter, the word "Islam" means "submission." Just as Saudis swear a *Bayah* to their king, Brothers submit fully to their leader and their cause; both are showing themselves committed to their Islamic ideology. The difference between the two, and the reason the latter oath is problematic, is that in Saudi Arabia the citizens are essentially doing what citizens of any other country do from the day they are born—accepting their government and its institutions as the law of the land, embracing their country's leadership as the body that binds and unites them—while Brotherhood members are submitting themselves to a body with no power, a body that watches over just a slim minority of the population and dreams and schemes of one day being able to rule based on Sharia.

In short, "the MB mimics some central features of a state in its hierarchical structure and the requirement for members to swear an exclusive oath of loyalty to the Murshid," Sir John Jenkins, former UK ambassador to the Kingdom, wrote in 2017. "However, it repudiates national identity and any loyalty other than that to the Murshid and God."[76]

RISE AND FALL OF TANZEEM

This rigid, familial hierarchy may help explain why the MB's primary attempt at international institution building failed. After the release of the Supreme Guide, or Murshid, Mustafa Machhour from prison in 1973, he and several other members of Nizam Al-Khass noticed that foreign MB branches, in Jordan and the Gulf, for instance, had prospered, while the Egyptian MB had withered under Nasser. They hit on a way to reinvigorate the movement, according to Pargeter:

They could see that whilst they were being stifled by the Egyptian regime, the international environment offered distinct opportunities that they could use not only to strengthen their influence within the movement as a whole, but also to increase the authority of their own particular clique within the Egyptian branch. As such they took steps to begin bringing the other branches under their control.[77]

For the most part, MB affiliates function as local chapters of the larger group based in Egypt. But in reality, especially after the crackdown during the Nasser years, each branch acts independently, with little oversight. Led by Machhour, the Egyptian MB group sought to engage and develop the web of MB-linked groups across the region and in Europe, and in doing so revive the Egyptian MB. The group chose a new leader and demanded that the leaders of the foreign branches come to Cairo to swear *baya* to the new Murshid, whose identity remained secret. "They imagined themselves as the real leaders of all the Ikhwan in the Arab world because Egypt for them was the real leadership of the movement as a whole," said former Syrian MB leader Issam Al-Attar. "They wanted to make the Murshid everything in the movement."[78]

All of this was finalized in a 1982 document called The Internal Salute, creating the international MB, called Tanzeem Al-Dawli, or more commonly just Tanzeem, to oversee the various branches and affiliates via a General Guidance Bureau, with Islamic input from a General Shura Council.[79] The Internal Salute outlined how the Supreme Guide in Egypt would serve as the head of the international MB. Most MB chapters outside Egypt were members of the international body and accepted the leadership of the MB in Egypt. This document formalized these ties between Cairo and other branches across the Arab world, handing the Egyptian MB more control and greater access to finances, while making the international branches formally bound to the center.

In the years that followed, this cost the Brotherhood many members, as those who did not wish to be at the mercy of Cairo simply left the group. Then came Iraq's 1990 invasion of Kuwait, which plunged the international Brotherhood into disarray, challenging its administrative and ideological unity. Some members' loyalties lay with Iraq, others' with the suffering in Kuwait. The Brotherhood ended up mildly condemning the invasion while strongly objecting to the presence of U.S. troops in the region and to Arab troops working alongside the West.

As detailed in Chapter 5, the divisions spurred the Kuwaiti Ikhwan to split from the international Tanzeem, a major blow that caused serious financial repercussions as Kuwait had been an important source of funds. This episode demonstrated the difficulties of being an international movement, highlighting how political realities can be different for the citizens of each country.

Due to its secrecy and vague mission, Tanzeem has been among the MB's more contentious issues almost since its creation. "There even seems to be confusion within the Brotherhood itself as to what exactly the international Tanzeem is and what role it plays," Alison Pargeter writes in her 2013 book *The Muslim Brotherhood*. "Whilst some Ikhwani talk about it as if it were an active component of the Brotherhood, part of its transnational identity that is actively directed from Cairo, others dismiss it as little more than a co-ordinating body, with no significant function."[80]

If the decline of Tanzeem started in 1990, the September 11 attacks marked its death. Post-9/11, the Brotherhood sought to downplay its

Islamist image, which was being linked to Al-Qaeda and the horrors of international terrorism. "Suddenly the world began to focus its attentions on the various Islamist movements," writes Pargeter, "and what had until then been considered as domestic opposition groups now came to be viewed by some as part of a global Islamist network that threatened the whole of Western civilisation."[81]

MB leaders sought to give the impression that the Tanzeem was a loose network with no power over decisions at the local level—which soon became a self-fulfilling prophecy. MB member Kamal Helbawy said Tanzeem is merely about "international coordination," while Aboul Fotouh has said Tanzeem existed primarily in the minds of Westerners.[82] Nevertheless, today there's still an informal hierarchy. The salient fact remains that Cairo proved unable to centralize decision-making and coordinate international MB activity, spurring schisms and leading to extremist organizations like Al-Qaeda. The Tanzeem still exists, but makes little impact, according to Aron Lund, former nonresident fellow in the Middle East Program at the Carnegie Endowment:

> Theoretically, the international leadership can overturn decisions taken by the national chapters, but historically, most attempts to intervene in local affairs have ended in splits and defections. The international leadership therefore remains weak and seems to serve mostly as a discussion forum and coordinating body for national groups.[83]

SALAFIST UNITY

Saudi Arabia also had a period of reckoning during the 1990–1991 Gulf War, yet how it resolved it shows the stark contrast between Salafism and the ideology of the Brotherhood. The Sahwa movement originated in the late 1950s and early 1960s, as thousands of Brotherhood members fled Egypt and arrived in the Kingdom. From the start, they saw Wahhabism as problematic. Even so, a cross-pollination of MB ideology and Wahhabist ideas spurred the creation of an Islamic dissent movement, which was dominated by Brotherhood members. Several different strains of Sahwa emerged, but all were inspired by MB teachings, according to Saad Al-Faqih, a Saudi dissident with ties to Al-Qaeda who was heavily influenced by the movement and now heads the Movement for Islamic Reform in Arabia.[84]

It is crucial to note that the religious opinions of important quietist Salafist thinkers in the Kingdom at this time, like Hadith expert Al-Albani, were not popular among the MB-inspired Sahwa. "Those who made him [Al-Albani] their absolute reference are the Sahwa's sworn enemies," said Hegghammer and Lacroix, who called this group neo-Ahl Al-Hadith, in reference to the medieval school that inspired Al-Albani. "The neo-Ahl Al-Hadith's main adversary was the Sahwa. . . .

They would justify this opposition by referring to Al-Albani and his stand on the Muslim Brotherhood."[85]

The neo-Ahl Al-Hadith brought together Al-Albani's views to build a thorough argument against the MB and the Sahwa. In a 1982 pamphlet, a prominent neo-Ahl Al-Hadith disciple argued that because the MB disliked Ulema, did not have any Ulema members, and forbid MB members from attending the courses of Ulema, the MB was largely ignorant of religious knowledge and preferred positions of power to the Sunna.[86]

Similarly, Al-Albani criticized the Brotherhood and the Sahwa for being more interested in politics than in Islam and religious interpretation, and said his priorities were precisely the opposite. "In the present circumstances, the good policy is to stay away from politics,"[87] he would say. This harkens back to Commins's thoughts mentioned earlier in this chapter, of how Wahhabists sought religious purity and understanding while MB-inspired terrorists like Al-Zawahiri and bin Laden were more about vengeance. In a 1977 lecture in Madinah, Al-Albani acknowledged that all Muslims wanted an Islamic state, but disagreed on the best way to get there. Opposing the MB tendency toward violence, he believed this dream could be made real through Da'wa.[88]

As detailed in Chapter 5, many MB and Sahwa figures, like Mohammed Qutb and Abdullah Azzam, were given key posts across academia and the education system, as well as in government ministries. Al-Faqih points to three key developments that further extended the reach and influence of Sahwa in the Kingdom: the Grand Mosque seizure of 1979, the Iranian Revolution that same year, and the Saudi leadership's support for sending Saudi mujahideen to fight the Soviets in Afghanistan in the 1980s.[89] All of these events encouraged the Saudi government to appease and assist Islamists, specifically the Sahwa, in their effort to encourage a conservative society and a greater role for the clergy. Combined with their positions of influence, this deeper government backing enabled their ideas to take deep root within Saudi education and Saudi society. As Sir John Jenkins says, "this diverse regional movement— known as the Islamic Sahwa ('awakening')—came in the 1990s to pose a powerful ideological challenge to existing dispensations [of the Saudi state]."[90]

This explains why many blame the Saudi religious establishment for rampant extremism in the Kingdom from the 1990s through 2010. But the truth, according to Sciences Po scholar Stéphane LaCroix, is that "the consciously totalizing conception of Islam owes more to the thinking of the Muslim Brotherhood than to traditional Wahhabism (or Salafism)."[91]

As explained in Chapter 5, the cooperation between Saudi and Sahwa leaders began to sour with Iraq's 1990 invasion of Kuwait. Hussein annexed the Gulf state, becoming the first Arab nation in modern history to invade another Arab nation without provocation, and the reasoning was that the leader of that state, Kuwait, deserved to be overthrown. The MB supported Hussein's problematic invasion and planned overthrow, which is perhaps unsurprising as it aligned with their revolutionary thinking.

Within Kuwait, people faced food scarcity, restricted movement, mass arrest, summary executions, and torture. Saudi leaders were well aware that Hussein might next make a move for the Kingdom, and they knew their defenses were likely no match for one of the region's best militaries. Strict Wahhabi ideology forbids seeking assistance from non-Muslims, even for self-defense. However, to avoid putting millions of Saudis through the horrors faced by Kuwaitis and to put an end to the suffering of fellow Muslims in a neighboring state, Saudi leaders decided that security and humanity were more pressing than Islamic fidelity. King Fahd invited the U.S. military to deploy on Saudi soil, from which they would then be able to force Hussein's troops to withdraw from Kuwait.

Sahwa scholars, led by Sheikh Salman Al-Awda and Sheikh Safar Al Hawali, accused Saudi leaders of religious hypocrisy for allowing infidel U.S. forces onto Saudi soil. They saw it as an embarrassment for Saudis to require a foreign military for protection. In 1991, Sahwa clerics delivered a twelve-point Letter of Demands, calling for reform, including the creation of an advisory council. Despite the horrors taking place in Kuwait, certain Sahwa and MB leaders continued to support the Iraqi takeover. To Saudi leaders who had welcomed exiled MB members fleeing oppression in Egypt a few decades prior, their support of Saddam Hussein's unjust oppression of fellow Muslims and Gulf citizens marked an act of betrayal. "The former crown prince and later interior minister Nayef bin Abdulaziz bitterly spoke about the Brotherhood's betrayal and began to gradually eliminate the group's concepts from the society," wrote Saudi journalist Mashari Althaydi.[92]

Saudi authorities responded by throwing the Sahwa leaders in jail. But the next year, King Fahd enacted the Basic Law of Governance, which established a sixty-person, royally appointed Shura Council. The council marries the Islamic principle of consultation with the desire for political participation. It can propose new laws, question cabinet members, lead five-year development plans, and review policies before approval. In the years that followed, a number of civil society groups emerged, and the Saudi leadership welcomed many of the Sahwa leaders back into the fold, including Abdulmohsen Al-Awaji, Sheikh Salman Al-Awda, and Sheikh Safar Al-Hawali.

Around this time, Saudi leaders began to fully understand the threat posed by the Brotherhood and the Sahwa movement. Prince Khaled Al-Faisal was among the first to grasp the troubling designs of the Sahwa movement, attacking its theological educational basis when its leaders were at the height of their influence, with many in top positions at universities and schools across the Kingdom. In 2006, Prince Khaled, as governor of the southern province of Assir, spoke about the troubling trend of the Sahwa and the extremist current linked to Al-Qaeda that had been spreading through the Kingdom, particularly within the school curriculum, via MB-linked faculty.

"There is a trend that wants to remove us from our religion, and there is a current that wants to remove us from our lands, both of which are the destruction of our religion, our countries and our societies," he told a 2006 seminar organized by the Saudi education ministry.[93] He went on to explain that together, the Sahwa and the jihadist current represent:

> an extremist movement within Saudi Arabia that wants to keep the country in ignorance, in darkness, and is preventing its natural development. This movement is made of two groups. The first, the genuine mind of darkness that claim that any development is contrary to the teachings of Islam (Jihadis). The second, are the ones that used our religion politically to purposely keep Saudis from properly educating themselves and progressing (MB-inspired Sahwa). . . . These two groups are teaching our children how to become suicide bombers in mind and spirit to detonate themselves. Whereas our children should be taught how to make their minds explode in ingenuity and analytical thinking based on a sound progressive education.[94]

In the years that followed, the Kingdom pushed any remaining MB-linked figures out of academia and key positions in the education system and rid the curriculum of books promoting MB ideology. As highlighted by Prince Khalid, much of this indoctrination was put in place by MB members working in the Saudi education system in the 1950s through the 1980s. The MB sees education as the optimal route to control the thinking and direction of a society, using the classroom as an entry point to indoctrinate children. The lack of tolerance for other faiths or other schools of Islamic thought, to cite just one example, no longer has any place in the Kingdom.

"We have recognized that a comprehensive, modern and open educational system—with new and revised textbooks—is fundamental to the growth and prosperity of our country," Prince Turki Al-Faisal, then Saudi ambassador to the United States, wrote in *USA Today* in 2006. "A thoughtful revision of this system is necessary, and indeed well underway."[95] Saudi leaders—guided by true Salafist principles—have in the past two decades made great strides in eradicating radical, MB-linked teachings from school instruction and ridding the system of incendiary teachers who urged students to violence and agitation.

Further, in the last few years, Sahwa scholars have begun to recognize their errors and repent, and the movement seems to have ended. "I apologise in the name of the Sahwa to the Saudi society for the mistakes that were not related to Islam and for the extreme fatwas," longtime Sahwa cleric Sheikh Ayidh Al-Qarni, who has nineteen million Twitter followers, said on a Saudi talk show in May 2019.[96] The fifty-nine-year-old explained that he had done a great deal of research into Islamic texts and understood Islam much better than when he was a young scholar. "Our religion is a religion of peace, safety and mercy," he said. "I apologize to Saudi society for the mistakes that have contradicted the Qur'an and Sunnah, and contradicted the tolerance of Islam, a moderate religion. I am today supportive of the moderate Islam, open to the world, which has been called for by Crown Prince Mohammed bin Salman."[97]

A few years ago, Jamal Khashoggi explained the Saudi state's response to the Sahwa this way: "In this case," he told me, "the state showed its control and confidence by first releasing the Sahwa leaders after years in prison, slowly forgiving them, and then completely re-integrating them back into the mainstream."[98] In essence, the Salafist state has also solidified its monopoly over religious law. Discussions about theology are acceptable in the Kingdom, to an extent. What is unacceptable is independent Islamic clerics issuing fatwas, which could potentially conflict with the Islamic interpretations of the Ulema. In order to maintain the bond between the state, the ideological descendants of Wahhab, and the majority of citizens who have sworn a *bayah*, only members of the Ulema are able to issue fatwas in Saudi Arabia.

This is why King Abdullah in 2010 issued a royal decree making the Ulema the only body that could legally issue public fatwas. A key reason for this is to ensure that only qualified, truly learned, and non-radical scholars of Islam are able to guide citizens' lives, to ensure their interpretations are accurate and do not encourage suffering. "We must rely only on Prophets and Messengers of all religions who have conveyed the messages given to them by the Creator of these faiths," Mohammed Al-Issa, secretary-general of the Muslim World League, said in 2018. "The religion of God came as a mercy to mankind; it was not revealed to cause their misery and be a reason for wars and calamities."[99]

In short, the view of the Salafi establishment in Saudi Arabia on fatwas prevents scholars (or MB leaders) from calling for random acts of violence or revolution. "By monopolizing fatwa issuance, the state—which ostensibly wanted to protect Saudi society from unqualified or extremist scholars—abolished the 'free market of fatwas' that would have otherwise provided a variety of interpretations and left it to citizens to evaluate each fatwa's value and legitimacy," Abdullah Alaoudh, Senior Fellow at Georgetown University's Prince Alwaleed Bin Talal Center for Christian-Muslim Understanding, wrote for the Carnegie Endowment in April 2018.[100]

In May 2018, Ambassador Bertrand Besancenot, diplomatic advisor to the French government and France's special presidential envoy to the GCC, told me: "The Kingdom is going through a revitalization process that is very much informed by a new awareness about the essence of Salafism—that it offers a moderate, quietist, peaceful form of Islam that stands in stark contrast to the extremist doctrines being espoused by various terrorist organizations."[101]

Now that much of the Kingdom's governance is being overseen by Crown Prince Muhammad bin Salman, this Salafist revitalization is expanding. In October 2017, he promised the Kingdom would return to "what we were before—a country of moderate Islam that is open to all religions and to the world."[102] The social rules being implemented in Saudi Arabia today—for instance, as of June 2018, women have the right to drive—are, according to the crown prince, a reflection of true Islam.

Some may snicker at this remark, but the Islam laid down by the Prophet Mohammed empowered women. In seventh-century Arabia, female infanticide was common. Yet abiding by the word of Allah as expressed in the Quran, the Prophet abolished the practice, calling a girl's birth a "blessing." He gave women the right to own property and inherit. The Prophet instituted that women needed to assent to marriage and had the right to divorce their husbands—an unprecedented move at that time. More than two centuries ago, Sheikh Abdul Wahhab also made clear the importance of women in a true Islamic society. "He who denies the right of a woman in inheritance is an infidel, because he does not believe in all that is in the Qur'an."[103]

This is Salafism. Yet now that women in Saudi Arabia have gained the right to drive and to attend mixed events such as football games or concerts or movies in theaters, the latest propaganda from MB-inspired Al-Qaeda aims to spur a backlash to the crown prince's reforms among conservative Muslims in the Kingdom.[104]

That's because rebellion, violence, and oppression are the MB's bread and butter. The absence of any real vision regarding the Brotherhood's views of Sharia reflects the weakness of its ideology when it comes to governance and jurisprudence. "The traditional Brotherhood model has three primary characteristics that are strictly incompatible with law, order and stability: it is revolutionary, conspiratorial and transnational," writes Hussein Ibish of the Arab Gulf States Institute.[105] From its earliest days, the Brotherhood was not concerned with the precise nature of how an Islamic state was organized, save for the fact that it was built on sharia. It has long been more concerned about vengeance, about ridding the Muslim world of Western influence at any cost rather than embracing true Islam. Focused on settling old scores and community outreach rather than building institutions, the Brotherhood has very little of the institutional understanding needed to run a twenty-first century state.

Few who understand this were surprised that in the days following the horrific 2019 Easter Sunday bombings in Sri Lanka, which killed more than 250 people in the deadliest terrorist attack in the world since 9/11, a clear link was made between the perpetrators and the Muslim Brotherhood. ISIS soon claimed the attack. But their operator on the ground was Zahran Hashim, leader of the Sri Lankan division of Jamaat Al-Tawhid Al-Watania, a little-known extremist group based in Chennai, India, and led by Salman Al-Nadwi, who was mentored by MB scholar Yusuf Al-Qaradawi and has sworn his loyalty to ISIS leader Abu Bakr Al-Baghdadi.[106] Hashim is said to have recently spent some time in Tamil Nadu, likely visiting Al-Nadwi and the Indian leadership of the organization.[107]

As the MB has in recent years shown its true colors again and again, the ideology of the Kingdom has gone in the other direction. Saudi leaders and religious scholars have of late gone so far as to deny that there is such a thing as Wahhabism, which is true. Wahhab was a scholar who returned Islam to the ways in which it had been practiced by its original founders, or the Salaf. So Wahhabism doesn't really exist per se; what exists is Salafism.

And this means that as much as Saudi Salafism is an embrace of the ideas of Sheikh Wahhab, it is also a return to the origins of Islam. As in those days, this "quiet and non-political" Salafism "dictates that we should obey and hear the ruler."[108] Crucially, if some Salafists turn violent and rebellious, it is because "they have been infected by the ideas of the Muslim Brotherhood."[109]

A more robust sense of Salafism's ability to ideologically counter the terrorist agenda of the Muslim Brotherhood is taking hold in the Kingdom. These days, many agree with the former foreign minister of Jordan, who told me in March 2018: "I think Saudi Arabia has a great opportunity to reinvigorate and unite most of the Arab and wider Muslim worlds through a renewed dedication to their basic Salafist principles that have a wide appeal."[110]

In his book *The Superiority of Islam*, Sheikh Abdul Wahhab warned of "the vicissitudes Islam will undergo, and the virtues of those who hold fast to its true principles."[111] In the next chapter, I will bring the dissonance between the Salafism typified by the Saudi state and the so-called Salafism incorrectly ascribed to or claimed by the MB into clear, personal focus. I will detail the life and ideas of the close friend and associate with whom I began this chapter—a man who struggled with being a Muslim Brother while also wanting to be loyal to his native Saudi Arabia, a man who was an ardent Salafist unable to renounce an organization that openly violated the peaceful precepts of his faith.

CHAPTER 9

The Case of Jamal Khashoggi

The tragic case of Jamal Khashoggi, a close friend and colleague of mine for over fifteen years, who was murdered on October 2, 2018, in the Saudi consulate in Istanbul, highlights just how difficult and complicated it is to address the Muslim Brotherhood, particularly from a Saudi standpoint. As just discussed, Saudi Arabians, like the majority of Gulf citizens, are conservative Muslims and Sunnis. This explains why the Kingdom and its neighbors were so welcoming to exiled MB members in the 1950s and 1960s—they were persecuted conservative Sunni Muslims whose beliefs were not at all foreign.

Similarly, we have Jamal Khashoggi, who in his early years as a student and then as a journalist was also a member of the MB. This was during the 1980s and early 1990s, when the Kingdom itself was more open to and accepting of the MB and before the Saudi government and citizens began to appreciate the inherently revolutionary and violent nature of the Brotherhood and grasp the grave threat the group posed to the state. And like the Kingdom, Jamal too came to understand that the MB was not the solution. He still had strong sympathies with the MB, even in his later years, but he generally sided with the Saudi state. For decades, he worked for the Saudi government, as an advisor and media activist. He was a patriot who wanted to have it both ways. However, in his later years, he may have lost his way, to some extent, particularly in regard to cooperating and interacting with adversarial countries to Saudi Arabia, Qatar and Turkey in particular.

But let me be clear: Jamal Khashoggi's horrendous murder was entirely undeserved and absolutely indefensible. It was also wholly inconsistent with the way the Saudi state operates. Jamal was murdered by a group of Saudi agents. When King Salman was personally informed of this macabre incident, he personally stepped in and ordered the jailing of the entire team that was involved in the killing. As of June 2019, five of them, so far, are facing a capital punishment verdict.

Jamal's life, however tragic, might serve as a cautionary tale. He loved his homeland, toiled for years with government officials, and worked to reform, improve, and modernize the Kingdom. Meanwhile he quietly maintained sympathies to an organization that advocated revolution and hoped to upend the state and bring down the monarchy. Those sympathies ultimately proved his undoing. This chapter takes a closer look at his story and his killing and examines what it might mean for the MB, Saudi Arabia, the Gulf, the region, and the world.

A LIFE WELL LIVED

From his earliest days, Jamal Khashoggi was a bundle of contradictions. He was born in October 1958 in the Saudi holy city of Madinah to a family of Turkish origins. His father ran a fabric shop, but his great uncle, Mohammed Khashoggi, had served as a personal physician to the Kingdom's founder, King Abdulaziz. One of his second cousins was the well-known international businessman Adnan Khashoggi.

Jamal studied Islamic theology in his youth, yet also embraced liberal thinking. He attended college in Saudi Arabia and then in the United States, at Indiana State University, and, after earning his graduate degree in political science in 1982, returned home to Jeddah. Within a few years, he had begun working as a reporter, first with the English-language *Saudi Gazette* and the Arabic outlet *Okaz* and later with the London-based Arabic outlets *Al-Sharq Al-Awsat* and *Al-Hayat*.[1]

Those years after the Islamic Revolution in Iran were heady days for political Islam, and Jamal became enamored with Brotherhood thinking, particularly the idea of eliminating Western influence in Arab lands and building a new Islamic society. Delving into MB ideology was mostly an intellectual exercise for Jamal and, as was his contradictory and peace-loving nature, he tried to turn Osama bin Laden away from violence.[2]

Jamal was religious from a young age. He repeatedly told me that he was a "political Salafi." And yet, he was also very involved in the ideology of the Brotherhood and publicly supported the campaign to send aid to the mujahideen in Afghanistan, a cause in which he firmly believed. As a journalist, he was sensitive to the situation in Afghanistan and supported the fighters there. At the same time, he fully and always associated himself with the Saudi state. He was proud of what it had achieved.

So, *Okaz* sent Jamal to cover the war in Afghanistan between the Soviet Union and the Afghan mujahideen, where he sympathized with his Muslim brethren. He also came into contact with the theologians who created Al-Qaeda and its dogmatic strain of Islamism, and he was known to the current Al-Qaeda chief Ayman Al-Zawahiri as a journalist. An infamous photo that ran alongside a 1988 Khashoggi story from Afghanistan shows the young reporter holding a rocket-propelled grenade launcher and smiling alongside mujahideen fighters from across the Arab world. More importantly, he knew well Al-Qaeda's chief Osama bin Laden and Al-Qaeda co-founder, the Palestinian theologian Abdullah Azzam.[3] Of course, it's important to note that at that time, the Afghan mujahideen were backed by the CIA as well as the General Intelligence Presidency (GIP), the Kingdom's main foreign intelligence agency. Thus, Khashoggi's apparent support for bin Laden was in the late 1980s aligned with U.S. and Saudi policy.

Jamal also worked to help his fellow Muslims. Barnett Rubin, a leading expert on Afghanistan and director of the Center for International Cooperation at New York University, recalls Jamal telling him how he once helped a European humanitarian group unload a shipment of aid for Afghan refugees in Peshawar, Pakistan: "One of his Arab Islamist comrades asked him why he was cooperating with the *kuffar* (non-believers)," Rubin wrote for *War on the Rocks* in October 2018.[4] " 'Because these *kuffar* are giving millions of dollars of goods to the Afghan refugees,' he answered. 'Are you?' "

At some point in the 1990s, Jamal stopped going to MB meetings, but he continued to embrace some MB thinking, including its commitment to political Islam and anti-Western rhetoric. It was around this time, when Jamal had distanced himself from the MB and began taking on leadership roles in media ventures and advising certain Saudi officials, that he and I met. We were both American educated and working for the Saudi leadership and became fast friends. Over some two decades, we became quite close. We collaborated and partnered on numerous political and media projects, usually offering a Saudi perspective on regional events, such as a 2013 CNN piece about the conflict in Syria.[5]

As his contradictions became clear, Jamal became much more sensitive to criticism and defensive. Depending on to whom he was speaking— a top Saudi official, a Saudi activist, an Arab official, an American official, or a Western journalist—he would adapt the stance most likely to avoid ruffling his interlocutor's feathers and put him in good stead. He largely lived a "normal" establishment life, working as an editor of *Al Watan* newspaper (which has a senior member of the royal family on its board as chairman) and as the media advisor to Saudi Arabia's ambassador at the time to London and then Washington, DC. Yet when I was working in London and DC and Jamal was there as well, the MB was a secondary issue compared to the other much more pressing things we were dealing with politically. It wasn't seen to possess the level of threat that local governments came to ascribe to it after the Arab revolutions of 2011. So it was a time where one could openly discuss having some sympathies for the MB without it being too verboten or risky.

And so our conversations, which often turned to his struggles, were free and open. He was faithful to his country and his king, but he still felt strong ties to the Brotherhood as well. He realized that you can't be for them one day and then not for them another. He recognized that the "MB is like a virus that gets into your blood," and it is very hard to get rid of. Yet he was always very careful not to criticize the leaders or actions of the group. Yes, he believed the Brotherhood was ultimately the right solution to the problems in the Arab world, yet he also knew that you can't have it both ways. He knew that the Brotherhood was a revolutionary organization and that the established monarchies of Saudi Arabia, Jordan, Morocco, and the Arab Gulf states were entirely unacceptable to them. I pointed out this contradiction often to him, and he admitted it was a contradiction, yet he simply didn't know what to do about it.

These contradictions are endemic to many supporters of the MB. They find it impossible to put their thoughts into perspective when it comes to their relationship to the organization and how that relates to their other loyalties. They say they're for democracy, yet they turn a blind eye to the MB's anti-democratic actions. They say they're against violence, yet they excuse the MB's forays into terrorism. And in the case with Jamal, who operated at the highest levels of political life, this ambivalence caused him to become a threat to himself because he was unable to properly explain what he stood for. No, he was not a threat of any sort to the Saudi state, but his inability to make that clear inevitably made him a prime target on a very unfortunate list of so-called dissidents put together by a certain royal court advisor by the name of Saud Al-Qahtani.

That said, this "middle of the road" approach worked well for Jamal because he was never being deceitful or dishonest. For decades, he held contradictory views: believing at the same time in the freedom and progress of the West and in its problematic, overly permissive society; sympathizing with the MB and even jihadis while also supporting the Saudi monarchy; working as an advisor to Saudi royals while being critical of certain Saudi foreign policy initiatives and supporting the MB actions in Egypt and Libya.

While Jamal eventually renounced his MB membership, he never turned his back on its ideology. In how he handled this, there are signs of what it means to be a "MB member." One doesn't carry a card. One doesn't have to go to meetings or pledge allegiance to any figure or anthem or symbol. So it is a fluid situation, hard to pin down. It is often expressed in a simple sympathy for some of the goals of the organization, or an adherence to some of the dictates of its ideology.

For instance, Jamal had a real passion for taking down all the corrupt Arab governments, especially after 2011, yet he refused to have a conversation about how the MB itself was also corrupt. He would never admit that they were no better, that they too were power-hungry, that they had no real plan. He was never able to be convinced that they were as bad as what they opposed. It was as if it would be too personally and psychologically traumatic to do so. It was as if his support for them was subconscious, existing alongside beliefs that are highly contradictory to what the MB actually stands for. Such was the case with Jamal and is the case with many others.

No, Jamal was not an MB member. Yet, some of his writings, his public support for "ideological thugs," such as Qaradawi, and his tendency to speak from his emotions had ramifications. And I often told him that. The man I knew would never truly support someone as shallow, close minded, racist, and ignorant as Al-Qaradawi. His experience in America, starting at the university in Indiana, had made him enamored of America, of progress, and of humanitarianism. He wanted to live in America, to master English, and to be a member of a society based on freedom and equality, and no true MB member would ever do that. Yet his MB sympathies lingered, deep, in the back of his mind, and he couldn't let them go.

This was Jamal, and it's no secret. As a *New York Times* headline put it shortly after his death, "For Khashoggi, a Tangled Mix of Royal Service and Islamist Sympathies."[6] In his Khashoggi obituary for *The Guardian*, Ian Black wrote of Jamal's "ambivalent status within Saudi society and vis-a-vis the regime: he was too Islamist for secular-minded liberals but too liberal for traditional conservative Wahhabis."[7]

An oversimplification, but broadly accurate. While his embrace of political Islam and patriotism kept him in good standing with Saudi leadership, his liberal mindedness, as well as his MB sympathies, often led to clashes with his patrons, even before the so-called Arab Spring. In 2003, for instance, he was forced to resign as editor-in-chief of *Al-Watan* after just fifty-four days because he had criticized the Saudi Ulema and was therefore seen as too progressive.[8] He began working as media advisor to Prince Turki Al Faisal, and then after four years he returned as *Al-Watan* editor but resigned in 2010 after another controversial editorial.[9]

This became a pattern, with Jamal accepting top positions with Saudi leaders or Saudi-backed news outlets before falling from grace due to his troubling, often critical views. In 2015, Crown Prince Salman became king and Jamal was appointed to run Prince Alwaleed bin Talal's new venture, the Bahrain-based Al-Arab news channel, which was meant to compete with Qatar's Al Jazeera. Instead, it was shut down on the day of its launch after broadcasting an interview with a Bahraini Shia dissident who had openly campaigned for the overthrow of the Bahraini monarchy.[10] We tried our utmost (he had asked for my assistance with Bahraini officials) in the following weeks to convince the Bahraini authorities to lift the ban, but to no success. The ban was never lifted.

A senior Bahrain official summed it up to me when I kept pressing him to intervene with King Hamad: "The problem is that Jamal doesn't think he did anything wrong. The only apology we have received is from HRH Prince Alwaleed to his Majesty and from you to me and others on his behalf."

Jamal had been attacked, vilified, and even abused in the Saudi media for several years, and that came to a head on December 20, 2015, when the Kingdom of Saudi Arabia's Ministry of Foreign Affairs released the following statement inspired and initiated by royal court advisor Al-Qahtani:

> In response to what has been circulated by media reports, an official source at the Ministry of Foreign Affairs has stressed that Jamal Khashoggi; Nawaf Obaid and Anwar Ishqi have nothing to do with any government agency and they don't reflect the viewpoint of the Government of the Kingdom of Saudi Arabia.
>
> "Their views reflect their personal viewpoints," the source said.
>
> Jamal Khashoggi is a Saudi journalist, columnist, author and the general manager and editor-in-chief of Al Arab News Channel which was launched in February 2015 but shut down after just one day.
>
> Nawaf Obaid is a Saudi academic and media commentator. He is a visiting fellow and associate instructor at Harvard University's Belfer Center for Science and International Affairs.
>
> Anwar Ishqi is also a Saudi media commentator and a former officer in the Saudi Arabian military.
>
> All three have been known to comment on Saudi affairs in Arab and international media.[11]

Jamal felt personally and professionally attacked. He took it deeply to heart. He felt betrayed and embarrassed that such a statement had to be made. And it was then that he started to change.

By contrast, while I too took the statement personally, my response was much more measured. I could tell it was very personal in nature. I knew it was someone higher up that had approved the message. And I could tell that the best response was no tangible response at all. The statement felt somewhat inconsequential to me as I had already packed up, moved my family, and left Riyadh in the summer of 2012 after having fallen out with the royal court's chief at the time, Khaled Al-Tuweijri, the person responsible for having brought Qahtani into government by making him his private media secretary. He also started allowing Qahtani to begin bullying and threatening numerous Saudi journalists, including, of course, Jamal. And it's important to note that Qahtani is Al-Tuweijri's creation, not the crown prince's.

Overall, I felt it was just best for Jamal to be quiet, accept it, and move on. But not Jamal. He stirred up a fuss to no end that ultimately hurt him more. And he knew he had to leave the Kingdom. He knew he had no future in Saudi Arabia.

UPRISINGS ALTER THE LANDSCAPE

Due to a wise and courageous intervention by Saudi Arabia's former information minister, Dr. Awad Al Awad, in August 2017, just over a year before his killing, Jamal tweeted his grateful loyalty to Crown Prince

Mohammed bin Salman for being allowed to return to writing his column for *Al Hayat* newspaper, giving media interviews, and tweeting.[12] The very next month, he was banned again, this time for good, for emphatic supportive interviews and tweets toward Al-Qaradawi and the MB. That's when he began writing for the *Washington Post*'s opinion page.

It should be known that Jamal had a limited grasp of written English, and hence when he was at the *Washington Post*, he had two people (not one as the *Post* previously reported) helping him edit and write his pieces, and these two people made his articles much more critical of the Kingdom than Jamal himself would ever have been were he writing in Arabic. The second person was a new acquaintance of Jamal since the time he settled in Washington, DC, and shared strong beliefs and ties to the MB parent organization in Egypt and to senior MB cadres in Qatar. In short, people other than Jamal wrote his *Washington Post* pieces, even though it was those pieces (translated back into Arabic) that inevitably brought the ire of Al-Qahtani and his coterie of thugs to a head.

Jamal's Brotherhood sympathies drove him out of the Kingdom, and it may have been those same sympathies that prodded Qahtani to order that ridiculous rendition that went so terribly and horrifically wrong at the Saudi General Consulate in Istanbul. It could even be said that he became something of an embodiment of the MB during his final year in exile. He was always changing and evolving, impossible to pin down, presenting a nice public face and loyalty to the Saudi leadership, but in private outlining a more nuanced and changing position.

Once he left the Kingdom, Jamal began to be approached by a certain Qatari emissary who claimed he wanted to provide him with the necessary support to do work on Saudi Arabia and its new leadership. This issue became a point of deep contention between him, his lifelong best friend, and me. We pointed out to him that he never attacked Qatar or Turkey in his writings, though they stood to benefit from his critical work on Riyadh. His best friend even correctly countered that Jamal was a Saudi and thus had much more interest in the success of the reform plans in the Kingdom than in their failures.

On that note, it's also important to point out that Jamal ultimately never received money from the Qatari embassy or any other Qatari-affiliated entity before his murder. In fact, I know from my dealings with his family that he had to re-mortgage his house in Virginia to pay for his new small apartment in Turkey. No one on the dole from Doha would have to go to such extremes to raise enough money to get a flat in Istanbul.

But at the same time, he had over the years written about Afghanistan, Syria, Iran, Gulf relations, and more. What kept him, a veteran journalist with a powerful platform, from speaking out against Turkey's jailing of tens of thousands of people, including hundreds of journalists in recent years? He was, after all, planning to marry a Turk and make the country his new home. Perhaps it was his MB sympathies, as well as some promised private support from Doha (that never materialized), that kept him silent on this issue.

His columns during this period suggest that Jamal had begun to feel that Crown Prince Mohammed bin Salman was less a reformer than a dictator. "The brash and abrasive young innovator has not encouraged or permitted any popular debate in Saudi Arabia about the nature of his many changes," he wrote in *The Guardian* in March 2018. "He appears to be moving the country from old-time religious extremism to his own 'You-must-accept-my-reform' extremism, without any consultation."[13]

At the same time, he remained a supporter of the Kingdom until the end. Jamal defended the Saudi leadership with its decision to execute Shia religious leader Nimr Al-Nimr, which was condemned by many international observers. "Nimr called for a foreign power to be in charge in Saudi Arabia, that is major treason," he said, appearing on Al Jazeera's Inside Story.[14] Even in 2018, he still rejected the label of dissident, because his criticisms were inspired by love and hope for his homeland. "I am an independent journalist using his pen for the good of his country," is how he put it.[15]

Jamal simply had a different perspective on reform, on what was best for Saudi Arabia. Karen Elliott House, veteran journalist and author of *On Saudi Arabia: Its People, Past, Religion, Fault Lines—and Future,* shared some of Khashoggi's private statements to her, about the Kingdom, in a November 2018 op-ed in the *Wall Street Journal.* "As my acquaintance Mr. Khashoggi wrote in his last email to me, two months before his death: 'If we spend our valuable reserve and income on unchecked expensive projects that we and the world don't need, that could bankrupt Saudi Arabia and add to its serious problems. . . . We need some form of checks and balance to assure [Prince Mohammed] succeeds.'"[16]

Around the time he wrote that email to House, he wrote supportively of the MB at length in one of his final *Washington Post* columns:

The eradication of the Muslim Brotherhood is nothing less than an abolition of democracy and a guarantee that Arabs will continue living under authoritarian and corrupt regimes. In turn, this will mean the continuation of the causes behind revolution, extremism and refugees—all of which have affected the security of Europe and the rest of the world. Terrorism and the refugee crisis have changed the political mood in the West and brought the extreme right to prominence there. There can be no political reform and democracy in any Arab country without accepting that political Islam is a part of it. A significant number of citizens in any given Arab country will give their vote to Islamic political parties if some form of democracy is allowed. It seems clear then that the only way to prevent political Islam from playing a role in Arab politics is to abolish democracy, which essentially deprives citizens of their basic right to choose their political representatives.

Shafeeq Ghabra, a professor of political science at Kuwait University, explains the problem in this way: "The Arab regimes' war on the Brotherhood does not target the movement alone, but rather targets those who practice politics, who demand freedom and accountability, and all who have a popular base in society."[17]

Unfortunately, Jamal failed to see the contradiction. In essence, he was arguing that marginalizing and eradicating the MB was also a taking away of Arab peoples' voices, of eliminating their chance to have a say in the leadership of their countries. This not only ignores the MB's lengthy history of violence and revolution but also elides the reality that the MB, when it was able to come to power, as in Egypt, soon began to make authoritarian decisions that curbed the voice of the people. Thus, the MB was guilty of doing precisely what Khashoggi said Arab leaders were doing in seeking to destroy the MB. And yet, most likely because of his Islamist sympathies, he saw this reality through rose-colored glasses:

> The coup in Egypt led to the loss of a precious opportunity for Egypt and the entire Arab world. If the democratic process had continued there, the Muslim Brotherhood's political practices could have matured and become more inclusive, and the unimaginable peaceful rotation of power could have become a reality and a precedent to be followed.[18]

None of this is meant to defend what happened to Jamal. The facts presented here are meant to highlight how he, in his last few years, even while remaining a Saudi patriot at heart, embraced an ideology that may have offered hope to many millions of Arabs, but also had a history of violence and revolution, and was viewed, in all Arab Gulf countries but one, as a threat to national security. He told me several times a week that leaving his children and Saudi Arabia to live abroad had been the most difficult decision of his life, and he clearly meant it. But this sentiment often failed to appear in his writings. I kept reminding him, along with his other lifelong friend in Jeddah, that with each new article or interview he did, the gulf between him and his country widened.

QATAR AND TURKEY AFTER KHASHOGGI

One immediate result of the killing is that the partnership between Qatar and Turkey appears to have strengthened, with the two committed to closer cooperation as Ankara becomes Doha's conduit for MB-related policies.

Weeks after the killing, Qatari Emir Sheikh Tamim bin Hamad Al-Thani met with Turkish president Erdogan in Istanbul, where the two reiterated the close bond between their countries and their joint stance against the Saudi-led bloc. "The Turkish nation showed intense efforts to break the blockade and sanctions targeting its Qatari brothers," said Turkey's leader.[19] Sheikh Tamim expressed a desire to boost all forms of cooperation, and the two countries agreed to build an international communication and public relations partnership—a mechanism sure to empower their anti-Saudi stance, particularly as it will involve MB-friendly Al Jazeera and Turkey's state-run news channel, TRT World.[20]

Turkey agreed on the sale of weapons to Qatar and to training the Qatari military—support Doha has sought since the imposition of the blockade in mid-2017. The timing was excellent for Ankara, which is currently staring down its first recession in nearly a decade. "The Middle East's biggest economy is on track to cap this year with two consecutive quarters of contraction—or a technical recession—in a sign the lira's crash in August and the ensuing spike in borrowing costs are proving nearly as damaging for Turkey's prospects as a failed coup attempt did two years ago," *Bloomberg* wrote in December 2018.[21]

Possibly responding to Ankara's economic troubles, Qatar agreed to boost its investments in Turkey's military and industry. And it should be noted that the duo's November 2018 summit came two months after Sheikh Tamim gifted Turkey's leader a lounge-filled Boeing 747-8 worth $400 million as a symbol of his "special love for Erdogan."[22]

In Istanbul, the two leaders also discussed their "need to approach the Trump administration regarding its stance towards the Muslim Brotherhood," sources told *Arab Weekly*, which added:

> Both Doha and Ankara, which are closely connected to the Muslim Brotherhood, are interested in convincing the US administration to be more accommodating towards the Islamist organisation, despite calls in the US Congress to consider it a terrorist group. . . . Doha and Ankara see this dialogue as a means to "counter accusations of terrorism levied against branches of the organisation by Egypt, the UAE and Saudi Arabia," as well as a way "to formulate a new vision for future cooperation between Washington and the organisation."[23]

Turkish sources also told *Arab Weekly* that Ankara and Doha hoped to avoid further escalation with the Kingdom and instead find opportunities for dialogue.[24] This was something of a surprise, as many observers believe Ankara, with its drip-drip-drip of leaks on the Khashoggi killing, had sought to put increasing pressure on Saudi Arabia and possibly weaken the position of the crown prince, undermining the monarchy.

Consider the depiction of Saudi Arabia in Turkey's government-friendly media outlets. Ibrahim Karagul is the editor-in-chief of Turkey's *Yeni Şafak* newspaper, which is widely seen as close to the Turkish government. Karagul is from Turkey's northeast Black Sea region, as are Erdogan and many senior government officials, and his columns are often seen as expressing the concerns of those in power in Ankara. In the past, Karagul has echoed the anti-Western rhetoric of Erdogan, with whom Khashoggi was of course friendly. Karagul has said that the United States is Turkey's real enemy and plans to "divide and destroy Turkey" by working with the PKK and ISIS.[25]

Shortly after the Khashoggi killing, Karagul wrote: "Saudi Arabia and the United Arab Emirates are playing a very dangerous game. They are openly taking steps that will signify the declaration of war against Turkey."[26] Karagul claims the Gulf pair financed the July 2016 coup attempt in Turkey, gave millions of dollars in funding to the Kurdistan Workers' Party, or PKK, which has fought a decades-long insurgency against Ankara, and is now working with the United States and Israel to spark a Turk-Arab war. He called Saudi crown prince Mohammed bin Salman and the UAE's Mohammed bin Zayed the "hitmen of the Western invasion," urging his readers: "Stop these two men! Stop these two crown princes! . . . Arab people, Arab streets, Arab political elites, intelligentsia, journalists, troops, businessmen, and everyone who is in their right mind: stand up! Exile these two traitors from your lands."[27]

Not surprisingly, Turkey views the Khashoggi killing as a hostile act on its soil on the part of Saudi Arabia, a blatant violation of its sovereignty. The tensions between Saudi Arabia and Turkey have increased considerably following the Kingdom's labeling of the MB as a terrorist group in 2014, Mohammed bin Salman's accession to crown prince the following year, and the 2017 blockade against Qatar. Thus, the killing increased already existing tensions and seemed to hand Erdogan the moral high ground in what he views as a regional rivalry with the Kingdom for Muslim leadership.

Yet an article in *The Atlantic* around this time entitled "The Irony of Turkey's Crusade for a Missing Journalist" pointed out that, "under Erdogan, the government has crushed dissent and dismantled the free press."[28] "The rift between Turkey and Saudi Arabia that emerged in the context of Jamal's death at the hands of Saudi agents in Istanbul—while carefully managed by both sides—is emblematic of this broader rivalry," wrote Hamid and Mandeville.

Erdogan's prime objective, with his measured and calculated response to the Khashoggi killing, is surely to pressure Saudi Arabia to lift the blockade on Qatar and weaken the stance of the anti-MB coalition, which also includes the UAE and Egypt, among others. But Turkey has trodden lightly thus far and is likely to continue to do so, according to Soner Cagaptay, director of Turkey research at the Washington Institute for Near East Policy and author of *The New Sultan: Erdogan and the Crisis of Modern Turkey*. "The Turkish president does not want a rift with the Saudis because of his deference for the Saudi king," Cagaptay told *The Atlantic*, "as well as because it will almost certainly rupture the already brittle Turkish economy."[29]

Erdogan's second objective, many agree, is to drive a wedge between King Salman and the crown prince, possibly leading to the latter's demotion. In March 2018, the crown prince referred to Turkey as part of a "triangle of evil," which also includes Iran and Qatar.[30] In his much-anticipated speech to Turkey's parliament on the Khashoggi killing, the

Turkish president spoke with great respect about King Salman, calling him the Custodian of the Two Holy Places, yet never once mentioned Crown Prince Mohammed bin Salman.

Just as Saudi Arabia is ever concerned about the threat of the MB, Turkey's efforts to seek out supporters of the Gulen movement—the group it blames for the July 15, 2016, coup attempt—appear at times all-consuming. No surprise, then, that Ankara's hunt soon became part of its Khashoggi response. A November 2018 NBC News report said that Turkey had told Washington it would be willing to end its efforts to pressure Saudi Arabia if the United States agreed to extradite the Muslim preacher behind the movement, Fethullah Gulen, who has been living in Pennsylvania for more than twenty years and has a green card. "According to four people interviewed by NBC, the White House has instructed the Justice Department, the FBI and the Department of Homeland Security to find a way to remove Fethullah Gulen, a former ally-turned-foe of Turkish President Recep Tayyip Erdogan," read the report.[31] A year later, there has been no further news on the matter, so it may have been merely a hopeful request on the part of Turkey and no more.

Two weeks after the killing, *The Atlantic*'s Krishnadev Calamur argued that the door remained open to a compromise in which the Saudi-led coalition would end the Qatar blockade and allow Turkey, though not Qatar, to continue its support for the MB and its affiliates.[32] By the year's end, however, the Trump administration had repeatedly voiced its strong support for the Saudi leadership—any compromise involving the Qatar blockade or Gulf states relenting in regard to the MB seemed highly unlikely, if not completely off the table. In addition, Riyadh relayed to Turkey that it would not under any circumstances be extraditing Saudi citizens to Turkey to face justice in the Khashoggi murder case.[33]

In December 2018, Riyadh hosted the annual GCC summit, which Qatari Emir Sheikh Tamim did not attend—just as Saudi and Emirati leaders did not attend the previous summit in Kuwait. But Qatar did send representatives, a sign of its continued commitment to the bloc even after the blockade and further tensions related to the Khashoggi killing, and GCC states issued a joint communique expressing their commitment to regional stability and economic integration.[34] Even Mahjoob Zweiri, who is director of the Gulf Studies Center at Qatar University and thus likely to take Qatar's side in the matter, acknowledges the importance of the GCC, highlighting how the United States and the EU see the council as vital to keeping the Gulf secure from Iran.[35]

U.S.-SAUDI RELATIONS AFTER KHASHOGGI

Six weeks after the killing, with the investigation all but concluded, U.S. president Donald Trump issued a statement on U.S.-Saudi relations following the Khashoggi killing. Primarily, he reiterated the strong bond

between the two nations, which goes back to an iconic 1945 meeting between FDR and King Abdulaziz, and highlighted the $450 billion Saudi
Arabia had committed to spend and invest in the United States, including
$110 billion on military equipment.

"The crime against Jamal Khashoggi was a terrible one," Trump wrote.
"We have taken strong action against those already known to have participated in the murder." He went on to say that "representatives of Saudi
Arabia say that Jamal Khashoggi was an 'enemy of the state' and a member of the Muslim Brotherhood." It is more than likely that Khashoggi's
repeated criticisms of the Saudi leadership in the past two years, combined with his plan to move to Istanbul, in close contact with his friend
President Erdogan, could increase Turkey's ability to promote the Islamist
agenda throughout the Arab world. This may have been what spurred
Saudi officials to act. To be clear, this would not make his brutal murder
defensible; it would merely help to explain the thinking behind this terrible rendition gone so wrong by Saudi agents.

Even as a handful of senior Republican U.S. senators pushed President
Trump to take a harder line toward the Kingdom in regard to Jamal's killing, other American institutions understood that the actions of a few Saudis were not the actions of a country or its king. In an internal report, for
instance, an associate vice provost urged the prestigious Massachusetts
Institute of Technology in December 2018 to retain its close ties to Saudi
Arabia in the wake of the killing.[36] Analysts from a number of prominent
think tanks also spoke out in favor of continued close ties with the Kingdom. "Mr. Trump understands the centrality of Riyadh in the effort to
counter a rising Iran and he is rightly unwilling to allow the murder of
Mr. Khashoggi to imperil that strategy," Michael Doran, a senior fellow
at the Hudson Institute, and Tony Badran, a research fellow at the Foundation for Defense of Democracies, wrote in a *New York Times* op-ed in
November 2018.[37]

They went on to explain that if the president listened to his critics and
sanctioned Saudi Arabia or called for the demotion of the crown prince,
this would only weaken the crown prince's position and possibly embolden his enemies and destabilize the Kingdom, undermining U.S. interests. "Punishing the de facto leader of Saudi Arabia will not bring justice
for Mr. Khashoggi," they add, "nor will it make Saudi Arabia a more de-
pendable ally. It will simply diminish the influence of the United States
and embolden its enemies."[38]

Washington did not condone the Khashoggi killing. On the contrary, the
White House took action in response, barring twenty-one Saudi suspects
from entering the United States and imposing sanctions on seventeen Saudis, as per the Magnitsky Human Rights Accountability Act.[39] And the
administration remains open to further measures if more facts come to
light. Several members of the Trump team—including Defense Secretary
James Mattis,[40] White House Senior Advisor, and Trump's son-in-law

Jared Kushner[41]—have come under criticism for their continued support of Saudi Arabia or their unwillingness to directly link the Saudi crown prince to the murder.

But most key figures agree that sanctioning the Crown Prince, or calling for his departure, and significantly damaging U.S.-Saudi relations on the foundation of such unpersuasive evidence would be a bad move. U.S. secretary of state Mike Pompeo supports a strong U.S.-Saudi partnership even after the Khashoggi killing. "Degrading U.S.-Saudi ties would be a grave mistake for the national security of the U.S. and its allies," he argued in a November 2018 *Wall Street Journal* op-ed:

> The kingdom is a powerful force for stability in the Middle East. Saudi Arabia is working to secure Iraq's fragile democracy and keep Baghdad tethered to the West's interests, not Tehran's. Riyadh is helping manage the flood of refugees fleeing Syria's civil war by working with host countries, cooperating closely with Egypt, and establishing stronger ties with Israel. Saudi Arabia has also contributed millions of dollars to the U.S.-led effort to fight Islamic State and other terrorist organizations. Saudi oil production and economic stability are keys to regional prosperity and global energy security.
>
> Is it any coincidence that the people using the Khashoggi murder as a cudgel against President Trump's Saudi Arabia policy are the same people who supported Barack Obama's rapprochement with Iran—a regime that has killed thousands world-wide, including hundreds of Americans, and brutalizes its own people? Where was this echo chamber, where were these avatars of human rights, when Mr. Obama gave the [Iranian] mullahs pallets of cash to carry out their work as the world's largest state sponsor of terrorism? Saudi Arabia, like the U.S.—and unlike these critics—recognizes the immense threat the Islamic Republic of Iran poses to the world. Modern-day Iran is, in Henry Kissinger's term, a cause, not a nation. Its objectives are to spread the Islamic revolution from Tehran to Damascus, to destroy Israel, and to subjugate anyone who refuses to submit, starting with the Iranian people. An emboldened Iran would spread even more death and destruction in the Middle East, spark a regional nuclear-arms race, threaten trade routes, and foment terrorism around the world.[42]

Some analysts, such as Tolga Tanis of Yahoo! News, expected Washington to use the Khashoggi killing to pressure Saudi Arabia to end the blockade of Qatar.[43] That has not come to pass. In her *Wall Street Journal* op-ed, which examines the Trump administration's predominantly friendly response to Saudi Arabia in the wake of the Khashoggi killing, Karen Elliott House described what she sees as "the most persuasive argument for Saudi Arabia's continuing importance to the U.S.," which is that "without the ruling Al-Saud family, things inside the kingdom could get much worse. The House of Saud could be replaced by a version of Islamic State or by chaos of the sort that is engulfing Syria. Either scenario would further destabilize the Middle East."[44]

CONCLUSION

On June 19, 2019, a one-hundred-page report on the killing of Jamal was released by Agnes Callamard, the UN's special rapporteur. In it, she presents an extensive narrative of the events and individuals relevant to the crime and claims to have analyzed the evidence in this narrative on the basis of international human rights law. The killing itself, she says, violated six different international laws, and Saudi Arabia's failure to rigorously investigate the crimes violated four more. She thus calls for other states to take up their responsibility in addressing the murder, for, as she ultimately declares, "Saudi state agents, 15 of them, acted under cover of their official status and used state means to execute Mr. Khashoggi. . . . His killing was the result of elaborate planning involving extensive coordination and significant human and financial resources. It was overseen, planned and endorsed by high-level officials. It was premeditated."[45]

The investigation by the Saudi public prosecutor into the murder of Jamal is ongoing, so not only is it not proper for me to comment on the case in depth but it is also not the purpose of this book. I will say, however, that there is a very troubling discrepancy between what Ms. Callamard learned through her investigation and what I learned through mine. While I have seen a copy of the transcript that the Turkish authorities have shared with a select group of countries and individuals, including Ms. Callamard, there is a critical difference. In her report, Ms. Callamard quotes two Saudi officers discussing what they plan on doing to Jamal once he enters the consulate:

At 13:02, inside the Consulate, Mr. Mutreb and Dr. Tubaigy had a conversation just minutes before Mr. Khashoggi entered. Mr. Mutreb asked whether it will *"be possible to put the trunk in a bag?"* Dr. Tubaigy replied *"No. Too heavy."* He expressed hope that it would *"be easy. Joints will be separated. It is not a problem. The body is heavy. First time I cut on the ground. If we take plastic bags and cut it into pieces, it will be finished. We will wrap each of them."* "Leather bags." There was a reference to cutting skin. Dr. Tubaigny also expressed concerns: *"My direct manager is not aware of what I am doing. There is nobody to protect me."* At the end of the conversation, Mr. Mutreb asked whether *"the sacrificial animal"* has arrived. At 13:13, a voice said "he has arrived." In these recordings heard by the Special Rapporteur, Mr. Khashoggi's name was not mentioned.[46]

I have two things to say in regard to this item in the report. First, I should point out that I am the one that socially introduced Jamal to General Maher Mutreb when Maher was a young bright intelligence officer serving at the Saudi embassy in London during the years 2002–2006. I mention this only to indicate my intimate history with the scene surrounding Jamal and those in the Kingdom who interacted with him. Second, in the original transcript I read, there was no mention of such a discussion between Mutreb and Tubaigy. In fact, I asked the officials in the country that gave me access to the transcript if they had seen this particular part, and they said it was the first they had heard of it. They followed up by inquiring of their Turkish counterparts, and the response was that any more details had now become unavailable.

Further, the Turks have refused—for some unknown reason—to share the recordings of their numerous hours of eavesdropping on the Saudi General Consulate in Istanbul. Instead they have transcribed sections of the recordings into transcript format in order to recreate from the audio what transpired in the consulate when Jamal entered it that fatal day. The hours of audio recorded prior to Jamal entering the consulate have not to my knowledge ever been shared. Yet it's a very small part of that very audio that Ms. Callamard heard and that would be critical to determining if indeed there was a viable premeditated plan to assassinate Jamal or if it was a rendition gone terribly and tragically wrong.

That being said, one can see how Jamal Khashoggi serves as a metaphor or case study on the MB. From the 1980s through 2000, the MB and Jamal were accepted in the Kingdom, as were the pro-Islamist views of Jamal. But in the years after 9/11, as Islamists' tendency toward violence became clear, and particularly after the Arab uprisings, the ground underneath the MB and Jamal began to shift.

A sharp, insightful journalist, Jamal often altered his views to fit the situation, even while appearing to maintain his sympathy with MB ideology. He was about to marry a Turkish woman and live in Istanbul. So is there little wonder that he never condemned Turkey's jailing of hundreds of his journalist colleagues in recent years? Perhaps this oversight was linked to his friendship with President Erdogan and their shared MB sympathies. Combine this with the fact that the MB, which Turkey and Qatar clearly supported, had in recent years revealed its revolutionary tendencies, and it seems inevitable that Jamal would at some point be seen by unworldly and unsophisticated Saudi officials, such as Al-Qahtani, as a national security threat and enemy of the state.

This, again, is not to say he deserved in the least to be murdered. It is merely to say that it is understandable if, in this period of unpredictable regional crises, Saudi security officials came to view Jamal as a problematic figure with questionable loyalties—just as U.S. federal agents might view a Muslim American who had voiced support for the views of MB's theological chief Al-Qaradawi. The way the situation ended was tragic.

Ultimately, what Jamal went through showed me what a maximalist organization the MB is. You cannot be half in and half out. Its vision consumes its believers, and somehow they are able to live with the contradictions. It is like a cult, in a sense. You simply believe, and if there are problems inherent in the belief, you just overlook them, because you are a believer. It is core to your identity. And I kept telling him—the struggle you are going through will destroy you. At one point—and this is a matter of public record—I urged him to publish an article making it clear that he was not a member of the Muslim Brotherhood, that he was loyal to his country, and that he renounced the MB's views. But he told me "no." He said it didn't matter, that "they" wouldn't believe him.

What more can one say? He was one of my closest friends and colleagues for over fifteen years and will be deeply missed. Those who knew and loved him are now left waiting on justice. And in my opinion, justice will eventually be served.

CHAPTER 10

Geostrategic Consequences of the Muslim Brotherhood's Failure

After more than ninety years of existence, the Brotherhood's chances of gaining and holding power in the Middle East have been reduced—more than eight years after the so-called Arab Spring—to near zero. The MB has worn out its welcome in most of the Arab world, which is precisely why in April 2019 the Trump administration announced that it had begun working to designate the Brotherhood a foreign terrorist organization.

The MB's response to its marginalization has been to meddle in the region's various crises. Following several chapters about Brotherhood failures in the various subregions of the Middle East, this chapter breaks down how the Qatar-backed MB has exacerbated the violence and chaos in the region by getting involved in several regional crises, altering the playing field in Syria, Yemen, and Palestine as well as in Iraq, Libya, Jordan, and Egypt, and examines how the MB's role has forced the United States, Saudi Arabia, and its Gulf allies into more difficult positions in the region.

To do so, I will first present each of the key regional crises individually before considering several together, with U.S. involvement, toward the end. Yet none should be considered in a vacuum. Due to complex regional geopolitics, these crises crisscross and are often better understood as part of a regional whole. For example, the Trump administration is expected to have a hard time pushing any reasonable peace plan in the Middle East mainly because Israeli policy and rhetoric have taken a sharp shift to the far right in the past decade-plus, thanks partly to the aggressions of MB-affiliate Hamas, which is backed by Qatar and Turkey. Thus, the blockade on Qatar aims to curb Brotherhood-inspired plans and political projects across the region, as well as help key players move toward a solution to the Israeli-Palestinian conflict. Similarly, the policies of Saudi Arabia and its Arab allies in Syria are as much about negating

Assad in Syria as they are about Iran and its emerging alliance with Russia. In post-Bashir Sudan and mid-2019 Libya, Gulf rivals are global players jockeying for influence. As much as anything, this chapter will aim to separate the strands of an increasingly complicated region before weaving them back together to present a more comprehensive depiction of the geopolitical complexities.

ARAB WORLD'S SLOW-MOTION COLLAPSE

Let us begin with, and later return to, the mother of all regional crises: Syria. As of June 2019, a few months after ISIS had been evicted from its last remaining stronghold in the northeast, the conflict was winding down and global powers were circling to secure their spheres of influence. Assisted by Turkey, Qatar, and Iran, the MB still hoped to wield real influence in the fractured Syrian state.

Perhaps because the MB had been a thorn in the side of his father Hafez thirty years before, Bashar Al-Assad largely blamed the MB for the mass protests that began to pop up in Syria in early 2011. Whether they had been involved or not, Syrian MB leaders spied an opportunity, and the group soon moved to gain political influence in the Syrian National Council and military might among the militias battling the regime (see Chapter 4).

With a significant presence in political opposition groups, in activist outfits, and in many fighting battalions, the MB's reach among those opposing Assad quickly became considerable. The MB's strong funding and appeal in the war's early years likely extended the Syrian conflict, leading to more death and destruction. During this time, hundreds of MB members were able to sneak back into Syria. Since 2017, however, the MB's influence has waned, particularly as the Assad regime has solidified control over most of the country. Post-Morsi, its reputation has fallen, and it is no longer able to recruit as it could before.

Meanwhile, Saudi Arabia and the UAE have worked together to undermine MB influence in the Syrian opposition, both politically and militarily. The United States has backed its Gulf allies, maintaining the position that the Syrian war is deserving of U.S. commitment "as long as Iranian troops are outside Iranian borders," U.S. national security advisor John Bolton said in October 2018.[1] This means that, as of late 2018, U.S. policy in Syria is not about countering ISIS, as it had been for years, but about containing Iran. This includes supporting aligned militias, increased diplomatic efforts, and withholding aid for reconstruction from areas where Iranian forces have been operating. This is covered in greater detail in the Iran section later in this chapter.

In December 2018, the United States had about 2,000 troops in Syria when President Trump suddenly announced that ISIS had been defeated and that U.S. forces would soon withdraw. Defense Secretary James Mattis and the then U.S. special envoy to the anti-ISIS coalition Brett McGurk resigned in the days following the announcement.[2] The withdrawal was soon delayed and then amended, with the United States deciding to leave a force of 400 divided between the mooted northeast safe zone and the southern base at Al-Tanf.[3]

In October 2018, seeking to act as a bulwark against further Iranian aggression, Saudi Arabia handed $100 million to the United States to stabilize Syrian territories formerly held by ISIS but now under the control of U.S.-allied Kurdish militia (the People's Protection Units, or YPG, the military arm of the Syrian Democratic Forces, or SDF).[4] Turkey has long opposed U.S. support for the YPG, which it views as an extension of Kurdish insurgents in Turkey (the Kurdistan Workers' Party, or PKK). Ankara would like to control the proposed buffer zone, aiming to isolate the YPG and expose it to the type of devastating assault that Turkish officials have repeatedly vowed. In January 2019, UAE state minister for foreign affairs Gargash condemned that safe zone plan, arguing that Ankara was conflating Kurdish nationalism with terrorism.[5]

A top former U.S. envoy spied a bigger problem. In the May/June 2019 issue of *Foreign Affairs*, McGurk urged Trump and the United States to reconsider their Syria withdrawal plans. He argued that the U.S. military presence, in holding off any Turkish attack, gave American diplomats the time they needed to secure a deal that could satisfy Turkey and protect the Kurds. "Withdrawing before such an arrangement is in place risks a catastrophe, a Turkish invasion that would lead to massive civilian displacement, fracture the SDF, and create a vacuum in which extremist groups such as ISIS would thrive," McGurk wrote.[6]

Washington, he continued, "should make clear to Ankara that a Turkish attack on the SDF, even after the U.S. withdrawal, will carry serious consequences for the U.S.-Turkish relationship."[7] With assistance from Saudi Arabia, UAE military advisors have helped prepare PKK and YPG officials for a possible Turkish assault.[8] As of April 2019, Ankara had reportedly begun reaching out to Bashar Al-Assad—whose relations with Erdogan had been ice-cold since the war began—to negotiate a plan for northeast Syria and the Kurds. Syrian and Turkish military and intelligence officials began meeting soon after this, and Al-Assad had expressed his willingness to meet Erdogan, according to Mehmet Yuva, a Syrian academic at the University of Damascus.[9]

That month was a fateful one for the post-Arab Spring hangover that continues to reverberate and further destabilize the region. In Africa, long-ruling presidents Abdelaziz Bouteflika of Algeria and Omar Al-Bashir of Sudan were forced out of office just as General Khalifa Haftar's Libyan National Army launched a full assault on the UN-backed MB-linked government in Tripoli. Meanwhile, over in Washington, the Trump administration, as mentioned, announced that it had begun working to designate the Brotherhood a foreign terrorist organization, a move that, if completed, would have a massive impact on the group's operations, on the policies of Qatar and Turkey, and on relations across the Gulf and the Middle East.

Largely incapacitated since a 2013 stroke, Bouteflika, who was elected president in 1999 and helped stabilize Algeria after years of civil war, resigned after weeks of protests calling for the end of his regime. After as many as 200,000 people died in the conflict, Bouteflika had restored peace and oversaw an average of 5 percent annual economic growth for a decade and a half. Lawmakers made a few constitutional changes during the Arab upheavals of 2011, handing greater rights to minorities, for instance. But his regime was ultimately undone by the collapse in the price of oil and the resulting financial crisis, analysts largely agree.

In late 2018, the head of Algeria's MB affiliate, the Movement of Society for Peace, also known as Hamas, had warned about the collapse of state institutions.[10] Bouteflika's departure, which was followed by weeks of protests calling for all members of the ruling elite to step down, opened the door again to the country's Islamists; it was their rise that spurred the civil war nearly thirty years ago. "His political demise will deepen uncertainty in the North African OPEC member," wrote *Bloomberg*. "With his departure, a longstanding North African bulwark against terrorism and illegal migration to Europe enters uncharted territory."[11]

Similarly, Al-Bashir was ousted that same month by the Sudanese military following months of protests. Two days later, as protests continued, the military announced that Al-Bashir's National Congress Party would be barred from the transitional government.[12] Al-Bashir had initially come to power in 1989 thanks in part to his ideologue Hassan Al-Turabi, who had been the leader of Sudan's MB affiliate when the group was dissolved in 1969.[13] Al-Turabi had argued that Islamism would sweep away all differences and unite the country.[14] That, of course, did not happen, and Sudan faced a twenty-year civil war that led to the horrific violence in Darfur, in 2007, and the creation of South Sudan four years later. Meanwhile, Al-Turabi made Sudan a safe haven for jihadists, hosting Osama bin Laden and Ayman Al-Zawahiri in the early 1990s.[15]

In recent years, Sudan has been one of the few regional governments to maintain good relations with both Turkey and Gulf states like Saudi Arabia and the UAE. Turkey, which had invested millions in Sudan and built up strong relations with the MB-linked Islamist regime, lost an ally with the end of Al-Bashir's reign. In the days after the coup, pro-government media outlets in Turkey went so far as to claim that Saudi Arabia was behind the coup.[16] This was of course untrue and served mainly to highlight how the regime had encouraged MB-linked Islamist actors at home and abroad. "If removing Al-Bashir from power was like winning a battle, then winning the war will be the elimination of the remnants of a regime that enabled the Muslim Brotherhood, in all its hues and outer cloaks, to infiltrate sensitive positions in the Sudanese state, especially related to education, culture and security," Khairallah Khairallah, Lebanese analyst and former foreign editor for Beirut-based Arabic news outlet *Annahar*, wrote for *Arab Weekly*.[17]

Though Al-Bashir had sided with Iran for years, he had recently shifted his regional stance. In 2016, Sudan contributed 1,000 soldiers to the Saudi-led fight in Yemen. That troop contribution soon grew and spurred some $3.6 billion in Sudan investments from the Kingdom and the UAE.[18] By early 2019, some 14,000 Sudanese soldiers were fighting with the Saudi-led coalition in Yemen. Days after Al-Bashir's overthrow, Sudanese officials confirmed that the troops would remain in Yemen[19] and Saudi Arabia, and the UAE announced a $3 billion aid package for Sudan, including a $500 million cash infusion, in an effort to help stabilize the country and its troubled currency.[20] Saudi Arabia and the UAE appeared to have friends in high places: the head of the transitional military council, Lieutenant General Abdel Fattah Al-Burhan, commanded Sudanese troops in Yemen that helped protect Emirati forces, while his deputy also commanded forces in Yemen and is seen as an ally of the Kingdom and the UAE.[21] In May 2019, a month after Al-Bashir's overthrow, the Sudanese army and protest leaders agreed to a three-year transition period to install a civilian government.[22]

Meanwhile, after victories over Islamist militias in Derna and Benghazi, General Hafter launched a major assault on Tripoli in early April 2019, reinvigorating Libya's civil war in its ninth year.[23] Much like Sudan, an array of players is fighting for influence amid the continuing violence in post-Qaddafi Libya (see Chapter 2). Doha has funded Turkey's arms shipments to the MB-linked Libya Dawn coalition based in Tripoli, in direct violation of a UN embargo. In May, General Haftar's army said it had downed a reconnaissance drone in Libya's Jufra region that it been supplied by Turkey to armed forces loyal to the Tripoli-based government.[24] Libyan analyst Mohamed Eljarh agreed, speculating that the drones had likely been a gift from Erdogan.[25]

Saudi Arabia, the UAE, Egypt, France, and Russia have been supporting the army of General Haftar, who met with King Salman in Riyadh just days before launching his Tripoli assault. The United States has also lined up against the Islamists, possibly thanks to the lobbying efforts of Saudi and Egyptian leaders.[26] Days after Haftar began his assault, President Trump said that he had spoken with Haftar and supported his efforts to fight terrorism.[27] The UN recognizes the Tripoli-based government, which came to power after denying the 2014 election results and maintains close ties to Turkey and Qatar.[28] "With no swift victory in sight in the battle for Tripoli, Libya risks another round of protracted war that could be aggravated by the fact that it is as much a domestic fight as it is a multi-layered proxy war," James M. Dorsey, senior fellow at Singapore's S. Rajaratnam School of International Studies, wrote a few weeks after Haftar began his assault.[29]

One group playing a key role in Libya is the followers of Rabee Al-Madkhali, an octogenarian Salafist scholar from Saudi Arabia. The movement gained ground in the Gulf and in Egypt toward the end of the twentieth century, in part as a response to the MB. Echoing the theology of Sheikh Abdul Wahhab, the main tenant of the movement is absolute loyalty to a country's Muslim leader, even if the leader has committed injustice against his people.[30] Qaddafi initially invited Madkhalis to Libya in the 1990s to ward off an Islamist threat, and the movement has since grown, with support from the Kingdom.

As of mid-2019, Madkhali units were fighting within Haftar's army, while, on the opposing side, Madkhalis controlled much of the security sector for the Tripoli-based government. The movement also controlled more mosques in Libya than any other group, and ran dozens of schools, according to Libyan doctoral researcher Bashir Al-Zawwawi.[31] Makdhali clerics across the country generally speak out against terrorism, urge Libyans to support Haftar and his Libyan National Army, and oppose the MB and other Islamists. "As the leadership in Riyadh and Abu Dhabi seek to stifle political activism throughout the Maghreb, the quietist Salafists across North Africa will prove to be useful allies against the backdrop of Muslim Brotherhood activities throughout the region," Giorgio Cafiero and Theodore Karasik wrote for *Gulf State Analytics* in early 2019.[32]

These proxy conflicts, in Egypt, Libya, Syria, and Sudan, regularly ripple across the region. In April 2019, for instance, Turkish authorities in Istanbul arrested two men who, according to an unnamed Turkish official, had confessed to spying for the UAE.[33] The report added that authorities thought they might be linked to the death of Jamal Khashoggi, the previous October, as one of the men had arrived soon after his murder.[34] Two weeks after their arrest, when a prison guard found one of the men dead in his cell, Turkish authorities revealed that the men were Palestinians, not Emirati, as some reports had suggested, and offered more details. "The two men were detained earlier this month and told the police that they were asked by UAE authorities," said a *Bloomberg* report, "to spy on members of the Muslim Brotherhood and Hamas, the Palestinian group that controls the Gaza Strip, according to a senior Turkish official who asked not to be identified because details of the probe haven't been made public."[35] Turkey's state broadcaster TRT added that the man who had died, Zaki Hasan Mubarak, was a fifty-five-year-old retired major general and senior intelligence official.[36]

But that was just one side of the story. In an interview the next day, Mubarak's son Youssef said his father was a political science professor who had gone to Istanbul looking for work.[37] He also said his father's lawyer had told the family that Mubarak's trial had been scheduled to start that week and that his father would likely be released soon. "Why would he commit suicide then?" Youssef said in an interview with Al Arabiya, calling for an international investigation into his father's death.

"He has become a scapegoat of a political struggle and Turkey is using him to cover its failures."[38]

Two weeks later, Mubarak's family received his body, which had been shipped from Turkey. His brother told Al Arabiya that an autopsy, which could help determine the cause of death, was likely impossible because the body cavity had been emptied.[39] "It is impossible to dissect the body again because there is nothing left inside, the body is completely empty," said Zakaria Mubarak, adding that the body showed signs of torture. "I did not even recognize my brother," he added. "They performed dissection throughout his body, even his tongue had been removed and replaced with cotton."[40]

Without further information, it is impossible to ascertain whether the men were everyday Palestinians in Istanbul looking for work, as the son argued, or did have some connection to the UAE and the regional MB divide, as Turkish officials said. One possibility is that their arrest was a response to the detention, a few days before, of two Turkish restaurant workers by the forces of General Haftar in Libya. Volkan Altinok and Mehmet Demir were accused by Haftar authorities of spying and working as foreign mercenaries.[41] Thus, the arrest of the Palestinian men in Istanbul, charged with spying for the UAE, could have been a tit-for-tat response. Whatever the realities behind these successive detentions in Libya and Turkey, this incident makes clear that the MB-focused rivalry between the Saudi-led Arab bloc and the Qatar/Turkish partnership continues to expand and evolve.

The United States appeared to firmly choose its side at the end of April 2019, when *The New York Times* broke the story that, following a meeting earlier that month with Egyptian president El-Sisi, President Trump decided to designate the MB a foreign terrorist organization.[42] "The president has consulted with his national security team and leaders in the region who share his concern, and this designation is working its way through the internal process," said White House press secretary Sarah Huckabee Sanders.[43] This may have been in part a response to the Kingdom's greater commitment to the United States in recent years. From 2009 to 2013, Saudi Arabia represented less than 5 percent of international U.S. arms sales, according to the Stockholm International Peace Research Institute. From 2014 to 2018, however, Saudi Arabia received more than 22 percent of U.S. arms exports, a more than fourfold increase that means billions of dollars and thousands of jobs for U.S. defense industries.[44]

Washington designating the MB a terrorist group would mean U.S. sanctions on MB-linked groups and their numerous members worldwide, including travel and business restrictions against people and businesses with Brotherhood links. National Security Advisor John Bolton and Secretary of State Mike Pompeo were said to be staunch supporters of the move, while many in the Pentagon and among national security and diplomatic corps were looking for an alternative move, according to the *Times* report.[45] The vast majority of Brotherhood experts see designating the MB as problematic at best, largely because it is not a single body but rather a loosely affiliated global network of political parties, national groups, and religious organizations.[46] Government lawyers have pointed out that the MB does not meet the legal criteria for a terrorist designation and that implementing it would be all but impossible.[47] What, many wonder, might happen to the likes of Tunisia's Ennahda party, which is affiliated with the MB but has run a coalition government and never been directly tied to radical violence? And what would become of U.S. military partnerships with Turkey and Qatar, both of which are strong MB supporters?

Some analysts fear that designating the MB could enable the region's autocrats and assist legitimate terrorist groups like ISIS and Al-Qaeda. Andrew Miller, a former State Department official now at the Project on Middle East Democracy, said designating the MB "would undercut the strength of actual designations against terrorist groups."[48] Others worry that the designation would undermine U.S. relations with the Muslim world. Yasin Aktay, a Turkish columnist known to be close to President Erdogan, argued that the designation would be a blow to U.S. credibility: "Such a decision by the U.S. carries the risk of being perceived as a total declaration of war against not only this organization but Islam," he wrote in May 2019.[49] Whatever the merits of the move, designating the MB as a whole could lead to more problems than solutions, as explained by Robin Simcox, the Margaret Thatcher Fellow at the Heritage Foundation:

> Labeling the group a terrorist organization would be a tricky needle to thread. For starters, here in the U.S., the government has, unfortunately, chosen to engage with Muslim Brotherhood legacy groups like the Council on American-Islamic Relations. Even the Trump administration has done so. Overseas, the U.S. is forced to engage Muslim Brotherhood-linked groups because they are part of various governments. Labeling the group a terrorist organization could, for instance, end up including President Recep Tayyip Erdogan's Justice and Development Party in Turkey, Ennahda in Tunisia, parts of the Kuwaiti National Assembly, and the ruling Justice and Development Party in Morocco. These parties may in fact be Islamist authoritarians. Some have even facilitated terrorist activities (for example, Erdogan initially supported elements of Al-Qaeda fighting against Syrian dictator Bashar Assad). Their ideology must certainly be challenged, and democratic alternatives carefully promoted. But it would be a bridge too far, politically, to call them terrorist groups.[50]

Hussein Ibish of the Arab Gulf States Institute sees the MB as a sort of gateway drug to terrorism. "If only one in 10 Brotherhood members graduates to Al-Qaeda, that is one too many," he wrote for *The National* in May 2019, weighing the U.S. designation. "The group's ideology is still the fount of many of the basic ideas and aims, such as the restoration of a caliphate, that animate the most violent Sunni extremists."[51]

Rather than blacklisting the entire octopus-like organization, Simcox, Ibish, and other analysts recommend designating violent MB affiliates and offshoots. The United States has in fact been doing this for some time. The State Department designated MB-affiliated Hamas a terrorist group in 1997, and in January 2018 labeled two MB offshoots in Egypt, Liwa Al-Thawra, and Harakat Sawa'd Misr, as specially designated global terrorists.[52] This label enables the Treasury Department to freeze and block their assets, alongside additional sanctions, but it is less far-reaching than a foreign terrorist organization designation.

In a series of May 2019 tweets, Jonathan Schanzer, senior vice president of research at the Foundation for Defense of Democracies, advocated a similar approach to designating the MB affiliates as terrorist groups:

> There are MB offshoots in places like Libya and Yemen that almost certainly meet criteria. Designate them ASAP. Then keep looking for other MB nodes that contribute to or finance violence. It's what we should be doing, anyway.[53] I'm hearing from friends on the Hill that opponents of the MB think targeting MB branches instead of the entire network is a cop out. What they should understand is that step-by-step approach doesn't preclude a broad designation. It actually helps us get there, if facts support.[54]

However U.S. policy plays out, this move on the part of the White House is a clear sign that more moderate voices on the MB, like former defense secretary James Mattis and former secretary of state Rex Tillerson, have lost out to those who advocate stronger measures. This list includes Bolton and Pompeo, who called for the MB to be designated in 2015, when he was a Congressman. Victoria Coates, senior director of Middle East policy on the National Security Council, which is leading an interagency process to explore the move, is also in favor of designating the MB.[55] "Some advisers to Mr. Trump have for years viewed the Brotherhood as a radical faction that is secretly infiltrating the United States to promote extremist Islamic law. They see the proposed terrorist designation as an opportunity to finally take action against the movement," said *The New York Times.*[56]

This marks a major policy shift in Washington, particularly as this group of officials also seems to support greater alignment with the Kingdom and a more hawkish stance toward Iran. Indeed, earlier in April, Pompeo pushed through a terrorist designation for the IRGC. And within a week of the White House announcement on the MB came word that the United States had dispatched Patriot missiles and a warship to the Gulf in response to a threat from Iran.[57]

GULF SECURITY UNDER THREAT

In the Gulf, it is not only Iran that has been meddlesome and problematic of late. As already heavily documented, Qatar's desire to wield outsized influence and an over-inflated sense of Islamic importance has resulted in its decades-long support for the Brotherhood. In the wake of the so-called Arab Spring, this marriage has put Doha in real trouble and thrown Gulf relations into crisis since the imposition of the blockade in mid-2017 (see Chapter 7).

Meanwhile, Qatar's Gulf neighbors have put their MB issues in order (see Chapter 5 for more details), whereas Doha has allowed the MB to infiltrate its government, its academic system, and its media arm, Al Jazeera, and refused to change its ways despite more than five years of pressure from Saudi Arabia, its Arab Gulf allies, and Egypt. Beyond its borders, Qatar's support for the MB often determines foreign policy, and much of its international spending is about supporting MB affiliates. As laid out in Chapter 4, Qatar coordinated with the Syrian MB to push aside a coalition figure who favored negotiations with the Assad regime, instead appointing Brotherhood figure Ghassan Hito as head of Syria's government-in-exile—a move that may have significantly extended the conflict, increasing bloodshed.

Troubling as that may seem, Qatar's backing of Hamas, with the help of its ally, Turkey, is much worse. Qatar's billions in aid over the past dozen years has enabled the MB-affiliated terrorist group to continue to remain in power in Gaza, dividing the Palestinian territories, boosting the death toll, and bringing progress toward peace to a halt. Hamas continues to support armed struggle against Israel, though it no longer calls for Israel's destruction and has expressed its willingness to agree to a state within the 1967 borders. That doesn't mean Hamas has gone soft. On the contrary, the group still refuses to participate in politics and exacerbates tensions by frequently attacking Israel, with missile barrages and incendiary balloons sent from Gaza into Israel, often claiming self-defense.[58]

But its newest tactic is its most monstrous: Hamas has begun organizing protests and mixing its attackers in with protesters, as in the deadly May 2018 riots at the Gaza border fence.[59] As a result of its so-called March of Return strategy, detailed in Chapter 4, every day Palestinians are now in danger of being killed or linked to terrorism, or both, merely for taking part in what they had been told would be a simple protest along the Gaza border with Israel. In reality, the demonstrations are part of Hamas's scheme to pump up the death toll in an effort to increase international sympathy for their cause.[60]

Even a Palestinian Authority official called the protest organizers "frauds who send women, children, and youths to their deaths."[61] Here's how James Phillips, senior research fellow on the Middle East at the Heritage Foundation, described Hamas's tactics:

As part of its "Great March of Return" propaganda offensive that began in March, Hamas has mobilized Palestinian civilians as human shields to hide systematic efforts to dismantle the border fence and stage a mass infiltration of Israel that could threaten thousands of Israeli civilians along the border. Hamas literally has used smoke and mirrors to disguise its assault on the border, which has included the use of firearms, explosive devices, Molotov cocktails, firebomb kites, and incendiary balloons.[62]

The result is a vicious cycle: Hamas attacks push Israel to take a more hawkish stance, which is soon backed by the United States, which makes Hamas see violence as the only solution. Peace hasn't seemed this distant in decades, thanks to Hamas. What may surprise some is that as Israel has taken a tougher line—a stance backed by the Trump administration's decision to move the U.S. embassy to Jerusalem—Hamas's popularity has ticked up. The White House has been planning to release a Middle East peace plan, but neither the Palestinian Authority nor Hamas is willing to engage with Washington following the embassy move and it's not clear when that might change.

As an MB affiliate, Hamas is a maximalist organization that demands complete allegiance to even its most questionable and troubling policies. Of course, it is reasonable that one would sympathize with the suffering of Palestinians within the Gaza Strip (see Israeli actions and policies detailed in Chapter 4). But there's a vast gulf between having sympathy and perhaps actively working to move key players toward peace and stability, and taking a blowtorch to the situation with missile attacks and disguising terrorists as civilian protesters to beef up the death toll. The most obvious result of this policy is a more hawkish Israel and a more distant peace. Israeli officials like Prime Minister Binyamin Netanyahu are no longer even discussing Palestinian statehood.[63]

"The best proof of the Muslim Brotherhood's incompetence is what's happening in the Gaza Strip," Lebanese analyst Khairallah Khairallah wrote in April 2019. "Hamas captured the Strip in June 2007 and has no intention of relinquishing power despite the numerous disasters it brought onto the besieged people of Gaza. Hamas has done nothing besides serving Israel's political interests by burying the Palestinian national project."[64]

Of course, Hamas is not solely responsible for this policy. Despite Israel's blockade of Gaza, in place since 2007, and the evisceration of its economy, Hamas will not be leaving the scene anytime soon because of backing from foreign groups. Hamas's actions in recent years have driven away the support of most every Muslim country—except, that is, the region's primary so-called "resistance" actors: Qatar, its ally Turkey, and their emerging friend, Iran. Tehran has been giving Hamas an annual $70 million in aid, along with $30 million given to Islamic Jihad, for years.[65] Unsurprisingly, ties between the two have improved since Hamas's regional marginalization began in spring 2018.[66] Security Studies Group's senior vice president David Reaboi wrote about Qatar's extensive support for Hamas in May 2019: "The Gulf emirate bankrolls the group's massive communications support network, including the institutions, media outlets and influencers that comprise most of anti-Israel activism globally."[67]

As many as a dozen Hamas military leaders live in perfect safety in Turkey, where President Erdogan has repeatedly asserted that Hamas is not a terrorist group, as labeled by the United States and its allies, but a political party.[68] An investigation by Israeli security services, Shin Beth, found that a company set up by Hamas in Turkey had collected and laundered millions of dollars donated to Hamas, by people in Turkey and other countries, before sending it to Gaza.[69] Another Turkish firm, owned by a retired Turkish general named Adnan Tanriverdi who in late 2018 was named an advisor to Erdogan, has also helped finance Hamas and even given Hamas military leaders access to major weapons expos.[70]

But the leading Hamas supporter is Qatar, which handed the group more than $1.1 billion from 2012 to 2018.[71] Qatar has been propping up Hamas since an initial $250 million payment in 2008, paying in recent years to keep the lights on in Gaza as well as the salaries of Hamas terrorists.[72] In March 2019, in a surprise move, Doha said that it would no longer finance Hamas and would instead put its aid toward reconstruction projects.[73] This was likely just a feint, particularly as it came just a week after Qatar's ambassador to Gaza met Hamas's leader in Gaza.[74] And even if Qatar has put an end to its direct payments to Hamas, this would in all likelihood just mean that it had begun diverting its Hamas financing through Turkey, with which it has signed billions of dollars' worth of deals across several industries in the last few years (see Chapter 6).

Israel is well aware of these connections, of how Qatar helps Turkey help Hamas in Gaza. In May 2019, in response to missile fire, Israel Defense Forces bombed a building that hosted the Gaza offices of Turkey's state-run Anadolu news agency.[75] The IDF said the building held Hamas military intelligence and security offices. Jonathan Schanzer of the Foundation for Defense of Democracies wondered if Turkey were somehow involved:

> If Israel is correct that terror activity was taking place in this building, it raises important questions: Did Anadolu know about it? Was the state-owned Turkish news agency involved in any way? . . . Turkey is a known and self-described supporter of Hamas. Many Hamas operatives and fundraisers are actually based in Turkey. Reports suggest that Turkey is helping Hamas build military capacity in Lebanon. How hard is it to do so in Gaza?[76]

This is precisely why making any progress toward Middle East peace is not just about pushing Israel and the Palestinians toward a deal. It is also about Qatar and its allies. That trio of Hamas enablers is equally responsible for the raging animosity within Israel and the Palestinian territories as of mid-2019. So, the problem of Hamas is as much a Qatar issue as it is an Israeli one. The more the Israelis continue their hawkish policies toward Gaza, the longer Hamas will be around, getting funded by Qatar and its allies.

Of course, Saudi Arabia, Egypt, and their respective Arab allies have repeatedly urged Doha to stop funding Hamas, to no avail, which is one of the reasons for their blockade on Qatar.[77] Truce talks between Hamas and Israel have been off and on, prodding Hamas leader Ismail Haniyeh to say in August 2018 that the end of the blockade is "around the corner."[78] Whether the Gaza blockade stays in place or ends, Qatar-backed Hamas appears set to continue to terrorize Israel and exacerbate tensions and hostilities for years to come.

It goes without saying that the United States is always going to be in Israel's corner, and, in March 2019, President Trump officially recognized the Golan Heights, which Syria views as occupied, as Israeli territory. Israel seized the highlands along the border in the 1967 Six-Day War. Turkey and Iran, as well as Russia, soon condemned the move, which seemed further evidence of Israeli and American unwillingness to offer carrots and encourage peace talks.[79] The United States appears ready to stand fully behind Israel without any push toward peace, as long as Hamas remains committed to terrorism.

Of course, there will never be any real movement toward a resolution without a drastic change in Israeli policy. Yet until Qatar and its allies, Turkey and Iran, stop funding the terrorism of Hamas, Israel has little reason to soften its stance. One feeds into the other, and it's clear that turning off the Qatari spigot to Hamas is crucial to finding a way toward a sustainable resolution.

In that regard, the Kingdom should continue to work with the United States and its Gulf allies to undermine Hamas and support the Palestinian Authority, looking to ultimately bring both sides—a non-MB-linked Palestinian leadership and Israel—to the negotiating table. Meanwhile, Saudi leaders could repeat their demand that Qatar halt payments to Hamas, including any made via Turkey, and remain ready to call for talks and lay out an updated peace plan when the time is right.

Meanwhile, in Yemen, the Saudi-led coalition and Qatar are in rare alignment against the Houthi rebels. MB-linked Al-Islah has long been a social and political force. Many leading Yemeni politicians and military figures are al-Islah members or allies. In 2017, Yemeni president Abdrabbuh Mansur Hadi appointed Ali Mohsen Al-Ahmar, an Al-Islah leader, as deputy president, and Al-Islah ally Abdul-Aziz Al-Maflahi as governor of Aden. The UAE condemned these moves.[80] But they may not have been Hadi's idea. Sanaa-based Yemeni journalist Nasser Arabyee, who has written for the Carnegie Endowment, believes the MB has been pressuring Hadi to do its bidding, in return for continued Islamist support.[81] The MB oversees some forty militias across the country, which have allied with AQAP in an effort to defeat the Houthis, according to Arabyee.[82]

Al-Islah has been involved in the war from the start, backed by Qatar and Saudi Arabia. Riyadh views Al-Islah as a tool to help unite Sunni military forces against the Iran-backed Houthis and agreed to work with

Al-Islah only once the group vowed to sever all ties with the MB and Al-Qaeda. The UAE has been supporting the Southern Transitional Council's so-called Security Belt, which has launched anti-terror operations against Al-Islah—though both are fighting the Houthis. In October 2017, STC authorities arrested a handful of Al-Islah militants and seized C4 explosives and rocket-propelled grenades.[83]

That same month, an Aden police officer said Qatar was encouraging al-Islah fighters to attack the UAE-backed forces.[84] This might explain why two years before, in December 2015, the UAE hired mercenaries to kill local Al-Islah leader Anssaf Ali Mayo (the plot failed).[85] In 2016, several Al-Islah officials turned up dead. "There is a widespread belief on the ground that the UAE is behind the assassination of Al-Islah officials and activists," Elisabeth Kendall, a Yemen scholar at the University of Oxford, told *Buzzfeed News*.[86]

By late 2017, the Qatar-UAE dispute over Al-Islah was starting to undermine the Saudi-led coalition's efforts to push back the Houthis and restore Yemen's government. So, in December, Sheikh Mohammad bin Zayed and Crown Prince Mohammad bin Salman met the leader of Al-Islah, Mohammad Al-Yadoumi, in Riyadh.[87] Soon after, Al-Yadoumi de-linked Al-Islah from the MB, telling Asharq Al-Awsat that the party had no links to the group and that it fully supported the Saudi-led coalition against the Houthis. These tensions are still playing out as of mid-2019. That April, Saudi Arabia and the UAE announced $200 million in aid for Yemen, providing food, medicine, and other necessary supplies for the people of the war-torn country during the holy month of Ramadan.[88] The next month, Houthi rebels began withdrawing from three key Red Sea ports, as per an agreement brokered by the UN in Sweden the previous December. The UK's *Independent* called it a "major breakthrough" that could lead to the end of the war.[89]

Finally, in April 2019, the chief of Qatari armed forces announced that the Qatari military had performed joint exercises in Doha not just with U.S. forces, stationed at Al-Udeid, but with Turkish troops as well.[90] This was a clear reminder that Turkish troops have remained in Qatar since the imposition of the blockade, which was accompanied by a list of demands that included shutting down the Turkish base and ceasing all military co-operation with Turkey within Qatar.[91]

All of these oppositional policies, in Yemen and Gaza, within the Gulf, and regarding the MB, have opened a vast division in the Gulf, which is underscored by the June 2017 blockade. Two years later, the crisis shows little sign of ending, as Doha continues to underestimate the problematic nature of the MB and refuses to meet the trio's demands. If supporting the MB has indeed become second nature to Qatar, part of its very character as a state, as argued in Chapter 7, then this division could last years, even decades.

What would it mean for the Gulf if the rift turns out to be long last-ing? Might we see greater animosity, even the outbreak of war? It's unthinkable that Doha would ever consider an attack on much more powerful Riyadh, and all the main players are U.S. allies, so direct con-flict seems difficult to imagine. At the same time, the trio does see the MB as an existential threat, so if Qatar remains recalcitrant, push may come to shove. As King Salman made clear in a June 2018 letter to Ma-cron, if Qatar were to ever deploy to threatening defense systems, "the kingdom would be ready to take all necessary measures . . . including military action."[92]

The likeliest fallout of the rift—decreased regional trade and a fractured GCC—would be problematic, but not apocalyptic. For the Kingdom, its best bet is to continue to work with its other Arab Gulf allies to marginal-ize and ostracize a recalcitrant Doha and stress to the international com-munity its unwillingness to work with its regional allies. Saudi leaders could highlight to the Trump administration, which is primarily focused on containing Iran, how Qatar's friendly relations with Tehran, combined with support for terrorists, undermine these efforts. This could lead to greater pressure from Washington, where National Security Advisor John Bolton has already publicly called for the United States to declare the MB a terrorist group and urge Qatar to do the same.

As detailed in Chapter 7, Doha has since the blockade begun growing closer in the Saudi-Iranian divide toward Tehran, as part of an emerging triumvirate with Turkey. Qatar has long had amicable relations with Iran, with which it shares the world's largest natural gas field. Iran helped re-route Qatari flights after the blockade, while Turkey has provided some $800 million in weapons deals, placed soldiers in Qatar, and agreed to build a naval base.[93] Doha now sees the Kingdom as a bigger security threat than Iran, according to risk analyst Giorgio Cafiero,[94] which is deeply problematic since as of April 2019 the United States views the Iran Revolutionary Guard Corps (IRGC) as a terrorist organization.[95]

Qatar hosts the United States' largest military base in the region, at Al-Udeid, which means Doha could never join a military alliance with Iran, or the IRGC in particular. But that does not mean it cannot continue to align its policies with those of its MB proxy, Turkey, and the Shia revolu-tionaries in Tehran. Even if temporary and predicated on desperation, as mentioned in Chapter 7, this troubling new regional axis has the potential to further destabilize the region, with its meddling in a handful of regional crises.

THE UNITED STATES AND IRAN

On the topic of Iran, that revanchist nation has seen the Syrian war as yet another opportunity to project power in the region and boost its flagging economy. Tehran's commitment there is about securing its primary client state and leading the country's rebuilding, so it will be difficult to budge. IRGC forces have not only been fighting in Syria for years but also helped train and equip local militias.[96]

Yet Saudi Arabia is also pitching in. In October 2018, the Kingdom sent the United States $100 million to help stabilize Syria.[97] This is all part of the United States' effort to pull back across the region and enable regional governments, particularly Saudi Arabia, to take the lead in stabilizing Arab states. "Saudi Arabia has now agreed to spend the necessary money needed to help rebuild Syria," Trump tweeted in December 2018. "Isn't it nice when immensely wealthy countries help rebuild their neighbors rather than a Great Country, the US, that is 5000 miles away."[98]

But Washington has not removed itself completely from the regional tug-of-war. The Trump administration has begun to move more aggressively against Iran, including lifting the Iran nuclear deal, ending oil waivers, and labeling the IRGC a terrorist group.[99] It also announced on July 18, 2019, that it was sending 1,000 more troops to the region.[100] However, the sanctions will not be as impactful as they might have been if the West were united. Britain, France, and Germany dislike the Trump administration policy on Iran, and as of late 2018 the EU and China were said to be developing a financial mechanism that would enable companies to skirt U.S. sanctions and enable trade in other currencies or barter.[101] Still, U.S. treasury secretary Steve Mnuchin expects that sanctions will in time reduce Iran's oil exports to nothing. "I don't expect we will get to zero in November but I do expect we will eventually get to zero," he said just before the sanctions hit.[102]

The new sanctions are expected to provide a boost to Saudi Arabia, which has lots of room to increase output, unlike most other oil producers, according to a May 2019 *Bloomberg* article headlined "The Winner from Trump's Iran Sanctions is Saudi Arabia."[103] Within days of that article appearing, attempts were made to undercut Saudi oil exports, most likely by Iran-backed players. First, two Saudi oil tankers, along with an Emirati and a Norwegian tanker, were attacked by unknown assailants and sustained significant damage near the Strait of Hormuz, the world's most important narrow passage for oil shipments.[104] Saudi Arabian energy minister Khalid Al-Falih described the incident as a deliberate attempt to "undermine the freedom of maritime navigation, and the security of oil supplies to consumers all over the world."[105]

In the days before the attacks, Israeli intelligence had warned the United States of Iran's intention to strike Saudi vessels, a senior Middle Eastern intelligence official told *The New York Times*.[106] U.S. national security agencies also believed Iranian proxies may have been behind the tanker attack.[107] Two days after that maritime assault, two Saudi Aramco pumping stations along the Kingdom's East-West pipeline were damaged by drone fire, forcing a temporary shutdown. Prince Khalid bin Salman, the Saudi vice defense minister, tweeted that the attacks were "ordered by the regime in Tehran, and carried out by the Houthis."[108] The next day, Yemen's Houthi-run Masirah TV said the group had carried out the drone attacks in response to continued aggression and blockade.[109] In the wake of these aggressions, Saudi leaders called Arab League and GCC meetings, and the Kingdom said it hoped to avert war but remained ready to respond with force.[110]

Renewing strong sanctions and terror-designating the IRGC mark a significant step forward in containing and marginalizing Iran and undermining its regime, which has been wreaking havoc across the region for decades. This meddling continues, and continues to expand. In April 2019, for instance, Bahrain authorities jailed 138 people and revoked their citizenship for plotting with the IRGC to form a terrorist group within Bahrain.[111] That same month, Tehran designated all U.S. troops in the Middle East as terrorists, a clear response to the U.S. designation of the IRGC.[112]

Just a few weeks prior, former British prime minister Tony Blair published an op-ed in the *Washington Post* expressing support for the Trump administration's ending of the Iran nuclear deal and increased pressure on Tehran. He detailed Iran's meddling across the region and laid out how its opponents should respond:

> The ayatollahs may have kept to the letter of the deal, but they have intensified their malign policies around the region. In Syria they have helped save the Assad regime despite its savagery, in Lebanon they exercise power through Hezbollah, and in Iraq they seek to undermine the country's independence. In Yemen they support the Houthi assault on the legitimate government, in the Gulf they do all they can to destabilize governments (especially Bahrain), and in the Palestinian territories they support the most intransigent and violent groups. And where Israel is concerned, they implacably oppose not only government policy but also the country's very existence.
>
> Where Iran is exercising military interference, it should be strongly pushed back. Where it is seeking influence, it should be countered. Where its proxies operate, it should be held responsible. Where its networks exist, they should be disrupted. Where its leaders are saying what is unacceptable, they should be exposed. Where the Iranian people—highly educated and connected, despite their government—are protesting for freedom, they should be supported. . . . 40 years of disappointment should make us clear-eyed. The revolution has made Iran the single biggest destabilizing force in the Middle East.[113]

The United States is indeed working to curb Iranian support for foreign proxies, including in Syria, in Yemen, and in Lebanon with Hezbollah. Containing and pushing back Iran in Syria would likely require more U.S. troops, as well as forward operating bases—a sizable commitment from an America that seems less interested in foreign entanglements, particularly in light of the planned U.S. withdrawal. Former U.S. envoy to the anti-ISIS coalition Brett McGurk argued in the May/June 2019 issue of

Foreign Affairs that the Syrian strategy Trump dismantled by withdrawing troops offered the United States its only real chance to prevent an ISIS resurgence, check the ambitions of Iran and Turkey, and negotiate a favorable post-war settlement.[114]

In late 2018, Egypt, UAE, and Bahrain, backed up by Saudi Arabia, began moving to bring Syria back into their fold, despite the distastefulness of the Bashar Al-Assad regime, in an effort to reduce Iran's significant influence there. Syria was expected to be readmitted to the Arab League, from which it had been expelled in 2011 over Assad's violent response to protests, sometime in 2019. The move is in large part about Assad's strong stance against Islamist outfits like the MB, according to Tobias Schneider, a research fellow at Berlin's Global Public Policy Institute.[115]

But it is also about—much like the Kingdom's support for Syrian reconstruction—curbing Iranian and Qatari influence in Syria.[116] The United States is well aware of the very real threat posed by an Iran in control of Syria and understands that Tehran also manages thousands of fighters from other countries, like Afghanistan.[117] If these fighters are pushed out of Syria, they could end up in other regional proxy wars—like in Yemen, for instance. So there's a bit of whack-a-mole to the Iran containment in Syria.

In Yemen, the United States remains committed to assisting the Saudi-led coalition to halt the advance of Iran-backed Houthis in Yemen—a position it may not need to hold much longer, since Houthis began to withdraw in May 2019. The United States has provided billions of dollars' worth of arms, along with intelligence, training, and refueling to the Yemen coalition, including 70 percent of recent Saudi weapons purchases.[118] The Pentagon understands that collateral damage does occur, despite the best efforts of well-trained armed forces teams, and remains confident that its assistance helps reduce civilian casualties.

Meanwhile, the UN has called the situation in Yemen the world's worst humanitarian crisis, with some 80 percent of the population in need of assistance and protection in early 2019.[119] Still, without U.S. training and assistance, the civilian death toll would likely be much higher. Crown Prince Mohammed bin Salman is close to Trump's Middle East advisor, and son-in-law, Jared Kushner, who sees him and the Kingdom as critical to the United States' efforts to contain Iran and support Israel. Due in part to that relationship, there's little question the Trump administration will continue to work with the Kingdom to address the biggest issues in the region, namely Iran and extremism.

On that note, when the Trump administration announced it wanted to designate the MB a terrorist organization, Iran and Turkey quickly condemned the move, with Ankara arguing that designating the Brotherhood would promote anti-Islamism.[120] Tehran's condemnation was a reminder that the Iranian regime's ideology is linked to that of the MB, with both inspired by the ideas of Sayyid Qutb. "Qutb was an influential figure among Iranian revolutionaries," Yusuf Unal, Fulbright Doctoral Fellow at Emory University specializing in early modern Iran, wrote in November 2016.[121]

Another Trump administration step against Iran is its decision to deny waiver extensions to the eight countries that had been buying Iranian crude. This was not only a move against the Islamist government in Turkey, which has relied on Iranian oil, but was also a move in favor of the Kingdom and its allies, as Washington tapped Saudi Arabia and the other Arab OPEC members to replace Iran's supply. "Saudi Arabia and others in OPEC will more than make up the Oil Flow difference in our now Full Sanctions on Iranian Oil," Trump tweeted in April 2019.[122] Saudi Oil Minister Khalid Al-Falih said the Kingdom would consult with fellow OPEC members about the waivers, but did not expect any need to quickly boost production.[123] UAE officials shared a similar view. "The two Gulf powerhouses are committed to doing their part to upend Tehran's economy and ideally marginalise its influence in the greater region," Jareer Elass, a Washington-based energy analyst, wrote for *Arab Weekly*.[124]

Iran has also seen its influence growing in Iraq amid an expected departure or reduction of U.S. troops. In March 2019, momentum was building within Iraq's parliament to evict U.S. troops, "an outcome that would leave Iraq's political future in the hands of neighboring Iran."[125] As of that date, the United States had some 5,200 troops in Iraq, advising and supporting Iraqi forces in the fight against ISIS, which had essentially come to an end with ISIS's defeat that same month. Within days of that defeat, a group of mostly Iran-backed deputies in Iraq's parliament began preparing a draft law calling for the full withdrawal of U.S. troops.[126] The next month, while Iraqi Prime Minister Adel Abdul Mahdi visited Tehran, Ayatollah Ali Khamenei urged Iraq to evict U.S. troops "as soon as possible." [127]

Then, in May, the United States announced the evacuation of all nonessential personnel from its Baghdad embassy, citing an unspecified threat from Iran.[128] By this time, ExxonMobil had evacuated its personnel from Basra, and Bahrain had evacuated its embassies in both Iran and Iraq.[129] Days after the U.S. evacuation, a rocket exploded in the Green Zone, not far from the U.S. embassy. It appeared to have been targeting the embassy, and an Iraqi counterterrorism official said it had been fired by an Iran-backed militia, Kataib Hezbollah, which in 2018 threatened to attack U.S. forces.[130]

The Kingdom has also begun making moves to reduce Iran's influence in Iraq. Saudi and Iraqi officials have agreed to reopen the Arar land border crossing to trade in October 2019.[131] That April, an Iraqi delegation visited Riyadh and left with a Saudi commitment to invest $1 billion in Iraq's economy and open a consulate in Baghdad.[132] State-backed Saudi broadcaster MBC plans to launch a dedicated Iraq channel. "We want to help Iraq be a strong country," Ibrahim Al-Nahas, a member of the Saudi

Shura Council's Foreign Affairs Committee, told *Bloomberg* in May 2019, adding that a Saudi rapprochement with Iraq "will decrease the influence of Iran."[133] Former British prime minister Tony Blair remembers Tehran's response to the end of the Saddam Hussein regime in neighboring Iraq, which was intended to foster a sovereign democracy. "Iran set about fomenting strife in Iraq and using the demise of Hussein to establish a network of influence in Iraq and expand regional hegemony," he wrote.[134]

As summer 2019 loomed, the United States continued its maximum pressure campaign on Iran. In May, the White House announced that a planned deployment to the Gulf of an aircraft carrier strike group and Air Force bombers was in response to an increased threat from Iran. "The United States is not seeking war with the Iranian regime, but we are fully prepared to respond to any attack," National Security Advisor Bolton said in a statement.[135] Days later, in a revision to military plans ordered by Bolton and other hardliners on Iran, Acting Defense Secretary Patrick Shanahan presented a plan that would send up to 120,000 troops to the Middle East if Tehran were to either attack U.S. forces or accelerate its work on nuclear weapons.[136]

This move appeared to highlight the rising influence of Bolton and Secretary of State Pompeo. James Mattis's resignation as Defense Secretary in December 2018 left Bolton as the administration's strongest voice on Iran. He has worked for years to weaken the regime and encourage a coup in Iran. In 2016, he gave a speech to Mujahideen-e-Khalq, an Iranian exile group dedicated to toppling Iran's theocracy. "The regime in Tehran needs to be overthrown at the earliest opportunity!" Bolton advised.[137]

Recent reports suggest that, amid a troubled economy, Iranians are growing tired of the corruption of the regime. After floods ravaged much of the country in April 2019, the Iranian Red Crescent made a call for donations. Many Iranians contributed, but many preferred to find their own ways to help. "I don't trust any of these government organizations," Masoud, a fruit-store owner in Tehran, told Al-Monitor. "We have heard so much news about thefts and embezzlements that we have to be stupid to give our money to these organizations again."[138] Masoud mentioned Mahmoud Reza Khavari, former chairman of Iran's state-owned Bank Melli, the largest bank in Iran, who fled to Canada in 2011 after embezzling some $2.6 billion.[139]

Iran's oil exports have been cut in half, as of May 2019, and seem likely to decline further.[140] The economy is expected to shrink a shocking 6 percent in 2019, as unemployment climbs above 15 percent.[141] Growing distrust of government and Iran's ruling elite is likely to lead to greater anger and frustration. "The opposition to the regime has widened," Bolton said in a May 2019 *New Yorker* profile. "There have been riots. You don't always read about this in the Western press, because they don't let reporters see it."[142] Both Bolton and Pompeo say the United States does not officially seek the overthrow of the Iranian government. Nevertheless, during a May 2019 podcast interview, Pompeo was asked if he thought Iran's leaders could alter their behavior enough to satisfy the White House. He responded that they could not. "I think what can change is the people can change the government," he said. "What we're trying to do is create space for the Iranian people."[143]

The United States appears to be making space for its allies in the region. By mid-2019, the new sanctions against Iran had made a clear impact, undermining Tehran's reach and the power of its proxies, particularly in Syria and Lebanon. "Iran's ability to finance allies such as Hezbollah has been curtailed. Hezbollah, the best funded and most senior of Tehran's proxies, has seen a sharp fall in its revenue and is being forced to make draconian cuts to its spending," said the *Washington Post*: "Fighters are being furloughed or assigned to the reserves, where they receive lower salaries or no pay at all, said a Hezbollah employee with one of the group's administrative units. Many of them are being withdrawn from Syria."[144]

This is precisely why Tehran and its proxies have begun to make a show of force—the sanctions are starting to hurt. The attacks on Saudi oil tankers, the drone attacks on the Saudi pipeline, and the missile shot into Baghdad's Green Zone—these are all signs of increasing desperation and hostility. "A potential conflict much larger than Iranian-backed Shia militias throwing mortar fire at the now fortress-like U.S. Embassy appears to be brewing amid credible intelligence coupled with heated anti-American rhetoric," Anne Speckhard and Ardian Shajkovci of the International Center for the Study of Violent Extremism, wrote for the *Daily Beast* in late May.[145]

Few expect war to break out between the United States and Iran, but in mid-2019 tensions between the two were as high as they have been in decades. This explains why the Trump administration in late May declared an emergency in order to bypass Congress and expedite more than $8 billion in arms sales to countries including Saudi Arabia and the UAE to help them deter "the malign influence" of Iran.[146] All-out conflict would likely be a disaster, at least in the short term, so Washington is helping its allies take the lead in regional security. The silver lining to this standoff is that there is no longer any question that the United States fully grasps, and is willing to respond to, Iran's regional ambitions and provocations.

Indeed, in March 2019, the United States organized a summit in Warsaw, Poland, to discuss with more than fifty allies possible joint strategies against Iran. A collection of European and Middle East officials attended the event, but one Arab country was conspicuous by its absence.[147] Qatar sent no officials to the event, again highlighting its unwillingness to stand against terrorist actors in the region. This made it clear that Qatar's support of the MB and acceptance of Iranian meddling is no longer just a Gulf or regional issue. It's also a concern for the United

States, as it could potentially torpedo the Trump plan to build a collective security architecture. The Middle East Strategic Alliance (MESA), which President Trump first announced at the May 2017 Riyadh summit, envisions the GCC states, Egypt, and Jordan aligning with the United States to target Iran. Creating a regional defense structure fits with the U.S. goal of scaling back its presence in the region while aiming to curb Iranian expansion and the creeping influence of Russia and China. But without Qatar, home to the largest U.S. base in the region, MESA could be dead on arrival.

Part of the goal of MESA is getting U.S. partners to invest more in their defenses, as Saudi Arabia, the UAE, Qatar, and Bahrain have done of late—purchasing more weapons in recent years than any other country grouping in the world. The Kingdom has also been making significant defense purchases for economically fragile Egypt. Another key aspect of the alliance would be its usefulness in bringing Israel and the Palestinians together to find peace. "The United States also counts on MESA's coordinated action to support its 'deal of the century' in the Israeli-Palestinian conflict," Yasmine Farouk, visiting fellow in the Middle East Program at the Carnegie Endowment, wrote in February 2019.[148] But this of course is an impossibility as long as Qatar refuses to end its support for Hamas.

Tim Lenderking, U.S. deputy assistant secretary of state for Arabian Gulf affairs, has said that, in addition to Iran, the alliance would focus on counterterrorism and "coordinating conflict management from Syria to Yemen."[149] Thus, Doha's support for the MB and its affiliates and its stubborn refusal to join the anti-Iran coalition are doubly undermining conflict resolution in Syria, Libya, and the Palestinian territories, and greatly enabling terrorism. In October 2018, the Qatari foreign minister was right when he said, "the real challenge facing the U.S.-led alliance is to solve the Gulf crisis."[150]

By May 2019, the international momentum appeared to be building against Qatar and its support for terrorists and their ideology. That month, a video report on AJ+ was found to be deeply anti-Semitic, questioning the truth about the Holocaust and arguing that the Zionist movement had benefited from it.[151] After a backlash on social media, Al Jazeera suspended the two journalists behind the report.[152]

Many analysts called on Doha to do more. "Don't be fooled by suspending a couple of journalists! Anti-Semitism there is so deeply entrenched, institutional and right from the top of the state," tweeted Ghanem Nusaibeh, chair of Muslims against anti-Semitism and a former Harvard fellow.[153] "For us as Muslims fighting anti-Semitism, the fight is much tougher than amongst non-Muslims. Not only is anti-Semitism rampant in mainstream media like Al Jazeera, it receives much funding from Qatar & few non-Muslims prepared to stand against Qatar's Al Jazeera & Muslim Brotherhood."[154]

The crucial step in resolving the crisis is convincing Qatar to end its support for terrorist organizations, particularly MB-linked groups. But this goal proved too much for retired U.S. general Anthony Zinni. In January 2019, he left his special envoy post, which had two roles, ending the Gulf dispute and building MESA. He told the *Washington Post* that his talks "did not make any progress"[155]—a sad commentary on the current reality in the Gulf, on the anti-Iran fight, and on the future prospects of an effective U.S.-backed security architecture for the region. "The resolution of the GCC rift must precede any talks about the establishment of a regional alliance," Farouk, of the Carnegie Endowment, wrote in February 2019.[156] Two months later, Egypt pulled out of the MESA initiative, expressing doubt about its seriousness.[157]

In addition to Qatar's recalcitrance, the United States must also deal with the fact that several of its regional partners have differing strategic priorities. One is Turkey, which, as previously outlined, considers the United States' Syrian Kurdish partner, the YPG, a terrorist outfit. This, along with its purchase of a Russian missile-defense system, which its NATO allies see as a security threat, has helped spur Turkey's shift away from the West and toward an alliance with Qatar and Iran. Analysts generally agree that the White House has been slow to react to this new reality. "Turkey has been outside the NATO tent for a decade now," Eric Edelman, former U.S. ambassador to Turkey and head of Turkey program at the Foundation for Defense of Democracies, and Jonathan Schanzer, senior vice president of research at FDD, wrote for the *Wall Street Journal* in May 2019:

> It is the largest external headquarters for the terrorist group Hamas in the Middle East. It has supported the worst jihadist actors in the Syrian civil war, including some linked to al Qaeda and Islamic State. From 2012–15, at the height of the effort to force Iran to relinquish its nuclear ambitions, the Turks were involved in a massive sanctions evasion scheme that netted Iran an estimated $20 billion.
>
> Meanwhile, Turkey has descended into authoritarianism domestically. The government in Ankara is now the world's top jailer of journalists. It has held Americans and other Westerners hostage. Mr. Erdogan has a personal stranglehold on the media and the judiciary. Whatever is left of the country's democratic process is groaning under the weight of Mr. Erdogan's efforts to manipulate it—as he demonstrated by his government's recent nullification of the March 31 Istanbul mayoral election.[158]

Edelman and Schanzer said U.S. officials had shown great patience with Ankara, but that it was time to take a stand against its problematic policies. Hussein Ibish of the Arab Gulf States Institute largely echoed this view: "Now that Turkey is no longer a U.S. partner in the Middle East and has an agenda that clashes with the interests of the U.S. and its Israeli and Arab allies, changes in U.S. attitudes are required," Ibish wrote for

Bloomberg in March 2019.[159] Ibish advised U.S. officials to seek out alternatives to Incirlik military base in southern Turkey, reduce military cooperation, and leverage U.S. cooperation for Ankara's commitment to the U.S.-led regional alliance.

The fact is, at this point Erdogan is weakened politically and Turkey is in deep economic crisis. "Turkey's economy is in the tank, leaving the strongman president exposed," Zach Vertin, nonresident fellow in the Brookings Institution's Foreign Policy program, wrote for Lawfare Blog in May 2019:

> After years of impressive growth, economic micro-mismanagement and Erdogan's sweeping institutional changes prompted a major downturn last summer. Bad turned to worse when the Turkish lira plummeted in eye-popping fashion, a freefall he attempted to blame on foreign conspirators. Investor confidence has waned while inflation, unemployment and prices have soared. Operating budgets and humanitarian aid allocations—an area in which Turkey previously led the world—have been slashed, curtailing agendas of all kinds, including in foreign policy.[160]

As Turkey shifts eastward and loses influence, Washington appears to be aligning more closely with the Saudi-led bloc against Qatar. Reversing the previous U.S. policy, the Trump administration has been supportive of General Haftar and his assault on Tripoli, with Trump talking to Haftar over the phone in April 2019 regarding their "shared vision" for Libya.[161] Some analysts have argued against this position, fearing the outbreak of greater violence and instability.[162] But Neville Teller, longtime Middle East analyst and author of several books, including *The Chaos in the Middle East: 2014–2016*, sees it differently: "The one politico-military figure in today's Libya possibly able to regain mastery of the situation and bring an end to the state of anarchy is Khalifa Haftar," he wrote soon after the assault began, in April 2019. "He appears to have the power and leadership qualities that Libya seems to require at the present time."[163]

Trump's shift in Libya has some wondering if he will also align with his Gulf allies in Sudan, where Saudi Arabia and the UAE have worked to maintain and even strengthen relations with the new military leadership after the overthrow of Omar Al-Bashir. Both have invested heavily in Sudan in recent years, including billions in agricultural investments to boost their domestic food supply. They also seek to gain a Red Sea beachhead in Africa; maintain Sudan's 14,000-troop presence in Yemen; and counter Turkey, Qatar, and Iran. In March 2018, Qatar signed a $4 billion deal with Al-Bashir to develop Suakin Island, on the Red Sea, and enable Turkey to build a naval base there.[164] With their Sudan investments, the Kingdom and the UAE also aim to keep MB-linked organizations, which had considerable strength and freedom in Sudan before the Arab uprisings, from toppling the new leadership, spurring waves of violence and destabilization, as in Syria and Libya.

The jockeying for influence in Sudan, particularly by Gulf states and their allies, is likely to continue through 2019 and beyond. "So many of the issues that are important to the Gulf seem to cluster in Sudan: the Iran issue, the Muslim Brotherhood, Yemen, the Red Sea coast, food security," Elizabeth Dickinson, an expert in the Arabian Peninsula for the International Crisis Group, told the *Wall Street Journal* in April 2019. "Everyone feels that Sudan is the country you need to have in your corner."[165]

RESOLVING THE CRISES

As for resolving the crisis in the Gulf, closer Saudi-U.S. ties may be crucial in forcing Qatar to budge. Already, Arab and U.S. counterterrorism officials have been working together to find and stop extremist preachers in the Gulf and across the Middle East who may be inciting violence.[166] Such increased bilateral cooperation suggests an opportunity. Although its problematic role in the region has been reduced, Qatar continues to back MB-linked groups in Libya, Gaza, and Syria, and encourage Saudi, Gulf, and other Arab dissidents, as detailed throughout the book. The Qataris seem to have decided to base their national security and foreign policy on the ironclad belief that they will face no credible military threat as long as the United States maintains a massive airbase in their country.

One way around this is for Riyadh to make an arrangement with Washington, that in the event of a Saudi-led invasion of Qatar, U.S. troops would remain at Al-Udeid and stay out of the fight as long as the invading forces take all the necessary precautions to avoid hitting the U.S. military installation. Considering the vast increase in Saudi defense purchases in recent years and the strategic consequences for U.S. posture in the region, Trump administration officials might offer a willing ear. Once U.S. officials agree to allow a limited Saudi-led invasion, with the objective of capturing key figures in Doha before swiftly withdrawing, Qatar will appreciate the seriousness of the threat and back down from its problematic policies. It is an extreme step, one that could unsettle Arab Gulf relations for decades, but short of such an aggressive stance the stalemate is likely to continue indefinitely.

To best ensure regional security, Saudi leaders could take advantage of the Kingdom's position of influence and make certain that no MB-affiliated party ever comes to power in the region again. However problematic some of today's governments across the Arab and Muslim worlds may be, the Brotherhood is not the solution, as we have seen throughout this book. The focus should be on making a repeat of the Morsi catastrophic failure in Egypt impossible. To be clear, this is not in any way an expression of support for El-Sisi or his model. It is instead a negation of the theory that the Qatar-backed MB offers the best route to a vibrant future for the Arabs and Muslims around the world.

The choice for Arabs and Muslims should not be between El-Sisi total-itarianism and MB revolution because both are unsustainable and will eventually collapse. A key reason Qatar and Turkey are increasingly iso-lated is because they are unable to end their misguided policy of support-ing MB groups; they have yet to realize that these groups are incompatible with stability and tend to sow violence and discord. Rather than being supported, they must be confronted, combated, and ultimately defeated.

After years of misunderstanding, the world is beginning to fully ap-preciate the true nature of the MB. Arab senior officials, especially the Saudis and Emiratis, for example, were deeply troubled by Obama's em-brace of Egyptian president Morsi. Saudi State Minister for Foreign Affairs Adel Al-Jubeir told *The New York Times'* Roger Cohen that with Obama, how could anyone "not come to the conclusion that you want the Mus-lim Brotherhood to take over the region?"[167] So it's been a major positive change to see the emergence of Trump's new national security policy that calls for the United States to declare the MB a terrorist group in part to pressure Qatar and Turkey.

This is all part of a broader shift in the prevailing political winds. In the coming decade, the MB problem is likely to be addressed with the same level of regional and international intensity directed at Al-Qaeda and ISIS. The Islamist agenda that the MB has represented for nearly a century seems to be on its last legs, because of the MB's repeated political failures, its connections to extremism and terror, and the renewed attention and energy that the United States along with Saudi Arabia and its Arab allies are paying to the problems inherent in the MB grand domination project.

part of Qatar to attempt to overthrow various Arab governments via support of the MB. Ample evidence has been provided to support the view that this conspiracy has been a conscious, intentional policy of the Qataris for some time. Only recently, with the implementation of the Saudi-led embargo, have the Qataris' incendiary actions come home to roost.

While every Arab state mentioned in this book has struggled to extricate the MB from its borders due to its profuse links to terrorism and the fact that it serves as an ideological source for Al-Qaeda and ISIS, Qatar has continued to send hundreds of millions of dollars to MB affiliates and members around the world. In the 1990s, as outlined earlier, Al-Qaradawi, who had long taken control of the Qatari educational system, began extensive discussions with Sheikh Hamad regarding political Islam and their mutual desire to spread it around the Arab world. Then, with the creation of Al Jazeera in 1996, Al-Qaradawi became an Arab superstar, spreading his MB-inspired ideology around the region. He spoke out against the various Arab leaders of the day, as well as political developments in numerous countries. His revolutionary message was embraced by a large listening public, even as it lacked a coherent vision for the future.

Qatar supported his message with extensive funding of various MB affiliates, especially in Egypt, Gaza (Hamas), Libya, and Syria. And now, the Qataris have found a new home base in Turkey, which is all too happy to use the MB as a conduit through which it can foment the overthrow of other Arab nations so that it can jump into a leadership position in the Arab world. The MB's message—strengthened after the so-called Arab Spring both ideologically and by increased financial commitments from Qatar—that the governments of the region are all corrupt and need to be overthrown locked in its powerful financial backer in the Qataris, who saw it as their religious duty and political mission to promote the MB's revolutionary zeal. And now that Turkey is in the game, as well as Iran, two large, relatively powerful nations are also on the Qatari bandwagon.

Qatar has done little to change its foreign policy in line with the demands of the Saudi-led bloc, though it has changed in other ways, seemingly in an attempt to appease the international community and keep its economy growing. Actions have included trying to make itself attractive to investment from Western and Asian countries, signing a counterterrorism memorandum with the United States, pledging to keep its promise to invest $45 billion in the United States between 2015 and 2020, improving labor laws, and allowing 100 percent foreign ownership of companies in all sectors.[2]

While these steps may be welcome to some, they have done little to rend the deep rift in the GCC. As far as Qatar's Gulf neighbors are concerned, these are bandages placed on areas where there is not even a wound. The real wound is Qatar's conspiracy to overthrow Arab governments via the

MB, as detailed extensively in this book. And on that note, Qatar's continued support for the MB in a sense proves the main thesis of MB failure that underpins this book. MB groups throughout the region have had to learn to operate in a more forbidding regional political landscape since the overthrow of Morsi in Egypt due to their own policy incompetence, penchant for violence, and inability to work within established governmental systems.

In many countries, the MB affiliate has endeavored to show it belongs and that it can work within the current system. As mentioned earlier, in countries where the MB chapter has a political foothold and parliamentary representation, it has often signaled this willingness by showing complete loyalty to the current leadership and disconnecting itself from the Egyptian MB and broader MB ideology. Then, of course, there are countries like Saudi Arabia, the UAE, and Egypt, where the MB has been labeled a terrorist group and exists today only underground and along the margins, but has otherwise been outlawed and eviscerated in recent years.

On that note, I will conclude by giving a brief analysis of the status of and prognosis for the MB in each country covered in this book, and doing so alphabetically, I will begin with Algeria. The Algerian army, which won the civil war against armed Islamist groups in the 1990s, has no intention of allowing MB-linked groups to gain power, particularly after seeing the destruction created by MB-affiliated parties in Egypt and Libya. Algerian MB affiliate MSP and smaller parties have learned to play by the rules of the game and position themselves for survival within a constrained political sphere. In early 2019, the army listened to the demands of the people and ousted Bouteflika's corrupt regime. In the days ahead, they are unlikely to allow any MB-influenced actors to gain any real influence. Thus, the future for the MB in Algeria is best described as bleak.

In Bahrain, however, the MB affiliate, Al-Menbar, is an established political party with some representation in parliament. It has been able to sustain ties with senior members of the Bahraini royal family by endeavoring to appear loyal and beholden to their rule. As long as Al-Menbar continues to adhere to the rules that govern its existence, its chances of survival look fair if it can maintain its measure of influence as it struggles against the fact that Bahrain is beholden to Saudi Arabia and thus forbidden from enabling any MB-linked actor to gain real power.

In Egypt, the situation is best described as very bleak. The MB has faced the region's most extreme crackdown as a result of its failed conspiracy while in power, in 2012–2013. Though we have seen a slight softening toward the MB since 2018, the percentage chance that the El-Sisi government will alter its position on the MB is near zero. The Egyptian leadership understands, perhaps more than that of any other state, the very real threat posed by the Brotherhood, particularly as the movement has again embraced violence in recent years. The army is in full control of the state, and it remains vehemently anti-Ikhwan. With the death of Morsi in mid-2019, the overall view of the MB could be said to align with the view of his rule: "His presidency seemed guided by greed and the benefit of his group rather than one of finding common ground. It was messy, bloody, and unstable."[3]

However, El-Sisi is not helping matters in the long run. Regardless of foreign pressures, Egypt under his rule will not cease to treat the MB harshly. Nevertheless, "by ousting, arresting, putting on show trial and criminally neglecting until his death a man whose presidency lasted just 12 months, the Egyptian military . . . made a hero out of a villain. It also transformed a hugely unpopular leader into the stuff of legend."[4] In short, Egypt not only will continue its attempts to be free of the MB but also must inevitably seek freedom from the oppressive military rule that makes even the MB seem to some, at times, like an attractive alternative.

Looking at Iraq, the MB's prognosis seems somewhat better. Iraq's MB affiliate, IIP, is a legitimate political party that has adapted to the unique demographic realities in Iraq, where Sunnis are a minority, and gained some representation in parliament. Though it has lost popularity in recent years as Sunni groups have lost influence in Baghdad, IIP works well with groups representing other religious and ethnic communities. The IIP has begun distancing itself from the MB of late in an effort to erase from its reputation the idea that its failures during the U.S.-led occupation drove Sunnis to violent groups like ISIS. As a Sunni party, it will always have its limitations in Iraq. But as long as it continues to keep its distance from any violent groups, it will remain as a political option for a segment of Iraq's Sunnis.

Likewise, Jordan's IAF is a savvy MB affiliate that has to some extent mirrored sister organizations in Morocco and Tunisia in its ability to moderate its stance within the Jordanian political scene, and thus it has a fair chance at surviving. It is represented in the Jordanian legislature and serves as an opposition party that is nonetheless loyal to King Abdullah and the Jordanian monarchy. It has not been able to distance itself as much from the MB core tenets as the North African chapters, in large part because of its close links to Hamas. But it has been able to survive within a narrow political space and preserve for now the MB franchise in Jordan. However, in recent years, the splintering of the Jordanian MB into at least four different factions has led to a loss of traction, particularly among the country's youth.

Like the IAF, Kuwait's Hadas is a well-established MB affiliate that has morphed into an important political party in the National Assembly. However, although it still maintains some core MB tenets, Hadas broke with the Egyptian Brotherhood nearly three decades ago because of the latter's support for Saddam Hussein's invasion. As in Bahrain and Jordan, Hadas will remain a legitimate political party as long as it remains loyal and beholden to the country's monarchy. It has done precisely that in recent years since the overthrow of Morsi in Egypt and the regional sea change toward the MB, which has led Emir Sheikh Jaber to push back against pressures from the Saudi-led coalition to disband and outlaw them. For that reason, its prognosis is good.

In Libya, the presence of MB-affiliated parties and other Islamist groups has played a significant role in the continuation of the Libyan civil war, which has torn the country in two. Leading the anti-Islamist side, and supported by Saudi Arabia, the UAE, Egypt, Russia, France, and, to a lesser extent, the United States, General Khaled Haftar controlled some 90 percent of the country as of mid-2019 and appeared set to take Tripoli and dislodge the Islamist government there. If that were to happen, a Haftar-led government would undoubtedly endeavor to keep any MB-linked figures from gaining power. But as of writing, the MB has a key role in the UN-backed government in Tripoli, so its future looks good.

Also in Northern Africa, Morocco's MB affiliate, PJD, has been able to transform itself into a national party and gain acceptance with a sizeable portion of the population. As with Tunisia's Ennahda, this enabled it to become a main party in the legislature and help form and head a government. But let's not forget, as in other regional monarchies, this is only possible as long as the PJD makes its subservience clear. It also must continue to reiterate that it is solely part of the national construct, with no pan-Arab or pan-Islamic revolutionary aims, so while its future prognosis looks fair, today's PJD barely qualifies as an MB affiliate.

Moving on to Oman, like Iraq, that state does not have a Sunni majority but rather an Ibadi majority, and hence the ground for any MB presence to take root is very limited. Particularly after the arrest of several hundred MB members in the 1990s, MB-linked groups have had near-zero presence in Oman. Considering regional geopolitics and Oman's demographics, the MB is unlikely to gain much ground in Oman anytime soon.

As for the all-important Palestine, the perennial question hovering over Hamas, the MB affiliate in Gaza, is what its role might be if and when a Palestinian state is established. This, however, is almost impossible to answer today, when the peace process is non-existent, and Hamas continues to be a lead agitator. If Hamas fails to reform and follow the example of sister organizations in Tunisia and Morocco, it will continue to be treated as a pariah and a movement predicated on terrorism, and the troubles will continue for Palestinians. Due to the rigidity of the structure of Hamas, it is highly unlikely that it will ever become a mainstream political party. However, as of mid-2019 Hamas continues to hold considerable power in Gaza and appears unwilling to relinquish it anytime soon.

As for Qatar, it no longer has an MB affiliate, since it was outlawed in 1999, but the group has, to some extent, remade Qatar into its own private fiefdom—a launch pad to extend itself into the UAE and to influence the Qatari leadership to follow pro-MB policies across the region and the world. Qatar's Gulf neighbors have begun to stand strongly against these policies, highlighting the destructive role the MB and its affiliates have played in the region. The embargo against Qatar is the direct result of this stance, and it is unlikely to end as long as Doha maintains its committed support for the MB. In short, the future looks good for the MB in Qatar.

Moving on to Saudi Arabia. A considerable portion of this book has been devoted to explaining the complexities and intricacies of the unique relationship between the MB and the kingdom due to the latter's large presence in the political landscape of the Middle East and its central role in the Islamic religion. What is clear is that the Saudis feel betrayed by the MB and its somewhat unofficial affiliate: the Sahwa movement. After clearing the Kingdom of MB affiliates and leaders in the recent decades, the new Saudi leadership is committed to eradicating any remaining ideological and theological remnants of Sahwa and MB education in the Kingdom, making its future there quite bleak.

The prognosis for the MB in Sudan is also bleak. The group won't recover anytime soon from its close affiliation with and support of Bashir. In essence, the military will make sure that no MB affiliate ever comes into power after the disastrous years of Bashir and Turabi.

Furthermore, due to the likely victory in the Syrian civil war of Assad and his allies, the outlook is not good for Syria's MB affiliates. Although MB figures were able to insert themselves within the Syrian opposition and gain outsized influence within both political opposition and armed groups, they have ended up without any real gains in Syria itself. If Assad is ever to be overthrown, the MB is likely to play a role, but the outcome of the Syrian civil war suggests that even then it will not be the central power it has long envisioned for itself.

By contrast, Tunisia represents the best example of how an MB affiliate has been able to pre-empt the regional wave of hostility with a makeover. Although Ennahda led the Tunisian government shortly after the overthrow of Ben Ali, it voluntarily ceded power to the liberal coalition and rebranded itself as a national party, separating its Brotherhood roots from its politics to fit in with the emerging political scene. So long as it continues to present itself as a purely national entity, distinct from the MB, Ennahda is likely to survive and remain a party to reckon with.

Then there is Turkey, which was not covered here as a nation with an MB affiliate, but which nonetheless, as this book has shown, now plays an important role in its evolution. Although Turkey is not an Arab country, it "is more isolated than ever in the Middle East,"[5] and technically does not have a domestic MB-affiliated party, its ruling AKP was inspired by the MB and maintains a similar ideology. More importantly, since the overthrow of Morsi, Turkey has welcomed dozens of exiled MB leaders and more closely aligned its policies with those of the region's lead MB-backer, Qatar. As of mid-2019, Egyptian MB figures operate at least two MB-linked television stations out of Istanbul, where MB-inspired Hamas maintains an office and is supported by businesses close to the Erdogan

government. Barring the Trump administration designating the MB a terrorist outfit, Brotherhood members and affiliates will continue to find safe
haven and support in Turkey, where they can recuperate, promote their
cause, and plot out their next steps, all thanks to the considerable power
of an MB-inspired ruling party.

Perhaps the UAE alone rivals Saudi Arabia and Egypt for its disdain
for the MB and its understanding of the group's violent and revolutionary
nature. Emirati leaders have never forgiven the local MB affiliate, Al-Islah,
for having attempted to insert itself and influence the country's political
future. Al-Islah has been disbanded, and any trace of MB educational and
theological influence has been eliminated. Thus, the MB's future in the
UAE is very bleak indeed.

Finally, there is Yemen. Due to its unique current situation, the MB
affiliate there will have a role in the future of the country after the civil
war. However, it will not be a leadership role. Al-Islah's chance to lead in
Yemen, as with many MB affiliates in other countries, is now nothing but
history.

Addendum

INTELLIGENCE AND SECURITY AGENCIES

The following is a list of intelligence and security agencies and their acronyms used in the book:

1) Bahrain

   NSA (National Security Agency)/Main intelligence and security agency

2) France

   DGSE (Direction General de la Securite Exterieure)/Main foreign intelligence agency

   DGSI (Direction General de la Securite Interieure)/Main domestic security agency

   DRM (Direction du Renseignement Militaire/Main military intelligence agency

3) Germany

   BND (Bundesnachrichtendienst)/Main foreign intelligence agency

   BfV (Bundesamt fur Verfassungsschutz)/Main domestic intelligence agency

4) Jordan

   GID (General Intelligence Directorate)/Main intelligence and security agency

5) The Netherlands

   AIVD (Algemene Inlichtingen-en Veiligheidsdienst)/Main foreign and security agency

   MIVD (Militaire Inlichtingen-en Veiligheidsdienst)/Main military intelligence agency

6) Saudi Arabia

GIP (General Intelligence Presidency)/Main foreign intelligence agency

SSP (State Security Presidency)/Main domestic intelligence agency

7) Switzerland

NDB/SRC/FIS (Nachrichtendienst des Bundes/Service de Renseignement de la Confederation)/Main intelligence security agency

8) The United Kingdom

SIS/MI6 (Secret Intelligence Service)/Main foreign intelligence agency

SSS/MI5 (Secret Security Service)/Main domestic intelligence agency

9) The United States

CIA (Central Intelligence Agency)/Main foreign intelligence agency

FBI (Federal Bureau of Investigation)/Main domestic security agency

DIA (Defense Intelligence Agency)/Main military intelligence agency

Notes

INTRODUCTION

1. Martyn Frampton, *The Muslim Brotherhood and the West: A History of Enmity and Engagement* (Cambridge, MA: The Belknap Press of Harvard University Press, 2018), 24.

2. Khalil al-Anani, "The Salafi-Brotherhood Feud in Egypt," *Al-Monitor*, February 21, 2013, https://www.al-monitor.com/pulse/originals/2013/02/muslim-brotherhood-salafist-feud-in-egypt.html

3. David D. Kirkpatrick, "Egypt's New Leader Takes Oath, Promising to Work for Release of Jailed Terrorist," *The New York Times*, June 29, 2012, https://www.nytimes.com/2012/06/30/world/middleeast/morsi-promises-to-work-for-release-of-omar-abdel-rahman.html

4. Khalil al-Anani, "The Salafi-Brotherhood Feud in Egypt," *Al-Monitor*, February 21, 2013, https://www.al-monitor.com/pulse/originals/2013/02/muslim-brotherhood-salafist-feud-in-egypt.html

5. *Ibid.*

6. David D. Kirkpatrick, "Raising Questions Within Islam after France Shooting," *The New York Times*, January 8, 2015, https://www.nytimes.com/2015/01/09/world/europe/raising-questions-within-islam-after-france-shooting.html

7. *Ibid.*

8. *Ibid.*

9. Avi Spiegel, "Succeeding by Surviving: Examining the Durability of Political Islam in Morocco," *The Brookings Institute*, August 2015, https://www.brookings.edu/wp-content/uploads/2016/07/Morocco_Spiegel-FINALE.pdf

10. Sarah H. Louden, "Political Islam in Tunisia: A History of Repression and a Complex Forum for Potential Change," *Mathal* 4, no. 1 (2015), https://ir.uiowa.edu/cgi/viewcontent.cgi?article=1060&context=mathal

11. Mehdi Mabrouk, "Tunisia: The Radicalization of Religious Policy," in *Islamist Radicalization in North Africa: Politics and Process*, ed. George Joffé (New York, NY: Routledge, 2012).

12. James Legge, "Tunisia Shocked by Assassinations: Opposition Leaders Mohamed Brahmi and Chokri Belaid Killed with the Same Gun," *Independent*, July 26, 2013, https://www.independent.co.uk/news/world/africa/tunisia-shocked-by-assassinations-opposition-leaders-mohamed-brahmi-and-chokri-belaid-killed-with-8733972.html

13. Mohamed Bechri, "Tunisia's Security-First Policy at a Crossroads," *Fikra Forum* (blog), The Washington Institute, July 23, 2014, https://www.washingtonin stitute.org/policy-analysis/view/tunisias-security-first-policy-at-a-crossroads

14. Larbi Sadiki, "Why Is Tunisia's Ennahda Ditching Political Islam?" Al Jazeera, May 24, 2016, https://www.aljazeera.com/news/2016/05/tunisia-en nahda-ditching-political-islam-160524094550153.html

15. Itzchak Weismann, "Democratic Fundamentalism? The Practice and Discourse of the Muslim Brothers Movement in Syria," *The Muslim World*, January 19, 2010, https://onlinelibrary.wiley.com/doi/abs/10.1111/j.1478-1913.2009.01298.x

16. Eyal Zisser, "Syria, the Ba'th Regime and the Islamic Movement: Stepping on a New Path?" *The Muslim World* 35 (2005): 48–50.

17. Nathan Brown, Amr Hamzawy, and Marina Ottaway, *Islamist Movements and the Democratic Process in the Arab World: Exploring the Gray Zones* (Washington, DC: Carnegie Endowment for International Peace, 2006), https://carnegieendow ment.org/files/cp_67_grayzones_final.pdf

18. Khetam Malkawi, "Authorities Close More Muslim Brotherhood Offices, Others to Follow," *The Jordan Times*, April 14, 2016, http://www.jordantimes.com/news/local/authorities-close-more-muslim-brotherhood-offices-others-follow

19. *Ibid.*

CHAPTER 1

1. Pulp Ark, "The History of the Muslim Brotherhood in 3 Minutes," YouTube video, 3:09, November 25, 2012, https://www.youtube.com/watch?v=0N-5uGF9eYs

2. https://www.theglobeandmail.com/news/world/the-crumbling-of-egypts-muslim-brotherhood/article15370983/

3. Brian Farmer, *Understanding Radical Islam: Medieval Ideology in the Twenty-First Century* (New York, NY: Peter Lang, 2007), 83.

4. Carrie Rosefsky Wickham, *The Muslim Brotherhood: Evolution of an Islamist Movement* (Princeton, NJ: Princeton University Press, 2013).

5. Martyn Frampton, *The Muslim Brotherhood and the West: A History of Enmity and Engagement* (Cambridge, MA: The Belknap Press of Harvard University Press, 2018), 20.

6. *Ibid.*, 19.

7. "The Egyptian Muslim Brotherhood: Building Bases of Support," *Directorate of Intelligence at Central Intelligence Agency*, May 1986, https://www.cia.gov/library/readingroom/docs/CIA-RDP88T00096R000200240001-4.pdf

8. Richard Paul Mitchell, *The Society of the Muslim Brothers* (New York, NY: Oxford University Press, 1993).

9. Martyn Frampton, *The Muslim Brotherhood and the West: A History of Enmity and Engagement* (Cambridge, MA: The Belknap Press of Harvard University Press, 2018), 15.

10. Carrie Rosefsky Wickham, *The Muslim Brotherhood: Evolution of an Islamist Movement* (Princeton, NJ: Princeton University Press, 2013), 23.

11. Martyn Frampton, *The Muslim Brotherhood and the West: A History of Enmity and Engagement* (Cambridge, MA: The Belknap Press of Harvard University Press, 2018), 21.

12. Ḥasan al-Bannā and Charles Wendell, *Five Tracts of Hasan al-Banna a Selection from the Majmu at Rasā'il al-Imâm al-Shahid Ḥasan al-Banna* (Berkeley, CA: University of California Press, 1978).

13. *Ibid.*

14. Alison Pargeter, *The Muslim Brotherhood: From Opposition to Power* (London, England: Saqi Books, 2013), 20.

15. David Kirkpatrick, *Into the Hands of the Soldiers: Freedom and Chaos in Egypt and the Middle East* (New York, NY: Penguin, 2018), 122–123.

16. Jacob Landau, *Pan-Islam: History and Politics* (New York, NY: Routledge, 2016), 224.

17. Martyn Frampton, *The Muslim Brotherhood and the West: A History of Enmity and Engagement* (Cambridge, MA: The Belknap Press of Harvard University Press, 2018), 36.

18. *Ibid.*, 47.

19. *Ibid.*

20. *Ibid.*, 48.

21. *Ibid.*, 52.

22. Alison Pargeter, *The Muslim Brotherhood: From Opposition to Power* (London, England: Saqi Books, 2013), 182.

23. *Ibid.*, 198.

24. *Ibid.*

25. Christopher Dickey, "The Real Reasons Saudi Crown Prince Mohammed bin Salman Wanted Khashoggi 'Dead or Alive,' " *Daily Beast*, October 21, 2018, https://www.thedailybeast.com/the-real-reasons-saudi-crown-prince-moham med-bin-salman-wanted-khashoggi-dead

26. Martyn Frampton, *The Muslim Brotherhood and the West: A History of Enmity and Engagement* (Cambridge, MA: The Belknap Press of Harvard University Press, 2018), 31.

27. *Ibid.*, 46–47.

28. *Ibid.*, 45–46.

29. *Ibid.*, 81–82.

30. *Ibid.*, 81–82.

31. *Ibid.*, 69.

32. Tarek Masoud, *Counting Islam: Religion, Class, and Elections in Egypt (Problems of International Politics)* (New York, NY: Cambridge University Press, 2014).

33. Martyn Frampton, *The Muslim Brotherhood and the West: A History of Enmity and Engagement* (Cambridge, MA: The Belknap Press of Harvard University Press, 2018), 120.

34. David Kirkpatrick, *Into the Hands of the Soldiers: Freedom and Chaos in Egypt and the Middle East* (New York, NY: Penguin, 2018), 124.

35. Martyn Frampton, *The Muslim Brotherhood and the West: A History of Enmity and Engagement* (Cambridge, MA: The Belknap Press of Harvard University Press, 2018), 123.

36. *Ibid.*, 146.

37. David Kirkpatrick, *Into the Hands of the Soldiers: Freedom and Chaos in Egypt and the Middle East* (New York, NY: Penguin, 2018), 124.

38. Martyn Frampton, *The Muslim Brotherhood and the West: A History of Enmity and Engagement* (Cambridge, MA: The Belknap Press of Harvard University Press, 2018), 96.

39. *Ibid.*, 146.

40. Sayyid Qutb, *In the Shade of the Quran* (United Kingdom: Islamic Foundation, 2009).

41. Martyn Frampton, *The Muslim Brotherhood and the West: A History of Enmity and Engagement* (Cambridge, MA: The Belknap Press of Harvard University Press, 2018), 124.

42. Arnaud de Borchgrave, "Commentary: Geopolitical Amnesia," *UPI*, August 19, 2013, https://www.upi.com/Top_News/Opinion/de-Borchgrave/2013/08/19/Commentary-Geopolitical-amnesia/79351376885700/

43. Martyn Frampton, *The Muslim Brotherhood and the West: A History of Enmity and Engagement* (Cambridge, MA: The Belknap Press of Harvard University Press, 2018), 97.

44. *Ibid.*, 203.

45. *Ibid.*, 204.

46. Carrie Rosefsky Wickham, *The Muslim Brotherhood: Evolution of an Islamist Movement* (Princeton, NJ: Princeton University Press, 2013), 27.

47. Ian Johnson, "Washington's Secret History with the Muslim Brotherhood," *New York Review Daily*, February 5, 2011, https://www.nybooks.com/daily/2011/02/05/washingtons-secret-history-muslim-brotherhood/

48. David Kirkpatrick, *Into the Hands of the Soldiers: Freedom and Chaos in Egypt and the Middle East* (New York, NY: Penguin, 2018), 124–125.

49. Martyn Frampton, *The Muslim Brotherhood and the West: A History of Enmity and Engagement* (Cambridge, MA: The Belknap Press of Harvard University Press, 2018), 295.

50. David Kirkpatrick, *Into the Hands of the Soldiers: Freedom and Chaos in Egypt and the Middle East* (New York, NY: Penguin, 2018), 125.

51. *Ibid.*, 124–125.

52. Martyn Frampton, *The Muslim Brotherhood and the West: A History of Enmity and Engagement* (Cambridge, MA: The Belknap Press of Harvard University Press, 2018), 322.

53. David Kirkpatrick, *Into the Hands of the Soldiers: Freedom and Chaos in Egypt and the Middle East* (New York, NY: Penguin, 2018), 119.

54. *Ibid.*, 119–120.

55. *Ibid.*, 128–129.

56. Alison Pargeter, *The Muslim Brotherhood: From Opposition to Power* (London, England: Saqi Books, 2013), 40.

57. Martyn Frampton, *The Muslim Brotherhood and the West: A History of Enmity and Engagement* (Cambridge, MA: The Belknap Press of Harvard University Press, 2018), 330.

58. *Ibid.*, 332.

59. Holly Fletcher, "Egyptian Islamic Jihad," *Council on Foreign Relations* (2008), accessed June 6, 2018, https://www.cfr.org/backgrounder/egyptian-islamic-jihad

60. Naguib Mahfouz, *Sugar Street: The Cairo Trilogy, Volume 3*, 2nd ed. (New York, NY: Random House, 2011).

61. Martyn Frampton, *The Muslim Brotherhood and the West: A History of Enmity and Engagement* (Cambridge, MA: The Belknap Press of Harvard University Press, 2018), 305.

62. Carrie Rosefsky Wickham, *The Muslim Brotherhood: Evolution of an Islamist Movement* (Princeton, NJ: Princeton University Press, 2013) quoted in Nawaf Obaid, "The Muslim Brotherhood: A Failure in Political Evolution," *Intelligence Project* (2017), https://www.belfercenter.org/sites/default/files/files/publica tion/Muslim%20Brotherhood%20-%20final.pdf

63. David Kirkpatrick, *Into the Hands of the Soldiers: Freedom and Chaos in Egypt and the Middle East* (New York, NY: Penguin, 2018), 122–124.

64. John Jenkins, "The Gulf and the Muslim Brotherhood," Oxford Gulf and Arabian Peninsula Studies Forum, https://www.oxgaps.org/files/commentary_-_jenkins.pdf

65. Martyn Frampton, *The Muslim Brotherhood and the West: A History of Enmity and Engagement* (Cambridge, MA: The Belknap Press of Harvard University Press, 2018), 24.

CHAPTER 2

1. "The Muslim Brotherhood in Algeria," *Crethi Plethi* (blog), January 2012, http://www.crethiplethi.com/the-muslim-brotherhood-in-algeria/global-islam/2012/

2. Omar Ashour, "Islamist De-Radicalization in Algeria: Successes and Failures," Middle East Institute, November 1, 2008, https://www.mei.edu/publica tions/islamist-de-radicalization-algeria-successes-and-failures

3. David Ottaway, "Algeria: Bloody Past and Fractious Factions," in *The Islamists Are Coming*, ed. Robin Wright (Washington, DC: Woodrow Wilson Center Press, 2012).

4. Omar Ashour, "Islamist De-Radicalization in Algeria: Successes and Failures," Middle East Institute, November 1, 2008, https://www.mei.edu/publica tions/islamist-de-radicalization-algeria-successes-and-failures

5. "Algeria's Government Alters Its Relationship with Islamists," *Worldview*, *Stratfor*, December 19, 2014, https://worldview.stratfor.com/article/algerias-gov ernment-alters-its-relationship-islamists

6. Omar Ashour, "Islamist De-Radicalization in Algeria: Successes and Failures," Middle East Institute, November 1, 2008, https://www.mei.edu/publica tions/islamist-de-radicalization-algeria-successes-and-failures

7. David Ottaway, "Algeria: Bloody Past and Fractious Factions," in *The Islamists Are Coming*, ed. Robin Wright (Washington, DC: Woodrow Wilson Center Press, 2012).

8. Vish Sakthivel, "Political Islam in Post-Conflict Algeria," Hudson Institute, November 2, 2017, https://www.hudson.org/research/13934-political-islam-in-post-conflict-algeria

9. David Ottaway, "Algeria: Bloody Past and Fractious Factions," Wilson Center, August 27, 2015, https://www.wilsoncenter.org/article/algeria-bloody-past-and-fractious-factions

10. Cameron Glenn, "Challenges for Algeria's Islamist Parties," Wilson Center, September 2, 2014, https://www.wilsoncenter.org/article/challenges-for-algerias-islamist-parties

11. Vish Sakthivel, "Political Islam in Post-Conflict Algeria," Hudson Institute, November 2, 2017, https://www.hudson.org/research/13934-political-islam-in-post-conflict-algeria

12. "Largest Islamist Movement in Algeria Refuses to Join the Government," *Middle East Monitor*, May 15, 2017, https://www.middleeastmonitor.com/20170515-largest-islamist-movement-in-algeria-refuses-to-join-the-government/

13. QatariLeaks قطريليكس, "Algerian Muslim Brotherhood; Qatar's Devastating Tool," YouTube video, 1:25, May 22, 2018, https://www.youtube.com/watch?v=Cd_BYcU134g

14. *Ibid.*

15. Anonymous (former director of the French Direction Generale de la Securite Exterieure) in discussion with the author, November 25, 2017, Boston, MA.

16. *Ibid.*

17. Egypt Today staff, "Int'l Branches of Muslim Brotherhood Mobilize to Rescue Qatar," *Egypt Today*, June 19, 2017, https://www.egypttoday.com/Article/2/8180/Int%E2%80%99l-branches-of-Muslim-Brotherhood-mobilize-to-rescue-Qatar

18. QatariLeaks قطريليكس, "Algerian Muslim Brotherhood; Qatar's Devastating Tool," YouTube video, 1:25, May 22, 2018, https://www.youtube.com/watch?v=Cd_BYcU134g

19. Egypt Today staff, "Int'l Branches of Muslim Brotherhood Mobilize to Rescue Qatar," *Egypt Today*, June 19, 2017, https://www.egypttoday.com/Article/2/8180/Int%E2%80%99l-branches-of-Muslim-Brotherhood-mobilize-to-rescue-Qatar

20. *Ibid.*

21. "Largest Islamist Movement in Algeria Refuses to Join the Government," *Middle East Monitor*, May 15, 2017, https://www.middleeastmonitor.com/20170515-largest-islamist-movement-in-algeria-refuses-to-join-the-government/

22. *Ibid.*

23. Dalia Ghanem, "The Future of Algeria's Main Islamist Party," *Carnegie Middle East Center*, April 14, 2015, https://carnegie-mec.org/2015/04/14/future-of-algeria-s-main-islamist-party-pub-59769

24. Omar Ashour, "Libya's Muslim Brotherhood Faces the Future," *Brookings*, March 9, 2012, https://www.brookings.edu/opinions/libyas-muslim-brotherhood-faces-the-future/

25. *Ibid.*

26. Abdul Sattar Hatita, "Libya Recollections: Gaddafi's Amnesty for Muslim Brotherhood Leaders," *Asharq Al-Awsat*, February 18, 2018, https://aawsat.com/english/home/article/1179196/libya-recollections-gaddafis-amnesty-muslim-brotherhood-leaders

27. *Ibid.*

28. Mary Fitzgerald, "Introducing the Libyan Muslim Brotherhood," *Foreign Policy*, November 2, 2012, https://foreignpolicy.com/2012/11/02/introducing-the-libyan-muslim-brotherhood/

29. Sasha Toperich, "Libya: The Muslim Brotherhood's Last Stand?" *Huffington Post*, December 6, 2017, https://www.huffpost.com/entry/libya-the-muslim-brotherhoods-last-stand_b_5618001

30. Muslim Brotherhood Terrorist Designation Act of 2015, S. 2230, 114th Cong. (2015).

31. Al Arabiya Staff, "Libyan Army: Qatar Transports Armed ISIS Militants from Syria to Libya," *Al Arabiya*, October 2, 2017, https://english.alarabiya.net/en/News/gulf/2017/10/02/Libyan-army-Qatar-transporting-armed-ISIS-militants-from-Syria-to-Libya.html

32. "Libya's Muslim Brotherhood Break Their Silence, Respond to Haftar's Accusations," *Middle East Monitor*, February 22, 2017, https://www.middleeastmonitor.com/20170222-libyas-muslim-brotherhood-break-their-silence-respond-to-haftars-accusations/

33. David Roberts, "Behind Qatar's Intervention in Libya," *Foreign Affairs*, September 28, 2011, https://www.foreignaffairs.com/articles/libya/2011-09-28/behind-qatars-intervention-libya

34. *Ibid.*

35. Jonathan Schanzer, "Qatar's Support of the Worst of the Worst in Libya Must End," *Newsweek*, August 6, 2017, https://www.newsweek.com/qatar-support-worst-worst-libya-must-end-646280

36. Al-Masry Al-Youm, "Qatar's Support to Terrorist Groups in Libya 'Will Not Pass without Charge': Hafter," *Egypt Independent*, June 1, 2017, https://ww.egyptindependent.com/qatar-support-terrorist-groups-libya/

37. Ian Black, "Qatar Admits Sending Hundreds of Troops to Support Libya Rebels," *The Guardian*, October 26, 2011, https://www.theguardian.com/world/2011/oct/26/qatar-troops-libya-rebels-support

38. Jonathan Schanzer, "Qatar's Support of the Worst of the Worst in Libya Must End," *Newsweek*, August 6, 2017, https://www.newsweek.com/qatar-support-worst-worst-libya-must-end-646280

39. *Ibid.*

40. *Ibid.*

41. Al-Masry Al-Youm, "Qatar's Support to Terrorist Groups in Libya 'Will Not Pass without Charge': Hafter," *Egypt Independent*, June 1, 2017, https://ww.egyptindependent.com/qatar-support-terrorist-groups-libya/

42. "New Report Ties Qatar and Muslim Brotherhood to Libyan Rebel Leader Who Supported ISIS," *The National*, August 30, 2018, https://www.thenational.ae/world/mena/new-report-ties-qatar-and-muslim-brotherhood-to-libyan-rebel-leader-who-supported-isis-1.765368

43. Mohammed el-Araby, "Muslim Brotherhood and al-Qaeda in Libya Reject French Initiative," *Al-Arabiya*, May 28, 2018, https://english.alarabiya.net/en/News/north-africa/2018/05/28/Muslim-Brotherhood-and-al-Qaeda-in-Libya-reject-French-initiative.html

44. Zvi Mazel, "Erdogan's Grand Plan: Is Libya Next?" *The Jerusalem Post*, January 7, 2019, https://www.jpost.com/Opinion/Erdogans-grand-plan-Is-Libya-next-576631

45. Ahmed Eljechtimi, "Libya Complains of Arms Cargo from Turkey, Joint Investigation Launched," Reuters, December 22, 2018, https://www.reuters.com/article/us-libya-turkey/libya-complains-of-arms-cargo-from-turkey-joint-investigation-launched-idUSKCN1OL0G3

46. "Libya, Algeria Slam Turkey over Arms Shipment," *Asharq Al-Awsat*, December 24, 2018, https://aawsat.com/english/home/article/1517566/libya-algeria-slam-turkey-over-arms-shipment

47. Zvi Mazel, "Erdogan's Grand Plan: Is Libya Next?" *The Jerusalem Post*, January 7, 2019, https://www.jpost.com/Opinion/Erdogans-grand-plan-Is-Libya-next-576631

48. *Ibid.*

49. *Ibid.*

50. "IN PICTURES: Attempt to Smuggle Turkish Weapons into Libya Foiled," *Al Arabiya*, January 8, 2019, https://english.alarabiya.net/en/News/north-africa/2019/01/08/IN-PICTURES-Attempt-to-smuggle-Turkish-weapons-into-Libya-foiled.html

51. "Libyan Investigator of Turkish Weapon Shipment Survives Assassination Attempt," *218 News*, January 7, 2019, https://en.218tv.net/2019/01/07/libyan-investigator-of-turkish-weapon-shipment-survives-assassination-attempt/

52. *Ibid.*

53. Michael Rubin, "Turkey's Libya Gambit," *The National Interest*, January 11, 2019, https://nationalinterest.org/feature/turkeys-libya-gambit-41242

54. Amr Hamzawy, *Party for Justice and Development in Morocco: Participation and Its Discontents* (Washington, DC: Carnegie Endowment for International Peace, 2008), https://carnegieendowment.org/files/cp93_hamzawy_pjd_final1.pdf

55. *Ibid.*

56. Myriam Catusse and Karam Karam, *Returning to Political Parties? Political Party Development in the Arab World* (Beirut, Lebanon: Presses de l'Ifpo, 2018), 10.

57. *Ibid.*

58. Ashraf Nabih El Sherif, "Institutional and Ideological Re-construction of the Justice and Development Party (PJD): The Question of Democratic Islamism in Morocco," *Middle East Journal* 66, no. 4 (Autumn 2012): 660–682, https://www.jstor.org/stable/23361622

59. *Ibid.*

60. The New Arab & agencies, "Scandals Mount for Morocco's Muslim Brotherhood Ahead of Elections," *The New Arab*, August 26, 2016, https://www.alaraby.co.uk/english/indepth/2016/8/26/scandals-mount-for-moroccos-muslim-brotherhood-ahead-of-elections

61. Avi Spiegel, "Succeeding by Surviving: Examining the Durability of Political Islam in Morocco," Project on U.S. Relations with the Islamic World at Brookings, Working Paper (August 2015).

62. Mohamed Daadaoui, "Of Monarchs and Islamists: The 'Refo-lutionary' Promise of the PJD Islamists and Regime Control in Morocco," *Middle East Critique* 26, no. 4 (2017): 355–371, https://www.tandfonline.com/doi/abs/10.1080/19436149.2017.1366122

63. Peter Mandaville and Shadi Hamid, *Islam as Statecraft: How Governments Use Religion in Foreign Policy* (Washington, DC: The Brookings Institute, 2018).

64. *Ibid.*

65. Anonymous (former Director of the French Direction Generale de la Securite Exterieure) in discussion with the author, November 25, 2017, Boston, MA.

66. "The Muslim Brotherhood in Morocco," *Crethi Plethi* (blog), January 2012, http://www.crethiplethi.com/the-muslim-brotherhood-in-morocco/global-islam/2012/

67. Avi Spiegel, "Succeeding by Surviving: Examining the Durability of Political Islam in Morocco," Project on U.S. Relations with the Islamic World at Brookings, Working Paper (August 2015).

68. Anne Wolf, *Political Islam in Tunisia: The History of Ennahda* (New York, NY: Oxford University Press, 2017), 32.

69. *Ibid.*, 33.

70. Noureddine Jebnoun, *Tunisia at the Crossroads: An Interview with Sheikh Rachid al-Ghannouchi* (Washington, DC: Alwaleed Center for Muslim-Christian Understanding, 2017), https://issuu.com/georgetownsfs/docs/noureddine_jeb noun_tunisia_at_the_c

71. Anne Wolf, *Political Islam in Tunisia: The History of Ennahda* (New York, NY: Oxford University Press, 2017), 38.

72. Alaya Allani, "The Islamists in Tunisia Between Confrontation and Participation: 1980–2008," *The Journal of North African Studies* 14, no. 2 (2009): 257–272, http://www.righttononviolence.org/mecf/wp-content/uploads/2012/08/arti cle-alaya-PDF.pdf

73. *Ibid.*

74. Anne Wolf, *Political Islam in Tunisia: The History of Ennahda* (New York, NY: Oxford University Press, 2017), 46.

75. Noureddine Jebnoun, *Tunisia at the Crossroads: An Interview with Sheikh Rachid al-Ghannouchi* (Washington, DC: Alwaleed Center for Muslim-Christian Understanding, 2017), https://issuu.com/georgetownsfs/docs/noureddine_jeb noun_tunisia_at_the_c

76. Anne Wolf, *Political Islam in Tunisia: The History of Ennahda* (New York, NY: Oxford University Press, 2017), 50.

77. *Ibid.*

78. *Ibid.*, 54.

79. *Ibid.*, 54, 66.

80. *Ibid.*

81. Monica Marks, "Tunisia's Ennahda: Rethinking Islamism in the Context of ISIS and the Egyptian Coup," Project on U.S. Relations with the Islamic World at Brookings, Working Paper (August 2015).

82. Mehdi Mabrouk, "Tunisia: The Radicalization of Religious Policy," in *Islamist Radicalization in North Africa: Politics and Process*, ed. George Joffé (New York, NY: Routledge, 2012).

83. Anne Wolf, *Political Islam in Tunisia: The History of Ennahda* (New York, NY: Oxford University Press, 2017), 101.

84. Tarek Amara and Andrew Hammond, "Violence Erupts After Tunisian Islamists Win Vote," Reuters, October 27, 2011, https://www.reuters.com/article/us-tunisia/violence-erupts-after-tunisian-islamists-win-vote-idUS TRE79Q32V20111027

85. Anne Wolf, *Political Islam in Tunisia: The History of Ennahda* (New York, NY: Oxford University Press, 2017), 139–140.

86. *Ibid.*, 154–155.

87. *Ibid.*

88. "Ennahda Is 'Leaving' Political Islam," Wilson Center, May 20, 2016, https://www.wilsoncenter.org/article/ennahda-gives-political-islam

89. Maajid Nawaz, "Tunisia Started the Arab Revolts, Now It's Beat Back the Islamist Tide," *Daily Beast*, June 1, 2016, https://www.thedailybeast.com/tunisia-started-the-arab-revolts-now-its-beat-back-the-islamist-tide?ref=scroll

90. Monica Marks, "Tunisia's Ennahda: Rethinking Islamism in the Context of ISIS and the Egyptian Coup," Project on U.S. Relations with the Islamic World at Brookings, Working Paper (August 2015).

91. "People in Turkey Becoming Less Religious—Konda Research," *Ahval News*, January 3, 2019, https://ahvalnews.com/religion/people-turkey-becoming-less-religious-konda-research#

92. *Ibid.*

93. *Ibid.*

94. Ahmed Nadhif, "Tunisia's Salafis: The Muslim Brotherhood's Other Face of Political Islam," *7D News*, November 15, 2018, https://7dnews.com/news/tunisia-s-salafis-the-muslim-brotherhood-s-other-face-of-political-islam

95. Rebecca Koch, "Islam and Politics in Tunisia: How Did the Islamist Party Ennahda Respond to the Rise of Salafism in Post-Arab Spring Tunisia and What Are Possible Explanatory Factors of This Reaction?" (unpublished paper, Paris School of International Affairs, 2014), https://www.sciencespo.fr/kuwait-program/wp-content/uploads/2018/05/KSP_Paper_Award_Spring_2015_KOCH_Rebecca.pdf

96. Monica Marks, "Tunisia's Ennahda: Rethinking Islamism in the Context of ISIS and the Egyptian Coup," Project on U.S. Relations with the Islamic World at Brookings, Working Paper (August 2015).

97. Kevin Sullivan, "Tunisia, after Igniting Arab Spring, Sends the Most Fighters to Islamic State after Syria," *Washington Post*, October 28, 2014, https://www.washingtonpost.com/world/national-security/tunisia-after-igniting-arab-spring-sends-the-most-fighters-to-islamic-state-in-syria/2014/10/28/b5db4faa-5971-11e4-8264-deed989ae9a2_story.html

98. Sondos Asem, "From Uprisings to Political Crisis: How Tunisia's Democracy Came to Be at Risk," *Middle East Eye*, December 11, 2018, https://www.middleeasteye.net/news/uprisings-political-crisis-how-tunisias-democracy-came-be-risk

99. James Legge, "Tunisia Shocked by Assassinations: Opposition Leaders Mohamed Brahmi and Chokri Belaid Killed with the Same Gun," *Independent*, July 26, 2013, https://www.independent.co.uk/news/world/africa/tunisia-shocked-by-assassinations-opposition-leaders-mohamed-brahmi-and-chokri-belaid-killed-with-8733972.html

100. Kevin Sullivan, "Tunisia, after Igniting Arab Spring, Sends the Most Fighters to Islamic State after Syria," *Washington Post*, October 28, 2014, https://www.washingtonpost.com/world/national-security/tunisia-after-igniting-arab-spring-sends-the-most-fighters-to-islamic-state-in-syria/2014/10/28/b5db4faa-5971-11e4-8264-deed989ae9a2_story.html

101. Mohamed Bechri, "Tunisia's Security-First Policy at a Crossroads," *Fikra Forum* (blog), The Washington Institute, July 23, 2014, https://www.washingtoninstitute.org/policy-analysis/view/tunisias-security-first-policy-at-a-crossroads

102. Kevin Sullivan, "Tunisia, after Igniting Arab Spring, Sends the Most Fighters to Islamic State after Syria," *Washington Post*, October 28, 2014,

Conclusion

And so the story comes to an end. It is, as one can see, an ultimately tragic tale. It is a tale of an organization that had, perhaps at first, noble and good intentions, but which, as history unfolded and more and more players became involved in the game, inevitably grew corrupt. It fell victim to its own ineptitudes and ambitions. It failed, and in its failure it brought many down with it. In essence, the Muslim Brotherhood is now "fragmented and weakened geographically, generationally and hierarchically . . . the senior leadership is in jail and broadly urging caution, the youth are either angry at what they see as the failures of the leaders and attracted to more militant tactics, or convinced political ambition was a mistake altogether and focused on preaching."[1]

Yet, even though the MB has failed politically in the Arab world, it is still able to wreak havoc. A few MB-affiliated groups have been able to participate in parliamentary politics by stripping away their entire Islamist agenda. But for the most part, the Arab nations of the Middle East and North Africa, especially after the overthrow of Morsi, seem politically closed to the MB. The group's next phase in the region will require a new strategy, or perhaps an old one, and social and political ambitions of a different order.

If one can speak of success relative to the MB, it is only within two contexts: the context of those affiliates that have given up so much of the MB agenda that they can barely be called an MB affiliate and the context of Qatari support that has kept the group's life support on well past when it should have been reasonably unplugged. Indeed, as this book has made abundantly clear, there has been a conspiracy in place for decades on the

https://www.washingtonpost.com/world/national-security/tunisia-after-ignit
ing-arab-spring-sends-the-most-fighters-to-islamic-state-in-syria/2014/10/28/
b5db4faa-5971-11e4-8264-deed989ae9a2_story.html

103. *Ibid*.

104. *Ibid*.

105. James Legge, "Tunisia Shocked by Assassinations: Opposition Leaders
Mohamed Brahmi and Chokri Belaid Killed with the Same Gun," *Independent*, July
26, 2013, https://www.independent.co.uk/news/world/africa/tunisia-shocked-
by-assassinations-opposition-leaders-mohamed-brahmi-and-chokri-belaid-
killed-with-8733972.html

106. Aaron Zelin, "Tunisian Jihadism Five Years After Ansar al-Sharia," The
Washington Institute, September 16, 2018, https://www.washingtoninstitute.org/
policy-analysis/view/tunisian-jihadism-five-years-after-ansar-al-sharia

107. Mohamed Ali Ltifi, "Does Tunisia's Police Protection Bill Go Too Far?"
Al-Monitor, November 26, 2017, https://www.al-monitor.com/pulse/originals/
2017/11/tunisia-bill-repress-attacks-armed-forces.html

108. Hany Ghoraba, "Tunisian Ennahda's 'Secret Apparatus' Draws Compari-
sons to Brotherhood Origins," *IPT News*, November 9, 2018, https://www.investi
gativeproject.org/7699/tunisia-ennahda-secret-apparatus-draws

109. Mohamed Ali Ltifi, "Does Tunisia's Police Protection Bill Go Too Far?"
Al-Monitor, November 26, 2017, https://www.al-monitor.com/pulse/originals/
2017/11/tunisia-bill-repress-attacks-armed-forces.html

110. Sondos Asem, "From Uprisings to Political Crisis: How Tunisia's Democracy Came to Be at Risk," *Middle East Eye*, December 11, 2018, https://www.middlee
asteye.net/news/uprisings-political-crisis-how-tunisias-democracy-came-be-risk

111. *Ibid*.

112. Mohamed Ali Ltifi, "Does Tunisia's Police Protection Bill Go Too Far?"
Al-Monitor, November 26, 2017, https://www.al-monitor.com/pulse/originals/
2017/11/tunisia-bill-repress-attacks-armed-forces.html

113. Samer Al-Atrush, "An Arab Street Caught Between Hope and Despair as
Strike Looms," *Bloomberg*, January 16, 2019, https://www.bloomberg.com/news/
articles/2019-01-17/an-arab-street-caught-between-hope-and-despair-as-strike-
looms

114. Aaron Zelin, "Tunisian Jihadism Five Years After Ansar al-Sharia," The
Washington Institute, September 16, 2018, https://www.washingtoninstitute
.org/policy-analysis/view/tunisian-jihadism-five-years-after-ansar-al-sharia

115. *Ibid*.

116. Sudarsan Raghavan, "Tunisia Feared the Return of Militants from Abroad.
The Threat Now Is Those Who Never Left," *Washington Post*, September 8, 2018,
https://www.washingtonpost.com/world/tunisia-feared-the-return-of-mil
itants-from-abroad-the-threat-now-is-those-who-never-left/2018/09/07/aaf
a6c84-aacf-11e8-9a7d-cd30504ff902_story.html

117. Aaron Zelin, "Tunisian Jihadism Five Years After Ansar al-Sharia," The
Washington Institute, September 16, 2018, https://www.washingtoninstitute
.org/policy-analysis/view/tunisian-jihadism-five-years-after-ansar-al-sharia

118. "Sudan's Islamists: From Salvation to Survival," *International Crisis Group*
briefing, no. 19 (March 2016), https://d2071andvip0wj.cloudfront.net/b119-su
dan-s-islamists-from-salvation-to-survival.pdf

119. "Muslim Brotherhood in Sudan," *Oxford Islamic Studies Online*, accessed June 25, 2019, http://www.oxfordislamicstudies.com/article/opr/t125/e1641

120. Stig Jarle Hansen and Atle Mesøy, "The Muslim Brotherhood in the Wider Horn of Africa," *Norwegian Institute for Urban and Regional Research*, no. 33 (December 2009), https://www.researchgate.net/publication/265191361_The_Muslim_Brotherhood_in_the_Wider_Horn_of_Africa

121. *Ibid.*

122. *Ibid.*

123. Associated Press, "Hassan al-Turabi, Sudan Opposition Leader Who Hosted Osama bin Laden, Dies," *The Guardian*, March 5, 2016, https://www.theguardian.com/world/2016/mar/06/hassan-al-turabi-sudan-opposition-leader-who-hosted-osama-bin-laden-dies

124. Stig Jarle Hansen and Atle Mesøy, "The Muslim Brotherhood in the Wider Horn of Africa," *Norwegian Institute for Urban and Regional Research*, no. 33 (December 2009), https://www.researchgate.net/publication/265191361_The_Muslim_Brotherhood_in_the_Wider_Horn_of_Africa

125. *Ibid.*

126. *Ibid.*

127. "Muslim Brotherhood in Sudan," *Oxford Islamic Studies Online*, accessed June 25, 2019, http://www.oxfordislamicstudies.com/article/opr/t125/e1641

128. Stig Jarle Hansen and Atle Mesøy, "The Muslim Brotherhood in the Wider Horn of Africa," *Norwegian Institute for Urban and Regional Research*, no. 33 (December 2009), https://www.researchgate.net/publication/265191361_The_Muslim_Brotherhood_in_the_Wider_Horn_of_Africa

129. "Muslim Brotherhood in Sudan," *Oxford Islamic Studies Online*, accessed June 25, 2019, http://www.oxfordislamicstudies.com/article/opr/t125/e1641

130. "National Islamic Front," Military, GlobalSecurity.org, accessed June 25, 2019, https://www.globalsecurity.org/military/world/sudan/political-parties-nif.htm

131. Stig Jarle Hansen and Atle Mesøy, "The Muslim Brotherhood in the Wider Horn of Africa," *Norwegian Institute for Urban and Regional Research*, no. 33 (December 2009), https://www.researchgate.net/publication/265191361_The_Muslim_Brotherhood_in_the_Wider_Horn_of_Africa

132. *Ibid.*

133. Jamal Mahjoub, "My Father Died Before He Could See al-Bashir Fall," *The New York Times*, April 12, 2019, https://www.nytimes.com/2019/04/12/opinion/my-father-died-before-he-could-see-bashir-fall.html

134. Stig Jarle Hansen and Atle Mesøy, "The Muslim Brotherhood in the Wider Horn of Africa," *Norwegian Institute for Urban and Regional Research*, no. 33 (December 2009), https://www.researchgate.net/publication/265191361_The_Muslim_Brotherhood_in_the_Wider_Horn_of_Africa

135. "Turkey Sends Militants to Sudan and Then into Libyan City of Sirte to Join Al Qaeda—Anti-terror Agency," *soL International*, March 19, 2018, https://news.sol.org.tr/turkey-sends-militants-sudan-and-then-libyan-city-sirte-join-al-qaeda-anti-terror-agency-174315

136. Mustafa Gurbuz, "How Saudi Arabia Outmanoeuvred Turkey in Sudan," *Ahval News*, June 11, 2019, https://ahvalnews.com/geopolitics/how-saudi-arabia-outmanoeuvred-turkey-sudan#

137. "Turkey Temporarily Granted Ancient Ottoman Red Sea Port in Sudan for Rebuilding," *Sputnik*, December 26, 2017, https://sputniknews.com/africa/2017 12261060333479-erdogan-red-sea-port-sudan-restoration-ottoman-empire/

138. Carol Morello, "U.S. Lifts Sanctions on Sudan, Ending Two Decades of Embargo," *Washington Post*, October 6, 2017, https://www.washingtonpost.com/world/national-security/us-lifts-sanctions-on-sudan-ending-two-decades-of-em bargo/2017/10/06/aac1bd22-86d5-434e-9a21-1e0d57a72cb0_story.html

139. Mustafa Gurbuz, "How Saudi Arabia Outmanoeuvred Turkey in Sudan," *Ahval News*, June 11, 2019, https://ahvalnews.com/geopolitics/how-saudi-ara bia-outmanoeuvred-turkey-sudan#

140. Matina Stevis-Gridneff and Summer Said, "As Sudan Grapples with a Post-Bashir Future, Regional Powers Circle," *Wall Street Journal*, April 27, 2019, https://www.wsj.com/articles/as-sudan-grapples-with-a-post-bashir-future-re gional-powers-circle-11556362800

141. *Ibid.*

142. Khalid Abdelaziz, "Saudi Arabia, UAE to Send $3 Billion in Aid to Su-dan," Reuters, April 21, 2019, https://www.reuters.com/article/us-sudan-pro tests/saudi-arabia-uae-to-send-3-billion-in-aid-to-sudan-idUSKCN1RX0DG

143. Amr Emam, "Sudan Likely to Hand Over Muslim Brotherhood Members to Egypt," *The Arab Weekly*, June 9, 2019, https://thearabweekly.com/sudan-like ly-hand-over-muslim-brotherhood-members-egypt

144. *Ibid.*

145. Peter Beaumont and Zeinab Mohammed, "Sudan: What Future for the Country's Islamists?" *The Guardian*, May 2, 2019, https://www.theguardian.com/world/2019/may/02/sudan-what-future-for-the-countrys-islamists

CHAPTER 3

1. David Kirkpatrick, *Into the Hands of the Soldiers: Freedom and Chaos in Egypt and the Middle East* (New York, NY: Penguin, 2018), 116.

2. Muhammad Hasanayn Haykal, *Autumn of Fury: The Assassination of Sadat* (New York, NY: Random House, 1983), 226.

3. *Ibid.*, 253.

4. "The Egyptian Muslim Brotherhood: Building Bases of Support," *Director-ate of Intelligence at Central Intelligence Agency*, May 1986, https://www.cia.gov/library/readingroom/docs/CIA-RDP88T00096R000200240001-4.pdf

5. Martyn Frampton, *The Muslim Brotherhood and the West: A History of Enmity and Engagement* (Cambridge, MA: The Belknap Press of Harvard University Press, 2018), 339.

6. Muhammad Hasanayn Haykal, *Autumn of Fury: The Assassination of Sadat* (New York, NY: Random House, 1983), 254.

7. "The Egyptian Muslim Brotherhood: Building Bases of Support," *Director-ate of Intelligence at Central Intelligence Agency*, May 1986, 2, https://www.cia.gov/library/readingroom/docs/CIA-RDP88T00096R000200240001-4.pdf

8. *Ibid.*

9. *Ibid.*

10. *Ibid.*, 4.

11. Elizabeth Iskander Monier and Annette Ranko, "The Fall of the Muslin Brotherhood: Implications for Egypt," *Middle East Policy Council* 20, no. 4 (Winter 2013), http://www.mepc.org/fall-muslim-brotherhood-implications-egypt

12. "The Egyptian Muslim Brotherhood: Building Bases of Support," *Directorate of Intelligence at Central Intelligence Agency*, May 1986, https://www.cia.gov/library/readingroom/docs/CIA-RDP88T00096R000200240001-4.pdf

13. *Ibid.*

14. Alison Pargeter, *The Muslim Brotherhood: From Opposition to Power* (London, England: Saqi Books, 2013), 54–56.

15. *Ibid.*

16. David Kirkpatrick, *Into the Hands of the Soldiers: Freedom and Chaos in Egypt and the Middle East* (New York, NY: Penguin, 2018), 37.

17. Anonymous (former Arab ambassador to Egypt between 2011 and 2016) in discussion with the author, January 20th, 2019, Paris, France.

18. CNN Wire Staff, "Egyptian Police Crack Down on Second Day of Protests," *CNN*, January 27, 2011, http://edition.cnn.com/2011/WORLD/africa/01/26/egypt.protests/index.html

19. Amira Nowaira, "Egypt's Day of Rage Goes On. Is the World Watching?" *The Guardian*, January 27, 2011, https://www.theguardian.com/commentisfree/2011/jan/27/egypt-protests-regime-citizens

20. Anonymous (former senior State Department envoy involved in the Egyptian transition between 2011 and 2014) in discussion with the author, May 5, 2018, Boston, MA.

21. Jamal Khashoggi (former Al Hayat and Washington Post Columnist) in discussion with the author, April 12, 2017, London, England.

22. Abdel Moneim Aboul-Fotouh, "'All They Can Do Is Kill'," interview by Christoph Reuter. *Spiegel Online*, August 19, 2013, https://www.spiegel.de/international/world/islamist-party-leader-aboul-fotouh-on-military-power-grab-in-egypt-a-917303.html

23. Kristen Chick, "Candidate Aboul Fotouh Highlights Diversity of Egypt's Islamists," *Christian Science Monitor*, May 18, 2012, https://www.csmonitor.com/World/Middle-East/2012/0518/Candidate-Aboul-Fotouh-highlights-diversity-of-Egypt-s-Islamists

24. David Kirkpatrick, *Into the Hands of the Soldiers: Freedom and Chaos in Egypt and the Middle East* (New York, NY: Penguin, 2018), 127.

25. Issandr El Amrani, "Why Khairat al-Shater Is Running," *Arabist* (blog), April 2, 2012, https://arabist.net/blog/2012/4/2/why-khairat-al-shater-is-running.html

26. David Kirkpatrick, *Into the Hands of the Soldiers: Freedom and Chaos in Egypt and the Middle East* (New York, NY: Penguin, 2018), 129.

27. Anonymous (former ambassador to Egypt between 2011 and 2016) in discussion with the author, January 20, 2019, Paris, France.

28. Dina Samak, "Will El-Shater Nomination Split Egypt's Brotherhood?" *Ahram Online*, April 4, 2012, http://english.ahram.org.eg/NewsContent/1/64/38392/Egypt/Politics-/Will-ElShater-nomination-split-Egypts-Brotherhood.aspx

29. Bradley Hope, "Khairat Al Shater—Muslim Brotherhood Power Broker and Now Target of Egyptian Anger," *The National*, July 2, 2013, https://www.thenational.ae/world/mena/khairat-al-shater-muslim-brotherhood-power-broker-and-now-target-of-egyptian-anger-1.597207

30. Jamal Khashoggi (former Al Hayat and Washington Post Columnist) in discussion with the author, April 12, 2017, London, England.

31. Bessma Momani, "Why Egypt Needs Space from Morsi," *Brookings*, February 25, 2013, https://www.brookings.edu/opinions/why-egypt-needs-space-from-morsi/

32. Peter Hessler, "The Showdown," *New Yorker*, July 15, 2013, https://www.newyorker.com/magazine/2013/07/22/the-showdown-2

33. Ian Black, "Mohammed Morsi: Brotherhood's Backroom Operator in the Limelight," *The Guardian*, May 25, 2012, https://www.theguardian.com/world/2012/may/25/mohammed-morsi-muslim-brotherhood

34. Bradley Hope, "Khairat Al Shater—Muslim Brotherhood Power Broker and Now Target of Egyptian Anger," *The National*, July 2, 2013, https://www.thenational.ae/world/mena/khairat-al-shater-muslim-brotherhood-power-broker-and-now-target-of-egyptian-anger-1.597207

35. David Kirkpatrick, *Into the Hands of the Soldiers: Freedom and Chaos in Egypt and the Middle East* (New York, NY: Penguin, 2018), 158.

36. Maggie Michael, "Egypt's New Leader Claims Revolution's Mantle," *The Times of Israel*, July 3, 2012, https://www.timesofisrael.com/egypts-new-leader-claims-revolutions-mantle/

37. David Kirkpatrick, *Into the Hands of the Soldiers: Freedom and Chaos in Egypt and the Middle East* (New York, NY: Penguin, 2018), 159.

38. *Ibid.*, 160.

39. Abdel-Rahman Hussein, "Egypt Defence Chief Tantawi Ousted in Surprise Shakeup," *The Guardian*, August 13, 2012, https://www.theguardian.com/world/2012/aug/12/egyptian-defence-chief-ousted-shakeup

40. Rasha Abdulla, *Egypt's Media in the Midst of Revolution* (Washington, DC: Carnegie Endowment for International Peace, 2014), https://carnegieendowment.org/files/egypt_media_revolution.pdf

41. Peter Hessler, "Tahrir Square Turns Against Morsi," *New Yorker*, November 24, 2012, https://www.newyorker.com/news/news-desk/tahrir-square-turns-against-morsi

42. David Kirkpatrick, *Into the Hands of the Soldiers: Freedom and Chaos in Egypt and the Middle East* (New York, NY: Penguin, 2018), 178.

43. Elizabeth Iskander Monier and Annette Ranko, "The Fall of the Muslim Brotherhood: Implications for Egypt," *Middle East Policy Council* 20, no. 4 (Winter 2013), http://www.mepc.org/fall-muslim-brotherhood-implications-egypt

44. Peter Beaumont, "Protests Erupt Across Egypt After Presidential Decree," *The Guardian*, November 23, 2012, https://www.theguardian.com/world/2012/nov/23/protests-egypt-presidential-decree

45. Tarek Masoud, *Counting Islam: Religion, Class, and Elections in Egypt (Problems of International Politics)* (New York, NY: Cambridge University Press, 2014).

46. David Kirkpatrick, *Into the Hands of the Soldiers: Freedom and Chaos in Egypt and the Middle East* (New York, NY: Penguin, 2018), 186.

47. Eric Trager and Marina Shalabi, "The Brotherhood Breaks Down," The Washington Institute, January 17, 2016, https://www.washingtoninstitute.org/policy-analysis/view/the-brotherhood-breaks-down

48. Mohammed Mido, "مظاهرات قصر الاتحادية," 4/12/2012 YouTube video, 8:52, December 5, 2012, https://www.youtube.com/watch?v=MECAKJf-gkU; Kareem

Abd El-Wahab, "احداث قصر الاتحادية شارع الخليفة المأمون," YouTube video, 8:26, December 6, 2012, https://www.youtube.com/watch?v=Xqr4JYdg9mI

49. David Kirkpatrick, *Into the Hands of the Soldiers: Freedom and Chaos in Egypt and the Middle East* (New York, NY: Penguin, 2018), 188.

50. Associated Press in Cairo, "Morsi Supporters Clash with Protesters Outside Presidential Palace in Cairo," *The Guardian*, December 5, 2012, https://www.theguardian.com/world/2012/dec/05/morsi-supporters-protest-presidential-palace-cairo

51. Zainab Magdy, "The 'Feminism' of Patriarchy in Egypt," *openDemocracy*, December 5, 2013, https://www.opendemocracy.net/en/5050/feminism-of-patriarchy-in-egypt/

52. *Ibid.*

53. David Kirkpatrick, *Into the Hands of the Soldiers: Freedom and Chaos in Egypt and the Middle East* (New York, NY: Penguin, 2018), 197.

54. *Ibid.*, 194–195.

55. "Egypt nearing collapse, warns army," *DW*, January 29, 2013, https://www.dw.com/en/egypt-nearing-collapse-warns-army/a-16559039

56. Fawaz bin Mohammed Al Khalifa (Bahrain's ambassador to the UK) in discussion with the author, December 5, 2018, London, England.

57. Patrick Kingsley, "Egyptian Police Go on Strike," *The Guardian*, March 10, 2013, https://www.theguardian.com/world/2013/mar/10/egypt-police-strike

58. Associated Press, "Thousands of Egyptians Across Country Protest Morsi," *Times of Israel*, April 6, 2013, https://www.timesofisrael.com/egyptians-across-country-protest-morsi/

59. Evan Hill and Muhammad Mansour, "Egypt's Army Took Part in Torture and Killings During Revolution, Report Shows," *The Guardian*, April 10, 2013, https://www.theguardian.com/world/2013/apr/10/egypt-army-torture-killings-revolution

60. David Kirkpatrick, *Into the Hands of the Soldiers: Freedom and Chaos in Egypt and the Middle East* (New York, NY: Penguin, 2018), 212.

61. *Ibid.*

62. Walaa Hussein, "Egypt's Tamarod Outlives Its Purpose," *Al-Monitor*, May 8, 2015, https://www.al-monitor.com/pulse/originals/2015/05/egypt-tamarod-movement-political-campaign-mubarak-sisi.html

63. Neil Ketchley, "How Egypt's Generals Used Street Protests to Stage a Coup," *Washington Post*, July 3, 2017, https://www.washingtonpost.com/news/monkey-cage/wp/2017/07/03/how-egypts-generals-used-street-protests-to-stage-a-coup/

64. News Wires, "Egypt's Luxor Governor Resigns After Controversy," *France 24*, June 23, 2013, https://www.france24.com/en/20130623-egypt-luxor-islamist-governor-adel-al-Khayat resigns-Mohammed-Morsi

65. MEE Correspondent, "Egypt and the Coup: Inside the 11 Days That Toppled Morsi," *Middle East Eye*, July 3, 2018, https://www.middleeasteye.net/news/egypt-and-coup-inside-11-days-toppled-morsi

66. Daniel Steinvorth, "Morsi and Precipice After Disastrous Year," *Spiegel Online*, July 2, 2013, https://www.spiegel.de/international/world/egyptian-army-gives-morsi-of-muslim-brotherhood-a-48-hour-ultimatum-a-908823.html

67. MEE Correspondent, "Egypt and the Coup: Inside the 11 Days That Toppled Morsi," *Middle East Eye*, July 3, 2018, https://www.middleeasteye.net/news/egypt-and-coup-inside-11-days-toppled-morsi

68. Richard Engel (RichardEngel), "Sources #army in Charge State TV Building. Staff Being Told to Go Home Early, Leaving Only Essential Personnel. #egypt," Twitter post, July 3, 2013, 5:32 A.M., https://twitter.com/RichardEngel/statuses/352404601368092673

69. Paul Taylor, "ElBaradei Party Asks Army to Save Egyptians from 'Mad' Morsi," Reuters, July 3, 2013, https://www.reuters.com/article/us-egypt-protests-elbaradei/elbaradei-party-asks-army-to-save-egyptians-from-mad-morsi-idUSBRE9620D120130703

70. Connor Simpson, Dashiell Bennett, and Abby Ohlheiser, "Tahrir Square Erupts in Cheers as Morsi Is Removed from Office," *The Atlantic*, July 3, 2013, https://www.theatlantic.com/international/archive/2013/07/egypt-morsi-deadline/313649/

71. David Kirkpatrick, "Army Ousts Egypt's President; Morsi Is Taken into Military Custody," *The New York Times*, July 3, 2013, https://www.nytimes.com/2013/07/04/world/middleeast/egypt.html

72. Anthony DeRosa (Anthony), "Arrest Warrants Issued for 300 Members of Muslim Brotherhood—Egypt State Newspaper Al-Ahram," Twitter post, July 3, 2013, 4:01 P.M., https://twitter.com/Anthony/status/352562887698550787

73. Connor Simpson, Dashiell Bennett, and Abby Ohlheiser, "Tahrir Square Erupts in Cheers as Morsi Is Removed from Office," *The Atlantic*, July 3, 2013, https://www.theatlantic.com/international/archive/2013/07/egypt-morsi-deadline/313649/

74. Arab News, "King Abdullah Congratulates New Egyptian Leader," *Arab News*, July 4, 2013, http://www.arabnews.com/news/456958

75. Patrick Werr, "UAE Offers Egypt $3 Billion Support, Saudis $5 Billion," Reuters, July 9, 2013, https://www.reuters.com/article/us-egypt-protests-loan/uae-offers-egypt-3-billion-support-saudis-5-billion-idUSBRE9680H020130709

76. Connor Simpson, Dashiell Bennett, and Abby Ohlheiser, "Tahrir Square Erupts in Cheers as Morsi Is Removed from Office," *The Atlantic*, July 3, 2013, https://www.theatlantic.com/international/archive/2013/07/egypt-morsi-deadline/313649/

77. David Kirkpatrick, *Into the Hands of the Soldiers: Freedom and Chaos in Egypt and the Middle East* (New York, NY: Penguin, 2018), 242.

78. *Ibid.*, 256–257.

79. Ashraf El-Sherif, *The Egyptian Muslim Brotherhood's Failures* (Washington, DC: Carnegie Endowment for International Peace, 2014), https://carnegieendowment.org/files/muslim_brotherhood_failures.pdf

80. *Ibid.*

81. Tarek Masoud, *Counting Islam: Religion, Class, and Elections in Egypt (Problems of International Politics)* (New York, NY: Cambridge University Press, 2014).

82. *Ibid.*

83. *Ibid.*

84. *Ibid.*

85. Bradley Hope, "Khairat Al Shater—Muslim Brotherhood Power Broker and Now Target of Egyptian Anger," *The National*, July 2, 2013, https://www.thenational.ae/world/mena/khairat-al-shater-muslim-brotherhood-power-broker-and-now-target-of-egyptian-anger-1.597207

86. *Ibid.*

87. Elizabeth Iskander Monier and Annette Ranko, "The Fall of the Muslim Brotherhood: Implications for Egypt," *Middle East Policy Council* 20, no. 4 (Winter 2013), http://www.mepc.org/fall-muslim-brotherhood-implications-egypt

88. Khalil al-Anani, "The Salafi-Brotherhood Feud in Egypt," *Al-Monitor*, February 21, 2013, https://www.al-monitor.com/pulse/originals/2013/02/muslim-brotherhood-salafist-feud-in-egypt.html

89. Elizabeth Iskander Monier and Annette Ranko, "The Fall of the Muslim Brotherhood: Implications for Egypt," *Middle East Policy Council* 20, no. 4 (Winter 2013), http://www.mepc.org/fall-muslim-brotherhood-implications-egypt

90. *Ibid.*

91. John Jenkins, "Three Things Western Analysts Get Wrong about the Middle East," *Arab News*, June 15, 2019, http://www.arabnews.com/node/1511206

92. Shadi Hamid, "The Massacre That Ended the Arab Spring," *The Atlantic*, August 14, 2017, https://www.theatlantic.com/international/archive/2017/08/arab-spring-rabaa-massacre/536847/

93. Thoraya Obaid (former UN Under-Secretary-General for Population Affairs, and executive director of the UN Population Fund) in discussion with the author.

94. Yasmine Saleh and Tom Finn, "More Than 200 Dead after Egypt Forces Crush Protest Camps," Reuters, August 13, 2013, https://www.reuters.com/article/us-egypt-protests/more-than-200-dead-after-egypt-forces-crush-protest-camps-idUSBRE97C09A20130814

95. Patrick Kingsley, "Egypt's Rabaa Massacre: One Year on," *The Guardian*, August 16, 2014, https://www.theguardian.com/world/2014/aug/16/rabaa-massacre-egypt-human-rights-watch

96. Bethan McKernan, "Rabaa Massacre: Five Years on Egypt Struggles with Legacy of Single Biggest Killing of Protesters in Modern History," *Independent*, August 14, 2018, https://www.independent.co.uk/news/world/middle-east/egypt-rabaa-massacre-cairo-muslim-brotherhood-abdel-fattah-al-sisi-ibrahim-halawa-a8491821.html

97. Heba Farouk Mahfouz et al., "Witnessing a Massacre," *Mada Masr*, August 14, 2017, https://madamasr.com/en/2017/08/14/feature/politics/witnessing-a-massacre/

98. Saba Elbalad, "علي مسئوليتي—أبو هاشم المنشق عن الاخوان يتحدث لاول مرة ويفضح اسرار التنظيم الارهابي," YouTube video, 2:31:52, August 11, 2018, https://www.youtube.com/watch?v=I7fvwSJuugw

99. *Ibid.*

100. "US Congressmen Tried to Designate the Muslim Brotherhood as Terrorist," *Ikhwan Info*, November 4, 2015, http://www.ikhwan.whoswho/en/archives/740

101. Eric Trager, *Arab Fall: How the Muslim Brotherhood Won and Lost Egypt in 891 Days* (Washington, DC: Georgetown University Press, 2016), 228.

102. Saba Elbalad, "علي مسئوليتي—أبو هاشم المنشق عن الاخوان يتحدث لاول مرة ويفضح اسرار التنظيم الارهابي," YouTube video, 2:31:52, August 11, 2018, https://www.youtube.com/watch?v=I7fvwSJuugw

103. *Ibid.*

104. Mohammed Mostafa, "Egypt al-Sisi—The Life of the People," Blog post, http://www.tutcn.com/2018/01/21_11.htm

105. Thoraya Obaid in discussion with author, October 3, 2018.

106. Mohammed Mostafa, "Egypt al-Sisi—The Life of the People," Blog post, http://www.tutcn.com/2018/01/21_11.htm

107. *Ibid.*

108. *Ibid.*

109. *Ibid.*

110. Jason Brownlee, "Morsi was No Role Model for Islamic Democrats," Middle East Institute, July 17, 2013, http://education.mei.edu/content/morsi-was-no-role-model-islamic-democrats

111. Tarek Masoud, *Counting Islam: Religion, Class, and Elections in Egypt (Problems of International Politics)* (New York, NY: Cambridge University Press, 2014).

112. *Ibid.*

113. Eric Trager, "Where Did They Go Wrong?" *Cipher Brief*, August 12, 2016, https://www.washingtoninstitute.org/policy-analysis/view/where-did-they-go-wrong

114. "Changes in U.S. Diplomacy," Baker Institute for Public Policy, November 26, 2012, https://www.bakerinstitute.org/news/one-man-one-vote-one-time/

115. Sada Elbalad, "على مسئوليتي—اعتراف الإرهابي عادل حبارة بارتكابه مجزرة رفح," YouTube video, 2:14, December 10, 2016, https://www.youtube.com/watch?v=1GJKdo86DuE

116. Omar Fahmy, Stephen Kalin, and Catherine Evans, "Egypt Carries Out First Execution of Mursi Supporter," Reuters, March 7, 2015, https://www.reuters.com/article/us-egypt-execution-islamist-idUSKBN0M30AU20150308

117. Louisa Loveluck, "Sisi Says Muslim Brotherhood Will Not Exist Under His Reign," *The Guardian*, May 5, 2014, https://www.theguardian.com/world/2014/may/06/abdel-fatah-al-sisi-muslim-brotherhood-egypt

118. "Egypt: Torture Epidemic May Be Crime Against Humanity," *Human Rights Watch*, September 6, 2017, https://www.hrw.org/news/2017/09/06/egypt-torture-epidemic-may-be-crime-against-humanity#

119. David Kirkpatrick, *Into the Hands of the Soldiers: Freedom and Chaos in Egypt and the Middle East* (New York, NY: Penguin, 2018), 297.

120. Hassan Hassan, "The Arab Winter Is Coming," *The Atlantic*, November 3, 2018, https://www.theatlantic.com/ideas/archive/2018/11/where-us-middle-east/574747/

121. Egypt Today staff, "Egypt Blacklists 600 Persons for Funding Muslim Brotherhood: Sources," *Egypt Today*, May 15, 2019, http://www.egypttoday.com/Article/1/70433/Egypt-blacklists-600-persons-for-funding-Muslim-Brotherhood-sources

122. Elizabeth Iskander Monier and Annette Ranko, "The Fall of the Muslim Brotherhood: Implications for Egypt," *Middle East Policy Council* 20, no. 4 (Winter 2013), http://www.mepc.org/fall-muslim-brotherhood-implications-egypt

123. Michael Crowley, "Trump to Welcome Egypt's Dictator," *Politico*, April 2, 2017, https://www.politico.eu/article/trump-to-welcome-egypts-dictator/

124. Tarek Masoud, *Counting Islam: Religion, Class, and Elections in Egypt (Problems of International Politics)* (New York, NY: Cambridge University Press, 2014).

125. David Kirkpatrick, *Into the Hands of the Soldiers: Freedom and Chaos in Egypt and the Middle East* (New York, NY: Penguin, 2018), 292.

126. *Ibid.*, 293.

127. Mokhtar Awad, "The Rise of the Muslim Brotherhood," Hudson Institute, November 6, 2017, https://www.hudson.org/research/13787-the-rise-of-the-violent-muslim-brotherhood

128. *Ibid.*

129. Murtaza Hussain, "ISIS Recruitment Thrives in Brutal Prisons Run by U.S.-Backed Egypt," *The Intercept*, November 24, 2015, https://theintercept .com/2015/11/24/isis-recruitment-thrives-in-brutal-prisons-run-by-u-s-backed-egypt/

130. Elizabeth Iskander Monier and Annette Ranko, "The Fall of the Muslim Brotherhood: Implications for Egypt," *Middle East Policy Council* 20, no. 4 (Winter 2013), http://www.mepc.org/fall-muslim-brotherhood-implications-egypt

131. Mokhtar Awad, "The Rise of the Muslim Brotherhood," Hudson Institute, November 6, 2017, https://www.hudson.org/research/13787-the-rise-of-the-vio lent-muslim-brotherhood

132. *Ibid.*

133. *Ibid.*

134. *Ibid.*

135. Nawaf Obaid, "The Muslim Brotherhood: A Failure in Political Evolution," *Intelligence Project*, 2017, https://www.belfercenter.org/sites/default/files/files/publication/Muslim%20Brotherhood%20-%20final.pdf

136. Martyn Frampton, *The Muslim Brotherhood and the West: A History of Enmity and Engagement* (Cambridge, MA: The Belknap Press of Harvard University Press, 2018), 305.

137. Hazem Kandil, *Inside the Brotherhood* (Cambridge, England: Polity Press, 2015).

138. Mokhtar Awad, "The Rise of the Muslim Brotherhood," Hudson Institute, November 6, 2017, https://www.hudson.org/research/13787-the-rise-of-the-vio lent-muslim-brotherhood

139. Arwa Ibrahim, "'Our Peacefulness Is Not Stronger Than Bullets': Muslim Brotherhood Divisions," *Middle East Eye*, February 6, 2015, https://www.middlee asteye.net/features/our-peacefulness-not-stronger-bullets-muslim-brotherhood-divisions

140. Hassan Hassan (hxhassan), "Well, well, well: ISIS profiles three former Egyptian army officers who joined ISIS after the Rabaa massacre by Sisi. They were supporters of Morsi & helped in the rescue during the dispersing in 2013. Later on, they realized Morsi & MB were on 'the wrong path' & joined ISIS," Twitter post, December 6, 2018, 5:42 P.M., https://twitter.com/hxhassan/status/1070 855961131266048

141. *Ibid.*

142. Shadi Hamid, "Radicalization After the Arab Spring: Lessons from Tunisia and Egypt," *Brookings*, December 1, 2015, https://www.brookings.edu/research/radicalization-after-the-arab-spring-lessons-from-tunisia-and-egypt/

143. *Ibid.*

144. TRT World, "Interview with Ashraf Abdel Ghaffar of Muslim Brotherhood Over Egyptian Revolution," YouTube video, 4:19, January 25, 2016, https://www.youtube.com/watch?v=XVTz74x_Hf8

145. "صدى البلد، "صدي البلد | عماد أبو هاشم: المخابرات البريطانية هى المرشد الحقيقى للجماعة الإرهابية." YouTube video, 7:57, August 11, 2018, https://www.youtube.com/watch?v=x3 LGbqq-0fo

146. Anonymous (former Senior White House Advisor) in discussion with the author, September 25, 2018.

147. "Omar al-Bashir: Sudan Military Coup Topples Ruler After Protests," *BBC News*, April 11, 2019, https://www.bbc.com/news/world-africa-47891470

148. Amberin Zaman, "Tunisia's Democracy on Life Support as Politicians Squabble," *Al-Monitor*, January 23, 2019, https://www.al-monitor.com/pulse/originals/2019/01/tunisia-democracy-life-support-revolution-economy.html

149. *Ibid*.

150. Michael Crowley, "Did Obama Get Erdogan Wrong?" *Politico*, July 16, 2016, https://www.politico.com/story/2016/07/obama-turkey-225659

151. Eli Lake, "Trump Repeats Obama's Mistakes with Turkey," *Bloomberg Opinion*, October 12, 2017, https://www.bloomberg.com/opinion/articles/2017-10-12/trump-repeats-obama-s-mistakes-with-turkey

152. Cagan Koc, "Turkey Rules Out Asking for Help from the IMF," *Bloomberg*, February 1, 2019, https://www.bloomberg.com/news/articles/2019-02-01/turkey-says-its-path-won-t-cross-with-imf-economy-is-strong

153. Carlotta Gall, "Spurning Erdogan's Vision, Turks Leave in Droves, Draining Money and Talent," *The New York Times*, January 2, 2019, https://www.nytimes.com/2019/01/02/world/europe/turkey-emigration-erdogan.html

154. Ayla Jean Yackley, "Have Turkey's Produced a Challenger to Erdogan?" *Foreign Affairs*, April 12, 2019, https://www.foreignaffairs.com/articles/turkey/2019-04-12/have-turkeys-elections-produced-challenger-erdogan

155. Deborah Sontag, "The Erdogan Experiment," *The New York Times Magazine*, May 11, 2003, https://www.nytimes.com/2003/05/11/magazine/the-erdogan-experiment.html

156. Abdel Monem Said Aly, "The Truth About the Muslim Brotherhood," *Cairo Review*, no. 29 (2018): 89–99, https://cdn.thecairoreview.com/wp-content/uploads/2018/05/cr29-said-aly.pdf

157. Dennis Ross, "Islamists Are Not Our Friends," *The New York Times*, September 11, 2014, https://www.nytimes.com/2014/09/12/opinion/islamists-are-not-our-friends.html

158. "The Egyptian Muslim Brotherhood: Building Bases of Support," *Directorate of Intelligence at Central Intelligence Agency*, May 1986, https://www.cia.gov/library/readingroom/docs/CIA-RDP88T00096R000200240001-4.pdf

159. "Muslim Brotherhood Review: Main Findings, H.C. 679," December 17, 2015, https://web.archive.org/web/20151224103901/https://www.gov.uk/government/uploads/system/uploads/attachment_data/file/486932/Muslim_Brotherhood_Review_Main_Findings.pdf

160. John Jenkins, "The Gulf and the Muslim Brotherhood," *Oxford Gulf and Arabian Peninsula Studies Forum*, https://www.oxgaps.org/files/commentary_-_jenkins.pdf

161. Alison Pargeter, *The Muslim Brotherhood: From Opposition to Power* (London, England: Saqi Books, 2013), 186.

CHAPTER 4

1. *Ibid.*, 68–69

2. *Ibid.*, 69.

3. Thomas Pierret, "Syria: Old-Timers and Newcomers," in *The Islamists Are Coming*, ed. Robin Wright (Washington, DC: Woodrow Wilson Center Press, 2012).

4. *Ibid*.

5. Yvette Talhamy, "The Muslim Brotherhood Reborn: The Syrian Uprising," *Middle East Quarterly* 19, no. 2 (Spring 2012): 33–40, https://www.meforum
.org/3198/syria-muslim-brotherhood

6. *Ibid.*

7. Alison Pargeter, *The Muslim Brotherhood: From Opposition to Power* (London,
England: Saqi Books, 2013), 73.

8. *Ibid.*, 78.

9. *Ibid.*, 79–80.

10. Yvette Talhamy, "The Muslim Brotherhood Reborn: The Syrian Uprising," *Middle East Quarterly* 19, no. 2 (Spring 2012): 33–40, https://www.meforum
.org/3198/syria-muslim-brotherhood

11. Thomas Pierret, "Syria: Old-Timers and Newcomers," in *The Islamists
Are Coming*, ed. Robin Wright (Washington, DC: Woodrow Wilson Center Press,
2012).

12. Alison Pargeter, *The Muslim Brotherhood: From Opposition to Power* (London,
England: Saqi Books, 2013), 67.

13. Thomas Pierret, "Syria: Old-Timers and Newcomers," in *The Islamists
Are Coming*, ed. Robin Wright (Washington, DC: Woodrow Wilson Center Press,
2012).

14. Yvette Talhamy, "The Muslim Brotherhood Reborn: The Syrian Uprising," *Middle East Quarterly* 19, no. 2 (Spring 2012): 33–40, https://www.meforum
.org/3198/syria-muslim-brotherhood

15. Alison Pargeter, *The Muslim Brotherhood: From Opposition to Power* (London,
England: Saqi Books, 2013), 86.

16. "The Muslim Brotherhood in Syria," *Diwan* (blog), *Carnegie Middle East
Center*, February 1, 2012, https://carnegie-mec.org/diwan/48370?lang=en

17. Yasmina Allouche, "The 1982 Hama Massacre," *Middle East Monitor*, February 12, 2018, https://www.middleeastmonitor.com/20180212-the-1982-hama-
massacre/

18. Alison Pargeter, *The Muslim Brotherhood: From Opposition to Power* (London,
England: Saqi Books, 2013), 89.

19. *Ibid.*, 90.

20. Yvette Talhamy, "The Muslim Brotherhood Reborn: The Syrian Uprising," *Middle East Quarterly* 19, no. 2 (Spring 2012): 33–40, https://www.meforum
.org/3198/syria-muslim-brotherhood

21. Thomas Pierret, "Syria: Old-Timers and Newcomers," in *The Islamists
Are Coming*, ed. Robin Wright (Washington, DC: Woodrow Wilson Center Press,
2012).

22. Alison Pargeter, *The Muslim Brotherhood: From Opposition to Power* (London,
England: Saqi Books, 2013), 93.

23. *Ibid.*, 95.

24. Thomas Pierret, "Syria: Old-Timers and Newcomers," in *The Islamists Are
Coming*, ed. Robin Wright (Washington, DC: Woodrow Wilson Center Press, 2012).

25. Yvette Talhamy, "The Muslim Brotherhood Reborn: The Syrian Uprising," *Middle East Quarterly* 19, no. 2 (Spring 2012): 33–40, https://www.meforum
.org/3198/syria-muslim-brotherhood

26. *Ibid.*

27. Thomas Pierret, "Syria: Old-Timers and Newcomers," in *The Islamists Are
Coming*, ed. Robin Wright (Washington, DC: Woodrow Wilson Center Press, 2012).

28. Yvette Talhamy, "The Muslim Brotherhood Reborn: The Syrian Uprising," *Middle East Quarterly* 19, no. 2 (Spring 2012): 33–40, https://www.meforum.org/3198/syria-muslim-brotherhood

29. Thomas Pierret, "Syria: Old-Timers and Newcomers," in *The Islamists Are Coming*, ed. Robin Wright (Washington, DC: Woodrow Wilson Center Press, 2012).

30. Yvette Talhamy, "The Muslim Brotherhood Reborn: The Syrian Uprising," *Middle East Quarterly* 19, no. 2 (Spring 2012): 33–40, https://www.meforum.org/3198/syria-muslim-brotherhood

31. *Ibid.*

32. Anonymous (former French Special Envoy to the Syrian Opposition) in discussion with the author, November 25, 2018, Paris, France.

33. Hassan Hassan, "How the Muslim Brotherhood Hijacked Syria's Revolution," *Foreign Policy*, March 13, 2013, https://foreignpolicy.com/2013/03/13/how-the-muslim-brotherhood-hijacked-syrias-revolution/

34. *Ibid.*

35. Thomas Pierret, "Syria: Old-Timers and Newcomers," in *The Islamists Are Coming*, ed. Robin Wright (Washington, DC: Woodrow Wilson Center Press, 2012).

36. Hassan Hassan, "How the Muslim Brotherhood Hijacked Syria's Revolution," *Foreign Policy*, March 13, 2013, https://foreignpolicy.com/2013/03/13/how-the-muslim-brotherhood-hijacked-syrias-revolution/

37. Aron Lund, *Struggling to Adapt: The Muslim Brotherhood in a New Syria* (Washington, DC: Carnegie Endowment for International Peace, 2013), https://carnegieendowment.org/files/struggling_to_adapt_mb.pdf

38. Dasha Afanasieva, "Banned in Syria, Muslim Brotherhood Members Trickle Home," Reuters, May 7, 2015, https://www.reuters.com/article/us-syria-crisis-brotherhood-idUSKBN0NR20Y20150507

39. *Ibid.*

40. News Desk, "Erdogan Trying to Bring Muslim Brotherhood to Syria: Shaaban," *Al Masdar News*, February 22, 2019, https://www.almasdarnews.com/article/erdogan-trying-to-bring-muslim-brotherhood-to-syria-shaaban/

41. John Hudson, "Saudi Arabia Transfers $100 Million to U.S. Amid Crisis Over Khashoggi," *Washington Post*, October 17, 2018, https://www.washingtonpost.com/world/national-security/saudi-arabia-transfers-100-million-to-us-amid-crisis-over-khashoggi/2018/10/17/22b23ae1-c6a4-43a4-9b7d-ce04603fa6ab_story.html

42. Aron Lund, *Struggling to Adapt: The Muslim Brotherhood in a New Syria* (Washington, DC: Carnegie Endowment for International Peace, 2013), https://carnegieendowment.org/files/struggling_to_adapt_mb.pdf

43. Hana Jaber, "The Jordanian Muslim Brotherhood Movement: From Pillar of Monarchy to Enemy of the State," *Arab Reform Initiative*, October 18, 2017, https://archives.arab-reform.net/en/node/1124

44. *Ibid.*

45. Hana Jaber, "The Jordanian Muslim Brotherhood Movement: From Pillar of Monarchy to Enemy of the State," *Arab Reform Initiative*, October 18, 2017, https://archives.arab-reform.net/en/node/1124

46. Nathan Brown, Amr Hamzawy, and Marina Ottaway, *Islamist Movements and the Democratic Process in the Arab World: Exploring the Gray Zones* (Washington,

DC: Carnegie Endowment for International Peace, 2006), https://carnegieendow
ment.org/files/cp_67_grayzones_final.pdf

47. Nur Köprülü, "Is Jordan's Muslim Brotherhood Still the Loyal Opposition?"
Middle East Quarterly 24, no. 2 (Spring 2017), https://www.meforum.org/6560/is-
jordan-muslim-brotherhood-still-the-loyal

48. Hana Jaber, "The Jordanian Muslim Brotherhood Movement: From Pillar of
Monarchy to Enemy of the State," *Arab Reform Initiative*, October 18, 2017, https://
archives.arab-reform.net/en/node/1124

49. Nur Köprülü, "Is Jordan's Muslim Brotherhood Still the Loyal Opposition?"
Middle East Quarterly 24, no. 2 (Spring 2017), https://www.meforum.org/6560/is-
jordan-muslim-brotherhood-still-the-loyal

50. Hana Jaber, "The Jordanian Muslim Brotherhood Movement: From Pillar of
Monarchy to Enemy of the State," *Arab Reform Initiative*, October 18, 2017, https://
archives.arab-reform.net/en/node/1124

51. Nur Köprülü, "Is Jordan's Muslim Brotherhood Still the Loyal Opposition?"
Middle East Quarterly 24, no. 2 (Spring 2017), https://www.meforum.org/6560/is-
jordan-muslim-brotherhood-still-the-loyal

52. Hassan Abu Haniyeh, "Jordan's Strategy to Fragment the Muslim Brotherhood," *Middle East Eye*, April 19, 2016, https://www.middleeasteye.net/opinion/
jordans-strategy-fragment-muslim-brotherhood

53. Nael Masalha and Shadi Hamid, "More Than Just the Muslim Brotherhood:
The Problem of Hamas and Jordan's Islamic Movement," *Brookings*, February 6,
2017, https://www.brookings.edu/research/more-than-just-the-muslim-brother
hood-the-problem-of-hamas-and-jordans-islamic-movement/

54. Al Jazeera and Agencies, "Jordan Closes Muslim Brotherhood Headquarters in Amman," Al Jazeera, April 14, 2016, https://www.aljazeera.com/
news/2016/04/jordan-closes-muslim-brotherhood-headquarters-amman-160
413114049536.html

55. Khetam Malkawi, "Old Brotherhood Cries Foul as Internal Elections
Banned," *The Jordan Times*, March 29, 2016, http://www.jordantimes.com/news/
local/old-brotherhood-cries-foul-internal-elections-banned

56. Sean Yom and Wael Al-Khatib, "Islamists Are Losing Support in Jordan,"
Washington Post, May 17, 2018, https://www.washingtonpost.com/news/mon
key-cage/wp/2018/05/17/islamists-are-losing-support-in-jordan/

57. Nael Masalha and Shadi Hamid, "More Than Just the Muslim Brotherhood:
The Problem of Hamas and Jordan's Islamic Movement," *Brookings*, February 6,
2017, https://www.brookings.edu/research/more-than-just-the-muslim-brother
hood-the-problem-of-hamas-and-jordans-islamic-movement/

58. "Muslim Brotherhood-Led Coalition Wins Big in Jordan Local Polls," *Middle
East Monitor*, August 16, 2017, https://www.middleeastmonitor.com/20170816-
muslim-brotherhood-led-coalition-wins-big-in-jordan-local-polls/

59. *Ibid.*

60. Nael Masalha and Shadi Hamid, "More Than Just the Muslim Brotherhood:
The Problem of Hamas and Jordan's Islamic Movement," *Brookings*, February 6,
2017, https://www.brookings.edu/research/more-than-just-the-muslim-brother
hood-the-problem-of-hamas-and-jordans-islamic-movement/

61. Anonymous (former CIA Station Chief in Jordan) in discussion with the
author, March 15, 2019, Washington, DC.

62. Sean Yom and Wael Al-Khatib, "Islamists Are Losing Support in Jordan," *Washington Post*, May 17, 2018, https://www.washingtonpost.com/news/mon key-cage/wp/2018/05/17/islamists-are-losing-support-in-jordan/

63. *Ibid.*

64. Holly Fletcher, "Palestinian Islamic Jihad," *Council on Foreign Relations*, April 10, 2008, https://www.cfr.org/backgrounder/palestinian-islamic-jihad

65. Boaz Ganor, "Hamas—The Islamic Resistance Movement in the Territories," *Jerusalem Center for Public Affairs*, February 2, 1992, http://jcpa.org/article/ hamas-the-islamic-resistance-movement-in-the-territories/

66. *Ibid.*

67. Yaniv Kubovich, Bar Peleg, and Jack Khoury, "Seven Wounded After Gaza Rocket Hits House in Central Israel," *Hareetz*, March 25, 2019, https://www .haaretz.com/israel-news/explosion-reported-after-rocket-alert-blares-in-central-israel-1.7048055

68. "Gaza: Stop Rocket Attacks Against Israel Civilians," *Human Rights Watch*, March 1, 2011, https://www.hrw.org/news/2011/03/01/gaza-stop-rocket-attacks-against-israel-civilians#

69. David Kirkpatrick, *Into the Hands of the Soldiers: Freedom and Chaos in Egypt and the Middle East* (New York, NY: Penguin, 2018), 125.

70. "Israel and Occupied Palestinian Territories," Amnesty International, accessed May 25, 2019, https://www.amnestyusa.org/countries/israel-and-occu pied-palestinian-territories/

71. *Ibid.*

72. AP Archive, "Israeli PM Says Occupation Is 'Bad for Us and Them'," YouTube video, 1:45, July 23, 2015, https://www.youtube.com/watch?v=9fzlkrAfxB s&feature=youtu.be

73. Yumna Patel, "State Dept refers to Golan Heights and Palestinian Territories as 'Israeli-Controlled' Instead of 'Occupied' in Annual Human Rights Report," *Mondoweiss*, March 14, 2019, https://mondoweiss.net/2019/03/palestin ian-territories-controlled/

74. Miriam Berger, "Israel's Hugely Controversial 'Nation State' Law, Explained," *Vox*, July 31, 2018, https://www.vox.com/world/2018/7/31/17623978/ israel-jewish-nation-state-law-bill-explained-apartheid-netanyahu-democracy

75. "Rights Group Puts Gaza Death Toll at 1,284," *CBS News*, January 22, 2009, https://www.cbsnews.com/news/rights-group-puts-gaza-death-toll-at-1284/

76. "Gaza Crisis," Occupied Palestinian Territory, United Nations Office for the Coordination of Humanitarian Affairs, last modified October 15, 2014, https:// web.archive.org/web/20150725191044/http://www.ochaopt.org/content .aspx?id=1010361

77. Human Rights Watch, *World Report 2019* (United States: Human Rights Watch, 2019), 304–314.

78. "Palestinian Teen Killed, Scores Injured by Israeli Forces in Gaza Protests," *Palestine News Network*, April 13, 2019, http://english.pnn.ps/2019/04/13/pales tinian-teen-killed-scores-injured-by-israeli-forces-in-gaza-protests-2/

79. Matti Friedman, "Falling for Hamas's Split-Screen Fallacy," *The New York Times*, May 16, 2018, https://www.nytimes.com/2018/05/16/opinion/hamas-israel-media-protests.html

80. *Ibid.*

81. TOI Staff, "Hamas Co-founder Admits 'We Are Deceiving the Public' About Peaceful Protests," *Times of Israel*, May 17, 2018, https://www.timesofisrael.com/hamas-co-founder-admits-we-are-deceiving-the-public-about-peaceful-protests/

82. World Bank, "Cash-Strapped Gaza and an Economy in Collapse Put Palestinian Basic Needs at Risk," press release, September 25, 2018, http://www.worldbank.org/en/news/press-release/2018/09/25/cash-strapped-gaza-and-an-economy-in-collapse-put-palestinian-basic-needs-at-risk

83. *Ibid.*

84. TOI Staff, "35,000 Palestinians Left Gaza in 2018 via Egypt and Turkey—Report," *Times of Israel*, May 19, 2019, https://www.timesofisrael.com/35000-palestinians-left-gaza-in-2018-via-egypt-and-turkey-report/

85. Marie Huillet, "Gaza's Ruling Group Hamas Seeks Funding in Bitcoin to Combat Financial Isolation," *Cointelegraph*, January 30, 2019, https://cointelegraph.com/news/gazas-ruling-group-hamas-seeks-funding-in-bitcoin-to-combat-financial-isolation

86. Rushdi Abu Alouf, "Gazans Squeezed by Triple Taxes as Hamas Replaces Lost Income," *BBC News*, June 20, 2016, https://www.bbc.com/news/world-middle-east-36274631

87. Associated Press, "UN Halts Aid into Gaza After 'Hamas Theft'," *The Guardian*, February 6, 2009, https://www.theguardian.com/world/2009/feb/06/gaza-un-aid-hamas

88. "Hamas Is Exploiting Turkish Aid for Military Purposes," *Israel Ministry of Foreign Affairs*, March 21, 2017, https://mfa.gov.il/MFA/ForeignPolicy/Terrorism/Pages/Hamas-is-exploiting-Turkish-aid-for-military-purposes-21-March-2017.aspx

89. David Pollock, "The Surprising Opinions of Palestinians," The Washington Institute, June 7, 2017, https://www.washingtoninstitute.org/policy-analysis/view/the-surprising-opinions-of-palestinians

90. Nidal al-Mughrabi and Tom Finn, "Hamas Softens Stance on Israel, Drops Muslim Brotherhood Link," Reuters, May 1, 2017, https://www.reuters.com/article/us-palestinians-hamas-document/hamas-softens-stance-on-israel-drops-muslim-brotherhood-link-idUSKBN17X1N8

91. Klahil Gebara (former Senior Advisor to Lebanese Interior Minister Nohad Machnouck) in discussion with the author, February 7, 2019, Beirut, Lebanon.

92. *Ibid.*

93. Nael Masalha and Shadi Hamid, "More Than Just the Muslim Brotherhood: The Problem of Hamas and Jordan's Islamic Movement," *Brookings*, February 6, 2017, https://www.brookings.edu/research/more-than-just-the-muslim-brotherhood-the-problem-of-hamas-and-jordans-islamic-movement/

94. *Ibid.*

95. Taylor Luck, "How Trump Move on Jerusalem Throws a Lifeline to Muslim Brotherhood," *Christian Science Monitor*, December 18, 2017, https://www.csmonitor.com/World/Middle-East/2017/1218/How-Trump-move-on-Jerusalem-throws-a-lifeline-to-Muslim-Brotherhood

96. Tallha Abdulrazaq, "The Iraqi Islamic Party: Failing the Sunnis," *Middle East Eye*, May 27, 2015, https://www.middleeasteye.net/opinion/iraqi-islamic-party-failing-sunnis

97. Muhanad Seloom, "An Unhappy Return: What the Iraqi Islamic Party Gave Up to Gain Power," *Carnegie Middle East Center*, November 19, 2018,

https://carnegie-mec.org/2018/11/19/unhappy-return-what-iraqi-islamic-par
ty-gave-up-to-gain-power-pub-77747

98. "The Muslim Brotherhood: Genesis and Development," in *Ayatollahs, Sufis and Ideologues—State, Religion and Social Movements in Iraq*, ed. Faleh Abdul-Jabar (London, England: Saqi Books, 2002), 162–176.

99. Muhanad Seloom, "An Unhappy Return: What the Iraqi Islamic Party Gave Up to Gain Power," *Carnegie Middle East Center*, November 19, 2018, https:// carnegie-mec.org/2018/11/19/unhappy-return-what-iraqi-islamic-party-gave-up-to-gain-power-pub-77747

100. "The Muslim Brotherhood: Genesis and Development," in *Ayatollahs, Sufis and Ideologues—State, Religion and Social Movements in Iraq*, ed. Faleh Abdul-Jabar (London, England: Saqi Books, 2002), 162–176.

101. Graham Fuller, *Islamist Politics in Iraq after Saddam Hussein* (Washington, DC: United States Institute of Peace, 2003), https://www.usip.org/sites/default/files/sr108.pdf

102. *Ibid.*

103. Muhanad Seloom, "An Unhappy Return: What the Iraqi Islamic Party Gave Up to Gain Power," *Carnegie Middle East Center*, November 19, 2018, https:// carnegie-mec.org/2018/11/19/unhappy-return-what-iraqi-islamic-party-gave-up-to-gain-power-pub-77747

104. Graham Fuller, *Islamist Politics in Iraq after Saddam Hussein* (Washington, DC: United States Institute of Peace, 2003), https://www.usip.org/sites/default/files/sr108.pdf

105. *Ibid.*; "The Muslim Brotherhood: Genesis and Development," in *Ayatollahs, Sufis and Ideologues—State, Religion and Social Movements in Iraq*, ed. Faleh Abdul-Jabar (London, England: Saqi Books, 2002), 162–176.

106. Graham Fuller, *Islamist Politics in Iraq After Saddam Hussein* (Washington, DC: United States Institute of Peace, 2003), https://www.usip.org/sites/default/files/sr108.pdf

107. Tallha Abdulrazaq, "The Iraqi Islamic Party: Failing the Sunnis," *Middle East Eye*, May 27, 2015, https://www.middleeasteye.net/opinion/iraqi-islamic-party-failing-sunnis

108. Kyle Orton, "How Saddam Hussein Gave Us ISIS," *The New York Times*, December 23, 2015, https://www.nytimes.com/2015/12/23/opinion/how-saddam-hussein-gave-us-isis.html

109. Graham Fuller, *Islamist Politics in Iraq after Saddam Hussein* (Washington, DC: United States Institute of Peace, 2003), https://www.usip.org/sites/default/files/sr108.pdf

110. Syed Saleem Shahzad, "A Third Force Awaits U.S. in Iraq," *Asia Times*, March 1, 2003, http://www.hartford-hwp.com/archives/51/225.html

111. Graham Fuller, *Islamist Politics in Iraq After Saddam Hussein* (Washington, DC: United States Institute of Peace, 2003), https://www.usip.org/sites/default/files/sr108.pdf

112. *Ibid.*

113. Muhanad Seloom, "An Unhappy Return: What the Iraqi Islamic Party Gave Up to Gain Power," *Carnegie Middle East Center*, November 19, 2018, https:// carnegie-mec.org/2018/11/19/unhappy-return-what-iraqi-islamic-party-gave-up-to-gain-power-pub-77747

114. *Ibid.*

115. Tallha Abdulrazaq, "The Iraqi Islamic Party: Failing the Sunnis," *Middle East Eye*, May 27, 2015, https://www.middleeasteye.net/opinion/iraqi-islamic-party-failing-sunnis

116. Mustafa al-Kadhimi, "Iraq Protests Present Muslim Brotherhood with Opportunity," *Al-Monitor*, January 9, 2013, https://www.al-monitor.com/pulse/originals/2013/01/muslim-brotherhood-iraq.html

117. gmbwatch, "Iraqi Muslim Brotherhood Elects New Political Head," *Global Muslim Brotherhood Daily Watch*, https://www.globalmbwatch.com/2011/08/10/iraqi-muslim-brotherhood-elects-new-political-head/

118. Aymenn Jawad Al-Tamimi, "The Fortunes of the Muslim Brotherhood in Iraq," *Pundicity*, January 28, 2014, http://www.aymennjawad.org/14325/the-fortunes-of-the-muslim-brotherhood-in-iraq

119. Anonymous (former French Ambassador to Egypt) in discussion with the author, January 12, 2018, Paris, France.

120. *Ibid.*

121. Associated Press in Baghdad, "Iraq Vice-President Sentenced to Death Amid Deadly Wave of Insurgent Attacks," *The Guardian*, September 9, 2012, https://www.theguardian.com/world/2012/sep/09/iraq-vice-president-hashemi-death-sentence

122. Aymenn Jawad Al-Tamimi, "The Fortunes of the Muslim Brotherhood in Iraq," *Pundicity*, January 28, 2014, http://www.aymennjawad.org/14325/the-fortunes-of-the-muslim-brotherhood-in-iraq

123. *Ibid.*

124. Muhanad Seloom, "An Unhappy Return: What the Iraqi Islamic Party Gave Up to Gain Power," *Carnegie Middle East Center*, November 19, 2018, https://carnegie-mec.org/2018/11/19/unhappy-return-what-iraqi-islamic-party-gave-up-to-gain-power-pub-77747

125. Tallha Abdulrazaq, "The Iraqi Islamic Party: Failing the Sunnis," *Middle East Eye*, May 27, 2015, https://www.middleeasteye.net/opinion/iraqi-islamic-party-failing-sunnis

126. "Jamaa Islamiyya," Civil Society Knowledge Center, last modified February 27, 2015, https://civilsociety-centre.org/party/jamaa-islamiyya

127. *Ibid.*

128. Raphaël Lefèvre, "A New Direction for Lebanon's Muslim Brothers," *Diwan* (blog), *Carnegie Middle East Center*, February 11, 2016, https://carnegie-mec.org/diwan/62740

129. *Ibid.*

130. *Ibid.*

131. Klahil Gebara (former Senior Advisor to Lebanese Interior Minister Nohad Machnouck) in discussion with the author, February 7, 2019, Beirut, Lebanon.

CHAPTER 5

1. Mohamed Mokhtar Qandil, "The Muslim Brotherhood and Saudi Arabia: From Then to Now," *Fikra Forum* (blog), The Washington Institute, May 18, 2018, https://www.washingtoninstitute.org/fikraforum/view/the-muslim-brotherhood-and-saudi-arabia-from-then-to-now

2. John Jenkins, "The Gulf and the Muslim Brotherhood," *Oxford Gulf and Arabian Peninsula Studies Forum*, https://www.oxgaps.org/files/commentary_-_jenkins.pdf

3. Andrew Leber, "Rentier Islamism: Politics and Religion in Arab Gulf Societies," *The New Arab*, September 12, 2018, https://www.alaraby.co.uk/english/comment/2018/9/12/rentier-islamism-politics-and-religion-in-arab-gulf-societies

4. "Muslim Brotherhood Cited in Oman Plot," *United Press International*, August 30, 1994, https://www.upi.com/Archives/1994/08/30/Muslim-Brotherhood-cited-in-Oman-plot/6767778219200/

5. GlobalMB, "ANALYSIS: Another U.S. Muslim Brotherhood Figure Surfaces In Bahrain, Rise of Bahraini Brotherhood?" *Global Muslim Brotherhood Daily Watch*, August 31, 2007, https://www.globalmbwatch.com/2007/08/31/analysis-another-us-muslim-brotherhood-figure-surfaces-in-bahrain-rise-of-bahraini-brotherhood/

6. N. Janardhan, "Islamists Stay Clear of Terrorism in Oman," *Terrorism Monitor* (Jamestown Foundation) 4, no. 5 (2006), https://jamestown.org/program/islamists-stay-clear-of-terrorism-in-oman/

7. Omar Al Zawawi (advisor to Sultan Qaboos for Foreign Liaison) in discussion with the author, London, England.

8. Paul McLoughlin, "Indian Scholar 'Asked to Leave' Oman After Anti-Saudi Speech," *The New Arab*, September 24, 2017, https://www.alaraby.co.uk/english/news/2017/9/24/indian-scholar-asked-to-leave-oman-after-anti-saudi-speech

9. Kylie Moore-Gilbert, "A Band of (Muslim) Brothers? Exploring Bahrain's Role in the Qatar Crisis," Middle East Institute, August 3, 2017, https://www.mei.edu/publications/band-muslim-brothers-exploring-bahrains-role-qatar-crisis

10. Alex MacDonald, "Sunni Islamists Could Face Uphill Struggle in Bahrain Elections," *Middle East Eye*, November 20, 2014, https://www.middleeasteye.net/features/sunni-islamists-could-face-uphill-struggle-bahrain-elections

11. *Ibid.*

12. *Ibid.*

13. Kristin Smith Diwan, "The Future of the Muslim Brotherhood in the Gulf," *Washington Post*, February 10, 2015, https://www.washingtonpost.com/news/monkey-cage/wp/2015/02/10/the-future-of-the-muslim-brotherhood-in-the-gulf/

14. Alessandra Antonelli, "Bahrain: Four Islamists, Three Woman in New Parliament," *Ansamed*, December 1, 2014, http://www.ansamed.info/ansamed/en/news/sections/politics/2014/12/01/bahrain-four-islamists-three-women-in-new-parliament_48a9b6c7-f3f5-4437-938f-4c6ae0a95aa6.html

15. Fawaz bin Mohammed Al Khalifa (Bahrain's ambassador to the UK) in discussion with the author, July 12, 2018, London, England.

16. Courtney Freer, "Ikhwan Ascendant? Assessing the Influence of Domestic Islamist Sentiment on Qatari Foreign Policy" (memo, London School of Economics and Political Science, London, England, October 7, 2015), https://blogs.lse.ac.uk/mec/2015/11/26/ikhwan-ascendant-assessing-the-influence-of-domestic-islamist-sentiment-on-qatari-foreign-policy/

17. Anonymous (former Chief of Kuwait National Security Agency) in discussion with the author, October 25, 2019, Boston, MA.

18. Simon Tisdall, "Superpowers Unite Over Iraqi Invasion of Kuwait—Archive, 1990," *The Guardian*, August 3, 2018, https://www.theguardian.com/world/2018/aug/03/superpowers-unite-over-iraq-invasion-of-kuwait-1990#comments

19. *Ibid.*

20. Sunday Times Insight Team, "Rape of the Gulf," *Sunday Times*, August 5, 1990, https://www.margaretthatcher.org/document/110785

21. Michael Gordon and Special to the New York Times, "Iraq Army Invades Capital of Kuwait in Fierce Fighting," *The New York Times*, August 2, 1990, https://www.nytimes.com/1990/08/02/world/iraq-army-invades-capital-of-kuwait-in-fierce-fighting.html

22. Sunday Times Insight Team, "Rape of the Gulf," *Sunday Times*, August 5, 1990, https://www.margaretthatcher.org/document/110785

23. Michael Gordon and Special to the New York Times, "Iraq Army Invades Capital of Kuwait in Fierce Fighting," *The New York Times*, August 2, 1990, https://www.nytimes.com/1990/08/02/world/iraq-army-invades-capital-of-kuwait-in-fierce-fighting.html

24. "World Acts Against Iraqi Invasion of Kuwait," Weapons of Mass Destruction (WMD), GlobalSecurity.org, August 16, 1990, https://www.globalsecurity.org/wmd/library/news/iraq/1990/900816-151051.htm

25. Chris Hedges and Special to the New York Times, "After the War: Kuwait; At Home Amongst the Enemy, Kuwaitis Learned to Survive," *The New York Times*, March 5, 1991, https://www.nytimes.com/1991/03/05/world/after-the-war-kuwait-at-home-among-the-enemy-kuwaitis-learned-to-survive.html

26. *Ibid.*

27. *Ibid.*

28. Patrick Tyler, "Kuwaitis Scale Back Resistance Effort," *Washington Post*, October 5, 1990, https://www.washingtonpost.com/archive/politics/1990/z10/05/kuwaitis-scale-back-resistance-effort/5f04b295-cb4b-455f-88ef-7831913 43cea/

29. Human Rights Watch, "Iraq and Occupied Kuwait," in *World Report 1992* (United States: Human Rights Watch, 1992), https://www.hrw.org/reports/1992/WR92/MEW1-02.htm

30. Paul Koring, "The Missing Kuwaitis of Baghdad's Gulag," *The Globe and Mail*, December 23, 2002, https://www.theglobeandmail.com/news/world/the-missing-kuwaitis-of-baghdads-gulag/article4142930/

31. Chris Hedges and Special to the New York Times, "After the War: Kuwait; At Home Amongst the Enemy, Kuwaitis Learned to Survive," *The New York Times*, March 5, 1991, https://www.nytimes.com/1991/03/05/world/after-the-war-kuwait-at-home-among-the-enemy-kuwaitis-learned-to-survive.html

32. Anonymous (former Chief of Kuwait National Security Agency) in discussion with the author, September 17, 2018, London, England.

33. Nawal Sayed, "Qatari-Funded Muslim Brotherhood Tampering with Kuwait," *Egypt Today*, July 22, 2017, https://www.egypttoday.com/Article/2/13158/Qatari-funded-Muslim-Brotherhood-tampering-with-Kuwait

34. Scott Williamson and Nathan Brown, "Kuwait's Muslim Brotherhood Under Pressure," *Foreign Policy*, November 20, 2013, https://foreignpolicy.com/2013/11/20/kuwaits-muslim-brotherhood-under-pressure/

35. *Ibid.*

36. Anonymous (former Chief of Kuwait National Security Agency) in discussion with the author, September 17, 2018, London, England.

37. Sylvia Westall, "Egypt Says to Brotherhood Members Arrested in the Gulf," Reuters, March 12, 2014, https://www.reuters.com/article/us-egypt-brother

hood-gulf/egypt-says-two-brotherhood-members-arrested-in-the-gulf-idUSBRE
A2B23V20140312

38. Giorgio Cafiero, "Kuwait's Pragmatic Islamists," Middle East Institute,
February 8, 2017, https://www.mei.edu/publications/kuwaits-pragmatic-is
lamists

39. Courtney Freer, "Ikhwan Ascendant? Assessing the Influence of Domestic
Islamist Sentiment on Qatari Foreign Policy" (memo, London School of Economics and Political Science, London, England, October 7, 2015), https://blogs.lse
.ac.uk/mec/2015/11/26/ikhwan-ascendant-assessing-the-influence-of-domestic-
islamist-sentiment-on-qatari-foreign-policy/

40. Anonymous (former Chief of Kuwait National Security Agency) in discussion with the author, September 17, 2018, London, England.

41. *Ibid.*

42. Pekka Hakala, "Opposition in the United Arab Emirates," European Parliament Policy Department, November 15, 2012, http://www.europarl.europa
.eu/RegData/etudes/briefing_note/join/2012/491458/EXPO-AFET_SP(2012)49
1458_EN.pdf

43. Matthias Sailer, "Hardly a Ruler in Waiting," trans. Nina Coon, *Qantara.
de*, March 28, 2018, https://en.qantara.de/content/uae-foreign-policy-and-the-
crown-prince-of-abu-dhabi-hardly-a-ruler-in-waiting?nopaging=1

44. Anonymous (former British Secret Intelligence Service Counter Terrorism
Director) in discussion with the author, April 26, 2016, London, England.

45. Pekka Hakala, "Opposition in the United Arab Emirates," European
Parliament Policy Department, November 15, 2012, http://www.europarl
.europa.eu/RegData/etudes/briefing_note/join/2012/491458/EXPO-AFET_
SP(2012)491458_EN.pdf

46. "UAE and the Muslim Brotherhood: A Story of Rivalry and Hatred," *Fanack*, July 16, 2017, https://fanack.com/united-arab-emirates/history-past-to-pres
ent/uae-muslim-brotherhood/

47. Anonymous (former British ambassador to United Arab Emirates) in discussion with the author, September 17, 2018, London, England.

48. "Political Islam Country Snapshot: UAE," WikiLeaks Cable: 03ABUDHABI
3565_a, July 30, 2003, https://wikileaks.org/plusd/cables/03ABUDHABI3565_a
.html

49. "UAE and the Muslim Brotherhood: A Story of Rivalry and Hatred," *Fanack*, July 16, 2017, https://fanack.com/united-arab-emirates/history-past-to-pres
ent/uae-muslim-brotherhood/

50. Lori Plotkin Boghardt, "The Muslim Brotherhood on Trial in the UAE," policy analysis, The Washington Institute, April 12, 2013, https://www.washingtonin
stitute.org/policy-analysis/view/the-muslim-brotherhood-on-trial-in-the-uae

51. Anonymous (former British Secret Intelligence Service Counter Terrorism
Director) in discussion with the author, April 26, 2016, London, England.

52. *Ibid.*

53. Louise Ireland and Sami Aboudi, "UAE Islamist Group Denies Reports It
Has an Armed Wing," Reuters, September 23, 2012, https://uk.reuters.com/ar
ticle/uk-emirates-islamists/uae-islamist-group-denies-reports-it-has-an-armed-
wing-idUKBRE88M05X20120923

54. Anonymous (former British Secret Intelligence Service Counter Terrorism
Director) in discussion with the author, April 26, 2016, London, England.

55. Andrew Chappelle, "Abu Dhabi's Problem with the Muslim Brotherhood," Al Jazeera, May 26, 2018, https://www.aljazeera.com/news/2018/05/abu-dhabi-problem-muslim-brotherhood-180526105937656.html

56. Ian Black, "Emirati Nerves Rattled by Islamist's Rise," The Guardian, October 12, 2012, https://www.theguardian.com/world/on-the-middle-east/2012/oct/12/uae-muslimbrotherhood-egypt-arabspring

57. Patrick Werr, "UAE Offers Egypt $3 Billion Support, Saudis $5 Billon," Reuters, July 9, 2013, https://www.reuters.com/article/us-egypt-protests-loan/uae-offers-egypt-3-billion-support-saudis-5-billion-idUSBRE9680H020130709

58. Kareem Fahim, "Muslim Brotherhood Supporters Defy Egyptian Crackdown," The New York Times, December 27, 2013, https://www.nytimes.com/2013/12/28/world/middleeast/muslim-brotherhood-supporters-defy-egyptian-crackdown.html

59. Kristen Smith Diwan, "The Future of the Muslim Brotherhood in the Gulf," Washington Post, February 10, 2015, https://www.washingtonpost.com/news/monkey-cage/wp/2015/02/10/the-future-of-the-muslim-brotherhood-in-the-gulf/

60. "Visions of Gulf Security," Project on Middle East Political Science (George Washington University), no. 25 (March 2014), https://pomeps.org/wp-content/uploads/2014/03/Visions_of_Gulf_Security.pdf

61. Aram Roston, "A Middle East Monarchy Hired American Ex-Soldiers to Kill Its Political Enemies. This Could Be the Future of War," BuzzFeed News, October 16, 2018, https://www.buzzfeednews.com/article/aramroston/mercenaries-assassination-us-yemen-uae-spear-golan-dahlan

62. Habib Toumi, "Kuwait Former MP Sentenced for Insulting UAE," Gulf News, April 13, 2016, https://gulfnews.com/world/gulf/kuwait/kuwait-former-mp-sentenced-for-insulting-uae-1.1710578

63. Diane Bartz and Peter Cooney, "UAE Arranged for Hacking of Qatar Government Sites, Sparking Diplomatic Row: Washington Post," Reuters, July 16, 2017, https://www.reuters.com/article/us-usa-qatar-report/uae-arranged-for-hacking-of-qatar-government-sites-sparking-diplomatic-row-washington-post-idUSKBN1A200H

64. Mashari Althaydi, "Saudi Arabia: We Are All Brothers and Muslims," Al Arabiya, June 18, 2016, https://english.alarabiya.net/en/views/news/middle-east/2016/06/18/Saudi-Arabia-We-are-all-brothers-and-Muslims.html

65. Stéphane Lacroix, Awakening Islam, trans. George Holoch (Cambridge, MA: Harvard University Press, 2011).

66. Ibid.

67. Abdellatif El-Menawy, "Why These Snakes Have No Place in Our Classrooms," Arab News, March 24, 2018, http://www.arabnews.com/node/1272776

68. Abdullah Al-Othaymeen (former Secretary-General of the King Faisal International Prize) in discussion with the author, July 5, 2011, Riyadh, Saudi Arabia.

69. Mohamed Mokhtar Qandil, "The Muslim Brotherhood and Saudi Arabia: From Then to Now," Fikra Forum (blog), The Washington Institute, May 18, 2018, https://www.washingtoninstitute.org/fikraforum/view/the-muslim-brotherhood-and-saudi-arabia-from-then-to-now

70. Ibid.

71. Al Jazeera, "Saudi and the Brotherhood: From Friends to Foes," Al Jazeera, June 23, 2017, https://www.aljazeera.com/news/2017/06/saudi-brotherhood-friends-foes-170623093039202.html

72. Mike Kelvington, "Importing the Muslim Brotherhood: Creation of the "Sahwa" in Saudi Arabia," *Havok Journal* (blog), April 27, 2019, https://havok journal.com/world/middle-east/importing-muslim-brotherhood-creation-sah wa-saudi-arabia/

73. "Saudi Arabia to Purge Muslim Brotherhood Influence in Schools," *The New Arab*, March 22, 2018, https://www.alaraby.co.uk/english/news/2018/3/22/saudi-arabia-to-purge-muslim-brotherhood-influence-in-schools

74. Thomas Hegghammer and Stéphane Lacroix, *The Meccan Rebellion: The Story of Juhayman Al-'Utaybi Revisited* (n.p.: Amal Press, 2011), 36.

75. Prince Nayef of Saudi Arabia interviewed (in Arabic) by Kuwaiti Newspaper Al Siyasah on November 28, 2002.

76. خليجية, "رئيس المجلس العسكري لتنظيم القاعدة بالسعودية علي الفقعسي ضيف برنامج الليوان مع عبدالله." المديفر," YouTube video, 1:26:24, May 12, 2019, https://www.youtube.com/watch?v=pIHf3GeTRsE

77. John Jenkins, "The Gulf and the Muslim Brotherhood," *Oxford Gulf and Arabian Peninsula Studies Forum*, https://www.oxgaps.org/files/commentary_-_jenkins.pdf

78. Abdul Mohsen Al Akkas (former Saudi Minister of Social Affairs) in discussion with the author, July 12, 2009, London, England.

79. Courtney Freer, "From Co-optation to Crackdown: Gulf States' Reactions to the Rise of the Muslim Brotherhood During the Arab Spring" (memo for workshop "From Mobilization to Counter-Revolution: The Arab Spring in Comparative Perspective," London School of Economics, London, England, May 3–4, 2016), https://pomeps.org/2016/06/03/from-co-optation-to-crackdown-gulf-states-reactions-to-the-rise-of-the-muslim-brotherhood-during-the-arab-spring/

80. Stéphane Lacroix, "Saudi Arabia's Muslim Brotherhood Predicament" (memo for workshop "Visions of Gulf Security," Venice, Italy, March 9, 2014), https://pomeps.org/2014/03/20/saudi-arabias-muslim-brotherhood-predicament/

81. Al Jazeera, "Saudi and the Brotherhood: From Friends to Foes," Al Jazeera, June 23, 2017, https://www.aljazeera.com/news/2017/06/saudi-brotherhood-friends-foes-170623093039202.html

82. Habib Toumi, "How the Muslim Brotherhood Betrayed Saudi Arabia," *Gulf News*, June 7, 2017, https://gulfnews.com/world/gulf/saudi/how-the-muslim-brotherhood-betrayed-saudi-arabia-1.2039864

83. Abdullah Al-Othaymeen (former Secretary-General of the King Faisal International Prize) in discussion with the author, July 5, 2011, Riyadh, Saudi Arabia.

84. Elizabeth Dickinson, "Sire, How Much Would You Spend to Stop the Next Arab Spring?" *New Republic*, September 1, 2013, https://newrepublic.com/article/114542/silent-arab-springs

85. Stéphane Lacroix, "Saudi Arabia's Muslim Brotherhood Predicament" (memo for workshop "Visions of Gulf Security," Venice, Italy, March 9, 2014), https://pomeps.org/2014/03/20/saudi-arabias-muslim-brotherhood-predicament/

86. "Saudi Arabia to Purge Muslim Brotherhood Influence in Schools," *The New Arab*, March 22, 2018, https://www.alaraby.co.uk/english/news/2018/3/22/saudi-arabia-to-purge-muslim-brotherhood-influence-in-schools

87. "Saudi Dissident Al-Otaibi to Return Home," *World Bulletin*, March 17, 2015, https://www.worldbulletin.net/middle-east/saudi-dissident-al-otaibi-to-return-home-h156685.html

88. "(خليجية, "د. كساب العتيبي ضيف برنامج الليوان مع عبدالله المديفر (حكاية المعارضة السعودية."
YouTube video, 1:29:57, May 9, 2019, https://www.youtube.com/watch?time_
continue=340&v=BjSxmlz4rQ0

89. *Ibid.*

90. *Ibid.*

91. *Ibid.*

92. *Ibid.*

93. *Ibid.*

94. *Ibid.*

95. *Ibid.*

96. Julia Sora, "Saudi University Dismissing Muslim Brotherhood-Linked Academics," *Center for Security Policy*, September 28, 2017, https://www.centerforse
curitypolicy.org/2017/09/28/saudi-university-dismissing-muslim-brotherhood-
linked-academics/

97. Toby Matthiesen, "The Domestic Sources of Saudi Foreign Policy: Islamists and the State in the Wake of the Arab Uprisings," Project on U.S. Relations with the Islamic World at Brookings, Working Paper (August 2015).

98. Abdellatif El-Menawy, "Why These Snakes Have No Place in Our Classrooms," *Arab News*, March 24, 2018, http://www.arabnews.com/node/1272776

99. Habib Toumi, "Saudi Schools Free of Muslim Brotherhood Influence," *Gulf News*, September 22, 2018, https://gulfnews.com/world/gulf/saudi/saudi-
schools-free-of-muslim-brotherhood-influence-1.2281181

100. Staff writer, "Mohammed bin Salman, Trump Discuss Bin Laden's Ties to the Muslim Brotherhood," *Al Arabiya*, March 16, 2017, https://english.alarabiya
.net/en/features/2017/03/16/Mohammed-bin-Salman-Trump-discuss-Osama-
bin-Laden-s-ties-to-Muslim-Brotherhood.html

101. Anonymous (former Secretary-General of Gulf Cooperation Council) in discussion with the author, September 23, 2017, Geneva, Switzerland.

102. Bertrand Besancenot (former French Ambassador to Saudi Arabia) in discussion with the author, July 10, 2018, Paris, France.

103. David Roberts, "Qatar, the Ikhwan, and Transnational Relations in the Gulf" (memo for workshop "Visions of Gulf Security," Venice, Italy, March 9, 2014), https://pomeps.org/2014/03/18/qatar-the-ikhwan-and-transnational-relations-
in-the-gulf/

104. *Ibid.*

105. Bertrand Besancenot (former French Ambassador to Saudi Arabia) in discussion with the author, September 27, 2018, Paris, France.

106. David Roberts, "Qatar, the Ikhwan, and Transnational Relations in the Gulf" (memo for workshop "Visions of Gulf Security," Venice, Italy, March 9, 2014), https://pomeps.org/2014/03/18/qatar-the-ikhwan-and-transnational-
relations-in-the-gulf/

107. Bertrand Besancenot (former French Ambassador to Saudi Arabia) in discussion with the author, September 27, 2018, Paris, France.

108. Anonymous (former Senior Case Office in the Central Intelligence Agency's Near East Directorate) in discussion with the author, April 15, 2016, Washington, DC.

109. "Muslim Brotherhood in Qatar," *Counter Extremism Project*, n.d., https://
www.counterextremism.com/sites/default/files/mb_pdf/MB%20Branch_Qa
tar_043019.pdf

110. Eric Trager, "The Muslim Brotherhood Is the Root of the Qatar Crisis," *The Atlantic*, July 2, 2017, https://www.theatlantic.com/international/archive/2017/07/muslim-brotherhood-qatar/532380/

111. David Roberts, "Qatar, the Ikhwan, and Transnational Relations in the Gulf" (memo for workshop "Visions of Gulf Security," Venice, Italy, March 9, 2014), https://pomeps.org/2014/03/18/qatar-the-ikhwan-and-transnational-relations-in-the-gulf/

112. Marvine Howe, "Southern Yemen Blends Marxism with Islam and Arab Nationalism," *The New York Times*, May 25, 1979, https://www.nytimes.com/1979/05/25/archives/southern-yemen-blends-marxism-with-islam-and-arab-nationalism.html

113. Stig Jarle Hansen and Atle Mesøy, "The Muslim Brotherhood in the Wider Horn of Africa," *Norwegian Institute for Urban and Regional Research*, no. 33 (December 2009), https://www.researchgate.net/publication/265191361_The_Muslim_Brotherhood_in_the_Wider_Horn_of_Africa

114. *Ibid.*

115. Office of Public Affairs, "United States Designates bin Laden Loyalist," press release, *U.S. Department of the Treasury*, February 24, 2004, https://web.archive.org/web/20100314033922/http://www.treasury.gov/press/releases/js1190.htm

116. Stig Jarle Hansen and Atle Mesøy, "The Muslim Brotherhood in the Wider Horn of Africa," *Norwegian Institute for Urban and Regional Research*, no. 33 (December 2009), https://www.researchgate.net/publication/265191361_The_Muslim_Brotherhood_in_the_Wider_Horn_of_Africa

117. *Ibid.*

118. *Bilal Zenab Ahmed*, "Ghosts of the Left," *Jacobin*, August 27, 2015, https://jacobinmag.com/2015/08/yemen-conflict-southern-nationalism

119. Paul Dresch and Bernard Haykel, "Stereotypes and Political Styles," *International Journal of Middle East Studies* 27, no. 4 (November 1995), 405–431, https://web.archive.org/web/20160324050646/http://www.jstor.org/stable/176363

120. Stacey Philbrick Yadav, "Yemen's Muslim Brotherhood and the Perils of Powersharing," Project on US Relations with the Islamic World, Brookings Institute, August 2015, https://www.brookings.edu/wp-content/uploads/2016/07/Yemen_Yadav-FINALE.pdf

121. Stig Jarle Hansen and Atle Mesøy, "The Muslim Brotherhood in the Wider Horn of Africa," *Norwegian Institute for Urban and Regional Research*, no. 33 (December 2009), https://www.researchgate.net/publication/265191361_The_Muslim_Brotherhood_in_the_Wider_Horn_of_Africa

122. "The Islah Party," *Islamopedia Online*, accessed June 8, 2019, https://web.archive.org/web/20150407021704/http://www.islamopediaonline.org/country-profile/yemen/political-landscape/islah-party#

123. Stig Jarle Hansen and Atle Mesøy, "The Muslim Brotherhood in the Wider Horn of Africa," *Norwegian Institute for Urban and Regional Research*, no. 33 (December 2009), https://www.researchgate.net/publication/265191361_The_Muslim_Brotherhood_in_the_Wider_Horn_of_Africa

124. *Ibid.*

125. *Ibid.*

126. Katherine Zimmerman, "Militant Islam's Global Preacher: The Radicalizing Effect of Sheikh Anwar al Awlaki," *Critical Threats*, March 12, 2010, https://www.criticalthreats.org/analysis/militant-islams-global-preacher-the-radicalizing-effect-of-sheikh-anwar-al-awlaki

127. Stig Jarle Hansen and Atle Mesøy, "The Muslim Brotherhood in the Wider Horn of Africa," *Norwegian Institute for Urban and Regional Research*, no. 33 (December 2009), https://www.researchgate.net/publication/265191361_The_Muslim_Brotherhood_in_the_Wider_Horn_of_Africa

128. "Humanitarian Crisis in Yemen Remains the Worst in the World, Warns UN," *UN News*, February 14, 2019, https://news.un.org/en/story/2019/02/1032811

129. Toby Matthiesen, "The Domestic Sources of Saudi Foreign Policy: Islamists and the State in the Wake of the Arab Uprisings," Project on U.S. Relations with the Islamic World at Brookings, Working Paper (August 2015).

130. Stephen Snyder, "Saudi Arabia Is Buying More Weapons Than Ever Before," *PRI's The World*, March 27, 2019, https://www.pri.org/stories/2019-03-27/saudi-arabia-buying-more-weapons-ever

131. Isaac Chotiner, "A Middle Eastern-Studies Professor on His Conversations with Mohammed Bin Salman," *New Yorker*, April 8, 2019, https://www.newyorker.com/news/q-and-a/a-middle-eastern-studies-professor-interprets-mohammed-bin-salman

132. *Ibid.*

133. *Ibid.*

134. *Ibid.*

135. Anchal Vohra, "Hezbollah Isn't Iran's Favorite Proxy Anymore," *Foreign Policy*, June 4, 2019, https://foreignpolicy.com/2019/06/04/hezbollah-isnt-irans-favorite-proxy-anymore/

136. Bel Trew, "Yemen War: End to Fighting Could Be in Sight as Houthi Rebels Announce Withdrawal from Lifeline Port," *Independent*, May 11, 2019, https://www.independent.co.uk/news/world/middle-east/yemen-war-end-hodeidah-port-houthi-rebels-withdrawal-un-peace-deal-aid-a8909256.html

137. Anchal Vohra, "Hezbollah Isn't Iran's Favorite Proxy Anymore," *Foreign Policy*, June 4, 2019, https://foreignpolicy.com/2019/06/04/hezbollah-isnt-irans-favorite-proxy-anymore/

138. "Houthi Missile Attack on Saudi Arabia's Abha Airport Wounds 26," Al Jazeera, June 12, 2019, https://www.aljazeera.com/news/2019/06/houthi-missile-strike-saudi-arabia-abha-airport-wounds-26-190612090351880.html

139. Ali Barada and Abdulhadi Abtor, "UN Draft Resolution Condemns Houthi Attacks on Saudi Arabia," *Asharq Al-Awsat*, June 11, 2019, https://aawsat.com/english/home/article/1761846/un-draft-resolution-condemns-houthi-attacks-saudi-arabia

140. Fatima Alasrar (YemeniFatima), "1. #Houthis of #Yemen raised funds for #Hezbollah during the month of #Ramadan It's not the first time. Yet many found the news surprising. #Houthis' ties to #Hezbollah & #Iran are undeniable. This thread will clarify some misconceptions about this clandestine alliance," Twitter post, May 29, 2019, 1:09 P.M., https://twitter.com/YemeniFatima/status/1133827680988741632

141. Ali Mahmood, "UAE and Saudi Arabia Hold Talks with Yemen's Al Islah Party," *The National*, December 14, 2017, https://www.thenational.ae/world/mena/uae-and-saudi-arabia-hold-talks-with-yemen-s-al-islah-party-1.684549

142. Eleonora Ardemagni, "'Martyrs' for a Centralized UAE," *Carnegie Endowment for International Peace*, June 13, 2019, https://carnegieendowment.org/sada/79313

143. John Jenkins, "The Gulf and the Muslim Brotherhood," *Oxford Gulf and Arabian Peninsula Studies Forum,* https://www.oxgaps.org/files/commentary_-_jenkins.pdf

144. Abdulaziz Khoja (former Saudi Information Minister) in discussion with the author, July 27, 2012, Jeddah, Saudi Arabia.

145. Turki Al Faisal (former Saudi Intelligence Director and ex-ambassador to the United Kingdom and United States) in discussion with the author, December 15, 2017, Paris, France.

CHAPTER 6

1. Mamoun Fandy and Imarat Al Ikhwan, "إمارة «الإخوان» .. بقلم: مأمون فندي", *Asharq Al-Awsat,* August 4, 2017, http://www.sudanile.com/index.php/

2. Anonymous (former Counterterrorism Director for the Direction General de la Sécurité Extérieur) in discussion with the author, November 17, 2018, Paris, France.

3. Kyle Shideler, "Hamas-Tip of the Muslim Brotherhood Spear," *Center for Security Policy,* July 21, 2014, https://www.centerforsecuritypolicy.org/2014/07/21/hamas-the-tip-of-muslim-brotherhood-spear/

4. "From Europe to the Qatar-Turkey Axis: The Secret Project of the Muslim Brotherhood," interview of Souad Sbai, *Almaghrebiya,* December 15, 2018, https://almaghrebiya.it/2018/12/15/from-europe-to-the-qatar-turkey-axis-the-secret-project-of-the-muslim-brotherhood/

5. Lorenzo Vidino, *The New Muslim Brotherhood in the West* (New York, NY: Columbia University Press, 2010), 92.

6. Anonymous (Swiss Counterterrorism Advisor for the Federal Department of Foreign Affairs) in discussion with the author, October 10, 2018, Bern, Switzerland.

7. Melanie Colburn, "America's Devil's Game with Extremist Islam," *Mother Jones,* January/February 2006, https://www.motherjones.com/politics/2006/01/americas-devils-game-extremist-islam/

8. Robert Dreyfuss, "Cold War, Holy Warrior," *Mother Jones,* January/February 2006, https://www.motherjones.com/politics/2006/01/cold-war-holy-warrior/

9. *Ibid.*

10. Alison Pargeter, *The Muslim Brotherhood: From Opposition to Power* (London, England: Saqi Books, 2013), 109.

11. Robert Dreyfuss, "Cold War, Holy Warrior," *Mother Jones,* January/February 2006, https://www.motherjones.com/politics/2006/01/cold-war-holy-warrior/

12. *Ibid.*

13. Alison Pargeter, *The Muslim Brotherhood: From Opposition to Power* (London, England: Saqi Books, 2013), 110.

14. *Ibid.,* 117.

15. Robert Dreyfuss, "Cold War, Holy Warrior," *Mother Jones,* January/February 2006, https://www.motherjones.com/politics/2006/01/cold-war-holy-warrior/

16. Ian Johnson, "How a Mosque for Ex-Nazis Became Center of Radical Islam," *Wall Street Journal,* July 12, 2005, https://www.wsj.com/articles/SB111964664777469127

17. *Ibid.*

18. *Ibid.*

19. Alison Pargeter, *The Muslim Brotherhood: From Opposition to Power* (London, England: Saqi Books, 2013), 117.

20. *Ibid.*, 165.

21. Ian Johnson, "How a Mosque for Ex-Nazis Became Center of Radical Islam," *Wall Street Journal*, July 12, 2005, https://www.wsj.com/articles/SB11196 4664777469127

22. Ian Johnson, *A Mosque in Munich: Nazis, the CIA, and the Rise of the Muslim Brotherhood in the West* (New York, NY: Houghton Mifflin Harcourt, 2010).

23. Ian Johnson, "How a Mosque for Ex-Nazis Became Center of Radical Islam," *Wall Street Journal*, July 12, 2005, https://www.wsj.com/articles/SB111964 664777469127

24. Alison Pargeter, *The Muslim Brotherhood: From Opposition to Power* (London, England: Saqi Books, 2013), 169.

25. Ian Johnson, "In Germany, Harder Line Looms," *Wall Street Journal*, September 12, 2005, https://www.wsj.com/articles/SB112648932945637655

26. Ian Johnson, "How a Mosque for Ex-Nazis Became Center of Radical Islam," *Wall Street Journal*, July 12, 2005, https://www.wsj.com/articles/SB11196 4664777469127

27. Alison Pargeter, *The Muslim Brotherhood: From Opposition to Power* (London, England: Saqi Books, 2013), 164.

28. Raghida Bahnam, "Muslim Brotherhood in Germany: Greater Danger Than ISIS, Qaeda," *Asharq Al-Awsat*, January 7, 2019, https://aawsat.com/english/home/article/1535806/muslim-brotherhood-germany-greater-danger-isis-qaeda

29. *Ibid.*

30. *Ibid.*

31. *Ibid.*

32. Lorenzo Vidino, *The Muslim Brotherhood in Austria* (n.p.: George Washington University, 2017), https://extremism.gwu.edu/sites/g/files/zaxdzs2191/f/MB%20in%20Austria-%20Print.pdf

33. *Ibid.*

34. *Ibid.*

35. Anonymous (Swiss Counterterrorism Advisor for the Federal Department of Foreign Affairs) in discussion with the author, October 10, 2018, Bern, Switzerland.

36. Lorenzo Vidino, *The Muslim Brotherhood in Austria* (n.p.: George Washington University, 2017), https://extremism.gwu.edu/sites/g/files/zaxdzs2191/f/MB%20in%20Austria-%20Print.pdf

37. *Ibid.*

38. Alison Pargeter, *The Muslim Brotherhood: From Opposition to Power* (London, England: Saqi Books, 2013), 140.

39. *Ibid.*

40. *Ibid.*, 147.

41. Tarek Dahroug, "Qatar and the Brotherhood in Europe," *Al-Ahram Weekly*, no. 1350 (2017), http://weekly.ahram.org.eg/News/20781.aspx

42. *Ibid.*

43. Alison Pargeter, *The Muslim Brotherhood: From Opposition to Power* (London, England: Saqi Books, 2013), 142.

44. Anonymous (former Counterterrorism Director for the Direction General de la Sécurité Extérieur) in discussion with the author, November 17, 2018, Paris, France.

45. Anonymous (Senior Advisor for the Direction General de la Sécurité Intérieur) in discussion with the author, March 7, 2019, Paris, France.

46. Alison Pargeter, *The Muslim Brotherhood: From Opposition to Power* (London, England: Saqi Books, 2013), 154.

47. James Brandon and Raffaello Pantucci, "UK Islamists and the Arab Uprisings," Hudson Institute, June 22, 2012, https://www.hudson.org/research/9902-uk-islamists-and-the-arab-uprisings

48. Alison Pargeter, *The Muslim Brotherhood: From Opposition to Power* (London, England: Saqi Books, 2013), 158.

49. Pekka Hakala, "Opposition in the United Arab Emirates," European Parliament Policy Department, November 15, 2012, http://www.europarl.europa.eu/RegData/etudes/briefing_note/join/2012/491458/EXPO-AFET_SP(2012)491458_EN.pdf

50. Alison Pargeter, *The Muslim Brotherhood: From Opposition to Power* (London, England: Saqi Books, 2013), 161.

51. James Brandon and Raffaello Pantucci, "UK Islamists and the Arab Uprisings," Hudson Institute, June 22, 2012, https://www.hudson.org/research/9902-uk-islamists-and-the-arab-uprisings

52. Andrew Gilligan, "How the Muslim Brotherhood Fits into a Network of Extremism," *Telegraph*, February 8, 2015, https://www.telegraph.co.uk/news/worldnews/middleeast/11398538/How-the-Muslim-Brotherhood-fits-into-a-network-of-extremism.html

53. Pekka Hakala, "Opposition in the United Arab Emirates," European Parliament Policy Department, November 15, 2012, http://www.europarl.europa.eu/RegData/etudes/briefing_note/join/2012/491458/EXPO-AFET_SP(2012)491458_EN.pdf

54. *Ibid.*

55. James Brandon and Raffaello Pantucci, "UK Islamists and the Arab Uprisings," Hudson Institute, June 22, 2012, https://www.hudson.org/research/9902-uk-islamists-and-the-arab-uprisings

56. Nigel Morris and Ian Johnston, "Muslim Brotherhood: Government Report Concludes They Should Not Be Classified as a Terrorist Organization," *Independent*, March 15, 2015, https://www.independent.co.uk/news/uk/home-news/muslim-brotherhood-government-report-concludes-they-should-not-be-classified-as-a-terrorist-10109730.html

57. James Brandon and Raffaello Pantucci, "UK Islamists and the Arab Uprisings," Hudson Institute, June 22, 2012, https://www.hudson.org/research/9902-uk-islamists-and-the-arab-uprisings

58. *Ibid.*

59. Alison Pargeter, *The Muslim Brotherhood: From Opposition to Power* (London, England: Saqi Books, 2013), 108–109.

60. *Ibid.*, 136.

61. Anonymous (former Counterterrorism Director for the Direction General de la Sécurité Extérieur) in discussion with the author, November 17, 2018, Paris, France.

62. Lorenzo Vidino, *The New Muslim Brotherhood in the West* (New York, NY: Columbia University Press, 2010).

63. Paul Peachey and David Connett, "British Dissident Investigated over Colonel Gaffagi Plot to Assassinate Saudi King," *Independent*, March 26, 2016, https://www.independent.co.uk/news/uk/crime/british-dissident-investigated-over-colonel-gaddafi-plot-to-assassinate-saudi-king-a6952756.html

64. Patrick Tyler, "Two Said to Tell of Libyan Plot Against Saudi," *The New York Times*, June 10, 2004, https://www.nytimes.com/2004/06/10/world/two-said-to-tell-of-libyan-plot-against-saudi.html

65. *Ibid.*

66. Paul Peachey and David Connett, "British Dissident Investigated over Colonel Gaffagi Plot to Assassinate Saudi King," *Independent*, March 26, 2016, https://www.independent.co.uk/news/uk/crime/british-dissident-investigated-over-colonel-gaddafi-plot-to-assassinate-saudi-king-a6952756.html

67. Harvey Kushner, *The Future of Terrorism: Violence in the New Millennium* (Thousand Oaks, CA: Sage Publications, 1998), 54.

68. Federal Bureau of Investigation, "No Cash for Terror: Convictions Returned in Holy Land Case," November 25, 2008, https://archives.fbi.gov/archives/news/stories/2008/november/hlf112508

69. Yusuf al-Qaradawi, *Priorities of the Islamic Movement in the Coming Phase* (n.p.: Awakening Publications, 1992), 7.

70. Pulp Ark, "The History of the Muslim Brotherhood in 3 Minutes," YouTube video, 3:09, November 25, 2012, https://www.youtube.com/watch?v=0N-5uGF9eYs

71. *Ibid.*

72. *Ibid.*

73. *Ibid.*

74. Abdel Monem Said Aly, "The Truth about the Muslim Brotherhood," *Cairo Review of Global Affairs* (Spring 2018), https://www.thecairoreview.com/essays/the-truth-about-the-muslim-brotherhood/

75. Ola Salem and Hassan Hassan, "Arab Regimes Are the World's Most Powerful Islamophobes," *Foreign Policy*, March 29, 2019, https://foreignpolicy.com/2019/03/29/arab-regimes-are-the-worlds-most-powerful-islamophobes/

76. Mark Tighe, "Muslim App Banned for Containing Anti-Semitic Rhetoric," *Sunday Times*, May 12, 2019, https://www.thetimes.co.uk/edition/ireland/muslim-app-banned-for-containing-anti-semitic-rhetoric-lwp6s0r7p

77. Lorenzo Vidino, *The Muslim Brotherhood in Austria* (n.p.: George Washington University, 2017), https://extremism.gwu.edu/sites/g/files/zaxdzs2191/f/MB%20in%20Austria-%20Print.pdf

78. *Ibid.*

79. Alison Pargeter, *The Muslim Brotherhood: From Opposition to Power* (London, England: Saqi Books, 2013), 119–120.

80. Pekka Hakala, "Opposition in the United Arab Emirates," European Parliament Policy Department, November 15, 2012, http://www.europarl.europa.eu/RegData/etudes/briefing_note/join/2012/491458/EXPO-AFET_SP(2012)491458_EN.pdf

81. Alison Pargeter, *The Muslim Brotherhood: From Opposition to Power* (London, England: Saqi Books, 2013), 137.

82. *Ibid.*, 139.

83. *Ibid.*, 175.

84. Mohammed Mehdi Akef, interview by Al-Sharq Al-Awsat, December 12, 2005, in Alison Pargeter, *The Muslim Brotherhood: From Opposition to Power* (London, England: Saqi Books, 2013).

85. gmbwatch, "Father of U.K. Muslim Brotherhood Leader to Head New Iraqi Electoral Coalition," *Global Muslim Brotherhood Daily Watch*, October 20, 2009, https://www.globalmbwatch.com/2009/10/20/father-of-uk-muslim-brotherhood-leader-to-head-new-iraqi-electoral-coalition/

86. Jamie Prentis, "Manchester Bomber's Imam Linked to Muslim Brotherhood," *The National*, August 21, 2018, https://www.thenational.ae/world/europe/manchester-bomber-s-imam-linked-to-muslim-brotherhood-1.762459

87. Pekka Hakala, "Opposition in the United Arab Emirates," European Parliament Policy Department, November 15, 2012, http://www.europarl.europa.eu/RegData/etudes/briefing_note/join/2012/491458/EXPO-AFET_SP(2012)491458_EN.pdf

88. Lorenzo Vidino, *The Muslim Brotherhood in Austria* (n.p.: George Washington University, 2017), https://extremism.gwu.edu/sites/g/files/zaxdzs2191/f/MB%20in%20Austria-%20Print.pdf

89. Andrew Harrod, "Georgetown University Stumps for the Muslim Brotherhood," *American Spectator*, October 5, 2017, https://spectator.org/georgetown-university-stumps-for-the-muslim-brotherhood/

90. James Brandon and Raffaello Pantucci, "UK Islamists and the Arab Uprisings," Hudson Institute, June 22, 2012, https://www.hudson.org/research/9902-uk-islamists-and-the-arab-uprisings

91. Abdullah Al-Othaymeen (former Secretary-General of the King Faisal International Prize) in discussion with the author, July 5, 2011, Riyadh, Saudi Arabia.

92. *Verfassungsschutzbericht* (Berlin, Germany: German Federal Ministry of the Interior, 2005), 190.

93. Lorenzo Vidino, *The Muslim Brotherhood in Austria* (n.p.: George Washington University, 2017), https://extremism.gwu.edu/sites/g/files/zaxdzs2191/f/MB%20in%20Austria-%20Print.pdf

94. John Mintz and Douglas Farah, "In Search of Friends Among the Foes: U.S. Hopes to Work with Diverse Group," *Washington Post*, September 11, 2004, https://www.washingtonpost.com/archive/politics/2004/09/11/in-search-of-friends-among-the-foes/654a7d58-057b-4965-ab44-4b1045915086/

95. "Tunisian Islamist Leader Embraces Turkey, Praises Erbakan," *Turkish Daily News*, March 3, 2011, https://www.newsturkish.com/tunisian-islamist-leader-embraces-turkey-praises-erbakan-2011-03-03.html

96. Svante Cornell, "Erbakan, Kısakürek, and the Mainstreaming of Extremism in Turkey," Hudson Institute, June 4, 2018, https://www.hudson.org/research/14375-erbakan-k-sak-rek-and-the-mainstreaming-of-extremism-in-turkey

97. *Verfassungsschutzbericht* (Berlin, Germany: German Federal Ministry of the Interior, 2005), 65.

98. Gönül Tol and Yasemin Akbaba, "Islamism in Western Europe: Milli Görüş in Germany," *Interdisciplinary Journal of Research on Religion* 12, no. 6 (2016), https://pdfs.semanticscholar.org/debc/c1f4d543e579abc869364b1d247b528f505c.pdf

99. Peter Mandaville and Shadi Hamid, *Islam as Statecraft: How Governments Use Religion in Foreign Policy* (Washington, DC: The Brookings Institute, 2018),

https://www.brookings.edu/research/islam-as-statecraft-how-governments-use-religion-in-foreign-policy/

100. Ahval, "Shadi Hamid: Erdogan Shares a Similar School of Thought to the Brotherhood," Soundcloud audio, 25:25, May 1, 2019, https://soundcloud.com/ahvalnews/shadi-hamid-of-the-brookings

101. Anonymous (former Senior Case Officer for the Middle East in France's foreign intelligence agency) in discussion with the author, January 5, 2019, Megeve, France.

102. *Ibid.*

103. "Interview with al-Kharbwai," *Ikhbariya News*, November 9, 2017.

104. Peter Mandaville and Shadi Hamid, *Islam as Statecraft: How Governments Use Religion in Foreign Policy* (Washington, DC: The Brookings Institute, 2018), https://www.brookings.edu/research/islam-as-statecraft-how-governments-use-religion-in-foreign-policy/

105. Michelle Fitzpatrick, "Cologne Braces for Protests as Erdogan Opens Mega Mosque," *The Local*, September 29, 2018, https://www.thelocal.de/20180929/cologne-braces-for-protests-as-erdogan-opens-mega-mosque

106. Gonul Tol, "Turkey's Bid for Religious Leadership," *Foreign Affairs*, January 10, 2019, https://www.foreignaffairs.com/articles/turkey/2019-01-10/turkeys-bid-religious-leadership

107. David Lepeska, "Turkey Casts the Diyanet," *Foreign Affairs*, May 17, 2015, https://www.foreignaffairs.com/articles/turkey/2015-05-17/turkey-casts-diyanet

108. Anonymous (former Lebanese Prime Minister) in discussion with the author, September 10, 2017, Geneva, Switzerland.

109. David Lepeska, "Turkey Casts the Diyanet," *Foreign Affairs*, May 17, 2015, https://www.foreignaffairs.com/articles/turkey/2015-05-17/turkey-casts-diyanet

110. *Ibid.*

111. Gonul Tol, "Turkey's Bid for Religious Leadership," *Foreign Affairs*, January 10, 2019, https://www.foreignaffairs.com/articles/turkey/2019-01-10/turkeys-bid-religious-leadership

112. Janene Pieters, "Erdogan Calls on Dutch-Turks to Be More Politically Active," *NL Times*, May 21, 2018, https://nltimes.nl/2018/05/21/erdogan-calls-dutch-turks-politically-active

113. Lorenzo Vidino, "Erdogan's Long Arm in Europe," *Foreign Policy*, May 7, 2019, https://foreignpolicy.com/2019/05/07/erdogans-long-arm-in-europe-germany-netherlands-milli-gorus-muslim-brotherhood-turkey-akp/

114. Gonul Tol, "Turkey's Bid for Religious Leadership," *Foreign Affairs*, January 10, 2019, https://www.foreignaffairs.com/articles/turkey/2019-01-10/turkeys-bid-religious-leadership

115. Steven Merley, *Turkey, the Global Muslim Brotherhood, and the Gaza Flotilla* (Jerusalem, Israel: Jerusalem Center for Public Affairs, 2011), http://www.jcpa.org/text/Turkey_Muslim_Brotherhood.pdf

116. Gonul Tol, "Turkey's Bid for Religious Leadership," *Foreign Affairs*, January 10, 2019, https://www.foreignaffairs.com/articles/turkey/2019-01-10/turkeys-bid-religious-leadership

117. *Ibid.*

118. Steven Merley, *Turkey, the Global Muslim Brotherhood, and the Gaza Flotilla* (Jerusalem, Israel: Jerusalem Center for Public Affairs, 2011), http://www.jcpa .org/text/Turkey_Muslim_Brotherhood.pdf

119. Ahmed Charai, "Turkey's Foreign Policy Priorities Are Shifting," *National Interest*, February 7, 2019, https://nationalinterest.org/feature/turkeys-foreign-policy-priorities-are-shifting-43832

120. Eric Trager, "Congress, Don't Meet with the Muslim Brotherhood," *The Hill*, September 13, 2017, https://thehill.com/opinion/international/350346-congress-dont-meet-with-the-muslim-brotherhood

121. David Roberts, "Behind Qatar's Intervention in Libya," *Foreign Affairs*, September 28, 2011, https://www.foreignaffairs.com/articles/libya/2011-09-28/behind-qatars-intervention-libya

122. Ahmed Tolba and Ayman al-Warfalli, "Libyan PM Says Turkey Supplying Weapons to Rival Tripoli Group," Reuters, February 27, 2015, https://www .reuters.com/article/us-libya-security-turkey/libyan-pm-says-turkey-supplying-weapons-to-rival-tripoli-group-idUSKBN0LV1S120150227

123. Staff writer, "Official Says Qatar, Sudan and Turkey Are 'Triad of Terrorism' in Libya," *Al Arabiya*, June 29, 2017, https://english.alarabiya.net/en/News/gulf/2017/06/29/Libyan-army-complains-about-foreign-backed-domestic-terro rism-.html

124. "Turkey Sends Militants to Sudan and Then into Libyan City of Sirte to Join Al Qaeda—Anti-terror Agency," *soL International*, March 19, 2018, https://news .sol.org.tr/turkey-sends-militants-sudan-and-then-libyan-city-sirte-join-al-qaeda-anti-terror-agency-174315

125. Zvi Mazel, "Erdogan's Grand Plan: Is Libya Next?" *Jerusalem Post*, January 7, 2019, https://www.jpost.com/Opinion/Erdogans-grand-plan-Is-Libya-next-576631

126. *Ibid.*

127. Asharq Al-Awsat, "Libya, Algeria Slam Turkey over Arms Shipment," *Asharq Al-Awsat*, December 24, 2018, https://aawsat.com/english/home/arti cle/1517566/libya-algeria-slam-turkey-over-arms-shipment

128. Michael Rubin, "Turkey's Libya Gambit," *National Interest*, January 11, 2019, https://nationalinterest.org/feature/turkeys-libya-gambit-41242

129. Paul Iddon, "Turkey and Regional Rivals Clash in Libya," *Ahval*, April 16, 2019, https://ahvalnews.com/muslim-brotherhood/turkey-and-regional-rivals-clash-libya

130. *De erfenis van Syrië: Mondiaal jihadisme blijft dreiging voor Europa* (Amster-dam, Netherlands: General Intelligence and Security Service, 2018).

131. William Armstrong, "Dogu Eroğlu on Investigating ISIS Networks in Tur-key," *William Armstrong* (blog), *Wordpress*, October 16, 2018, https://armstrong william.wordpress.com/2018/10/16/dogu-eroglu-on-investigating-isis-net works-in-turkey/

132. Anne Speckhard and Ardian Shajkovci, "The ISIS Ambassador to Turkey," *Homeland Security Today*, March 18, 2019, https://www.hstoday.us/subject-mat ter-areas/terrorism-study/the-isis-ambassador-to-turkey/

133. Burak Ege Bekdil, "Turkey Targets Defense and Aerospace Exports to Counter Growing National Deficit," *Defense News*, March 13, 2019, https://www .defensenews.com/industry/2019/03/13/turkey-targets-defense-and-aerospace-exports-to-counter-growing-national-deficit/

134. Tuvan Gumrukcu, "Qatar's Emir Pledges $15 Billion Direct Investment in Turkey: Erdogan's Office," Reuters, August 15, 2018, https://www.reuters.com/article/us-turkey-currency-qatar/qatars-emir-pledges-15-billion-direct-investment-in-turkey-erdogans-office-idUSKBN1L01MX

135. Al Jazeera and News Agencies, "Erdogan Vows to Strengthen Cooperation with Qatar," Al Jazeera, January 13, 2019, https://www.aljazeera.com/news/middleeast/2019/01/erdogan-vows-strengthen-cooperation-qatar-190113132119164.html

136. Agence France-Presse, "Turkish President Erdogan Lashes Out at Sisi over Egypt Executions," *France 24*, February 24, 2019, https://www.france24.com/en/20190224-turkish-president-erdogan-lashes-out-sisi-over-egypt-executions

137. Nordic Monitor, "Commentary: Is Erdogan Selling Out His Islamist Brothers?" *Nordic Monitor*, February 2019, https://www.nordicmonitor.com/2019/02/commentary-is-erdogan-selling-out-his-islamist-brothers/

138. مكملين – أخبار, "مستشار الرئيس التركي ياسين أقطاي يوضح التفاصيل حول ترحيل الشاب المصري عبدالحفيظ إلى القاهرة," YouTube video, 11:14, February 5, 2019, https://www.youtube.com/watch?v=kbBCyK4nzXA

139. Paul Iddon, "Turkey and Regional Rivals Clash in Libya," *Ahval*, April 16, 2019, https://ahvalnews.com/muslim-brotherhood/turkey-and-regional-rivals-clash-libya

140. Yavuz Baydar, "For Turkey, It's a Choice between Ikhwanism and Ba'athist-Islamist Blend," *Ahval*, February 25, 2019, https://ahvalnews.com/erdogan/turkey-its-choice-between-ikhwanism-and-baathist-islamist-blend

141. Ahmed Charai, "Turkey's Foreign Policy Priorities Are Shifting," *National Interest*, February 7, 2019, https://nationalinterest.org/feature/turkeys-foreign-policy-priorities-are-shifting-43832

142. *Ibid.*

143. Gonul Tol, "Turkey's Bid for Religious Leadership," *Foreign Affairs*, January 10, 2019, https://www.foreignaffairs.com/articles/turkey/2019-01-10/turkeys-bid-religious-leadership

144. Michael Rubin, "Turkey's Libya Gambit," *National Interest*, January 11, 2019, https://nationalinterest.org/feature/turkeys-libya-gambit-41242

145. Anonymous (former Lebanese Prime Minister) in discussion with the author, September 10, 2017, Geneva, Switzerland.

146. Jonathan Ferziger and Fadwa Hodali, "Turkey's Erdogan Is All Over East Jerusalem," *Bloomberg*, September 20, 2018, https://www.bloomberg.com/news/articles/2018-09-20/turkey-s-erdogan-is-all-over-east-jerusalem

147. Tim Lowell and Mark Bentley, "How Much Is $15 Billion from Qatar Really Worth?" *Ahval*, August 29, 2018, https://ahvalnewstr.com/qatar-turkey/how-much-15-billion-qatar-really-worth

148. "Qatar Accused of Financing Muslim Brotherhood Activities in Europe," *The Arab Weekly*, October 29, 2017, https://thearabweekly.com/qatar-accused-financing-muslim-brotherhood-activities-europe

149. *Ibid.*

150. Christian Chesnot and Georges Malbrunot, "Le Qatar veut acheter de l'influence et peser sur l'Islam européen," *France Inter*, April 6, 2019, https://www.franceinter.fr/emissions/l-invite-du-week-end/l-invite-du-week-end-06-avril-2019

151. Damien McElroy, "Qatar 'Spent Huge Sums on Muslim Brotherhood Groups in Europe'," *The National*, April 5, 2019, https://www.thenational.ae/world/qatar-spent-huge-sums-on-muslim-brotherhood-groups-in-europe-1.845510

152. Anonymous (Senior Advisir for the Direction General de la Sécurité Intérieur) in discussion with the author, March 7, 2019, Paris, France.

153. Fawaz bin Mohammed Al Khalifa (Bahrain's ambassador to the UK) in discussion with the author, April 20, 2019, London, England.

154. Tarek Dahroug, "Qatar and the Brotherhood in Europe," *Al-Ahram Weekly* no. 1350 (2017), http://weekly.ahram.org.eg/News/20781.aspx

155. Christian Chesnot and Georges Malbrunot, "Le Qatar veut acheter de l'influence et peser sur l'Islam européen," *France Inter*, April 6, 2019, https://www.franceinter.fr/emissions/l-invite-du-week-end/l-invite-du-week-end-06-avril-2019

156. "Research Center for Islamic Legislation and Ethics," Hamad Bin Khalifa University, accessed May 26, 2019, https://www.hbku.edu.qa/en/cis/center/cile

157. Tarek Dahroug, "Qatar and the Brotherhood in Europe," *Al-Ahram Weekly* no. 1350 (2017), http://weekly.ahram.org.eg/News/20781.aspx

158. Anonymous (Swiss Counterterrorism Advisor for the Federal Department of Foreign Affairs) in discussion with the author, October 10, 2018, Bern, Switzerland.

159. Tarek Dahroug, "Qatar and the Brotherhood in Europe," *Al-Ahram Weekly* no. 1350 (2017), http://weekly.ahram.org.eg/News/20781.aspx

160. *Ibid.*

161. Anonymous (former Swiss Special Envoy and current ambassador) in discussion with the author, March 7, 2018, Bern, Switzerland.

162. *Ibid.*

163. "Qatar's Attempts to Justify Terror Financing Exposed," *Khaleej Times*, August 27, 2017, https://www.khaleejtimes.com/region/qatar-crisis/qatars-attempts-to-justify-terror-financing-exposed

164. Fawaz bin Mohammed Al Khalifa (Bahrain's ambassador to the UK) in discussion with the author, November 18, 2017, London, England.

165. Christian Chesnot and Georges Malbrunot, "Le Qatar veut acheter de l'influence et peser sur l'Islam européen," *France Inter*, April 6, 2019, https://www.franceinter.fr/emissions/l-invite-du-week-end/l-invite-du-week-end-06-avril-2019

166. Tarek Dahroug, "Qatar and the Brotherhood in Europe," *Al-Ahram Weekly* no. 1350 (2017), http://weekly.ahram.org.eg/News/20781.aspx

167. Christian Chesnot and Georges Malbrunot, "Le Qatar veut acheter de l'influence et peser sur l'Islam européen," *France Inter*, April 6, 2019, https://www.franceinter.fr/emissions/l-invite-du-week-end/l-invite-du-week-end-06-avril-2019

168. Tarek Dahroug, "Qatar and the Brotherhood in Europe," *Al-Ahram Weekly* no. 1350 (2017), http://weekly.ahram.org.eg/News/20781.aspx

169. Agence France-Presse, "Tariq Ramadan: Oxford Professor Facing Rape Charges Granted Conditional Release," *The Guardian*, November 15, 2018, https://www.theguardian.com/world/2018/nov/15/tariq-ramadan-oxford-professor-facing-rape-charges-granted-conditional-release

170. Christian Chesnot and Georges Malbrunot, "Le Qatar veut acheter de l'influence et peser sur l'Islam européen," *France Inter*, April 6, 2019, https://www.franceinter.fr/emissions/l-invite-du-week-end/l-invite-du-week-end-06-avril-2019

171. "Qatar Accused of Financing Muslim Brotherhood Activities in Europe," *The Arab Weekly*, October 29, 2017, https://thearabweekly.com/qatar-accused-financing-muslim-brotherhood-activities-europe

172. Tarek Dahroug, "Qatar and the Brotherhood in Europe," *Al-Ahram Weekly* no. 1350 (2017), http://weekly.ahram.org.eg/News/20781.aspx

173. *Ibid.*

174. *Ibid.*

175. Christian Chesnot and Georges Malbrunot, "Le Qatar veut acheter de l'influence et peser sur l'Islam européen," *France Inter*, April 6, 2019, https://www.franceinter.fr/emissions/l-invite-du-week-end/l-invite-du-week-end-06-avril-2019

176. Tarek Dahroug, "Qatar and the Brotherhood in Europe," *Al-Ahram Weekly* no. 1350 (2017), http://weekly.ahram.org.eg/News/20781.aspx

177. Christian Chesnot and Georges Malbrunot, "Le Qatar veut acheter de l'influence et peser sur l'Islam européen," *France Inter*, April 6, 2019, https://www.franceinter.fr/emissions/l-invite-du-week-end/l-invite-du-week-end-06-avril-2019

178. Tarek Dahroug, "Qatar and the Brotherhood in Europe," *Al-Ahram Weekly* no. 1350 (2017), http://weekly.ahram.org.eg/News/20781.aspx

179. David Lepeska. "Turkey Casts the Diyanet," *Foreign Affairs*, May 17, 2015, https://www.foreignaffairs.com/articles/turkey/2015-05-17/turkey-casts-diyanet

180. Francois Murphy, Ali Kucukgocmen, and Robin Pomeroy, "Austria to Shut Down Mosques, Expel Foreign-Funded Imams," Reuters, June 8, 2018, https://www.reuters.com/article/us-austria-politics-islam/austria-plans-to-shut-down-mosques-expel-foreign-funded-imams-idUSKCN1J40X1

181. "Proposed German Law Could Push Out Turkish Imams," *Ahval*, March 4, 2019, https://ahvalnews.com/turkey-eu/proposed-german-law-could-push-out-turkish-imams

182. Chase Winter, "German Intelligence Mulls Putting Largest Turkish-Islamic Group under Surveillance," *DW*, September 21, 2018, https://www.dw.com/en/german-intelligence-mulls-putting-largest-turkish-islamic-group-under-surveillance/a-45586282

183. Michelle Fitzpatrick, "Cologne Braces for Protests as Erdogan Opens Mega Mosque," *The Local*, September 29, 2018, https://www.thelocal.de/20180929/cologne-braces-for-protests-as-erdogan-opens-mega-mosque

184. Axel Spilcker, "Türkische Regierung lädt Extremisten in die Kölner Ditib-Zentralmoschee," *Focus*, January 8, 2019, https://www.focus.de/politik/deutschland/mehrtaegige-islamkonferenz-tuerkische-regierung-laedt-extremisten-in-die-koelner-ditib-zentralmoschee_id_10151660.html

185. "Brotherhood Connection: German State Puts Turkish Organization under Scrutiny," *Al Arabiya*, January 10, 2019, https://english.alarabiya.net/en/News/world/2019/01/10/Brotherhood-connection-German-state-puts-Turkish-organization-under-scrutiny.html

186. Christian Chesnot and Georges Malbrunot, "Le Qatar veut acheter de l'influence et peser sur l'Islam européen," *France Inter*, April 6, 2019, https://www.franceinter.fr/emissions/l-invite-du-week-end/l-invite-du-week-end-06-avril-2019

187. *Ibid.*

188. Giulio Meotti, "Qatar: "A Wolf in Sheep's Clothing': Bankrolling Islamism in Europe," *Gatestone Institute*, April 9, 2019, https://www.gatestoneinstitute.org/14042/qatar-europe-islamism-finance

189. "Qatar Accused of Financing Muslim Brotherhood Activities in Europe," *The Arab Weekly*, October 29, 2017, https://thearabweekly.com/qatar-accused-financing-muslim-brotherhood-activities-europe

190. Bertrand Besancenot (former French Ambassador to Saudi Arabia) in discussion with the author October 15, 2018, Paris, France.

191. Lorenzo Vidino, *The Muslim Brotherhood in Austria* (n.p.: George Washington University, 2017), https://extremism.gwu.edu/sites/g/files/zaxdzs2191/f/MB%20in%20Austria-%20Print.pd

192. "United States and Turkey Split over Muslim Brotherhood," *Ahval*, February 7, 2019, https://ahvalnews.com/muslim-brotherhood/united-states-and-turkey-split-over-muslim-brotherhood

CHAPTER 7

1. Jeffrey Goldberg, "Ashton Carter: Gulf Arabs Need to Get in the Fight," *The Atlantic*, November 6, 2015, https://www.theatlantic.com/international/archive/2015/11/ashton-carter-gulf-iran-isis/414591/

2. Peter Mandaville and Shadi Hamid, *Islam as Statecraft: How Governments Use Religion in Foreign Policy* (Washington, DC: The Brookings Institute, 2018), https://www.brookings.edu/research/islam-as-statecraft-how-governments-use-religion-in-foreign-policy/

3. *Ibid.*

4. Former French ambassador in discussion with the author, January 2, 2018, Paris, France.

5. Andrew Hammond, "Arab Awakening: Qatar's Controversial Alliance with Arab Islamists," *openDemocracy*, April 25, 2013, https://www.opendemocracy.net/en/north-africa-west-asia-qatars-controversial-alliance-with-arab-islamists/

6. Abdullah Al-Othaymeen (former Secretary-General of the King Faisal International Prize) in discussion with the author, April 11, 2014, Paris, France.

7. "Muslim Brotherhood in Qatar," *Counter Extremism Project*, n.d., https://www.counterextremism.com/sites/default/files/mb_pdf/MB%20Branch_Qatar_043019.pdf

8. Kristian Coates Ulrichsen, "Qatar: The Gulf's Problem Child," *The Atlantic*, June 5, 2017, https://www.theatlantic.com/international/archive/2017/06/qatar-gcc-saudi-arabia-yemen-bahrain/529227/

9. Robert Worth, "Egypt Is Arena for Influence of Arab Rivals," *The New York Times*, July 9, 2013, https://www.nytimes.com/2013/07/10/world/middleeast/aid-to-egypt-from-saudis-and-emiratis-is-part-of-struggle-with-qatar-for-influence.html

10. Abdulaziz Khoja (former Saudi Information Minister) in discussion with the author, October 18, 2016, London, England.

11. Kate Shuttleworth and Hazem Balousha, "Qatar Is Top Donor as $5bn Is Pledged to Rebuild Gaza," *The Guardian*, October 12, 2014, https://www.the guardian.com/world/2014/oct/12/gaza-rebuild-international-donors-israel-hamas-qatar

12. Tom Finn, "Qatar Says Gives $30 Million to Pay Gaza Public Sector Workers," Reuters, July 22, 2016, https://www.reuters.com/article/us-palestinians-gaza-qatar-idUSKCN1021AQ

13. Inna Lazareva, "Mossad Spy Who Saved Hamas Leader's Life Calls for Him to Seek Peace," *Telegraph*, August 24, 2014, https://www.telegraph.co.uk/news/worldnews/middleeast/israel/11052952/Mossad-spy-who-saved-Hamas-leaders-life-calls-for-him-to-seek-peace.html

14. Nic Robertson, Andrew Carey, and Tamara Qiblawi, "Hamas Leader Issues Direct Plea to Trump to Seize 'Historic Opportunity'," *CNN*, May 3, 2017, https://www.cnn.com/2017/05/03/middleeast/palestinian-hamas-khaled-meshaal/index.html

15. Bloomberg and Associated Press, "Hamas Leaders Meet in Gaza to Consider Ceasefire with Israel," *The National*, August 3, 2018, https://www.thenational.ae/world/mena/hamas-leaders-meet-in-gaza-to-consider-ceasefire-with-isra el-1.756614

16. Fawaz bin Mohammed Al Khalifa (Bahrain's ambassador to the UK) in discussion with the author, March 15, 2018, London, England.

17. Turki Al Faisal (former Saudi Intelligence Director and ex-ambassador to the United Kingdom and United States) in discussion with the author, December 15, 2017, Paris, France.

18. Former French ambassador in discussion with the author, January 2, 2018, Paris, France.

19. Anonymous (former British ambassador to several Middle Eastern countries between 2005 and 2015) in discussion with the author, April 15, 2018, London, England.

20. Turki Al Faisal in discussion with the author, August 15, 2018, Paris, France.

21. Anonymous (former British ambassador to several Middle Eastern countries between 2005 and 2015) in discussion with the author, April 15, 2018, London, England.

22. Talal bin Mohammed Al Khalifa (former President of Bahrain National Security Agency) in discussion with the author, October 5, 2018, London, England.

23. Ali Younes, "Analysis: Behind the Punishing Blockade Against Qatar," Al Jazeera, May 1, 2019, https://www.aljazeera.com/news/2019/04/analysis-punishing-blockade-qatar-190430154256454.html

24. Bertrand Besancenot (former French Ambassador to Saudi Arabia) in discussion with the author, July 10, 2018, Paris, France.

25. "Visions of Gulf Security," *Project on Middle East Political Science* (George Washington University), no. 25 (March 2014), https://pomeps.org/wp-content/uploads/2014/03/Visions_of_Gulf_Security.pdf

26. Anonymous (former British ambassador to several Middle Eastern countries between 2005 and 2015) in discussion with the author, April 15, 2018, London, England.

27. *Ibid.*

28. Ian Black, "Egypt's Overthrow of Morsi Creates Uncertainty for Islamists Everywhere," *The Guardian*, July 12, 2013, https://www.theguardian.com/world/2013/jul/12/egypt-morsi-islamists-uncertainty

29. Paul Alster, "Secret Document Appears to Show Qatar Payoffs to Key Morsi Cronies," *Fox News*, July 9, 2013, https://www.foxnews.com/world/secret-document-appears-to-show-qatar-payoffs-to-key-morsi-cronies

30. Patrick Markey, "Egypt Court Sentences Mursi to 25 Years in Qatar Spy Case," Reuters, September 16, 2017, https://www.reuters.com/article/us-egypt-court/egypt-court-sentences-mursi-to-25-years-in-qatar-spy-case-idUSKCN1BR0ES

31. Angus McDowall, Amena Bakr, and Ralph Boulton, "Leading Sunni Cleric Says in Fatwa Egyptians Should Back Mursi," Reuters, July 6, 2013, https://www.reuters.com/article/us-egypt-protests-qaradawi/leading-sunni-cleric-says-in-fatwa-egyptians-should-back-mursi-idUSBRE9650DN20130706

32. David Roberts, "Qatar and the Muslim Brotherhood: Pragmatism or Preference?" *Middle East Policy Council* 21, no. 3 (Fall 2017), https://www.mepc.org/qatar-and-muslim-brotherhood-pragmatism-or-preference

33. Anonymous (former Senior White House Advisor) in discussion with the author, September 25, 2018, Rome, Italy.

34. Bertrand Besancenot (former French Ambassador to Saudi Arabia) in discussion with the author, June 20 2018, Paris, France.

35. *Ibid.*

36. Anonymous (former Senior Case Office in the Central Intelligence Agency's Near East Directorate) in discussion with the author, April 15, 2016, Washington, DC.

37. Anonymous (Emiri Court Advisor) in discussion with the author, March 9, 2018, Geneva, Switzerland.

38. MsNajla1, "مكالمه سريه بين حمد بن جاسم ومعمر القذافي," YouTube video, 5:41, December 22, 2011, https://www.youtube.com/watch?time_continue=1&v=d503YP1_EMg

39. "What Did the Qataris Say About Saudi Arabia," *Gulf News*, March 17, 2014, https://gulfnews.com/world/gulf/qatar/what-did-the-qataris-say-about-saudi-arabia-1.1305178

40. Ramadan Al Sherbini and Sara Al Shurafa, "Prominent Saudi Preacher Apologises on TV for Years of 'Hardline' Islam," *Gulf News*, May 8, 2019, https://gulfnews.com/world/gulf/saudi/prominent-saudi-preacher-apologises-on-tv-for-years-of-hardline-islam-1.63817748

41. *Ibid.*

42. *Ibid.*

43. Borzou Daragahi, "Arab League Summit Is Held Despite Snubs," *Los Angeles Times*, March 30, 2008, https://www.latimes.com/archives/la-xpm-2008-mar-30-fg-arab30-story.html

44. MsNajla1, "مكالمه سريه بين حمد بن جاسم ومعمر القذافي," YouTube video, 5:41, December 22, 2011, https://www.youtube.com/watch?time_continue=1&v=d503YP1_EMg

45. *Ibid.*

46. https://www.reuters.com/article/us-saudi-usa-gulf/saudi-arabia-defies-u-s-pressure-to-end-qatar-row-after-khashoggi-killing-idUSKCN1NL1XM

47. Andrew Hammond, "Arab Awakening: Qatar's Controversial Alliance with Arab Islamists," *openDemocracy*, April 25, 2013, https://www.opendemocracy .net/en/north-africa-west-asia-qatars-controversial-alliance-with-arab-islamists/

48. Angus McDowall, "Saudis, UAE, Bahrain Withdraw Envoys from Qatar in Security Dispute," Reuters, March 5, 2014, https://www.reuters.com/article/us-gulf-qatar-ambassadors-idUSBREA240T620140305

49. David Kirkpatrick, "Muslim Brotherhood Says Qatar Ousted Its Members," *The New York Times*, September 13, 2014, https://www.nytimes.com/2014/09/14/world/middleeast/bowing-to-pressure-qatar-asks-some-muslim-brotherhood-leaders-to-leave.html

50. Former Saudi cabinet minister in discussion with the author, January 2018.

51. Emily Harris, "Why Israel Lets Qatar Give Millions to Hamas," *National Public Radio*, June 18, 2015, https://www.npr.org/sections/parallels/2015/06/18/414693807/why-israel-lets-qatar-give-millions-to-hamas

52. i24NEWS, "Qatar to Transfer $100 Million in Aid for Gaza Reconstruction," *i24 News*, February 13, 2017, https://www.i24news.tv/en/news/international/middle-east/137518-170213-qatar-to-transfer-100-million-in-aid-for-gaza-reconstruction

53. Clifford May, Robert Gates, and Jenna Lee, "Qatar and the Muslim Brotherhood's Global Affiliates: A New U.S. Administration Considers New Policies," Discussion Transcript, May 23, 2017, https://s3.us-east-2.amazonaws.com/defenddemocracy/uploads/documents/05-23-17_Gates_Keynote_(FINALFinal).pdf

54. Kersten Knipp, "Discord in the Persian Gulf: Qatar and the Muslim Brotherhood," *DW*, May 27, 2017, https://www.dw.com/en/discord-in-the-persian-gulf-qatar-and-the-muslim-brotherhood/a-39005743

55. Dexter Filkins, "A Saudi Prince's Quest to Remake the Middle East," *New Yorker*, April 2, 2018, https://www.newyorker.com/magazine/2018/04/09/a-saudi-princes-quest-to-remake-the-middle-east

56. Anonymous (former Senior Political Advisor for United States Central Command) in discussion with the author, June 10, 2018, Tampa, FL.

57. *Ibid*.

58. *Ibid*.

59. Eric Trager, "The Muslim Brotherhood Is the Root of the Qatar Crisis," *The Atlantic*, July 2, 2017, https://www.theatlantic.com/international/archive/2017/07/muslim-brotherhood-qatar/532380/

60. Habib Toumi, "How the Muslim Brotherhood Betrayed Saudi Arabia," *Gulf News*, June 7, 2017, https://gulfnews.com/world/gulf/saudi/how-the-muslim-brotherhood-betrayed-saudi-arabia-1.2039864

61. News Agencies, "Tillerson: Blacklisting Muslim Brotherhood Problematic," Al Jazeera, June 14, 2017, https://www.aljazeera.com/news/2017/06/tillerson-blacklisting-muslim-brotherhood-problematic-170614193311591.html

62. Jonathan Chait, "Trump Hired Bolton to Make Foreign Policy Exciting Again," *Intelligencer* (*New York Magazine*), March 23, 2018, http://nymag.com/intelligencer/2018/03/trump-hired-bolton-to-make-foreign-policy-exciting-again.html

63. "US Should Declare the Muslim Brotherhood a Terrorist Organization, Says John Bolton," *Arab News*, July 13, 2017, http://www.arabnews.com/node/1128816/middle-east

64. Charlie Savage, Eric Schmitt, and Maggie Haberman, "Trump Pushes to Designate Muslim Brotherhood a Terrorist Group," *The New York Times*, April 30, 2019, https://www.nytimes.com/2019/04/30/us/politics/trump-muslim-broth erhood.html?module=inline

65. Karen DeYoung and Ellen Nakashima, "UAE Orchestrated Hacking of Qatari Government Sites, Sparking Regional Upheaval, According to U.S. Intelligence Officials," *Washington Post*, July 16, 2017, https://www.washingtonpost .com/world/national-security/uae-hacked-qatari-government-sites-sparking-regional-upheaval-according-to-us-intelligence-officials/2017/07/16/00c46e54-6 98f-11e7-8eb5-cbccc2e7bfbf_story.html

66. Peter Salisbury, "The Fake-News Hack That Nearly Started a War This Summer Was Designed for One Man: Donald Trump," *Quartz*, October 20, 2017, https://qz.com/1107023/the-inside-story-of-the-hack-that-nearly-started-anoth er-middle-east-war/

67. Karen DeYoung and Ellen Nakashima, "UAE Orchestrated Hacking of Qatari Government Sites, Sparking Regional Upheaval, According to U.S. Intelligence Officials," *Washington Post*, July 16, 2017, https://www.washingtonpost .com/world/national-security/uae-hacked-qatari-government-sites-sparking-regional-upheaval-according-to-us-intelligence-officials/2017/07/16/00c46e54-6 98f-11e7-8eb5-cbccc2e7bfbf_story.html

68. TOI Staff and Agencies, "Qatari FM Insists Hamas 'A Legitimate Resistance Movement'," *Times of Israel*, June 10, 2017, http://www.timesofisrael.com/qatari-fm-insists-hamas-a-legitimate-resistance-movement/

69. Megan Wilson and Ellen Mitchell, "Qatar Brings Lobbyists into Gulf Showdown," *The Hill*, June 13, 2017, https://thehill.com/business-a-lobbying/337515-qatar-brings-lobbyists-into-gulf-showdown

70. Ann Simmons, "Accused of Funding Terrorism and Being Too Cozy with Iran, Qatar Says It Has Done No Wrong," *Los Angeles Times*, August 27, 2017, https://www.latimes.com/world/middleeast/la-fg-global-qatar-qa-20170 827-htmlstory.html

71. Iman Zayat, "Qatari Ties to Iran, Turkey Undermine Regional Security," *Arab Weekly*, December 16, 2018, https://thearabweekly.com/qatari-ties-iran-tur key-undermine-regional-security

72. Clifford May, Robert Gates, and Jenna Lee, "Qatar and the Muslim Brotherhood's Global Affiliates: A New U.S. Administration Considers New Policies," Discussion Transcript, May 23, 2017, https://s3.us-east-2.amazonaws.com/de fenddemocracy/uploads/documents/05-23-17_Gates_Keynote_(FINALFinal) .pdf

73. *Ibid*.

74. Mohammed bin Abdulrahman Al-Thani, interview by Gulf Affairs, in Oxford Gulf and Arabian Peninsula Studies Forum, "Foreign Policy Trends in the GCC States," *Gulf Affairs* (Autumn 2017): 36–39, https://www.oxgaps.org/files/ gulf_affairs_autumn_2017_full_issue.pdf

75. "Qatar Announces $150 Million Aid to Gaza," *MSN*, October 10, 2018, http://www.msn.com/en-xl/middleeast/top-stories/qatar-announces-dol lar150-million-aid-to-gaza/ar-BBOdibS

76. Oren Liebermann et al., "Suitcases of $15M in Cash from Qatar Bring Relief for Gaza," *CNN*, November 11, 2018, https://edition.cnn.com/2018/11/11/mid dleeast/gaza-qatar-humanitarian-intl/index.html

77. Reuters, "Qatar Pays Gaza Salaries to Ease Tensions," *Ynetnews*, September 11, 2018, https://www.ynetnews.com/articles/0,7340,L-5394624,00.html

78. Tom Wilson and Dan Williams, "Hamas Shifts Tactics in Bitcoin Fundraising, Highlighting Crypto Risks: Research," Reuters, April 26, 2019, https://uk.reuters.com/article/us-crypto-currencies-hamas/hamas-shifts-tactics-in-bitcoin-fundraising-highlighting-crypto-risks-research-idUKKCN1S20FA

79. Yoni Ben Menachem, "Muslim Brotherhood Religious Authority Resigns," *Jerusalem Center for Public Affairs*, November 15, 2018, http://jcpa.org/muslim-brotherhood-religious-authority-resigns/

80. Eric Trager, "The Muslim Brotherhood Is the Root of the Qatar Crisis," *The Atlantic*, July 2, 2017, https://www.theatlantic.com/international/archive/2017/07/muslim-brotherhood-qatar/532380/

81. Anonymous (former Prime Minister of Jordan) in discussion with the author, September 25, 2017, Amman, Jordan.

82. The National, "Russian Diplomat Reveals Influence of Muslim Brotherhood Scholar on Qatari Media," *The National*, April 21, 2018, https://www.thenational.ae/world/gcc/russian-diplomat-reveals-influence-of-muslim-brotherhood-scholar-on-qatari-media-1.723598

83. David Roberts, "Qatar, the Ikhwan, and Transnational Relations in the Gulf" (memo for workshop "Visions of Gulf Security," Venice, Italy, March 9, 2014), https://pomeps.org/2014/03/18/qatar-the-ikhwan-and-transnational-relations-in-the-gulf/

84. Bertrand Besancenot (former French Ambassador to Saudi Arabia) in discussion with the author, June 20 2018, Paris, France.

85. Courtney Freer, *Rentier Islamism: The Influence of the Muslim Brotherhood in Gulf Monarchies* (New York, NY: Oxford University Press, 2018).

86. Samir Salama, "How the Muslim Brotherhood Manipulated the Qatari Regime," *Gulf News*, July 30, 2017, https://gulfnews.com/world/gulf/qatar/how-the-muslim-brotherhood-manipulated-the-qatari-regime-1.2066309

87. Paul Wood, "'Billion Dollar Ransom': Did Qatar Pay Record Sum?" *BBC News*, July 17, 2018, https://www.bbc.com/news/world-middle-east-44660369

88. Anonymous (Swiss Counterterrorism Advisor for the Federal Department of Foreign Affairs) in discussion with the author, April 25, 2019, Bern, Switzerland.

89. David Roberts, "Qatar and the Muslim Brotherhood: Pragmatism or Preference?" *Middle East Policy Council* 21, no. 3 (Fall 2017), https://www.mepc.org/qatar-and-muslim-brotherhood-pragmatism-or-preference

90. Ahmed Ramadan, "Who Will Benefit from Qatar's Asylum Law?" *Al-Monitor*, June 13, 2019, https://www.al-monitor.com/pulse/originals/2019/06/qatar-asylum-law-legitimacy-egyptian-brotherhood-fugitives.html

91. Fawaz bin Mohammed Al Khalifa (Bahrain's ambassador to the UK) in discussion with the author, March 15, 2018, London, England.

92. Dominic Evans, "Saudi Prince Says Turkey Part of 'Triangle of Evil': Egyptian Media," Reuters, March 7, 2018, https://www.reuters.com/article/us-saudi-turkey/saudi-prince-says-turkey-part-of-triangle-of-evil-egyptian-media-idUSKCN1GJ1WW

93. "Interview with al-Kharbwai," *Ikhbariya News*, November 9, 2017.

94. Bertrand Besancenot (former French Ambassador to Saudi Arabia) in discussion with the author.

95. Damien McElroy, "US Advisers Quit Qatar Role as Emir Dines with Muslim Brotherhood Leader," *The National*, June 7, 2018, https://www.thenational.ae/world/gcc/us-advisers-quit-qatar-role-as-emir-dines-with-muslim-brotherhood-leader-1.737981

96. *Ibid.*

97. Liam Denning, "Qatar Leaving Is an Ominous Sign for OPEC," *Bloomberg*, December 3, 2018, https://www.bloomberg.com/opinion/articles/2018-12-03/qatar-leaving-opec-is-an-ominous-sign-for-opec

98. Marc Champion, "Qatar's Departure from OPEC Suggests Gulf Rift Is Here to Stay," *Bloomberg*, December 3, 2018, https://www.bloomberg.com/news/articles/2018-12-03/qatar-s-departure-from-opec-suggests-gulf-rift-is-here-to-stay

99. The New Arab & agencies, "Qatar Economy Still Growing Despite Saudi-Led Blockade, Says IMF," *The New Arab*, November 14, 2018, https://www.alaraby.co.uk/english/news/2018/11/14/qatar-economy-still-growing-despite-saudi-led-blockade-says-imf

100. David Kirkpatrick, "Emirati Prince Flees to Qatar, Exposing Tensions in U.A.E.," *The New York Times*, July 14, 2018, https://www.nytimes.com/2018/07/14/world/middleeast/emirati-prince-qatar-defects.html

101. Habib Toumi, "UAE, Bahrain Dismiss Misleading Statements About Qatar's Crisis," *Gulf News*, December 16, 2018, https://gulfnews.com/world/gulf/qatar/uae-bahrain-dismiss-misleading-statements-about-qatars-crisis-1.60970588

102. (AnwarGargash), د. أنور قرقاش، "أمير قطر في منتدى الدوحة يرفض التدخل في شؤونه الداخلية ويتمسك عبر سياسات بلاده بالتدخل في الشؤون الداخلية لجيرانه ودول المنطقة، ازدواجية تحمل بصمات الامير السابق، والمختصر اننا في ظل هيمنته لن نرى تغيرا جوهريا يتيح للقيادة الشابة إدارة الأمور بواقعية" Twitter post, December 15, 2018, 4:53 A.M., https://twitter.com/AnwarGargash/status/1073924079613284352

103. Peter Mandaville and Shadi Hamid, *Islam as Statecraft: How Governments Use Religion in Foreign Policy* (Washington, DC: The Brookings Institute, 2018), https://www.brookings.edu/research/islam-as-statecraft-how-governments-use-religion-in-foreign-policy/

104. Mohammed bin Abdulrahman Al-Thani, interview by Gulf Affairs, in Oxford Gulf and Arabian Peninsula Studies Forum, "Foreign Policy Trends in the GCC States," *Gulf Affairs* (Autumn 2017): 36–39, https://www.oxgaps.org/files/gulf_affairs_autumn_2017_full_issue.pdf

105. Ted Regencia, "Qatar-Gulf Rift: The Iran Factor," Al Jazeera, June 5, 2017, https://www.aljazeera.com/indepth/features/2017/06/qatar-gulf-rift-iran-factor-170605102522955.html

106. The Associated Press, "Turkey, Iran Help Qatar Thrive, One Year into Saudi-Led Blockage," *Hareetz*, June 18, 2018, https://www.haaretz.com/middle-east-news/turkey/qatar-crisis-turkey-iran-help-tiny-emirate-thrive-one-year-into-saudi-led-blockade-1.6177992

107. Marc Champion, "Qatar's Departure from OPEC Suggests Gulf Rift Is Here to Stay," *Bloomberg*, December 3, 2018, https://www.bloomberg.com/news/articles/2018-12-03/qatar-s-departure-from-opec-suggests-gulf-rift-is-here-to-stay

108. "Sheikh Tamim Denies Qatar Has Links to Terrorism," *Khaleej Times*, May 25, 2017, https://www.khaleejtimes.com/region/qatar/sheikh-tamim-denies-qatar-has-links-to-terrorism

109. Al-Monitor Staff, "Iran's FM Says Qatar 'Brought Saudi Arabia to Its Knees'," *Al-Monitor*, May 2, 2018, https://www.al-monitor.com/pulse/originals/2018/05/iran-zarif-amir-kabir-basij-attack-qatar-saudi-arabia-jcpoa.html

110. Peter Mandaville and Shadi Hamid, *Islam as Statecraft: How Governments Use Religion in Foreign Policy* (Washington, DC: The Brookings Institute, 2018), https://www.brookings.edu/research/islam-as-statecraft-how-governments-use-religion-in-foreign-policy/

111. *Ibid.*

112. The National, "Qatar Considers Iran Offer to Host World Cup Teams," *The National*, November 13, 2018, https://www.thenational.ae/world/gcc/qatar-considers-iran-offer-to-host-world-cup-teams-1.791299

113. Karen DeYoung and Dan Lamothe, "Qatar to Upgrade Air Base Used by U.S. to Fight Terrorism," *Washington Post*, July 24, 2018, https://www.washingtonpost.com/world/national-security/qatar-to-upgrade-air-base-used-by-us-to-fight-terrorism/2018/07/23/19e04c84-8eb7-11e8-b769-e3fff17f0689_story.html

114. Mohammed bin Abdulrahman Al-Thani, interview by Gulf Affairs, in Oxford Gulf and Arabian Peninsula Studies Forum, "Foreign Policy Trends in the GCC States," *Gulf Affairs* (Autumn 2017): 36–39, https://www.oxgaps.org/files/gulf_affairs_autumn_2017_full_issue.pdf

115. *Ibid.*

116. "Sheikh Tamim Denies Qatar Has Links to Terrorism," *Khaleej Times*, May 25, 2017, https://www.khaleejtimes.com/region/qatar/sheikh-tamim-denies-qatar-has-links-to-terrorism

117. Hussein Ibish, "Turkey Is Changing the Middle East. The U.S. Doesn't Get It," *Bloomberg Opinion*, March 14, 2019, https://www.bloomberg.com/opinion/articles/2019-03-14/turkey-is-changing-the-middle-east-the-u-s-doesn-t-get-it?srnd=politics-vp

118. *Ibid.*

119. *Ibid.*

120. Adelle Nazarian, "Qatar May Escalate Conflict with Saudi Arabia and the UAE with Turkish Troops," *Daily Caller*, February 24, 2019, https://dailycaller.com/2019/02/24/qatar-conflict-saudi-arabia-uae-turkish-troops/

121. Marc Champion, "Qatar's Departure from OPEC Suggests Gulf Rift Is Here to Stay," *Bloomberg*, December 3, 2018, https://www.bloomberg.com/news/articles/2018-12-03/qatar-s-departure-from-opec-suggests-gulf-rift-is-here-to-stay

122. Bülent Aras and Emirhan Yorulmazlar, "Turkey, Iran and the Gulf Crisis," *HSF Policy Brief* (Humanitarian Studies Foundation) 1, no. 3 (March 2018): 1–12, http://humsf.org/wp-content/uploads/2018/05/HSF_PolicyBrief_3.pdf

123. Ali Bakeer, "Testing the Turkey-Qatar Military Partnership," *The New Arab*, February 25, 2019, https://www.alaraby.co.uk/english/comment/2019/2/25/testing-the-turkey-qatar-military-partnership

124. *Ibid.*

125. "Russia in Talks Over S-400 Air-Defense Systems with Qatar, Saudi Arabia," *Daily Sabah*, February 19, 2019, https://www.dailysabah.com/defense/2019/02/19/russia-in-talks-over-s-400-air-defense-systems-with-qatar-saudi-arabia

126. Mohammed Alkhereiji and Kelly Kennedy, "Missile Defence System Sparks US-Russia Tensions in Middle East," *The Arab Weekly*, March 10, 2019, https://thearabweekly.com/missile-defence-system-sparks-us-russia-tensions-middle-east

127. Marc Champion, "Qatar's Departure from OPEC Suggests Gulf Rift Is Here to Stay," *Bloomberg*, December 3, 2018, https://www.bloomberg.com/news/articles/2018-12-03/qatar-s-departure-from-opec-suggests-gulf-rift-is-here-to-stay

128. *Ibid.*

129. Iman Zayat, "Qatari Ties to Iran, Turkey Undermine Regional Security," *The Arab Weekly*, December 16, 2018, https://thearabweekly.com/qatari-ties-iran-turkey-undermine-regional-security

130. Mohammed Ayoob, "The Regional Factors Bringing Turkey and Iran Together," *The Strategist* (blog), *Australian Strategic Policy Institute*, December 12, 2018, https://www.aspistrategist.org.au/the-regional-factors-bringing-turkey-and-iran-together/

131. Iman Zayat, "Qatari Ties to Iran, Turkey Undermine Regional Security," *The Arab Weekly*, December 16, 2018, https://thearabweekly.com/qatari-ties-iran-turkey-undermine-regional-security

132. Colin Clarke and Ahmet Yayla, "The United States Can't Rely on Turkey to Defeat ISIS," *Foreign Policy*, December 31, 2018, https://foreignpolicy.com/2018/12/31/the-united-states-cant-rely-on-turkey-to-defeat-isis-kurds-syria-ypg-erdogan/

133. Joost Hiltermann, "The Kurds Once Again Face American Abandonment," *The Atlantic*, August 30, 2018, https://www.theatlantic.com/international/archive/2018/08/syria-kurds-assad-ypg-isis-iraq/569029/

134. Samuel Ramani, "UAE Steps Up Anti-Turkey Efforts in Syria," *Al-Monitor*, February 25, 2019, https://www.al-monitor.com/pulse/originals/2019/02/uae-syria-turkey-containment-efforts-kurds-erdogan.html

135. *Ibid.*

136. *Ibid.*

137. News Service, "Saudi, UAE Step Up Support for PKK Terrorists in Northeast Syria," *Yeni Şafak*, December 1, 2018, https://www.yenisafak.com/en/news/saudi-uae-step-up-support-for-pkk-terrorists-in-northeast-syria-3467953

138. Dimitar Bechev, "Is Turkey Ready to Embrace Assad?" *Ahval*, March 7, 2019, https://ahvalnews.com/turkey-syria/turkey-ready-embrace-assad

139. Hussein Ibish, "Turkey Is Changing the Middle East. The U.S. Doesn't Get It," *Bloomberg Opinion*, March 14, 2019, https://www.bloomberg.com/opinion/articles/2019-03-14/turkey-is-changing-the-middle-east-the-u-s-doesn-t-get-it

140. "Middle East Entente: Tehran, Ankara and Doha Found Each Other," *Katehon*, December 28, 2018, http://katehon.com/article/middle-east-entente-tehran-ankara-and-doha-found-each-other

141. "Erdoğan Most Popular Foreign Leader in Kuwait, Poll Says," *Daily Sabah*, March 10, 2019, https://www.dailysabah.com/mideast/2019/03/10/erdogan-most-popular-foreign-leader-in-kuwait-poll-says

142. Hussein Ibish, "Turkey Is Changing the Middle East. The U.S. Doesn't Get It," *Bloomberg Opinion*, March 14, 2019, https://www.bloomberg.com/opinion/articles/2019-03-14/turkey-is-changing-the-middle-east-the-u-s-doesn-t-get-it

143. "From Europe to the Qatar-Turkey Axis: The Secret Project of the Muslim Brotherhood," interview of Souad Sbai, *Almaghrebiya*, December 15, 2018,

https://almaghrebiya.it/2018/12/15/from-europe-to-the-qatar-turkey-axis-the-secret-project-of-the-muslim-brotherhood/

144. "In Full: Qatar's Emir-Trump White House Post-Meeting Transcript," Al Jazeera, April 11, 2018, https://www.aljazeera.com/news/2018/04/full-qatar-emir-trump-white-house-post-meeting-transcript-180411073527099.html

145. Richard Miniter, "Why Is Our Ally Qatar Hosting Terrorists Like Hamas?" *Forbes*, April 28, 2017, https://www.forbes.com/sites/richardminiter/2017/04/28/why-is-our-ally-qatar-hosting-terrorists-like-hamas/#478409a421bd

146. Iman Zayat, "Qatari Ties to Iran, Turkey Undermine Regional Security," *Arab Weekly*, December 16, 2018, https://thearabweekly.com/qatari-ties-iran-tur key-undermine-regional-security

147. Armin Rosen, "Qatar's Efforts to Influence American Jews Continue to Unravel," *Tablet*, June 13, 2018, https://www.tabletmag.com/scroll/264132/qatars-efforts-to-influence-american-jews-continue-to-unravel

148. Ben Schreckinger, "Ex-Republican Fundraiser Accuses Lobbying Firm of Leaking Hacked Emails," *Politico*, January 24, 2019, https://www.politico.com/story/2019/01/24/elliott-broidy-republican-fundraiser-hacked-emails-1124067

149. U.S. Department of the Treasury, "United States Disrupts Large Scale Front Company Network Transferring Hundreds of Millions of Dollars and Euros to the IRGC and Iran's Ministry of Defense," press release, March 26, 2019, https://home.treasury.gov/index.php/news/press-releases/sm639

150. Alissa Rubin, "Iran's Revolutionary Guards: The Supreme Leader's Military-Industrial Complex," *The New York Times*, April 9, 2019, https://www.ny times.com/2019/04/09/world/middleeast/iran-revolutionary-guards-.html

151. *Ibid.*

152. AFP, "Saudi Arabia Hails US Terror Blacklisting of Iran Guard," *Times of Israel*, April 9, 2019, https://www.timesofisrael.com/saudi-arabia-hails-us-terror-blacklisting-of-iran-guards/

153. "Turkey, Qatar Object to U.S. Designation of Iran Revolutionary Guards as Terror Group," *Ahval*, April 10, 2019, https://ahvalnews.com/iran-us/turkey-qatar-object-us-designation-iran-revolutionary-guards-terror-group

154. Alissa Rubin, "Iran's Revolutionary Guards: The Supreme Leader's Military-Industrial Complex," *The New York Times*, April 9, 2019, https://www.nytimes.com/2019/04/09/world/middleeast/iran-revolutionary-guards-.html

155. Elif Erşen, "US Sanctions Take Heavy Toll on Iranian Economy," *Daily Sabah*, May 9, 2019, https://www.dailysabah.com/economy/2019/05/09/us-sanctions-take-heavy-toll-on-iranian-economy

156. Matt Egan, "David Petraeus: Iran's Economy Is in a 'Tailspin' and It Would Be 'Suicide' to Start a War with US," *CNN Business*, May 10, 2019, https://edition.cnn.com/2019/05/09/business/iran-sanctions-economy-petraeus/index.html

157. *Ibid.*

158. *Ibid.*

159. Sinem Koseoglu, "Iran Oil Sanctions to Hit Turkish Economy," Al Jazeera, May 5, 2019, https://www.aljazeera.com/news/2019/05/iran-oil-sanctions-hit-turkish-economy-190505054450884.html

160. Natasha Turak, "Turkey's Economy Is Spiraling—And a New Election Will Make Things Worse," *CNBC*, April 17, 2019, https://www.cnbc.com/2019/04/17/turkeys-economy-is-spiraling-as-erdogans-akp-requests-new-election.html

161. Dion Rabouin, "Turkey's Economy Is Getting Worse," *Axios*, May 7, 2019, https://www.axios.com/turkey-economy-recession-gdp-lira-48d8dfde-0f6a-4d9f-9a80-f5c00bd9093d.html

162. Bülent Aras and Emirhan Yorulmazlar, "Turkey, Iran and the Gulf Crisis," *HSF Policy Brief* (Humanitarian Studies Foundation) 1, no. 3 (March 2018): 1–12, http://humsf.org/wp-content/uploads/2018/05/HSF_PolicyBrief_3.pdf

163. Security Studies Group, "Qatar: US Ally or Global Menace?" Transcript, *Security Studies Group*, February 11, 2019, https://securitystudies.org/qatar-us-ally-or-global-menace-conference-transcript/

164. Dana Khraiche, "Saudi Prince Praises Qatar's Economy in Surprising Shift," *Bloomberg*, October 24, 2018, https://www.bloomberg.com/news/articles/2018-10-24/saudi-crown-prince-praises-qatar-s-economy-in-surprising-shift

165. Anonymous (former Senior Political Advisor for United States Central Command) in discussion with the author, June 10, 2018, Tampa, FL.

CHAPTER 8

1. Katherine Zimmerman, *America's Real Enemy: The Salafi-Jihadi Movement* (n.p.: American Enterprise Institute, July 2017), https://www.criticalthreats.org/wp-content/uploads/2017/07/Zimmerman_Americas-Real-Enemy-The-Salafi-Jihadi-Movement.pdf

2. Joshua Block, "Qatar Is a Financier of Terrorism. Why Does the U.S. Tolerate It?" *Los Angeles Times*, June 9, 2017, https://www.latimes.com/opinion/op-ed/la-oe-block-qatar-terrorism-syria-20170609-story.html

3. Assaf Moghadam, "The Salafi-Jihad as a Religious Ideology," *CTC Sentinel* 1, no. 3 (February 2008): 14–16, https://www.belfercenter.org/publication/salafi-jihad-religious-ideology

4. Matthew Taylor, "Don't Fear (All) Salafi Muslims," *Huffington Post*, January 22, 2016, https://www.huffpost.com/entry/dont-fear-all-salafi-muslims_b_9042496

5. Abdullah Al-Othaymeen (former Secretary-General of the King Faisal International Prize) in discussion with the author, December 8, 2015, Riyadh, Saudi Arabia.

6. Thomas Edward Lawrence, *Seven Pillars of Wisdom* (London, England: The Reprint Society, 1926).

7. Abd Allah Salih al-'Uthaymin, *Muhammad ibn 'Abd al-Wahhab: The Man and His Works* (London, England: I.B. Tauris, 2009), 55.

8. "Amr ibn Mohammad al-Faisal, Interview by Jihan El-Tahri," *PBS Frontline*, September 2003, https://www.pbs.org/wgbh/pages/frontline/shows/saud/interviews/amr.html

9. Abd Allah Salih al-'Uthaymin, *Muhammad ibn 'Abd al-Wahhab: The Man and His Works* (London, England: I.B. Tauris, 2009), 74.

10. Robert Vitalis, *American's Kingdom: Mythmaking on the Saudi Oil Frontier* (Stanford, CA: Stanford University Press, 2007), 40.

11. Mohammad bin Abdullah Al Suweilem (President of Citizens and Tribal Affairs at the Saudi Royal Court) in discussion with the author, 2010.

12. Jihan El-Tahri and Martin Smith, *House of Saud*, Documentary, Transcript, *PBS Frontline*, February 8, 2005, https://www.pbs.org/wgbh/pages/frontline/shows/saud/etc/script.html

13. Abd Allah Salih al-'Uthaymin, *Muhammad ibn 'Abd al-Wahhab: The Man and His Works* (London, England: I.B. Tauris, 2009), 92–93.

14. *Ibid.*, 99.

15. John Jenkins, "The Gulf and the Muslim Brotherhood," *Oxford Gulf and Arabian Peninsula Studies Forum*, https://www.oxgaps.org/files/commentary_-_jenkins.pdf

16. Abdullah Al-Othaymeen (former Secretary-General of the King Faisal International Prize) in discussion with the author, December 8, 2015, Riyadh, Saudi Arabia.

17. Turki Al Faisal (former Saudi Intelligence Director and ex-ambassador to the United Kingdom and United States) in discussion with the author, December 15, 2017, Paris, France.

18. John Jenkins, "The Gulf and the Muslim Brotherhood," *Oxford Gulf and Arabian Peninsula Studies Forum*, https://www.oxgaps.org/files/commentary_-_jenkins.pdf

19. Martyn Frampton, *The Muslim Brotherhood and the West: A History of Enmity and Engagement* (Cambridge, MA: The Belknap Press of Harvard University Press, 2018), 129.

20. *Ibid.*, 308.

21. Abd Allah Salih al-'Uthaymin, *Muhammad ibn 'Abd al-Wahhab: The Man and His Works* (London, England: I.B. Tauris, 2009), 133.

22. *Ibid.*, 134.

23. David Commins, *The Wahhabi Mission and Saudi Arabia* (London, England: I.B. Tauris, 2009), 148.

24. Tarek Masoud, *Counting Islam: Religion, Class, and Elections in Egypt (Problems of International Politics)* (New York, NY: Cambridge University Press, 2014).

25. Abd Allah Salih al-'Uthaymin, *Muhammad ibn 'Abd al-Wahhab: The Man and His Works* (London, England: I.B. Tauris, 2009), 101.

26. *Ibid.*, 105.

27. Abdel Monem Said Aly, "The Truth About the Muslim Brotherhood," *Cairo Review*, no. 29 (2018): 89–99, https://cdn.thecairoreview.com/wp-content/uploads/2018/05/cr29-said-aly.pdf

28. Abd Allah Salih al-'Uthaymin, *Muhammad ibn 'Abd al-Wahhab: The Man and His Works* (London, England: I.B. Tauris, 2009), 113.

29. *Ibid.*

30. Abdel Monem Said Aly, "The Truth About the Muslim Brotherhood," *Cairo Review*, no. 29 (2018): 89–99, https://cdn.thecairoreview.com/wp-content/uploads/2018/05/cr29-said-aly.pdf

31. *Ibid.*

32. David Commins, *The Wahhabi Mission and Saudi Arabia* (London, England: I.B. Tauris, 2009), 149.

33. *Ibid.*

34. *Ibid.*, 190.

35. Thomas Hegghammer and Stéphane Lacroix, *The Meccan Rebellion: The Story of Juhayman Al-'Utaybi Revisited* (n.p.: Amal Press, 2011), 204.

36. Abd Allah Salih al-'Uthaymin, *Muhammad ibn 'Abd al-Wahhab: The Man and his Works* (London, England: I.B. Tauris, 2009), 79.

37. *Ibid.*

38. Mohammed Al Issa, *Muslim World League in Kalima* (2018), 5.

39. Bernard Haykel and Cole Bunzel, "Messages to Arabia: Al-Qaida Attacks MBS and the Saudi Monarchy," *Jihadica* (blog), January 24, 2019, http://www.ji hadica.com/messages-to-arabia/

40. *Ibid*.

41. *Ibid*.

42. *Ibid*.

43. *Ibid*.

44. David Commins, *The Wahhabi Mission and Saudi Arabia* (London, England: I.B. Tauris, 2009), 149.

45. Steven Stalinsky, "Dr. Ahmad Al-Ruba'i: A Legacy of Reform," *Inquiry & Analysis Series* (Middle East Media Research Institute), no. 465 (February 9, 2009), https://www.memri.org/reports/dr-ahmad-al-rubai-legacy-reform

46. David Commins, *The Wahhabi Mission and Saudi Arabia* (London, England: I.B. Tauris, 2009), 172.

47. Abdel Monem Said Aly, "The Truth About the Muslim Brotherhood," *Cairo Review*, no. 29 (2018): 89–99, https://cdn.thecairoreview.com/wp-content/up loads/2018/05/cr29-said-aly.pdf

48. Nawaf Obaid, "The Myth of Saudi Support for Terrorism," *Washington Times*, July 21, 2016, https://m.washingtontimes.com/news/2016/jul/21/the-myth-of-saudi-support-for-terrorism/

49. Chris Hedges, "Reckoning with Failure in the War on Terror," *Common Dreams*, April 8, 2019, https://www.commondreams.org/views/2019/04/08/ reckoning-failure-war-terror

50. "Palestinian Islamic Jihad," Anti-Defamation League, accessed May 26, 2019, https://www.adl.org/resources/glossary-terms/palestinian-islamic-jihad

51. Journeyman Pictures, "The Muslim Brotherhood Exposed by a Former Member," YouTube video, 28:38, January 12, 2018, https://www.youtube.com/ watch?v=4BFUbE5kO0k

52. خليجية "رئيس المجلس العسكري لتنظيم القاعدة بالسعودية علي الفقعسي ضيف برنامج الليوان مع عبدالله"، المديفر," YouTube video, 1:26:24, May 12, 2019, https://www.youtube.com/ watch?v=pIHf3GeTRsE

53. John Hannah, "It's Time for Saudi Arabia to Stop Exporting Extremism," *Foundation for Defense of Democracies*, May 4, 2019, https://www.fdd.org/analy sis/2019/05/04/its-time-for-saudi-arabia-to-stop-exporting-extremism/

54. Josh Hammer (Josh_hammer), "I like a lot of what @FDD puts out, but this is a weird and outdated take. KSA has largely (not wholly) cleaned up its act. And MBS's KSA is now a key strategic ally against the real U.S. regional foe: The Iran-Qatar-Turkey-Muslim Brotherhood axis of destructive Islamism," Twitter, May 9, 2019, 7:57 A.M., https://twitter.com/josh_hammer/status/1126501 472315822080

55. Anthony Cordesman and Nawaf Obaid, *National Security in Saudi Arabia: Threats, Responses, and Challenges* (Washington, DC: Center for Strategic and International Studies, 2005), 273.

56. Bernard Haykel and Cole Bunzel, "Messages to Arabia: Al-Qaida Attacks MBS and the Saudi Monarchy," *Jihadica* (blog), January 24, 2019, http://www.ji hadica.com/messages-to-arabia/

57. Elizabeth Dickinson, "Rally Round the Flag in Riyadh," *Foreign Policy*, May 13, 2015, https://foreignpolicy.com/2015/05/13/rally-round-the-flag-in-riyadh/

58. Deborah Amos, "In Saudi Arabia, an Uphill Fight to Out-Shout the Extremists," *National Public Radio*, June 27, 2015, https://www.npr.org/sections/paral lels/2015/06/27/417162532/in-saudi-arabia-an-uphill-fight-to-out-shout-the-extremists

59. Tarek Masoud, *Counting Islam: Religion, Class, and Elections in Egypt (Problems of International Politics)* (New York, NY: Cambridge University Press, 2014).

60. Hazem Kandil, *Inside the Brotherhood* (Cambridge, England: Polity Press, 2015), 6.

61. Tarek Masoud, *Counting Islam: Religion, Class, and Elections in Egypt (Problems of International Politics)* (New York, NY: Cambridge University Press, 2014).

62. *Ibid.*

63. *Ibid.*

64. "The Egyptian Muslim Brotherhood: Building Bases of Support," *Directorate of Intelligence at Central Intelligence Agency* (May 1986), 6, https://www.cia.gov/library/readingroom/docs/CIA-RDP88T00096R000200240001-4.pdf

65. *Ibid.*, 4.

66. *Ibid.*, 5.

67. *Ibid.*

68. Richard Paul Mitchell, *The Society of the Muslim Brothers* (New York, NY: Oxford University Press, 1993), 198.

69. Alison Pargeter, *The Muslim Brotherhood: From Opposition to Power* (London, England: Saqi Books, 2013), 248.

70. Abdel Monem Said Aly, "The Truth About the Muslim Brotherhood," *Cairo Review*, no. 29 (2018): 89–99, https://cdn.thecairoreview.com/wp-content/uploads/2018/05/cr29-said-aly.pdf

71. Saba Elbalad, "علي مسئوليتي—أبو هاشم المنشق عن الاخوان يتحدث لاول مرة ويفضح اسرار التنظيم الارهابي," YouTube video, 2:31:52, August 11, 2018, https://www.youtube.com/watch?v=I7fvwSJuugw

72. Crane Brinton, John Christopher, and Robert Lee Wolff, *A History of Civilization, Vol. 2: 1715 to the Present* (New York, NY: Prentice Hall, 1955), 520.

73. Albion Ross, "Moslem Brotherhood Leader Slain as He Enters Taxi in Cairo Street," *The New York Times*, February 13, 1949, 5.

74. George W. Bush, "A Nation Challenged: President Bush's Address on Terrorism Before a Joint Meeting of Congress," *The New York Times*, Transcript, September 21, 2001, https://www.nytimes.com/2001/09/21/us/nation-challenged-president-bush-s-address-terrorism-before-joint-meeting.html

75. Abdel Monem Said Aly, "The Truth About the Muslim Brotherhood," *Cairo Review*, no. 29 (2018): 89–99, https://cdn.thecairoreview.com/wp-content/uploads/2018/05/cr29-said-aly.pdf

76. John Jenkins, "The Gulf and the Muslim Brotherhood," *Oxford Gulf and Arabian Peninsula Studies Forum*, https://www.oxgaps.org/files/commentary_-_jenkins.pdf

77. Alison Pargeter, *The Muslim Brotherhood: From Opposition to Power* (London, England: Saqi Books, 2013), 103.

78. *Ibid.*, 104.

79. Aron Lund, *Struggling to Adapt: The Muslim Brotherhood in a New Syria* (Washington, DC: Carnegie Endowment for International Peace, 2013), https://carnegieendowment.org/files/struggling_to_adapt_mb.pdf

80. Alison Pargeter, *The Muslim Brotherhood: From Opposition to Power* (London, England: Saqi Books, 2013), 103.

81. *Ibid.*, 54.

82. *Ibid.*, 103.

83. Aron Lund, *Struggling to Adapt: The Muslim Brotherhood in a New Syria* (Washington, DC: Carnegie Endowment for International Peace, 2013), https://carnegieendowment.org/files/struggling_to_adapt_mb.pdf

84. "Saudi Arabia's Islamic Awakening Could Be Facing Its Demise," *Fanack*, November 6, 2018, https://fanack.com/religions/saudi-islamic-awakening-sahwa-facing-demise/

85. Thomas Hegghammer and Stéphane Lacroix, *The Meccan Rebellion: The Story of Juhayman Al-'Utaybi Revisited* (n.p.: Amal Press, 2011), 217.

86. *Ibid.*

87. *Ibid.*

88. *Ibid.*

89. "Saudi Arabia's Islamic Awakening Could be Facing Its Demise," *Fanack*, November 6, 2018, https://fanack.com/religions/saudi-islamic-awakening-sahwa-facing-demise/

90. John Jenkins, "The Gulf and the Muslim Brotherhood," *Oxford Gulf and Arabian Peninsula Studies Forum*, https://www.oxgaps.org/files/commentary_-_jenkins.pdf

91. Stéphane Lacroix, *Awakening Islam*, trans. George Holoch (Cambridge, MA: Harvard University Press, 2011).

92. Mashari Althaydi, "Has 'Sahwa' Ended in Saudi Arabia?" *Al Arabiya*, November 3, 2017, https://english.alarabiya.net/en/views/news/middle-east/2017/11/03/Has-Sahwa-ended-in-Saudi-Arabia-.html

93. عبدالله البندر ,(a_albander) "أول من هاجم "الصحوة" فكرياً عندما كانوا في عز قوتهم ومنذ سنين طويلة في المدارس ومع التربويين هو الأمير خالد الفيصل، وهذا "الفيديو" عمره أكثر من 20 سنة عندما كان أميرا لمنطقة عسير. | تسمع هذا الحديث وكأنه الآن | #عايض_القرني_في_ليوان_المديفر" ,May 9, 2019 7:53 A.M., https://twitter.com/a_albander/status/1126500441703895043

94. *Ibid.*

95. Turki al-Faisal, *USA Today*, June 4, 2006, in *Contemporary Persian Gulf*, eds. P.R. Kumaraswamy and Md. Muddassir Quamar (Abingdon, England: Routledge, 2018).

96. Ramadan Al Sherbini and Sara Al Shurafa, "Prominent Saudi Preacher Apologises on TV for Years of 'Hardline' Islam," *Gulf News*, May 8, 2019, https://gulfnews.com/world/gulf/saudi/prominent-saudi-preacher-apologises-on-tv-for-years-of-hardline-islam-1.63817748

97. *Ibid.*

98. Jamal Khashoggi in discussion with the author, April 28, 2017, London, England.

99. Mohammed Al Issa, *Muslim World League in Kalima* (2018), 5.

100. Abdullah Alaoudh, "State-Sponsored Fatwas in Saudi Arabia," *Sada*, *Carnegie Endowment for International Peace*, April 3, 2018, https://carnegieendowment.org/sada/75971

101. Bertrand Besancenot (former French Ambassador to Saudi Arabia) in discussion with the author May 28, 2018, Paris, France.

102. Bethan McKernan, "Saudi Arabia's Crown Prince Promises Country Will Return to 'Moderate, Open Islam'," *Independent*, October 24, 2017, https://www.independent.co.uk/news/world/middle-east/saudi-arabia-crown-prince-mohammed-bin-salman-saud-moderate-islam-vision-2030-conference-a8017181.html

103. Abd Allah Salih al-'Uthaymin, *Muhammad ibn 'Abd al-Wahhab: The Man and His Works* (London, England: I.B. Tauris, 2009), 91.

104. Jesse Morton and Amarnath Amrasingam, "The Crown Prince of Riyadh vs. the Crown Prince of Jihad: Al-Qaeda Responds to Mohammed Bin Salman's Reforms," *War on the Rocks* (blog), May 17, 2018, https://warontherocks.com/2018/05/the-crown-prince-of-riyadh-vs-the-crown-prince-of-jihad-al-qaeda-responds-to-mohammed-bin-salmans-reforms/

105. Hussein Ibish, "A Strategic US Approach Is Required to Counter the Muslim Brotherhood," *The National*, May 4, 2019, https://www.thenational.ae/opinion/comment/a-strategic-us-approach-is-required-to-counter-the-muslim-brotherhood-1.857100

106. "Sri Lanka Attacks Plotters Have Links to Muslim Brotherhood Leader Qaradawi," *Middle East Online*, April 25, 2019, https://middle-east-online.com/en/sri-lanka-attacks-plotters-have-links-muslim-brotherhood-leader-qaradawi

107. P.K. Balachandran, "Obscure Group Jamaat al-Tawhid al-Watania Claims Responsibility for Lankan Blasts," *The Citizen*, April 23, 2019, https://www.thecitizen.in/index.php/en/NewsDetail/index/5/16780/Obscure-Group-Jamaat-al-Tawhid-al-Watania-Claims-Responsibility-for-Lankan-Blasts

108. "Saudi Arabia Turns Against Political Islam," *The Gulf* (special report), *The Economist*, June 21, 2018, https://www.economist.com/special-report/2018/06/21/saudi-arabia-turns-against-political-islam

109. *Ibid.*

110. Anonymous (former foreign minister of Jordan) in discussion with the author, March 17, 2018, Geneva, Switzerland.

111. Abd Allah Salih al-'Uthaymin, *Muhammad ibn 'Abd al-Wahhab: The Man and His Works* (London, England: I.B. Tauris, 2009), 83.

CHAPTER 9

1. Ian Black, "Jamal Khashoggi Obituary," *The Guardian*, October 19, 2018, https://www.theguardian.com/world/2018/oct/19/jamal-khashoggi-obituary

2. David Ignatius, "Jamal Khashoggi Chose to Tell the Truth. It's Part of the Reason He's Beloved," *Washington Post*, October 7, 2018, https://www.washingtonpost.com/opinions/global-opinions/jamal-khashoggi-chose-to-tell-the-truth-its-part-of-the-reason-hes-beloved/2018/10/07/4847f1d6-ca70-11e8-a3e6-44daa3d35ede_story.html

3. Patrick Poole (pspoole), "I didn't realize until yesterday that Jamal Khashoggi was the author of this notorious 1988 Arab News article of him tooling around Afghanistan with Osama bin Laden and al-Qaeda co-founder Abdullah Azzam. He's just a democrat reformer journalist holding a RPG with jihadists," Twitter post, October 12, 2018, 10:46 A.M., https://twitter.com/pspoole/status/1050804806997151745

4. Barnett Rubin, "The Jama Khashoggi I Knew," *War on the Rocks* (blog), October 26, 2018, https://warontherocks.com/2018/10/the-jamal-khashoggi-i-knew/

5. Nawaf Obaid and Jamal Khashoggi, "Syria Tragedy a Turning Point for West," *CNN*, September 16, 2013, http://linkis.com/blogs.cnn.com/a0v3

6. Ben Hubbard and David Kirkpatrick, "For Khashoggi, a Tangled Mix of Royal Service and Islamist Sympathies," *The New York Times*, October 14, 2018, https://www.nytimes.com/2018/10/14/world/middleeast/jamal-khashoggi-saudi-arabia.html

7. Ian Black, "Jamal Khashoggi Obituary," *The Guardian*, October 19, 2018, https://www.theguardian.com/world/2018/oct/19/jamal-khashoggi-obituary

8. AFP, "Khashoggi: From Saudi Royal Insider to Open Critic," *Jordan Times*, November 15, 2018, https://jordantimes.com/news/region/khashoggi-saudi-royal-insider-open-critic

9. Ian Black, "Jamal Khashoggi Obituary," *The Guardian*, October 19, 2018, https://www.theguardian.com/world/2018/oct/19/jamal-khashoggi-obituary

10. *Ibid.*

11. "Khashoggi, Obaid and Ishqi Do Not Speak for Saudi Government: Foreign Ministry," *Al Ekhbariya*, December 20, 2015, http://alekhbariya.net/en/node/1303

12. جمال خاشقجي, (JKhashoggi) "اعود للكتابة والتغريد، الشكر لمعالي وزير الاعلام لمساعيه الطيبة والشكر والولاء متصلان لسمو ولي العهد لا كسر في عهده قلمْ حر ولا سكت مغرد", Twitter post, August 12, 2017, 4:34 P.M., https://twitter.com/JKhashoggi/status/896515210135179265

13. Jamal Khashoggi and Robert Lacey, "The Crown Prince Doesn't Listen to Saudis—Why Would He Listen to Theresa May?" *The Guardian*, March 6, 2018, https://www.theguardian.com/commentisfree/2018/mar/06/crown-prince-saudis-theresa-may-britain-saudi-arabia-money

14. Mohammed Alzaher محمد آل زاهر, "I condemn the extrajudicial kill of #jamal-khashoggi despite the fact he stood with the #Saudi authority against the other Saudi dissidents. Here is jamal, @amnestygulf new star, endorsing an extrajudicial execution of a Saudi dissident condemned by the contradicted NGO itself," Twitter post, December 10, 2018, 10:15 P.M., https://twitter.com/alzahermm/status/1072374377545678848

15. Hatice Cengiz, "My Fiancé Jamal Khashoggi Was a Lonely Patriot," *The New York Times*, October 13, 2018, https://www.nytimes.com/2018/10/13/opinion/jamal-khashoggi-saudi-arabia-fiancee-mbs-murder.html

16. Karen Elliott House, "Rethinking Saudi Arabia," *Wall Street Journal*, November 30, 2018, https://www.wsj.com/articles/rethinking-saudi-arabia-1543595189

17. Jamal Khashoggi, "The U.S. Is Wrong About the Muslim Brotherhood—And the Arab World Is Suffering For It," *Washington Post*, August 28, 2018, https://www.washingtonpost.com/news/global-opinions/wp/2018/08/28/the-u-s-is-wrong-about-the-muslim-brotherhood-and-the-arab-world-is-suffering-for-it/

18. *Ibid.*

19. "Turkey and Qatar Prove to be True Friends, Says Erdoğan," *Hürriyet Daily News*, November 27, 2018, http://www.hurriyetdailynews.com/turkey-and-qatar-prove-to-be-true-friends-says-erdogan-139210

20. AW Staff, "Erdogan-Tamim Summit Sets Common Agenda for Turkey, Qatar," *The Arab Weekly*, November 30, 2018, https://thearabweekly.com/erdogan-tamim-summit-sets-common-agenda-turkey-qatar

21. Cagan Koc and Baris Balci, "Turkish Economy's Hard Landing Upsets Erdogan Electoral Play," *Bloomberg*, December 10, 2018, https://www.bloomberg.com/news/articles/2018-12-10/turkish-economy-sputters-after-lira-s-melt down-cripples-consumer

22. The National, "Qatar Gifts Turkey's Recep Tayyip Erdogan $400 Million Luxury Jet," *The National*, September 15, 2018, https://www.thenational.ae/world/gcc/qatar-gifts-turkey-s-recep-tayyip-erdogan-400-million-luxury-jet-1.770460

23. AW Staff, "Erdogan-Tamim Summit Sets Common Agenda for Turkey, Qatar," *The Arab Weekly*, November 30, 2018, https://thearabweekly.com/erdogan-tamim-summit-sets-common-agenda-turkey-qatar

24. *Ibid.*

25. Ibrahim Karagül, "US Is the Enemy for Turkey. One Day, Thousands of People Will Siege İncirlik as Well," *Yeni Şafak*, January 26, 2018, https://www.yenisafak.com/en/columns/ibrahimkaragul/us-is-the-enemy-for-turkey-one-day-thousands-of-people-will-siege-incirlik-as-well-2042300

26. Ibrahim Karagül, "This Is a Declaration of War Against Turkey. Arab Nations, We Are Warning You; Stop Those Two Crown Princes at Once! Topple Mohammed bin Salman! Understand that the Trap Has Been Set Against You!" *Yeni Şafak*, December 1, 2018, https://www.yenisafak.com/en/columns/ibrahimkaragul/this-is-a-declaration-of-war-against-turkey-arab-nations-we-are-warning-you-stop-those-two-crown-princes-at-once-topple-mohammed-bin-salman-understand-that-the-trap-has-been-set-against-you-2046787

27. *Ibid.*

28. Krishnadev Calamur, "The Irony of Turkey's Crusade for a Missing Journalist," *The Atlantic*, October 15, 2018, https://www.theatlantic.com/international/archive/2018/10/turkey-saudi-jamal-khashoggi/573052/

29. *Ibid.*

30. Dominic Evans, "Saudi Prince Says Turkey Part of 'Triangle of Evil': Egyptian Media," Reuters, March 7, 2018, https://www.reuters.com/article/us-saudi-turkey/saudi-prince-says-turkey-part-of-triangle-of-evil-egyptian-media-idUSKCN1GJ1WW

31. Frida Ghitis, "If Trump Sacrifices Fethullah Gulen to Protect Saudi Arabia, He Will Make a Mockery of the U.S. Extradition System," *Think*, NBC News, November 16, 2018, https://www.nbcnews.com/think/opinion/if-trump-sacrifices-fethullah-gulen-protect-saudi-arabia-he-will-ncna937281

32. Krishnadev Calamur, "The Irony of Turkey's Crusade for a Missing Journalist," *The Atlantic*, October 15, 2018, https://www.theatlantic.com/international/archive/2018/10/turkey-saudi-jamal-khashoggi/573052/

33. Tuqa Khalid, "Saudi Foreign Minister Rules Out Extraditing Suspects in Khashoggi Case," Reuters, December 9, 2018, https://www.reuters.com/article/us-saudi-khashoggi-turkey-extradition-idUSKBN1O80NW

34. Naser Al-Wasmi, "GCC Appoints New Chief of Joint Military Command at Riyadh Summit," *The National*, December 9, 2018, https://www.thenational.ae/world/gcc/gcc-appoints-new-chief-of-joint-military-command-at-riyadh-summit-1.800836

35. Farah Najjar, "A Fractured GCC Meets in Riyadh Amid Ongoing Crisis," Al Jazeera, December 9, 2018, https://www.aljazeera.com/news/2018/12/expect-year-gcc-summit-riyadh-181208122627452.html

36. Deirdre Fernandes, "MIT Should Keep Ties with Saudis, Internal Report Says," *Boston Globe*, December 6, 2018, https://www.bostonglobe.com/metro/2018/12/06/internal-report-recommends-mit-retain-its-saudi-ties/b43g8XVo HCvl4zbl64kieP/story.html

37. Michael Doran and Tony Badran, "Trump Is Crude. But He's Right About Saudi Arabia," *The New York Times*, November 21, 2018, https://www.nytimes.com/2018/11/21/opinion/trump-saudi-arabia-khashoggi.html

38. *Ibid.*

39. Mike Pompeo, "The U.S.-Saudi Partnership Is Vital," *Wall Street Journal Opinion*, November 27, 2018, https://www.wsj.com/articles/the-u-s-saudi-partnership-is-vital-1543362363

40. Agencies, "Mattis Faces Criticism After Comments in Khashoggi Case," *Daily Times*, December 8, 2018, https://dailytimes.com.pk/331030/mattis-faces-criticism-after-comments-in-khashoggi-case/

41. Tom O'Connor, "Jared Kushner Still Defended Saudi Crown Prince After Khashoggi Murder, After 'Friends' Exchanged Text Messages for 2 Years: Report," *Newsweek*, December 8, 2018, https://www.newsweek.com/kushner-defended-crown-prince-murder-text-messages-1250810

42. Mike Pompeo, "The U.S.-Saudi Partnership Is Vital," *Wall Street Journal Opinion*, November 27, 2018, https://www.wsj.com/articles/the-u-s-saudi-partnership-is-vital-1543362363

43. Tolga Tanis, "Ending the Qatar Blockage Might Be the Price Saudi Arabia Pays for Khashoggi's Murder," *Yahoo News*, November 3, 2018, https://www.yahoo.com/news/iranian-sanctions-deadline-looms-ending-qatar-blockade-might-price-saudi-arabia-pays-khashoggis-murder-170606165.html

44. Karen Elliott House, "Rethinking Saudi Arabia," *Wall Street Journal*, November 30, 2018, https://www.wsj.com/articles/rethinking-saudi-arabia-1543595189

45. Agnes Callamard, "Investigation into the Unlawful Death of Mr. Jamal Khashoggi," UN Human Rights Council, June 19, 2019, https://www.ohchr.org/EN/HRBodies/HRC/RegularSessions/Session41/Documents/A_HRC_41_CRP.1.docx

46. *Ibid.*

CHAPTER 10

1. Clin Clarke and Ariane Tabatabai, "America's Indefinite Endgame in Syria," *The Atlantic*, October 16, 2018, https://www.theatlantic.com/international/archive/2018/10/bolton-pledges-american-troops-syria-iran/573121/

2. Daniel Lippman et al., "Top US Envoy in Fight Against ISIS Resigns Over Trump's Syria Withdrawal," *Politico*, April 19, 2019, https://www.politico.eu/article/isis-trump-syria-withdrawal-brett-mcgurk-james-mattis/

3. Roberta Rampton and Idrees Ali, "In Reversal, U.S. to Leave a Total of About 400 Troops in Syria," Reuters, February 22, 2019, https://www.reuters.com/article/us-mideast-crisis-usa-troops/u-s-to-leave-a-total-of-about-400-troops-in-syria-official-idUSKCN1QB26K

4. John Hudson, "Saudi Arabia Transfers $100 Million to U.S. Amid Crisis Over Khashoggi," *Washington Post*, October 17, 2018, https://www.washingtonpost.com/world/national-security/saudi-arabia-transfers-100-million-to-us-amid-crisis-over-khashoggi/2018/10/17/22b23ae1-c6a4-43a4-9b7d-ce04603fa6ab_story.html

5. Samuel Ramani, "UAE Steps Up Anti-Turkey Efforts in Syria," *Al-Monitor*, February 25, 2019, https://www.al-monitor.com/pulse/originals/2019/02/uae-syria-turkey-containment-efforts-kurds-erdogan.html

6. Brett McGurk, "Hard Truths in Syria," *Foreign Affairs*, May/June 2019, https://www.foreignaffairs.com/articles/syria/2019-04-16/hard-truths-syria

7. *Ibid.*

8. Samuel Ramani, "UAE Steps Up Anti-Turkey Efforts in Syria," *Al-Monitor*, February 25, 2019, https://www.al-monitor.com/pulse/originals/2019/02/uae-syria-turkey-containment-efforts-kurds-erdogan.html

9. Mehmet Yuva, "Paranoyaklık ve . . . Esad Erdoğan buluşması olur mu?" *Aydinlik*, May 12, 2019, https://www.aydinlik.com.tr/paranoyaklik-ve-esad-erdogan-bulusmasi-olur-mu-mehmet-yuva-kose-yazilari-mayis-2019

10. "Brotherhood in Algeria Warns of Collapse of State Institutions," *Middle East Monitor*, October 2, 2018, https://www.middleeastmonitor.com/20181002-brotherhood-in-algeria-warns-of-collapse-of-state-institutions/

11. Caroline Alexander and Salah Slimani, "Ousted by Protests, Bouteflika Was Once Algeria's Savior," *Bloomberg*, April 2, 2019, https://www.bloomberg.com/news/articles/2019-04-02/ousted-by-protests-bouteflika-was-once-algeria-s-saviour

12. The New Arab, "Bashir's Former Ruling Party Barred from Transitional Government, Will Take Part in Future Elections," *The New Arab*, April 15, 2019, https://www.alaraby.co.uk/english/news/2019/4/15/bashirs-party-barred-from-transitional-government-military-council-says

13. Associated Press, "Hassan al-Turabi, Sudan Opposition Leader Who Hosted Osama bin Laden, Dies," *The Guardian*, March 5, 2016, https://www.theguardian.com/world/2016/mar/06/hassan-al-turabi-sudan-opposition-leader-who-hosted-osama-bin-laden-dies

14. Jamal Mahjoub, "My Father Died Before He Could See al-Bashir Fall," *The New York Times*, April 12, 2019, https://www.nytimes.com/2019/04/12/opinion/my-father-died-before-he-could-see-bashir-fall.html

15. Associated Press, "Hassan al-Turabi, Sudan Opposition Leader Who Hosted Osama bin Laden, Dies," *The Guardian*, March 5, 2016, https://www.theguardian.com/world/2016/mar/06/hassan-al-turabi-sudan-opposition-leader-who-hosted-osama-bin-laden-dies

16. Fehim Tastekin, "Erdogan Claims Sudanese Coup Actually Targeted Turkey," *Al-Monitor*, April 18, 2019, https://www.al-monitor.com/pulse/originals/2019/04/turkey-sudan-pro-akp-media-claim-saudi-arabia-behind-coup.html#ixzz5lXnPreNH

17. Khairallah Khairallah, "Sudan Needs a New Generation of Leaders," *The Arab Weekly*, April 28, 2019, https://thearabweekly.com/sudan-needs-new-generation-leaders

18. Matina Stevis-Gridneff and Summer Said, "As Sudan Grapples with a Post-Bashir Future, Regional Powers Circle," *Wall Street Journal*, April 27, 2019, https://www.wsj.com/articles/as-sudan-grapples-with-a-post-bashir-future-regional-powers-circle-11556362800

19. MEE and agencies, "Sudan Pledges to Continue Supporting Saudi-Led Coalition in Yemen," *Middle East Eye*, April 15, 2019, https://www.middleeasteye.net/news/sudan-pledges-continue-supporting-saudi-led-coalition-yemen

20. Khalid Abdelaziz, "Saudi Arabia, UAE to Send $3 Billion in Aid to Sudan," Reuters, April 21, 2019, https://www.reuters.com/article/us-sudan-protests/saudi-arabia-uae-to-send-3-billion-in-aid-to-sudan-idUSKCN1RX0DG

21. Matina Stevis-Gridneff and Summer Said, "As Sudan Grapples with a Post-Bashir Future, Regional Powers Circle," *Wall Street Journal*, April 27, 2019, https://www.wsj.com/articles/as-sudan-grapples-with-a-post-bashir-future-re gional-powers-circle-11556362800

22. "Sudan Crisis: Military and Opposition Agree Three-Year Transition," *BBC News*, May 15, 2019, https://www.bbc.com/news/world-africa-48276764

23. "Ankara Voices Concern Over 'Increasing Tension' in Libya," *Ahval*, April 7, 2019, https://ahvalnews.com/libya-turkey/ankara-voices-concern-over-increas ing-tension-libya

24. "«الجفرة في طيار بدون طائرة إسقاط يعلن «المسماري»," *Al-Wasat*, May 16, 2019, http://alwasat.ly/news/libya/245140

25. Borzou Daragahi, "Libya: UN-Backed Government Defending Capital from Warlord Haftar Now Using Drones on Front Lines," *Independent*, May 15, 2019, https://www.independent.co.uk/news/world/middle-east/libya-capital-khalifa-haftar-drones-war-khaled-el-meshri-a8915246.html

26. Vivian Salama, Jared Malsin, and Summer Said, "Trump Backed Libyan Warlord After Saudi Arabia and Egypt Lobbied Him," *Wall Street Journal*, May 12, 2019, https://www.wsj.com/articles/trump-backed-libyan-warlord-after-saudi-arabia-and-egypt-lobbied-him-11557668581

27. Steve Holland, "White House Says Trump Spoke to Libyan Commander Haftar on Monday," Reuters, April 19, 2019, https://www.reuters.com/article/us-libya-security-trump/white-house-says-trump-spoke-to-libyan-commander-haftar-on-monday-idUSKCN1RV0WW

28. Ergun Babahan, "Fehim Taştekin: Turkey Is Part of the Problem in Libyan Conflict," *Ahval*, April 8, 2019, https://ahvalnews.com/libya-turkey/fehim-tastekin-turkey-part-problem-libyan-conflict

29. James Dorsey, "Tripoli Battle Prolongs Libya Conflict," *Firstpost* (blog) 1, no. 14 (April 26, 2019), https://www.firstpost.com/blogs/world-blogs/global/tripoli-battle-prolongs-libya-conflict-6522051.html

30. Theodore Karasik and Giorgio Cafiero, "Libyan General Haftar's Visit to Saudi Arabia," *Gulf State Analytics*, n.d., https://gulfstateanalytics.com/libyan-general-haftars-visit-to-saudi-arabia/

31. Francesca Mannocchi, "Saudi-Influenced Salafis Playing Both Sides of Libya's Civil War," *Middle East Eye*, December 9, 2018, https://www.middleeasteye .net/news/saudi-influenced-salafis-playing-both-sides-libyas-civil-war

32. Theodore Karasik and Giorgio Cafiero, "Libyan General Haftar's Visit to Saudi Arabia," *Gulf State Analytics*, n.d., https://gulfstateanalytics.com/libyan-general-haftars-visit-to-saudi-arabia/

33. "Turkey Arrests Suspected UAE Spies in Istanbul," *BBC News*, April 19, 2019, https://www.bbc.com/news/world-middle-east-47991187

34. *Ibid.*

35. Firat Kozok, "Turkey Says Alleged U.A.E. Spy Committed Suicide in Prison," *Bloomberg*, April 29, 2019, https://www.bloomberg.com/news/articles/2019-04-29/alleged-u-a-e-spy-commits-suicide-at-turkish-prison

36. "Turkey Says UAE 'Spy' Committed Suicide in Prison, Family Demands Investigation," *Indian Express*, April 29, 2019, https://indianexpress.com/article/world/turkey-says-uae-spy-committed-suicide-5701045/

37. "بمقتله تحقق دولية لجنة أطلب بتركيا: القتيل الفلسطيني ابن," *Al Arabiya*, April 29, 2019, https://tinyurl.com/yywsblb

38. *Ibid.*

39. Staff writer, "'The Body Is Completely Empty': Family of Palestinian Who Died in Turkish Jail," *Al Arabiya*, May 16, 2019, https://english.alarabiya.net/en/features/2019/05/16/-The-body-is-completely-empty-Family-of-Palestinian-who-died-in-Turkish-jail.html#

40. *Ibid.*

41. "Two Men Held in Libya Are Not Spies, Say Turkish Officials," *Ahval*, May 1, 2019, https://ahvalnews.com/libya-turkey/two-men-held-libya-are-not-spies-say-turkish-officials

42. Charlie Savage, Eric Schmitt, and Maggie Haberman, "Trump Pushes to Designate Muslim Brotherhood a Terrorist Group," *The New York Times*, April 30, 2019, https://www.nytimes.com/2019/04/30/us/politics/trump-muslim-brotherhood.html

43. *Ibid.*

44. Pieter Wezeman et al., "Trends in International Arms Transfers, 2018," *SIPRI*, March 2019, https://www.sipri.org/sites/default/files/2019-03/fs_1903_at_2018.pdf

45. Charlie Savage, Eric Schmitt, and Maggie Haberman, "Trump Pushes to Designate Muslim Brotherhood a Terrorist Group," *The New York Times*, April 30, 2019, https://www.nytimes.com/2019/04/30/us/politics/trump-muslim-brotherhood.html

46. Brookings (BrookingsInst), "There is not a single American expert on the Muslim Brotherhood who supports designating them as a terrorist group, says @shadihamid," Twitter post, April 30, 2019, 6:50 A.M., https://twitter.com/BrookingsInst/status/1123223076785750017

47. Eric Schmitt et al., "On Muslim Brotherhood, Trump Weights Siding with Autocrats and Roiling Middle East," *The New York Times*, May 6, 2019, https://www.nytimes.com/2019/05/06/world/middleeast/muslim-brotherhood-trump.html

48. *Ibid.*

49. Yasin Aktay, "What Would Trump Guided by Sisi Bring Upon the US?" *Yeni Şafak*, May 4, 2019, https://www.yenisafak.com/en/columns/yasinaktay/what-would-trump-guided-by-sisi-bring-upon-the-us-2047033

50. Robin Simcox, "Should the Muslim Brotherhood Be Labeled Terrorists?" *Heritage Foundation*, May 2, 2019, https://www.heritage.org/terrorism/commentary/should-the-muslim-brotherhood-be-labeled-terrorists

51. Hussein Ibish, "A Strategic US Approach Is Required to Counter the Muslim Brotherhood," *The National*, May 4, 2019, https://www.thenational.ae/opinion/comment/a-strategic-us-approach-is-required-to-counter-the-muslim-brotherhood-1.857100

52. Office of the Spokesperson, "State Department Terrorist Designations of Ismail Haniyeh, Harakat al-Sabireen, Liwa al-Thawra, and Harakat Sawa'd Misr (HASM)," media note, *United States Department of State*, January 31, 2018, https://www.state.gov/state-department-terrorist-designations-of-ismail-haniyeh-harakat-al-sabireen-liwa-al-thawra-and-harakat-sawad-misr-hasm/

53. Jonathan Schanzer (JSchanzer), "My approach is pretty simple. There are MB offshoots in places like Libya and Yemen that almost certainly meet criteria. Designated them ASAP. Then keep looking for other MB nodes that contribute to or finance violence. It's what we should be doing, anyway," Twitter post, May 1, 2019, 1:35 P.M., https://twitter.com/JSchanzer/status/1123687463476781056

54. Jonathan Schanzer (JSchanzer), "I'm hearing from friends on the Hill that opponents of the MB think targeting MB branches instead of the entire network is a cop out. What they should understand is that step-by-step approach doesn't preclude a broad designation. It actually helps us get there, if facts support," Twitter post, May 1, 2019, 1:50 P.M., https://twitter.com/JSchanzer/status/112369123 1379374080

55. Eric Schmitt et al., "On Muslim Brotherhood, Trump Weights Siding with Autocrats and Roiling Middle East," *The New York Times*, May 6, 2019, https://www.nytimes.com/2019/05/06/world/middleeast/muslim-brotherhood-trump.html

56. *Ibid.*

57. "US Sends Patriot Missile System to Middle East Amid Iran Tensions," *BBC News*, May 11, 2019, https://www.bbc.com/news/world-us-canada-48235940

58. Scott Neuman, "Israeli Airstrikes Hit Gaza After Hamas Launches Rocket Attacks," *National Public Radio*, August 9, 2018, https://www.npr.org/2018/08/09/637004199/israeli-airstrikes-hit-gaza-after-hamas-launches-rocket-attacks

59. Yoav Zitun and Elior Levy, "61 Killed in Gaza Riots; IAF Strikes Multiple Hamas Targets," *Ynetnews*, May 14, 2018, https://www.ynetnews.com/articles/0,7340,L-5260097,00.html

60. Matti Friedman, "Falling for Hamas's Split-Screen Fallacy," *The New York Times*, May 16, 2018, https://www.nytimes.com/2018/05/16/opinion/hamas-israel-media-protests.html

61. Amos Yadlin and Ari Heistein, "Hamas Incites Violence to Hide Its Own Shortcomings," *Ynetnews*, May 14, 2018, https://www.ynetnews.com/articles/0,7340,L-5260612,00.html

62. James Phillips, "Hamas Hides Behind Smoke and Mirrors to Attack Israel," *Heritage Foundation*, May. 17, 2018, https://www.heritage.org/middle-east/commentary/hamas-hides-behind-smoke-and-mirrors-attack-israel

63. Dalia Hatuqa, "How the Gulf States Got in Bed with Israel and Forgot About the Palestinian Cause," *Foreign Policy*, March 28, 2019, https://foreignpolicy.com/2019/03/28/how-the-gulf-states-got-in-bed-with-israel-and-forgot-about-the-palestinian-cause-netanyahu-oman-chad-uae-saudi-arabia-mohammed-bin-salman-qatar-bahrain/

64. Khairallah Khairallah, "Sudan Needs a New Generation of Leaders," *The Arab Weekly*, April 28, 2019, https://thearabweekly.com/sudan-needs-new-generation-leaders

65. Elior Levy, "Iran's $100 Million Aid to Hamas and Islamic Jihad," *Ynetnews*, March 8, 2018, https://www.ynetnews.com/articles/0,7340,L-5321985,00.html

66. Adnan Abu Amer, "What Is Behind the Hamas-Iran Rapprochement?" Al Jazeera, July 26, 2018, https://www.aljazeera.com/indepth/opinion/hamas-iran-rapprochement-180725150509789.html

67. David Reaboi, "Qatar Shows Two Faces to the World," *Jewish Journal*, May 22, 2019, https://jewishjournal.com/cover_story/298975/qatar-shows-two-faces-to-the-world/

68. Burak Bekdil, "Hamas: Turkey's Longtime Love," *Gatestone Institute*, February 22, 2018, https://www.meforum.org/7217/hamas-turkey-longtime-love

69. Amos Harel, "Shin Bet: Hamas Funneling Terror Funds to West Bank, Gaza Through Turkey," *Haaretz*, February 12, 2018, https://www.haaretz.com/israel-news/shin-bet-accuses-turkey-of-facilitating-hamas-money-laundering-1.5810563

70. Omer Dostri, "Hamas Activities in Turkey Against Israel," *Jerusalem Institute for Strategy and Security*, August 3, 2018, https://jiss.org.il/en/dostri-hamas-activities-in-turkey-against-israel/

71. Yaniv Kubovish, "With Israel's Consent, Qatar Gave Gaza $1 Billion Since 2012," *Haaretz*, February 10, 2019, https://www.haaretz.com/middle-east-news/palestinians/.premium-with-israel-s-consent-qatar-gave-gaza-1-billion-since-2012-1.6917856

72. Arutz Sheva Staff, "Report: Qatar Transferring Funds to Hamas—via Israel," *Arutz Sheva*, October 6, 2018, https://www.israelnationalnews.com/News/News.aspx/252835

73. Jack Rosen, "Qatar's Break with Hamas Shapes Up Mideast Politics," *Jerusalem Post*, March 24, 2019, https://www.jpost.com/Opinion/Qatars-break-with-Hamas-shakes-up-Mideast-politics-584379

74. "Qatari Ambassador Meets Hamas Leader Sinwar in Gaza," *Middle East Monitor*, March 13, 2019, https://www.middleeastmonitor.com/20190313-qatari-ambassador-meets-hamas-leader-sinwar-in-gaza/

75. Oliver Holmes, "Turkey Condemns 'Israeli Terrorism' for Bombing News Agency in Gaza," *The Guardian*, May 5, 2019, https://www.theguardian.com/world/2019/may/05/turkey-condemns-israeli-terrorism-for-bombing-news-agency-in-gaza?CMP=share_btn_tw

76. Jonathan Schanzer (JSchanzer), "The reason I raise this: Turkey is a known and self-described supporter of Hamas. Many Hamas operatives and fundraisers are actually based in Turkey. Reports suggest that Turkey is helping Hamas build military capacity in Lebanon. How hard is it to do so in Gaza?" Twitter post, May 5, 2019, 7:23 A.M., https://twitter.com/JSchanzer/status/1125043314175168512

77. AFP, "Hamas 'Shocked' by Saudi Call on Qatar to Halt Funds," *Times of Israel*, June 7, 2017, https://www.timesofisrael.com/hamas-shocked-by-saudi-call-on-qatar-to-halt-funds/

78. Al Jazeera and News Agencies, "Hamas: End to Israel's Gaza Blockade 'Around the Corner'," Al Jazeera, August 21, 2018, https://www.aljazeera.com/news/middleeast/2018/08/hamas-israel-gaza-blockade-corner-180821134707824.html

79. "Turkey, Iran, Russia Condemn US Move on Golan Heights," *TRT World*, April 27, 2019, https://www.trtworld.com/turkey/turkey-iran-russia-condemn-us-move-on-golan-heights-26204

80. Kelly Thornberry, "The UAE's Divisive Strategy in Yemen," *RealClearDefense*, April 24, 2018, https://www.realcleardefense.com/articles/2018/04/24/the_uaes_divisive_strategy_in_yemen_113364.html

81. "Yemen's Muslim Brotherhood Chooses Extremism," *Al-Ahram Weekly*, no. 1177 (December 2013–January 2014), http://weekly.ahram.org.eg/News/4959.aspx

82. *Ibid.*

83. Matthew Hedges, "Saudi Distances Itself from Yemen's Muslim Brotherhood," *Fair Observer*, November 16, 2017, https://www.fairobserver.com/region/middle_east_north_africa/saudi-arabia-yemen-muslim-brotherhood-latest-middle-east-news-16661/

84. MEE Correspondent, "Brothers No More: Yemen's Islah Party Faces Collapse of Aden Alliances," *Middle East Eye*, October 21, 2017, https://www.middleeasteye.net/news/brothers-no-more-yemens-islah-party-faces-collapse-aden-alliances

85. Aram Roston, "A Middle East Monarchy Hired American Ex-Soldiers to Kill Its Political Enemies. This Could Be the Future of War," *BuzzFeed News*, October 16, 2018, https://www.buzzfeednews.com/article/aramroston/mercenaries-assassination-us-yemen-uae-spear-golan-dahlan

86. *Ibid.*

87. Saeed Al Batati, "Yemen's Islah Party Distances Itself from Brotherhood," *Gulf News*, January 9, 2018, https://gulfnews.com/world/gulf/yemen/yemens-islah-party-distances-itself-from-brotherhood-1.2154324

88. "Saudi Arabia, UAE Give Yemen $200m in Aid for Ramadan," *Middle East Monitor*, April 8, 2019, https://www.middleeastmonitor.com/20190408-saudi-arabia-uae-give-yemen-200-million-in-aid-for-ramadan/

89. Bel Trew, "Yemen War: End to Fighting Could be in Sight as Houthi Rebels Announce Withdrawal from Lifeline Port," *Independent*, May 11, 2019, https://www.independent.co.uk/news/world/middle-east/yemen-war-end-hodeidah-port-houthi-rebels-withdrawal-un-peace-deal-aid-a8909256.html

90. "Turkish, US, Qatari Forces Hold Joint Air Drill in Doha," *Hürriyet Daily News*, April 28, 2019, http://www.hurriyetdailynews.com/turkish-us-qatari-forces-hold-joint-air-drill-in-doha-142988

91. Al Jazeera and News Agencies, "Arab States Issue 13 Demands to End Qatar-Gulf Crisis," Al Jazeera, July 12, 2017, https://www.aljazeera.com/news/2017/06/arab-states-issue-list-demands-qatar-crisis-170623022133024.html

92. Mohammed Alkhereiji, "Missile Defence System Sparks US-Russia Tensions in Middle East," *The Arab Weekly*, March 10, 2019, https://thearabweekly.com/missile-defence-system-sparks-us-russia-tensions-middle-east

93. Ali Bakeer, "Testing the Turkey-Qatar Military Partnership," *The New Arab*, February 25, 2019, https://www.alaraby.co.uk/english/comment/2019/2/25/testing-the-turkey-qatar-military-partnership

94. Marc Champion, "Qatar's Departure from OPEC Suggests Gulf Rift Is Here to Stay," *Bloomberg*, December 3, 2018, https://www.bloomberg.com/news/articles/2018-12-03/qatar-s-departure-from-opec-suggests-gulf-rift-is-here-to-stay

95. Alex Ward, "Trump Just Labeled Iran's Revolutionary Guard a Terrorist Organization. But It Could Backfire," *Vox*, April 8, 2019, https://www.vox.com/2019/4/8/18300239/iran-trump-irgc-terrorist-pompeo

96. Ali Alfoneh, "The War in Syria is Transforming the IRGC into an Expeditionary Force," Blog post, *Arab Gulf States Institute in Washington*, December 5, 2018, https://agsiw.org/the-war-in-syria-is-transforming-the-irgc-into-an-expeditionary-force/

97. Ben Hubbard, "Saudi Arabia Delivers $100 Million Pledged to U.S. as Pompeo Lands in Riyadh," *The New York Times*, October 16, 2018, https://www.nytimes.com/2018/10/16/world/middleeast/saudi-arabia-money-syria.html

98. Donald Trump (realDonaldTrump), "Saudi Arabia has now agreed to spend the necessary money needed to help rebuild Syria, instead of the United States. See? Isn't it nice when immensely wealthy countries help rebuild their neighbors rather than a Great Country, the U.S., that is 5000 miles away. Thanks to Saudi A!" Twitter post, December 24, 2018, 9:23 A.M., https://twitter.com/realDonaldTrump/status/1077253411358326785

99. Alex Ward, "Trump Just Labeled Iran's Revolutionary Guard a Terrorist Organization. But It Could Backfire," *Vox*, April 8, 2019, https://www.vox.com/2019/4/8/18300239/iran-trump-irgc-terrorist-pompeo

100. Joyce Karam, "US to Send 1,000 More Troops to Middle East," *The National*, June 18, 2019, https://www.thenational.ae/world/mena/us-to-send-1-000-more-troops-to-middle-east-1.875715

101. Elizabeth Rosenberg, "The EU Can't Avoid U.S. Sanctions on Iran," *Foreign Affairs*, October 10, 2018, https://www.foreignaffairs.com/articles/europe/2018-10-10/eu-cant-avoid-us-sanctions-iran

102. Lesley Wroughton, "Mnuchin Says It Will Be Harder for Iran Oil Importers to Get Waivers," Reuters, October 21, 2018, https://www.reuters.com/article/us-iran-nuclear-sanctions-mnuchin/mnuchin-says-it-will-be-harder-for-iran-oil-importers-to-get-waivers-idUSKCN1MV0OF

103. Julian Lee, "The Winner from Trump's Iran Sanctions? Saudi Arabia," *Bloomberg Opinion*, May 12, 2019, https://www.bloomberg.com/opinion/articles/2019-05-12/the-winner-from-trump-s-iran-sanctions-saudi-arabia

104. Vivian Yee, "Claim of Attacks on 4 Oil Vessels Raises Tensions in Middle East," *The New York Times*, May 13, 2019, https://www.nytimes.com/2019/05/13/world/middleeast/saudi-arabia-oil-tanker-sabotage.html

105. Nada Altaher and Ben Westcott, "Four Ships Targeted in Mystery 'Sabotage Attack,' Says UAE," *CNN*, May 13, 2019, https://edition.cnn.com/2019/05/12/middleeast/uae-cargo-ship-sabotage-intl/index.html

106. Vivian Yee, "Claim of Attacks on 4 Oil Vessels Raises Tensions in Middle East," *The New York Times*, May 13, 2019, https://www.nytimes.com/2019/05/13/world/middleeast/saudi-arabia-oil-tanker-sabotage.html

107. "U.S. Believes Iran Proxies May Be Behind Tanker Attacks—Official," Reuters, May 14, 2019, https://www.reuters.com/article/saudi-oil-usa-iran-proxies/us-believes-iran-proxies-may-be-behind-tanker-attacks-official-idUSL2N22Q0SB

108. Aya Batrawy, "Saudis Blame Iran for Drone Attack Amid Calls for US Strikes," *AP News*, May 16, 2019, https://www.apnews.com/028d1755bdbb4e90ae0a92a68ff14d39

109. Ghaida Ghantous, Paul Tait, and Clarence Fernandez, "Houthi-Run TV Says Yemeni Group Targeted Vital Saudi Installations," May 14, 2019, https://www.reuters.com/article/us-yemen-security-saudi/houthi-run-tv-says-yemeni-group-targeted-vital-saudi-installations-idUSKCN1SK0I4

110. Marwa Rashan and Stephen Kalin, "Trump, Saudi Arabia Warn Iran Against Middle East Conflict," Reuters, May 18, 2019, https://www.reuters.com/article/us-saudi-oil-emirates-tanker/saudi-arabia-says-seeking-to-avert-war-ball-in-irans-court-idUSKCN1SP01C

111. Staff writer, "Bahrain Sentences 138 Individuals on Terror Charges," *Al Arabiya*, April 16, 2019, https://english.alarabiya.net/en/News/gulf/2019/04/16/Bahrain-sentences-138-individuals-on-terror-charges.html

112. Alex Ward, "Iran Labels All US Troops in the Middle East 'Terrorists'," *Vox*, April 16, 2019, https://www.vox.com/2019/4/16/18410646/iran-usa-terrorist-middle-east-irgc

113. Tony Blair, "Don't Make the Mistake of Dismissing Iran's Ideology," *Washington Post*, February 8, 2018, https://www.washingtonpost.com/opinions/2019/02/08/dont-make-mistake-dismissing-irans-ideology/

114. Brett McGurk, "Hard Truths in Syria," *Foreign Affairs*, May/June 2019, https://www.foreignaffairs.com/articles/syria/2019-04-16/hard-truths-syria

115. Bethan McKernan and Martin Chulov, "Arab League Set to Readmit Syria Eight Years After Expulsion," *The Guardian*, December 26, 2018, https://www .theguardian.com/world/2018/dec/26/arab-league-set-to-readmit-syria-eight-years-after-expulsion?CMP=share_btn_tw

116. Bilge Nesibe Kotan, "Why Is Saudi Arabia Funding Reconstruction in Syria Instead of the US?" *TRT World*, December 26, 2018, https://www.trtworld .com/mea/why-is-saudi-arabia-funding-reconstruction-in-syria-instead-of-the-us-22837

117. Colin Clarke and Ariane Tabatabai, "America's Indefinite Endgame in Syria," *The Atlantic*, October 16, 2018, https://www.theatlantic.com/internation al/archive/2018/10/bolton-pledges-american-troops-syria-iran/573121/

118. Stephen Snyder, "Saudi Arabia Is Buying More Weapons Than Ever Before," *PRI's The World*, March 27, 2019, https://www.pri.org/stories/2019-03-27/ saudi-arabia-buying-more-weapons-ever

119. "Humanitarian Crisis in Yemen Remains the Worst in the World, Warns UN," *UN News*, February 14, 2019, https://news.un.org/en/story/2019/02/ 1032811

120. Saeed Abdelrazek and Mohamed Nabil Helmy, "Iran, Turkey Reject Trump's Move to Classify Muslim Brotherhood as Terrorist Organization," *Asharq Al-Awsat*, May 2, 2019, https://aawsat.com/english/home/article/1704771/iran-turkey-reject-trump%E2%80%99s-move-classify-muslim-brotherhood-terrorist

121. Yusuf Ünal, "Sayyid Quṭb in Iran: Translating the Islamist Ideologue in the Islamic Republic," *Journal of Islamic and Muslim Studies* 1, no. 2 (November 2016): 35–60, https://www.jstor.org/stable/10.2979/jims.1.2.04?seq=1#page_scan_ tab_contents

122. Donald Trump (realDonaldTrump), "Saudi Arabia and others in OPEC will more than make up the Oil Flow difference in our now Full Sanctions on Iranian Oil. Iran is being given VERY BAD advice by @JohnKerry and people who helped him lead the U.S. into the very bad Iran Nuclear Deal. Big violation of Logan Act?" Twitter post, April 22, 2019, 6:37 A.M., https://twitter.com/realDon aldTrump/status/1120320642686038016

123. Jareer Elass, "How Saudi Arabia, UAE Will Stabilise the Oil Market," *The Arab Weekly*, April 28, 2019, https://thearabweekly.com/how-saudi-arabia-uae-will-stabilise-oil-market

124. *Ibid.*

125. Geneive Abdo, "Iraq Prepares to Evict U.S. Troops," *Foreign Policy*, March 20, 2019, https://foreignpolicy.com/2019/03/20/iraq-prepares-to-evict-u-s-troops/

126. Qassim Abdul-Zahra and Zeina Karam, "Why Iraq's President Says There's No Serious Opposition to US Troops in His Country," *Military Times*, March 31, 2019, https://www.militarytimes.com/flashpoints/2019/03/31/ why-iraqs-president-says-theres-no-serious-opposition-to-us-troops-in-his-country/

127. "Iran's Khamenei Urges Iraq to Force Out US Troops 'As Soon As Possible'," *Middle East Monitor*, April 7, 2019, https://www.middleeastmonitor.com/20190407-irans-khamenei-urges-iraq-to-force-out-us-troops-as-soon-as-possible/

128. Edward Wong, "U.S. Orders Partial Evacuation of Embassy in Baghdad," *The New York Times*, May 15, 2019, https://www.nytimes.com/2019/05/15/us/ politics/us-iraq-embassy-evacuation.html

129. Anne Speckhard and Ardian Shajkovci, "Is Iran Testing Trump with Little Attacks in Iraq, Saudi Arabia, and the Persian Gulf?" *Daily Beast*, May 20, 2019, https://www.thedailybeast.com/is-iran-testing-trump-with-little-attacks-in-iraq-saudi-arabia-and-the-persian-gulf

130. *Ibid.*

131. Abbas Al Lawati and Donna Abu-Nasr, "Saudi Arabia Makes Friends with an Old Enemy," *Yahoo Finance*, May 9, 2019, https://finance.yahoo.com/news/saudi-arabia-makes-friends-old-040104184.html

132. *Ibid.*

133. *Ibid.*

134. Tony Blair, "Don't Make the Mistake of Dismissing Iran's Ideology," *Washington Post*, February 8, 2018, https://www.washingtonpost.com/opinions/2019/02/08/dont-make-mistake-dismissing-irans-ideology/

135. Edward Wong, "Citing Iranian Threat, U.S. Sends Carrier Group and Bombers to Persian Gulf," *The New York Times*, May 5, 2019, https://www.nytimes.com/2019/05/05/world/middleeast/us-iran-military-threat-.html

136. Eric Schmitt and Julian Barnes, "White House Reviews Military Plans Against Iran, in Echoes of Iraq War," *The New York Times*, May 13, 2019, https://www.nytimes.com/2019/05/13/world/middleeast/us-military-plans-iran.html?module=inline

137. Dexter Filkins, "John Bolton on the Warpath," *New Yorker*, April 29, 2019, https://www.newyorker.com/magazine/2019/05/06/john-bolton-on-the-warpath

138. Saeid Jafari, "Iran Floods Further Add to Public Mistrust of Government Organizations," *Al-Monitor*, April 27, 2019, https://www.al-monitor.com/pulse/originals/2019/04/iran-floods-public-mistrust-mismanagement-society-state.html#ixzz5mZxvNPAv

139. *Ibid.*

140. Elif Erşen, "US Sanctions Take Heavy Toll on Iranian Economy," *Daily Sabah*, May 9, 2019, https://www.dailysabah.com/economy/2019/05/09/us-sanctions-take-heavy-toll-on-iranian-economy

141. Matt Egan, "David Petraeus: Iran's Economy Is in a 'Tailspin' and It Would Be 'Suicide' to Start a War with US," *CNN Business*, May 10, 2019, https://edition.cnn.com/2019/05/09/business/iran-sanctions-economy-petraeus/index.html

142. Dexter Filkins, "John Bolton on the Warpath," *New Yorker*, April 29, 2019, https://www.newyorker.com/magazine/2019/05/06/john-bolton-on-the-warpath

143. Mike Pompeo, "Intelligence Matters," Interview by Michael Morell, Transcript, *CBS News*, May 1, 2019, https://www.cbsnews.com/news/transcript-mike-pompeo-talks-with-michael-morell-on-intelligence-matters/

144. Liz Sly and Suzan Haidamous, "Trump's Sanctions on Iran Are Hitting Hezbollah, and It Hurts," *Washington Post*, May 18, 2019, https://www.washingtonpost.com/world/middle_east/trumps-sanctions-on-iran-are-hitting-hezbollah-hard/2019/05/18/970bc656-5d48-11e9-98d4-844088d135f2_story.html

145. Anne Speckhard and Ardian Shajkovci, "Is Iran Testing Trump with Little Attacks in Iraq, Saudi Arabia, and the Persian Gulf?" *Daily Beast*, May 20, 2019, https://www.thedailybeast.com/is-iran-testing-trump-with-little-attacks-in-iraq-saudi-arabia-and-the-persian-gulf

146. Zachary Cohen and Ryan Browne, "Trump Declares Emergency to Expedite Arms Sales to Saudi Arabia and UAE," *CNN*, May 24, 2019, https://edition.cnn.com/2019/05/24/politics/trump-arms-sales-saudi-arabia-uae/index.html

147. Noa Landau, Amir Tibon, and Jack Khoury, "Netanyahu to Join Arab Leaders at U.S.-hosted Mideast Conference in Poland," *Haaretz*, February 12, 2019, https://www.haaretz.com/israel-news/.premium-netanyahu-to-attend-divisive-mideast-conference-in-poland-1.6931908

148. Yasmine Farouk, "The Middle East Strategic Alliance Has a Long Way to Go," *Carnegie Endowment for International Peace*, February 8, 2019, https://carnegieendowment.org/2019/02/08/middle-east-strategic-alliance-has-long-way-to-go-pub-78317

149. Mina Al-Oraibi and Joyce Karam "Exclusive: Mesa to Include Nine Countries While Prioritising Iran Threat," *The National*, September 26, 2018, https://www.thenational.ae/world/mena/exclusive-mesa-to-include-nine-countries-while-prioritising-iran-threat-1.774415

150. "GCC News Roundup: Gulf States' Foreign Ministers Meet with Pompeo, GCC Military Budget to Reach $100 Billion (September 1–30)," *Brookings*, October 1, 2018, https://www.brookings.edu/blog/up-front/2018/10/01/gcc-news-roundup-gulf-states-foreign-ministers-meet-with-pompeo-gcc-military-budget-to-reach-100-billion-september-1-30/#cancel

151. Seth Frantzman, "Al Jazeera Suspends Two Journalists for Questioning the Holocaust," *Jerusalem Post*, May 20, 2019, https://www.meforum.org/58561/aljazeera-suspends-2-journalists-for-holocaust-denial

152. "Al Jazeera Suspends Journalists for Holocaust Denial Video," *BBC News*, May 20, 2019, https://www.bbc.com/news/world-middle-east-48335169

153. Ghanem Nuseibeh (gnuseibeh), "I tweeted this last year, about the extreme anti Semitism of Aljazeera. Don't be fooled by suspending a couple of journalists! Anti Semitism there is so deeply entrenched, institutional and right from the top of the state," Twitter post, May 20, 2019, 1:07 A.M., https://twitter.com/gnuseibeh/status/1130384606761504769

154. Ghanem Nuseibeh (gnuseibeh), "For us as Muslims fighting anti Semitism, fight is much tougher than amongst non Muslims. Not only is anti Semitism rampant in mainstream media like Aljazeera, it receives much funding from Qatar & few non Muslims prepared to stand against Qatar's Aljazeera & Muslim Brotherhood," Twitter post, May 19, 2019, 12:25 P.M., https://twitter.com/gnuseibeh/status/1130192692087054336

155. Karen DeYoung, "U.S. Special Envoy Working on Persian Gulf Disputes Steps Down," *Washington Post*, January 8, 2019, https://www.washingtonpost.com/world/national-security/us-special-envoy-working-on-persian-gulf-disputes-steps-down/2019/01/08/9e24a846-1364-11e9-90a8-136fa44b80ba_story.html

156. Yasmine Farouk, "The Middle East Strategic Alliance Has a Long Way to Go," *Carnegie Endowment for International Peace*, February 8, 2019, https://carnegieendowment.org/2019/02/08/middle-east-strategic-alliance-has-long-way-to-go-pub-78317

157. Stephen Kalin and Jonathan Landay, "Exclusive: Egypt Withdraws from U.S.-Led Anti-Iran Security Initiative—Sources," Reuters, April 10, 2019, https://www.reuters.com/article/us-usa-mesa-egypt-exclusive/exclusive-egypt-withdraws-from-us-led-anti-iran-security-initiative-sources-idUSKCN1RM2WU

158. Eric Edelman and Jonathan Schanzer, "Trump Can't Afford to Go Soft on Turkey," *Wall Street Journal Opinion*, May 15, 2019, https://www.wsj.com/articles/trump-cant-afford-to-go-soft-on-turkey-11557960028

159. Hussein Ibish, "Turkey Is Changing the Middle East. The U.S. Doesn't Get It," *Bloomberg Opinion*, March 14, 2019, https://www.bloomberg.com/opinion/articles/2019-03-14/turkey-is-changing-the-middle-east-the-u-s-doesn-t-get-it?srnd=politics-vp

160. Zach Vertin, "Turkey and the New Scramble for Africa: Ottoman Designs or Unfounded Fears?" *Lawfare* (blog), May 19, 2019, https://www.lawfareblog.com/turkey-and-new-scramble-africa-ottoman-designs-or-unfounded-fears

161. Steve Holland, "White House Says Trump Spoke to Libyan Commander Haftar on Monday," Reuters, April 19, 2019, https://www.reuters.com/article/us-libya-security-trump/white-house-says-trump-spoke-to-libyan-commander-haftar-on-monday-idUSKCN1RV0WW

162. Yousuf Eltagouri, "Trump's Embrace of Haftar Will Reignite Libya's Proxy War," *Foreign Policy Research Institute*, April 25, 2019, https://www.fpri.org/article/2019/04/trumps-embrace-of-haftar-will-reignite-libyas-proxy-war/

163. Neville Teller, "Khalifa Hafter: Libya's Problem, Or Its Saviour?—OpEd," *Eurasia Review*, April 13, 2019, https://www.eurasiareview.com/13042019-khalifa-hafter-libyas-problem-or-its-saviour-oped/

164. John Davison, "Sudan, Qatar to Sign $4 Billion Deal to Manage Red Sea Port—Ministry," Reuters, March 26, 2018, https://www.reuters.com/article/us-sudan-qatar/sudan-qatar-to-sign-4-billion-deal-to-manage-red-sea-port-ministry-idUSKBN1H22WH

165. Matina Stevis-Gridneff and Summer Said, "As Sudan Grapples with a Post-Bashir Future, Regional Powers Circle," *Wall Street Journal*, April 27, 2019, https://www.wsj.com/articles/as-sudan-grapples-with-a-post-bashir-future-regional-powers-circle-11556362800

166. John Hannah, "It's Time for Saudi Arabia to Stop Exporting Extremism," *Foundation for Defense of Democracies*, May 4, 2019, https://www.fdd.org/analysis/2019/05/04/its-time-for-saudi-arabia-to-stop-exporting-extremism/

167. Roger Cohen, "The Prince Who Would Remake the World," *The New York Times*, June 21, 2018, https://www.nytimes.com/2018/06/21/opinion/sunday/saudi-arabia-women-drivers.html

CONCLUSION

1. Salma Islam, "Morsi's Death in Egypt Puts Diminished Muslim Brotherhood Back in Spotlight," *Los Angeles Times*, June 24, 2019, https://www.latimes.com/world/la-fg-egypt morsi-muslim-brotherhood-20190624-story.html

2. Jane Kinninmont, "The Gulf Divided: The Impact of the Qatar Crisis," *Middle East and North Africa Programme*, May 2019, https://www.chathamhouse.org/sites/default/files/publications/research/2019-05-30-Gulf%20Crisis_0.pdf

3. Mosa'ab Elshamy (mosaaberizing), "His presidency seemed guided by greed and the benefit of his group rather than one of finding common ground. It was messy, bloody, and unstable. The army watched as people, many who voted him, asked for the military to step in," Twitter post, June 17, 2019, 2:21 P.M., https://twitter.com/mosaaberizing/status/1140731091604713474

4. Khaled Diab, "Mohamed Morsi Was an Unpopular, Incompetent Hack. Egypt Has Made Him a Martyr," *Washington Post*, June 20, 2019, https://www.washingtonpost.com/outlook/2019/06/20/mohamed-morsi-was-an-unpopular-incompetent-hack-egypt-has-made-him-martyr/

5. Soner Cagaptay, "Erdogan's Failure on the Nile," *Cairo Review of Global Affairs*, Spring 2019, https://www.washingtoninstitute.org/policy-analysis/view/erdogans-failure-on-the-nile

Index

About the Author

NAWAF OBAID, PhD, is an author, academic, and a former Saudi Arabian government adviser. He coauthored *National Security in Saudi Arabia: Threats, Responses, and Challenges* (Praeger, 2005) with Anthony Cordesman. His articles and editorials have appeared in numerous publications, including *The New York Times*, *The Washington Post*, CNN, and *Foreign Policy*; from 2012 to 2018 he was a visiting fellow and adjunct lecturer at the Harvard Kennedy School.